Dedicated to:

Pastor Jeff O'Neil (29 Sep 1937- 25 Jan 2019)
& Mrs Shirley O'Neil

"We must talk!" he urged, when he saw my awkwardness as I tried to answer his
question: "So you sing the psalms?"

We will have much to talk and sing about when we are reunited before our Saviour who sang:
"Thou wilt shew me the path of life: in thy presence is fulness of joy; at thy right hand there are
pleasures for evermore" (Ps 16:11).

" For both he that sanctifieth and they who are sanctified are all of one:

for which cause he is not ashamed to call them brethren, Saying,

I will declare thy name unto my brethren, in the midst of the church

will I sing praise unto thee"

—Hebrews 2:11-12—

Contents

The Songs of Christ:

A Devotional, Cantorial-Christological Commentary on the Psalms

Volume 1 of 2

(Book I-III: Psalms 1-89)

JJ Lim

THE SONGS OF CHRIST:
A Devotional, Cantorial-Christological Commentary on the Psalms
by JJ Lim

This edition is first published in June 2019 by
Pilgrim Covenant Church
Blk 203B, Henderson Road, #07-07, Singapore 159546.

Cover photo by Mrs Shirley O'Neil: Pastor Jeff O'Neil fishing for salmon on
Garynahine River, Isle of Lewis, Outer Hebrides, Scotland.
Where is Pastor Jeff in the photograph?

Release 0.027 dated 07 December 2021

Foreword

It is with pleasure that I commend to your edification and spiritual enjoyment Rev Lim's latest book, *The Songs of Christ*.

In its pages of this book Pastor Lim leads us with him into a deeper appreciation of Christ in the Psalms. There is perhaps no greater need, or blessing, for a believer than to grow in appreciation of that spiritual and mystical, yet real and inseparable union and communion believers have with Christ as their Head in grace and glory[1]... in every trial and triumph on their pilgrimage heavenward. Every comfort flows from this union. To unfold, through clear and sound exegetical principles, the communion that is ours to enjoy with Christ in *all* the Psalms, and in a way that engenders worshipful trust ... that is a blessing indeed.

Believing souls desire to follow closely upon the one who says: "... all things..., which were written in ... the psalms, concerning me. Then opened he their understanding, that they might understand the scriptures" (Luke 24:44-45).

This little book is also very timely for the Church in a day when the singing of Psalms has fallen on hard times.

> If one had to choose one single pragmatic concern back of the decline of Psalmody in the Reformed churches, it would be that its people, through indolence and lack of instruction, gradually came to the point where they no longer saw Christ in the Psalms.

That was Michael Bushell's assessment in his excellent book, *The Songs of Zion* (p. 97).

William Romaine, writing around 1800, identified that same lack as the principle reason for American Christianity replacing Psalms with human compositions:

> "It is not difficult to account for this strange practice. Our people had lost sight of the meaning of the Psalms. They did not see their relation to Jesus Christ. This happened when vital religion began to decay among us, more than a century ago."[2]

Our experience certainly supports this assessment. Presbyterian and Reformed churches, for the most part, have abandoned the Psalms in favour of human compositions. The argument we hear repeatedly is that Jesus is not in the Psalms, and the Psalms don't breathe the Spirit of Christ. Therefore, it is argued, Christians must (through the Spirit of Christ which we now enjoy in this New Testament age), write Christian hymns and spiritual songs that are Christ-centred and honouring to the Lord Jesus, and reflective of His Spirit.

---

[1] *Westminster Larger Catechisms* 65,66.

[2] Cited from Bushell, p. 97.

This line of reasoning shows (among many other things) a lamentable superficiality and lack of appreciation of the relation of the Psalms to Jesus Christ, and to His mystical body. There is a sad failure to see Christ in the Psalms.

Thank God, there are in still some Presbyterian and Reformed Churches who do see Christ in the Psalms and practice exclusive Psalmody.

The Songs of Christ encourages Psalm singers to look to the spirituality of their worship in song. We don't do this, we trust, because we are old-fashioned and cling to traditions from the past. Nor is it because we have to ... as if the biblical principle that regulates God's worship (what is not required by God in Scripture is forbidden) stops us doing what we *want*. If that were true of us, it would only be a matter of time before the Psalms give way to human compositions. We sing Psalms, we trust, because we know that the Psalms are divinely inspired and in a category all of their own. And, may it be, that we all do so because we can still see Christ in the Psalms. If that is true of us it is a great blessing!

That is not, however, something that we can reasonably hope would continue in our generations, if "indolence and lack of instruction", against which Bushell warns, gradually brings us to the point where we no longer see Christ in the Psalms.

There is reason to feel some measure of urgency about this matter, we believe. It is distinctly possible that our children and youth, singing Psalms with us in family worship and in the solemn assembly on the Lord's day, do not see Christ in the Psalms as they could, and we aren't really teaching them how to! This will leave them open to replacing the Psalms with something new and understandable. For they will want to sing songs in which they can see Christ! If that isn't the Psalms, then something else will be looked for. That is not unreasonable to expect.

It is possible that those of us who have been added to the church and to Psalmody along with "the church package" have not yet learned to see Christ in the Psalms. This can be true for us when we have been many years in the church. To be singing Psalms when we do not understand them is not a comfortable position. It must leave us unsatisfied and confused – or struggling with what can feel like "a tradition that needs updating." The Church that cares for us in this situation will want to open our eyes to understand and see Christ in the Psalms. If it doesn't, then it would seem reasonable to assume that Psalmody is just a tradition – and the sooner it is jettisoned the better!

And it is possible that those of us who have lived all, or most of, our days in the practice of exclusive Psalmody see Christ but dimly, and when we aren't clear on how to understand and interpret the Psalms, our experience of the wonder and blessing of the Psalms can be hindered. We wouldn't want to lose the Psalms, but we certainly could do with understanding them better. The fathers who are heads of their home, and custodians of the souls of their family, will sense a need here.

Perhaps those of us who are ministers, elders or deacons will be among those who would profit most from a much clearer sight of Christ in the Psalms. It is, after all, for the shepherds not only to feed the flock, but to guard it against that which will harm.

Who cannot see, in such circumstances, (which are rather "ordinary" and perfectly understandable as we are busy with other important truths of our Christian faith and life in the day to day needs of) that quite unwittingly a church can slide away from that vital spirituality that enables it to see Christ in the Psalms? Who cannot see how needful it is for a church to gird itself up to hold its ground against, what really is, a tsunami of man-centred modernization sweeping through the churches?

History shows that to lose sight of Christ in the Psalms leads to the Psalms being washed out of the Worship.

Our churches are not immune to this. We are certainly not above, or somehow stronger or better than the once mighty churches that have lost Christ in the Psalms, or are in the process of losing Him.

The Songs of Christ are a welcome encouragement in many ways.

Pastor Chris Connors
Evangelical Presbyterian Church of Australia

Preface:
The Pervasive Christology of the Psalms

Few of us will dispute that Christ is the key to all Scripture. Christ Himself told His disciples after He rose from the dead:

> "These are the words which I spake unto you, while I was yet with you, that all things must be fulfilled, which were written in the law of Moses, and in the prophets, and in the psalms, concerning me" (Lk 24:44).

Then we are told:

> He "opened... their understanding, that they might understand the Scriptures, and he said to them, Thus it is written, and thus it behoved Christ to suffer, and to rise from the dead the third day" (Lk 24:45-46).

The Law, the Prophets and the Psalms: this was how the Jews divided the Hebrew Old Testament. When the Lord speaks of the Law, the Prophet and the Psalms, He is referring to the whole Old Testament. All of Scripture, including the Old Testament, point to Christ. They point particularly to His suffering, death and resurrection.

So, all the Old Testament is, in a sense, Christological or Messianic. But I submit to you that the entire book of Psalms is Christological in a *special* way that goes beyond all the other parts of the Old Testament. What do I mean? In a word, it is my contention that each Psalm is either about Christ or contains the word of Christ as the main speaker, or the head of the party speaking. I believe this is how the apostles viewed the Psalms, and this is how the Holy Spirit wants us to view the Psalms.

This contention may be verified by proving five propositions.

- First, we must show that there are some Psalms that are clearly Messianic beyond all other parts of the Old Testament.

- Secondly, we must show that there are Psalms which *do not* appear to be Messianic but is taken to be so in the New Testament. If we can show this, we will understand why most of the Early Church Fathers sought to interpret *every* Psalm evangelically or Messianically.

- Thirdly, we must show that there are Psalms, which were clearly written upon particular occasions in David's life, which are also clearly Messianic. If we can show this, then we will understand that interpreting the Psalms Messianically does not violate the rules of historical-grammatical hermeneutics.

- Fourthly, we must show that the so-called Imprecatory Psalms are also Messianic. If we can show this, then we would remove the first major objection to seeing that every verse and passage in the Psalms can be interpreted with a reference to Christ.

- Fifthly, we must show that even penitential Psalms can be interpreted Messianically. If we can show this, then we would have removed the second major objection to seeing that every verse and passage in the Psalms can be interpreted with a reference to Christ.

1. There Are Psalms that Are
Clearly Messianic

Consider Psalm 2. This is a very familiar Psalm, but it is also a difficult Psalm for many. Most scholars believe that this Psalm was written on the occasion of David's coronation in Jerusalem around 1040 BC.

When we read this Psalm, many questions cross our minds. For example, we ask:

- Who is this "anointed" in verse 2?

- Who is this "king" that is referred to in verse 6?

- Who is the "me" in verse 7 who says "the LORD hath said unto me, Thou art my Son; this day have I begotten thee"?

- Who is this "thou" in verse 9, who "shalt break them with a rod of iron" and "dash them in pieces like a potter's vessel"?

- Who is "Son" in verse 12, whom the kings should kiss "lest he be angry, and [they] perish from the way, when his wrath is kindled but a little"?

Liberal and unbelieving scholars will say: Surely the answer is David.

But the Christian, filled with the Spirit, knows otherwise. Why? Because the New Testament, which is inspired by the Holy Spirit quotes this Psalm in reference to Christ!

For example, in Acts 4:25-26, we have a record of the early believers praying. What is unique about this prayer is that they were using the words of the first two verses of Psalm 2 to refer to the exaltation of Christ and the opposition that was raised against His gospel.

Then in Acts 13, we have a sermon of the Apostle Paul, which was recorded under the inspiration of the Holy Spirit. In verse 33, he says:

> "God hath fulfilled the same unto us their children, in that he hath raised up Jesus again; as it is also written in the second Psalm, Thou art my Son, this day have I begotten thee."

Paul was quoting from Psalm 2:7. This same verse is quoted again in Hebrews 1:5 and again in Hebrews 5:5 as referring to Christ, the only begotten Son of God.

I believe it is not difficult for us (who live under the New Covenant) to see that Psalm 2 is entirely about Christ.

When we realise this is the case, then we see that there is something extremely unique about this Psalm compared to all other parts of the Old Testament.

- In *no* other books of the Old Testament, with the exception of the Song of Solomon, do we find the explicit words of Christ, as in verse 7: "the LORD hath said unto ME, Thou art my Son; this day have I begotten thee."

- And in *no* other books of the Old Testament, do we find a record of words spoken directly to Christ as in verse 9: "THOU shalt break them with a rod of iron; thou shalt dash them in pieces like a potter's vessel."

Psalm 2 is therefore Messianic in a way that surpasses most of the other portions of the Old Testament. But the question we must ask is: To what extent is the book of Psalms

Messianic? Some scholars say that there are only thirteen Messianic Psalms.[3] But is that correct? What about the "my" and "I" of say, Psalm 3 and Psalm 4? Do they refer to Christ too? Do we have any basis to believe that they may also be interpreted as referring to Christ?

I believe we have a basis. Indeed, I believe that every Psalm is Christological or Messianic. One of the major reasons I believe this is right is that...

2. There Are Psalms that Are Messianic but Not Obviously so

Psalm 2 is obviously Messianic. Its content leads us to think that it is about Christ; and the New Testament confirms that it is about Christ.

But what about Psalm 8? When we read Psalm 8, it appears to us to be setting forth the pre-eminence of man compared to the rest of creation. Verses 4-5 read:

> "[4] What is man, that thou art mindful of him? and the son of man, that thou visitest him? [5] For thou hast made him a little lower than the angels, and hast crowned him with glory and honour" (Ps 8:4-5).

But what does the inspired New Testament teach us? Consider Hebrews 2:6-9:

> "[6] But one in a certain place testified, saying, 'What is man, that thou art mindful of him? or the son of man, that thou visitest him? [7] Thou madest him a little lower than the angels; thou crownedst him with glory and honour, and didst set him over the works of thy hands: [8] Thou hast put all things in subjection under his feet.' [quoting Psalm 8:4-5]. For in that he put all in subjection under him, he left nothing that is not put under him. But now we see not yet all things put under him [i.e. under man]. [9] But we see Jesus, who was made a little lower than the angels for the suffering of death, crowned with glory and honour; that He by the grace of God should taste death for every man."

What is the apostle saying? He is saying, is he not, that Psalm 8 is not really about the pre-eminence of man? It is rather about Jesus Christ. Christ was made a little lower than the angels in that He took on human flesh to suffer and die for us. But now He is crowned with glory and honour.

Psalm 8 is, therefore, a Christological Psalm.

Or consider Psalm 19. There is no indication from the Psalm that it has anything to do with Christ. It seems to be about the material heavens, or about the cycle of the sun and moon. Verse 4 reads:

> "Their line is gone out through all the earth, and their words to the end of the world. In them hath he set a tabernacle for the sun."

This seems to be speaking merely about how the glory of God is displayed to the whole world through the rising and setting of the sun.

But what does the inspired commentary in the New Testament say? Turning to Romans 10:17-18, we read:

---

[3] These are Psalms 2, 8, 16, 22, 40, 45, 69, 72, 89, 102, 109, 110, 132

"So then faith cometh by hearing, and hearing by the word of God. But I say, Have they not heard? Yes verily, their sound went into all the earth, and their words unto the ends of the world."

Paul is quoting from Psalm 19:4. He has a very different idea of what the verse means, doesn't he? He tells us that Psalm 19:4 is not just about natural revelation brought about by the glory of the sun. It is rather about the Gospel radiating from the Sun of Righteousness!

Psalm 19 is a Christological Psalm.

Or if these are not convincing enough, consider Psalm 102. If you read Psalm 102 by itself, it is highly unlikely that you will conclude that it is Christological, for there is nothing in it to indicate that it is anything other than a "Prayer of the Afflicted." But how would the Holy Spirit have us interpret it? In Hebrews 1, the inspired writer is seeking to show that Christ is superior to the angels. He quotes Psalm 45:6-7 as the words of the Father to the Son (Heb 1:8-9). Psalm 45 is generally acknowledged as a Messianic Psalm, so this is not so surprising. But he goes on to quote Psalm 102:25-27 as also the words of the Father to the Son:

"And, Thou, Lord, in the beginning hast laid the foundation of the earth; and the heavens are the works of thine hands: [11] They shall perish; but thou remainest; and they all shall wax old as doth a garment; [12] And as a vesture shalt thou fold them up, and they shall be changed: but thou art the same, and thy years shall not fail" (Heb 1:10-12).

Now, this is surprising! But this must be the correct interpretation: for it is given under inspiration. To conclude otherwise would be to charge the apostle of misusing Scripture, at the very least. But if this is the correct interpretation, then the natural way to interpret Psalm 102:1-24 will be to see them as the words of the Son to the Father (for it cannot also be the words of the Father to the Son, seeing it is a word of prayer as indicated in verse 1).

Thus Psalm 102 is clearly Christological. It even contains the words of Christ in the first person!

Neither Psalm 8, 19 or 102 give any hint that they are Messianic. And yet the inspired New Testament teaches us that they are all Messianic! Surely, we must submit to the infallible interpretation of the Holy Spirit!

Where does this lead us to? Does it not lead us to think about the other Psalms? If even Psalms 8, 19 and 102 are Messianic when there seems to be no indication that they are so, then what about Psalms 3, 4 or 5 which can easily be interpreted in the context of the Lord's suffering? Does this not lead us to conclude that there is a great possibility that all the Psalms are Messianic?

Indeed, does it not lead us to wonder if the apostles, in fact, presupposed the Messianic character of the entire book of Psalms? There is no indication that they picked and chose verses that are clearly Messianic to support their doctrine. It appears rather that they understood the Psalms—as the Jews in the days of the Lord did—that they were all Messianic.

Does this not explain why the Apostle Paul exhorts us:

"Let the WORD OF CHRIST dwell in you richly in all wisdom; teaching and admonishing one another in psalms and hymns and spiritual songs, singing with grace in your hearts to the Lord" (Col 3:16)?

There were no human inspired hymns and songs in the days of the Apostle Paul. Paul was, no doubt, referring to the Psalms. The Greek words for "psalms", "hymns" and "songs" were all used in the Greek translation of the Psalms to refer to the Psalms.

The Apostle Paul would have us memorise the Psalms that we may admonish one another with them. But notice how he speaks of the Psalms as being the word of Christ. "Let the WORD OF CHRIST dwell in you richly in all wisdom," says the apostle.

It is no wonder that the Early Church Fathers, almost unanimously spoke of the Psalms as entirely Messianic. We know, for example, that Chrysostom, Tertullian, Jerome, Ambrose, Augustine, and Hilary, all interpreted the Psalms Messianically. It was Tertullian of the 3rd century who says: "almost all the Psalms are spoken in the person of Christ, being addressed by the Son to the Father, that is, by Christ to God."

But what about the Psalms that were clearly written upon some specific occasions in the life of David? Surely these Psalms cannot be Messianic? But no, for we see that...

3. There Are Psalms Which Have Clear Historical Occasions, Which Are Unquestionably Messianic

Consider Psalm 18. The preface of Psalm 18 tells us that it is:

"A Psalm of David, the servant of the LORD, who spake unto the LORD the words of this song in the day that the LORD delivered him from the hand of all his enemies, and from the hand of Saul."

But we know from the New Testament that this Psalm is clearly Messianic. Look at Romans 15:8-9:

"^{8} Now I say that Jesus Christ was a minister of the circumcision for the truth of God, to confirm the promises made unto the fathers: ^{9} And that the Gentiles might glorify God for his mercy [i.e. in Jesus Christ]; as it is written, For this cause I will confess to thee among the Gentiles, and sing unto thy name."

Now if you do a careful study of this verse, you will realise that the apostle is, in fact, quoting Psalm 18:49. Psalm 18, in other words, is not just about David's deliverance from Saul, but the greater David's deliverance from death. He died for our sins. He rose again for our justification that He might call a people unto Himself; that He might confess the greatness and mercy of His Father amongst the Gentiles.

Psalm 18 has a clear historical occasion, but it is also Christological!

Likewise, there is Psalm 41. This Psalm was clearly written by David upon the occasion of his betrayal by his beloved son Absalom and his trusted counselor Ahithophel. Verse 9 reads:

"Yea, mine own familiar friend, in whom I trusted, which did eat of my bread, hath lifted up his heel against me" (Ps 41:9).

How does the New Testament refer to this Psalm? Consider the words of the Lord Himself in John 13:18:

"I speak not of you all: I know whom I have chosen: but that the scripture may be fulfilled, He that eateth bread with me hath lifted up his heel against me."

Notice how the Lord speaks of Psalm 41 as referring to his own persecution, and how Psalm 41:9 is to be fulfilled in His own betrayal by Judas Iscariot?

Clearly then, Psalm 41 is also Christological, though it has a clear historical occasion.

Both Psalms 18 and 41 have clear historical backgrounds, but they are both Messianic!

What does this lead us to think? Does it not lead us to conclude that the Lord of Providence, so directed the life of David so that his experience foreshadowed the experience of Christ; and his feelings expressed in the Psalms, reflect the feelings of Christ in His humiliation and exaltation?

It cannot be otherwise. It cannot be that Christ picked out a few verses, out of context, to refer to Himself. It is inconceivable that the Holy Spirit would interpret any verse out of context in order to have it refer to Christ. And it is unreasonable to think that in a single Psalm, without any change in immediate context, the first-person pronouns sometimes can refer to Christ and sometimes cannot. Is it not much safer to conclude that really, all the first-person pronouns can be applied to Christ?

But what about words of imprecation, and words of penitence? Surely, they cannot be Messianic. I believe they can, for in the first place, ...

4. There Are Psalms Which Are Imprecatory, Which Are Messianic

Some think that words of imprecation or curses cannot possibly flow from the holy lips of our gentle Saviour. But what does the Scripture say?

Consider the famous imprecatory Psalm—Psalm 69. Look at the words of imprecation against the adversaries of the psalmist (v. 23-25):

> "[23] Let their eyes be darkened, that they see not; and make their loins continually to shake. [24] Pour out thine indignation upon them, and let thy wrathful anger take hold of them. [25] Let their habitation be desolate; and let none dwell in their tents."

Could these fearful words have been spoken by our gentle Saviour? Could it reflect the wish of our Saviour? Surely this Psalm cannot be Messianic! But look at verses 20-21:

> "[20] Reproach hath broken my heart; and I am full of heaviness: and I looked for some to take pity, but there was none; and for comforters, but I found none. [21] They gave me also gall for my meat; and in my thirst they gave me vinegar to drink."

It is obvious, is it not? The first-person pronoun, "I," in this Psalm does not primarily point to David, but to the Lord Jesus Christ in His suffering on the cross. Nowhere are we informed that David was given vinegar and gall to quench his thirst, whereas it happened to the Lord at the cross (Mt 27:34).

What we have then, is the fact that the imprecations recorded in this Psalm are, in fact, the words of Christ. So, the Apostle Peter was correct to apply the curse in Psalm 69:25 to Judas Iscariot as one who epitomised the Lord's enemies. We see this in Acts 1:20, in his inaugural sermon.

Now then, if the imprecations in Psalm 69 can, and should be taken as the words of Christ our Saviour, what is there to prevent us from understanding the words of imprecation in other Psalms as describing the prayers of our Lord?

The insistence that Christ could not have uttered words of imprecation, is simply not biblical! In fact, unless we recognise the imprecations of the Psalms as the word of Christ, we may end up with the idea that God approves our having personal enemies, and entertaining personal imprecations against them! The reality is that only Christ is qualified to say, "I hate them with perfect hatred" (Ps 139:22). Only Christ perfectly qualifies to judge His enemies as being truly the enemies of God, and therefore is perfectly just to call imprecations against them!

But what about words of penitence? Christ was tempted in all points like as we are, and yet without sin. How could words that ask God for forgiveness be ascribed to the Lord, whether directly or typically?

5. Penitential Psalms May also Be Interpreted Messianically

This is indeed a difficulty. And it is such a difficulty that many sound commentators recoil from saying they could possibly have poured forth out of the lips of our holy Saviour.

How could words of confession and pleas for forgiveness be attributed to the Lord who never sinned?

I believe they could be, for two reasons.

First, there are Psalms containing words of penitence which are indisputably Messianic. We know that they are Messianic because the New Testament quotes the words of the Psalmist as being the words of the Lord: for example, Psalms 40[4] and Psalm 69[5]. Both of these Psalms contain words of penitence.

Look at Psalm 40:12:

> "For innumerable evils have compassed me about: mine iniquities have taken hold upon me, so that I am not able to look up; they are more than the hairs of mine head: therefore my heart faileth me."

And look at Psalm 69:5:

> "O God, thou knowest my foolishness; and my sins are not hid from thee."

Now, it does not make reasonable sense to say that these verses do not belong to the Lord, while the "Messianic" verses (in the same Psalms) belong to Him. Doing so would involve reading our own whims and fancies into the Scripture.

As such, we have to conclude that these penitential verses could be attributed to the Lord, and, in fact, should be interpreted as words belonging to Him, and ultimately spoken by Him.

But what does that do to our theology that Christ is sinless? Well, let me assert secondly, there is a very good theological ground to attribute words of penitence in the Psalms to our sinless Lord.

This is because all our sin was imputed to the Lord as He suffered as a substitutionary sacrifice on our behalf. This is taught in many places in the Scriptures. For example:

The Apostle Paul says: "Christ hath redeemed us from the curse of the law, being made a curse for us: for it is written, Cursed is every one that hangeth on a tree" (Gal 3:13).

---

[4] cf. v. 6-8; Heb 10:5-7

[5] cf. v. 4; Jn 15:25; v. 9; Jn 2:17, Rom 15:3, Col 3:16; v. 21, Mt 27:34

Now, you must realise that the Lord Jesus was not simply paying for our sin theoretically. No, He took the guilt of our sin upon Himself and suffered for it on the cross. Just as Adam's guilt was imputed to all mankind, so the guilt of the elect was imputed to Christ (Rom 5:15-17).

Christ was accounted as a sinner in God's sight as He suffered on the cross. He was suffering for sins, "the just for the unjust" (1 Pet 3:18). He was not suffering as a righteous man should suffer. Though He had no sin, He was suffering the pains of hell as the "most guilty man" who ever lived. This is why He was, as it were, forsaken of the Father, and He cried out: "My God, my God, why hast thou forsaken me?" (Ps 22:1).

If I could enumerate my sins: there on the cross, Christ my Lord was suffering the punishment due to every one of them. And not only my sin, but the sin of all the elect throughout the ages, including David's.

Now, the words of penitence in the Psalms can all be taken as expressions of the Lord's grief and sorrow as He hung on the cross, bearing our sin. Thus, the words "my sin is ever before me... against thee, thee only, have I sinned," may be taken as expressing the enormous grief, sorrow and pain that we all ought to feel for our sin.

George Horne in his excellent Christological commentary on the Psalms agrees with this view. Alluding to the writings of the ancient Fathers, he says:

> Christ in the day of his passion standing charged with the sin and guilt of his people, speaks of such their sin and guilt, *as if they were his own*, appropriating to himself those debts, for which, in the capacity of a surety, he had made himself responsible.[6]

Christ our Lord, in other words, suffered on our behalf. He suffered also the feeling of guilt though He was Himself without sin.

Psalm 51 is a Penitential Psalm. It was written by David after he committed adultery with Bathsheba. It is most easily interpreted as being the words of David. But dare we say they are not the words of Christ when David, according to the Apostle Peter, wrote under the direction of the Spirit of Christ who was in him signifying and testifying "beforehand the sufferings of Christ, and the glory that should follow" (1 Pet 1:11).

Could not the Lord of providence have so ordered the life of David that his experience foreshadowed the experience of Christ? Is it not likely that the feelings that David expressed in Psalm 51 were written as a reflection of how our Lord must have felt on our behalf when He bore our guilt on the cross of Calvary?

Conclusion

We have, I believe, sufficiently demonstrated our case:

- We have shown that there are some Psalms that are clearly Messianic beyond all other parts of the Old Testament.

- We have shown that there are Psalms which *do not* appear to be Messianic, but are taken to be so in the New Testament.

- We have shown that there are Psalms which were clearly written upon particular occasions in David's life, which are clearly Messianic.

---

[6] *Commentary on the Psalms* (Old Paths, 1997), xix; italics mine.

- We have shown that the so-called imprecatory Psalms are also Messianic.

- Finally, we showed that even penitential statements can be interpreted Messianically.

What do we say to all these things? I believe we can conclude, quite safely, through them, that all the Psalms are uniquely Messianic and can be interpreted Messianically.[7]

There are some who say that only those verses which are quoted in the New Testament are Messianic. But that would be a restrictive, mechanical view.

When the Holy Spirit teaches us that one verse in the Psalm is spoken by the Messiah, and there is no change in person, what should we conclude but that He is the speaker throughout the Psalm? It goes against reason and context to think that Christ is the speaker of one statement and then deny that the next statement may be attributed to Him.

So, we can conclude that the whole Psalm can and should be ascribed to Him. But if Christ is the speaker in a Psalm, then what is there to prevent us from applying another Psalm to Christ when it is written with the same background, or contain the same, or similar substance with the Psalm already accepted as Messianic?

What I am saying is that it is unreasonable to suppose that the only parts of the Psalms that should be interpreted Messianically are those which are explicitly quoted as Messianic in the New Testament. In fact, it is perfectly reasonable to assume that every Psalm has a Messianic import.

Some of the Psalms speak of the Church of Christ; some are the confessions of the Church of Christ; some refer to Christ Himself in the third person; some address Christ in the second person; but there are many in which the speaker may be taken to be Christ Himself.

In saying this, we are not saying that the historical context in which the Psalms were written are not important. Psalm 2 was written perhaps on the occasion of David's coronation. Psalm 18 was written when God had delivered David out of the hand of Saul. Psalm 51 was written after David fell into sin with Bathsheba. But could not the Lord of Providence, so direct the life of David so that his experience foreshadowed the experience of Christ; and his feelings expressed in the Psalms reflect the feelings of Christ in His humiliation and exaltation?

---

[7] Remarkably, the renowned Hebrew scholar, Dr Bruce Walke had come to a similar conclusion in a process that, no doubt, led him closer to the Reformed Faith in some areas. He writes: "In all fairness, it seems as though the writers of the New Testament are not attempting to identify and limit the psalms that prefigure Christ but rather are assuming that the Psalter as a whole has Jesus Christ in view and that this should be the normative way of interpreting the psalms....

I conclude, therefore, that both the nonhistorical and   undisciplined method of interpreting the psalms and the Antiochian principle of allowing but one historical meaning that may carry with it typical significance are inadequate hermeneutical principles for the interpretation of the psalms. In place of these methods, therefore, I would like to argue for a canonical process approach in interpreting the psalms, an approach that does justice both to the historical significance(s) of the psalms and to their Messianic significance. Indeed, I shall argue that from a literary and historical point of view, we should understand that the human subject of the psalms-whether it be the blessed man of Psalm 1, the one proclaiming himself the son of God in Psalm 2, the suffering petitioner in Psalms 3-7, the son of man in Psalm 8--is Jesus Christ. By the canonical process approach I mean the recognition that the text's intention became deeper and clearer as the parameters of the canon were expanded. Just as redemption itself has a progressive history so also older texts in the canon underwent a correlative progressive perception of meaning as they became part of a growing canonical literature" (Bruce K. Waltke, "A Canonical Process Approach to the Psalms," in *Tradition and Testament: Essays in Honor of Charles Lee Feinberg,* ed. John S. Feinberg and Paul D. Feinberg (Chicago: Moody, 1981), 7.

Christ is the greater David. When we read and sing the Psalms, then, we must have an eye particularly on Christ. Let us sing His word cheerfully. Let us memorise them. Let us sing them gratefully. The Lord has promised that when we sing the Psalms, He would, as it were, be in our midst to sing with us (see Heb 2:12, cf. Ps 22:22). Indeed, He would not only join us, but would lead us as our Priestly King, for the Psalms are really His songs. As Dr Michael LeFebvre points it out in his excellent book, *Singing the Songs of Jesus*, "When you sing Psalms, you are actually singing the songs of Jesus, with Jesus as your songleader."[8] This is the theology of worship that may be derived from the Psalms, especially from Psalm 24.

Although many of the Psalms may be used by believers to express their own experiences, the personal use of the Psalms is legitimate only because of the union that the Church has with Christ. Thus, for example, Psalm 24:3-4 says: "Who shall ascend into the hill of the LORD? or who shall stand in his holy place? He that hath clean hands, and a pure heart" (Ps 24:3-4a). Who is he that has clean hands and a pure heart? No doubt, only the Lord Jesus Christ! It is only through Him and in union with Him that our worship may ascend unto God, who is transcendently holy. "I am the way, the truth, and the life: no man cometh unto the Father, but by me," says our Saviour (Jn 14:6).

This is the reason for this rather brief, unscholarly and unpolished "commentary" of the Psalms, which is really a compilation of studies delivered at the PCC Prayer Meetings on Friday evenings between 2004 and 2012. We call it a Christological commentary for obvious reasons. We call it a cantorial commentary even though the English text expounded is the KJV, because our comments made herein are largely guided by the underlying principle that they are the Songs of our King, which He designed for us to sing in union with Him as our Worshipper-in-Chief. May the LORD our God, Christ our Prophet, Priest and King, and His Spirit bless this feeble effort for the glory of His name through the biblical and intelligent worship of His people! Amen.

—*JJ Lim*

---

[8] Michael LeFebvre, *Singing the Songs of Jesus: Revisiting the Psalms* (Ross-Shire: Christian Focus, 2010), 50.

Acknowledgements

All praise and thanks be to the LORD God Triune who has made this work possible by His ordination, redemption, providence and illumination.

Special thanks to my wife and children who bore with me as I laboured, sometimes at the expense of family time, to get this book ready over several years.

I am deeply indebted to the officers and members of Pilgrim Covenant Church, Singapore, who heard and critique my initially extempore comments, and later, prepared expositions of the Psalms during weekly prayer meetings. Thank you for your patience and often helpful comments!

Last, but not least, I would like to thank those who helped to proofread this work including my daughter, Anna, who made a valiant attempt at proofreading before the pressures of school work overwhelmed her resolve; aunty Janet Ng, who although unable to join us for public worship, painstakingly and prayerfully read through and corrected any typographical and grammatical errors she could find in the draft; sister Winnie Lee whose sharp eye spotted more typos as she read the initial release of the book with her daughter Lois; sister Bee Ha who not only culled out more errors, but pointed out the long and complex sentences that needed revision; Mr Peter Best who spotted more grammatical glitches and made helpful recommendations; as well as the *PCC Bulletin* team who proofread the initial versions of the expositions. Any remaining errors in this work are, without exception, mine.

—*JJ Lim, July 2019*

Psalm 1:
The Righteous One's Blessedness

The Book of Psalms is the inspired hymnbook of the Church. It may be known as the Song Book of the Kingdom because it comprises the songs of Christ given for His Church to sing in union with Him.[9] King David is known as "the sweet psalmist of Israel" (2 Sam 23:1). But David wrote in the Spirit of Christ so that the Psalms are not just the songs of David, but the songs of Christ, the greater David. Writing to the Colossians, the Apostle Paul says:

> "Let the word of Christ dwell in you richly in all wisdom; teaching and admonishing one another in psalms and hymns and spiritual songs, singing with grace in your hearts to the Lord" (Col 3:16).

The Greek terms, psalms, hymns and spiritual songs were all used in the Septuagint to refer to the Psalms. The Septuagint is a Greek translation of the Old Testament used by most of the apostles and apostolic believers.

The Holy Spirit would have us fill our hearts with the words of Christ in the Psalms so that we may sing not only in worship, but in admonishment and instruction to one another.

This background is essential if we are to appreciate the Psalms more fully. Psalm 1 is no exception. Many have commented that this is like the introduction to the whole book of Psalms, and for good reasons. In this Psalm you will find a description of the righteous man in contra distinction to a wicked man. But who is the righteous man? The Apostle Paul—paraphrasing Psalm 14 and 53—says: "There is none righteous, no not one" (Rom 3:10).

So, who is the righteous man? Well, the answer is obvious, isn't it? Paul is not saying that there is absolutely no one at all righteous: for there is one who is truly righteous in the eyes of God, even Jesus Christ the righteous (1 Jn 2:1). And besides, the Scriptures also teach us that the righteousness of Christ is imputed to those who believe in Him so that as Jesus Christ is the Righteous One, all who believe in Him are righteous ones in God's sight. And not only so, they are infused with the righteousness of Christ, in regeneration and sanctification, so that they have a real beginning in righteousness that is growing day by day.

Psalm 1, and all the other Psalms, therefore, is about the Lord Jesus Christ, directly and absolutely; and it is about believers united to him, indirectly and subjectively.

So, when we talk about the Righteous or Righteous One in this Psalm and all the Psalms following, we are speaking about Christ; and what the Christian ought to be and has begun to be.

Psalm 1 may be entitled *"The Righteous One's Blessedness."* In it we are given to sing three things about the Righteous One which conduce to His blessedness:

1. v. 1-2   His Attitude

2. v. 3-4   His Significance

3. v. 5-6   His Destiny

---

[9] "When you sing the Psalms, you are actually singing the songs of Jesus, with Jesus as your songleader....it is in the biblical Psalms alone that Jesus himself, our priestly king, leads our sung proclamations in the presence of the Father" (Michael LeFebvre, *Singing the Songs of Jesus: Revisiting the Psalms* [Ross-shire: Christian Focus Publications, 2010], 50-51)

1. His Attitude

¹ Blessed is the man that walketh not in the counsel of the ungodly, nor standeth in the way of sinners, nor sitteth in the seat of the scornful. ² But his delight is in the law of the LORD; and in his law doth he meditate day and night.

To be blessed, simply stated, is to be happy. Every person has a natural, God-given desire to be happy. Therefore, every man will seek his own happiness. Many will seek happiness by acquiring power, wealth and health. Many will also seek it by way of food, drinks and entertainment. This is why these industries are so huge. But all these will only create a sense of happiness in the body. They do not produce a truly lasting blessedness that touches the soul.

True blessedness, as we are given to sing in this Psalm, is to be found in the way of the Lord.[10] And mind you, this way is not defined by the physical actions of walking, standing and sitting. You see, verses 1 and 2 must go together since they are connected by the comparative disjunction, "but." Verse 2 is about attitude; therefore verse 1 would naturally also be about attitude.

Four things are said about the attitude of the truly blessed man in these two verses. Three of them are negative, and one of them is positive.

- Firstly, the Righteous One does not WALK with the ungodly. That is, He does not go along with them. He does not take advice from them on how to live. He does not live according to the principles adopted by the ungodly.

- Secondly, the Righteous One does not STAND in the way of sinners. Not only does He not go along with sinners, He does not agree with them. He does not take a stand with them.

- Thirdly, the Righteous One does not SIT in the seat of the scornful. That is, He does not judge anything according to the ungodly, scornful standards of the wicked. Note how the terms *"ungodly"*, *"sinners"* and *"scorners"* are used synonymously to describe the wicked. The wicked, often, does not only have a low regard for the Law of God, but actually despises God's Word. And therefore, his judgement is always wicked, whereas the righteous would judge righteous judgement.

- But fourthly and conversely, the THOUGHTS of the righteous are shaped by the word of God. His delight is not in the ways of the world, but in the Law of the LORD. The wicked has no regard for God's Word. He either ignores it; or he pours scorn on it. He refuses to obey God's Law. Not so the righteous.

The Righteous One delights in the Law of the LORD. He thinks about God's Word. He meditates on it day and night. The word translated "meditate" (הָגָה, *hagah*) is a special word. It does speak of meditation, but not *silent* meditation. Most likely, this is a reference to singing the Law. The Psalter, of which Psalm 1 begins, is really a means provided for us, as it were, to sing the Law.

---

[10] For the purpose of consistency and clarity, we shall, throughout this book, refer to the Truine God, Jehovah as LORD, per the KJV; and the Messiah, Christ Jesus as "Lord." The son of God is, of course, the second Person of the Trinity, and so we must know that when we refer to the LORD it does not exclude Him; but when we refer to the Lord, we are usually referring to Christ as the God-Man, or as our Mediatorial King.

Christ our Lord, quite clearly, fits perfectly the description of one who loves the Law and meditates or sings the Law. He is called the Word of God (Jn 1:1). He was full of the word of God. He, no doubt, meditated on the word of God. He spoke the word of God in all situations. He sang the Law with His disciples. He interpreted and applied the word of God. He obeyed the word of God. He fulfilled the word of God. He lived the word of God. He is the Word of God.

Christ Jesus our Lord is the only one who fulfils the second verse of the Psalms absolutely and perfectly.

And He alone perfectly fulfils the first verse too! Yes, He did dine with sinners and publicans, and even with Pharisees, but He would never take His stand with them nor walk in their ways, nor judge anything according to their standards as we are sometimes tempted to do. Instead, He exposes their wickedness by His righteousness. This is why Malachi calls Him "the Sun of Righteousness" (Mal 4:2).

It is in this way, that our Saviour finds perfect blessedness.

But all who are united to Him, and who name His name will also find true blessedness in the same way! His yoke is easy and His burden is light (Mt 11:30). They find His commandments not grievous (1 Jn 5:3). They love Him, because they know the love of God (1 Jn 4:19). But those who walk otherwise find life to be an unending drudgery: for their sins are bound into a yoke (Lam 1:14). They find life meaningless and joyless. They hate God. They have no sense of God's love for His children.

As believers in this world, though we are not of this world, we are bound to have interactions with the wicked. The question is: Are we like the Lord Jesus—refusing to take a stand with the wicked, to walk in their ways or to judge according to their standard? Are we striving to be holy as Christ is holy?

All of us, who name the name of Christ, ought to imitate the Lord; and we will by God's grace become more and more like the Lord. Little by little, day by day, the Holy Spirit is working in us to make us hate sin and love God more and more. In this way, we are enabled, more and more, to sing this Psalm with sincerity in regard to ourselves.

2. His Significance

³ And he shall be like a tree planted by the rivers of water, that bringeth forth his fruit in his season; his leaf also shall not wither; and whatsoever he doeth shall prosper.

The Righteous One is like a tree. But it is not just any tree. He is not a tree which bears no fruit and sheds his leaves in winter. He is not like the Oak Tree which bears a fruit, which is more or less useless except to squirrels; and also sheds its leaves in winter.

The Righteous One is an evergreen tree. He does not shed His leaves in winter and He bears useful fruits. He is like an Olive Tree which is evergreen and bears a sweet and useful fruit.

Indeed, Christ is more than an Olive Tree. He is, rather, more like the Tree of Life described by the Apostle John in Revelation 22:

> "In the midst of the street of it, and on either side of the river, was there the tree of life, which bare twelve manner of fruits, and yielded her fruit every month [including the winter months]: and the leaves of the tree were for the healing of the nations" (Rev 22:2).

The Tree of Life in Revelation 22 may or may not be Christ Himself; but it is certainly a symbol and type of the ministry of the Lord Jesus Christ.

Christ alone fully and perfectly fulfils the analogy of the fruitful evergreen tree by the river.

During His earthly ministry, He bore much fruit with His life. The blind were made to see, the lame walked, the deaf heard, the dumb spoke, the lepers were cleansed, and the dead rose. And sinners were converted! Whatever He did, prospered in the hands of God. And God was greatly glorified. The Father was pleased with Him. He was reliable and trustworthy.

And He was consistently so. Even His death brought much fruit: for it is by His death, that we have life.

Who but Christ truly fulfils this third verse of the Book of Psalms?

But thank God that those who are united to Christ and bear His name, have the ability to imitate Him because His Spirit dwells in them. Those who are living in imitation of the Lord will be valuable members in society; in their families, in their schools, in their workplaces, in their churches, and indeed in the kingdom of God.

By contrast, the ungodly is like the chaff (v. 4).

⁴ The ungodly are not so: but are like the chaff which the wind driveth away.

Chaff refers to the lightweight bits of seed head or husks that must be separated from the grain before they are used for food.

In ancient days, when a wheat farmer harvests his crop, he will not only thresh the sheaves to get the grain, he will winnow what remains. For after threshing, a lot of chaff and straw will remain in the grain pile. What the farmer then does is to rake away the straw, and wait for the wind to blow. When the wind starts to blow, he will toss the grain into the air. The wind will blow away the light and valueless chaff.

The wicked is like the chaff. They are ultimately light and valueless. They do not produce any truly useful fruit in God's eyes. Whatever fruit they have are poisonous, like the fruit of the pong pong tree or that of the yellow oleander. They have no positive significance.

Do you feel your life to be significant and valuable? If not, it could just be because you have been walking in the way of the wicked. One who is united to Christ will have the attitude of Christ. He will make use of the means of grace that Christ appointed for him; and he will have a fruitful and meaningful life. He will be like a tree planted by the river that remains green and fruitful, through all the changing scenes of life, like his Master.

And he will have a destiny of joy as he shares in his Master's blessedness. Consider therefore, the destiny of the Righteous One...

3. His Destiny

⁵ Therefore the ungodly shall not stand in the judgment, nor sinners in the congregation of the righteous. ⁶ For the LORD knoweth the way of the righteous: but the way of the ungodly shall perish.

The word *"therefore"* tells us of consequences as well as destiny. *"Therefore the ungodly shall not stand in the judgment, nor sinners in the congregation of the righteous."*

The Bible tells us in many places that there is a judgement day. "It is appointed unto men once to die, but after this the judgment," says the apostle to the Hebrews (Heb 9:27). "For God shall bring every work into judgment, with every secret thing, whether *it be* good, or whether *it be* evil," says Solomon, after warning against living a life lived under the sun without regard to God (Ecc 12:14).

The Lord Jesus Himself tells us in His parable of the Sheep and Goats, Matthew 25:

[31] When the Son of man shall come in his glory, and all the holy angels with him, then shall he sit upon the throne of his glory: [32] And before him shall be gathered all nations: and he shall separate them one from another, as a shepherd divideth *his* sheep from the goats: [33] And he shall set the sheep on his right hand, but the goats on the left...

Then the King will say to the sheep: "Come ye blessed of my Father, inherit the kingdom prepared for you from the foundation of the world" (v. 34); whereas He will say to the goats: "Depart from me, ye cursed, into everlasting fire..." (v. 41).

The "blessed of [the] Father" are, no doubt, the righteous ones united to Christ! They will stand at the right hand of the King as His sheep. They are the congregation of the righteous that would inherit the kingdom of God. This kingdom was prepared for them from the foundation of the world. This is why we are given to sing in verse 6, "*the LORD knoweth the way of the righteous.*" The LORD knows because He planned it. He knows because He watches over it. He knows because He is lovingly directing their steps as they seek to walk in His ways.

The ungodly and unrighteous are not so. They "*shall not stand in the judgment.*" They will not stand "*in the congregation of the righteous.*"

In the day of judgement, they will not stand with the congregation of the righteous on the right hand of the throne of Christ. They will stand on the left hand. Nay, they will be bowing down, and cringing in shame and fear. For they know that they have wasted their lives away and they have no answer to give to the Lord. Their proud ways have come to an end. They will perish with their ungodly way: "*the way of the ungodly shall perish.*"

Conclusion

What is your life, dear reader?

Are you living in imitation of the Lord Jesus Christ that you may be an evergreen fruit tree by the riverside? By nature, we are all useless bits of chaff tossed to and fro by the wind; but in Christ we can be a useful, evergreen and fruitful tree by the riverside.

All believers have been planted by the riverside. We can draw refreshment and strength from the Spirit of Christ. We have been blessed that we may be a blessing. Only when we are a blessing to others will we be truly significant and truly happy; for only then will we be living a life that counts.

Shall we not walk in gratitude and thanksgiving with Christ our Saviour, who made such a life possible for us by His life and death as our Covenant Head? Shall we not strive to be like Him, that we may enjoy His blessedness that we sing about in this Psalm? And shall we not sing this Psalm in union with Christ often, to exhort and encourage each other to this end. Amen. Ω

Psalm 2:
The Righteous One's Anointing

Psalm 2 is all about the only begotten Son of God, the Lord Jesus Christ, the King of the Church. Hardly anyone in the history of the Church has any doubt that this is the case.

It is a Psalm appointed by our King for us to sing with Him about His own ordination as our King; and to rehearse the will of His Father for Him, for the Church, and for the world.

We may entitle it *"The Righteous One's Anointing."*

It can be divided naturally into four strophes.

- The 1st strophe is from verses 1-3, and speaks of how the world rages against the Messiah.

- In the 2nd strophe from verses 4-6, we read of God's response to their raging.

- The 3rd strophe is from verses 7-9, where we see the Messiah's response.

- In the 4th strophe from verse 10 to the end, we read of a charge to the proud and mighty. This charge is issued by the Lord to the world through the Church.

With this in mind, we may outline this Psalm thus:

1.	v. 1-3	The World's Raging
2.	v. 4-6	The Father's Laugh
3.	v. 7-9	The Son's Rejoinder
4.	v. 10-12	The Church's Call

1. The World's Raging

¹ Why do the heathen rage, and the people imagine a vain thing? ² The kings of the earth set themselves, and the rulers take counsel together, against the LORD, and against his anointed, saying, ³ Let us break their bands asunder, and cast away their cords from us.

Christ is the Anointed of the LORD. The Hebrew word for "anointed" is מָשִׁיחַ (*mâshîyach*), from which we get the transliteration Messiah. The word "Christ" comes from the Greek word Χριστός (*Christos*) which means "anointed one."

The heathen, the people of the world and their leaders, are raging against God and His Son, the Messiah. What is it to rage? The word rendered "rage" (רָגַשׁ, *ragash*) speaks of loud clamoring, violent commotion or public agitation. Why are they raging? They are raging against God and His Son because they feel that they are being hemmed in and held ransom by God's Laws. His ways are disagreeable to them. *"Let us break their bands asunder, and cast away their cords from us,"* they exclaim.

How do they rage in reality? They rage when they crucified the Lord who came to deliver man from sin (Acts 4:26-27). They rage when they persecute the servants of the Lord (cf. Acts 4:18, 23-26). They rage whenever they speak as if God does not exist, or God does not care. They rage whenever they call evil good and good evil. They rage when they seek to legalise homosexual marriages. They rage when they try to take away the death penalty for violent crimes. They rage when they insist that abortion is a right and not murder. They rage when immorality and wickedness are paraded as entertainment. They rage when employers exploit employees. They rage when churches are burned. They rage when they campaign for atheism and evolution.

The world cares not for God or for Christ. They do not want His rule. They want to break away from Him. Like Adam, our first father, they imagine that freedom and enjoyment are found in living according to their own desires and standards. They consider any restriction based on God's Word to be bondage. But despite what they say, Christ and His Gospel do not bound men, any more than wings do to birds.

What will be God's response? His response will be to laugh.

2. The Father's Laugh

The world is throwing a tantrum. In a certain way it looks funny. It is like a little spider waving its arms, and raving and ranting against a giant. What will the giant do? What will the Creator of the heaven and earth do?

> [4] *He that sitteth in the heavens shall laugh: The Lord shall have them in derision.* [5] *Then shall he speak unto them in his wrath, and vex them in his sore displeasure.* [6] *Yet have I set my king upon my holy hill of Zion.*

God will laugh!

Were it not for the fact that the world is raging against the thrice holy God, the Creator of the heaven and earth, their raging would indeed be funny to behold.

But the world is raging against their Creator to whom they owe respect and honour. Like a little spoilt brat, they are throwing their tantrum, thinking that the Father will not do anything.

Therefore, God will visit them with His wrath! He will put down their rebellion. He will punish the world for their raging and rebellion. One word from Him, and the world will be silent forever.

But God is merciful and longsuffering. "[6] *Yet have I set my king upon my holy hill of Zion,*" He says. Instead of destroying the world, He sets up His Son as the King upon the holy hill of Zion. That is, He has appointed Christ as King and Ruler over His Church. The holy hill of Zion is the Church.

God is withholding His wrath, not willing that any of those appointed to salvation should perish. He is calling upon the world to repent and to return to Him.

He is calling them not with the sword or with threatening, but with the Gospel of peace of the Lord Jesus Christ.

Christ is on His holy hill, ruling His people by His grace; in order that His people, as a city set upon a hill, may beckon the world to abandon its raging, to come and seek a peace that will endure unto all eternity.

What does Christ say?

3. The Son's Rejoinder

> [7] *I will declare the decree: the LORD hath said unto me, Thou art my Son; this day have I begotten thee.*

These are the words of Christ speaking about what the Father said unto Him. "*Thou art my*

Son; this day have I begotten thee," says the Father to the Son. Now, take note that the Father does not say, "This day have I begotten thee, therefore thou art my Son." He says, "Thou art my Son, this day have I begotten thee." Christ is the eternally begotten Son of God, but there is a sense in which He was begotten in time. In particular, this verse seems to speak of His being begotten in time.

What does He mean? Thankfully, we have an inspired commentary on this verse from the lips of the Apostle Paul. We read this in Acts 13:30-33:

> "³⁰ But God raised him from the dead: ³¹ And he was seen many days of them which came up with him from Galilee to Jerusalem, who are his witnesses unto the people. ³² And we declare unto you glad tidings, how that the promise which was made unto the fathers, ³³ God hath fulfilled the same unto us their children, in that he hath raised up Jesus again; as it is also written in the second Psalm, Thou art my Son, this day have I begotten thee."

In other words, when the Father says to the Lord, "*Thou art my Son, this day have I begotten thee,*" He is speaking metaphorically about His resurrection from the dead.

The resurrection is like a new birth.

Christ Jesus is seated on the throne on the holy hill of Zion because He laid down His life for His Church. Indeed, He rose again from the dead and is seated at the right hand of the throne of God. The writer of Hebrews speaks of how Christ, having laid down His life to purge our sin, is seated at the right hand of the majesty on high and upholding all things by the word of His power (Heb 1:1-3).

And Christ has the promise of His Father to have whatever He prays for. He has promised Him that all the world will be brought in subjection to Him upon His request:

> ⁸ *Ask of me, and I shall give thee the heathen for thine inheritance, and the uttermost parts of the earth for thy possession.* ⁹ *Thou shalt break them with a rod of iron; thou shalt dash them in pieces like a potter's vessel.*

Whatever the Son asks the Father, He will give. If He would ask the Father to withhold His hand of mercy today, the world will perish.

The fact is Christ is in control. The only reason why the world is still raging is because Christ is interceding on behalf of His elect. Christ laid down His life for us. He is ruling the world for our good and for the glory of God.

Well, beloved brethren, when we look at the world in turmoil and we see the heathen and even professing believers raging against God, it is easy for us to become discouraged. It is easy for us to become disillusioned.

What is the solution to such discouragement? The solution is to think about Christ. It is to remember that He is on the throne, having laid down His life for us. He is in control; and one day every knee will bow and every tongue confess that He is LORD (Phil 2:10-11). In that day, every wrong will be righted; every injustice dealt with; and every tear will be wiped away. And those who are united to Christ will not only rule with Christ, but share in His glory (Rev 2:26-28).

What shall we do with this knowledge? Shall we not exhort one another? Shall we not call the world to bow down before the LORD?

4. The Church's Call

[10] *Be wise now therefore, O ye kings: be instructed, ye judges of the earth.* [11] *Serve the LORD with fear, and rejoice with trembling.* [12] *Kiss the Son, lest he be angry, and ye perish from the way, when his wrath is kindled but a little. Blessed are all they that put their trust in him.*

Here is a call to the kings and judges, to the mighty and proud of the world. When we sing the Psalms, we not only exhort and encourage one another, we are calling upon all who hear us with the word of God.

The world is foolishly raging against the LORD. We who know better must not remain silent. We must call the world to repentance. One of the ways we must do so is by singing the word of God and by our testimony in private conversations and public declarations.

We must call the world to be wise. We must call the world to serve the LORD. And not just serve the LORD, but serve Him with a filial fear. And we must call the world to rejoice in the LORD. And not just to rejoice, but rejoice with trembling. We must serve the LORD and rejoice in Him for who He is.

We must call the world to kiss the Son, to embrace Him as their King and Saviour. We must warn the world that though Christ will receive all who come unto Him in contrition, His patience has a limit. There will come a day when His anger will burn against all who remain unrepentant. The day is called, in the Book of Revelation, The Day of the Wrath of the Lamb.

Let us, therefore, as the body of Christ, warn the world. Let us call for repentance. But let us encourage all to trust in Christ: *"Blessed are all they that put their trust in him."* This must be the desire of our hearts as we call upon all who will heed our entreaty to *"Kiss the Son,"* so that they and we ourselves will enjoy the blessedness of the Son.

Conclusion

True happiness is not found in the freedom of the world. The freedom of the world is the freedom of a fish swimming in the toxic water of a polluted river. The fish is slowly dying.

True happiness can only be found in Christ. Let us trust Him. Let us call the world to trust in Him; and let us apply the call to ourselves. We must submit to His rule with love mingled with fear. He is our King and Saviour. Amen Ω

Psalm 3:
The Righteous One's Safety
in the Midst of Foes

Psalm 3 is hardly ever regarded as a Messianic Psalm. David wrote it when he fled from Absalom his son who wanted to take over the throne.

But David, no doubt, wrote in the Spirit of Christ. David was a type of Christ in many respects. His experiences and emotions reflected what our Lord Himself went through in His days of humiliation.

For this reason, when you have gone through the book of Psalms, you will realise that almost every one of them could have been taken by our Lord in His lips, to apply to some particular situation during His own earthly life.

Indeed, some of the Psalms—such as Psalm 22—can hardly be applied to David, whereas they so clearly fitted into the earthly life of our Lord.

This is perhaps why the apostles generally understood that the Psalms refer to Christ, and that He is speaking about Himself in them. Thus, we have a good basis to believe that the Holy Spirit intends for us, when we read or sing the Psalms, to understand them as being directly applicable to the Lord Himself. It is in this way that the Lord is said to join us in the congregation, nay, lead us, to sing when we sing the Psalms (Heb 2:12).

We therefore agree with Andrew Bonar, who noting that this Psalm may be known as "a prayer of the Messiah," remarks:

> Every member of Christ may use it... We feel as if sympathy were more sure to us, when we know that the Lord Jesus himself once was in circumstances when such a ... hymn expressed his state and feelings; for now every believer can say, "My Head once used this Psalm; and while I used its strains, his human heart will recall the day of his humiliation, when himself was comforted thereby."

Bearing this in mind, let us consider this Psalm, by thinking about how it applies to our Lord in the first place; and how we may apply it to ourselves in the second place. We may entitle it *"The Righteous One's Safety in the Midst of Foes."* As the Righteous One found comfort in it, righteous ones united to Him may find the same comfort in Him through it.

We may discern three sections in this Psalm. As there are three *selahs* in it, we may expect the logical strophes or sections to correspond nicely with their placement; but for some reason, they do not match up so well. The first section is from verses 1-2, where we are given to sing about the Lord's persecution. In the second section, verses 3-6, we are given to share in the Lord's confidence. Finally, in verses 7-8, we have an expression of the Lord's petition.

1. v. 1-2   The Lord's Persecution

2. v. 3-6   The Lord's Confidence

3. v. 7-8   The Lord's Prayer

1. The Lord's Persecution

[1] *LORD, how are they increased that trouble me! many are they that rise up against me.* [2] *Many there be which say of my soul, There is no help for him in God. Selah.*

During our Lord's earthly ministry, He initially made many friends. He was healing the sick, casting out demons and feeding the multitude. Many people were drawn to Him.

But as He began to teach hard doctrine, more and more people began to forsake Him (cf. Jn 6:66). And not only so, but more and more turned against Him (cf. Jn 8:31, 59). Eventually our Lord had more enemies than friends. "*LORD, how are they increased that trouble me! many are they that rise up against me!*" our Lord must have cried.

Oh, how these enemies of our Lord taunted Him! Remember how they insulted him: "Say we not well that thou art a Samaritan, and hast a devil?" (Jn 8:48). Recall how they mocked Him: "He saved others; himself he cannot save" (Mk 15:31). "He trusted in God; let him deliver him now, if he will have him: for he said, I am the Son of God" (Mt 27:43).

Would not our Lord have taken the words of the Psalm in His lips, "*Many there be which say of my soul, There is no help for him in God*" (v. 2).

Now, none of us will fully understand the grief of our Lord, as His enemies increased in number and their hostility increased in intensity, for He is the holy Son of God.

But all who are the disciples of Christ will taste of the same kind of persecution to some degree. Our Lord says:

"[18] If the world hate you, ye know that it hated me before it hated you. [19] If ye were of the world, the world would love his own: but because ye are not of the world, but I have chosen you out of the world, therefore the world hateth you. [20] Remember the word that I said unto you, The servant is not greater than his lord. If they have persecuted me, they will also persecute you; if they have kept my saying, they will keep yours also" (Jn 15:18-20).

How should we comfort ourselves when we are persecuted? We may comfort ourselves by recalling and meditating on God's Word. We may especially comfort ourselves by singing the word of Christ, remembering that He suffered similarly for our sakes.

At the same time, let us remember our Lord's confidence in His Father.

2. The Lord's Confidence

[3] *But thou, O LORD, art a shield for me; my glory, and the lifter up of mine head.* [4] *I cried unto the LORD with my voice, and he heard me out of his holy hill. Selah.*

In the Psalms and indeed in the whole of Scripture, the name of God, Jehovah, can apply to God Triune, to the Father, to the Son or to the Holy Ghost.

When the word was taken in the lips of our Lord, it would usually apply to the Father or to the Triune God as represented by the Father.

The Lord Jesus was persecuted and tormented. But He never did lose hope. His eyes were constantly on His Father. He knew that His Father would hear His prayer. He therefore looked to His Father to protect Him as a shield, and to exalt and encourage Him. "*Thou, O LORD, art a shield for me; my glory, and the lifter up of mine head*" (v. 3).

When all things around Him taunt Him to hang His head in sorrow, the thought of His Father's glory and love alone would have lifted up His head. The lifter up of His head is His Father. Thus, in His High Priestly Prayer, He prayed:

"[4] I have glorified thee on the earth: I have finished the work which thou gavest me to do.

^{5} And now, O Father, glorify thou me with thine own self with the glory which I had with thee before the world was" (Jn 17:4-5).

Our Saviour prayed. He prayed long meditative prayers such as in His High Priestly Prayer. He also prayed urgent, ejaculatory prayers with audible cries (v. 4a). Are we not told in Hebrews 5:7 that "in the days of his flesh", He "offered up prayers and supplications with strong crying and tears unto him that was able to save him from death, and was heard in that he feared"?

As our Saviour prayed, so we must pray. As He cried with passion, so ought we to cry. As the Father was a shield unto His Son, so He is a shield unto us in His Son. Indeed, the Son is a shield unto us especially in taking upon Himself all the darts that should pierce our hearts with sorrows because of our sin. As the Father glorified His only begotten Son, so He will glorify His adoptive sons with Him (cf. 1 Jn 3:2). As the Father lifted up His Son's head, so He lifts up our head in Him, especially when we are given the assurance that we can do all things through Him who strengthens us (Phil 4:13).

Our Saviour was heard (v. 4b). He found the peace in His heart that enabled Him to sleep each night despite the dangers all around Him, verse 5:

^{5} I laid me down and slept; I awaked; for the LORD sustained me. ^{6} I will not be afraid of ten thousands of people, that have set themselves against me round about.

As He is fully human, our Lord needed to rest. But how was He to sleep when so many problems beset Him? How was He to rest when so many enemies were in His life? The Lord was able to sleep because He trusted in His Father. He knew His Father would sustain and protect Him. As long as His time was not yet come, He knew that nothing could touch Him.

So, He slept in the storm, not afraid of the great wind and waves. So, He slept in the midst of persecution and enmity, not afraid even if ten thousand people who hated Him surrounded Him. He slept peacefully each time He laid down His head to sleep.

Such was His confidence in His Father. Such is the confidence we may have in Him as our elder brother.

But our Lord was not sanguine or insouciant. He did not have a care-less attitude. He was able to rest not because He did not care about what would happen to Him. It was rather that He had full confidence in His Father. This is why He would have us memorialise in song His prayer to the Father. For even as He acknowledged how He was able to rest unafraid, He called unto His Father to arise for Him.

Consider therefore, His prayer.

3. The Lord's Prayer

^{7} Arise, O LORD; save me, O my God: for thou hast smitten all mine enemies upon the cheek bone; thou hast broken the teeth of the ungodly. ^{8} Salvation belongeth unto the LORD: thy blessing is upon thy people. Selah.

He calls upon His Father with the encouragement that He always hears His prayer. God does not close His eyes to the wicked works of the enemies of His children.

The enemies of God's children inevitably think that they can do what they do with impunity. So, they mock God's children or use innuendos to sneer at them. Or they speak evil of God's children behind their backs. They take advantage of them thinking that they would not retaliate.

Well, it is true that God's children will probably not retaliate; for they know that vengeance belongs to the Lord.

But God will retaliate. He will arise to deliver His people. He will arise with fierce wrath against their enemies. He does not only give them a slap in the face, He gives them a knockout punch. *"He smites the ungodly upon the cheek bone, he breaks their teeth."*

God's dealings with the enemies of His people testify of His wrath against them. So, David prayed that the LORD again arise on his behalf; so, the Lord prayed unto His Father that He would arise on His behalf.

Are you facing much persecution and afflictions, dear reader? Be sure that the Lord has not forsaken you. He will never leave you nor forsake you.

He will not turn a blind eye to all the wicked things that have been said and done against you, who are beloved of the LORD.

He has promised to arise for you, for salvation belongs to Him; and His blessings are reserved for His people.

So, trust Him; so, plead with Him according to His promise. You do not need to suffer in silence when you are persecuted or when you are taken advantage of.

Learn from your Saviour who, when He was reviled, reviled not; but committed Himself to His Father (1 Pet 2:23).

Are you troubled by many things, dear child of God? Have you been unable to sleep at night because those worries keep replaying in your mind? Oh, will you not learn to do as your Saviour did and commit all things to the hand of your heavenly Father; and then lay down your head and sleep—not allowing those things that trouble you to continue to play in your hearts and minds, so that you have no rest.

Conclusion

Thank God for this 3rd Psalm. As our Lord was safe in the midst of foes and troubles; so too we who hope in the name of the Lord can have peace in the midst of foes and tribulations.

Let us remember that as our Lord faced persecution and trouble, so all who are united to Him and following in His footsteps can expect the same. But just as our Lord walked confidently with the Father as His shield, His glory and the Lifter of His head, so let us walk with the same faith and confidence that we may rest soundly each night as our Lord did. And as our Lord prayed, so let us learn to pray, believing that our prayers will be heard because of God's great love for us, for Christ's sake. Amen. Ω

Psalm 4:
The Righteous One's Rest in Perplexity

In times of perplexity and distress we often find it difficult to sleep. I remember an occasion when on a Saturday evening, my computer crashed before I printed out my sermon notes for the next day! I worked all night to recover my notes to no avail. When I was compelled to get some sleep, I had a difficult time sleeping. I had no peace. The whole week of work seemed to have gone down the drain. All I could do was to rely on my memory to preach the sermon. So I was running the sermon through my mind, trying to recall it. And then, when I manage to catch some sleep, it was a troubled sleep with dreams involving ghosts—I think because we were working with a *Norton* recovery utility known as "Ghost"!

It was a difficult night. But in the morning as I began to meditate on Psalm 4, I realised I could have peace in the LORD despite the perplexity that plagued me the whole night!

Notice how this Psalm begins with perplexity:

[1] Hear me when I call, O God of my righteousness: thou hast enlarged me when I was in distress; have mercy upon me, and hear my prayer.

And look at how it ends in verse 8:

[8] I will both lay me down in peace, and sleep: for thou, LORD, only makest me dwell in safety.

We may entitle this Psalm *"The Righteous One's Rest in Perplexity."* The Righteous One is Christ, even as righteous ones are those who are united to Christ and therefore are imputed with a righteousness acceptable to God.

Psalm 4 was probably penned by David on the same occasion as Psalm 3, seeing that there are much similarities between both Psalms. If so, it was borne out of the deepest anguish that a mere man can experience: For what deeper grief can afflict a godly man than that his own son whom he loves not only rebells against him, but stirs up others to do the same. Nevertheless, David's experience pales in comparison with what our Lord went through. Yet, we need not doubt that David was given the painful experience so that He might pen, under inspiration, but with affection, the immense grief that the greater David would endure on our behalf. Thus, we can be sure that it would have been used by the Lord Himself as He faced great perplexity in His earthly ministry. In fact, the Lord, of all men, would have faced most intensely, the perplexity, frustration and exasperation alluded to in this Psalm. His distress was far more profound than what anyone of us would have experienced.

The Lord had hardly begun His ministry when a multitude of people tried to kill Him (Lk 4:29). They hated His message. And if this is not perplexing enough, the Lord knew from prophecy that His own disciples would betray Him and the rest would forsake Him in His hour of need. How perplexed can a person be? Our Lord, no doubt, would have sung or meditated on the words of this Psalm as He went through those days of anguish. This, after all, is His own song, which was inspired by His Spirit, that the Church through the ages may sing in union with Him. He would have us to sing, no doubt, to reflect on what He experienced for our salvation; and to exhort one another to imitate Him when we are called to take up our cross to "fill up that which is behind of the afflictions of Christ" (Col 1:24).

And as our Lord used those words so we too can use them in times of perplexity, whether it has to do with people, or circumstance, or machine. Whatever the circumstance of perplexity may be in our life, we can come to this Psalm and meditate on it to encourage ourselves in the LORD.

This Psalm has four parts. Like the previous Psalm, they do not correspond well to the musical divisions suggested by the "selahs." You see, the word "Selah" actually breaks the Psalm into strophes; but often these strophes do not correspond to logical sections in the Psalm as far as content is concerned. Does this not show us that the words of the Psalm has priority over its musical structure, unlike in the case of modern hymnody, in which words are forcibly fitted into predetermined structures?

The Scottish Psalter reflects the biblical priority of content over musical structure by dropping the *selahs* altogether. It is, after all, nearly impossible, in an English translation, to match the musical strophes with the logical paragraphs very nicely all the time.

In any case, these are the divisions we can derive by analysing the content of the Psalm:

1. v. 1   The Righteous One's Cry Unto the LORD
2. v. 2-3   The Righteous One's Chagrin
3. v. 4-5   The Righteous One's Counsel to the Godly
4. v. 6-8   The Righteous One's Words of Comfort

As mentioned: the Righteous One is Christ, whereas we are righteous ones in Him. What He experienced for us, we can experience in Him. Consider, then, this Psalm according to these divisions and see how they ought to encourage us in our times of trials.

1. The Righteous One's Cry

¹ Hear me when I call, O God of my righteousness: thou hast enlarged me when I was in distress; have mercy upon me, and hear my prayer.

Here the Righteous One, Christ our Lord cries to the Father in a moment of distress. Notice how even as He cries unto the Father to hear Him, He reminds Himself of how the Father heard Him in the past, and that the Father never fails: *"Thou hast enlarged me when I was in distress."*

We may paraphrase and enlarge on how our Lord might have prayed:

"I felt very constricted. I was stuck. I felt like I was between two brick walls—not knowing how to get out of the situation... But you have enlarged me, you gave me freedom in my heart. Now LORD, hear me again. Hear my prayers as I am in this present strait, for I cry unto you with the assurance that you can and will deliver."

As our Lord was delivered, so we too can expect the LORD to deliver. When we cry unto the Father, we can cry on the basis not just that He has delivered us in the past, but on the basis that He has delivered our Head, who laid down His life for us. We have tremendous assurance to cry out unto the LORD.

Are you, dear child of God, facing a time of distress? Are you in a perplexing situation, wondering what is going to happen next? Do you find yourself tired and yet unable to sleep as tears flood your eyes and a thousand thoughts swirl in your mind? Flee to Christ. By Him, go to the Father!

2. The Righteous One's Chagrin

² O ye sons of men, how long will ye turn my glory into shame? how long will ye love vanity, and seek after leasing? Selah. ³ But know that the LORD hath set apart him that is godly for himself: the LORD will hear when I call unto him.

It can be extremely perplexing for a child of God to deal with people who are disagreeable or with the enemies of the gospel. If you ever deal with such persons, you will, no doubt, feel vexed by the things that you have to hear.

Such was the experience of our Lord at the cross, only that it involves not just a vexation, but a turning of the glory of the Righteous One into shame. The Righteous One trusted the LORD. He trusted in the Father. But enemies derided Him: "He trusted in God, let him save himself, then deliver us. Let him prove that He is indeed the Son of God!" In so doing, they added grief to His already difficult circumstance.

"How long?" the Lord asks. How long will you love vanity and seek after idleness, or seek after the idols of this world without recognizing that there is one living and true God, who alone is in control? Know you not that the LORD has set apart him that is godly for Himself?

As the Righteous One expresses His chagrin over the sons of man who dishonour God in their failure to acknowledge His Son; He, at the same time, tells them to look and see how the LORD would deal kindly with those who are walking according to His ways.

The righteous need not be jealous over the prosperity of the wicked. Nor should the righteous succumb under the evil suggestions of the wicked when they mock: "You trust in the Lord, now see what you have got. The Lord is not hearing your prayer." We must not succumb to their temptations. Though we are exasperated at what they say, we must turn unto the Lord, and yet again acknowledge that He is in control. And we should bravely remind the wicked: There is *one* living and true God. Do you not fear God?

3. The Righteous One's Counsel

⁴ *Stand in awe, and sin not: commune with your own heart upon your bed, and be still. Selah.* ⁵ *Offer the sacrifices of righteousness, and put your trust in the LORD.*

Now what do we do when we fall into times of perplexity? Very often, when we are perplexed, our tempers become very short. We become very impatient. Is that not true? When you face frustration you become very impatient. You become very angry easily over little things here and there. But what does the Lord teach us? The Righteous One who was tempted in all points like as we are, yet without sin, calls upon us in such a circumstance to *"Stand in awe, and sin not"* (v. 4). What does *"Stand in awe"* mean? Remarkably, there is a reference to this verse in the New Testament though it is not obvious to many of us. In fact, this verse is quoted directly, word-for-word from the Septuagint translation in Ephesians 4:26a in the words, "Be ye angry, and sin not." But the original Hebrew is translated in our English version as *"Stand in awe, and sin not."* How do they connect? "Be ye angry..." versus *"Stand in awe"*? How can the same Hebrew expression be translated so differently?

Well, the connection lies in the fact that when you are angry you are actually amazed. You are amazed and you allow those feelings of amazement to rise up and boil in your heart. This is anger. So what the Righteous One is telling us is this: "There may be times when you are so amazed to the point that you are angry, but do not sin."

There is such a thing as righteous anger. Our Lord was angry when He saw the people selling doves and changing money in the temple courtyard. He was so angry, that He made a whip and drove the people out. Did He sin? Of course not! It was righteous anger. Our Lord was tempted in all points like as we are yet without sin. But He was angry. So anger itself is not necessarily wrong. But do not be angry to the point of sin.

In times of great perplexity, you may get angry. But realise that it is very easy to slide into sin in such situations. Think about it. The computer breaks down. You get angry. What are you angry with? The computer is a dumb thing. You can't get angry with it. So in the final analysis you are really angry with God—because God is He who is in control over all things, and providentially bringing all things to pass. So your anger becomes sin.

Similarly, you can be angry with another person unjustly. Maybe he made a mistake unintentionally. Unfortunately his mistake got you into trouble and inconvenience. And so you get angry. Who are you angry with? Is it with the person who made the mistake? But it was an accident! So you are angry unjustly! You sinned! But the Lord reminds us in this circumstance, "Watch your heart." You may be angry, but sin not. Not only that, but do not let the sun go down upon your wrath. Commune with your own heart upon the bed and be still in the night.

Well, that was what I failed to do. Lying there in the night, I was not angry, but I was restlessly tossing and turning. When I finally managed to sleep, it was a disturbed sleep. We must learn to lie down. Be still. Trust in the Lord that He would bring all things to pass and that all would turn out well for those who trust in Him.

When that becomes clear, we must offer the sacrifices of righteousness (v. 5). Praise the LORD, and trust Him. *Put your trust in the LORD.* Worship Him in your perplexity. Our Lord did so. And we must learn to do so as we consider...

4. The Righteous One's Comfort

[6] There be many that say, Who will shew us any good? LORD, lift thou up the light of thy countenance upon us.

Who will show us any good? *The LORD* will show us good. And indeed, we can have the confidence that whatever happens, He is working all things together for our good. Does not the word of God assure us of that? So we call unto the LORD, "Lift up Your countenance upon us. Smile upon us. Give us grace to trust in you, and to know that you are in control." Then will we be able to speak of what the LORD has done for us with that joyful assurance that the Righteous One had:

[7] Thou hast put gladness in my heart, more than in the time that their corn and their wine increased.

When you are in perplexity, as you cry unto the LORD to look down upon you with His heavenly smile, remember how He has in time past blessed you. And He has given you *much more* to enjoy than in the times when the corn and wine of our fathers increased.

In those ancient agricultural days, when the harvest was good, and there was a lot of corn and wine, people were smiling all the time. But we know that the Lord has given us far more than those things to enjoy. So what if we are perplexed for a moment in our present life? Have we not greater reasons to trust our heavenly Father? Has He not given us the glorious hope that one day all tears and sorrows will pass away? In that day, there will be no more perplexity, no more pain, no more sorrow. And so with that thought, we must do as our Covenant Head was able to do, namely, to sleep in the storm.

[8] I will both lay me down in peace, and sleep: for thou, LORD, only makest me dwell in safety.

Conclusion

Thou, LORD, enablest me to dwell in safety. Whatever the circumstance in my life, I know thou knowest best. My Saviour testified of that in His worst trials for my sake. And therefore I will sleep in peace. Help me, LORD. Amen. Ω

Psalm 5:
The Righteous One's Morning Meditations

Psalm 5 is not usually known as a Messianic Psalm. But the words in it certainly fit the lips and experience of our Lord, even better than it fitted David.

David was, no doubt, a man of prayer. He, no doubt, sought the LORD in prayer in the morning, as described in verse 3. But there is no reference in the historical accounts that he rose up early to pray. In contrast, our Lord was known to arise very early to pray, even before the sun arose.

We read in Mark 1:35, for example, "And in the morning, rising up a great while before day, He went out, and departed into a solitary place, and there prayed."

Similarly, if you read the Gospel accounts, you will not find any direct references to the Lord praying with loud crying in the fear of God. And yet the writer of Hebrews makes a strong point that He did so. We read this in Hebrews 5:7:

> "Who [i.e. the Lord Jesus] in the days of his flesh, when He had offered up prayers and supplications with strong crying and tears unto Him that was able to save Him from death, and was heard in that He feared."

Now, the word translated "crying" is the word κραυγῆς (*kraugēs*), which speaks of loud cries or even shrieking or shouting. Our Lord prayed with loud cries according to this verse.

Where did the apostle get this idea? Perhaps he was thinking about the Garden of Gethsemane. But if you read the account of our Lord in the Garden of Gethsemane, you will not find anything that suggests our Lord was praying with loud cries. Where then did the idea come from?

Could it be from Psalm 5? Look at verse 2: "*Hearken unto the voice of my cry.*" Interestingly, the word translated "cry" here occurs only once in the Hebrew Bible, and it is translated in the Septuagint (the Greek translation of the Old Testament) using the word κραυγῆς (*kraugēs*) which is exactly the word used in Hebrews 5:7!

And look at verse 7b: "in thy *fear* will I worship towards thy holy temple." The apostle to the Hebrews tells us that the Lord Jesus "offered up prayers and supplications with strong crying and tears ...and was heard in that He *feared*" (Heb 5:7).

Does it not appear that the writer of Hebrews, writing under inspiration, must have understood Psalm 5, as he does all the other Psalms, as not merely describing the experience of David, but rather the experience of Christ? David was but a type of Christ. By the providence of God, David was given experiences that would enable him to write about the inner feelings of Christ in the days of His flesh.

We may discern four sections in this Psalm:

1.　v. 1-3　　　An Earnest Plea

2.　v. 4-7　　　An Expression of Confidence in God's Hatred for Evil and Love for the Righteous

3.　v. 8-10　　　A Prayer for Guidance and Protection

4.　v. 11-12　　　An Exhortation Based on These Thoughts

With this in mind, and for our purpose in this study, let us glean three lessons from this

Psalm under the theme *"The Righteous One's Morning Meditations."* This is, after all, a Psalm which Christ would have us sing with Him and meditate with Him that there be synchrony between His heart and ours; and between His practice and ours.

First, let us consider how our Lord prayed in the morning.

1. Our Lord's Practice of Prayer

When we consider that Psalm 5 is not merely about David, but about our Lord Jesus in the days of His flesh, it is not difficult to see how this Psalm actually fills in some of the blanks that are left out in the Gospel accounts in regard to our Lord's earthly ministry.

In particular, when you read the Gospel accounts about the Lord getting up in the morning to pray, do you not wonder how our Lord prayed and what He prayed? Well, this Psalm gives us an idea.

This Psalm opens with an indication of how our Lord prayed. He prayed early. He prayed earnestly and with strong crying. He prayed aloud. He did not only petition His Father. He prayed conversationally. *"Give ear to my words, O LORD, consider my meditation,"* He says.

This was how our Lord prayed in the days of His flesh. He was the Son of God; and He was extremely busy. But He prayed. He did not just shoot a few arrows to heaven. No, no; He took time to enjoy fellowship with His Father. He told His Father about His fears and sorrows. He acknowledged who His Father is, and praised Him for how He deals with man.

His petitions were made with appropriate augmentations and arguments. *"[8] Lead me, O LORD, in thy righteousness because of mine enemies; make thy way straight before my face."* Notice how He appeals to the Father to lead Him: not in any way, but in righteousness. Notice how He calls upon His Father to consider His enemies. Our Lord had many enemies during the days of His flesh.

His prayers were conversations with His Father, but His prayers were not flippant. He worshipped with "fear" (v. 7). He was always reverential towards His Father. Never did He come to the Father sleepily and perfunctorily.

Oh, may we learn from the example of our Lord how we ought to pray.

This is our first lesson from this Psalm.

But now let's consider the things that move our Lord to pray in this Psalm: namely, His thoughts about man and God's relationship with them.

So our second lesson from this Psalm must be our Lord's attitude towards the wicked.

2. Our Lord's Attitude Towards the Wicked

We live in a day when political correctness is demanded of all public figures. Our Lord was not politically correct. He was simply correct. He was not afraid to call a snake, a snake; and a sheep, a sheep. He does not speak of snakes as legless sheep. He identifies them for what they are, for this is how God views them.

[4] For thou art not a God that hath pleasure in wickedness: neither shall evil dwell with thee. [5] The foolish shall not stand in thy sight: thou hatest all workers of iniquity. [6] Thou shalt destroy them that speak leasing: the LORD will abhor the bloody and deceitful

man....

⁹ For there is no faithfulness in their mouth; their inward part is very wickedness; their throat is an open sepulchre; they flatter with their tongue.

Our Lord, you must realise is not simply speaking about some people He did not like. He is speaking about the wicked in general.

Notice how the Apostle Paul quotes verse 9 in Romans 3:13.

"Their throat is an open sepulchre; with their tongues they have used deceit; the poison of asps is under their lips" (Rom 3:13).

Paul is, in the context, speaking about the natural man. "All men are by nature like that!" He is saying. In fact, "there is none righteous, no not one" (Rom 3:10).

It is clear, then, that in Psalm 5, the Lord is not merely speaking about some extraordinarily wicked person. He is speaking about the natural man in general.

All men are, by nature, wicked and hateful to God.

The Lord Jesus did not try to minimise God's hatred for the wicked. Even the elect are children of wrath before their conversion. How much more the reprobate?

How should we respond to this truth? Surely, we must not respond by showing hatred to unbelievers. No, no; the Lord Jesus Himself teaches us that our heavenly Father sends the rain and the sunshine on the just and the unjust. And He teaches us to be kind and merciful even to the wicked.

But this truth that our Lord teaches us should shape our prayers. How should we pray for the wicked? Surely, we must never pray that God will bless them temporarily, without praying for their conversion.

We should, in fact, in our prayer for unbelievers acknowledge how they are hateful to God, as our Lord did. And we must also be prepared to pray that the LORD will deal with the wicked in a robust way as our Lord does, verse 10:

¹⁰ Destroy thou them, O God; let them fall by their own counsels; cast them out in the multitude of their transgressions; for they have rebelled against thee.

But our Lord does not only think about the wicked. He thinks also about the righteous. So our third lesson must be on our Lord's attitude towards the righteous.

3. Our Lord's Attitude
Towards the Righteous

But who are the righteous? We just saw that there are none righteous, no not one. Who then are the righteous?

Well, the righteous are those who trust in the LORD:

¹¹ But let all those that put their trust in thee rejoice: let them ever shout for joy, because thou defendest them: let them also that love thy name be joyful in thee. ¹² For thou, LORD, wilt bless the righteous; with favour wilt thou compass him as with a shield.

The righteous are not righteous in themselves. They are righteous on account of Christ. They are righteous because God defends them from His own wrath. They are righteous because God has compassed them with, as it were, a shield.

Who is this shield? This shield is the Lord Jesus Christ Himself. He took on the arrows of God's wrath on our behalf.

Let us remind ourselves of how deeply our Lord loved us and was determined to bless us. In this Psalm, He would have us join Him to call upon God to bless us. He desires that we be able to shout for joy. But it is not just an empty desire. It is a desire that He made possible. We were wicked children of wrath. He laid down His life for us that we may be righteous in the sight of God. He died that we may have life. He became a curse for us in order that we may have God's blessing. He cried in pain that we might shout for joy.

What shall we do in the light of this truth? Shall we not turn away from sin? He hates sin so much, that He laid down His life to cleanse us of it. Shall we not resolve to lay down our life for Him, and for one another? Shall we not take positive steps to make sure that we can indeed live for Him?

Conclusion

Christ our Lord prayed fervently. He prayed for Himself that He might be guided in God's way. He prayed for the wicked—that God would glorify Himself by dealing with the wicked. And He prayed for the saints—that God would bless them. And in order that His prayers might be heard, He laid down His life that His Father might deal with Him as He would deal with the wicked—that having satisfied His wrath, He might receive us as a people whose sins have been paid for.

Thank God for Christ our Lord. Thank God that because of Him, we are not consumed. Shall we not love Him? Shall we not trust Him and serve Him joyfully. Shall we not sing in union with Him of His own experience, that by His Spirit working in us we might be transformed into His image, by the renewing of our minds? Amen. Ω

Psalm 6:
The Righteous One's "Rebuke Me Not"
when Sorely Chastised

Psalm 6 is one of seven Psalms known as Penitential Psalms. (The others are Pss 32, 38, 51, 130, 140 & 143). Penitential Psalms are often spoken of as if they are mutually exclusive to Messianic Psalms. It is thought that since the Messiah is altogether holy, He would have no occasion to ask the Father for mercy or to withhold His hand of chastisement.

But I am not comfortable with this view. I believe that this Psalm, as with all the other Psalms, is Messianic in one way or another. I agree with Andrew Bonar that this Psalm is not of David, but of the Son of David; for "the grief is too deep for any other." Bonar adds: "David may have been led by the Holy Ghost to write it when in anguish of soul, as well as suffering of body; through such a bruised reed the Spirit of God may have breathed. But surely he meant to tell of One greater than David—'the Man of Sorrows.'"

The Prophet Isaiah, speaking of the ministry of the Lord, says, "Surely he hath borne our griefs, and carried our sorrows: yet we did esteem him stricken, smitten of God, and afflicted" (Isa 53:4). Our Lord bore the griefs and sorrows that belong to us on account of our sin. He experienced what we ought to have experienced for our sin. Our heart is too cold and hardened to respond to sin in a way that is pleasing and acceptable to our holy heavenly Father. Christ our Lord took not only our punishment upon Himself, but our penitence too.

With this in mind, we see that this Psalm has essentially two parts: In verses 1-7, we see our Lord prostrated in the Garden of Gethsemane, crying unto His Father for mercy. In verse 8-10, we see Him, arising and declaring victory in His Father. Here is the *"Righteous One's 'Rebuke Me Not' when Sorely Chastised."* He is being chastised or, in fact, punished for the sin of His people.

    1.v. 1-7   A Cry for Mercy

    2.v. 8-10   A Cry of Deliverance

Consider first the cry of mercy of our Lord that reflects His anguish as He headed to the cross, and particularly as He paused in the Garden of Gethsemane to pray.

1. A Cry for Mercy

¹ O LORD, rebuke me not in thine anger, neither chasten me in thy hot displeasure.

Our Lord is bearing our sin. Upon Him is heaped the guilt of our sin. The wrath of His Father is hot against Him as a result. He knows that His Father is perfectly just to be angry with Him for He is our representative. But that does not make the punishment any less painful. And so He cries, "O LORD, rebuke me not." He is not saying He does not deserve the rebuke, but simply that He dreads the rebuke deeply. Did not He say in the Garden of Gethsamane: "O my Father, if it be possible, let this cup pass from me" (Mt 26:39)? The sentiments of the two petitions are equivalent.

² Have mercy upon me, O LORD; for I am weak: O LORD, heal me; for my bones are vexed.

He said to His disciples: "the spirit indeed is willing, but the flesh is weak" (Mt 26:41). I wonder if He was only referring to His disciples; or was He not also referring to Himself? For the word that is translated "willing", πρόθυμος (*prothumos*) is not one of the usual words for "willing" (βούλομαι [*boulomai*], εὐδοκέω [*eudokeō*]). It is rather a word that means "ready." In the two other occasions it is used in the New Testament, it is translated as "ready": "Watch ye and pray, lest ye enter into temptation. The spirit truly is *ready*, but the flesh is weak" (Mk 14:38); and "I am *ready* to preach the gospel to you that are at Rome also" (Rom 1:15).

Being fully man, our Lord would no doubt have felt the burden upon His flesh. In His divine Spirit, He was ready to go to the cross. But His flesh was weak. He must have felt empty in His stomach. He must have felt an aching in His bone. "*For my bones are vexed,*" He says. Do you not feel the same when great trouble comes upon your soul?

The Lord said: "the spirit truly is ready, but the flesh is weak." Perhaps he is not just speaking about His disciples. Perhaps He is suggesting that in His Spirit, He is prepared to go to the cross; but there is apprehension in His flesh.

But of course, it was not just His flesh that was vexed, but His soul as well:

> ³ *My soul is also sore vexed: but thou, O LORD, how long?* ⁴ *Return, O LORD, deliver my soul: oh save me for thy mercies' sake.*

Did not the Lord tell His disciples: "My soul is exceeding sorrowful, even unto death" (Mt 26:38)?

So here in verse 5, we see the Lord saying:

> ⁵ *For in death there is no remembrance of thee: in the grave who shall give thee thanks?*

Oh, how our Lord must have been tried as He anticipated the cross: for He knew that as He tasted death on behalf of His people, He would experience a season of deep darkness, when memories of God's mercy would be clouded by a sense of His wrath.

And He knew that if He were given over to the power of death, then neither He nor the Church will have occasion to give thanks unto the LORD.

> ⁶ *I am weary with my groaning; all the night make I my bed to swim; I water my couch with my tears.* ⁷ *Mine eye is consumed because of grief; it waxeth old because of all mine enemies.*

Our Lord certainly did not pray with dry eyes. No, no; the burden of sin and the assault of the wicked one upon His soul could not be borne without tears.

As He wept in sympathy with Mary, the sister of Lazarus; so He must have wept in the Garden of Gethsemane as He considered how He would be forsaken not only by His disciples, but, as it were, even by His Father.

But "weeping may endure for a night, but joy cometh in the morning" (Ps 30:5). So, in this Psalm, even as He anticipates the terror of the cross, our Lord looks forward to the deliverance that comes in answer to prayer. And so the Psalm concludes with...

2. A Cry of Deliverance

> ⁸ *Depart from me, all ye workers of iniquity; for the LORD hath heard the voice of my weeping.* ⁹ *The LORD hath heard my supplication; the LORD will receive my prayer.* ¹⁰ *Let all mine enemies be ashamed and sore vexed: let them return and be ashamed suddenly.*

The Father will always hear the prayer of His beloved Son. So our Lord confidently exclaims to those who would torment Him: "*Depart from me, all ye workers of iniquity*" (v. 8).

Do not these words sound familiar? Turn to Matthew 7:

"[21] Not every one that saith unto me, Lord, Lord, shall enter into the kingdom of heaven; but he that doeth the will of my Father which is in heaven. [22] Many will say to me in that day, Lord, Lord, have we not prophesied in thy name? and in thy name have cast out devils? and in thy name done many wonderful works? [23] And then will I profess unto them, I never knew you: *depart from me, ye that work iniquity*" (Mt 7:21-23).

Are these words not exactly the same? Well, turn to Luke 13:27. Here is a parable intended to teach exactly the same thing as in Matthew 7. What does the master of the house, who represents the Lord say? *"Depart from me, all ye workers of iniquity."*

Our Lord was led to the cross by the workers of iniquity. But these workers of iniquity do not stand alone. They are, as it were, representatives of all workers of iniquity throughout the ages. They comprise Jews and Gentiles; heathen and professing Christians. In Matthew 7, our Lord is clearly referring to those who would call Him Lord, Lord; or professing believers.

But make no mistake. It is not only false believers who will be sent off to eternal damnation.

All who oppose Christ, and all who refuse to submit to Him, are likewise the enemies of Christ. They will be sent away. Not only so, but everything in this world that is opposed to godliness and everything that Satan makes use of today, to bring shame to the name of Christ, will be destroyed. In that day, every knee will bow and every tongue will confess that Jesus is Lord. In that day, the war of the ages will come to a glorious end.

The prayer of our Lord would, in that day, be fully answered. What a wonder it will be as God's people behold their Saviour and themselves vindicated and exalted!

Conclusion

Although the Lord has taken upon Himself our grief and sorrow, He has given us His Spirit so that we may have a godly response when we fall into sin. At such times, rather than bottling up our grief, let us learn to express our sorrow with the words of this Psalm.

As we sorrow, let us remember that our Lord sorrowed on our behalf. We know that though we ought to sorrow, our tears can never wash away our sin as Rome teaches they can. No, no; even our repentance and sorrow are tainted with sin.

But thank God that we have a sympathetic Great High Priest, who was in all points tempted like as we are, yet without sin. And not only so, but though He did not fall into sin as we did, He felt the grief that we should be feeling so that we may know the restorative hand of our Father, though our repentance is tainted with pride.

Thank God we can sing this Psalm as a people united to Christ; whose sins have been forgiven for Christ's sake; who can plead with Christ, *"O LORD, rebuke me not"* even though we can't be certain we do not deserve the rebuke.

Are you discouraged because of sin? Are you struggling because you feel the hand of God's chastisement upon you? May I encourage you to meditate on the suffering and victory of our Lord as given in this Psalm? Let the words of this Psalm inspire you to pray with assurance, that you have a sympathetic high priest who fully understands your sorrows and grief. Look to Him with full confidence, and believe that all your struggles will come to an end, in the day that your heavenly Father completes His answer to the prayer of His Son for you. Amen. Ω

Psalm 7:
The Righteous One's Response to Slander

Psalm 7 was written by David under inspiration, when his heart was smarting in pain because of the words of Cush the Benjamite as the title suggests. Who is Cush the Benjamite? Well, the word Cush means "black" or "Ethiopian." So, some commentators suggest that it refers to the black-hearted Saul. But it is interesting to note that sin and wickedness are not usually represented by black colour in the Scripture. It is rather represented by red; whereas black represents suffering (SS 1:6; Jer 8:21; Isa 1:18).

Well, more likely Cush refers to someone who was in league with Saul the Benjamite; and who had apparently slandered David before Saul.

It was his slander that prompted David to write this "song of the slandered saint."

This title was suggested by Charles Spurgeon. It is a song that Christians who feel that they have been unjustly slandered can take up.

To be slandered is to be maligned or insulted by someone behind your back. This, as you can appreciate can be a very painful experience.

But it was also Spurgeon who pointed out that if someone were to say something bad about him to another, he would not get too upset because his slanderer could have said much worse things about him if only he knew the whole truth about him.

Is it not a fact that the things that anyone who slanders us say about us cannot be compared to what he could have said if he can read our hearts and our memories.

But if that is so, how can we honestly sing the words in verse 8: *"judge me, O LORD, according to my righteousness, and according to mine integrity that is in me"*?

Well, we can sing these words only because this song is no ordinary song. It was written in the Spirit of Christ. It is written to reflect what Christ the greater David would suffer in His own earthly life. It is a song that Christ would have often taken on His lips, or at least in His heart, in the days of His suffering. It is only because these words are the words of Christ that we can sing them with honesty as a people united to Him.

Were it not for the fact that Christ's righteousness covers us, we would be foolish to sing — *"judge me, O LORD, according to my righteousness"*: because all my righteousnesses are but filthy rags in the sight of God. But because of the righteousness of Christ imputed and imparted to us, we can sing these words of Christ with confidence.

With this in mind, let us consider this Psalm briefly under the theme *"The Righteous One's Response to Slander."*

This Psalm has five parts:

1.	v. 1-2	Danger Stated
2.	v. 4-5	Innocence Avowed
3.	v. 6-9	Judgement Called for
4.	v. 10-16	Divine Justice Affirmed
5.	v. 17	Concluding Praise

1. Danger Stated

¹ O LORD my God, in thee do I put my trust: save me from all them that persecute me, and deliver me: ² Lest he tear my soul like a lion, rending it in pieces, while there is none to deliver.

Here we see the Righteous One, our Lord crying out unto His Father to deliver Him from those who persecute Him (v. 1). He was charged with blasphemy; He certainly did not blaspheme. He was said to be a Sabbath breaker; He alone was the exemplary Sabbath-keeper. He was said to have claimed to be able to rebuild the temple in Jerusalem in three days if it were torn down; He was referring to His own death and resurrection.

Our Lord was maligned and falsely accused. His persecutors were ready, as it were, to tear His soul like a lion tears his prey apart (v. 2). Indeed, our Lord's words suggest that He feels that they are already starting to do that. When we find out that someone has slandered us before others, is that not how we feel?

I have felt slandered many times. I think every minister will experience it. There were times when I felt that someone had stabbed me from behind and twisted the blade. Other times I feel like a lion has pounced on my soul.

What to do at such times? Our Lord committed Himself to His Father. When He was reviled, He reviled not in return. He does not play the game of tit for tat. He goes to the Father, singing and meditating the words of this and other Psalms.

But He can only have comfort and assurance to pray in this way, in the knowledge that He is innocent of the wickedness that His enemies are guilty of. So from verses 3-5, He avows His innocence.

2. Innocence Avowed

³ O LORD my God, if I have done this; if there be iniquity in my hands; ⁴ If I have rewarded evil unto him that was at peace with me; (yea, I have delivered him that without cause is mine enemy:) ⁵ Let the enemy persecute my soul, and take it; yea, let him tread down my life upon the earth, and lay mine honour in the dust.

Confident of His innocence, our Lord asks His Father to examine Him to see if He has slandered or if there is iniquity in His hands.

If He had slandered or rewarded evil unto Him that was at peace with Him, He would willingly submit Himself to be persecuted by His enemies, to be trampled underfoot by them.

But the fact is, as can be seen in the parenthesis in verse 4, He even delivered or spared those who without cause were His enemies.

David who penned this Psalm, twice preserved the life of Saul who was persecuting him without cause. He could have killed Saul, once in the wilderness of En Gedi, and once in the plain. But he did not.

So too our Lord—by whose Spirit, David wrote—delivered those who persecuted Him without cause. He could have called upon a million angels to strike them dead. But instead He prays for them: "Father, forgive them for they know not what they do."

Our Lord loved us who were His enemies so much that instead of punishing us for our sin, He laid down His life for us.

It is for this reason that we must learn to lay down our lives for one another. We must follow the footsteps of our Lord as the Apostle Peter reminds us. If we are going to be able to use His Psalms with a clear conscience, we must be imitators of Christ. We must not ever engage in slander, or to render evil for good. If we cannot say anything good about someone, it may be best for us not to say anything.

Our Lord sets us the example. Compared to what His persecutors were doing to Him, He was very kind to them. And because of His kindness towards them, how absolutely unjustified it would be for them to continue to persecute Him.

Therefore, the Lord calls for judgement against them. "Vengeance belongs unto me," says the LORD. Our Lord as the Son of Man therefore refused to take revenge against His slanderers, but committed them to His Father.

3. Judgement Called for

[6] *Arise, O LORD, in thine anger, lift up thyself because of the rage of mine enemies: and awake for me to the judgment that thou hast commanded.*

We must not assume that our heavenly Father does not care when we are slandered. No, no; He is angry. As the Father was angry against those who slandered His only begotten Son, so we know that He is angry against those who slander His adoptive sons and daughters.

As our elder brother cried to the Father to arise for Him, so we must do likewise.

We must plead with the Father that He does so, so that His name may be magnified and His people drawn to Him (v. 7).

We must plead with the Father, that He distinguishes between the wicked and the just, in His acts of providence (v. 8-9). Our Lord is of course perfectly just. He was tempted in all points like as we are and yet without sin. He alone can stand when the Father judges according to righteousness. He alone is righteous in God's eyes.

We who are united with Christ can plead the righteousness of Christ, imputed to us in justification, when we are persecuted on account of our faith. At the same time, we may plead the righteousness of Christ imparted to us in sanctification.

Those who are united to Christ by faith have Christ's righteousness both imputed and imparted to them. We can therefore honestly sing these words, calling upon the Father to arise for us, to judge us according to our righteousness, or rather the righteousness of His Son imputed and imparted to us.

When we so pray or sing the Psalms, we must do so with full confidence that the Father will indeed deal justly.

This is why the fourth section of the Psalm affirms the justice of God...

4. Divine Justice Affirmed

[10] *My defence is of God, which saveth the upright in heart.* [11] *God judgeth the righteous, and God is angry with the wicked every day.*

God's love and care is particular. He does not stand up for the wicked or for slanderers. He stands up for the upright and righteous. He is angry at the wicked every day.

The wicked can expect that their wicked devices will eventually turn to their disadvantage. They are digging a pit for themselves (v. 15). They are, in modern idiom, "shooting their own foot."

Those who slander God's children can expect to do themselves more harm eventually.

This is the assurance that our Lord had. It was an assurance that translated into reality: for those who persecuted Him and continued to do so eventually faced the full wrath of divine justice.

"The Son of man indeed goeth, as it is written of him: but woe to that man by whom the Son of man is betrayed! good were it for that man if he had never been born" (Mk 14:21).

Woe unto those who clamoured for His blood by slander and refused to repent of their wickedness, for God is perfectly just and He will see to it that justice is meted out.

For this reason, we must learn to praise the LORD in the midst of our perplexity!

5. Concluding Praise

His execution of perfect justice, and His vindication of His children and punishment of the wicked give great reasons for God's children to praise Him.

^{17} I will praise the LORD according to his righteousness: and will sing praise to the name of the LORD most high.

Our Lord must have meditated on these words in His hour of suffering. He would shortly experience the darkness of the cross. But His confidence in the Father and His perfect justice gave Him hope.

His hope was not an empty hope, but a firm assurance that gave Him a strong reason to praise the Father.

Conclusion

You may not, at the moment, be suffering from slander as was our Lord; but very few, if any, of us, will go through life without experiencing being slandered at one time or another. Sometimes the slander could even originate from friends we once trusted. Or it may originate from our colleagues or bosses.

What do we do when we are slandered? What should we do when we are badly hurt? Let us remember how our Lord was slandered on our behalf. Let us remember how our Lord conducted Himself in a praiseworthy manner and committed Himself to His Father. Let us remember this Psalm. Let us sing it; and let us meditate on it.

But let us sing this Psalm especially in corporate worship, in union with our Mediator, that our hearts may be filled with gratitude and praise towards Him. Let us do so that we may feel something of what He felt, as we encourage one another to be imitators of Him. Amen. Ω

Psalm 8:
The Righteous One's Meditation
on God's Condescension
to the Son of Man

Psalm 8 is a favourite Psalm of the children. When you first read it, it will *not* appear to be a Messianic Psalm. It appears to be a Psalm about the pre-eminence of man compared to the rest of creation. You may even wonder if it has anything to do with Christ.

Indeed, I believe that many commentators would also dispute that it is Messianic—were it not for the fact that the New Testament makes it clear that it is about Christ. We will see how this is so in a moment.

But for now, let us understand that this is a Psalm of praise. Notice how this Psalm begins and ends with the same words:

¹ O LORD our Lord, how excellent is thy name in all the earth! (v. 1a, v. 9).

This is the thesis of this Psalm. The word "excellence" speaks of greatness, majesty and glory. If God's name is great, majestic and glorious, then it is a name to be praised.

This Psalm is therefore a hymn of praise. The reasons why we should praise the LORD are sandwiched between the opening and closing verses. What are the reasons?

We may enumerate three reasons:

1. v. 1-2   He has ordained praise out of the mouths of infants

2. v. 3   He has made the vast universe

3. v. 4-9   He has exalted man to a position of honour in Christ

Here is *"The Righteous One's Meditation on God's Condescension to the Son of Man."*

1. He Has Ordained Praise
out of the Mouths of
Infants

¹ᵇ...who hast set thy glory above the heavens. ² Out of the mouth of babes and sucklings hast thou ordained strength because of thine enemies, that thou mightest still the enemy and the avenger.

The LORD has set His glory above the heavens. That is to say: He is infinitely more glorious and excellent than the heavens and its inhabitants. The noblest of creatures and those that shine most brightly in heaven cannot be compared to the Lord.

So great is the glory of God that even babes and infants praise Him. It is one thing to have the highest and mightiest of angels praise God; it is quite another thing to have babes and infants praise Him.

Which is more glorious? To have babes and infants praise Him, or to have the mighty angels praise him? I submit to you that it is more glorious to have babes and infants praise Him. Why? Because angels are made to recognise glory, whereas infants must grow to understand glory.

An accomplished musician can draw much applause by playing a beautiful piece of music on his highly tuned and polished violin. But if a poor beggar boy walks onto stage and plays the same piece of music on his fiddle, he would no doubt draw a more vigorous applause from those who understand the significance of what is going on.

So, God has not only ordained that angels should praise His name, but also infants and sucklings. He would especially use infants and sucklings to praise Him when His enemies rise against His Son like a flood.

You will remember how our Lord referred to this verse. He had entered Jerusalem for the last time, sitting on the colt of an ass. The multitude cried out "Hosanna to the Son of David!" Then when He entered the temple, the children cried out the same thing: "Hosanna to the Son of David!" When the chief priests and scribes complained to our Lord about it, He replied:

> "Yea; have ye never read, Out of the mouth of babes and sucklings thou hast perfected praise?" (Mt 21:16b)

Our Lord was citing Psalm 8:2. So great is God's glorious condescension that He would choose to use, not the voice of angels, but that of the babes and sucklings of fallen men, to silence His enemies (v. 2).[11]

The praises of the babes and sucklings ought to silence the enemies of the Lord with shame.

The praises of the babes and sucklings ought also to stir us to praise the LORD more enthusiastically. You know there are times when I feel myself too tired to lift up my voice to praise the LORD. But when I hear the children praising Him loudly (even if it is out of tune), it just lifts my spirit and spurs me to truly praise Him. He has ordained praise out of the lips of babes and infants. Let us take our cue from them!

Secondly, we should also praise the LORD for He has made the vast universe.

2. He Has Made the Vast Universe

In verses 3-4, we are given to sing with our Lord:

> *³ When I consider thy heavens, the work of thy fingers, the moon and the stars, which thou hast ordained; ⁴ What is man, that thou art mindful of him? and the son of man, that thou visitest him?*

What He is saying is: When I look at the night sky and behold the glory of the moon and stars, I cannot but wonder at why you should pay attention to man —when we are such puny worthless creatures.

Herein then are two reasons to praise the LORD. The first is God's greatness as displayed in His creation; and the second is God's condescension in caring for man.

We will look at the second reason in our next point, but do you not see how when we look at God's vast universe, we cannot but lift up our hearts to praise Him?

> "The heavens declare the glory of God; and the firmament sheweth his handywork" (Ps 19:1)

---

[11] It is possible that Christ is suggesting that He is, in fact, Jehovah whom Psalm 8 is directed to, and indeed there is a sense in which the Psalm is directed to Him, for He is the second person of the Trinity. However, it is more likely that Christ is simply highlighting the fact that God would often use the praises of infants to put to silence His enemies. It will, after all, make little sense for us to understand this Psalm as being directed to Christ if we are to understand the "son of man" (v. 4) as having ultimate reference to Christ as we shall see.

David is looking at the heavens. It is a clear, cloudless day. The moon is shining full bright. The myriad of stars has come out in full force. It is an awesome sight that we are unlikely to see in modern Singapore because of light pollution. Well, David could have seen perhaps two or three thousand stars. But some astronomers have estimated that there are more than 100 billion stars in the Milky Way alone, and there are possibly 2 trillion (i.e. a 2×10^{12}) *galaxies* in the observable universe!

And every one of these galaxies, and stars, and planets and moons are delicately crafted by God's fingers! Oh, how shall we not be overwhelmed by the glorious wonder of God! How great thou art! How excellent is Thy name in all the heavens!

This then is the second reason given in this Psalm why we must praise the LORD. We must praise Him; nay, our hearts are lifted up to praise Him by the knowledge of His glory displayed in His vast universe.

Finally, the third reason we must praise the LORD is that...

3. He Exalted Man to a Position
of Honour in Christ

⁴ What is man, that thou art mindful of him? and the son of man, that thou visitest him? ⁵ For thou hast made him a little lower than the angels, and hast crowned him with glory and honour. ⁶ Thou madest him to have dominion over the works of thy hands; thou hast put all things under his feet: ⁷ All sheep and oxen, yea, and the beasts of the field; ⁸ The fowl of the air, and the fish of the sea, and whatsoever passeth through the paths of the seas.

Now, when we read these words, the first impression we will get is that David is speaking about how God has shown favour to man and exalted him to a position of honour over the rest of creation. Man is made but a little lower than angels, and unto man has been committed dominion over all the creatures that God has made, whether they be land animals or birds or fishes or marine creatures.

In a certain way this is true, but this is not the whole truth: for the inspired commentary of this Psalm in the New Testament teaches us that this Psalm is not about man in general, but about the Son of Man, Christ Jesus.

Consider Hebrew 2:6-9:

"⁶ But one in a certain place testified, saying, 'What is man, that thou art mindful of him? or the son of man, that thou visitest him? ⁷ Thou madest him a little lower than the angels; thou crownedst him with glory and honour, and didst set him over the works of thy hands: ⁸ Thou hast put all things in subjection under his feet.' [quoting Psalm 8:4-5].

For in that he put all in subjection under him, he left nothing that is not put under him. But now we see not yet all things put under him [i.e. under man]. ⁹ But we see Jesus, who was made a little lower than the angels for the suffering of death, crowned with glory and honour; that He by the grace of God should taste death for every man" (Heb 2:6-9).

What is the apostle saying? He is suggesting: When you read Psalm 8, you may think that the "son of man" refers to man in general. And you may think that God has put all things in creation in subjection under mankind. But do you not see? It has not happened. God has not put all things under mankind. Neither has He crowned mankind with glory and honour!

On the other hand, you will see how the Lord Jesus Christ fits into the description of the "son of man" in the Psalm like a hand into a glove:

⁹ But we see Jesus, who was made a little lower than the angels for the suffering of death, crowned with glory and honour; that He by the grace of God should taste death for every man.

The point is clear, is it not? Psalm 8 is not really about the pre-eminence of mankind. It is rather about the pre-eminence of the Son of Man. Christ was made a little lower than the angels in that He took on human flesh to suffer and die for us. But now He is crowned with glory and honour.

The title "son of man" was Christ's favourite self-designation. It occurs 81 times in the Gospels, and every time it is used by our Lord to refer to Himself. By comparison, the title "son of God" occurs only 28 times, and Christ uses it to describe Himself only 5 times!

The title "son of man" does not always refer to Christ in the Old Testament. But in this Psalm, it is ultimately about Him. It speaks of the dominion or kingship of Christ over all of Creation!

There is a reference to sheep and oxen in the farms, the wild animals in the fields and forests, the birds in the air and the fish and all marine creatures (v. 7-8). The Lord rules over all these. But it is clear that this is not an exhaustive list. The fact is His dominion is without bounds.

But what has that got to do with us, that we should praise the LORD for this reason. It has to do with us because Christ is given dominion over all of Creation, not for Himself, but for us.

Look at Hebrews 2:9 again. The apostle, commenting on verses 4 and 5 of our text, says:

> "But we see Jesus, who was made a little lower than the angels for the suffering of death, crowned with glory and honour; that He by the grace of God should taste death for every man" (Heb 2:9).

Christ the God-Man is the King that God crowned for man. But He is a king unlike any other. He was a suffering king. He was made a little lower than angels, specifically so that He might suffer and die in order to pay for the penalty due to His people.

He came for His people. He came to lay down His life for every one of His sheep. He came to suffer and die for us.

But He came not only to lay down His life for us. He came as our King. So He would have us sing with Him unto the Father:

> *"Thou madest him to have dominion over the works of thy hands; thou hast put all things under his feet"* (v. 6).

Why is Christ given dominion over creation? It is for the sake of the Church!

The Apostle Paul makes this very clear in Ephesians 1:22:

> "And [God] hath put all things under his feet, and gave him to be the head over all things to [i.e. for] the church."

Christ has been given dominion over all things, spiritual and material, for the sake of the Church! In other words, Christ the God-Man has been appointed by God to be the administrator of all things in the universe for the good of His Church.

Unto Christ has been committed the rule of the entire universe. Christ is sitting on the right hand of the throne of God in heaven. The apostle to the Hebrews tells us that Christ has been appointed heir of all things and He is upholding all things by the word of His power (Heb 1:2-3).

What is man that God should be mindful of us, that He sent Christ His son to die for us and also to live for us and to rule the universe for us. And not only to rule for us, but to restore us that we may rule with Him and exercise the dominion over creation according to God's appointment. What is man that we should have such great privileges!

Is this not a good reason to praise the Lord?

⁹ O LORD our Lord, how excellent is thy name in all the earth!

Conclusion

This is Psalm 8. As we sing it in union with the Son of Man, let us do so with a heart filled with awe and gratitude.

Children, you must praise the LORD enthusiastically. God has ordained that you praise Him and lead the adults to praise Him.

Brethren, you must praise Him. Take the cue from the children; and take the cue from the book of nature to praise the LORD.

God has, as it were, written three books: The Book of Revelation (the Bible); the book of Providence; and the Book of Nature. Psalm 8 points us to the book of nature. This book reminds us of the greatness of God's wisdom, power and condescension. This book will stir our hearts to praise the LORD if only we will take time to read it. Let us praise Him as we behold His wondrous Creation.

But most of all, let us praise Him for His wondrous grace in sending Christ our Lord to live for us, to suffer for us, to die for us and to be our King.

Praise the LORD for our King; for He is not only a great Ruler, He is the King of kings who is compassionate, kind and understanding. He rules with our best interest in heart, for He shares in our nature. He is the Son of Man. Amen. Ω

Psalm 9:
The Righteous One's
Prayer of Vindication

Psalm 9 shows itself to be a Messianic Psalm in a rather unique way. It provides a hint in its title, and confirms it in the text.

The title of the Psalm reads: "To the chief Musician upon Muth-labben, A Psalm of David." The words 'Muth-labben' mean "the death of the son."

Which son? It cannot be David's illegitimate son through Bathsheba, for this Psalm is neither a dirge nor a penitential Psalm.

Neither can the son refer to Absalom who died in the hands of Joab after he rose in rebellion against David—for there is no sense of sorrow in this Psalm. The tone in this Psalm is that of triumph and victory.

Some have suggested that the son here must refer to Goliath per the Aramaic translation; but Goliath is nowhere else referred to as "the son," whether in the Old Testament or the New Testament.

Who then is this son referred to in the title?

I believe He is none other than the Son of David; the Son of God, the Son of Man, the Lord Jesus Christ.

The death of the Lord Jesus Christ signals the victory of God over sin: for at the cross, the Lord crushed the head of the Serpent. The resurrection of Christ signalled the end of the wicked one and his kingdom. The resurrection of Christ is spoken of in verse 13:

> Have mercy upon me, O LORD; consider my trouble which I suffer of them that hate me, thou that liftest me up from the gates of death.

These words were, no doubt, spoken by David in the Spirit of Christ. They are the words of Christ which He has appointed for His Church to sing with Him, to plead with the Father to vindicate His and His Church's labours for His glory.

Since the time that Christ rose from the dead, the Church has been looking forward to His return and final vindication, when every knee will bow and every tongue confess that Jesus is LORD, when the wicked one shall forever be destroyed.

This is the theme of this Psalm: The Justice of God displayed in the vindication of the Redeemer. This is *"The Righteous One's Prayer of Vindication."*

It has essentially three parts:

    1.v. 1-8   A Word of Adoration

    2.v. 9-12   A Word of Confession

    3.v. 13-20 A Word of Petition

1. A Word of Adoration

[1] *I will praise thee, O LORD, with my whole heart; I will shew forth all thy marvellous works.* [2] *I will be glad and rejoice in thee: I will sing praise to thy name, O thou most High.*

These words immediately tell us that this Psalm is a Psalm of praise.

It is a Psalm that reminds us of the death of the Lord as its title suggests. But the death of the Lord is the death of deaths, and therefore we cannot meditate on the death of the Lord and its consequences without lifting up our hearts to praise the LORD.

Here in the first six verses of this Psalm, we are reminded to do just that, even as our Lord lifts up His eyes to praise His Father. Why does He praise?

The reason is that God is just. Man is made in the image of God, and therefore we have a natural sense of morality and justice, which to a degree remains after the Fall. And yet, we so often see the wicked trampling and triumphing over the just.

Our Lord's persecution and crucifixion is a prime example. Read the Gospel accounts superficially and it may appear that those who pursued and killed our Lord went away scot-free. Only Judas Iscariots, it seems, met with justice when he took his own life.

What about the rest? What about a great multitude of people throughout the ages who mock the name of Christ and persecute His people? The answer is found in verses 3-4:

> [3] *When mine enemies are turned back, they shall fall and perish at thy presence.* [4] *For thou hast maintained my right and my cause; thou satest in the throne judging right.*

God is a God of justice. Though for a moment He seems to overlook sin, He does not forget, and He will not leave any sin undealt with. In eternity, there will be no occasion for anyone to cry out unto the LORD for justice. He will deal with the wicked thoroughly and perfectly (v. 5).

No sinner whose sins are not dealt with by the LORD can come before His all-seeing eyes and not perish (v. 6).

All whose sin against the Son of God is not washed away by His own blood will face destruction at the Great Day of Judgement: for God is a righteous and just Judge. His throne is a throne of judgement and justice (v. 7).

On account of this fact, we see the Lord confessing that His Father is worthy of praise and trust.

2. A Word of Confession

> [9] *The LORD also will be a refuge for the oppressed, a refuge in times of trouble.* [10] *And they that know thy name will put their trust in thee: for thou, LORD, hast not forsaken them that seek thee.* [11] *Sing praises to the LORD, which dwelleth in Zion: declare among the people his doings.*

God is a refuge for the oppressed. He was a refuge to the Son of God. He is a refuge to the sons of man.

Because He is a just and holy God, we can have the confidence that He will indeed hear our cries and our sighs.

Indeed, as He who is seated at the right hand of the Father was persecuted and treated unjustly, we can be sure that we will have a hearing before the Father: for Christ is our Mediator.

He it is who calls us to praise the Father for His mercy and justice in this Psalm. He it is that exhorts us to trust Him.

He is our mediator. We have double confidence to trust in the Father!

Therefore, dear reader, whatever the trial you may be going through in your life, remember that God is not only sovereign but just and compassionate.

He will bless you. He will watch over you. He will never allow injustice against you to remain unresolved. He may not deal with it presently, but He will definitely deal with it at the Day of the Lord Jesus Christ.

Therefore fret not. Do not allow what you perceive to be injustice against you to overwhelm you with sadness or anger. Indeed, do not place your hope in a just outcome in this life, or that hope may become your idol, as you find your joy conditioned upon its fulfilment. Therefore, cast aside those silver idols in your pockets that weigh you down as you run the race. Look unto Jesus! Trust Him! Commit your cares unto Him. He is no debtor to justice.

He says in verse 18:

> For the needy shall not alway be forgotten: the expectation of the poor shall not perish for ever.

Finally, consider our Lord's Petition, which we are given to sing with Him.

3. A Word of Petition

In His hour of need, the Lord prays for Himself.

> [13] Have mercy upon me, O LORD; consider my trouble which I suffer of them that hate me, thou that liftest me up from the gates of death: [14] That I may shew forth all thy praise in the gates of the daughter of Zion: I will rejoice in thy salvation.

Notice how He prayed. He did not insist that His Father deal with His persecutors immediately. Indeed, on the cross, He cried out on behalf of His elect amongst those who clamoured for His blood: "Father forgive them for they know not what they do."

How does the Lord pray? He asks His Father to have mercy upon Him, to consider His trouble. He acknowledges that His Father will lift Him up from the grave in order that He may show forth His praises in the gates of the daughters of Zion.

The gates of Zion is a reference to the public worship of God's people. "The LORD loveth the gates of Zion more than all the dwellings of Jacob" (Ps 87:2). God delights in the public worship of His people more than their private worship.

So what our Lord is saying here is the same as in Psalm 22:

> "I will declare thy name unto my brethren: in the midst of the congregation will I praise thee" (Ps 22:22);

or Psalm 40:

> "I have not hid thy righteousness within my heart; I have declared thy faithfulness and thy salvation: I have not concealed thy lovingkindness and thy truth from the great congregation" (Ps 40:10).

Each of these verses speaks of what the Lord would do when He was raised from the dead. He would glorify the Father in the congregation of the saints. His human nature would, indeed, ascend and be in session at the right hand of the throne of God. But remember that He is united to us not only in the soul, but in the body as well (cf. 1 Cor 6:15; WSC 37); therefore, when we gather for worship in His name, He worships in our midst, as it were, as our Worshipper-in-Chief!

In other words, the Lord is in these words pleading for His Father's intervention for the sake of the glory of the Father! He is praying that He may be lifted up so that He may praise the Father in union with His body, the Church, when we gather for worship in the power of the Resurrection.

Today, when we sing the same Psalm in union with our Saviour, we are reflecting on what He suffered for us, and acknowledging that His attitude under persecution is exemplary and worthy of our appropriation.

His attitude, simply stated, is *Soli Deo Gloria*. The glory of the Father forms the basis of the petitions of our Lord.

This is clear in the rest of the Psalm too.

In verse 16, the LORD Jehovah is known by the judgement which He executes. He will send the wicked to hell, verse 17; and He will vindicate the needy and poor in Christ, verse 18.

In verse 19, our Lord petitions His Father to arise for His own name's sake. "*Let not man prevail,*" He says. Let not man continue in his wicked ways. Let not man continue to shame Your name by living in ways that suggest that You do not exist or do not see. Rather, put man to shame so that all the world may know that they are but men (v. 20). Man is a proud creature who is always striving for autonomy to his own hurt.

Satan tempted Eve by saying that she could be like God—knowing good and evil. Essentially, he was telling her that she needed not take instructions from God: she could be like God.

Adam fell for the same ruse and took of the forbidden fruit. Today, the majority of mankind have the same attitude. They have no fear of God. They imagine that they are gods.

Our Lord, therefore, prays as He concludes this Psalm:

> "*Put them in fear, O LORD: that the nations may know themselves to be but men*" (Ps 9:20).

Our Lord's desire for the world must be our desire too. Oh how little we have prayed the way that the Lord has prayed!

Conclusion

Notice how our Lord prayed. He was praying in the context of persecution and injustice against Him. Yet His prayer is not centred upon Himself, but upon the Father.

He praises the LORD for His perfect justice; He confesses that He has every reason to trust Him; and He prays that He will glorify His own name by continuing to act justly, and by humbling man that man may fear Him and know that He is God.

May the Lord teach us how to pray likewise; both when we feel overwhelmed by a sense of being unjustly treated, and when we are perplexed by the things we see happening in the world—where evil is called good, and good evil. May we own our Lord's words and become more like Him, by the power of the Spirit, as we sing His song in union with Him. Amen. Ω

Psalm 10:
The Righteous One's Plea for the Godly

We have seen that Psalm 9 is clearly a Messianic Psalm that alludes to the death and resurrection of the Messiah, to crush the head of the Serpent and his ungodly vipers who have risen up against Him and His seed.

Psalm 10 is so similar in content and tone, that the Septuagint translates it as a continuation of Psalm 9. But the difference between the two Psalms is that Psalm 9 emphasises the ruin of the ungodly; while Psalm 10 emphasises the guilt of the ungodly. Psalm 9 speaks of how God will triumph over the ungodly; Ps 10 speaks of how terribly guilty the ungodly are and calls upon God to deal with them.

This Psalm has essentially two parts. In the first part, verses 1-11, the Righteous One, as it were, paints a picture of the ungodly before His Father. In the second part, verses 12-18, the Righteous One appeals to the Father to interpose on behalf of the godly.

    1. v. 1-11   A Picture of the Ungodly

    2. v. 12-18   A Plea for the Godly

1. A Picture of the Ungodly

God sees all things. But there are times when it appears that the wicked have a free reign to do what they want; and God does not seem concerned.

It is like a robbery is going on; but at a distance is the police chief. He sees what is going on, but he does nothing. It is like a child is being beaten up by another; the father is standing at a distance. He sees what is going on but does nothing. When we see the wicked doing wicked deeds with apparent impunity, do we not wonder why God does not seem to do anything?

It must have been at such a time that the psalmist penned the words of this Psalm. This is a Psalm that our Lord must surely have meditated on when he saw injustice and wickedness all around Him, both against Him and against His saints during His earthly ministry.

¹ Why standest thou afar off, O LORD? why hidest thou thyself in times of trouble?

Why dost Thou stand apart, O LORD?

The wicked seems to be doing many things.

v. 2 —He persecutes the poor in his pride. He looks down on the poor. They are of no use to him, so he despises and persecutes them.

v. 3 —He boasts about the lusts of his heart, and blesses the covetous, calling good evil and evil good.

v. 4 —He has no regard for God; God is not in all his thoughts. He thinks only of himself and his own prosperity.

v. 5 —His ways are always grievous; he is arrogant. He thinks he is always right.

v. 6 —He boasts that nothing can shake him. He is over-confident.

v. 7 —His mouth is full of cursing and deceit. He cheats. He curses those who point out his wickedness.

v. 8-10 —He is full of scheming and underhanded methods by which he crushes the poor and takes advantage of them.

v. 11 —He says in his heart: God has forgotten; He is hiding His face; He will never see it.

He has no fear of God. He has no compassion for the poor. He cares only for himself.

When the Righteous One sees this happening, and He knows that God is holy and sovereign, He will, no doubt, feel a holy indignation on behalf of God's name.

> ¹ *Why standest thou afar off, O LORD? why hidest thou thyself in times of trouble?*

He is not asking the Father to explain Himself, we must realise. It is an expression of desire that the Father would deal with the wicked, that justice may prevail upon the earth.

This desire is explicitly stated in the second part of this Psalm, where the Messiah pleads for the godly:

2. A Plea for the Godly

> ¹² *Arise, O LORD; O God, lift up thine hand: forget not the humble.*

The humble are those who are afflicted, helpless and poor in spirit. "Blessed are the poor in spirit: for theirs is the kingdom of heaven," says our Lord (Mt 5:3). "Whosoever therefore shall humble himself as this little child, the same is greatest in the kingdom of heaven" (Mt 18:4).

Not everyone who is poor materially is humble. Many who are poor are so headstrong and proud: they have no need of God. They care not for the prayers of the Messiah.

The Messiah is not concerned about them. They can take care of themselves. The Messiah is concerned about the humble, that is, those who know that they are nothing, have nothing and deserve nothing good.

Christ pleads on behalf of them. He desires that the Father should act on their behalf. They are too weak to lift a hand against the proud and wicked. But God's arms are not too short to deal with them. "*Arise, O LORD; O God, lift up thine hand: forget not the humble.*"

But why? Why should God do so? Why should God arise on behalf of the humble?

Firstly, because the wicked contemn or revile God's name by their actions and words (v. 13). He challenges God arrogantly: "*Thou wilt not require it!*" You will not call me to account. You will not do anything. I defy you to show that you can do anything to me!

Oh such arrogance!

So, God should arise on behalf of the humble because the wicked is holding God in contempt.

Secondly, God should arise on behalf of the humble because He Himself sees what is going on:

> ¹⁴ *Thou hast seen it; for thou beholdest mischief and spite, to requite it with thy hand:*

LORD, Thou art not unaware of what is going on. Indeed, as Habakkuk puts it:

> "Thou art of purer eyes than to behold evil, and canst not look on iniquity: wherefore lookest thou upon them that deal treacherously, and holdest thy tongue when the wicked devoureth the man that is more righteous than he?" (Hab 1:13).

But thirdly, God should arise against the wicked on behalf of the poor because the poor have committed themselves unto Him, and He is the helper of the fatherless (v. 14).

The poor and humble are helpless to help themselves, O LORD. Wouldst not Thou arise on their behalf to help them?

> [15] Break thou the arm of the wicked and the evil man: seek out his wickedness till thou find none.

LORD, do not hold back Thy wrath. Deal severely with the wicked who mock Thy name.

Will the LORD indeed arise? Yes, He will. We must believe that. We may not see it today. But we must live by faith, not by sight. "One day is with the Lord as a thousand years, and a thousand years as one day" (2 Pet 3:8).

The fact that God will not deal with the wicked today does not mean that He will not deal with them. Rather God is allowing them to store up wrath against the day of wrath.

The prayer of the Messiah will be heard. "Thou hearest me always," says the Lord, in John 11:42.

So as we conclude this Psalm, we are given to confess with our Lord, in no uncertain terms of what will happen. This is in the future, but the situation is reported in the present and past tense.

It is like we are being transported to the end of history that we might look back to see what is ahead of us today:

> [16] The LORD is King for ever and ever: the heathen are perished out of his land. [17] LORD, thou hast heard the desire of the humble: thou wilt prepare their heart, thou wilt cause thine ear to hear: [18] To judge the fatherless and the oppressed, that the man of the earth may no more oppress.

The day is coming. As certainly as the fact that Christ has already come, the day is coming when God will arise for the poor and humble, against the proud and wicked.

In that day, only the poor in spirit, the humble in heart and the godly will remain in the garden of the LORD, to enjoy Him and their eternal inheritance forever and ever. The wicked will be no more. There will be no more proud people. There will be no more evil and persecution. There will be no more tears and sorrows.

Justice and equity will pervade the earth. Praise be to the LORD!

Conclusion

Beloved reader, what is this Psalm to you?

This Psalm assures me that the Lord cares. There is a lot of injustice in this world, but we must not allow it to grip us or to overwhelm us. We must cast our cares upon the Lord and continue to live honestly and humbly, remaining poor in spirit.

We must not crave to get back against those who exploit the poor. Leave it in the hands of the LORD.

Have you been unjustly treated in school or at work? Leave it in the hand of the LORD. He will take care of it. Only continue to trust Him and hope in Him. Only in this way will you be like Christ, "Who, when he was reviled, reviled not again; when he suffered, he threatened not; but committed himself to him that judgeth righteously" (1 Pet 2:23). Amen. Ω

Psalm 11:
The Righteous One's
Trial of Faith

Psalm 11 must have been written by David at a time when his faith was sorely tried. But this Psalm was, no doubt, written in the Spirit of Christ, for David had no righteousness in and of himself. All our righteousnesses are but filthy rags in the sight of God (Isa 64:6). And yet he writes, verse 7: *"For the righteous LORD loveth righteousness; his countenance doth behold the upright."*

If David were not writing the words of Christ, in the Spirit of Christ, he would be declaring his own relative righteousness as being good enough for a holy God, who is of purer eyes than to behold evil (Hab 1:13); and then either he is contradicting himself in Psalm 14:2-3, or the Apostle Paul misapplied his words in Romans 3:10 to teach universal total depravity.

We have, no doubt, that this Psalm contains the words of Christ, the Righteous One. God by His providence appointed for David to experience some of the sufferings that our Lord would experience, that He might pen the words that would fill the mind of our Lord at His incarnation, especially during the times when His confidence was sorely tried.

We may, as such, entitle this Psalm *"The Righteous One's Response to Assault on His Faith;"* or more briefly, *"The Righteous One's Trial of Faith."*

Believers, including David, are righteous ones on account of the representation and Spirit of the Righteous One. We may therefore sing this Psalm confidently, in union with Him, and even apply it to our own trials when the situation calls for it.

This Psalm has two parts. The first 3 verses paint a picture of the Righteous One's trial of faith; while the second part contains an expression of the Righteous One's confidence.

1.   v. 1-3   The Righteous One's Temptation
2.   v. 4-7   The Righteous One's Confidence

1. The Righteous One's Temptation

[1] In the LORD put I my trust: how say ye to my soul, Flee as a bird to your mountain? [2] For, lo, the wicked bend their bow, they make ready their arrow upon the string, that they may privily shoot at the upright in heart [3] If the foundations be destroyed, what can the righteous do?

"Fly away! Hide in the mountain! Why go headlong into danger? The wicked are ready to kill you. You are righteous, but what can you do when the foundations are destroyed—when the wicked has no regards to authority or moral principles or established rules of law; what can you do?"

Who is saying all these things? Sometimes, in our darkest hours, the old man within us arises to give us what sounds like sound advice. "Give up the fight—run away. It is not worth it; you can't win anyway."

But our Lord does not have an old man. He is perfectly righteous. The voice of temptation, in the case of our Lord, came from outside: "How say ye to my soul..." The Hebrew is very specific and our translators picked it up. *"How say ye,"* not "How say thee." ("thee" is singular; "ye" is plural). There were voices from without tempting our Lord to flee from danger.

One day, when the Lord was in Jerusalem, the Pharisees came to Him and said: "Get thee out, and depart hence: for Herod will kill thee" (Lk 13:31). We doubt that the Pharisees were speaking out of concern. Most likely, it was out of jealousy. They were seeking to frighten the Lord to abandon His ministry.

But the Pharisees were not the only ones who tried to dissuade the Lord from His work. Even His disciples did that, albeit more mildly. When for example, the Lord wanted to go into Judaea to see Lazarus and his sisters, His disciples said to Him: "Master, the Jews of late sought to stone thee; and goest thou thither again?" (Jn 11:7-8).

But the Lord would not be moved by the voice of temptation.

¹ In the LORD put I my trust: how say ye to my soul, Flee as a bird to your mountain?

If I put my trust in the LORD, why should I be frightened? Why should I flee? God is sovereign, is He not? The LORD is in control, is He not? Shall I not continue to serve him courageously?

Our Saviour once said: "If the world hate you, ye know that it hated me before *it hated* you" (Jn 15:18). If we love the Lord and walk in His footsteps, it is almost inevitable that we will be faced with similar temptation to flee from doing right. When, for example, someone who is being queried in a church discipline case issues a veiled threat to destroy the church if his sins are exposed, what do we feel in our hearts, but what the Lord must have felt?

¹ In the LORD put I my trust: how say ye to my soul, Flee as a bird to your mountain?

May the Lord give us the courage that He had, to do as He would do at such times of temptation!

2. The Righteous One's Confidence

⁴ The LORD is in his holy temple, the LORD's throne is in heaven: his eyes behold, his eyelids try, the children of men.

The LORD is in His throne room, the holy temple. He is seated on high. He sees all things that are happening. He even sees through the heart of everyone.

"His eyes behold, his eyelids try, the children of men." Man may say all they want and do all they want, but the LORD sees the attitude and intention of their heart.

He upholds the righteous and puts down the wicked.

The Lord Jesus and all who are united to Him have no fear, therefore, even if the foundations be broken: for no one can break the authority of God.

⁵ The LORD trieth the righteous: but the wicked and him that loveth violence his soul hateth. ⁶ Upon the wicked he shall rain snares, fire and brimstone, and an horrible tempest: this shall be the portion of their cup. ⁷ For the righteous LORD loveth righteousness; his countenance doth behold the upright.

The LORD hates the wicked. He will not allow them to prosper in their wicked work. Moreover, He will judge them and vindicate His children.

His adoptive children are, no doubt, not righteous in themselves; but in Christ they are righteous and are being made righteous. They have been imputed with the righteousness of Christ, and are being imparted with the righteousness of Christ.

They are, therefore, righteous in the eyes of the Father. He looks down upon them with pity. His countenance does behold them with love and concern.

As the Lord Jesus went about His earthly ministry in the confidence of His Father's watchful and loving eyes, so anyone who is righteous in Christ may also go about the Lord's work and walk with courage and confidence.

We must not allow temptations, whether internal or external, to turn us out of the way to flee to the mountains—to run away from the problems, but to deal with them with the Lord's strength. We must walk by faith, not by sight. Sight tells us that all is lost: give up! Faith shows us that victory and blessings awaits the righteous.

Conclusion

May the Lord help us, that when we feel weak, we may know that His grace is sufficient for us and that his power is made perfect in our weakness.

May we sing this Psalm, in union with our Saviour, not only that our hearts may be filled with gratitude to Him for all that He went through for us, but that we may find comfort in our own trials as we walk with Him. Amen. Ω

Psalm 12:
The Righteous One's Confidence in God's Words over Man's Words

"Sticks and stones may break my bones but words will never hurt me," so goes a common idiom. But is it really true that words will never hurt?

The fact is: Words do hurt! We can pretend that they do not hurt or we can rationalise the hurt away, but we cannot escape the reality that it is often words that hurt the most. This is so in the civilised society that we dwell in. It was not very different in the days of David; or of the Lord, the greater David.

Psalm 12 is a Psalm about war of words. It is a Psalm that our Covenant Head has provided by His Spirit to be a balm to our soul, when the words of the wicked or when wicked words strike at our hearts, and cause pain and sorrow. It is a Psalm that our Lord would have us sing in union with Him, to encourage and exhort one another *vis-à-vis* the reality that sin of the tongue can bring much pain to the communion of saints.

Let us look at this Psalm briefly under two headings:

1.   v. 1-4, 8   The Problem

2.   v. 5-7   The Solution

1. The Problem

David in this Psalm is expressing his exasperation and frustration on account of the speech of those around him. He was experiencing a taste of what the Lord Jesus would endure during His earthly ministry.

As our Lord, like David earlier, listened to the speech of the people around Him, He must have felt quite exasperated. There appears to be a lack of seriousness and sincerity in their conversation. Hypocrisy, innuendos and flattery appear to rule the day:

> *² They speak vanity every one with his neighbour: with flattering lips and with a double heart do they speak.*

With their tongues they speak flattery and boast proud things (v. 3). They have no regard for God (v. 4). They oppress the poor and trample the needy (v. 5).

And there are so many of them that it seems almost like everyone is like that.

> *¹ Help, LORD; for the godly man ceaseth; for the faithful fail from among the children of men.*

> *⁸ The wicked walk on every side, when the vilest men are exalted.*

This was the cry of David and of the greater David. This was also the cry of such godly men as Moses and Elijah.

> "The children of Israel have forsaken thy covenant, thrown down thine altars, and slain thy prophets with the sword; and I, even I only, am left; and they seek my life, to take it away" cried Elijah (1 Kgs 19:10).

This is the cry and feeling, no doubt, of every child of God who is in this world, but not of this world.

This Psalm, therefore, may be taken up by every child of God especially when we are troubled or hurt by the words of man. As our Lord was troubled by the hypocrisy and lies of the scribes and Pharisees, so we too can expect to be troubled on every side by unruly tongues. We too can often feel very vexed in the spirit, and very lonely. Unless our speech and manner of speech are no different from the rest of the world, we will feel exasperated by unruly tongues.

But as we cry out unto the LORD with the words of our Lord, we can be sure of His help; for He has promised to do so.

2. The Promise

5b Now will I arise, saith the LORD; I will set him in safety from him that puffeth at him.

Can we trust the words of the LORD? Of course we can! We often cannot trust the words of man. Man's words are full of insincerity, innuendos, hidden agendas, half truth and flattery. Even when man tells the truth, he is not always able to keep his promises.

But God is able.

6 The words of the LORD are pure words: as silver tried in a furnace of earth, purified seven times.

The words of the Lord are pure words.

"God is not a man, that he should lie; neither the son of man, that he should repent: hath he said, and shall he not do it? or hath he spoken, and shall he not make it good?" (Num 23:19).

God will keep His word. He promises to arise for the poor (v. 5). He has promised to shelter them from the strong blasts of those who afflict them. He will keep His word.

7 Thou shalt keep them, O LORD, thou shalt preserve them from this generation for ever.

Who is the "them" referred to here? The Hebrew is very clear. The "them" in verse 7 points back to "the poor" and "the needy" in verse 5, rather than to the *"words of the LORD"* in verse 6.[12]

We are, in other words, given here to sing in acknowledgement of the LORD's preservation of the poor and needy, who are being oppressed by the proud and flattering!

God will arise for them. He will preserve them from the multitude of ungodly persons who surround them.

He will even restrain the growth of wickedness on their behalf.

8 The wicked walk on every side, when the vilest men are exalted.

"Promotion cometh neither from the east, nor from the west, nor from the south. But God is the judge: he putteth down one, and setteth up another" (Ps 75:6-7).

For the sake of the righteous and the poor, the LORD will withhold the promotion of the

---

[12] We must not take verse 7 out of context to mean that God will preserve His word and that He will preserve it in the King James Bible. This is the error the Seventh Day Adventists and disagreeable authors such as Peter Ruckman and D.A. Waite. No honest and reputable commentators we know of support their opinion.

In the Hebrew, the word translated "words" in verse 6 is in the feminine plural; whereas the pronouns in verse 7 are in the masculine plural and singular, which matches with the masculine plural and singular used to described the poor and the needy in verse 5.

vilest. He will not allow injustice and wickedness to prevail. He will restrain and cut off all those who are guilty of such wickedness. He has promised that He will do so.

Conclusion

The war of words is but a facet of the war of the ages. It is inevitable that as we dwell in this sin-drenched world, we will hear words that do not please our ears and words that hurt us.

And words do hurt us. Worse still, words often translate into hurtful actions so that the disciples of the Lord would often feel oppressed and intimidated in the world of arrogant people.

But thank God for His firm promise that He will preserve His people. He preserved our holy Saviour as He walked through the world of sin for us. So we can be sure that He will preserve us.

Let us trust Him. Let us find our refuge in Him when things around us afflict our souls. By the grace of God, let us not allow ourselves to be defeated by the words of man. Rather, let us be healed by the gracious promises of the LORD as we enter the experience of His Son, and take up His words in our lips that we may express our assurance of His Father's help, in union with Him. Amen. Ω

Psalm 13:
The Righteous One's
"LORD, How Long?"

Psalm 13 may be known as *"The Righteous One's 'LORD, How Long?'."*

Notice the repetition of the question, "how long?"

- *^{1} How long wilt thou forget me, O LORD? For ever?*
- *^{1b} How long wilt thou hide thy face from me?*
- *^{2} How long shall I take counsel in my soul, having sorrow in my heart daily?*
- *^{2b} How long shall mine enemy be exalted over me?*

This Psalm must have been written by David at a time when great darkness was over his soul. It was darkness which could be felt. The hours were long. The nights were wearisome. The burden upon his soul was heavy.

Was David in the wilderness of Judea running away from Saul, while waiting on the promises of God that he would be king one day?

Or was he already king, but experiencing a season of spiritual depression due to the discontent and murmuring amongst the people stirred up by his son Absalom?

We don't know. But one thing we know: David was writing in the Spirit of Christ.

During His earthly ministry, our Lord experienced such darkness upon His soul that David could not even have imagined.

It was the darkness of the Father's abandonment on the cross. Our Lord was bearing our sin on the cross. Our guilt was upon Him so much so that His Father, as it were, turned His face from Him. For three hours, even the sun refused to shine. For three hours, all that our Lord saw of His beloved Father was His angry face—so much so that at the end of the three hours, He cried out: "Eli, Eli, lama sabachthani?" "My God, my God, why hast thou forsaken me?" (Mt 27:46).

All through His earthly life, not once do we read of our Lord calling His Father as "God" but always as "Father": so intimate is His relationship with His Father. But now on the cross, forsaken by His Father because of the guilt He is bearing, He cries out in anguish "My God, my God!"

But this darkness upon His soul did not begin only at the cross: for even as He anticipated the cross, He was already deeply troubled. He told his disciples: "My soul is exceeding sorrowful, even unto death" (Mt 26:38).

He wrestled so much in prayer that night that His perspiration fell to the ground like great drops of blood. He cried unto His Father, "If it be possible, take this cup from me. Yet not my will but thy will be done."

The words of Psalm 13 must have been part of His meditation throughout this time. We can discern three elements in it:

1. v. 1-2   His Anxiety

2. v. 3-4   His Plea

3. v. 5-6   His Confidence

1. His Anxiety

¹ How long wilt thou forget me, O LORD? For ever?

¹ᵇ How long wilt thou hide thy face from me?

² How long shall I take counsel in my soul [i.e. how long do I have to talk to myself], having sorrow in my heart daily?

²ᵇ How long shall mine enemy be exalted over me?

Can you see how these words take on fresh meanings once we understand them as the words of the Righteous One, our Lord?

Our Lord is not a stoic. He knows and He feels the pains and anxiety that we feel as He waits upon God for deliverance.

But our Lord is not faithless as many of us are. When He asks "how long?" He is not asking for an answer. There is no doubt in His heart at all that the Father will deliver Him. He is, rather, expressing His desire that the period of darkness may be as short as possible.

So we are given to sing in the second part of the Psalm:

2. His Plea

³ Consider and hear me, O LORD my God: lighten mine eyes, lest I sleep the sleep of death; ⁴ Lest mine enemy say, I have prevailed against him; and those that trouble me rejoice when I am moved.

Consider the plea of our Lord. He cries unto His Father to hear His plea.

He has one plea in this Psalm: *"Lighten mine eyes!"* (v. 3). This is His plea. *"Lighten mine eyes,"* or "Give light to my eyes." Take away the darkness from my soul that I may again enjoy the brightness of Thy heavenly smile. Our Lord was silent in His lips but not in His heart during the three hours of darkness! He would have used this Psalm on many occasions as He walked in a world ravaged and darkened by sin, but He would, no doubt, have meditated on these words as He hung in darkness to purchase light for His people.

The rest of the verses contain His arguments why He desired to be heard:

³ᵇ lest I sleep the sleep of death;

⁴ᵃ Lest mine enemy say, I have prevailed against him; and

⁴ᵇ [Lest] those that trouble me rejoice when I am moved.

Now, although these reasons may appear to be selfish and self-centred, they are not. Although it is legitimate to defend one's name (for a good name is better to be chosen than great riches) our Lord was not only concerned about His own name, but for His Father's name. He had trusted in His Father, and His tormentors had mocked Him for doing so. Therefore, they, and all heaven and earth, must now see that His faith is not in vain. Thus, our Lord concludes with a word of confidence.

3. His Confidence

⁵ But I have trusted in thy mercy; my heart shall rejoice in thy salvation [i.e. deliverance]. ⁶ I will sing unto the LORD, because he hath dealt bountifully with me.

Lighten my eyes, lest I sleep the sleep of death and my enemies rejoice over my fall—whereas I have trusted in Thy mercy.

It is like the Lord saying: "Not just for my sake, Father; but for Thy glory's sake, wouldst Thou lift me out of my gloom: for I have trusted in Thee. Grant that I may yet have occasion to rejoice in Thy deliverance."

Those of us who have had occasion of experiencing darkness upon our soul take note: It is not wrong to desire to see the sunshine behind the dark clouds. It is not wrong to ask for the dark clouds to be driven away. As our Lord cried for deliverance, let us learn likewise to cry for deliverance.

Our Lord desired to see the light, and His prayers were answered.

When the hours of darkness were over, the sun began to shine again. And when His confidence was restored, He cried out, "It is finished," and unto His Father He said: "Father, into thy hands I commend my spirit" (Lk 23:46), and having said thus, He gave up the ghost.

Three days later, our Lord rose from the dead, and eventually ascended up to heaven.

> [6] I will sing unto the LORD, because he hath dealt bountifully with me.

Our Lord must have sung these words even before He was raised from the dead. But such was His confidence in His Father that He could speak in the past tense: "*he hath dealt bountifully with me.*"

The Lord will always deal bountifully with all those who rest in Him.

Conclusion

Are you, dear believer, experiencing some trials and suffering in your soul?

Is it due to a physical illness? Or is it depression in your soul? Is it a sad circumstance in your life? Are you faced with a failure? A sick child? A wayward son? A quarrelsome mother-in-law? A bedbound and demented father? Fail not to cry out unto the Lord: "O Lord, How long?"

Our Lord cried out: "O Lord, How long?" and was heard.

David cried out "O Lord, How long?" and was heard.

Our fathers in the faith have cried out "O Lord, how long?" and they have been heard.

I think of John Calvin. He was a man afflicted with many illnesses. Theodore Beza spoke of how he was afflicted by headaches, fevers, gout, ulcerated haemorrhoids, colic, etc. But while he was oppressed by so many diseases, no man ever heard him utter a word unbecoming of a man of firmness, far less unbecoming a Christian. But he was often seen raising his eyes towards heaven, and saying, "O Lord, how long?"

Fret not, beloved brethren, when dark clouds overshadow your soul. Cry out unto the Lord, "O Lord, how long?" Yes, cry unto Him for deliverance, but remember to wait upon Him patiently. You will not know how long you have to wait. But you must know that your deliverance is drawing near, and your light affliction is but for a moment, and it is working for you a far more exceeding and eternal weight of glory through Christ your King. Amen. Ω

Psalm 14:
The Righteous One's
Censure of Atheism

Psalm 14 is one of the dark and gloomy Psalms. It is quoted in the New Testament by the Apostle Paul in another dark but well-known passage, where he speaks about the depravity of man, viz., Romans 3:10-11:

> "As it is written, There is none righteous, no, not one: There is none that understandeth, there is none that seeketh after God" (Rom 3:10-11).

Paul is quoting from Psalm 14:1, 3. He is, under the inspiration of the Holy Spirit, suggesting that what David says in the Psalm is true of all mankind through the ages.

David might have written this Psalm at a time when he was very discouraged as he beheld the darkness and sin of all the people around him. We don't know when exactly it was. It could have been before he became king when he was being pursued by Saul in the wilderness and when the people who supported him were the off-scouring of society.

Or it might have been after he became king, as the reference to salvation coming out of Zion may suggest.

Whatever may be the case, we can be sure that this Psalm is the word of Christ. While David could in some sense speak of Israel as being "my people" (v. 4), it is Christ alone who can speak of the Church throughout the ages as "my people."

If this Psalm is merely the word of David, its scope would be very small, and the validity of what is said, very limited. After all, who is David to judge that there is none that seeketh after God and none that doeth good? Even if David were referring only to Israel, he, as a sinner, has no moral basis to make such a sweeping judgement.

But Christ who is without sin has every right. And when He speaks of "my people" He is speaking of the seed of the woman throughout the ages, in contrast to the seed of the serpent.

We may entitle this Psalm *"The Righteous One's Censure of Atheism."* We may outline it as follows:

1. v. 1-4 The Present Time

2. v. 5-7 The Time to Come

1. The Present Time

[1] *The fool hath said in his heart, There is no God. They are corrupt, they have done abominable works, there is none that doeth good.*

These are words that the Righteous One has given for us to sing in union with Him. What He is saying is a stubborn reality that came with the Fall. It was true during Noah's time; it was true in David's time; it was true in the first century. It remains true in our time. Man is made in the image of God. There are no natural atheists. But there are many practical atheists— both inside and outside the church. They say in their heart: *"There is no God."* They do not want to be accountable to God. So they try to convince themselves that there is no God in order that they may live in any way they choose.

The result is they live as if God does not exist. They are corrupt in their thoughts and speech.

They do abominable things. Indeed, as they do not do anything in the fear of God, they cannot do good.

But they are foolish. "They are fools," says the Lord. Only fools will say that there is no God.

Where are these fools to be found? They are found everywhere. In fact, the Apostle Paul suggests that every natural man is a fool because of the Fall. The Fall renders every natural descendant of Adam spiritually dead. Only in Christ can anyone have spiritual life.

Therefore, in the eyes of God, there is none righteous, no not one:

> [2] *The LORD looked down from heaven upon the children of men, to see if there were any that did understand, and seek God.*

Look! It is Jehovah who is doing the searching. He did not send a man or an angel, for they might unintentionally miss someone.

God Himself is looking down with burning eyes that pierce through the heart and soul of man. No corner of the earth is hid from His all-seeing eyes. No period of history is spared His scrutiny as He searches for the one that understands, and seeks Him by his own inclination and power.

Are there any righteous? Are there any with spiritual understanding? Are there any that seeks God? No, not one! There is none at all!

> [3] *They are all gone aside, they are all together become filthy: there is none that doeth good, no, not one.*

There is none that does good, no not one. The Fall has made man altogether filthy. They have all turned aside from the path of righteousness. They are no longer walking in the way of holiness. All their righteousnesses is as filthy rags in the sight of God.

The irony is that they do not see it nor acknowledge their iniquity. Instead, they continue to live and do wickedly. And their wickedness has touched the apple of God's eyes, the people of the LORD:

> [4] *Have all the workers of iniquity no knowledge? who eat up my people as they eat bread, and call not upon the LORD.*

It is hard to imagine that the workers of iniquity should not know the way of truth. But it is a fact. They have fooled themselves into living without God.

It is hard to imagine that the workers of iniquity should not be awakened from their foolishness just by looking at the stark difference between their lives and the lives of those who are redeemed by the Lord. But it is a fact they are not only often unmoved by the righteous lives of the saints, but they trample them underfoot.

They eat them up like they eat bread. They call not upon the LORD, and they think nothing about taking advantage of the saints.

But the time is coming when this will come to an end. Our Lord sees it clearly.

2. The Time to Come

He sees it as if it is right before His eyes as something that has already happened:

> [5] *There were they in great fear: for God is in the generation of the righteous.* [6] *Ye have shamed the counsel of the poor, because the LORD is his refuge.*

The fools and wicked in the world are cringing in fear when they had before instilled fear upon the righteous. They had mocked the poor when they testified that their dependence and refuge is the LORD. They shamed their counsel (v. 6).

But now the LORD will laugh at them. They were foolish, proud and self-sufficient. But now they are cringing in fear calling upon the mountains and the rocks to cover them for the Day of the Wrath of the Lamb is come.

In Psalm 53, which is almost word for word identical with this Psalm, we have an apocalyptic description of that day:

> "There were they in great fear, where no fear was: for God hath scattered the bones of him that encampeth against thee: thou hast put them to shame, because God hath despised them" (Ps 53:5).

That dreadful day will see the end of hope for the foolish.

But while we long for that day, we must desire too that the foolish may be made wise so that deliverance for the righteous comes in this life.

It is with this desire, that we echo the Lord's words:

> ⁷ *Oh that the salvation of Israel were come out of Zion! when the LORD bringeth back the captivity of his people, Jacob shall rejoice, and Israel shall be glad.*

Oh that salvation of Israel would come out of Zion! Oh that the LORD will redeem Israel through the ministration of the word coming out of Zion!

There are many in Israel, or in the visible church who are, sadly, as yet foolish, who would unconscionably take advantage of the poor. But these are not without hope as long as they are within reach of the sword of the Spirit issuing forth from the throne of Zion—the throne or pulpit of Christ.

Oh that the LORD would give salvation to Israel. Oh that the LORD would change the foolish in Israel into the wise by His grace.

What a joy it will be for God's people when that happens. Oh, shall we not pray? Shall we not pray for genuine conversion in the church?

Shall we not pray for each other's conversion? Conversion is repentance of sin and faith in the LORD. We need more repentance. We need more faith.

Shall we not pray for the conversion of our little ones in whose heart foolishness is bound?

If the LORD will revive us and drive out all our foolishness, oh, what a blessing it will be upon the church!

- The ministry will have less heartache.

- The members will enjoy walking in the way of the LORD without the burden of guilt.

- And more will be willing to serve the LORD with their time and resources.

- The elders will be able to spend more time to encourage the members positively rather spending so much time on church discipline.

- The deacons will be able to serve the LORD with joy seeing that their work is greatly appreciated.

- Misunderstandings resulting from children's foolishness will be minimised.

- Tears that flow due to apostasy of covenant children will start to dry up.
- There will be more who will be willing to put their hands to the plough and sickle and enter into the harvest fields.
- And the name of the LORD will be greatly magnified as God's people join together to worship Him; even as we anticipate the day of the restoration of all things, when the whole congregation throughout the ages will stand together in an eternal Hallelujah, with Christ our Worshipper-In-Chief visibly leading us.

Conclusion

Let us pray, O righteous ones in Christ, to this end.

7 Oh that the salvation of Israel were come out of Zion! when the LORD bringeth back the captivity of his people, Jacob shall rejoice, and Israel shall be glad. Amen. Ω

Psalm 15:
The Righteous One's
Holy Character

Psalm 15 is not a very popular Psalm. It is seldom sung and seldom quoted. Neither is it usually known to be Messianic. But it is not difficult to see that it is indeed so, once we get into it. We may entitle it *"The Righteous One's Holy Character."*

We may meditate on it under three headings:

1. v. 1   Who Is He
2. v. 2-5b   Who He Is
3. v. 5c   Who We Should Be

1. Who Is He

The Psalm begins with:

> ^{1} *LORD, who shall abide in thy tabernacle? who shall dwell in thy holy hill?*

The tabernacle and the holy hill are, no doubt, figures of the dwelling place of God—namely heaven.

Who may abide or dwell in heaven? Who may take up residence in the brightness of heaven in all its glorious splendour before the transcendently holy God of whom the prophet Habakkuk declares: "Thou art of purer eyes than to behold evil, and canst not look on iniquity" (Hab 1:13a)? Even the holy seraphim had to cover their eyes and their feet in His presence.

What hope then has man when we are told in the previous Psalm:

> "There is none that doeth good... They are all gone aside, they are altogether become filthy: there is none that doeth good, no not one" (Ps 14:1, 3).

And in case anyone should think that David was employing the language of hyperbole, let us be clear that the Apostle Paul's inspired doctrine of Total Depravity in Romans 3:10-12 is based on these verses. If David was speaking hyperbolically, Paul had misused Scripture! But the Scripture cannot be broken.

There is none amongst mere men, amongst those who descended by ordinary generation from Adam, who can abide in the tabernacle of God or dwell in His holy hill.

But thank God there is one who did not descend by ordinary generation, who is fully man as we are, even the Lord Jesus Christ, our elder brother.

*   This is He who is called "Jesus Christ the righteous" (1 Jn 2:1) by the Apostle John.
*   This is He who is the "Holy One and the Just" (Act 3:14) to the Apostle Peter.
*   This is He "who knew no sin" (2 Cor 5:21) to the Apostle Paul.
*   This is He who is "holy, harmless, undefiled, separate from sinners, and made higher than the heavens" (Heb 7:26) to the writer of Hebrews.

Who shall abide in the tabernacle of God? Who shall dwell in His holy hill? None, but Jesus Christ, who alone is perfectly upright and righteous.

Psalm 15 is about this Man—this man of men, or rather this man of God, the God-Man. This

Psalm describes the personal character of our Lord Jesus Christ. It describes what He is like—especially during His earthly ministry.

So consider...

2. Who He Is

a. He Is Pure in Deeds

² He that walketh uprightly, and worketh righteousness,

Walking and working: these are terms that describe our external deeds. These are things which we do with our hands and feet.

Our Lord is upright and righteous in outward deeds. He is upright and righteous in His heart. And since out of the heart "are the issues of life" (Prov 4:23), our Lord is upright and righteous in all that He does.

He did not at any point transgress the Law of God in all that He did. Some of the Jews charged Him for breaking the Sabbath. But they knew that they had no basis for their charge. For when He was tried before Annas, and Caiaphas, and Pilate, and Herod, none could prove He had broken any law—whether civil or religious. The Jews had to resort to false witnesses to indict Him.

Our Lord is sinless in action. He did not break the Law, and He did good whenever the opportunity arose. Thus, it could not be said that He failed the Law.

He walked uprightly and worked righteously. Oh, how we should imitate Him—so that we may be blameless before God and man.

b. He Is Pure in Thoughts

²ᵇ and speaketh the truth in his heart.

What is the speech of the heart but the thought? "Out of the abundance of the heart the mouth speaketh," says our Lord (Mt 12:34). Speech is an overflow of our thoughts.

The thoughts of our Lord are truth and faithfulness. He does not entertain falsehood. He does not allow sinful thoughts. Sinful thoughts are either based on falsehood or wrong reasoning. Righteous thoughts are founded upon truth and right reasoning.

Our Lord is pure and perfect in His thought life. He was tempted in all points like as we are, yet without sin (Heb 4:15).

Were it not that His thought life is as pure as His outward life, would His Father have been pleased with Him? Would His Father have accepted His sacrifice? We are taught in Psalm 44 that God "knoweth the secrets of the heart" (Ps 44:21).

Our Lord hid no secret from His Father. He had no secret sin. He had no sin even in His thoughts.

c. He Is Pure in Speech

³ He that backbiteth not with his tongue, nor doeth evil to his neighbour, nor taketh up a reproach against his neighbour.

Our catechism teaches us that we sin in words, deeds and thoughts (*WSC* 82). We have seen how our Lord is perfectly righteous in thoughts and deeds. What about His speech? His speech is also without sin!

He does not backbite with His tongue. He does not talk bad about anyone behind His back—where the subject cannot defend himself. He does not slander.

Nor does He cast a slur on His neighbour.

He does not do evil to His neighbour by gossips or by spreading falsehood. He does not render evil for evil. The Apostle Peter reminds us that guile was not found in His mouth, and that when He was reviled, He reviled not again; when He suffered, He threatened not, but committed Himself to Him that judges righteously (1 Pet 2:22-23).

It is particularly on this point that Christ has set us an example, that we should follow in His steps (1 Pet 2:21). How many of us can resist the lust of the flesh to poke at anyone who has provoked us? Our Lord reviled not in turn when He was reviled.

d. He Is Pure in Relationships

⁴ In whose eyes a vile person is contemned; but he honoureth them that fear the LORD.

Our Lord is not only pure in heart and conduct. He is careful with His friends. Yes, He was called "a friend of publicans and sinners" (Mt 11:19).

But are we not all sinners? He is a friend to the publicans and sinners because they feared God, and confessed their sin before God. They were His sheep, and they heard His voice and followed Him. He is a friend to all such who fear the LORD. He honours them with blessings which He has received from His Father.

On the other hand, He would have nothing to do with the proud Pharisees and scribes. They are vile in God's sight and vile in His sight. They love the honour of men. Our Lord tells us that…

> "…they make broad their phylacteries, and enlarge the borders of their garments, And love the uppermost rooms at feasts, and the chief seats in the synagogues, And greetings in the markets, and to be called of men, Rabbi, Rabbi" (Mt 23:5-7).

They are contemptible in our Lord's eyes. He would not flatter them. He would not be their friend. He called them white-washed tombs and a brood of vipers.

Our Lord, in other words, valued His friends according to their relationship with God, not according to their temporal status, wealth, education or religiosity.

e. He Is Pure in Promises

⁴ᵇ He that sweareth to his own hurt, and changeth not.

Our Lord is a man of His word. He made many promises, and He kept His promises even when they hurt. The greatest of His promises was, of course, His promise unto His Father in the eternal Covenant of Grace.

Our Lord covenanted to take on human flesh, to suffer on behalf of those whom the Father gave Him. He promised to die on their behalf to pay for their sin. It was a most painful promise to keep. But He kept it all to the jot and tittle.

He suffered the pains of hell for you and I who belong to Him.

f. He Is Pure in the Use of
Worldly Possession

⁵ He that putteth not out his money to usury,

The Law of Moses forbids the Israelites from lending money to other Israelites for interest (Ex 22:25; Lev 25:35-37). The law does not forbid charging a reasonable interest for strangers and aliens.

But our Lord would no doubt not put his money to usury at all. We read of Him and His disciples *giving*, but we do not read of them *lending*, much less earning interest through loans. He had no interest in being paid for doing good. Were He willing to put His money to usury, He would have been willing to make a lot of money selling bread and fish to the four and five thousand.

This is what charging interest is all about. It is about helping the poor for a fee. Our Lord was interested in doing good. He had no interest in making money out of the poor. Indeed, the gospel accounts indicate that the apostolic band under the leadership of the Lord gave to the poor routinely: for why else would they be indignant that Mary's ointment was not sold and given to the poor (cf. Mk 14:5)?

"It is more blessed to give than to receive" (Acts 20:35), says our Lord. "Freely ye have received, freely give" (Mt 10:8). This was His principle of life and ministry. He exemplified it by giving His life for us.

g. He Is Pure in Justice

⁵ᵇ nor taketh reward against the innocent.

The word rendered "reward" here refers to a bribe. In ancient days and even today, there are unscrupulous people who will take bribes to testify against the innocent. The more you pay them, the more they are willing to support your case against another—however innocent he may be.

Our Lord would not take bribes. He would not pervert the course of justice. He has no respect of persons. He deals with everyone equally. Just as He would not do good for material gains, He does not pervert justice for material gains. Just as it is His life's principle to do good *unconditionally*; so it is His life's principle to do justice *uncompromisingly*.

Now, we have no record of our Lord, being asked to take bribes against the innocent during His earthly ministry. But we do have examples of how He lived out the same principle, which would have kept Him from taking any bribes to pervert justice. Do you not see how He refused to give face to the ungodly rich and powerful? He told them plainly that they were wicked and heading for destruction. Do you not see how He sided with the repentant sinners and publicans? Do you not see how He rebuked Simon the Pharisee for his wicked thoughts against the unnamed woman who washed His feet with her tears? Do you not see how He cared not what the religious Jews would say when He went into Samaria to preach to the Samaritans? Do you not see how He refused to honour the wicked Herod with an answer, not to mention with the miracles that he wanted to see? Although our Lord was innocent, He refused to do anything that might in any way be seen as perverting justice.

Most of all, do you not see how our Lord did not compromise justice, but bore the full brunt of God's wrath against us—in order to satisfy divine justice.

In the Garden of Gethsemane, our Lord pleaded with His Father: "If it were possible, take this cup away from me." But we must not think that He was asking His Father to compromise justice. No, no; "if it were possible" must be understood as "if it were possible by any way that will fully satisfy divine justice."

Our Lord would not take bribes against the innocent. By the same principle, He would likewise not seek the reduction of punishment for the guilty.

We were guilty. He laid down His life to pay for our penalty—in full—that we might be reconciled to God.

3. Who We Should Be

The description in the preceding verses matches no one perfectly but Christ. Yet as we conclude, we are given to sing: "*He that doeth these things shall never be moved.*"

It is evident that here is a challenge and exhortation to one another to do these things (cf. Col 3:16); as well as a promise of divine blessedness for those who do.

But how can this exhortation and promise have any meaning for us if it is impossible for us to do as described? Well, it can have meaning because Christ is the Head of the Church and the Church is His Body. Those who believe in Him are united to Him and covered by His righteousness in justification, and therefore regarded as righteous in God's sight. What Christ did in His earthly walk is accounted to them. And not only so, the Spirit of Christ indwells them so as to make them more and more like Christ.

Thus, this Psalm does not only describe what believers united to Him should be, but provides us with the portrait of Christ so that we may behold His glory and be "changed into the same image from glory to glory, even as by the Spirit of the Lord" (2 Cor 3:18b).

What a blessing is this Psalm to the Church!

Conclusion

¹ LORD, who shall abide in thy tabernacle? Who shall dwell in thy holy hill?

Who? But the Lord Jesus Christ who is pure in deeds, thoughts, and words, friendship, promises, possession and justice.

This is He who is holy, righteous and just. This is He who alone has the words HOLINESS TO THE LORD engraved upon His mitre (Ex 28:36). This is He who may abide in the tabernacle of God.

None of us may of ourselves abide in the tabernacle of God. None of us have a right to heaven.

But thanks be to God; He came as a representative of His people. He came so that God might not deal with us as our sin deserves.

Shall we not thank the Lord? Shall we not seek His grace to be transformed by the renewing of our mind, to be conformed to His image, knowing that only those who are holy, and righteous, and just may finally be found in the tabernacle of God? Has it not been written concerning heaven:

"And there shall in no wise enter into it any thing that defileth, neither whatsoever worketh abomination, or maketh a lie: but they which are written in the Lamb's book of life" (Rev 21:27)?

If you are a disciple of Christ, you will enter into the heavenly tabernacle of God on the basis of the righteousness and holiness of Christ, not on the basis of your holiness. You will enter in because your name is written in the Lamb's book of life. But at the same time as you enter, you will, no doubt, rejoice that by the work of the Spirit and by means of the Scriptures such as this Psalm, you bear a semblance to the Lord awaiting to receive you, to lead you into the everlasting abode He has prepared for you! Amen. Ω

Psalm 16:
The Righteous One's
Satisfaction with His Lot

Psalm 16 is a well-known Messianic Psalm. No one disputes that it is Messianic not because its content leaves us without doubt that it is Messianic, but because the New Testament makes it very clear that the speaker of this Psalm is Christ Himself.

Notice how the Apostle Peter quotes Psalm 16:8-11 in Acts 2:25-28. Then he adds:

"[29] Men and brethren, let me freely speak unto you of the patriarch David, that he is both dead and buried, and his sepulchre is with us unto this day. [30] Therefore being a prophet, and knowing that God had sworn with an oath to him, that of the fruit of his loins, according to the flesh, he would raise up Christ to sit on his throne; [31] He seeing this before spake of the resurrection of Christ, that his soul was not left in hell, neither his flesh did see corruption. [32] This Jesus hath God raised up, whereof we all are witnesses" (Acts 2:29-32).

King David died, and he was buried, and he saw corruption. Therefore, David could not be speaking about himself. The Scripture cannot be broken. He must be speaking about the Messiah, the Lord Jesus Christ who was raised from the dead.

The Apostle Paul confirms this interpretation in Acts 13:35, where he quotes Psalm 16:10:

"[35] Wherefore he saith also in another psalm, Thou shalt not suffer thine Holy One to see corruption. [36] For David, after he had served his own generation by the will of God, fell on sleep, and was laid unto his fathers, and saw corruption: [37] But he, whom God raised again, saw no corruption" (Acts 13:35-37).

But if this Psalm is about the resurrection of Christ, then the first person pronouns in it must refer to Christ: for the resurrection mentioned is not spoken of in the third person, but in the first person. See Psalm 16:10-11a, for example:

"*For thou wilt not leave **my** soul in hell; neither wilt thou suffer thine Holy One to see corruption. [11] Thou wilt shew **me** the path of life...*"

Christ, in other words, is speaking about His own resurrection!

Psalm 16, is therefore, without controversy, a Messianic Psalm. David wrote in the Spirit of Christ, and the speaker in the Psalm is Christ Himself.

It is difficult to give a title to this Psalm, but we concur with Andrew Bonar that a good title would be: "*The Righteous One's Satisfaction with His Lot*." Likewise, we agree with Bonar that Psalm 17 may, in tandem, be called "The Righteous One's Dissatisfaction with This Present World."

Psalm 16 is about our Lord's contemplation of the privileges that He enjoys because of His relationship with His Father. He is looking at those who have been pursuing strange gods, and He laments the sorrows that await them (v. 4).

He Himself was dwelling in this present world of pain, suffering, sorrow and persecution. He was deeply dissatisfied with the situation in the world. Psalm 17 makes that very clear.

But yet there was a satisfaction in Him. It was a satisfaction that transcended the situation He was in. He had joy and peace because He knew God.

Let's look at this Psalm briefly that we may more fully appreciate the satisfaction of our Lord and how we too, as a people united to Him, may share in this satisfaction.

Four things are expressed in this Psalm, namely:

1. v. 1   The Lord's Prayer to the Father
2. v. 2-6   The Lord's Sufficiency in the Father
3. v. 7-9   The Lord's Confidence in the Father
4. v. 10-11   The Lord's Hope in the Father

1. The Lord's Prayer
to the Father

[1] Preserve me, O God: for in thee do I put my trust.

Notice how our Lord does not take for granted that His Father will preserve Him. If anyone has the right to take the Father's love and preservation for granted it is the Son, and yet, He makes it a matter of prayer to ask His Father to preserve Him.

How much more, we who are adoptive sons and daughters of the Father should learn to do the same.

Let us, therefore, learn to do so every day lest we be lulled to live presumptuously and atheistically.

Let us pray each day:

- "LORD, preserve my health that I may serve thee, for in thee do I put my trust."

- "Preserve my faith that I may walk with Thee."

- "Preserve my church that we may glorify thee."

2. The Lord's Sufficiency
In The Father

[2] O my soul, thou hast said unto the LORD, Thou art my Lord: my goodness extendeth not to thee; [3] But to the saints that are in the earth, and to the excellent, in whom is all my delight.

The Lord Jesus Christ came to do His Father's will. He did not come to do good to His Father. No one can do good to the Father who is perfectly good and sufficient. When we praise the Father, we do not add to His goodness or glory. Rather, we acknowledge and manifest His glory.

It was the same for the Son. He came not to do good to the Father. His goodness extends not to the Father. He came to do good, rather, to the saints (v. 3)—the holy ones, the elect of God.

He came to do good to us. He delights in us not because we are worthy but because the Father has elected us. Our Lord came for us to bless us.

He did not come for idolaters, who hate Him and who vex His spirit.

[4] Their sorrows shall be multiplied that hasten after another god: their drink offerings of blood will I not offer, nor take up their names into my lips.

Take note that the "their" in this verse does not refer to the godly of verse 3, but to those who pursue after false gods. Our Lord does not approve of their worship. He would not take their names in His lips before the Father as He would do in the case of those in whom He delights. He laments their sorrow and destruction, but it is not for Him to bless all those who will remain the enemies of God.

On the other hand, for those who have been given to Him by the Father, our Lord has a blessing. This is what He says in verses 5-6:

> [5] *The LORD is the portion of mine inheritance and of my cup: thou maintainest my lot.* [6] *The lines are fallen unto me in pleasant places; yea, I have a goodly heritage.*

Our Lord came to purchase a goodly heritage not for Himself but for those He delights in. Because He loves His Father, and He came to do His Father's will, He knows that the blessing He would receive and distribute is unlimited.

It is as if God Himself is His inheritance and cup. He has a goodly heritage and His cup is overflowing. He came to secure all these not for Himself, but for His children.

So we too, as co-heirs with Christ, may enjoy the confidence and blessings that He enjoys.

This heritage which awaits us is a spiritual heritage. While we may be poor in this life, we are really rich in God because of Christ our Lord.

So, let us take the words of our Lord in our lips:

> "*The LORD is the portion of mine inheritance... The lines are fallen unto me in pleasant places; yea, I have a goodly heritage.*"

"The LORD is my portion,... therefore will I hope in him" (Lam 3:24).

3. The Lord's Respite
in the Father

[7] *I will bless the LORD, who hath given me counsel: my reins also instruct me in the night seasons.* [8] *I have set the LORD always before me: because he is at my right hand, I shall not be moved.* [9] *Therefore my heart is glad, and my glory [or soul] rejoiceth: my flesh also shall rest in hope.*

Our Lord is facing persecution and dangers in His life daily as He goes about doing His Father's will. He is daily vexed in the spirit by those who fear not God and serve Him not, but serve themselves, or false gods, or materialism and worldliness.

Yet the Lord has satisfaction and respite in His soul. How is He able to have such peace in His heart? He is able because He is in constant communion with His Father—not only in the day, but in the night seasons (v. 7).

His eyes are set on His Father. He is not flustered by the troubles He faces day by day because His eyes are fixed on His Father. "*I have set the LORD always before me*" (v. 8a). He knows that the Father is with Him in all His trials. He knows His Father is ready and able to help at all times. "*He is at my right hand, I shall not be moved,*" he says (v. 8b). [13]

---

[13] Who is this "he" in the phrase "He is at my right hand"? If the speaker is Christ, then this "he" must refer to God the Father. But the ascended Christ is seated at the right hand of the Father, so the Father is, as it were, on His left! So this verse must not be taken to refer to Christ's sitting at the right hand of the Father, but to the readiness, ability and power of the Father to help at any time. The right hand is the hand of power and readiness.

Therefore He is able to rejoice and to rest in hope (v. 9).

Every believer should have the same kind of peace and respite as our Lord. Indeed, we have even greater reasons to rejoice and hope—for Christ our Lord has already come. He suffered and died for us, and He is seated at the right hand of the throne of the Father, interceding for us.

So let us fix our eyes on our Lord as He fixed his eyes on the Father. "He that hath seen me hath seen the Father," says our Lord. When we look at Jesus the Author and Finisher of our faith, we will be doing exactly what our Lord did.

Let us fill our hearts with the promises of God, our tongues with the praise of God, and our eyes with Christ—that we may run our Christian race with joy, peace, confidence, and hope.

4. The Lord's Hope
in the Father

[10] *For thou wilt not leave my soul in hell; neither wilt thou suffer thine Holy One to see corruption.* [11] *Thou wilt shew me the path of life: in thy presence is fulness of joy; at thy right hand there are pleasures for evermore.*

These are the verses that make this Psalm so well known. What is our Lord saying in these verses?

Our Lord is the Holy One. He is speaking about what the Father will do for Him.

He knows that He came to do His Father's will, which includes dying on the cross as the Lamb to take away the sin of His people.

That thought will at one point bring our Lord very low; for in the Garden of Gethsemane, He cried out unto the Father: "If it be possible, take this Cup from me, but not my will, but thy will be done."

But our Lord's confidence in the Father was never diminished. He dreaded the thought of being forsaken by His Father on the cross, but He knew that in so far as His human life is concerned, His Father would not leave Him in the state of death or the grave.

That is how the word "hell" in our text is to be understood. Our Lord Jesus was under the power of death for three days. For three days, His soul was separated from His body. Now, we often think nothing about it, but do you realise that this separation was an undesirable humiliation for our Lord?

Otherwise, our Lord would not rejoice in saying: "thou wilt not leave my soul in hell."

Our Lord was not looking forward to the state of death. He was fully man. Being separated from his body is not something He could ever get used to.

When we get to heaven, we can be sure that we will not get used to living without a body. Like the souls of the martyrs in Revelation 6, we will be asking the Lord, "How long, O Lord, holy and true, dost thou not judge and avenge our blood..." (Rev 6:10)? How long before our Messiah returns as Judge and King? How long before our bodies are raised from the ground?

The state of separation between body and soul is a state of humiliation. This is why traditional Reformed theology speaks of glorification as happening not at death, but at the resurrection!

Our Lord was in a state of humiliation during the three days when His body was in the grave.[14] We must not think that because His soul had gone to heaven that He was in a state of exaltation. No, no; our Lord was still being humbled for our sins.

But thank God, His Father would not leave His soul in that state.

And neither would He suffer His Holy One to see corruption. It was enough that our Lord should die. His suffering the wrath of God and His dying on the cross was sufficient to pay the penalty due for our sin.

There was no need for His body to see corruption. He did not have sinful flesh like us. No doubt, He came in the "likeness of sinful flesh" (Rom 8:3). But His body was not the instrument of sin, nor was it defiled by sin—original or actual. His body was holy. There was no need for it to suffer corruption.

Thus, the Father would not allow it to see corruption. He was preserved from decay until He rose on the first day of the week.

Our Lord refers to His resurrection in verse 11:

> [11] Thou wilt shew me the path of life: in thy presence is fulness of joy; at thy right hand there are pleasures for evermore.

These words are very rich. It speaks of the fullness of our Lord's joy when He was raised from the dead. Remember that though He committed His soul unto His Father upon His death, it was not until His body was raised that He enjoyed the fullness of joy.

When a body is raised from the dead, it is freed from all wants. A soul in heaven, which is without its body will want its body, but a soul in heaven united to its body cannot want anything more. There is fullness of joy.

Today, we can have a cup full of joy mingled with gall which we must enjoy with tears. In the day we leave this world, our cup of joy will no longer be mingled with gall, but neither shall we enjoy it with tears of joy, for our bodies will be suffering corruption in the grave.[15] But in that great and glorious day of the Resurrection, we will be immersed in an ocean of joy unmingled with any feelings of want.

Let us observe three things from our Lord's testimony of how He basked in the fullness of joy. Consider the way, the source and the duration of our Lord's joy.

First, observe that there is a **way** to the fullness of joy, namely—*"the path of life." "Thou wilt shew me the path of life."* What is the *"path of life"*? In this context, the path of life is not referring to the Christian walk. It refers, rather to the way of resurrection. This is the path to the fullness of joy. We will not have fullness of joy until then.

Secondly, observe what is the **source** of the fullness of joy. *"In thy presence is fulness of joy; at thy right hand there are pleasures for evermore,"* says our Lord. What is the source of the fullness of joy? What is the source of pleasures for evermore?

It is God. Notice how our Lord speaks of God as being the source of joy? *"In thy presence is fullness of joy"* speaks about joy derived from fellowship with God. *"At thy right hand there*

---

[14] Cf. *WLC* 50.

[15] A man who lost his limbs in this life can be full of joy and contentment, but he knows that his joy will never be complete until he has his limbs again.

are pleasures," on the other hand, speaks of God commanding His blessing.

Our Lord was not only anticipating heaven. He was anticipating the joy of fellowship with God and of receiving His blessings.

God is our Lord's chiefest joy. It was His chiefest joy during His earthly ministry, it remained His chiefest joy when He returned to heaven.

Our Lord's resurrection was not the chiefest joy. His resurrection only enabled Him to enjoy God's fellowship and blessing fully—as the God-Man.

Heaven as a place was not our Lord's chiefest joy. His source of joy is the Father Himself. Heaven is a place of joy because the Father is there. Were it not for the Father's presence and fellowship with Him, heaven could not bring the fullness of joy for our Lord.

There is fullness of joy in heaven, because God is there.

But now, notice *thirdly*, the **duration** of our Lord's joy. "*At thy right hand there are pleasures for evermore.*" The fullness of joy that our Lord would enjoy in heaven will last forevermore.

Heaven is not merely a place of never-ending existence. If it were merely a place of never-ending existence, it would be a boring place: for we would soon find nothing in heaven new or pleasurable.

Only fellowship with God who is infinite and unchangeable can give man the fullness of joy and everlasting pleasure.

Because of God's fellowship and blessing, our Lord, as the God-Man can enjoy everlasting pleasure for all eternity.

Such was the joy that our Lord was anticipating even as He thought of His impending death. It was this hope that gave our Lord satisfaction and confidence as He headed to the cross to do His Father's will.

Conclusion

This hope that our Lord enjoyed is available to all who are united to Him. As we can share in our Lord's sufficiency and confidence in the Father, let us also share in His hope.

This hope is not a mere wish. The Christian hope speaks of a reality to come.

As our Lord was resurrected from the dead, so all who are united to Him would one day be raised.

This world is not our home. The trials in this life do not characterise our life. It is but a phase we have to pass through. Our life is destined to be a life of the fullness of joy everlasting.

Oh let us not allow the dark clouds of our day to rob us of our joy and satisfaction in God. Let us rather, with genuine hope, continue to run the Christian race, following the example of our Saviour as He walked through life in the fear and love of His Father for our sake. Amen. Ω

Psalm 17:
The Righteous One's Dissatisfaction with This Present World

We saw in our last study that Psalm 16 may be titled: *"The Righteous One's Satisfaction with His Lot."*

The Righteous One is Christ in the first place, and all believers united to Him in the second place. The Righteous One says in Psalm 16:

> "The LORD is the portion of mine inheritance and of my cup: thou maintainest my lot. The lines are fallen unto me in pleasant places; yea, I have a goodly heritage" (Ps 16:5-6).

But now coming to Psalm 17, we see that it may be titled: *"The Righteous One's Dissatisfaction with this Present World."*

He says, verses 13-14:

> "Arise, O LORD, disappoint him, cast him down: deliver my soul from the wicked, which is thy sword: From men which are thy hand, O LORD, from men of the world, which have their portion in this life..." (Psalm 17:13-14).

This Psalm was written as a prayer by David. But it was surely written in the Spirit of Christ. Christ, much more than David, would have felt the deep dissatisfaction in regard to this sinful world during His earthly sojourn.

This Psalm, therefore, reveals something of our Lord's perplexity and His communications with His Father in regard to the vexation of His soul, as He lived amongst sinful men in an imperfect world.

This Psalm, as such, gives expression to the groaning of our hearts as a people indwelt with the Spirit of Christ, who are in this world but not of this world.

We may discern the following structure in it:

1. Prologue (v. 1 6)
2. Petitions
    a. Encouragement (v. 7)
    b. Protection (v. 8-12)
    c. Imprecation (v. 13-14)
3. Concluding confession (v. 15)

1. Prologue

The Psalm begins in verse 1 with a prologue in the form of a petition unto the Father to be heard:

> [1] Hear the right, O LORD, attend unto my cry, give ear unto my prayer, that goeth not out of feigned lips. [2] Let my sentence come forth from thy presence; let thine eyes behold the things that are equal.

Here our Lord calls unto His Father, to attend to the cry and meditations of His heart. You can perhaps sense the perplexity of our Lord in these words. Notice how He speaks of His prayer as coming out of unfeigned lips. Is this not a reflection of the fact that many around

Him speak with pretence and insincerity? Notice also how our Lord asks His Father to judge Him according to His omniscient eyes and to vindicate Him (v. 2)? Does this not reflect how the world is full of injustice? There are those who unjustly accuse us of wrong-doing. There are many who will question our motives when they disagree with us. There are many who will judge us unfairly without proper knowledge, without giving us an opportunity to answer.

If you have experienced perplexity, our Lord experienced it much more acutely.

But our Lord was able to cry unto the Father with such sincerity because no guile was found in Him. He was in all points tempted like as we are, yet without sin (v.3). He sinned neither in thought, nor in word (v. 3), nor in deed (v. 4). But our Lord was not haughty. He cries unto His Father (v. 5):

> [5] *Hold up my goings in thy paths, that my footsteps slip not.*

Oh how we must learn to imitate our Lord if we would commune in sincerity with the Father on our frustrations with this present world. Oh how we must humble ourselves to seek the Lord's help to uphold us from falling into sin.

Only then can we, wholeheartedly, take up the words of verse 6 into our lips:

> [6] *I have called upon thee, for thou wilt hear me, O God: incline thine ear unto me, and hear my speech.*

What does our Lord request of His Father?

2. Petitions

Essentially, He requests three things: (a) Encouragement, (b) Protection, and (c) Imprecation.

a. Encouragement

First, He asks His Father to demonstrate His marvellous lovingkindness:

> [7] *Shew thy marvellous lovingkindness, O thou that savest by thy right hand them which put their trust in thee from those that rise up against them.*

The word lovingkindness here is a special word that refers to God's covenant mercies towards His people. Out of His lovingkindness, the Father has often arisen to help His children against their enemies.

The Lord desired that His Father should show the wonder of His great love towards Him at this time of His need.

This is a legitimate prayer. At times when we are most perplexed by the world, and we feel almost ready to give up, the only thing that can lift us up is if the LORD displays His wondrous love towards us in a distinct and discernible way.

In the case of our Lord, His Father spoke from heaven to confirm His love: "This is my beloved Son, in whom I am well pleased" (Mt 3:17).

What will it be in our case? Maybe a kind word from a brother or sister. Maybe blessing received. In my own experience, when I am most discouraged and crying out unto the Father, the Father has mercifully displayed tokens of His mercy by way of conversion and repentance. For example, when discouragement comes through severe criticism and I feel myself crushed, then the LORD comes along and with a word of gratitude through the lips of someone who is not known to be charitable or someone who has long resisted the truth, but now sees it clearly.

So dear reader, when you feel perplexed and discouraged by the things happening around you, cry out to the LORD to show His marvellous lovingkindness, to display the wonders of His love.

This is the first thing that our Lord asked of His Father.

b. Protection

Secondly, He asked to be protected from His enemies and the devices of the wicked one (v. 8-9):

> [8] *Keep me as the apple of the eye, hide me under the shadow of thy wings,* [9] *From the wicked that oppress me, from my deadly enemies, who compass me about.*

The apple of the eye refers to the pupil of the eye.[16] If anyone tries to touch the pupil of your eye, what will you do? You will react instantly to protect your eye, won't you?

Similarly, when an eagle is nesting, do not ever try to touch the chicks, or you will get a painful shock.

The Lord desired for His Father to protect Him as a man will protect his pupil or as an eagle would protect her chicks.

Our Lord had many enemies. Remember, for example, how when He returned to preach in the synagogue at Nazareth, many wanted to kill Him by pushing Him down a cliff.

But the Lord's time was not yet. And so the Father protected Him so that He was able to walk through the crowd unharmed.

So it is with us. Today we may not have many enemies who will harm us physically. But Satan is ever our enemy, and he is using all means to try to harm us. He will use, for example, circumstances and words to hurt us.

Words may seem very harmless, but I think most of us would have enough experience of being hurt by words, that we know how damaging words can be.

Shall we not then ask the LORD to protect us from all words that hurt and tear down? Let us take heed lest we fall. Let us not pretend that we are strong and can take whatever comes our way. Let us ask the Father, as our Lord did, to protect us.

He will protect us for His Son's sake. He may do so in many ways such as by helping us to have a positive attitude and a godly response, or by enabling us to come out of the difficult circumstance a better person. Whatever may be the case, He will help, if only we will cry to Him.

This is the second thing we must learn from our Lord's prayer.

---

[16] Literally, the Hebrew (שָׁמְרֵנִי כְּאִישׁוֹן בַּת־עָיִן) may be translated "Keep me as the little man—the daughter of [your] eye" in reference to the little reflection that one sees of himself in the eye of another if he stands close enough to him. It may, therefore, imply a plea to be kept under God's watchful and intimate care.

c. Imprecation

The *third* thing in our Lord's prayer is more offensive than defensive. Verse 13:

> [13] *Arise, O LORD, disappoint him, cast him down: deliver my soul from the wicked, which is thy sword:* [14] *From men which are thy hand, O LORD, from men of the world, which have their portion in this life...*

Not only does the Lord ask His Father to display His lovingkindness and to protect Him as the apple of His eyes; He ask His Father to deal with His enemies.

His enemies are those whose lives comprise merely the things of this present world. They care not for righteousness. They care not for others. Their portion is in this life. They have wealth, and substance and even children, but they remain ungrateful to the LORD. They forget that all things that they possess come from the LORD.

They live wickedly and deal wickedly with the righteous. Our Lord understands that they do not have the right to do what they do. He cries out unto His Father to disappoint them or to frustrate their plans.

Too long have we assumed that the wicked have the right to do what they do! Too long have our tongues remained silent. Too long have we allowed the wicked to triumph over the righteous and trample the name of the LORD!

But silence is not good. It will only embolden the wicked. What shall we do? Well, no where does the word of God teach us to call for a mass demonstration or to resort to violence. No, no; the only approved means is prayer. We must pray as our Lord prayed that the Father will arise against the wicked.

3. Concluding Confession

[15] *As for me, I will behold thy face in righteousness: I shall be satisfied, when I awake, with thy likeness.*

This world that we live in cannot give us the peace, joy and satisfaction that we desire to have. For here, we do not have a continuing city. This is not our home. Our home is in heaven: the celestial city where Christ is. Only when we awake at the Resurrection shall we be satisfied (v. 15).

But we do not need to go through this life stoically. We ought rather to go through this life prayerfully. Let us pray as our Lord teaches us: (1) that God will show forth His great love towards us through fitting tokens of mercy; (2) that God will protect us as the apple of His eyes; and (3) that God will rise up against the wicked and wickedness.

May the Lord grant us that in this way, we may be, not only theoretically but by experience, more than conquerors through Christ who loves us. Amen. Ω

Psalm 18:
The Righteous One's
Thanksgiving for Deliverance

The inspired title of this Psalm indicates that it was written by David after the LORD delivered him from the hand of all his enemies, including Saul.

So this Psalm is a song of gratitude for victory by the warrior-king who was at last ruling the nation in peace.

The words of this Psalm appear also in 2 Samuel 22 with what may be known as editorial differences. It is very probable that an early version of the song is recorded under inspiration in 2 Samuel 22; whereas Psalm 18 contains the final version inspired by the Holy Spirit for use in public worship. This being the case, what we have in Psalm 18 is appointed for public singing; whereas what is in 2 Samuel 22 is designed for reading.

This is one of the reasons why we do not sing the other songs appearing in the Bible. They are simply not intended for public worship throughout the ages; for if they were, they would have been incorporated by the Spirit into the Psalter.

Now, although this Psalm was written by David, it was no doubt written in the Spirit of Christ, so that the words that appear belong to Christ in a special and direct manner.

We say this for good reasons.

First, the Apostle Paul quotes verse 49 of this Psalm in Romans 15:8-9 to indicate that this Psalm has to do with the salvation of the Gentiles in the name of Christ, rather than merely about the enemies of David.

Secondly, some of the words in this Psalm are clearly words that only Christ could say with a clear conscience. For example, verses 20-21:

> "20 *The LORD rewarded me according to my righteousness; according to the cleanness of my hands hath he recompensed me.* 21 *For I have kept the ways of the LORD, and have not wickedly departed from my God.*"

Who but Christ could have spoken these words with full confidence?

With these two considerations in mind, and looking at its content, we can understand this Psalm as the word of thanksgiving of Christ after He returned victorious from the grave.

This Psalm has four major parts: From verses 1-3, the Lord extols the greatness of God as His Rock, Fortress, Deliverer and Help. From verses 4-24, the Lord describes the sorrow and distress He was in, and how the Father delivered Him through a mighty show of power. From verses 25-45, the Lord rejoices in the victory over darkness and enmity that the Father granted Him. From verses 46-50, the Lord leads all His people, including the Gentiles, to give praise and thanks unto God for all that He has done for Him.

We may outline the Psalm as follows:

1. v. 1-3   The LORD Is My Rock
2. v. 4-24   The LORD Is My Reward
3. v. 25-45   The LORD Will Light My Candle
4. v. 46-50   The LORD Will Be Exalted

In this short study, we shall not be able to examine this Psalm in detail. Instead, let us take a couple of verses from each of these 3 sections to meditate for a moment.

1. The LORD Is My Rock

[1] *I will love thee, O LORD, my strength.* [2] *The LORD is my rock, and my fortress, and my deliverer; my God, my strength, in whom I will trust; my buckler, and the horn of my salvation, and my high tower.*

Our Saviour, the beloved Son of God, more than any other man in the history of mankind can say that He loves the LORD. His is a perfect love: for God is love. He Himself is sovereign God, but He humbled Himself to take on the nature of man, even man that is dependent on God for His being, movement and life. It is in this dependence that the reality that the LORD is His strength finds meaning. And it is in this reality that those He came to represent, can sing in union and sympathy with Him, especially after they are enabled by Him to respond to the love of God, to love Him in return. It is in this reality that we can identify with His "I" and "my" in this Psalm. What is true of Him as our Covenant Head, becomes true of us by the power of His Spirit.

Notice the sevenfold description of the LORD as His rock, His fortress, His deliverer, His strength, His buckler, His horn and His high tower. And so the LORD is my, and your rock, fortress, deliverer, strength, buckler, horn and high tower.

"The LORD is my rock." Three times in this Psalm (v. 31, 46) and twenty times in the whole book of Psalms is the LORD referred to as the Rock. Why is He a Rock? He is our Rock because He alone is unchanging and fully dependable. He provides stability and security for us.

And the LORD is also *"my fortress."* Why is He a fortress? He is a fortress because He is a strong and high place to hide in. When I feel defenceless; when I have nowhere to flee from all my troubles, it is only to the LORD my fortress I can flee. It is far safer and comforting to hide in the LORD than to hide in a man-made fortress, or to go far from the maddening crowd.

And the LORD is also my *deliverer*. Not only does the LORD hide as a fortress, He delivers as a King.

And the LORD is my *strength*. The word used here paints the picture of a mighty rocky cliff. Those of us who have had the opportunity to behold massive cliffs, whether in Grand Canyon, in Wales, or in Norway, or elsewhere, would no doubt have felt a sense of awe as we came to a fresh realization of just how small we are. God is to us a mighty cliff. He is our strength; we can trust Him for while we are weak, He is immensely strong.

And the LORD is also my *buckler*. This word rendered "buckler" is usually translated as "shield." Three times in this Psalm is the LORD described as our buckler or shield. Our LORD protects us from the assaults of the wicked one. Moreover, in Christ, we are also shielded from the wrath of God.

And the LORD is the *horn* of my salvation. Horns are symbols of strength and authority. God is the Captain of our salvation in Christ.

And finally, the LORD is my high *tower*. In Him I have protection from the enemies, and in Him I can see with eyes of faith what others cannot see. "Call unto me, and I will answer thee, and shew thee great and mighty things, which thou knowest not" (Jer 33:3).

David knew and experienced the Father's protection and help at the time when he was deeply distressed. He was able to experience the LORD's help because he learned to turn his eyes away from himself and from the circumstances surrounding him. He learned to turn his eyes to the LORD. So too our Lord Himself turned His eyes to the Father when He was perplexed and sorrowing because of the circumstances surrounding Him.

What about you, dear Christian? Whatever difficulties you may be going through in life, remember that the LORD is your Rock, your Fortress, your Deliver, your Strength, your Buckler, your Horn and your High Tower. Therefore, confidently call upon Him *who is worthy to be praised*" (v. 3), in the knowledge that He will deliver you from His and your enemies.

2. The LORD Is My Reward

David experienced the dramatic deliverance of the LORD out of sorrows and distress that brought him near to death. This great deliverance is described in terms of smoke and fire, and hail stone, and lightning and thunder (v. 4-19).

This poetic description may seem to some to be an over dramatization of what happened to him. But no, these are ultimately the words of the greater David. David's experience is but a shadow of what our Saviour experienced. Did not the deliverance of our Lord actually involve an earthquake, the opening of the grave, the appearance of angels and even the resurrection of the dead?

Even then, the picture of deliverance painted in earthly terms, in this Psalm, is really accommodated to our feeble understanding, and does not fully convey the significance of all that He experienced.

David was delivered out of life-threatening situations; the greater David was delivered out of death which the whole army of the seed of the serpent orchestrated, thinking that he would have victory over Him. But none could defeat Him to whom the Father delights (v. 19b). "This is my beloved Son, in whom I am well pleased," says the Father (Mt 3:17).

Our Saviour understood this full well. So He appoints for us to sing with Him, verse 20:

> "The LORD rewarded me according to my righteousness; according to the cleanness of my hands hath he recompensed me. [21] For I have kept the ways of the LORD, and have not wickedly departed from my God."

We noted how these words cannot fully apply to sinful man including David. God is of purer eyes than to behold evil. All our righteousnesses are as filthy rags before His eyes.

If God is to reward us according to our own righteousness or according to the cleanness of our hands, we will get nothing of the blessings of God, but only His curses.

No, no; these verses can only be taken in the lips of our Saviour according to His own merits. He alone had clean hands (v. 20). He alone kept the ways of the LORD perfectly (v. 21). He alone had the judgements of God before Him at all times (v. 22). He walked blamelessly and kept Himself from all sin (v. 23).

All others can take these words only through union with Christ. So when we sing verse 20 or verse 24, we must do so, with eyes of faith set upon Christ before us as our Worshipper-in-Chief. In this way, we may sing the words we are given to sing as words that pertain to Christ primarily and to ourselves secondarily. We may, for example, understand verse 24 as it applies to ourselves in this way:

"Therefore [on account of what Christ has done] hath the LORD recompensed me according to my righteousness [which is the righteousness of Christ imputed to me in justification and imparted to me in sanctification]; according to the cleanness of my hands [which are washed by the Spirit of Christ and the blood of Christ] in His eyesight."

Thank God for Christ Jesus our Lord. He was tempted in all points like as we are, yet without sin.

Because of His righteousness and the cleanness of His hands, He was fit to represent us at the cross of Calvary. At Calvary, He died not for His own sin, but for our sins.

Now then, our salvation is entirely on account of His work. And yet, He promises to reward us. He died and rose again in order that He might give gifts to us.

"And, behold, I come quickly; and my reward is with me, to give every man according as his work shall be" (Rev 22:12).

He rewards us out of grace. But of course, this does not mean that we can therefore live as we like—for those whom God will reward are those who will seek first the kingdom of God. "Seek ye first the kingdom of God and His righteousness and all these things shall be added unto you" (Mt 6:33).

We must seek first His kingdom. But thank God that He will not cast us out because our striving and seeking are imperfect. Thank God that we can resort to Christ our Rock as He resorted to His Rock the Father.

Thank God that He does not whip us to make us holy, but He draws us with cords of love by giving us the righteousness of Christ and a promise of His reward.

3. The LORD Will Light
My Candle

The LORD is perfectly just and perfectly righteous, therefore He will not reward the wicked with good and the righteous with evil. He will deal with the Righteous One and the righteous ones in Him according to their kindness, blamelessness and purity. He will deal with the wicked according to their wickedness (v. 25-26).

Therefore, He will not allow the righteous to remain in darkness.

[28] *For thou wilt light my candle: the LORD my God will enlighten my darkness.*

These words are so familiar to us that it is difficult to explain it without spoiling its beauty.

What does it mean to *"light my candle"*? "What does it mean to *"enlighten my darkness"* or to *"turn my darkness into light"*? No doubt, candle or lamp, is a metaphor to speak about a life of joy or brightness. Job says:

"How oft is the candle of the wicked put out! and how oft cometh their destruction upon them! God distributeth sorrows in his anger" (Job 21:17).

The LORD will light my candle or keep my candle burning speaks of how He will sustain my life and enable me to enjoy His blessing in this life. He will make *"my feet like hinds' feet and setteth me upon high places"* (v. 33).

Not only does the LORD protect us from harm and dangers as it pertains to this life; He also watches over our souls to enable us to live a victorious Christian life.

It is a fact that our lives are full of ups and downs. It is a known fact that many people sink into long periods of darkness and depression. This happens to both believers and unbelievers. Unbelievers have no one to turn to. But thank God that believers can turn to the LORD.

Indeed, God is able to sustain our peace and joy. He is able to keep our candle burning. And He is able to turn my darkness into light in that He alone can give me joy and brightness when dark clouds are over my head and I sorrow and grieve over some sad turn of events in my life.

Our LORD is very kind and loving towards us. He will not allow His children who cry out unto Him to remain in sorrow and distress and depression. He will help. As the Father encouraged the Son in the Garden of Gethsemane by sending Him a myriad of angels; so the Son who intercedes for us, will send help from His Father's throne.

Thank God that whatever depressing circumstance in life we may go through—the LORD will light our candle and He will turn our darkness, however dark it may be, into light! By His help, we shall have victory over all difficulties. We shall *"run through a troop"*, we shall *"leap over a wall"* (v. 29). We shall be victorious in the battles we have been appointed to fight in whatever form they make take (v. 30-45).

4. The LORD Will Be Exalted

[46] *The LORD liveth; and blessed be my rock; and let the God of my salvation be exalted.*

As mentioned, verse 49 is quoted by the Apostle Paul in Romans 15:8-9 as being a promise of the Lord Jesus Christ to give thanks and praise God amongst the Gentiles. Therefore, this whole concluding strophe of praise, and indeed, the whole Psalm must be understood as the word of Christ. He came to glorify God (Jn 17:4-5). He glorified the Father not only by a perfect walk, but by proving that the Father lives and that He will save all those who put their trust in Him. Our Lord has no need of salvation from sin, but as the God-Man in His humiliation, He had need of strength and deliverance (v. 47-48).

Because He did receive strength and deliverance as the Anointed One representing His people (v. 50), He calls upon all of us to bless and exalt the LORD with Him. And He has given us the words to do so!

Conclusion

This is Psalm 18 in a nutshell. Oh may the words of this Psalm encourage us to persevere on in our pilgrim walk though the way may often be gloomy and dark. When the shadows of dark providence fall over our path, let us think about Christ our Rock and how He is a very present help in trouble. Let us remember how He went through the same valley of shadows, and how He triumphed over the darkness. Let us, therefore, confidently take the next step singing in our heart:

"The Lord will light my candle so,
    that it shall shine full bright:
The Lord my God will also make
    My darkness to be light" (v. 28 in metre)

The Lord is your Reward who has promised to bless. As the Father kept His candle burning through His darkest hours, so He will keep your candle burning and turn your darkness into light. Amen. Ω

Psalm 19:
The Righteous One's
Twin-Books of Nature & Law

Psalm 19 is another of the Psalms that does not appear to be Messianic and is hardly ever regarded as Messianic by any commentator.

However, as we study this Psalm and compare Scripture with Scripture, you will realise that the Apostle Paul, writing under inspiration, actually regarded this Psalm as being about the Messiah and His Gospel (cf. Rom 10:17-18; Ps 19:4). This Psalm, as is the case with all others, is the "word of Christ" (Col 3:16) which He has appointed for us to sing in union with Him, not only in prayer and praise, but to exhort and encourage one another.

Looking at the Psalm itself, we can discern two main divisions. The first division (v. 1-6) has to do with the natural or general revelation of God. It deals, in other words, with the Book of Nature. The Second division (v. 7-14) has to do with the supernatural or special revelation of God. It deals, in other words, with the Book of Law. As Christ is the Word or Revelation of God, we know that both of these modes of revelation may be attributed to Him, and thus, both of these books are His books.

So we may entitle this Psalm "The Righteous One's Twin-Books of Nature and Law." The Righteous One is, of course, Christ. But so closely united is He with His saints that all who are united to Him may appropriate His words into their own lips as righteous ones. Thus, this is also our song, so much so, that we may honestly and affectively sing the first-person experiences and requests in it (cf. v. 11-14). Let us bear this in mind as we consider this Psalm according to the outline already alluded to:

1.   v. 1-6   The Book of Nature

2.   v. 7-14   The Book of Law

1. The Book of Nature

[1] *The heavens declare the glory of God; and the firmament sheweth his handywork.* [2] *Day unto day uttereth speech, and night unto night sheweth knowledge.*

The heavens here refer not to the dwelling place of angels. It describes rather the vastness of our sky and the expanse of space.

When we look up into the sky, whether in the day, or in the night, we cannot help but be filled with a sense of awe as we realise just how small we are.

In the day, the beauty of the clouds, the brilliance of the sun and blueness of the sky testify of the wisdom and greatness of God.

In the night, the vastness of space, the profound darkness and the scintillation of stars testify of the wonder and awesome creative power of God. But more than that, the "*day unto day*" and "*night unto night*" movement of the sun, the moon and the stars bear witness of God's providential power in all its wisdom and care. The wonderment that we are called to rejoice in is not in a completed work of art, but rather in God's ongoing work on the cosmic mural.

Day unto day, and night unto night, the sky bears testimony of the work of God's hands and declares His greatness and power as the Creator, Sustainer and Governor of the universe, and of life.

This is the message of nature. God's Creation is one long and eloquent sermon on the glory of God. And it is a sermon that is heard by all mankind throughout the ages, verse 3:

> *³ There is no speech nor language, where their voice is not heard. ⁴ Their line is gone out through all the earth, and their words to the end of the world.*

The message of Creation is heard and understood by men, women and children throughout the ages:

> "For the invisible things of him from the creation of the world are clearly seen, being understood by the things that are made, even his eternal power and Godhead; so that they are without excuse" (Rom 1:20).

But does this message have anything to do with the Gospel? Well, it seems that it does not. It seems that it is only a general message about the existence and power of God. But this is not how the Apostle Paul understands it.

Consider Romans 10:17-18:

> "So then faith cometh by hearing, and hearing by the word of God. But I say, Have they not heard? Yes verily, their sound went into all the earth, and their words unto the ends of the world."

Paul is quoting from Psalm 19:4.

He has a very different perspective of what the verse means, doesn't he? He tells us that Psalm 19:4 is not just about natural revelation brought about by the glory of the sun. It is rather about the Gospel radiating from the Sun of Righteousness!

Looking back at Psalm 19, verse 4b, we see a reference to the sun.

> *⁴ᵇ In them hath he set a tabernacle for the sun, ⁵ Which is as a bridegroom coming out of his chamber, and rejoiceth as a strong man to run a race. ⁶ His going forth is from the end of the heaven, and his circuit unto the ends of it: and there is nothing hid from the heat thereof.*

On the surface, this is a poetic description of how the sun is like a bridegroom emerging from his nuptial bedroom, and like a strong runner conquering the road ahead. In this imagery, we are reminded firstly, of the life-giving power of the sun even as the bridegroom rejoices in the generations that will proceed from him; and secondly, of the relentless conquest of the sun as it swallows up the darkness, inch by inch. But the Apostle Paul is telling us that there is more to it. He teaches us under the inspiration of the Spirit that David is not only writing about the physical sun, but about the Sun of Righteousness, the bridegroom of the Church, His bride.

The fact that all men in the world throughout the ages have heard the language of the cosmic sun, bears testimony to that fact that the Jews of the Old Testament, and indeed all men today, are without excuse when they refuse to believe in the Gospel.

The Gospel was preached to the Jews for several thousand years before Christ came (Heb 4:2). The Jews could as well excuse themselves for not having heard of Christ as they could claim to have not seen the sun.

Today, after so many thousand years, the same may be said of the vast majority of the people in the world. Hardly anyone at all in the world has not heard about Christ and the Gospel. They may not have heard the Gospel in its fullness and purity, but to claim not to have heard about Christ is almost as good as claiming not to have seen and felt the sun.

Indeed, even if suppose they have not heard of Christ or have heard only a very distorted view of Christ, they have no excuse for not seeking Him, for the Lord's book of nature testifies of His glory and power (Rom 1:20). If man would take heed to the message of Creation, and so seek the Creator, they would be found of the Lord! And they would have found new life as the darkness in hearts is driven away by the Sun of Righteousness.

Nevertheless, since the language of nature is not so clear and is subject to interpretation, God in His mercy caused that His word be inscripturated in a way that can be passed down accurately from generation to generation.

This is what the second part of this Psalm is about.

2. The Book of Law

[7] *The law of the LORD is perfect, converting the soul: the testimony of the LORD is sure, making wise the simple.* [8] *The statutes of the LORD are right, rejoicing the heart: the commandment of the LORD is pure, enlightening the eyes.* [9] *The fear of the LORD is clean, enduring for ever: the judgments of the LORD are true and righteous altogether.*

Notice how *"the Law of the LORD"* is also known as His *"testimony," "statutes," "commandment," "fear,"* and *"judgments"* here. The Law, which we are here given to sing about, in other words, is not merely a collection of dos and don'ts. It is rather, a reference to all of God's word or self-revelation, especially as it pertains to His eternal plan for the glory of His Son through the redemption of His people. This is what the statutes and ordinances of the Old Testament—whether of priesthood, or vestments, or sacrifices, or altars, or feasts—are all about. This is what the sacred history of the Gospel accounts, as well as the apostolic expositions in the New Testament are all about.

God's word is perfect, sure, pure, clean, endures forever and are true and righteous altogether.

God's word converts the soul, makes the simple wise, rejoices the heart, and enlightens the eyes. It accomplishes, in the hand of the Spirit, what Creation is no longer adequate to do due to the Fall. It is as such, verse 10:

[10] *More to be desired are they than gold, yea, than much fine gold: sweeter also than honey and the honeycomb.*

I wonder how many of us can say these words with full sincerity? But I am sure we can all testify of how it has changed us, made us wiser, given us direction and brought us peace, joy and hope in our lives.

Is not the word of God more to be desired than gold? The Bible is worth far more than its weight in pure gold. And it is sweeter than the honey and the honeycomb, for it delights not just the tongue for a moment, but the soul for all eternity.

And it is not just a notion or a feeling, for it is a fact that without the word of God, our lives will be lived in constant dangers and frustration. The word of God is God's instruction manual for us.

We must not doubt that as long as we are living according to the word of God, our lives would be full of joy, peace, love and hope. A lot of unhappiness, quarrels, chaos and frustrations in life are really a result of our neglecting to read and obey God's word. God would speak to us by His word, but we refuse to take heed and so go into harm's way.

Thus, the Lord gives us to sing with Him:

> [11] *Moreover by them is thy servant warned: and in keeping of them there is great reward.* [12] *Who can understand his errors? cleanse thou me from secret faults.* [13] *Keep back thy servant also from presumptuous sins; let them not have dominion over me: then shall I be upright, and I shall be innocent from the great transgression.*

"*Secret faults*" (v. 12) refer to sin of ignorance in distinction to presumptuous sin. The servant, in so far as he is not named, may be understood as Christ, the Righteous One, and all who are united to Him. The Righteous One, of course, had no sin, but He was tempted in all points like as we are, and He had to learn obedience (Heb 5:8; 4:15).

Yes, even the Son of God must learn obedience as the God-Man. How does He learn obedience? "*By them*" (v. 11), i.e. by the word of God! Christ, the God-Man, we must remember, had to learn. For though He is a divine person, His divine nature is by His choice routinely in repose so that He might walk as our sympathetic representative. Thus, He would learn as we learn. He learned by the word of God and by the Spirit bringing to His mind the word of God.

If that is so, then how much more, we who are the adopted children of God must learn the same way? Unless we learn the word of God and live according to the word of God, we shall stumble and fall, and bring upon ourselves much misery; and we shall sin against God in ignorance and presumption.

But the keeping of God's word, on the other hand, brings much blessing.

The Lord Jesus says: "But seek ye first the kingdom of God, and his righteousness, and all these things shall be added unto you" (Mt 6:33).

To seek the kingdom of God and His righteousness is to seek to walk according to God's word.

God is a promise-keeping God. If we find our life to be miserable or frustrating in some ways—we ought to ask ourselves wherein have we or our family failed to keep God's word?

Conversely, if we have been saturating ourselves with God's word and walking in His way, we will find ourselves enjoying the richness of the word of God so that you cannot but praise the LORD even when trials abound.

We will find the word of God precious. We will find it sweeter than the honey and the honeycomb. We will find ourselves extolling the LORD not only for His wonderful Creation, but also for His wonderful word. We will find ourselves taking upon our lips with sincerity the words of our Saviour:

> [14] *Let the words of my mouth, and the meditation of my heart, be acceptable in thy sight, O LORD, my strength, and my redeemer.*

What a wonder that these words should be taken upon the holy lips of the Righteous One, our Saviour! He came to do the Father's will. His Father was His Strength and Kinsman-Redeemer who would lift Him out of the grave when His sacrifice on behalf of His people is accomplished. But He came for the purpose of worship. He would worship the Father in His pilgrim walk as the God-Man; He would worship the Father through His Church united to Him as their Head and Mediator.

If we were to take these words upon our lips in and of ourselves, we know we fall short of the glory of God, and so neither our words nor our meditation could be acceptable to God. But as a people united to Christ, covered with His righteousness and filled with His Spirit of righteousness, singing in union with Christ, we know that the desire of our hearts to please God will be heard.

Conclusion

This is Psalm 19.

Oh may the Lord grant us that we may sing this Psalm with fresh appreciation of the mercies of God towards us in revealing Himself to us through His Creation and His word. What a marvel that His word, Christ, by whom He created all things and by whom He reveals all truths, should give us a song to sing in union with Him about these two books!

Oh may the Lord grant us that we may appreciate both of these books more.

Those of us who tend to ignore the Book of Natural Revelation ought to go out more and to open our eyes to see what the LORD has made. We ought to think about what message the LORD has for us through His Creation whether it pertains to the course of the sun, the clouds, the trees, the seas, the streams, the insects, the birds, the breezes, the mosses, the leaves, etc.

Those of us who love nature but are confused about the Book of Special Revelation ought to read and meditate on the Bible more. The Bible is an amazing book. The truth in it makes the simple wise and converts the soul that hitherto lies in sin. The Bible opens the eyes of all who would, to behold what a wonderful God we serve! In particular, it reveals Christ not only in the third person, but open His heart to us that we may walk and sing in union with Him in our pilgrim journey towards the Celestial City where we will celebrate God, world without end! Oh what a lovely book we have in our hand. When my tongue is still and I can no more taste the sweetness of honey and the honeycomb, my soul will still sing of the sweetness of this book, and of Christ who inspires it, and who is revealed in it. Amen. Ω

Psalm 20:
The Righteous One's
Send-Off Song

Psalm 20 is a Psalm unlike any other. It is composed in the language of benediction and prayer. We do not know the occasion in which it was originally written. Luther calls it a "battle-cry." Others suppose that this Psalm must have been written to express the feeling and expectation of the people on the Day of Atonement—as they waited anxiously for the high priest to emerge from the Holy of holies.

But whatever the original setting for this Psalm might have been, those of us who read it with evangelical eyes cannot help but notice how it fits into our Lord's passion and eventual ascension. This, then, is how we will look at this Psalm in this study. We may entitle it *"The Righteous One's Send-off Song."* It contains the words of Christ given to the Church in anticipation of the horrors of the cross. It is not difficult to imagine how in our Lord's hour of loneliness—when He was in the Garden of Gethsemane—that these words, which He has long appointed for His Church to sing, would have encouraged Him.

Yes, His closest disciples were exhausted and sleeping, but had not His Church been singing the Psalm for the last one thousand years to encourage Him in anticipation of this day of days. And it is not difficult to imagine that the saints already in heaven would have been given a view of what was going on, down on earth. If today we can see things happening on the other side of the world without the need for omniscience, what is so difficult for saints who have departed to see what the Saviour was doing in His hour of need. In 1 Peter 1:12, we have a picture painted for us of the angels in heaven leaning over the parapet of heaven to see what the Lord was doing on the earth. Surely it is not difficult to imagine the saints made perfect doing the same.

Perhaps Hebrews 12:1 is more literal than we allow it to be. It does not take much imagination, does it, to picture the saints in heaven watching what was going on, and singing the words of this Psalm to encourage the Lord?

Neither is it difficult to suppose that when the angels were finally sent to minister to the Lord, in the Garden, they would have told Him of how the saints made perfect were singing this Psalm and crying out unto the Father to support Him, their Saviour. Not that our Saviour, the God-Man, would not know.

Today, we sing this same Psalm in union with our risen Saviour to reflect upon the pregnant and poignant hours as He stepped towards the cross for us and shortly after that.

This Psalm has 2 parts. In verses 1-5, we see the people sending their Messiah off to the cross; and calling a blessing upon Him. In verses 6-9, we see the people receiving their Messiah back.

1. v. 1-5   Sending off the Messiah
2. v. 6-9   Receiving the Messiah Back

1. Sending off
the Messiah

¹ The LORD hear thee in the day of trouble; the name of the God of Jacob defend thee; ² Send thee help from the sanctuary, and strengthen thee out of Zion; ³ Remember all thy offerings, and accept thy burnt sacrifice; Selah.

The saints know that their Saviour is heading to the cross for their sin. He is going to fight the big battle against Satan, and against death on behalf of His people. They cannot go, because they will be consumed by the wrath of God. He alone must go. They are sending Him, the way Jacob sent his sons to Egypt to find salvation for the family. Only that He is going alone, with empty hands. There is nothing they can give Him to bring along. They can only go with Him in prayer.

> [1] *The LORD hear thee in the day of trouble; the name of the God of Jacob defend thee;* [2]*Send thee help from the sanctuary, and strengthen thee out of Zion;* [3] *Remember all thy offerings, and accept thy burnt sacrifice; Selah.*

The LORD, the heavenly Father, will hear their cry. He will remember mercy in His wrath. He will send help. He will remember the offerings of the Lord. He will accept the Lord's sacrifice. The Lord is offering Himself, as it were, as a burnt sacrifice for the sins of His people. The Father will receive His offering indeed. And He will give Him the desires of His heart.

> [4] *Grant thee according to thine own heart, and fulfil all thy counsel.*

At first sight, we may wonder: Did the Father give our Lord the desires of His heart? Did not the Lord say: "If it be possible, take this cup away from me"? Is this not the desire of His heart? But no, for the Lord also add: "Yet not my will, but thy will be done." It was the desire of our Lord that the Father's will would be fully fulfilled. He came to do His Father's will.

> "Sacrifice and offering thou wouldest not, but a body hast thou prepared me: In burnt offerings and sacrifices for sin thou hast had no pleasure. Then said I, Lo, I come (in the volume of the book it is written of me,) to do thy will, O God" (Heb 10:5-7)

The overwhelming desire of our Lord is to fulfil the will of the Father. Because He did so, His people might rejoice in His salvation:

> [5] *We will rejoice in thy salvation, and in the name of our God we will set up our banners: the LORD fulfil all thy petitions.*

Because He conquered death and sin, we have the assurance that the LORD is on our side and that we are more than conquerors through Christ who petitions the Father on our behalf.

The Lord's victory is secured because He has no sin; and because He is heading to the cross as the God-Man. So in this Psalm, we not only see the Messiah being sent off to the cross, we see Him being received back by His people.

2. Receiving the Messiah Back

> [6] *Now know I that the LORD saveth his anointed; he will hear him from his holy heaven with the saving strength of his right hand.*

Who is this "I"? No doubt this "I" is Christ Himself. This is Christ singing in the midst of the Church as the Captain of our salvation (cf. Ps 22:22; Heb 2:12, 10). He refers to Himself in the third person because He is singing about Himself with us! He, the Messiah went to the cross. The ancient serpent bruised His heel. But He crushed the serpent's head.

The sun refused to shine, the Father turned His face away from Him. But the sun did not remain in hiding, and the Father turned His face again towards Him in love. He died, but three days later, He rose again. Victory! Victory! Christ has conquered death! Christ has paid for our sin.

> ⁶ *Now know I that the LORD saveth his anointed; he will hear him from his holy heaven with the saving strength of his right hand.*

The anointed one is the Messiah (which is the Hebrew for "Anointed One", just as "Christ" is the Greek for "Anointed One"). His sacrifice for sin is accepted. He has made satisfaction. The Father heard His cries. The Father restored Him to life with the saving strength of His right hand, or His hand of power. He rose to heaven, and is seated at the right hand of the power of God. He is now, as it were, the right-hand man of God. By Him the Father rules the entire universe. He is seated at the right hand of the Father as the God-Man, upholding the world by the word of His power.

> ⁷ *Some trust in chariots, and some in horses: but we will remember the name of the LORD our God.* ⁸ *They are brought down and fallen: but we are risen, and stand upright.*

Note the change in first person pronoun to the plural, which signifies the Church joining with the Lord in a melodious exclamation! We will trust the LORD God our Father. We enjoy victory with Christ. As He rose from the grave, we rose with Him. As He who is our King conquered, so we shall conquer. We are more than conquerors through Him that loved us (Rom 8:37). Therefore, we will not trust in man or in the devices of man. Those who trust in the arm of flesh, shall fail.

> ⁹ *Save, LORD: let the king [the King of kings] hear us when we call.*

What a privilege we have that Christ is our King, for He is the Son of God. And He was tempted in all points like as we are, yet without sin. What a privilege it is to have our prayers heard through Him! What a privilege it is to have our prayers mediated by our Lord who understands our needs better than we do ourselves, who is compassionate towards our failures.

Conclusion

What a Psalm! What is this Psalm to you, fellow Christian? This Psalm helps me, firstly to feel for the Lord as I meditate on His going to the cross. I know I should be the one to have gone to the cross. But I know that I would have perished had I gone. I know Christ my Saviour deserved not the suffering that He endured. But I know He went for me. He went for me even before I could join the church to sing those words of encouragement, to strengthen Him as He went to the cross. I owe Him my all.

This Psalm also helps me, secondly, by giving me the assurance that the Father will hear my prayer because Christ my Lord went to the cross for me, and He rose victorious, and is seated at the right hand of the Father in my nature to intercede for me. Some will trust in chariots and horses; some will trust in man and money; some will trust in medicine and supplements; but I will trust in the Lord.

This Psalm helps me, finally, by encouraging me that I am not alone in my trials. As Christ the Anointed One was supported by the Church as he went to the cross, so as one anointed with His Spirit, I know that when I go through trials, that Christ and His Church will be supporting me (cf. 1 Cor 12:26-27).

You, beloved brother or sister in Christ, are an anointed one by your union with Christ. Are you going through a time of trial as you bear the cross of Christ? May the words of this Psalm encourage you as you consider how your King suffered much more for you. Amen. Ω

Psalm 21:
The Righteous One's
Song of Triumph

Psalm 21 is a joyful and triumphant Psalm. It is not difficult to see how it is a Messianic Psalm that continues with the theme of Psalm 20.[17] In Psalm 20, we see the Lord heading to the cross. The Church was singing the Psalm to send Him off, in anticipation of receiving Him back again after His sacrifice of Himself. In Psalm 21, the Lord has returned from the dead. He has conquered death. He has crushed the head of the Serpent. The Church is therefore celebrating.

This is *"The Righteous One's Song of Triumph"* that He has appointed for His righteous ones, the Church, to sing in union with Him, in praise and thanksgiving unto the Father. It has two stanzas. In the first, we are given to sing in praise and thanksgiving to the Father for the success of His Son, the Messiah, in the cosmic war that He came to fight (cf. Gen 3:15). In the second stanza, we are given to praise and magnify the Messiah, our King.

1. v. 1-7   The Church Thanks the Father
2. v. 8-13   The Church Magnifies the Son

1. The Church Thanks
the Father

¹ The king shall joy in thy strength, O LORD; and in thy salvation how greatly shall he rejoice!
² Thou hast given him his heart's desire, and hast not withholden the request of his lips. Selah.

The king is none other than Christ, the King of kings and Lord of lords. The King was going to battle. He was going to fight against sin and the ancient serpent. He would win the battle. The people of God began to sing this song even before the Lord went to the cross. This explains the future tense in verse 1: *"The king shall joy in thy strength, O LORD; and in thy salvation how greatly shall he rejoice!"*

But victory is certain. Victory was sure upon the decree of God and the everlasting covenant between the Father and the Son in eternity. Victory will be complete in the day when Christ returns again in His glory—when every knee will bow and every tongue confess that Jesus is LORD (Phil 2:10). But victory was sealed at Calvary—upon the Lord's going to the cross and rising again from the dead.

² Thou hast given him his heart's desire, and hast not withholden the request of his lips.

Remember how in Psalm 20, the Church encourages the Messiah with the words: "The LORD... grant thee according to thine own heart, and fulfil all thy counsels" (v. 4). Do you see how the Father's answer is now acknowledged? *"² Thou hast given him his heart's desire, and hast not withholden the request of his lips."* Indeed, the Father who loves the Son with

---

[17] By contrast it actually challenges our moral senses to think of this Psalm as being primarily about David because the only time we read of a crown of gold being set upon his head (as in v. 3) was during the conquest of Rabbah (2 Sam 12:30; 1 Chr 20:2). But this was also when David committed such unconscionable atrocities against the enemies he captured (see 2 Sam 12:31; cf. Ps 21:9), that commentators and translators scramble to sanitise David's actions. Indeed, it is very likely that this event occurred during the nine months between David's sin of adultery and murder, and his confrontation by the Prophet Nathan (cf. 2 Sam 11:1; 12:26). David was walking in unrepentance and wickedness as a backslidden man in those days. Whether or not this Psalm was written upon the occasion, David did not deserve its accolades at all.

an infinite love could not but run ahead of Him to bless Him:

3 For thou preventest [i.e. went ahead of] him with the blessings of goodness: thou settest a crown of pure gold on his head. 4 He asked life of thee, and thou gavest it him, even length of days for ever and ever.

Christ our Lord went to do the Father's will on the cross. His desire has always been that the Father's will would be fulfilled. The will of the Father, which is also His will, is that He suffers and dies on behalf of His people to reconcile them to God. But of course, His desire must also have been to rise from the dead and to live on in the fellowship of God forever.

The Lord, as the God-Man would not take it for granted that He would rise from the dead. He would ask His Father. He asked for life and the Father heard Him. He raised Him from the dead. He would live forever and ever in heaven as the God-Man, as the apostle to the Hebrews reminds us:

"23 And they truly were many priests, because they were not suffered to continue by reason of death: 24 But this man, because he continueth ever, hath an unchangeable priesthood" (Heb 7:23-24).

But in that He rose from the dead, He was highly exalted:

5 His glory is great in thy salvation: honour and majesty hast thou laid upon him. 6 For thou hast made him most blessed for ever: thou hast made him exceeding glad with thy countenance. 7 For the king trusteth in the LORD, and through the mercy of the most High he shall not be moved.

The best commentary for these words is found in the epistle of Paul to the Philippians in chapter 2:

He "being in the form of God, thought it not robbery to be equal with God: *7 But made himself of no reputation, and took upon him the form of a servant, and was made in the likeness of men: 8 And being found in fashion as a man, he humbled himself, and became obedient unto death, even the death of the cross. 9 Wherefore God also hath highly exalted him, and given him a name which is above every name: 10 That at the name of Jesus every knee should bow, of things in heaven, and things in earth, and things under the earth; 11 And that every tongue should confess that Jesus Christ is Lord, to the glory of God the Father" (Phil 2:6-11).*

Need we say more? The Spirit has spoken. The Son humbled Himself. The Father exalted Him on high. He trusted the Father through His humiliation. He was lifted up, never to bow down ever again. He is King of kings, Lord of lords. He is ruling over all; and He will manifest Himself powerfully in the Last Day.

So the Church blesses Him:

2. The Church Magnifies
the Son

8 Thine hand shall find out all thine enemies: thy right hand shall find out those that hate thee. 9 Thou shalt make them as a fiery oven in the time of thine anger: the LORD shall swallow them up in his wrath, and the fire shall devour them. 10 Their fruit shalt thou destroy from the earth, and their seed from among the children of men.

The Lord would be vindicated. All power is given unto Him in heaven and on earth. Many hated Him during His earthly ministry. They clamoured for His blood. They poured scorn upon Him. "He saved others, but cannot save Himself. He claims to be the Son of God, let Him come down from the cross, then we will believe Him," they mocked.

Today, many continue to hate Him and His Church. They speak disparagingly of Him. They ridicule theology and Bible history. They sneer at His people and even try to kill them. They blaspheme His name. But these will be met with final justice and eternal condemnation— these and their children who do not repent.

Lord, thou art God! Thou wilt vindicate thine own name.

> [11] *For they intended evil against thee: they imagined a mischievous device, which they are not able to perform.* [12] *Therefore shalt thou make them turn their back, when thou shalt make ready thine arrows upon thy strings against the face of them.*

It is a fearful thing to fall into the hands of an angry God. Those who spit in the face of the Lord and clamour for His blood thought that they were trampling underfoot a weakling. They thought that they could easily get away with it. But they are wrong, for the arrow of the Lord is aimed at their heart. Who can run away when the Son of man has His arrows aimed at him?

It will be a terrible day for those who oppose the Lord! But for those who trust in Him, it will be a day of joy and gladness. The vindication of the Lord's name will add to our joy. So we sing in conclusion:

> [13] *Be thou exalted, LORD, in thine own strength: so will we sing and praise thy power.*

Notice how the King is now the LORD! In that day, every tongue will confess that Jesus is LORD (cf. Phil 2:11).

Be thou exalted, Oh LORD Jesus. Be exalted in thine own strength and power, for there is none who is higher and more powerful, who can exalt Thee. Thou art the sovereign God. Thou art omnipotent, infinite, eternal and unchangeable. We will sing and praise Thy power.

Conclusion

Life in this world can be very depressing. It is depressing when unhappy things happen to us. It is depressing when we see problems in the church. It is depressing when we see the name of Christ ridiculed by unbelievers and blasphemed by professing believers. It is even more depressing when we see our covenant children straying before they make confession of faith or apostatising after that. It is depressing when we find ourselves struggling against sin and failing. But the Scripture teaches us to rejoice and to rejoice again. What shall we do to lift up our spirit?

Well, we know of no better way than to look to Christ. This is why the Psalms are so precious to us. The Psalms bring Christ before our eyes and before our hearts.

Psalm 21 is an especially comforting Psalm to us because of the language of triumph in it. In this Psalm Christ is lifted up so high, that everything in the world becomes small and insignificant. With Christ my King on the throne I need not fear anything, and really, I need not get depressed over anything. With Christ my King on the throne, I know that all things will work together for my good and for His Church's well-being. Christ has conquered and is conquering. He will be highly exalted. He will manifest His glory over the entire world. Blessed be His name! Ω

Psalm 22:
The Righteous One's
Crucifixion Song
or Messiah Bearing the Cross & Wearing the Crown

I believe that all the Psalms are Messianic in one way or another. But Psalm 22 is *the* most famous of the Messianic Psalms. Hardly anyone in the history of the church will disagree that this Psalm is a prophecy concerning the deepest sufferings of the Lord Jesus Christ on the cross of Calvary. Yes, some think that David was originally describing his own sufferings, while others believe that this Psalm refers exclusively and originally to Christ. But all agree that only the sufferings of the Lord Jesus Christ can fully explain the language used in this Psalm.

This Psalm is quoted numerous times in the Gospels to show how the sufferings of the Lord Jesus Christ fulfilled ancient prophecies. Therefore, I believe we should interpret the first-person pronouns in this Psalm to be all referring to the Lord Jesus Christ, without a need to apply to David as a type. So, we agree with Matthew Henry that...

> "In singing this psalm we must keep our thoughts fixed upon Christ, and be so affected with His sufferings—as to experience the fellowship of them, and so affected with His grace—as to experience the power and influence of it."

This is how we must look at this Psalm in this study. We may name it: *"The Righteous One's Crucifixion Song"* or *"Messiah Bearing the Cross & Wearing the Crown."*

It is easy to see that this Psalm has two main parts. From verse 1 to verse 21, we are given a glimpse of the Messiah's suffering. From verse 22 to the end, we are given a vision of the Messiah entering into His glorious kingdom.

1. v. 1-21   Messiah's Suffering
2. v. 22-31   Messiah's Glory

1. Messiah's Suffering

In this first section, we see the Lord's suffering as wave upon wave of sorrow sweeps over Him as He hangs on the cross. In fact, if you read the passage carefully, you will discern three waves of sorrow sweeping over the Lord.

We must realise that these three waves did not necessarily sweep over the Lord consecutively while the Lord was on the cross. But they represent the sorrow that attended His soul.

The first wave contains the painful words of our Lord which He cries after the three hours of darkness:

¹ *My God, my God, why hast thou forsaken me?*

The Lord spoke these words in Aramaic: "Eli eli lama sabathani." Christ our Lord, the eternal son of God is on the cross as our representative. He is bearing our sin. He is suffering the wrath of God on our behalf. Our guilt has been imputed to Him. For that reason, He is, at that moment, the most guilty person who ever lived. It was to underscore that, that for three hours the sun refused to shine. During those three hours, all that our Lord saw of the Father was His back and His angry face. At the end of the three hours our Lord cried out: "My God, my God, why hast thou forsaken me?"

At no time during our Lord's earthly ministry, did the Lord Jesus address His Father as "God" but always as "Father." But here in His hour of dereliction, sensing only His Father's wrath, He cries out: *"My God, my God, why has Thou forsaken me."*

But even as the Lord experiences His darkest hours, He does not give up hope. He finds encouragement in the fact that God is a holy God, who has proven Himself to be merciful in the history of His people:

⁴ Our fathers trusted in thee: they trusted, and thou didst deliver them. ⁵ They cried unto thee, and were delivered: they trusted in thee, and were not confounded.

But our Lord is not only afflicted because of the Father's wrath. He is afflicted by His own people mocking Him.

⁶ But I am a worm, and no man; a reproach of men, and despised of the people. ⁷ All they that see me laugh me to scorn: they shoot out the lip, they shake the head, saying, ⁸ He trusted on the LORD that He would deliver him: let Him deliver him, seeing He delighted in him.

This is the second wave of sorrow that is sweeping over His soul. He is mocked and ridiculed by the priests, and by the people who have been misled by the priests, as well as those who are disappointed that He did not free them from Roman dominion as they had expected.

But once again, our Lord triumphs over it. He takes comfort that His life is in the hand of His Father. His Father gave Him human flesh. His Father gave Him life as the God-Man:

⁹ But thou art He that took me out of the womb: thou didst make me hope when I was upon my mother's breasts. ¹⁰ I was cast upon thee from the womb: thou art my God from my mother's belly.

In times of great distress and confusion, it is always helpful for us to remember that we are creatures of dust, who exist only by the sovereign power of God. If we understand that, then it will not matter anymore what others say about us, so long as we are doing the Lord's will. But that does not mean that it would be the end of our pain and sorrow in this world. Our Lord experienced not just mental anguish, but physical torment.

¹² Many bulls have compassed me: strong bulls of Bashan have beset me round. ¹³ They gaped upon me with their mouths, as a ravening and a roaring lion.

The Lord is surrounded by fierce and unreasonable people. His friends have fled or are kept at a distance. All around Him are people who want Him dead, or are doing their duty to kill Him. They mock Him and scold Him. They gnash their teeth at Him because of their jealousy. They surround Him like lions, and bulls, and dogs (v. 16). They stripped Him of His garment, stretched Him out on a wooden cross, and nailed Him to it, hands and feet, to the cross:

¹⁶ For dogs have compassed me: the assembly of the wicked have inclosed me: they pierced my hands and my feet. ¹⁷ I may tell all my bones: they look and stare upon me. ¹⁸ They part my garments among them, and cast lots upon my vesture.

They hung our Lord on the cross to die a slow and excruciating death. He is stretched and impaled in a most painful and humiliating manner. He is exposed to the elements. He is in pain and bleeding profusely. He can hardly breathe. You can count His rib bones. But below, the soldiers are casting lots for His garments, the only possessions He had. He would die of exposure, exhaustion, blood loss and dehydration.

¹⁴ I am poured out like water, and all my bones are out of joint: my heart is like wax; it is melted in the midst of my bowels. ¹⁵ *My strength is dried up like a potsherd; and my tongue cleaveth to my jaws; and thou hast brought me into the dust of death.*

It is in thirst our Lord cries out "I thirst." But though His body is drying up, He is still full of the Spirit. He does not despair, but turns again to His Father in prayer (v. 19-21). He calls upon His Father to be near Him and to deliver Him. What an example for us!

Our Lord, full of faith, knows that the Father will hear His prayer. He knows that the Father will raise Him from the dead. So this poignant Psalm ends not with a poignant note, but with a triumphant chorus.

2. Messiah's Glory

²² *I will declare thy name unto my brethren: in the midst of the congregation will I praise thee.*

Our Lord anticipated that His Father would accept His sacrifice and He would rise from the dead. He would join, nay lead, His people to worship the Father. The writer to the Hebrews quotes these words when He says:

"¹¹ For both He that sanctifieth and they who are sanctified are all of one: for which cause He is not ashamed to call them brethren, ¹² Saying, I will declare thy name unto my brethren, in the midst of the church will I sing praise unto thee" (Heb 2:11-12).

Our Lord went to the cross in our flesh. He lived and died for us. He died because of our sin. He bore our sin. Therefore, He is not afraid to call us His brothers and sisters, even though we sin against God and fall short of His glory. Instead, He calls us to join Him to praise the Father. Indeed, He laid down His life for that very purpose: That as lively stones united to Him, the Chief Corner Stone, we may, as the temple of God, offer up spiritual sacrifices pleasing to God (cf. 1 Pet 2:4-10). Thus, He assures us of the Lord's blessings as we join Him to worship the Father:

²³ *Ye that fear the LORD, praise him; all ye the seed of Jacob, glorify him; and fear him, all ye the seed of Israel. ²⁴ For He hath not despised nor abhorred the affliction of the afflicted; neither hath He hid His face from him; but when He cried unto him, He heard.*

The Father heard the cry of our Saviour. He will surely hear our cry too. He did not despise nor abhor the affliction of the afflicted. He heard and answered Him when He cried to Him. So we can be sure He will also hear us when we cry unto Him.

But now the foremost thought in our Saviour's mind is the joy of praising the Father with His Church redeemed by His blood:

²⁵ *My praise shall be of thee in the great congregation: I will pay my vows before them that fear him. ²⁶ The meek shall eat and be satisfied: they shall praise the LORD that seek him: your heart shall live for ever.*

Our Lord paid His vows. He came to fulfil His covenant vow to lay down His life for His people. He came to redeem a great congregation to worship the Father. They shall live forever and they shall be contented in the Lord. And this would be true not just for His people who are already in the covenant, but for as many as the Lord our God shall call:

²⁷ *All the ends of the world shall remember and turn unto the LORD: and all the kindreds of the nations shall worship before thee. ²⁸ For the kingdom is the LORD's: and He is the governor among the nations.*

He is the King of kings and Lord of lords. When He has laid down His life, He would be exalted to the right hand of the Father as He is appointed ruler and governor over all the affairs of the universe.

At the cross, He secured victory over the devil. He crushed the head of the serpent. But the serpent is threshing about in its dying throes. The war is won, but there are mopping-up battles to be fought. Christ our Lord is powerfully directing the battles. All power is given unto Him in heaven and on earth. The Apostle Paul is referring to this mopping-up operation when He says in 1 Corinthians 15:24:

"[23] But every man in His own order: Christ the firstfruits; afterward they that are Christ's at His coming. [24] Then cometh the end, when He shall have delivered up the kingdom to God, even the Father; when He shall have put down all rule and all authority and power. [25] For He must reign, till He hath put all enemies under His feet. [26] The last enemy that shall be destroyed is death" (1 Cor 15:23-26).

In that day, when He shall destroy death forever, every knee will bow and every tongue will confess that He is Lord. Or as the Lord says in verse 29:

[29] *All they that be fat upon earth shall eat and worship: all they that go down to the dust shall bow before him: and none can keep alive His own soul.*

In that day, there will be none refusing to bow: for either they will bow in adoration and love, or they will bow in fear and trepidation. Rich or poor, powerful or weak, all will bow down to worship Him. But whatever might be the case, a seed shall serve Him.

[30] *A seed shall serve him; it shall be accounted to the Lord for a generation.* [31] *They shall come, and shall declare His righteousness unto a people that shall be born, that He hath done this.*

This seed refers to those who are spiritually united to Christ. Paul says:

"Now to Abraham and His seed were the promises made. He saith not, And to seeds, as of many; but as of one, And to thy seed, which is Christ" (Gal 3:16).

The seed of Christ will serve the Lord in their generation and they will declare to their children and their children's children about what Christ has done. Eventually, all the elect will be called. Then as a generation, even the seed of Christ, they shall serve the Father forever and ever.

Conclusion

What a blessing!

What a wonderful Psalm. This Psalm begins with the darkest and most painful of human experiences ever: for the God-Man suffered as no man ever suffered. But the same Psalm ends with the most glorious and joyous of human experiences ever: for the God-Man is exalted and all His elect are united to Him to enjoy Him forever and ever.

The darkest and most painful experience was suffered by our Lord. The brightest and most joyous experience will be ours and our children's. But oh, at what expense and love! Christ suffered infinitely in order that we might have perfect bliss for all eternity.

May the Lord grant us that we may, out of gratitude for Him, worship Him and serve Him with all our soul, heart, mind and strength, until the day we rest fully in Him to enjoy Him forever and ever. Amen. Ω

Psalm 23:
The Righteous One's Shepherd Psalm

For some strange reason, Psalm 23 is not normally classified as a Messianic Psalm. But it is not difficult to see how it is indeed Messianic or perhaps better, Christological.

In the first place, the New Testament speaks of the Lord Jesus as the Good Shepherd (Jn 10:11), the Chief Shepherd (1Pt 5:4) and the Great Shepherd (Heb 13:20). As we look at the content of this Psalm, we can see how this Psalm is given by our Good Shepherd for His sheep and lambs to sing about Him. He is the Son of God and our Messiah. It is perfectly fitting for us to direct our praises to Him as well as to the Father and to the Spirit.

In the second place, we can also see how our Lord Himself would have used these words to encourage Himself under the care of His Father during His earthly ministry. It is no coincidence that He is called the "Lamb of God," for He took upon Himself our nature to live and die for us. So it is no coincidence that in the same place where our Lord calls Himself our Good Shepherd, He says: "As the Father knoweth me, even so know I the Father: and I lay down my life for the sheep" (Jn 10:14-15). Is not the Lord saying, "As the Father knew and led me, so I know and will lead you. I became the Lamb in order that I may be your Shepherd" (cf. Rev 7:17)? It is in this way that we can see a clear connection between Psalm 22 and Psalm 24. Psalm 22 is about the death of Christ, while Psalm 24 is about His ascension. Psalm 23 straddles between the two. Notice His meditation on His death (v. 4)! We think of how Christ would have meditated on His entire life, death and subsequent resurrection using this Psalm as He hung on the cross.

So then, this Psalm is Messianic both in that it is given for us to sing about our Messiah, and that it was used by the Messiah. We may note that the LORD (Jehovah) was to our Lord (Jesus), the Father representing God-Triune; but to us, in the context of this Psalm, God-Triune is represented by the Son.

In any case, in this study, we want to consider briefly how Christ is our Shepherd as He is painted in this Psalm. There are a number of ways to outline this Psalm, but since it is so rich, we may simply enumerate what our Lord is to us, being our Shepherd, just as His Father is to Him, as He became a sheep for us:

1. v. 1   He Is Our Provider
2. v. 2a   He Is Our Peacemaker
3. v. 2b   He Is Our Preserver
4. v. 3a   He Is Our Physician
5. v. 3b   He Is Our Pilot
6. v. 4   He Is Our Protector
7. v. 5   He Is Our Prince
8. v. 6   He Is Our Patron

1. He Is Our Provider

¹ The LORD is my shepherd; I shall not want.

As the Father was a Shepherd to Christ, so Christ is a Shepherd to all united to Him by faith. I can sing this Psalm in the first person because the first person "I" is first of all Christ, and secondarily all who are united to Him by faith.

With Christ as our Shepherd, we shall not lack anything—temporal or spiritual. Christ our Shepherd will see to it. He is Jehovah Jireh.

> "For ye know the grace of our Lord Jesus Christ, that, though He was rich, yet for your sakes He became poor, that ye through His poverty might be rich" (2Cor 8:9).

We can and should be contented.

Do we find ourselves lacking in spiritual gifts and graces? We can go to the LORD and ask of Him. He has taught us to ask for the Holy Spirit.

Do we find ourselves lacking materially? He has taught us to pray to His Father, "give us this day our daily bread."

Christ is my Provider, I shall not want.

2. He Is Our Peacemaker

^{2a} *He maketh me to lie down in green pastures:*

A shepherd turned pastor once taught that a sheep will only lie down when four conditions are satisfied: freedom from fear; freedom from antagonism within the flock, freedom from irritants like parasites and flies, and freedom from hunger. It is not difficult to see how these ovinological conditions may be translated to spiritual conditions. For example, while flies might irritate the sheep, the sheep of Christ might be irritated by careless and hurtful words that fly around us.

Christ, the Sheep of sheep, experienced all these things for our sake, but by His faith found peace in His Father. So it is with us. Christ frees us from the fear that comes with guilt on account of sin. Guilt translates into a fear of God as well as a fear of man. Christ our Shepherd gives us peace—peace with God, peace with man: Peace that the world does not understand. He does so by removing our guilt.

And Christ our Lord by His word and spirit brings us peace within the flock by making us love one another.

Moreover, though many cares and accusations irritate us and give us no rest, in Christ we can have peace: for He calls us to cast our burdens upon Him and assures us that all things are working together for our good.

Most of all, He feeds us. He feeds us with His word to comfort and encourage us, so that we are able to rest in Him in a restless world.

Christ is my Peacemaker; He makes me to lie down in green pastures.

3. He Is Our Preserver

^{2b} *He leadeth me beside the still waters.*

As sheep need to drink water in order to survive, so spiritual sheep need to drink if we are to persevere on in our journey. Christ, the Lamb of God, found refreshment through the anointing of the Spirit which the water represents (cf. Jn 7:38). So as our Shepherd He leads us to where we may be refreshed spiritually.

As sheep will not drink from rushing water, so we will not find refreshment in this busy world except we come apart with Christ to go beside the still waters.

So Christ leads us each day to the closet or to the mountainside where we can be alone with

Him and we can pray. Were it not for Christ setting us an example and instructing us to do so, we would not do so. But when we follow Him, and come apart for prayer, oh what refreshment we find for our souls.

He is our Preserver. He preserves me by encouraging me to pray and to enjoy the ministry of His Spirit.

4. He Is Our Physician

3a He restoreth my soul:

Sheep are prone to wander. If there is a hole in their fence, they would leave the flock in search of greener pastures even if out there is a semi-arid desert.

Christ our elder sheep never wanders; but we are prone to wander. While we may not feel grief and loss when we wander, our elder brother does. Where does He find the healing and restoration that He needs as the head of the flock responsible for us? He finds it, no doubt, in His Father.

Are we not prone to wander? We are prone to wander from the flock and from the green pastures that our Shepherd placed us in. We are prone to wander from Christ who loves us so.

But Christ loves us more than to allow us to get ourselves into danger. He would leave the ninety-nine to look for us. He would restore us by admonishment, by church discipline and by painful providence.

He bears the pain I ought to feel even as He seeks to restore my soul. Thank God for my Shepherd's love for me.

5. He Is Our Pilot

3b He leadeth me in the paths of righteousness for His name's sake.

The ancient shepherd had to lead the flock from one place to another to graze. Sometimes the paths can be dangerous and difficult. But He leads them on.

So the Father leads Christ through the most treacherous terrain that He might procure righteousness for us. So Christ leads us on in our journey to the Celestial City. He leads us in the paths of righteousness by guiding us with His word. "Thy word is a lamp unto my feet and a light unto my path" (Ps 119:105). He gives us the Holy Spirit to keep us in the way of holiness.

He does so for His name's sake: for at the end of our journey, He will present us to the Father as the trophies of His redeeming grace. Then will His name be greatly magnified and we shall share in His glory forever and ever.

Thank God that Christ does not leave me alone to fight the spiritual battle and to run the Christian race. "I am with you alway," He assures me (Mt 28:20).

I thank Thee, Lord, for leading me as the Pilot and Captain of my salvation!

6. He Is Our Protector

4 Yea, though I walk through the valley of the shadow of death, I will fear no evil: for thou art with me; thy rod and thy staff they comfort me.

Whenever the flock of sheep is on the move, it faces many dangers. Wolves and lions may be waiting in the shadows to pounce upon them. But with the shepherd guiding them with his rod and protecting them with his staff, they need fear no evil.

Our Saviour became a sheep that He might experience the fear of death on our behalf. Because of what He did, we need not fear what evil may come our way. Especially, we need not fear when death approaches.

Death can be a very frightful experience for a person without Christ—for he goes alone and he knows not where he is going.

But death for the saint need not be fearful. When it is time for me to die, my only concern will be those I leave behind, my dear wife, my children, my beloved brothers and sisters in the Lord, and all whose lives may be affected by my departure. But I know that death is but a portal into heavenly glory.

And I know I will not need to enter through the door alone, for Christ, whose experience is captured in this Psalm, will be with me.

7. He Is Our Prince

[5] *Thou preparest a table before me in the presence of mine enemies: thou anointest my head with oil; my cup runneth over.*

At the beginning of this Psalm, we were pictured as sheep being led from one pasture to another. But now the sheep is no longer wandering.

They have come to a place of rest. We are now being taken care of in a very personal way. The shepherd makes a table. He lays the food on the table – that's what shepherds do when they hand feed their sheep. If they throw the pellets on the ground especially in the wetter months, the sheep may get sick because of the bacteria in the soil.

And not only so, but the shepherd anoints the head of his sheep individually with oil and provides them plenty of water that their cups run over.

So it is with Christ the Lamb of God. When He had gone through the shadow of death, He came into the presence of the Father (cf. Lk 22:18). He would, as it were, dine with Him in the presence of His enemies. And so it will be with us, for we shall be His guests at His table (cf. Lk 22:30). We shall dine with Him.

All through our life's journey, He protects us from all harm and danger and enemies. When we have finally returned home, we shall still see our enemies, but none of them can touch us.

All through life's journey, we had an earnest of our eternal inheritance, even an anointing of the Holy Spirit. But now the Spirit is given to us in full. We are made perfect in the full enjoyment of Christ.

All through life's journey, our Shepherd provides us sufficiently for our needs so that we have no want. But now, He fills our cup full—brim-full—so that it overflows with spiritual blessing that we can enjoy for all eternity.

What a privilege it is to be a sheep of Christ! What assurance! What hope! And what longing, for Christ is also our patron for all eternity.

8. He Is Our Patron

[6] *Surely goodness and mercy shall follow me all the days of my life: and I will dwell in the*

house of the LORD for ever.

What is the greatest privilege that a sheep can enjoy? It is to be brought into the house of the shepherd to be cared for as a household pet or a member of the family.

So it is true with Christ as the God-Man. Forever and ever, He would dwell with the Father as the chief of the flock. So it will be with us. We shall be invited into the house of our Shepherd. We shall dwell with Him forever in the heavenly mansions that He has gone ahead to prepare for us (Jn 14:2).

What a lofty thought: Unworthy sinners being allowed to see their Creator in the beatific vision, and then enjoying the rapturous joy of heaven unhindered by any pain, sorrow or tears.

Yes, today we labour under much sorrow and discouragement due to weaknesses, failures and sin. But all that will be removed.

> "And God shall wipe away all tears from their eyes; and there shall be no more death, neither sorrow, nor crying, neither shall there be any more pain: for the former things are passed away" (Rev 21:4).

Instead of weeping, there will be laughter of wondrous joy beyond description. Instead of death, there will be life abundant, free and eternal. Instead of pain, there will be everlasting pleasures. Instead of sorrow, there will be the fullness of rejoicing and praise as we behold the glory of God in the face of Christ our Shepherd forever and ever.

Hope and faith will give way to sight, and we shall be ravished with the love of Christ our Shepherd forever and ever.

And the love of Christ shall overflow from our hearts so that every sheep will enjoy the company of other sheep perfectly. We will love one another perfectly.

There will be no more quarrels, misunderstanding, criticisms, accusations, fears, disappointments, suspicions, hypocrisy, slander, gossips, disrespect, jealousy, separation, or any such things.

There will only be love. Heaven is a place of love. The relationship between Christ and His sheep is love. The relationship between sheep and sheep is love. There is no relationship within heaven that cannot be described as love.

> *⁶ Surely goodness and mercy shall follow me all the days of my life: and I will dwell in the house of the LORD for ever.*

Conclusion

What a great Psalm! What a blessing it is just to think about it. May the Lord our Provider, our Peacemaker, our Preserver, our Physician, our Pilot, our Protector, our Prince, and our Patron—be greatly magnified as we sing these words in His praise, in union with Him!

May His Spirit encourage us too that we may walk with joy in the assurance that surely goodness and mercy shall follow us all the days of our lives, until the day we enjoy the raptures of heaven, as we behold the face of our Shepherd whose love for us knows no bounds.

Amen. Ω

Psalm 24:
The Righteous One's
Access to Heaven

Psalm 24 is so obviously a Messianic Psalm that it will probably surprise many of us to know that it is not classified as such by many modern commentators.

This Psalm might have been written by David to celebrate the occasion of the ark being brought up to Jerusalem from the house of Obed-Edom. But those who read it with spiritual evangelical eyes will no doubt see that the event is prophetic or typical of the Lord Jesus' ascension to heaven.

It is no coincidence that the Apostle Paul quotes another ascension Psalm, Psalm 68, to refer to the ascension of Christ in Ephesians 4:7-13 (cf. Ps 68:18).

Psalm 24 carries a similar theme. It may be entitled *"The Righteous One's Access to Heaven."* This title will become more obvious as we look at the content of the Psalm; and as you shall see, it actually provides us, in a nutshell, what biblical worship really is. It is a Psalm given by our Worshipper-in-Chief, for us to sing with Him in acknowledgment of God's wonderful provision for sinful creatures of dust to come into His holy presence to worship Him.

It has three distinct strophes. In the first strophe, from verses 1-2, we are given to sing of how the LORD alone is worthy of worship: for He is not only the Creator, but is the Governor over the world. In the second strophe, from verses 3-6, we are given to acknowledge that Christ alone is worthy to worship, and to receive blessings from God. And finally, in the third strophe, from verse 7 to the end, we are given to solemnly charge the gates of heaven to open for Christ, our King.

1. v. 1-2   The LORD is Worthy of Worship
2. v. 3-6   Christ is Worthy to Worship
3. v. 7-10   The Gates of Heaven Open for Christ

1. The LORD Is Worthy of Worship

[1] *The earth is the LORD's, and the fulness thereof; the world, and they that dwell therein.* [2] *For He hath founded it upon the seas, and established it upon the floods.*

The opening verse of this Psalm is quoted by the Apostle Paul in 1 Corinthians 10:26 to remind us that all things in this universe exist for the glory of God. *"The earth is the LORD's, and the fulness thereof."* The earth and all its inhabitants belong to the LORD.

The LORD, the I AM, is He who created the universe with the physical world represented initially by a water-covered earth (see Gen 1:1-2). The LORD is He who set the watery boundaries of every piece of land.

He is the sovereign Creator, Owner and Ruler over all things in the universe. He is not just the Ruler over the irrational creation: the mountains and rocks and rivers and animals; He is, especially, the Ruler over man.

And man, being created in the image of God, ought—of all creatures—to recognise their Creator and to worship Him as their God and King.

This is the implicit call of the opening two verses in this Psalm. It confronts us with our responsibility to worship the LORD our Creator as the Living and True God!

But who may worship Him—even Him, who as the Creator, stands outside creation, as the transcendently holy God?

2. Christ Is Worthy to Worship

³ Who shall ascend into the hill of the LORD? or who shall stand in His holy place? ⁴ He that hath clean hands, and a pure heart; who hath not lifted up His soul unto vanity, nor sworn deceitfully.

The "hill of the LORD" is a picture of heaven (Eph 4:10). To ascend into the hill of the LORD is essentially to come into the presence of the LORD to worship Him and to have fellowship with Him.

Who may worship the LORD, the transcendently holy Creator, Owner and Ruler over all things? The answer, as we are given to testify, is none other than "He who has clean hands and a pure heart, &c."

Are we to understand these qualifications relatively as referring to those who have *cleaner* hands and *purer* hearts? Surely not! If God is the holy Creator, then only He who is absolutely holy in heart and life is fit to worship Him! But there is none righteous, no not one amongst the children of Adam (Ps 14:1, Rom 3:10ff).

Who then may worship the LORD? Who, but Christ our Saviour! He alone has clean hands and a pure heart. He alone is holy and undivided in His heart, and pure in His deeds. There is no guile and hypocrisy in His heart. He does not lift His soul unto vanity. There are no idols in His life. The chief end in His life is to glorify God. He does not swear deceitfully. His yea is yea and nay is nay. He, alone, has the right to ascend the hill of God! He alone can stand in God's holy place.

He lived for us. He did not live for Himself. He sought not the pleasures of the world, for that was not what He came to do. He came to deliver us from the turmoil and bondage of the restless world. He came also to be our Worshipper-In-Chief to lead us to worship the Father. Thus, He says in Psalm 22:22: "I will declare thy name unto my brethren: in the midst of the congregation will I praise thee." He died for us, He rose again and He ascended, in order that He might receive and bestow upon us the gifts He came to purchase for us, especially the Holy Spirit who would dwell in us, by whom He would worship with us as Worship Leader, both spiritually and vicariously.

So we are given to sing in verse 5:

⁵ He shall receive the blessing from the LORD, and righteousness from the God of His salvation.

He shall receive of the Father in order to give gifts to men, as the Apostle Paul puts it (cf. Eph 4:8). These are the men, and women, and children who are accounted for a generation in Psalm 22. This is the generation that seeks Him:

⁶ This is the generation of them that seek Him, that seek thy face, O Jacob.

Jacob is but another name for Christ, for Jacob is synonymous with Israel which is the name of the people of God, the church. Christ is the head of the church, of which the people is the body.

Thus Matthew, in the New Testament, could apply a prophecy about Israel in the Old Testament to the Lord. Remember how the prophet Hosea quotes God as saying: "When Israel was a child, then I loved Him, and called my son out of Egypt" (Hosea 11:1). He is referring to the people. But Matthew tells us that this prophecy is fulfilled in God's calling the Lord out of Egypt after the death of Herod (Mt 2:15).

Israel, and so Jacob, is the typical name of Christ our Saviour. Our Saviour, our Redeemer, is He who came for us and after accomplishing His work on the cross, ascended up to heaven as the Captain of our salvation (Heb 2:10). He ascended that He might pour down His purchased gifts, even the gift of His Spirit upon His covenant people and all who seek Him and call upon His name. Indeed, we are the "captivity" that He led captive in His ascension (Eph 4:8): for as Paul reminds us, God "raised us up together, and made us sit together in heavenly places in Christ Jesus" (Eph 2:6).

In other words, Christ not only opened the way for us to enter heaven one day; He has, in fact, already brought His people to heaven. Thus, the apostle to the Hebrews reminds us that we have already come (as indicated by the Greek Perfect tense) unto Mount Zion, and unto the city of the Living God, the heavenly Jerusalem (Heb 12:22). We are already citizens of heaven, though there remains a not-yet element in our experience, and therefore until that time, we must enjoy heaven while on earth by worshipping within the gates of Zion.

How may we worship the Father when we do not have clean hands and a pure heart? Only by union with Christ! This is why we sing the Psalms, even the "Word of Christ" (Col 3:16). He is after all the true worshipper, and our Worshipper-in-Chief. It is only with Him leading us in worship, that the gates of heaven will open for our praise to ascend as sweet savour sacrifices.

Thus, we are given to call upon the gates of heaven to open not merely that Christ might return at His ascension, but that His praises accompanied by the praises of His people united to Him might ascend unto the Throne of God.

3. The Gates of Heaven Open for Christ

[7] *Lift up your heads, O ye gates; and be ye lift up, ye everlasting doors; and the King of glory shall come in.* [8] *Who is this King of glory? The LORD strong and mighty, the LORD mighty in battle.*

[9] *Lift up your heads, O ye gates; even lift them up, ye everlasting doors; and the King of glory shall come in.* [10] *Who is this King of glory? The LORD of hosts, He is the King of glory.*

It is hard to say anything that will not mar the beauty and loftiness of these words of exaltation. Christ has ascended. He was taken by a cloud and disappeared from the sight of His disciples watching His ascension. Like a ship disappearing over the horizon appears on another shore, so our Lord disappeared out of the sight of earth only to appear in a different dimension of existence.

Where does He appear when He disappeared from the sight of mortal man? He appears no doubt at the gates of the Celestial City.

A million angels must have accompanied Him. He went into battle. He has returned victorious. He led captivity captive. He is the King of glory. His name has been even more greatly magnified for He was made strong and mighty in battle. There is great celebration!

"Lift up your heads, O ye gates; and be ye lift up, ye everlasting doors!"

Open up, ye everlasting doors for the Son of Man to come in to take His rightful place by the Ancient of Days (Mk 14:62; Dan 7:13; Ps 110:1)!

Oh may we join in this refrain with triumph and gratitude! May we sing it, in celebration of the historical ascension that has already occurred. May we also sing it with boldness and gratitude in our hearts to charge heaven's gates to open for our worship led by our King to ascend to the throne of God!

Conclusion

This is Psalm 24. It is perhaps one of the most important Psalms to teach us about the theology of worship. Modern worship may be likened to congregational strength choir singing praises of man's composition unto God while Christ either stands in front to receive the praise, or stands by the side nodding His approval or shaking His head in disapproval in the case of songs that are heretical or unbiblical. But biblical worship has Christ as the Worshipper-in-Chief. Instead of a congregation strength choir singing their own songs, we have Christ singing His songs and the congregation singing with Him. This accords well with Psalm 22:22 (cf. Heb 2:12) and the theology of worship in Psalm 24.

And did not the Lord Himself say: "I am the way, the truth, and the life: no man cometh unto the Father, but by me" (Jn 14:6). This is not only applicable to our final entrance into heaven, it is surely applicable also to our spiritual entrance into heaven in worship. We know this to be the case in prayer, which is why we pray in the name of Christ. But we forget that it is also true in the element of praise. In prayer, the minister is given to use his own words guided by Scripture to pray in the name of Christ. But in praise, we are, nowhere, given the mandate to use our own words. We are, rather, to use the words appointed by our Lord, even the Psalms, the word of Christ, that we may sing with Him.

Therefore, let us use this Psalm to inform our intellect on how we ought to worship aright. At the same time, let us sing it to stir our affections to sing boldly and gratefully unto the LORD, our Creator and Redeemer. Let us do so in view of all that Christ the Captain of our salvation has done for us, is doing for us, and will do for us!

Amen. Ω

Psalm 25:
The Righteous Ones' Confidence
in the LORD's Mercies

Psalm 25 is the first of seven acrostic or alphabetical Psalms in the Scriptures. An acrostic Psalm is a Psalm which is arranged according to the Hebrew alphabet. The most famous of the acrostic Psalms is Psalm 119.

Psalm 25 is not perfectly acrostic in that not all the letters of the alphabet are represented. For example, there is no verse for the letter *Beth*. Verse 1 begins with *Aleph*; verse 2 begins with *Gimel* which is the third letter of the Hebrew alphabet. Why is this Psalm ordered alphabetically? It is ordered alphabetically, no doubt, as a memory device: for when you read this Psalm, you will find that almost every verse is significant and can stand by itself— much like in the book of Proverbs.

In fact, someone has said that this Psalm is really a collection of independent expressions of pious feelings. This is quite right. But this does not mean that this Psalm comprises some insignificant religious platitudes. On the contrary, there is much that is instructive and edifying in this Psalm. I believe this Psalm is Messianic, and can even be understood in the same way as we understand Psalm 22, that is, with Christ speaking in the first person. The difference is that in Psalm 22, Christ speaks as the head of the Church so that when we sing the Psalm in union with Him, we are singing His experience on our behalf; whereas here, He speaks not only as head but as member of the Church so that He takes up our experience in His lips. We may say that when we sing Psalm 22, we join our Saviour to sing His song. On the other hand, when we sing Psalm 25, our Saviour joins us to sing our song which He has written for us, His covenant people.

We may roughly organise this Psalm into seven parts, which we may outline as follows:

1. v. 1-3   Confident Trust
2. v. 4-5   Petition for Guidance
3. v. 6-7   Plea for Mercy
4. v. 8-10   Declaration of the Covenant Goodness of the LORD
5. v. 11   Petition for Pardon
6. v. 12-14   Celebration of God's Covenant Favour
7. v. 15-21   Prayer for Deliverance

Firstly, we are given to express our confidence in the LORD and to plead that we may not be disappointed.

1. Confident Trust

² *O my God, I trust in thee: let me not be ashamed, let not mine enemies triumph over me.*

Christ our Lord was tempted in all points like as we are (Heb 4:15), and therefore, He would certainly have used this prayer Himself. And if so, how much more, we who are His fallible members ought to learn the same prayer!

The Christian life is full of pitfalls and dangers. Our Lord warns us that if the world hates us, it is because it hated Him first. So as our Lord trusted His Father through all the dangers that attended His soul, let us learn to trust the Father. Let us especially trust Him, seeing that our

Head "endured the cross, despising the shame, and is set down at the right hand of the throne of God" (Heb 12:2). Let us plead God's covenant love that He may keep us from disappointment by supporting us under temptation and provocation of the enemies of the cross.

Secondly, from verses 4-5, we ask the LORD to guide us in the path of truth...

2. Petition for Guidance

⁴ Shew me thy ways, O LORD; teach me thy paths. ⁵ Lead me in thy truth, and teach me: for thou art the God of my salvation; on thee do I wait all the day.

Again, Christ our Lord would have prayed these words for "though He were a Son, yet learned He obedience by the things which He suffered" (Heb 5:8). He needed not salvation from sin, but He certainly needed deliverance from temptation and from the snares that wicked men laid in His paths.

As our Head prayed, so let us learn to do the same, especially as we have been plucked out of the way of death and enabled by our Head to walk with Him in the way of truth and righteousness. Shall we not, therefore, join our Saviour to ask the Father to show us His ways and to teach us His paths? He will teach us with His word and Spirit. The Word is like our map. The Spirit is our light. He illumines our minds so that we can read the road map with understanding. He will also teach us by His Son who has given us these words to sing with Him. He is the Author and Finisher of our faith: let us look to Him and follow after Him not only in words, but in life.

Thirdly, from verses 6-7, we are given to appeal to the LORD to have mercy towards us.

3. Plea for Mercy

⁶ Remember, O LORD, thy tender mercies and thy lovingkindnesses; for they have been ever of old. ⁷ Remember not the sins of my youth, nor my transgressions: according to thy mercy remember thou me for thy goodness' sake, O LORD.

How could our Saviour, who had no sin, ask for His sins of youth and His transgressions not to be remembered? Well, though He had no sin, He had taken our sin upon Himself. So He leads us to pray as we ought to—just as a father might pray with his children, "Lord, please forgive *our* naughtiness and our disobeying daddy's instruction." And though the father could not candidly pray with the first-person *singular* pronoun in this instance, our Saviour could, for He is truly united to us and have taken our guilt upon Himself.

So let us learn from our Lord to plead the Father's tender mercies and lovingkindness. Let us own our Lord's word which He gives us to pray that we may seek for forgiveness as we ought to. Oh may our Father not deal with us according to our sin, not because we do not deserve to be so dealt with, but because our Saviour took our sin upon Himself. So let us plead His covenant mercies and His goodness.

Fourthly, from verses 8-10, we are given to declare God's goodness towards His covenant people.

4. Declaration of the Covenant Goodness
of the LORD

⁸ Good and upright is the LORD: therefore will He teach sinners in the way. ⁹ The meek will He guide in judgment: and the meek will He teach His way. ¹⁰ All the paths of the LORD are mercy and truth unto such as keep His covenant and His testimonies.

This is a beautiful declaration. Sinners who are left to walk on their own, will rush headlong into eternal destruction. But the LORD is merciful. He will teach sinners the right way to live: Not all sinners, of course, but sinners who are represented by the Saviour who came for them. They are those whom our Saviour will enjoin to sing with Him. They are those whom our Saviour gives His Spirit to enliven with the graces of meekness, faith and repentance.

Those who thus have meekness sown, will repent of their sin and therefore be willing to learn the right way. Those the Father will further guide along in the path of justice, mercy and truth by His word and Spirit. They are those who keep His covenant and His testimonies. They are the ones who will declare God's goodness because they taste of His mercy and truth. This we will do, the Lord enabling us.

Fifthly, from verse 11, we are given a…

5. Petition for Pardon

[11] *For thy name's sake, O LORD, pardon mine iniquity; for it is great.*

This is another verse that convinces many that Christ could not have sung this Psalm, for Christ had no sin. But we must remember that though He had no sin, He was afflicted because of our sin. Our sins were imputed to Him. So He could surely take in His lips these words as well as the words in verse 18:

[18] *Look upon mine affliction and my pain; and forgive all my sins.*

As Christ our Lord cried unto the Father to look upon His affliction, and forgive our sin imputed to Him, so we must join Him to cry unto the Father to look upon our affliction and to forgive us our sin.

Though the afflictions that we suffer in this life may not be due to any particular sin we have committed, we must recognise that all affliction is a result of sin in general. Thus, we should be ready at all times to cry unto the Father in the words of this Psalm. But let us especially see to it that these words of Christ dwell richly in our hearts that when we face any form of affliction and pain—whether emotional or physical in this life, we may have something to sing for the comfort of our soul. James says, "Is any among you afflicted? Let Him pray. Is any merry? Let Him sing psalms" (Jas 5:13). Surely, He does not mean that we should only sing Psalms *when merry*, but rather that both prayer and Psalm singing ought to be used to express our emotional ebbs and flows.

Sixthly, from verses 12-14, we have a celebratory statement of faith with regard to the LORD's covenant blessing towards those who fear Him:

6. Celebration of
God's Covenant Favour

[12] *What man is He that feareth the LORD? Him shall He teach in the way that He shall choose.* [13] *His soul shall dwell at ease; and His seed shall inherit the earth.* [14] *The secret of the LORD is with them that fear him; and He will shew them His covenant.*

Our Saviour feared the LORD, His Father. Are we not told, that He, "in the days of His flesh, when He had offered up prayers and supplications with strong crying and tears unto Him that was able to save Him from death, … was heard in that He feared" (Heb 5:7). This, of course, is not a fear of dread and repulsion that desires to run away; but rather, a fear of love and reverence that desires to draw near.

Our Saviour, more than anyone else feared the LORD in this way, for He was not polluted by pride. So He feared the Father for us, and what blessings He received from the Father, He received for us: in order that we might enjoy them when we, by His Spirit and by imitation, fear the Father in union with Him.

Thus the Christian not only loves the Father, but fears Him too. Those who fear the Father will know the way and the blessing of the Lord. They will know the secret of the LORD, in that they have been taken into the confidence of the LORD, and given the wisdom and grace to understand God's ways. "Call unto me, and I will show thee great and mighty things that thou knowest not," says the LORD through Jeremiah (Jer 33:3). They will know the blessing of His covenant—of salvation in the home, and of prosperity both temporal and spiritual. They will enjoy God's blessings in a very real way.

Finally, from verse 15 to the end, we are given to conclude this Psalm with a swath of petitions, which recap all that has been said before, as we pray for deliverance from the troubles that beset us in this present life.

7. Prayer for Deliverance

[21] *Let integrity and uprightness preserve me; for I wait on thee.* [22] *Redeem Israel, O God, out of all His troubles.*

This is our Saviour's prayer. It is His prayer for Himself and for the people He came to redeem. So we who are His people may join Him to pray the same, recognising that though God will preserve and protect His people, He would generally do so in answer to their faith in Him and in the integrity and uprightness of their walk.

This is what we mean when we sing: "*Let integrity and uprightness preserve me; for I wait on thee.*" It is not our integrity and uprightness that will preserve us. It is God who will preserve us. But God will preserve only those who will walk in integrity and uprightness—in grateful response to the redeeming work of the Lord, whose integrity and uprightness alone are worthy.

So it is when the Church is seeking to follow after the Lord faithfully, that we can sing: "*Redeem Israel, O God, out of all His troubles.*" For as long as we are not walking with the Lord, in integrity and uprightness, then trouble is indeed good for us, for it will bring us to our knees, to depend on the LORD, whereas peace will make us complacent and prayerless.

Conclusion

This is Psalm 25. Have you, dear child of God, been striving to walk in the ways of the Lord?

You will not succeed, because sin ensures that while in this world, we shall fall short of the glory of God. But Christ your Saviour succeeded and this is His song which He has given for you to sing with Him. So if you are humbly striving and seeking and relying on Him, then you can be assured of God's covenant blessings.

God's blessing is not merely a display of His benevolence. It is God's blessing reserved for His covenant people, or the people who are united to His Son by faith, and by the sign and seal of the covenant. May the Lord hear our cries to deliver us out of trouble, according as we strive to walk in His ways! Amen. Ω

Psalm 26:
The Righteous One's
Resolution to Be Pure and Holy

Psalm 26 may be known as *"The Righteous One's Resolution to Be Pure and Holy."* When you read this song, you will realise that the singer is given to appeal very much to His own integrity and righteousness.

Verse 1 opens with *"Judge me, O LORD: for I have walked in mine integrity."* Verse 6 reads, *"I will wash mine hands in innocency,"* and verse 11: *"I will walk in mine integrity."*

Now, these words were written by David under the inspiration of the Holy Spirit. As a man who sought after God's own heart, David could, of course use these words to describe himself. Yes, he did sin grievously against the LORD on a number of occasions. But if you look at his life as a whole, you will see that he was indeed a man of integrity who walked in innocence.

And so too should every Christian!

But if we are honest with ourselves, we will find that there are many times when we will not be able to sing those words to refer to ourselves without any reservation. Indeed, if we put in a little more thought, we will realise that we fall short of the glory of God and sin not only in deeds and words, but in thoughts. This being the case, we cannot really, at any time, sing these words to refer to ourselves, with no qualification at all.

The only man who can use these words with a clear conscience, at all times, is our Lord Himself.

The rest of us can only use these words honestly because we are united to Him as our Head. We can only sing these words in the knowledge that the righteousness of Christ covers us and that God does not deal with us according to our sin, for He looks at us as a people covered with the righteousness of Christ.

So as Andrew Bonar puts it:

> In this Psalm, "our head speaks... as well as His members. We may consider Him as teaching His members to take up His words, and address them to the Father in His name."

With this in mind, we shall, in this study, look at this Psalm as the word of Christ, taking Christ to be the primary speaker in this Psalm.

We may break this Psalm into four parts:

1. v. 1-3   The Righteous One's Reflection
2. v. 4-8   The Righteous One's Resolve
3. v. 9-10   The Righteous One's Request
4. v. 11-12   The Righteous One's Repose

1. The Righteous One's Reflection

[1] *Judge me, O LORD; for I have walked in mine integrity: I have trusted also in the LORD; therefore I shall not slide.* [2] *Examine me, O LORD, and prove me; try my reins and my heart.*

Our Lord was tempted in all points like as we are, yet without sin. And it was not just that

He did not sin outwardly; He did not sin in deeds, words and thoughts.

This is why He could ask the Father to examine Him: to certify that He is indeed walking in integrity and not in hypocrisy. Our Lord was truly a man without guile, a man who says what He means and means what He says. Never did He say something to flatter anyone when in His heart He thought otherwise.

As believers we must imitate the Lord. Though we fail, we too must desire to be pure. For this purpose, we should examine ourselves. And we should ask the LORD to examine us. Of course, unlike the Lord, we should ask the Father to examine us not so much to certify us, as to lead us in the way of truth.

"^{23} Search me, O God, and know my heart: try me, and know my thoughts: ^{24} And see if there be any wicked way in me, and lead me in the way everlasting" (Ps 139:23-24)

In any case, our attitude should be as the Lord's attitude—as expressed in the reason for wanting to be examined:

^{3} *For thy lovingkindness is before mine eyes: and I have walked in thy truth.*

The Lord requests for examination because He desires to live a life of gratitude, occasioned by the knowledge of the covenant lovingkindness of the Father.

How often do you think about God's lovingkindness? And when you do so, do you ask the LORD to examine yourself? How often do you take heed to repent and walk in the right way when the Spirit through your conscience points you to the right way?

Let us imitate the Lord's example. Let us think about God's covenant lovingkindness towards us, and when we do so, let us examine ourselves to see how we have ungratefully fallen short of His expectation; and then seek the enablement of His Spirit to turn us back to the way of truth.

And let us, secondly, confess and follow the Lord's example in His resolution to keep Himself pure and holy.

2. The Righteous One's Resolve

^{4} *I have not sat with vain persons, neither will I go in with dissemblers. ^{5} I have hated the congregation of evil doers; and will not sit with the wicked. ^{6} I will wash mine hands in innocency:*

We have seen this attitude in Psalm 1. Our Lord does not look at holiness as a subjective thing. He calls sin, sin; and wickedness, wicked. He does not tell people who are evil: "You are OK, I love you." He is not politically correct. He is not a compromiser.

His resolve is that He will be pure. He resolves to keep His hands pure from wicked deeds. So He does not want complicity with anyone who has no regard for purity and holiness.

But why? Why does the Lord so resolve to keep Himself pure?

^{6b} *so will I compass thine altar, O LORD: ^{7} That I may publish with the voice of thanksgiving, and tell of all thy wondrous works. ^{8} LORD, I have loved the habitation of thy house, and the place where thine honour dwelleth.*

The Lord's reason is very simple: He desires to worship the Father with sincerity. He desires to sing the praises of God without hypocrisy. He loves the habitation of God's house. He does not want to worship God with a cloud over His conscience. For how can He enjoy God if He lives a hypocritical life? The LORD sees through His heart.

So let us likewise resolve to be pure and holy as the LORD is holy. Each time we come for prayer, each time we come for worship: let us resolve as the Lord does to approach the Father in sincerity.

Only those who approach the Father in sincerity in this life can expect to enjoy worship in the heavenly dwelling of God for all eternity.

It was because Christ Jesus our Lord lived such a life that He could confidently approach the Father.

3. The Righteous One's Request

⁹ Gather not my soul with sinners, nor my life with bloody men: ¹⁰ In whose hands is mischief, and their right hand is full of bribes.

As the Lord lives a righteous life, He desires to die a righteous death. He, therefore, petitions the Father not to take away His soul or life in the manner and occasions when the Father would judge the wicked—such as during wars or natural calamities.

Our Lord is not saying that He does not want to die with the wicked by His side: For as Isaiah would prophesy 300 years after this Psalm was written, that the Lord would make His grave with the wicked. He would, in particular, die between two malefactors. One of them would indeed repent, but the other would remain to His last breath a wicked blasphemer.

No, no; the Lord is asking to be looked upon uniquely. Though He would die a violent death, let it be known that He died not for His sin, for He had none.

¹¹ But as for me, I will walk in mine integrity: redeem me, and be merciful unto me.

He recognises that sometimes God in His wrath will sweep a multitude of people into eternity in a moment. Sometimes the children of God are caught up in the disasters too. Is it an earthquake, a tsunami, a typhoon, a hurricane, or a terrorist act? The child of God who lives distinctly from the wicked has the privilege of asking to be delivered from such mass destruction.

Think of Noah's flood: how God preserved Noah. Think of Sodom and Gomorrah: how Abraham prayed for His nephew Lot and God promised not to destroy the city if only ten righteous persons were found in it. God did, of course, destroy the city, but not before pulling Lot and his daughters out.

Therefore, if you are seeking to walk in the way of the Lord, you need not fear to be swept along with the multitude when God sends His judgment. Cry unto the LORD on the basis of your covenant union with Christ and on the integrity of your own walk. He is a prayer-hearing God. Even if for some reason, the LORD would have you be swept up in the general cataclysm, you can be sure that He will not suffer you to be rushed into a Christless eternity with a godless multitude.

It is in this confidence that the Lord has His repose or rest.

4. The Righteous One's Repose

¹² My foot standeth in an even place: in the congregations will I bless the LORD.

Because the Lord is perfectly righteous, He cannot fall. His foot is standing firm, as it were, on level ground. He knows that He will enjoy the eternal worship that the great congregation of God's people will enjoy for all eternity.

As a people united to Christ, we too can share in this confidence. As long as we are walking in integrity and trusting the LORD (v. 1), our feet will be on level ground. We shall not slide and fall.

Yes, today we may still fall because of the remnant of corruption that is in us. But one day, we shall be made perfectly righteous: then we shall never fall, and we shall enjoy worshipping the LORD in the great congregation of the Lord forever.

Conclusion

This is Psalm 26. Here we are given to sing, in union with the Righteous One, in respect to a holy and pure walk before the face of His Father.

We are given, in this way, an opportunity to consider our own attitude and life vis-à-vis our Lord's reflection of His own life, His resolve to be holy, His requesting the Father to deal with Him according to His integrity, and His resting in the confidence that all will be well for Him.

What is this Psalm to you? May it not be merely an interesting Psalm about the Lord! May it be that as we consider the Lord's life and attitudes, we may examine ourselves against His example and see if we are living the holy life that we desire?

Christ our Lord laid down His life for us, to redeem us out of a sinful and destructive life, which is neither glorifying to God nor satisfying to us.

Let us not be as a swine going back to the mud to wallow in it; rather, let us seek to live a life with Christ in the centre. Oh may it be that Christ be formed in our lives more and more so that our decisions are made according to His word, where our aim is His glory, where our motivation is His love, and where our example is Christ Himself.

May the LORD grant that as we meditate and sing this Psalm, we may, by the power of the Spirit of Christ, be spurred to be holy as He is holy! Amen. Ω

Psalm 27:
The Righteous One
Surrounded by Foes, and Forsaken by Friends

"The LORD is my light and my salvation." These opening words immediately lead us to think of Christ, the "true Light" (Jn 1:9) and our Saviour. Indeed, some think that these words could not have been sung by the Lord Jesus because of the reference to "salvation." The Lord does not need salvation since He had no sin, or so it is surmised. But the word "salvation" does not only refer to being "saved from sin." In fact, in the context, it is about deliverance from one's enemies. See verse 2! So these words could, no doubt, have been used by the Lord. But the question is: Does this Psalm describe the experience of Christ or that of a Christian? I believe it is both: For we must remember that the Church and Christ is one. Christ is the head; the Church is the body. As Andrew Bonar puts it: "David was taught by the Spirit to write the blessed experience of the Church and its Head."

This Psalm describes objectively, the experience of our Lord, and subjectively, the experience of every believer united to Him. We must sing it in union with our Saviour with an eye on what He went through on our behalf, and another eye on what our own responses ought to be.

Here is *"The Righteous One Surrounded by Foes, and Forsaken by Friends."* This theme may not seem obvious immediately, because this Psalm seems a lot more positive with the enrapturing references to the brightness and beauty of the LORD (v. 1, 4b), and the joy and delight of being in the presence of God and worshipping Him (v. 4a, 6). However, a closer look at the text will reveal that these glories are being revelled against a much more depressing backdrop. Indeed, this is part of the genius of this Psalm: for it is in the darkest nights that the brightness of heavenly glory and comfort shines most intensely and reassuringly to our souls. This, surely, is what our Saviour who gave us this Psalm, wants us to appreciate as we sing these strophes in union with Him.

1. v. 1-3   An Affirmation of Confidence in the LORD

2. v. 4-6   A Yearning for Delightful Communion with God

3. v. 7-12   A Plea to Hear His cry for Favour and Grace

4. v. 13-14   A Counsel to Wait on the LORD

1. An Affirmation

[1] *The LORD is my light and my salvation; whom shall I fear? the LORD is the strength of my life; of whom shall I be afraid?* [2] *When the wicked, even mine enemies and my foes, came upon me to eat up my flesh, they stumbled and fell.* [3] *Though an host should encamp against me, my heart shall not fear: though war should rise against me, in this will I be confident.*

Do not these words bring to mind the scene in the Garden of Gethsemane when Judas Iscariot came with a band of soldiers to arrest the Lord?

It was a dark and lonely night in the Garden of Gethsemane for our Lord. While His disciples slept, He was praying in regard to the intense suffering that was about to befall Him. "If it be possible, take this cup from me; yet not my will but thy will be done," our Lord beseeched His Father. So intense was our Lord in prayer that His sweat fell to the ground like great drops of blood. Then came Judas, with the band of soldiers carrying "lanterns and torches and weapons" (Jn 18:3) to arrest Him.

¹ The LORD is my light and my salvation; whom shall I fear? the LORD is the strength of my life; of whom shall I be afraid?

He asked them: "Whom seek ye?" They said, "Jesus of Nazareth." He said, "I am he"; and immediately, they "went backward, and fell to the ground" (Jn 18:6).

² When the wicked, even mine enemies and my foes, came upon me to eat up my flesh, they stumbled and fell.

Then they surrounded the Lord in such a threatening fashion that Peter raised his sword to cut off the ear of one of them. And the Lord had to stop him. We read: "Then said Jesus unto him, Put up again thy sword into his place: for all they that take the sword shall perish with the sword. Thinkest thou that I cannot now pray to my Father, and He shall presently give me more than twelve legions of angels?" (Mt 26:52-53).

³ Though an host should encamp against me, my heart shall not fear: though war should rise against me, in this will I be confident.

Can you see how beautifully these words express our Lord's experience in the night of His passion? Though our Lord was facing one of the most severe trials in His life, He was confident of His Father's deliverance.

Shall we not learn likewise to trust in Him through times of fear and uncertainty? Let us learn to be brave in the Lord. Believers should never be cringing cowards. In times of trial, let us learn to lift up our heads unto the Father. Indeed, as Christ our Lord—who was likewise tempted as we are—is seated at the right hand of the Father, let us go to the Father boldly in His name. Let us go to Him and hide in Him as our Lord did. For, consider His meditation on how He found peace and delight in the presence of His Father.

2. A Yearning

⁴ One thing have I desired of the LORD, that will I seek after; that I may dwell in the house of the LORD all the days of my life, to behold the beauty of the LORD, and to enquire in His temple.

What a beautiful statement of faith by our Lord. While He was confronted by His enemies and by the prospect of suffering and abandonment at the cross, He was thinking about the joy of being in communion with His Father.

What do you think about to encourage yourself in times of darkness and distress? Our Lord thought about the joy of fellowship with the Father. As He thought about the Father, all His troubles must have, as it were, melted away. Even in the midst of the trouble, the Father hides Him in His pavilion, in the secret of His tabernacle. Verse 5:

⁵ For in the time of trouble He shall hide me in His pavilion: in the secret of His tabernacle shall He hide me; He shall set me up upon a rock. ⁶ And now shall mine head be lifted up above mine enemies round about me: therefore will I offer in His tabernacle sacrifices of joy; I will sing, yea, I will sing praises unto the LORD.

It is not difficult for us to imagine how these words must have encouraged our Lord as the soldiers surrounded Him and bound Him up. These words are written in the future tense because they were written before the Lord's actual experience. But surely they must have resounded in the heart of our Lord, and brought Him comfort. Even as He was surrounded by angry men who would, as it were, eat Him up, He was hidden in the secret dwelling of the Lord, sheltered by the pavilion of His temple, and set upon a high rock. His captors must have pushed His head down physically as captors always do when leading their prisoners away. But spiritually, His head was lifted up and He was singing praises in His heart. He was, as it were, transported in the spirit to a different reality where He found comfort and joy in the presence of His Father.

Oh what an example of faith! Let us follow His lead. When things in our life begin to crash around us and everything seems unreal, let us not allow ourselves to sink in despondency. Let us go, rather, to the Father and hide in Him. We can do so in the spirit, even though the trial that is afflicting us is still troubling us.

Our Lord both meditated on the delight of communion with His Father, and petitioned Him at the same time.

3. A Plea

⁷ Hear, O LORD, when I cry with my voice: have mercy also upon me, and answer me. ⁸ When thou saidst, Seek ye my face; my heart said unto thee, Thy face, LORD, will I seek.

One of the most comforting thoughts when going through trials is the knowledge that the Father is in control and giving appropriate guidance.

So notice how the Lord desired of the Father that He continue to commune with Him: to answer Him, and to call out to Him. This was especially so as He was about to face the darkest hour in His work as Redeemer. He was about to go to the cross for the sin of His people. He knew that at the cross, the full weight of the guilt of His Church would be placed upon His shoulders. As He was sentenced by the earthly court in perfect *injustice*, so He was sentenced by the heavenly court in perfect *justice*, though not for His own sin, but rather for the sin of His people.

In this anticipation, our Lord would have cried out to His Father:

⁹ Hide not thy face far from me; put not thy servant away in anger: thou hast been my help; leave me not, neither forsake me, O God of my salvation.

Do these words not remind you of how our Lord cried on the cross: "My God, my God, why hast thou forsaken me?" The Father heard His prayer indeed, but for the sake of the elect He must suffer His wrath, or they would find no redemption.

So our Lord's prayer that He would not be forsaken must be understood according to what He said in the Garden: "Not my will, but thy will be done." The same goes for the petition in verse 12:

¹² Deliver me not over unto the will of mine enemies: for false witnesses are risen up against me, and such as breathe out cruelty.

Our Lord would indeed be delivered over to the will of His enemies through false witnesses and those who breathe out cruelty. But, though that might be the case, our Lord knew that the Father would not completely abandon Him even if all men, including His earthly father and mother were to forsake him:

¹⁰ When my father and my mother forsake me, then the LORD will take me up. ¹¹ Teach me thy way, O LORD, and lead me in a plain path, because of mine enemies.

The Father would not completely abandon Him. Even though He was delivered into the hands of His enemies, they were but instruments of His wrath. They were in His hands to accomplish His purpose.

So it is with those of us who are in Christ: God will never fully abandon us even when He has to chastise us for our sin. Our Lord was punished for our sin, yet the Father did not forsake Him completely. His wrath burned but for a moment.

God will not punish us for our sin, because He has already punished His Son for us. But He will sometimes chastise us, out of love for us. Let us be assured that His wrath will last but for a moment, and then weeping shall turn into joy.

So let us take heed to the Lord's exhortation…

4. A Counsel

[13] *I had fainted, unless I had believed to see the goodness of the LORD in the land of the living.* [14] *Wait on the LORD: be of good courage, and He shall strengthen thine heart: wait, I say, on the LORD.*

Had our Lord not believed in the Father, He would have fainted: not that He would literally faint, but that He would have given up, for weakness and fear. But our Lord believed. Love "believeth all things" (1 Cor 13:7). Greater love has no man than that of the Son for His Father! And so He was confident that He would see the goodness of the LORD whilst He was yet in the land of the living (cf. Isa 38:11), and that He would again live to see the goodness of the LORD even after He dies. That is: He was confident that He did not have to wait for death before He saw again the goodness of the LORD; and He was confident that He would rise again, and with Him, those whom He came to give life, abundant and free.

Did He not say: "It is finished"? Did He not say: "Father, into thy hands, I commend my spirit"? Our Lord did not give up. When the hours of darkness ended, He knew that His Father was still there. He knew that the Father had never given up on Him. He knew that His Father would keep His promises according to the Covenant of Grace.

Therefore, let us take heed to our Lord's counsel: Wait on the LORD. Be of good courage. He will strengthen your heart. If He appears to withdraw His countenance for a while, remember that there is a good reason for it, and that it would only be for a season. Wait on the LORD. He will, in His good time, bring cheer to your heart.

It will be soon. You will not have to wait for death to end your misery. You will know the blessings of the Lord in the land of the living. This was the confidence of our Saviour; this can be our confidence too. So seek Him in prayer; and wait patiently for Him.

Conclusion

Are you going through a difficult trial in your life, dear believer? Have you ever wondered why so many of the Psalms have to do with trials?

Is it not because "we must through much tribulation enter into the Kingdom of God" (Acts 14:22)? God appointed for us tribulations that we may learn to wait upon Him patiently. While we may not like the trials that try us, we must understand that they are for our long term and eternal good. And so we ought not to grumble against the LORD, but to rejoice in our trials.

And we are not to rejoice with a stoic indifference. We must follow the example and exhortation of our Lord and rejoice. We must do so as we wait upon the Lord. And while waiting, we may encourage ourselves by singing and meditating on His word, such as in this Psalm! May the Lord help us! Amen. Ω

Psalm 28:
The Righteous One's
Cry Against Temptation

The theme of Psalm 28 is not immediately obvious. John Brown sees it as David's cries for deliverance due to some distress. Andrew Bonar sees it as "the appeal and thanksgiving of the righteous as they view the tents of the ungodly." George Horne sees it as the Lord's prayer for deliverance from His enemies and for their destruction.

I am inclined to see this Psalm as *"The Righteous One's Cry Against Temptation to follow the way of the wicked."*

Though this Psalm was penned by David, he, no doubt, wrote the word of Christ (Col 3:16) under the inspiration of the Spirit of Christ (1 Pet 1:11). Christ was tempted in all points like as we are, yet without sin. So as He taught us to pray, "Lead us not into temptation," we know that He must have prayed likewise.

This Psalm gives us an insight into how He must have expanded the prayer: "Lead us not into temptation." It has two parts, which we may outline as follows:

1.   v. 1-5   Petition for Deliverance from Temptation
2.   v. 6-9   Thanksgiving for Deliverance

1. Petition for Deliverance from Temptation

To be tempted is to experience something very common to man. Our first parents fell because they were tempted. Since then, every person who knows the difference between right and wrong has experienced temptation.

However, very few of us take temptations very seriously. Most of us take them as they come; and when they come, we deal with them in a haphazard way. Very often, we resist or give in to them according to how we feel at the moment. We think very little about what is going on, and the consequence of our actions.

But our Lord is the perfect man. He was tempted in all points like as we are, yet without sin. And it is not because He was shielded from all temptation. Indeed, while we are shielded from all temptation except for what is common to man and what we are individually able to bear (1 Cor 10:13), Christ our Lord must have been tempted to an uncommon degree and in ways that none of us could have withstood.

We can imagine, for example, how intensely our Lord must have been tempted when He was wrongly accused by His enemies. When someone accuses us of something relating to our intentions or attitudes, very few of us (who are honest with ourselves), will be able to claim perfect innocence. But our Lord is perfectly clear in His mind. He knows that He has absolutely no evil intentions. This, no doubt, would have caused a sense of injustice to arise in His heart, so that perhaps He was tempted to make a strong counter-accusation, or even to put to silence His accuser. And He would be able to do so with perfect honesty. But if He did so, and He was perfectly capable of doing so, He would have sinned against God by breaking His own vow to suffer on behalf of His people; and He would have lost the opportunity to redeem them.

What then did our Lord do when He faced such temptations? He, no doubt, cried out unto the Father! And this Psalm, which is inspired by His Spirit, I believe, gives us an idea of how

He must have prayed.

Consider, *firstly*, His plea to be heard:

> [1] *Unto thee will I cry, O LORD my rock; be not silent to me: lest, if thou be silent to me, I become like them that go down into the pit.* [2] *Hear the voice of my supplications, when I cry unto thee, when I lift up my hands towards thy holy oracle.*

The Lord calls His Father "*my rock*" because He is immovable and dependable. What does the Lord mean when He says, "*be not silent to me*"? What He means is simply that He desires to be heard—not just heard as one making a noise, but heard as one crying for help. He desires to hear an answer from the Father—whether in words or in actions.

In other words, He desires a discernible response from His Father. It is like when a child asks something of his mother, but his mother is busy and does not reply. This can be extremely exasperating for the child.

The Father—no doubt—always hears Him. "Thou hearest me always: but because of the people which stand by I said it," says the Lord on another occasion (Jn 11:42). The Father always hears Him; but for our sakes—He prays as He does: that we may learn to plead with the Father.

But why does our Lord want to be heard? "[1b] *Lest, if thou be silent to me, I become like them that go down into the pit,*" He says.

Unless the Father hears and answers His prayer, He may be like them that go down into the pit. That is, that He may become like the wicked—perhaps beginning to live as if God does not exists, or being dragged into temptation and doing the things that the wicked do. This would, of course, not happen to Christ, the God-Man. But the God-Man prays as man should pray. And in prayer, man being a finite creature may support His petition with what He perceives will be the consequence if His prayer is not answered. This is what our Lord does in His first petition.

Secondly, consider His petition to be kept from temptation:

> [3] *Draw me not away with the wicked, and with the workers of iniquity, which speak peace to their neighbours, but mischief is in their hearts.*

That is: Do not allow me to go in the way of the wicked. Lead me not into temptation, but deliver me from evil. Allow me not to wander away from Thee, to follow the example of the wicked and the workers of iniquity. Workers of iniquity are those who are hypocrites, who say one thing, but mean another.

Remember how the Lord Jesus warns that in the Last Day, there will be many who say unto Him, "Lord, lord, have we not done many wonderful works in thy name?" And He would say unto them, "I never knew you," "depart from me, all ye workers of iniquity" (Lk 13:27).

Workers of iniquity are essentially those who are lawless and hypocritical.

The Lord desires not to be like unbelievers or like hypocrites who profess to believe, but are walking in sin. This is His second petition. He is mindful of the possibility of assimilating the ways of the wicked and beginning to do as they do. Though He will not sin despite being tempted sore, He does not take for granted that He will stand. He, therefore, asks His Father to protect Him from wandering.

Thirdly, consider how He asks the Father to deal with these wicked persons and hypocrites:

⁴ Give them according to their deeds, and according to the wickedness of their endeavours: give them after the work of their hands; render to them their desert.

The wicked and the hypocrites sometime appear to cruise along in life as if everything is fine. They deserve to be punished for their wickedness, but they seem to get away with their wicked deeds.

The Lord prays that the Father will take action against them—both for justice's sake, and so that others, including Himself may take warning.

The way of the wicked may seem very attractive to the child of God when it always appears so smooth.

So one of the means to remove the attractiveness of sinful ways is for the Father to deal with those who walk in that way; and for the child of God to meditate on how the Father hates their wicked deeds.

This is what the Lord is doing in verse 5:

⁵ Because they regard not the works of the LORD, nor the operation of His hands, He shall destroy them, and not build them up.

Here then are the three petitions of the Lord as He asked His Father to deliver Him from temptation.

First, He prays earnestly and sincerely for a response so that He is assured that His earnest request is heard. It is not simply a-matter-of-fact prayer.

Secondly, He prays that He may not be tempted to follow the example of the wicked and the hypocrite.

Thirdly, He prays that the Father would deal with the wicked and the hypocrites, that the righteous may be reminded of how God hates sinful ways.

Shall we not take heed to do the same as we ask the LORD to lead us not into temptation?

Shall we not pray with faith as the Lord did, and therefore, is able to rejoice in the fact that His Father hears and answers His cries...

2. Thanksgiving for Deliverance
from Temptation

⁶ Blessed be the LORD, because He hath heard the voice of my supplications.

It is easy when praying against temptation to take it lightly, or to think that God does not hear, or is not concerned about it.

Thank God for our Lord's assurance that His prayers are heard.

⁷ The LORD is my strength and my shield; my heart trusted in Him, and I am helped: therefore my heart greatly rejoiceth; and with my song will I praise Him.

The Father will protect and strengthen us against all temptation if only we would trust Him.

The Lord Jesus trusted Him, and was helped. Therefore, His heart greatly rejoiced and He overflowed with songs of praise.

Are you aware when God helps you to overcome a certain temptation, or a certain besetting sin in your life? Will you not rejoice and praise the LORD for His goodness towards you?

[8] *The LORD is their strength, and He is the saving strength of His anointed.*

The Anointed One is the Messiah (מָשִׁיחַ, *mâshîyach*). That is the Hebrew for Anointed. The Greek for Anointed One is *"Christos"* or Christ. The Father is the strength of the Anointed One and the people united to Him.

The Anointed One is He whose prayer is recorded in this Psalm. He sets us an example of praying for deliverance from temptation. But He does not stop there. He petitions on our behalf too, for Satan would sieve us as wheat.

This is how He ends the Psalm:

[9] *Save thy people, and bless thine inheritance: feed them also, and lift them up for ever.*

Save thy people. Save them from sin. Save them from wrath. Bless them. They are Thy inheritance. Feed them as a shepherd. Do not let them stray into the paths of wickedness and hypocrisy. Gather them when they stray. Lift them up when they fall. Carry them when they are too weak to follow. Do not forsake them. Be with them forever.

Thank God for this prayer of our Mediator. Thank God that the Father appointed Him as our Shepherd that we may be led by one who knows our frailty, having Himself been tempted in our flesh.

Conclusion

Psalm 28 is not a very well-known or well-used Psalm. But it deals with a theme that affects all of us: for we are all tempted to sin in many ways.

Let us pray that the LORD opens our eyes to see wherein we have sinned, and wherein we have behaved like the wicked and the hypocrites, that we may be kept from temptation.

Let us also learn from the Lord's example to pray earnestly and sincerely against falling into temptation. Let us ask the Lord to grant us a holy hatred for sin, especially our own sin! Let us pray that we may see through the ruse of the wicked one that we may not be led in the way of iniquity. Amen. Ω

Psalm 29:
The Righteous One's
Adoration in the Day of Storm

Psalm 29 is famously known as the Storm Psalm. It was probably composed by David under the inspiration of the Holy Spirit on a stormy night. We can imagine that on that day David might have gone out hunting in the wilderness of Kadesh. A storm began to brew, and he was forced to take shelter in a cattle stall.

As he sits there looking over a lake and surrounded by the forest, awesome streaks of lightning illumine the sky and land, accompanied by terrifying peals of thunder, and an intense outpouring of rain. It is as if our mighty God were speaking from heaven. Seven times in this Psalm, does David speak of the voice of the Lord in an apparent allusion to the thunderous peals. David is awe-struck and humbled; his heart is filled with adoration for the God of Wonder, and his lips overflow with praise.

This is why we call it a Storm Psalm, or more fully, *"The Righteous One's Adoration in the Day of Storm."* David, no doubt, wrote under the inspiration of the Spirit of Christ to give expression to the meditation of our Lord as He faced the storm of God's wrath at the cross of Calvary. In this way, the Church is also given a song to sing in union with Christ about the majesty of our great God, when storms whether physical or spiritual fall upon us.

We may divide it simply into three parts:

1. v. 1-2   A Call to Praise
2. v. 3-9   A Cause for Praise
3. v. 10-11   A Conclusion of Praise

1. A Call to Praise

[1] *Give unto the LORD, O ye mighty, give unto the LORD glory and strength.* [2] *Give unto the LORD the glory due unto His name; worship the LORD in the beauty of holiness.*

The mighty ones are the angels and all the mighty men of the world. None are so great as the LORD God Almighty. None deserve the praise and honour that our LORD deserves.

"Give unto the LORD." Our LORD does not need anything. When we sing, *"Give unto the LORD"*, the meaning of the word "give" is to "ascribe" or "declare." Ascribe unto the LORD glory and strength—praise and magnify Him for His glory and strength. Praise Him especially in the moments when His greatness is manifested, such as in a storm, or in the day of His revelation.

Praise Him. Lift up your voice and ascribe unto Him the glory due unto Him. Let all the world know that He is indeed great. And worship Him in the beauty of holiness. Worship Him not in the beauty of human devised artefacts of idolatry. Worship Him in the beauty and splendour of His holiness.

To be holy is to be transcendent or separated. God is holy for He is utterly other: that is, He is absolutely not a part of Creation. He is the Creator. He cannot really be represented by things created, whether by Himself or by man. His beauty cannot in the least way be captured by human art or description. Therefore, to worship Him in the beauty of holiness, we may only worship Him in the simplicity of worship that He has appointed in His word.

But let us be stirred up to worship Him by meditating on His power and greatness in the things that we see and hear. The thunderstorm is a very great example. David was inspired to write this Psalm because his heart was lifted up to God as he witnessed the storm.

Therefore, let us sing this Psalm to praise the LORD in stormy days, knowing that our Saviour who has promised to be with us always, will sing with us.

But let us also sing this Psalm in fair weather, bringing to mind how our Saviour weathered the storm for us, and triumphed over it.

Remember the occasion in the earthly ministry of our Lord, when He and His disciples were caught up in a storm. Remember what happened? The Lord was sleeping at the back of the boat when the storm started. The boat was beginning to be flooded. One of the disciples woke the Lord. What did He do? He stood up, and He rebuked the wind and the waves. And there was immediately a great calm.

What happened to the disciples when they saw this? We are told that they were exceedingly fearful, and they cried out one to another "What manner of man is this? That even the wind and the waves obey His commands?"

The disciples saw that Christ was the LORD, the everlasting King.

And so when we think about storms, it is hard for us not to think about the Lord Jesus Christ. Indeed, as our Lord has been appointed by the Father to be the administrator of the universe for our sakes, so we can indeed direct our praise to Him as our King.

This Psalm is a celebration of His greatness. It is a call to all men to meditate on the LORD's greatness and to praise Him: Father, Son and Holy Spirit, the One Mighty God!

And consider how God in His providence gives us cause to praise Him.

2. A Cause for Praise

³ The voice of the LORD is upon the waters: the God of glory thundereth: the LORD is upon many waters.

Over the lake, the sight and sound of lightning can be awesome. It is like the LORD Himself has come upon the waters and is speaking with a glorious voice.

⁴ The voice of the LORD is powerful; the voice of the LORD is full of majesty.

What David heard with his ear was the thunderous boom of the lightning. What he heard with his soul was the voice of God. If the thunder is majestic and powerful, how much more is the LORD full of power and majesty?

There is but a hiding of His power and majesty in the thunder and lightning. The noise of the thunder is but a whisper of God. The brightness of the lightning is but His shadow.

But still the power of the lightning is unmistakable....

⁵ The voice of the LORD breaketh the cedars; yea, the LORD breaketh the cedars of Lebanon.

It is possible that a lightning struck a cedar tree right before the eyes of David and it started to catch fire and to crash to the ground.

⁶ He maketh them also to skip like a calf; Lebanon and Sirion like a young unicorn. ⁷ The voice of the LORD divideth the flames of fire.

From a distance, the whole forest seems to come alive like dancing unicorns as the lightning streaks across the sky one after another, some of them hitting the trees in the distant. And the thunder is so loud that everything seems to shake.

[8] The voice of the LORD shaketh the wilderness; the LORD shaketh the wilderness of Kadesh.

But there in the cattle stall where David is taking shelter, even the animals are feeling uneasy about the display, so much so that the cows go into labour....

[9] The voice of the LORD maketh the hinds to calve, and discovereth the forests:

Outdoors, the lightning exposes everything; indoors every creature is affected. The cows are frightened into casting their calves. What about man?

Those who fear the Lord will not fear, nor will they merely be amazed by these sights and sounds. Instead, they will respond with worship.

This is why David says in the second part of verse 9...

... and in His temple doth every one speak of His glory.

Perhaps David is thinking about what the holy priests in the temple will be talking about as they also experienced the same great storm. He surmises that they would be talking about God's glory. For no one who fears the Lord, will behold such a wonderful display of God's power, and be unmoved by it. What's more, the priests are in the temple of God.

So, let us not allow any storm to blow pass without our hearts being lifted up to magnify the LORD, and to thank our Saviour who said to the storm: "Peace, be still!"

When we so exercise our hearts, we can be sure of peace in our hearts. Even though the storm is raging, we can have peace. Praise concludes with peace because praise acknowledges that He who brings the storm will also bring peace.

3. A Conclusion of Praise

[10] The LORD sitteth upon the flood; yea, the LORD sitteth King for ever.

The LORD sitteth on the flood—not literally; but that He is in control over the flood. He is the King of kings forever. He is King over all things including the storm, the wind, the waves and the lightning.

These things, whether literal or metaphorical, frighten us. They leave us with anxieties in our hearts.

Remember how Martin Luther was so frightened when a lightning bolt struck near him that he decided to become a monk.

But these things ought not to frighten us. Why should they frighten us when we know that our Saviour—who sings with us—triumphs over the final storm, and is seated at the right hand of God to be our Mediator?

Because of what He endured and did for us, we have peace:

[11] The LORD will give strength unto His people; the LORD will bless His people with peace.

The Lord will give us strength and peace not by a supernatural injection of adrenaline or Valium or anything like that. No, no; it will be through the Holy Spirit reminding us of who God is and what He has done, is doing, and will do for us.

The Holy Spirit works by bringing to remembrance the word of God that we have received. So let us hide these truths which are revealed in this Psalm in our hearts, that we may be prepared for stormy days.

Conclusion

Let us hide in our hearts the three interrelated things from this Psalm:

- *First*, let us remember that the loud thunder of nature are but the voice of the LORD. That is, let us understand that the LORD is sovereign. Everything in nature that is great and magnificent, is intended to serve as a reminder of the mighty power of God.

- *Secondly*, let it be lodged in our mind that however great a storm may be, Christ our Lord is greater. The wind and the waves obeyed Him. Whether it is a literal storm, or a stormy time in our life, let us understand that Christ is greater.

- *Finally*, let us never allow loud thunders in our experience to dislodge from our mind the confidence that the LORD will bless His people with peace for Christ's sake. That is, the LORD who is sovereign over all things will see to it that we will be protected from all things that are eternally harmful to us, and will bestow upon us things that are eternally good for us. This is His promise to His Son. Therefore, this is also His promise to all united to His Son. Amen. Ω

Psalm 30:
The Righteous One's
Song of Dedication of His Family

Psalm 30 has a rather descriptive title to indicate the occasion it was written: "*A Psalm and Song at the dedication of the house of David.*"

But what exactly is this house of David? Many commentators such as JA Alexander and Andrew Bonar hold that it refers to the dedication of the threshing floor of Ornan on Mount Moriah. The occasion, they surmise, was David's numbering of the troops, which incurred God's wrath. God sent a plague against the people in His wrath, but the plague stopped at the threshing floor of Ornan where David prepared to offer a sacrifice unto the Lord. When the LORD answered David by fire, David, in astonishment, exclaimed: "This is the house of the LORD God" (1 Chr 22:1).

This view fits very well with the content of the Psalm, especially, verses 6-7:

⁶ And in my prosperity I said, I shall never be moved. ⁷ LORD, by thy favour thou hast made my mountain to stand strong: thou didst hide thy face, and I was troubled.

The problem with this view, however, is that the title of this Psalm speaks of the "house of David," not "the house of the LORD."

Other commentators, such as Calvin, hold that this Psalm is about the dedication of the house of David (1 Chr 15:1; 17:1). In this case, this Psalm is about how God finally gave David rest after the tumultuous years of being pursued vehemently by Saul, as well as the conflicts of a divided kingdom for another seven years.

The problem with this view is that the term "house of David" occurs 24 other times in the Old Testament; but it is never used to describe the palace of David. It is always used to describe the dynasty or kingly line of David. For example in 2 Samuel 3:1, we read about the conflict that David faced while he was ruling in Hebron in these terms:

"Now there was long war between the house of Saul and the house of David: but David waxed stronger and stronger, and the house of Saul waxed weaker and weaker."

I would submit to you, then, that the "house of David" in the title of this Psalm refers to the kingly line and family of David.

This is consistent with the words of David's prayer recorded in 1 Chronicles 17:24:

"Let it even be established, that thy name may be magnified for ever, saying, The LORD of hosts is the God of Israel, even a God to Israel: and let the house of David thy servant be established before thee."

Psalm 30 could very well have been written for the same occasion as when David said this prayer. David was consecrating his house to the service of the Lord.

Now, this is significant because when we understand the "house of David" in this sense, we know that it includes not just the biological descendents of David, but all who are spiritually united to Christ, the greater David. After all, the house or lineage of David is but a type of the Church which is united to Christ, the King of kings. Thus Zechariah, referring to the ministry of the Lord, says:

"In that day there shall be a fountain opened to the house of David and to the inhabitants of Jerusalem for sin and for uncleanness" (Zech 13:1).

With this in mind, it is not difficult for us to see that Psalm 30, which David wrote in the Spirit of Christ, on the occasion of his dedication of his dynasty to the Lord, is ultimately about the dedication or consecration of the Church of Christ.

Indeed, it is not difficult to see how the words of this Psalm could have been taken in the lips of Christ our Lord upon His resurrection from the dead; whereupon, He dedicates His house, even His people unto the Father. Thus we may entitle it *"The Righteous One's Song of Dedication of His Family."* This is how we will look at this Psalm in this study.

This Psalm has four parts:

1. v. 1-3   Expression of Thanksgiving to the LORD
2. v. 4-5   Exhortation to Praise the LORD
3. v. 6-10   Explanation of Gratitude for the LORD's Mercy
4. v. 11-12   Exhilaration upon the LORD's Deliverance

1. Expression of Thanksgiving to the LORD (v. 1-3)

¹ I will extol thee, O LORD; for thou hast lifted me up, and hast not made my foes to rejoice over me. ² O LORD my God, I cried unto thee, and thou hast healed me. ³ O LORD, thou hast brought up my soul from the grave: thou hast kept me alive, that I should not go down to the pit.

The Lord Jesus, the greater David went to the cross for our sin. As part of His punishment due to our sin, He had to bear the insults and abuses of the unbelieving Jews and Gentiles. Indeed, they would put Him to death through a sham judicial process that saw Him condemned to die despite being pronounced innocent.

Our Lord laid down His life in order that we may have life. He died that we might die to sin. But the Father would not allow Him to remain in the grave, for He was perfectly righteous.

"O LORD, thou hast brought up my soul from the grave" (v. 3).

Our Lord cried unto the Father (v. 2). He prayed with sweat, like drops of blood, in the Garden of Gethsemane. No doubt, He did not only ask to be delivered from the bitter cup, if it were possible. No doubt, He prayed to be delivered from death when His atonement was completed. Our Lord was never presumptuous.

The Father heard His prayer. He lifted Him up from the grave. His enemies could not triumph over Him. So our Lord begins this Psalm with an expression of gratitude:

¹ I will extol thee, O LORD; for thou hast lifted me up, and hast not made my foes to rejoice over me.

If the worthy Son of God is inclined to praise and thank the Father, how much more should we unworthy sons of God learn to express our gratitude unto the LORD? And this is exactly what our Lord would have us join Him to do, in the next section of this Psalm:

2. Exhortation to Praise the LORD (v. 4-5)

⁴ Sing unto the LORD, O ye saints of his, and give thanks at the remembrance of His holiness. ⁵ For His anger endureth but a moment; in His favour is life: weeping may endure for a night, but joy cometh in the morning.

As our Lord gave thanks to the Father after His wrath was over-passed, so let us, as sons of God, join Him to do so.

Let us remember His holiness and justice by which He must deal with sin. He dealt with our Lord for our sin in order that we might be imputed with His righteousness, that we might have fellowship with Him.

But He would also deal with our sin by chastising us. He will not punish us according as our sin deserves, because He has already punished Christ our Lord. But He will chastise us in love. He will chastise us so that we may be holy as He is holy. God's chastisements always serve to sanctify us by cultivating patience, and by teaching us to trust in Him.

Nevertheless, these chastisements, as with the Lord's suffering for our sin, last but for a moment. "*Weeping may endure for a night, but joy cometh in the morning*" (v. 5b).

Even if the LORD brings us through a lifetime of chastisement, the joy that comes in the morning lasts for all eternity. Then shall we acknowledge that our weeping endures but for a night!

It is a fact that God does not allow us to be tempted beyond what we can bear (1 Cor 10:13). Therefore, in times of trials, let us turn our eyes unto the LORD with faith, knowing that He will only chastise us as much as we need and no more.

Are you going through a period of darkness and confusion—whether it is due to an illness of your own or of a loved one, or due to a loss, or due to a broken relationship, or depression? Remember to turn your eyes to the LORD in faith, believing that "*weeping may endure for a night, but joy cometh in the morning.*"

What a joy it will be when the brightness of God's countenance and favour shine on you again!

When that happens, let us not forget to sing; and sing cheerfully with grace in our hearts, giving thanks at the remembrance of His holiness and His patience towards us.

And let us also remember the LORD's mercy in our trials. Indeed, let us meditate on the purpose for which He sends us the trial as we reflect on His mercy towards us.

3. Explanation of Gratitude for the LORD's Mercy (v. 6-10).

[6] And in my prosperity I said, I shall never be moved. [7] LORD, by thy favour thou hast made my mountain to stand strong: thou didst hide thy face, and I was troubled.

When everything is well with us, we may indeed feel very confident that we will never be moved—God will not allow us to be moved. By the LORD's favour we are made to stand strong as a mountain (v. 7). Our Lord who was tempted in all points like as we are, would know the feeling without falling into the sin of complacency and self-boast.

But as soon as God hides His face, then we are troubled. It is human to be troubled when God hides His face. Our Lord was likewise troubled. Before the Garden of Gethsemane, our Lord did not appear to be much troubled by the trial that was about to come upon Him. But as the dark hour approached and the prospect of His Father, as it were, hiding His face loomed, He was greatly troubled in His heart.

Our Lord is fully human.

So we too may expect to be troubled when God hides His face from us. But that is part of our sanctification: for such troubles drive us onto our knees that we might seek the LORD in prayer even as our Lord did:

> [8] *I cried to thee, "O LORD; and unto the LORD I made supplication.* [9] *What profit is there in my blood, when I go down to the pit? Shall the dust praise thee? shall it declare thy truth?* [10] *Hear, O LORD, and have mercy upon me: LORD, be thou my helper."*

Now, we must not misunderstand that the Lord is saying that His blood has no value. That would be heretical! What He is saying here (in view of what He has already said in verse 3) is that if He remains under power of death, His death would be of no profit. To paraphrase, He would be saying: "What profit would there be in my death if I should go down to the pit and remain there? Shall it declare Thy truth that Thou art a just and holy God? Shall it testify that thy Son is sent that Thy house may praise thee, and fellowship with Thee for all eternity?" For this reason, the Apostle Paul teaches us that Christ is raised for our justification (Rom 4:25) and that the Resurrection is essential to the gospel (1 Cor 15:14-17).

The Lord prayed with an eye on the praise and glory of the Father; and the Father heard His prayer. Shall He not hear our cries for deliverance too if we learn to imitate His Son?

4. Exhilaration upon the LORD's Deliverance (v. 11-12)

> [11] *Thou hast turned for me my mourning into dancing: thou hast put off my sackcloth, and girded me with gladness;* [12] *To the end that my glory may sing praise to thee, and not be silent. O LORD my God, I will give thanks unto thee for ever.*

As long as the Lord was bearing our sin, He was mourning. He mourned when His friends forsook Him. He mourned when the Father turned His face from Him. He mourned when He gave up the ghost.

Weeping may endure but for a night, but joy comes in the morning.

As the experience of God's wrath turned into a celebration of His love, so our Lord's mourning turned into rejoicing.

Indeed, He would not be the only one who would be rejoicing. For all who are united to Him would be praising God with Him, using His word.

This is the glory of Christ. The glory of Christ is the Church. "Unto Him be glory in the church by Christ Jesus throughout all ages, world without end. Amen" (Eph 3:21).

The whole purpose of our Lord's suffering and resurrection is so that His Church might praise Him and not be silent. Christ has dedicated His Church to be an instrument of praise and thanksgiving unto God for all eternity.

David was inspired by the Spirit of Christ to write this Psalm on the occasion of the dedication of His house unto the Lord. But it is a song which our Lord must have inspired to express His dedication of His Church; and at His resurrection, He would no doubt have sung or meditated on it as He consecrated His Church unto His Father—to be an instrument of praise and thanksgiving for all eternity.

We shall thank and praise God in union with our Lord. We shall praise and thank Him in a way that no angel can, for the angels never experienced sin and forgiveness and restoration as we do. This is the purpose of the spiritual house of Christ, of which He is the chief corner stone and we are the lively stones (1 Pet 2:5-6).

Conclusion

This is Psalm 30. But let us conclude with three thoughts arising from it.

- *First*, let us remember that the Father's wrath endures but for a moment. Weeping may endure for a night, but joy comes in the morning. Therefore, if you are going through a dark patch in your life, do not despair. Joy is round the corner. The fact that you do not see it does not mean it is not there. As the Father delivered our elder brother, Christ our Lord, so He will deliver you. God has promised. In a moment, your affliction will be over and you shall be able to rejoice unhindered. Only believe.

- *Secondly*, let us remember this Psalm, to use it. Have you been delivered from a season of trial and darkness? This Psalm is a very appropriate Psalm for us. We are told that in 1559, John Calvin was sick and unable to preach for eight months. At the end of the period, when he was restored, he returned to the pulpit and one of the Psalms that he led the people to sing was Psalm 30. Let us remember to use this Psalm too.

- *Finally*, let us remember that the Church is the glory of Christ. Let us therefore pray for the Church. Let us pray for one another. And let us—as members of the Church—seek always the glory of Christ rather than our own glory or our own ambitions and benefits. Let us shine forth for Christ by loving Him and loving one another in the truth.

But let us remember, especially, that as the glory of Christ, we have been dedicated by our Lord to be the instrument of praise for all eternity.

Shall we not, therefore, begin today to praise and thank the LORD daily; and especially when we gather together as the body of Christ? Let us do so with joy (v. 5). It is an affront to God for us to sing such a joyful song with a mournful tune or with deadness in the heart. Therefore, let us seek the LORD's grace to sing unto Him cheerfully. May the Lord help us! Amen. Ω

Psalm 31:
The Righteous One's
Song of Repose in the LORD

Psalm 31 is not usually classed as a Messianic Psalm. But it is not difficult to see how this Psalm would have been taken up by the Lord in His soul during the quiet moments as He hung on the cross of Calvary. This is especially so, as the last of seven statements uttered audibly by the Lord on the cross was taken from this Psalm, even verse 5: "Unto thy hands I commend my spirit" (cf. Lk 23:46).

It has been conjectured that this Psalm was written by David after he was betrayed by the Ziphites to Saul (see 1 Sam 23:19-26). We cannot be sure of that. But we can be sure that David wrote it in the Spirit of Christ. And when we read this Psalm *vis-à-vis* the sufferings of our Lord on the cross, it becomes immensely so much the more meaningful and precious.

This, then, is how we must look at this Psalm in this study. We may entitle it *"The Righteous One's Song of Repose in the LORD."* It is a Psalm given by Christ, the Righteous One, for those united to Him as righteous ones, to sing with Him, in reflection of how He found peace in His heart, in the midst of the turmoil all around Him.

This Psalm has roughly four parts:

1. v. 1-13   A Petition for Deliverance
2. v. 14-18   A Declaration of Trust
3. v. 19-22   An Eruption of Thanksgiving
4. v. 23-24   An Exhortation to Others

1 A Petition for Deliverance

This Psalm opens with the Righteous One calling unto His Father to deliver Him in His righteousness:

> [1] *In thee, O LORD, do I put my trust; let me never be ashamed: deliver me in thy righteousness.*

God is not only just and holy, He is also righteous. His holiness prevents sinners from having fellowship with Him. His justice demands that sinners be punished. But His righteousness requires that He spares those who trust in Him.

Our Lord trusted in His Father perfectly. He went to the cross upon a covenant promise that He would be punished—only as much as is necessary to secure the redemption of His people.

But our Lord is not presumptuous about His deliverance. He cried unto His Father that He would, in His righteousness, keep His promise to deliver Him.

Thus, even as He commits His spirit unto His Father (v. 5), He petitions Him that He would deliver Him from the snares that His enemies have laid for Him (v. 2-4).

His enemies set traps for Him countless number of times. When our Lord allowed Himself to be arrested, they bound Him and demanded His crucifixion. They tried to silence Him with death. But our Lord could not be contained by death because God is His rock, defence, fortress and deliverer.

⁵ Into thine hand I commit my spirit: thou hast redeemed me, O LORD God of truth.

The enemies of the Lord Jesus thought that He was in their hands to do what they would to Him. But the Lord was still in control. He would commit His soul to none but His Father.

The word translated "truth" here speaks of faithfulness. God is faithful. He keeps His promises. Therefore, our Lord committed His spirit unto Him.

But as usual, our Lord does not petition His Father without context or arguments. The Father, of course, knows all things. But He delights to hear His Son and His adoptive sons and daughters tell Him about their struggles.

So our Lord supports His petition for deliverance with several arguments.

- He demonstrates His faith in the Father by expressing His hatred for lying vanities or idols (v. 6).

- He expresses His confidence in His Father by highlighting past deliverances which come to mind (v. 7-8).

- He delineates His present trouble and grief on account of His enemies and friends who mocked Him and forsook Him (v. 9-12). Even His disciples fled from Him.

- He asserts His integrity in the midst of slanders and plots against Him (v. 13).

Can you see how a study of the psalms will provide us with a glimpse of the Lord's thought life?

May we learn likewise to pray with godly arguments as our Lord did that we may enjoy the assurance that God hears and answers our prayers.

But our Lord does not only petition His Father. His meditation is rich. He declares His trust; He expresses His gratitude and thinks about others—as we shall see in the rest of this Psalm.

2. A Declaration of
Trust

¹⁴ But I trusted in thee, O LORD: I said, Thou art my God. ¹⁵ My times are in thy hand:…

We wonder how many times our Lord must have used this prayer. Though very few of His prayers are recorded for us in the Gospel, we read of the chief priests and scribes and elders mocking Him:

> "He trusted in God; let Him deliver Him now, if He will have him: for He said, I am the Son of God" (Mt 27:43).

It is apparent that our Lord must have taken the words of Psalm 31 in His prayers. Indeed, when He told His disciples, "my time is not yet full come" (Jn 7:8), and later "my time is at hand" (Mt 26:18), He was most probably thinking of Psalm 31:15: *"My times are in thy hand."*

Our Lord was fully aware that His time was completely in His Father's hands. And He trusted Him fully each step of the way. But that does not stop Him from expressing His desires unto His Father. He desired to be delivered from the hands of His enemies (v. 15b). His Father would answer His prayer by raising Him from the grave. He desired that His Father's face would shine upon Him again (v. 16). His Father would indeed receive Him again when His atonement for our sins was completed. He desired that He would not be ashamed, for shame is fitting only for the wicked (v. 17). His Father would indeed vindicate Him in His resurrection and exaltation. He desired that the liars, the wicked, and the proud be put to silence (v. 18). This would indeed happen not just through the condemnation of the wicked upon their death, but in the day of the wrath of the Lamb, when every knee shall bow and every tongue confess that Jesus is LORD.

He who trusts in the Father can desire as the Lord desired. Indeed, he who trusts in the Father does not need only to desire; for he may hope in the Father, for the Father will hear the outpouring of his heart.

For our Lord, hope was as good as reality. Therefore, even before it happened, His hope gave way to...

3. An Eruption of
Thanksgiving

[19] Oh how great is thy goodness, which thou hast laid up for them that fear thee; which thou hast wrought for them that trust in thee before the sons of men!

The Father is good! But He does not dispense His goodness to all without distinction. His blessings are especially reserved for all who trust in Him and fear Him. Paul says the same thing when he declares that all things work together for good to them that love God, to them who are the called according to His purpose (Rom 8:28). They are beloved by the Father. They are the ones whom the Lord Jesus came to live and die for.

Indeed, He died and rose from the dead that the sons of men might become the sons of God. This is why our Lord speaks now of the Father's goodness unto them, rather than unto Him. When the Father heard Him in His incarnation, it was partly for the sake of the elect for whom He came. They are in the world, but not of the world. Therefore, they would know the Father's special protection from wicked persons in the world (v. 20).

But above all, they would experience the Father's blessing, when He received the Son's sacrifice. Remember the three hours of darkness that our Lord experienced as He bore our guilt. Our Lord must have felt like David when he was trapped in a besieged city, as He experienced the wrath of God. But when the Father's face finally shone on Him again, and the sun began to shine again, He was again experiencing the assurance of the Father's love and kindness. Look at verse 21:

[21] Blessed be the LORD: for He hath shewed me His marvellous kindness in a strong city. [22] For I said in my haste, I am cut off from before thine eyes: nevertheless thou heardest the voice of my supplications when I cried unto thee.

At the end of the three hours of darkness, our Lord cried out using the words in Psalm 22: "My God, my God why hast thou forsaken me?" "*I said in my haste, I am cut off from before thine eyes.*"

The Gospel does not record the Father's answer. What we are told, however, is the Lord's cry of victory and contentment: "It is finished!"

The Father heard His cry: "*nevertheless thou heardest the voice of my supplications when I cried unto thee.*" He accepted His sacrifice. He must still die bodily so that bodily death might be conquered for His people. But the Sacrifice was essentially completed on the cross.

The Father has sealed His love unto His Son and unto His sons and daughters, who would come unto Him by faith in His Son!

What a marvel of love! How should we respond to Him but to love Him? "We love Him, because He first loved us," says John (1Jn 4:19). So our Lord concludes this Psalm with an exhortation to all the saints to love the LORD:

4. An Exhortation
to Others

²³ *O love the LORD, all ye His saints: for the LORD preserveth the faithful, and plentifully rewardeth the proud doer.*

The Psalms are given to us by our Lord not only that we may know how a godly heart should beat. It is given to us too that the word of Christ may dwell in us richly in all wisdom, teaching and admonishing one another in psalms and hymns and spiritual songs, singing with grace in our hearts to the LORD (Col 3:16). So this Psalm ends with a word of instruction.

Oh may we learn from our Lord's example, and take heed to His exhortation!

Let us love Him. Let us love the Father and the Spirit. The LORD will preserve those who are faithful to Him, and believe in the Son. He will deal with all our enemies and all things that bring grief to us.

One day, we shall not need to cry for help and deliverance anymore: for in that day, everything will be perfected. We shall be perfect. Those around us shall be perfect. The environment we dwell in will be perfect. Best of all, our enjoyment of God will be perfect. Therefore, verse 24:

²⁴ *Be of good courage, and He shall strengthen your heart, all ye that hope in the LORD.*

Run the Christian race courageously! All ye who hope in the LORD, run bravely! When you are weak, remember that His grace is sufficient for you; His power is made perfect in weakness, and you can do all things through Christ who strengthens you.

Christ, the Captain of your salvation, the Author and Finisher of your faith, has run ahead of you. He "for the joy that was set before Him endured the cross, despising the shame, and is set down at the right hand of the throne of God" (Heb 12:2).

Conclusion

Look to the Lord Jesus Christ! Consider how He was tempted in all points like as you are, and yet fell not into sin. But consider also how He suffered and how He petitioned His Father. He was not, as some suppose, impervious to suffering and fear. But He found courage in His Father's love. And so let us learn to do likewise—to petition the Father. Let us learn to do so in imitation of the Son who has also given us His experience in songs, that by His grace and the affecting power of singing, what is true of Him, may become true of us. Amen. Ω

Psalm 32:
The Righteous One's
Blessedness in the Way of Forgiveness

Psalm 32 is, together with the Psalm 51, the most famous of the Penitential Psalms.

It is believed that both of these Psalms were written by David after he was confronted by the prophet Nathan for his adultery with Bathsheba and the murder of her husband Uriah. Nathan had approached David with a parable about a rich man who killed the beloved lamb of a poor man to entertain a traveller. David had responded with anger that the rich man must pay fourfold. It was then that Nathan said: "Thou art the man!" David was immediately struck in his conscience and cried, "I have sinned against the LORD!" (2 Sam 12:13).

From that moment David was under deep conviction for his sins. In the days following, David wrote two Psalms, namely Psalms 32 and 51. Most likely, Psalm 51 was written immediately after Nathan the prophet rebuked him. The wordings of Psalm 51 suggest that he had not had the assurance of forgiveness though he was under deep conviction for his sin. But Psalm 32 was probably written later: when he had fully confessed his sins, and knew that he was forgiven. But in both Psalms, he expressed some of his feelings when he was under conviction. These are feelings that we can all identify with when we are under conviction of sin ourselves.

But could this Psalm be taken up in the lips of our Holy Saviour who was tempted in all points like as we are, and yet without sin? Could our Lord have sung it?

Listen to the wisdom of Andrew Bonar:

> We generally take up this Psalm as if it was for the members of Christ alone; but we should not forget that the Head himself traversed the way of forgiveness. He stood for us, in our room, in our very place. He stood as our substitute, and all the sins of "that great multitude which no man can number" were laid upon Him by imputation. So dreadful was His position, so truly awful did it seem to Him to be reckoned a sinner, that even this, apart from the wrath and curse, would have been sufficient to make Him cry, "O blessed is the man to whom the Lord doth not impute sin." He was dumb for our sakes; His bones wasted away; He groaned from day to day, and during the lonesome hours of midnight was kept awake by our woes.... In this state He acknowledged our sin; it was only ours He had to acknowledge; He spread it out before God on the cross; He continued to do so till it was forgiven Him as our substitute.

I agree wholeheartedly with Bonar. This Psalm was indeed written by David to express the blessedness he enjoyed as he experienced God's forgiveness following his grievous sin. But it was written in the Spirit of Christ in a way that would express the grief of our Lord as He bore our sin, and the blessedness He felt when His sacrifice was accepted on our behalf. So this Psalm, as the word of Christ, expresses the pain and joy of our Lord on the cross.

This Psalm is, of course, given also for the Church to sing in union with the Righteous One as a most perfect expression of the blessedness we experience when we become assured that God has forgiven us our sin for the sake of Christ Jesus our Lord.

In this study, therefore we want to look at how this Psalm applies both to Christ and to all who are united to Him. Here is *"The Righteous One's Blessedness in the Way of Forgiveness."* It has essentially four strophes, each terminating with a selah. A selah is probably a musical notation for a pause to reflect on the thought of the moment.

1. The Blessedness of
the Forgiven

Our Psalm begins with the word "blessed."

> *¹ Blessed is he whose transgression is forgiven, whose sin is covered. ² Blessed is the man unto whom the LORD imputeth not iniquity, and in whose spirit there is no guile.*

Actually, our English word "blessed" does not quite capture the intensity of the Hebrew word in the context (אֶשֶׁר, *esher*). The word is used as an interjection: "How happy!" So it speaks of intense joy or in other words, joy unspeakable.

The blessedness that comes with forgiveness is indescribable. It is joy unspeakable especially when it is experienced by a man *"in whose spirit there is no guile [or deceit]."* Why? Because such a man knows he is truly forgiven since God who sees through his heart can vouch for his sincerity. And there is no man that fits this description so perfectly as the Lord Himself. David might be described as such a man, when his web of lies was exposed and he repented of his deceit. But it seems almost incongruous for him to speak of himself as a man in whose spirit there is no guile at this juncture.

This blessedness of forgiveness is especially intense when there is a period of suffering on account of sin.

> *³ When I kept silence, my bones waxed old through my roaring all the day long. ⁴ For day and night thy hand was heavy upon me: my moisture is turned into the drought of summer.*

David, after he was confronted by Nathan, came under intense conviction of sin. He must have felt such a heavy burden upon his heart that he felt like his bones were aching and his energy was sapping away. But our Lord had experienced much more. His bones literally ached and He literally thirsted as He hung on the cross for our sin. And in those three hours of darkness when all He saw was His Father's wrath—how He must have felt the pains of hell multiplied a million times. It is no wonder that at the end of His ordeal, He cried out, "My God, my God, why hast thou forsaken me?"

Thank God that He was heard. Thank God that His sacrifice was accepted. "It is finished!" He exclaimed. Thank God that He would be raised from the dead as a token of the forgiveness He has procured for His Church. The blessedness He experienced must have been like that of one who has just been plucked out of hell and transported to heaven.

Today, we too can enjoy the same blessedness of forgiveness, for our guilt was lifted from us and heaped upon the Lord Jesus, and from there cast into the black hole of forgetfulness. Though I suspect that many of us would not know the intensity of the blessedness that our Lord, or even David experienced, we can surely sing with genuine gratitude in our heart— *"Blessed is he whose transgression is forgiven, whose sin is covered."*

Indeed, if you have never experienced such a blessing to any degree, then you should examine if your repentance from sin and confession of sin is genuine.

2. The Confession of
the Forgiven

5 I acknowledged my sin unto thee, and mine iniquity have I not hid. I said, I will confess my transgressions unto the LORD; and thou forgavest the iniquity of my sin.

Someone may object: "How could the Lord speak about His sin and iniquity, when He had no sin? So this Psalm cannot be Messianic!"

Our answer is that it is not only here that we see the Lord acknowledging iniquity. We see it also in the Psalms that are biblically and universally accepted as Messianic, such as Psalm 40. Psalm 40:12 reads:

> "For innumerable evils have compassed me about: mine iniquities have taken hold upon me, so that I am not able to look up; they are more than the hairs of mine head: therefore my heart faileth me."

The fact is Christ our Lord could acknowledge guilt because He took the guilt of our sin upon Himself. He bore it as if it is His own.

As He presented them before the Father, one by one, the burden of our guilt was also removed.

David, as a member of the Church, did the same and found relief in a forgiveness that has been purchased by the Messiah. So too we can experience the same relief.

Have you sinned against the Lord in any particular way, dear child of God? Is your burden so great, and do you feel that no one understands? The Lord understands and there is no sin too great that the Father cannot forgive: For He has already forgiven us in Christ. What needs to be done is for you to acknowledge your sin and confess your guilt unto Him.

What is it to confess our guilt? It is to lay it before the LORD. It is to acknowledge that we have sinned and deserve nothing but the wrath of God. As the Lord has already experienced the wrath of God due to us, shall we not take encouragement and seek His Fatherly forgiveness?

3. The Reflection of
the Forgiven

6 For this [for the fact that thou has forgiven my guilt and given me blessedness] shall every one that is godly pray unto thee in a time when thou mayest be found: surely in the floods of great waters they shall not come nigh unto him.

The flood in Noah's days was an outburst of God's judgement. All those who were overwhelmed in the great deluge were overwhelmed because they had remained in sin without repentance.

If God could forgive David for his sin of adultery and murder, if the Father could accept the sacrifice of His Son for such gross sins multiplied a million times, will He not forgive all who come unto Him? Will not the godly go to the Lord and find deliverance from the judgement of God? Will they not join our Lord in His eternal songs?

7 Thou art my hiding place; thou shalt preserve me from trouble; thou shalt compass me about with songs of deliverance.

May the Lord's reflection come true in our lives! When we experience the burden of guilt and anticipate that we would be overwhelmed when God judges sinners, let us crawl into the cleft of the rock which is Christ our Lord. Then shall we find refuge as our Lord found refuge in the Father's love and forgiveness.

4. The Instruction of
the Forgiven

[8] *I will instruct thee and teach thee in the way which thou shalt go: I will guide thee with mine eye.*

Who is this "I"? It does not seem to be David. Maybe it is the Father responding to the words of confessions and acknowledgment of the Son. But perhaps it is our Lord Himself. As He went to the cross for us, so He leads us by His example to walk in the way of forgiveness.

Let us follow the Lord when we fall into sin. Let us seek to respond to sin in the way that we should. Let us not be like a horse or mule which refuses to go to its owner unless it is dragged by the bit and bridle (v. 9).

In a certain way, David was like that in the one year after he sinned, before Nathan confronted him.

Let us rather flee quickly to the Lord. Let us, as such pray for a heart that is sensitive to the working of the Holy Spirit. Let us be quick to turn from our sin for many sorrows shall surround the wicked, whereas he who trusts in the Lord, shall be surrounded by the mercy of the LORD (v. 10).

[11] *Be glad in the LORD, and rejoice, ye righteous: and shout for joy, all ye that are upright in heart.*

The child of God should not be pulling a long face every day. He, of all men, can know the blessedness of God. He, of all men, can have real joy because forgiveness is what really matters.

When we sin against man, we feel a heavy burden in our hearts. We need to find the person to seek his forgiveness, but we know that that is not enough. Even if the person says, "I forgive you" a hundred times, there is still no satisfaction in our heart—until and unless we are assured of God's forgiveness.

And the good news is: If you are united to Christ and so may be known as a righteous one on account of His righteousness, you have already been forgiven for Christ's sake. And you have the warrant and encouragement of our Lord to go to the Father to seek His Fatherly forgiveness.

Conclusion

Go to Him, dear child of God. Go to Him and find peace and blessedness for your soul.

There is real forgiveness in Him because every sin that the Father will forgive has been paid for by His Son.

Your sins, past, present, and future, have been forgiven for Christ's sake. Learn, therefore, to go to the Father to seek His Fatherly forgiveness in the name of His Son. He will not deny you if you go to Him in sincerity: for He is a just and holy God. Amen. Ω

Psalm 33:
The Righteous One's Adoration
of the LORD

Psalm 33 is not very well known to many of us, unlike Psalm 32. Many of us will not be able to tell what this Psalm is about. One reason is perhaps because we are easily overwhelmed by the many things that are said in it so that we quickly lose track of its central theme. But Psalm 33 is really a very beautiful Psalm, once you understand its structure.

Is this Psalm Messianic? Well, there is no reason for us to doubt that it was given by our Messiah that we might join Him to sing in praise of His Father.

Andrew Bonar puts it beautifully when he says:

"It is a very simple Psalm, yet full of the feelings which a forgiven soul teems with. Never did any heart so abound in those feelings as the heart of the Lord Jesus; and his saints learn from Him. It is He who leads the praise in the great congregation (cf. Ps 22:22)".

This Psalm is indeed a Psalm of praise as the opening words, *"Rejoice in the LORD"* indicates. This is *"The Righteous One's Adoration of the LORD."*

It has three parts, which we may outline as follows:

1. v. 1-3   Call to Praise the LORD
2. v. 4-19   Reasons to Praise the LORD
    a.   His Character (v. 4-5)
    b.   His Creation-Work (v. 6-9)
    c.   His Counsels (v. 10-11)
    d.   His Care of the Church (v. 12-19)
3. v. 20-22   Response to the call to Praise the LORD

1. Call to Praise the LORD

[1] *Rejoice in the LORD, O ye righteous: for praise is comely for the upright.* [2] *Praise the LORD with harp: sing unto him with the psaltery and an instrument of ten strings.* [3] *Sing unto him a new song; play skilfully with a loud noise.*

Man is created righteous to the end that we may glorify and enjoy God. One of the highest ways in which we can glorify God is to praise Him with grateful hearts. But mankind has fallen into sin. All our righteousnesses have become filthy rags in the sight of God because there is none righteous, no not one. That is, no one, but He who is altogether righteous, even the Son of God.

He came to take away the sin of His people, to give them righteousness to the end that they may accomplish the purpose for which they were created. He came, in other words, that we may be righteous, so that we may rejoice in the LORD and praise Him in righteousness. Imputed with the righteousness of Christ and imbued with His righteousness by His Spirit, we are in the eye of God truly righteous. Our praise is truly acceptable to Him for Christ's sake. The praise of no one else is acceptable to God. For this reason, we are not only called to rejoice in the LORD and to praise Him; but we are given the words to do so in union with, and under the leadership of, the Righteous One of God.

Praise is comely. That is, praise is fitting and beautiful. It is the most suitable use of our tongues and emotions. It is our highest calling for which we are redeemed to fulfil.

In the Old Covenant, the Levites in the temple would worship God using instruments of various kinds, especially when the animal sacrifices were being offered. There is no indication that in the temple, they would sing with instruments when the animals were not being offered (cf. 2 Chr 29:26-29).

Under the New Covenant, musical instruments were done away with for formal worship, just as the sacrifices were done away with. For this reason, the Apostle Paul teaches us to speak to each other "in psalms and hymns and spiritual songs, singing and making melody in [our] heart to the Lord" (Eph 5:19).

The words, "making melody" translates a Greek word that literally means "plucking the strings of an instrument." Paul is telling us that our hearts should be our musical instrument. We should pluck our heartstrings as we sing.

This is how we must, as New Covenant saints, understand the word of Christ as He calls us to *"Praise the LORD with harp: sing unto him with the psaltery and an instrument of ten strings. [And to] play skilfully with a loud noise."*

Let us, therefore, not sing to the LORD mechanically as a matter of routine. Let us rather sing unto Him with understanding. And let us sing unto Him with joy and gladness in our hearts.

But how best may we praise the Lord with understanding and affection?

Our Lord gives us four reasons to praise the LORD, which cannot but move our hearts to praise Him with sincerity and gratitude.

2. Reasons to Praise the Lord

First, we should praise Him for...

a. His Character

[4] *For the word of the LORD is right; and all His works are done in truth.* [5] *He loveth righteousness and judgment: the earth is full of the goodness of the LORD.*

The LORD Jehovah is good, true, faithful, righteous and just. Whatever He says is right and true. He is the standard of truth. He is faithful to keep all His promises.

And if we would only open our eyes to see, and to think objectively, we will see that the earth is full of the goodness of the LORD: for every good and perfect gift comes from above.

Sinful man has a way of being blind to the goodness of God and being critical of the things that happen in Providence—blaming God for the worst things, and taking the best things for granted. But let God be true, and every man a liar. If God were to withhold His providential care of the world, and man be allowed to do what he wants to do without fear of repercussion, this world will not last a day.

The sun will refuse to shine. The winds will swirl uncontrollably. There will be droughts or floods. The seas will burst their banks. The insects and animals in the world will lose their restraint. Imagine being scorched by the sun, swept by the seas, choked by noxious gases, blinded by dust, and stung and bitten by insects constantly. And all these would be the least of your worries, for man will be gnashing at one another as they seek selfishly to ensure their own survival.

Thank God that this is not a present reality. Instead, do we not see the goodness of the LORD everywhere: in the rain and the sunshine, in the air that we breathe, and indeed, in all the things that we enjoy in this life? And not only so, but we will see that God is faithful and just. When He does send something that afflicts man, it is always because man deserves it, due to sin. God is just. The only reason why this sinful world can still enjoy much of the creation of God is that God has withheld His hand of judgement.

God is good, faithful, righteous and just. Let us praise Him for His character.

Secondly, let us praise Him for...

b. His Creation-Work

[6] *By the word of the LORD were the heavens made; and all the host of them by the breath of his mouth.* [7] *He gathereth the waters of the sea together as an heap: he layeth up the depth in storehouses.* [8] *Let all the earth fear the LORD: let all the inhabitants of the world stand in awe of him.* [9] *For he spake, and it was done; he commanded, and it stood fast.*

The LORD Jehovah made all things. The entire universe is made by Him. The ocean is made by Him. He made all things by the word of His power. Is that not sufficient reason to praise Him?

When we look at the beauty and greatness of Creation, we cannot but lift up our hearts to praise the LORD.

Only an atheist can look at the beauty of creation and remain unmoved by it.

God's children, therefore, must especially learn to praise the LORD for His wonderful Creation. Let us praise Him for being the wise and mighty Creator that He is.

And thirdly, let us praise Him for...

c. His Counsels

[10] *The LORD bringeth the counsel of the heathen to nought: he maketh the devices of the people of none effect.* [11] *The counsel of the LORD standeth for ever, the thoughts of his heart to all generations.*

The counsels of the LORD are His decrees. He is a sovereign God that accomplishes all that He decreed to do.

The heathen are opposed to Him. They want to do things according to their own fancies. Like the people in Babel of old, man has always sought to usurp the authority of God. But man can never succeed because God is sovereign.

As He disrupted the plan of man to build the tower of Babel, so He has continued to bring to naught the wicked devices of man. For example, man has sought to create life, but he has never succeeded. Man has tried to eradicate the Church and the Bible. But the more he tries, the more the Church has grown and today the Bible remains the all time best seller.

So man has tried to do away with the Sabbath. But over and over again, God demonstrates that those who do so, suffer many consequences: including health related problems and economic losses.

"[8] *For my thoughts are not your thoughts, neither are your ways my ways, saith the LORD.*

[9] For as the heavens are higher than the earth, so are my ways higher than your ways, and my thoughts than your thoughts" (Isa 55:8-9)

Shall we not praise the LORD for His wise and sovereign counsels?

Most of all, shall we not praise Him for ...

d. His Care of the Church

[12] *Blessed is the nation whose God is the LORD; and the people whom he hath chosen for his own inheritance.*

The nation whose God is the LORD, is the Church. She is the royal priesthood, a holy nation, a people belonging to God, a people chosen for God's own inheritance.

As a church, we must praise the LORD: for His eyes are upon us (v. 18). We are special in His eyes.

Yes, all men are alike—sinners (v. 13-15). No doubt, all men are given abilities by the LORD to accomplish many things through natural means. But no, man cannot guarantee success in all that he does, no matter how powerful and rich he may be, and no matter how effective his means may be. Promotion comes from the Lord:

[16] *There is no king saved by the multitude of an host: a mighty man is not delivered by much strength.* [17] *An horse is a vain thing for safety: neither shall he deliver any by his great strength.*

Unless God grants salvation, the great power of kings can achieve nothing. Unless God grants safety, the great strength of a horse will be useless. Unless God heals, all the most powerful medicine in the world cannot keep a person alive. Unless God by His providence warns of an impending earthquake, a nation can be completely swallowed up in a matter of seconds. Unless God delivers from hell, we shall be heading gleefully into it.

Thank God that while He does not promise deliverance to the heathen, He has promised it to His people, and especially to those who fear Him and love Him:

[18] *Behold, the eye of the LORD is upon them that fear him, upon them that hope in his mercy;* [19] *To deliver their soul from death, and to keep them alive in famine.*

Our LORD is watching over us. We must not doubt it. Yes, sometimes in this present life, we may not be cognizant of His deliverances, but they are no less real. Yes, our final deliverance is yet future, but faith and hope will one day give way to reality. One day we shall be raised from the dead. We will be freed from all our troubles whereas our enemies will face the justice of God.

God cares for us individually and corporately. We are the apple of His eye. And His eyes are upon all them that fear Him and hope in His mercy.

Shall we not praise Him?

So we have four reasons to praise Him. We should praise Him for His character, His creation-work, His counsel and His care. Shall we not stir our hearts by meditating on these things that we may cheerfully and gratefully praise the LORD with the same attitude as our Saviour?

3. Our Response to the Call
to Praise the LORD

This Psalm opens with a call to praise the LORD. This call is enlarged with four reasons. But now as the Psalm closes, we must respond to the call.

How shall we respond but to praise the LORD?

> [20] *Our soul waiteth for the LORD: he is our help and our shield.* [21] *For our hearts shall rejoice in him, because we have trusted in his holy name.* [22] *Let thy mercy, O LORD, be upon us, according as we hope in thee.*

Our LORD is our help and protector. He shields us from the evil that is due to sin. He even shields us from His own wrath through the Lord Jesus Christ, the Son of God, who took God's wrath due to us upon Himself. God is our shield in Christ. Christ is our Worshipper-In-Chief, leading us to praise the Father with Him.

Conclusion

We have many reasons to praise the LORD. Shall we not praise Him? Shall we not meditate on His character, His creation, His counsel and His care; and praise Him for all these?

Oh may the Spirit of the LORD bring these things to our remembrance constantly that our hearts may be lifted up to praise the LORD!

A praise-filled life is a life that most glorifies and enjoys God. On the other hand, a failure to recognise the greatness of God, and how worthy He is of our praise, may result in a self-centred life, together with all the problems associated with it, such as anxiety over the future, covetousness, quarrels over minor issues, etc.

If only we will take heed to the words of our Lord and start to meditate on how great God is, and praise Him from the bottom of our hearts, then the things of this world will grow strangely dim, our problems will become strangely trivial as faith, hope and love fill our hearts.

Thank God, therefore, for Psalm 33 which our Saviour has given to us to sing in union with Him, not only to praise the Father, but to exhort one another to live for Him. May the Lord help us! Amen. Ω

Psalm 34:
The Righteous One's Affectionate Cry
Under the Cross

Psalm 34 is not generally recognised as a Messianic Psalm by commentators who make use of the grammatical-historical method strictly. It was, according to the Jewish (and we believe, inspired) editors who affixed the title, written by David in recollection of the occasion *"when he changed his behaviour before Abimelech; who drove him away, and he departed."*

This occasion was recorded in 1 Samuel 21:10-15. David, you may recall, was on that occasion running away from Saul. He thought that he might seek refuge in Gath. But when he reached the city, the Philistines recognised him and brought him before King Achish, also known as Abimelech.

David feared for his life and we are told:

> "He changed his behaviour before them, and feigned himself mad in their hands, and scrabbled on the doors of the gate, and let his spittle fall down upon his beard" (1 Sam 21:13).

His ruse worked, and Achish quickly sent him away.

David, filled with thanksgiving that the LORD had delivered him, must have written this Psalm, as an expression of his gratitude to the LORD, for His protection and deliverance.

But this Psalm is certainly not about David only. Indeed, those who read this Psalm with an eye on the Lord, the greater David, should be able to see how this Psalm fits the experience of our Lord, much more perfectly than it fits David's experience.

Consider verses 6 and 7.

While we are not told that David cried when he was arrested by the soldiers of Achish, we are told the Lord in the Garden of Gethsemane cried unto the Father with "strong crying and tears" (Heb 5:7); and His perspiration fell to the ground like great drops of blood.

And who but the Lord could testify with certainty that the angel of the Lord encamps around them that fear Him. We are told specifically that an angel appeared unto Him from heaven to strengthen Him after His ordeal in the Garden (Lk 22:43). And when His disciples drew swords to resist His arrest, the Lord would say:

> "Thinkest thou that I cannot now pray to my Father, and he shall presently give me more than twelve legions of angels?" (Mt 26:53)

Or Consider verses 17 and 18.

Who but the Lord can claim to be righteous in and of Himself? The typical David was only truly righteous on account of the righteousness of the true David. Indeed, we wonder if the way that David reacted in fear before Achish was an entirely righteous response.

And why should David emphasise that not one of his bones was broken; whereas it is an important fact that none of the Lord's bones were broken despite the torture that He had to endure. This is in order to fulfil the Old Testament prophesy, and the fact that He is the paschal lamb of God (cf. Jn 19:36).

So Bonar says:

"Taking advantage of David's peculiar state and feelings, the Holy Ghost gives to the Church a song that might suit her Head, the true David when He came, and might equally suit every member."

Likewise, two other commentators, Dr Allix and Horsley say: "This Psalm containeth the praises which the Messiah gives to his Father for having delivered him out of all his sufferings." And "Messiah exhorts to holiness and trust in God, by the example of his own deliverance."

This is how we must see this Psalm in this study.[18] We may entitle it *"The Righteous One's Affectionate Cry Under the Cross."* It is the word of Christ, taken up in the lips of our Lord, and given to the Church, so that we may sing in union with Him, as He sings in sympathy with us. Although it is an acrostic Psalm, we may discern the following structure in it:

1. v. 1-7   Effusion of Praise for Deliverance
2. v. 8-10   Encouragement for All Who Fear the LORD
3. v. 11-14   Exhortation to the Young to Trust the LORD
4. v. 15-22   Explication of God's Care for the Righteous

1. Effusion of Praise for Deliverance

[1] I will bless the LORD at all times: his praise shall continually be in my mouth. [2] My soul shall make her boast in the LORD: the humble shall hear thereof, and be glad. [3] O magnify the LORD with me, and let us exalt his name together.

The famous Hebrew word *Halleluyah* is unique in that it is both a word of praise as well as a call to praise. This word is not used in this Psalm, but the idea is expressed in the first three verses. Here is a declaration of personal fervour and resolution to praise the Lord (v. 1-2) immediately followed by a call to join in praise (v. 3).

What occasioned such an effusion of grateful praise? The next three verses explain:

[4] I sought the LORD, and he heard me, and delivered me from all my fears. [5] They looked unto him, and were lightened: and their faces were not ashamed. [6] This poor man cried, and the LORD heard him, and saved him out of all his troubles.

As David was delivered from the hands of Achish, so our Lord was delivered from the clutches of the wicked one and his henchmen. He rose from the grave, and today, He is keeping His resolution to praise the Father continually (v. 1)—not only at the right hand of the throne of God, but in a special way, every time His Church assembles for worship (cf. Ps 22:22). David died and is no longer able to join us to praise the Father, but the Lord Jesus is with us by His Spirit.

When we sing praises unto the Father with the words of our Lord, we are joining Him to magnify the Father with Him in a very real way, for by His Spirit, He is with us always (Mt 28:20); and has promised to praise God in the midst of the Church (Heb 2:12).

---

[18] This is not to say that we will ignore the inspired title. It is rather a recognition that while the title gave the occasion for the composition of the Psalm, it is not intended to delimit how the Psalm is to be interpreted. Futato puts it astutely when he says: "We seem to be left with a certain ambivalence towards the historical information in the titles: it is canonical but cannot play much of a role in the interpretive process other than illustrating in a general way the kind of situation in which a given psalm arose.... Or, put yet another way, the historical information in the titles gives the impression that the psalms are time-bound, while the psalms themselves seem rather timeless" (Mark D. Futato, *Interpreting the Psalms: An Exegetical Handbook* [Grand Rapids: Kregel Publications, 2007], 122).

And indeed, it is often through the singing of His body, the Church, that the humble hears and is glad (v. 2). For this reason, we may be singing a Psalm of praise and yet we are exhorting and admonishing one another as the Apostle Paul instructs us (Col 3:16).

Let us, as the body of the Lord Jesus Christ seek heartily to praise the LORD in union with our Saviour and with one another. May we do so in public worship, in family worship, and even in our individual devotions! But let us also learn to use this Psalm in times of affliction, remembering that our Head was more severely afflicted, and has taught us that the best thing to do under affliction is to praise and thank the LORD.

Let us remember that as the Father delivered His Son, so shall He deliver all His adoptive sons and daughters, especially those who fear His name and cry out unto Him for deliverance:

⁷ The angel of the LORD encampeth round about them that fear him, and delivereth them.

As the angels of the LORD attended to our Saviour at the moments of His greatest need, so we can be sure that the angel of the LORD is never far from us, and is ready to intervene and deliver us from harm, as far as it shall serve for our good and the glory of God.

Those who fear the LORD, need fear no other, for the LORD will deliver them from all their fears. He will do so expeditiously, often with the intervention of His angel, or angels.

2. Encouragement for All Who Fear the LORD

⁸ O taste and see that the LORD is good: blessed is the man that trusteth in him.

What does the Lord mean? We can neither taste, nor see the LORD. Clearly, what the Lord would have us do is to learn firsthand that God is good.

It is like if you go to the market to buy an orange. The sign says: Sweet mandarins. You are not convinced. You ask the store holder: Is it sweet or sour? And the store holder says: "Oh, go ahead; take one, taste and see that it is indeed sweet."

This is what our Lord is telling us to do. The word of God says that God is good. But don't just take my word for it; come taste and see that the LORD is good!

How to taste and see that the LORD is good? We must begin by trusting Him. *"Blessed is the man that trusteth in him."* We must commit our anxieties to Him in prayer, and trust Him to deliver us and wait upon Him to deliver.

The LORD is a prayer-hearing God. He will hear our cries. He will deliver us.

But as we noted earlier, this assurance comes to all who fear the LORD. Thus, we are given to encourage one another, verse 9:

⁹ O fear the LORD, ye his saints: for there is no want to them that fear him.

What does it mean to fear the LORD?

There are two main shades of meaning for the word "fear" in the Scripture. One is a fear that wants to distance oneself. Many years ago, a friend and I, craving adventure, planned a night visit to an abandoned mansion in an off-shore island of Singapore. The building had an ominous attraction to us as we drew near. We saw many interesting things like bats and owls. But suddenly, we heard loud barking. When we turned around we saw a pack of dogs charging towards us.

I was instantly afraid. Fearing for my life, I grabbed my friend's arm and said: "Run!" But my friend who was almost 1.8 metres tall and stoutly built was so frightened that he froze on the spot. His legs could not carry him. I could not abandon him. So I stood with him. In a split second the dogs came. They saw my friend frozen stiff, were totally confused by the sight and started turning away. It was a good thing that he did not run: for had he run, the dogs would have chased.

Now, the fear that my friend and I experienced is the first kind of fear. This is a fear of harm and danger. We ought to have such a fear of God when we sin against Him. Adam and Eve feared the LORD when they fell into sin. That is why they hid themselves.

The second kind of fear in the Scripture is a fear that wants to draw near. This is akin to the fear that drew my friend and me to the abandoned mansion in the first place. That house looked very imposing and impressive even in the day. We were drawn to it.

This is the fear that a child, or even an adult, may experience, if he is invited to see someone important. It is a fear that wants to draw near. It is a fear of love.

This is the kind of fear that the Lord is exhorting us to cultivate. Yes, when we sin against God, we should have the fear of pain, if our conscience is not seared. But the fear of love, we do not naturally have.

It is given by the Spirit and we must cultivate it. How to cultivate it? We may cultivate it by seeking the LORD, and by meditating on the glory of God and the greatness of His promises.

Those who fear the LORD will enjoy God's blessings, both in temporal things and eternal things.

[10] *The young lions do lack, and suffer hunger: but they that seek the LORD shall not want any good thing.*

This is not to say that we will become rich. No, no; it is rather that we will have the blessing of contentment, or an assurance that the LORD is providing sufficiently for us.

3. Exhortation to the Young to Trust the LORD

[11] *Come, ye children, hearken unto me: I will teach you the fear of the LORD.*

Little children are often totally unaware of God and the fear of Him. This is why they think nothing of walking about during family worship or doing something else during public worship.

But the Lord Jesus is very patient with them. He suffered the little children to come unto Him: for unto such is the kingdom of God. But He would have us join Him, to teach them gently, the fear of the LORD.

The fear of the LORD is the beginning of wisdom and understanding. It is the ABC's of the Christian faith. Until and unless our children know the fear of the Lord, they will never truly know the LORD.

Children who grow up in an environment where worship is taken very lightly, will grow up to be strangers to our Holy God.

Let us, therefore, resolve with our Lord to teach our children the fear of God. Let us begin by ceasing to play with our children at worship. We all know it is very tempting to laugh at a child who is being cheeky at worship; but let us play with the child at the right time so that he knows that we are coming into the presence of the most holy God when we worship Him.

Let us also teach our children in the way that Moses instructs us in Deuteronomy 6: on how they should conduct themselves in the fear of the LORD. What shall we teach them? Verses 12-14 give us a good summary:

> [12] *What man is he that desireth life, and loveth many days, that he may see good?* [13] *Keep thy tongue from evil, and thy lips from speaking guile.* [14] *Depart from evil, and do good; seek peace, and pursue it.*

4. Explication of God's Care of the Righteous

> [15] *The eyes of the LORD are upon the righteous, and his ears are open unto their cry....* [17] *The righteous cry, and the LORD heareth, and delivereth them out of all their troubles.* [18] *The LORD is nigh unto them that are of a broken heart; and saveth such as be of a contrite spirit.* [19] *Many are the afflictions of the righteous: but the LORD delivereth him out of them all.* [20] *He keepeth all his bones: not one of them is broken. ...* [22] *The LORD redeemeth the soul of his servants: and none of them that trust in him shall be desolate.*

These are the verses that many of us will read to fellow believers who are ill or suffering some very difficult circumstances in life.

This is God's promise of deliverance from trouble. This promise has been kept over and over again. It was kept on behalf of our Lord (cf. v. 4-6).

It is the LORD's promise of readiness to hear our cry (v. 15), of ability to help (v. 16b), of comforting nearness (v. 18), of deliverance (v. 19), of protection (v. 20), and of trustworthiness (v. 22).

It is a promise to the righteous. Christ alone is the Righteous One, but all who are united to Him are covered with His righteousness, and therefore, may claim the same promise. It is a promise to those whose heart is broken, whose spirit is contrite in response to sin (v. 18). Because of sin in this world, they will suffer afflictions in this life, despite their being righteous in God's sight. But these afflictions are part of God's curriculum to cultivate our dependence upon Him, and our appreciation for Him.

How different is God's attitude towards the wicked:

> [16] *The face of the LORD is against them that do evil, to cut off the remembrance of them from the earth....* [21] *Evil shall slay the wicked: and they that hate the righteous shall be desolate.*

These are verses that we may feel uncomfortable reading by the hospital bed. Some of us would, no doubt, be tempted to skip them when reading this Psalm to encourage an afflicted brother or sister in Christ. But they are there, interspersing the words of comfort for a purpose. They are there, not only to fulfil the acrostic structure of the text. They are there, to remind us that God's care for His saints is particular and purposeful, rather than indiscriminate. He does not bless the wicked. He is not favourable towards them. Indeed He will punish them for their wickedness and for their hatred towards the righteous. Again who is the righteous? The Lord says: "If the world hate you, ye know that it hated me before *it hated* you" (Jn 15:18). Is it not likely, that our Lord had in mind Psalm 34:21?

But those words are there also to remind us that though our Lord enjoyed the favour of the Father, He actually suffered the wrath of the Father on our behalf, because of our sin. We are by nature wicked!

He went to the cross for our sakes. He suffered abandonment by the Father. For three hours of darkness, He saw nothing but the wrath of God. He knew nothing of the favourable presence of His Father.

Three hours later, our Lord cried, "My God, my God, why hast thou forsaken me." I believe our Lord cried these words at the end of the period—divinely appointed as sufficient to pay for our sin. Only then did He know again the presence of His Father so that He could commend His spirit into His loving hands.

Our Lord paid for our sin fully. Since that moment, men, women and children united to Him, need no longer doubt that God will never leave them nor forsake them.

Yes, sin may make us experience the Father's displeasure for a season. But no, even sin cannot separate us from the love of God that was sealed in the blood of our Saviour. As soon as we come before the LORD in humble repentance and contrition, so soon do we find the assurance of the Father's loving presence.

This is a promise that we must never doubt.

Conclusion

This is Psalm 34. May the Lord help us, that as we sing and meditate on these things, and pray about them, we may be transformed by the renewing of our minds. May we be provoked to resolve to do as our Lord did! May we be enabled to obey what He commands! May we experience the fulfilment of His promises in our lives! Amen. Ω

Psalm 35:
The Righteous One's Exasperation
Under the Cross

We do not know the historical occasion under which Psalm 35 was written. Some believe that it is connected to Psalm 34 which was originally written by David as he thought about how God delivered him from Achish. It is noted that both Psalms have a reference to the angel of the LORD (v. 5, 6), and to bones (v. 10).

But we cannot be sure. One thing is sure, however: This Psalm was written in the Spirit of Christ. While we may not be able to trace exactly where this Psalm fits into the life of David, it is not at all difficult to see how this Psalm describes vividly the experience and thoughts of our Lord as He headed to the cross.

In the same night in which He was betrayed, our Lord, while speaking to the disciples, quoted part of verse 19 in these words, "they hated me without a cause" (see Jn 15:25). He was describing what the scribes and chief priest were doing. They hated Him without cause, and were about to translate their hatred into murder.

In this Psalm, we see the Lord's grief at the way He was rewarded evil for good; and we see how He committed His impenitent enemies unto His Father's vengeance.

This is quite a long Psalm, which we may entitle, *"The Righteous One's Exasperation Under the Cross."* It has essentially three sections:

1. v. 1-10   Imprecations: The Lord's cry against His and His Father's enemies.

2. v. 11-16   Exasperation: The Lord's outpouring of His exasperation unto the Father in regard to the wicked enemies of His.

3. v. 17-28   Supplication: The Lord's plea to His Father to intervene, to destroy the wicked, and to bless the righteous.

1. Imprecations (v. 1-10)

¹ Plead my cause, O LORD, with them that strive with me: fight against them that fight against me. ² Take hold of shield and buckler, and stand up for mine help.

The word "plead" is translated from a Hebrew word (רִיב, *rîyb*) that describes a courtroom process.

Our Lord is calling unto the LORD, His Father, to take up His case, to make a righteous judgement about it, and to fight for Him. He can ask God to fight for Him because He is perfectly confident that He is perfectly righteous and innocent, whereas His enemies are entirely at fault.

⁷ For without cause have they hid for me their net in a pit, which without cause they have digged for my soul.

For this same reason, our Lord calls unto His Father to deal with His enemies.

³ Draw out also the spear, and stop the way against them that persecute me…

⁴ Let them be confounded and put to shame that seek after my soul.

Let them be turned back and brought to confusion that devise my hurt.

⁵ Let them be as chaff before the wind: and let the angel of the LORD chase them.

⁶ Let their way be dark and slippery: and let the angel of the LORD persecute them....

⁸ Let destruction come upon him at unawares; and

Let his net that he hath hid catch himself: into that very destruction let him fall.

Few of us dare to make such solemn imprecations: for every time we ask the LORD to condemn anyone for his sin, our own sin rises up in our conscience to cloud our mind, like the mud at the bottom of a pond being stirred up.

But Christ our Lord is without sin. And His relationship with the Father is one of profound intimacy. *"Say unto my soul, I am thy salvation,"* He requests His Father (v. 3b). Therefore, His request that the LORD deals with His enemies is as much a desire to see His name vindicated, as it is to have an occasion to praise His Father and to celebrate His greatness. This is what He says in verses 9-10:

⁹ And my soul shall be joyful in the LORD: it shall rejoice in his salvation....

Our Lord has every right to call imprecations upon His enemies. As a people united to Christ we too, may call imprecations against the enemies of God.

Yes, we may find ourselves unable to frame words of imprecation of our own, but we may certainly sing these words with our Lord. And we may certainly cry out unto the Father to plead our cause and to deal with our enemies, especially when we are persecuted for righteousness' sake, as our Lord was persecuted by His tormentors.

But none of us will ever experience the degree of pain and exasperation that our Lord experienced when He endured the cross on our behalf.

2. Exasperation (v. 11-16)

¹¹ False witnesses did rise up; they laid to my charge things that I knew not.

Our Lord had no sin. He had a conscience void of offence before God and before man. When He was dragged before Annas and then Caiaphas, neither of them could find any fault with Him. They bribed or persuaded some false witnesses to say something nasty about Him, but even they could not agree among themselves.

The most they could say was:

"We heard him say, I will destroy this temple that is made with hands, and within three days I will build another made without hands" (Mk 14:58).

Our Lord was not talking about the temple in Jerusalem; and neither did He say that He would destroy it. He was talking about His own body, and how after they had killed Him, He would rise again on the third day.

And not only did they accuse Him falsely, they rewarded Him evil for good (v. 12). This is so much the more wicked because our Lord had been extraordinarily kind towards many of those who were clamouring for His blood (v. 13-14). He wept with them that wept. He healed many who were sick. He delivered many possessed with demons. He fed many who were hungry. Many of them were total strangers but He dealt with them with uncommon kindness.

But sadly many of them abandoned Him as soon as they discovered that it was costly to follow Him. Some of them even joined in to clamour for His blood. Their eyes of gratitude were blindfolded by their sin.

Instead of grieving that our Lord was suffering under the hands of wicked men, they rejoiced. They seem to say: "If he would not accede to our demand to be a king, to supply all our needs, why bother to have him around. Away with him! Crucify him! Crucify him!"

These, the enemies of our Lord, were like a pack of wild animals surrounding Him, snapping at Him, gnashing their teeth and waiting to tear Him apart (v. 15-16).

Sadly, most of them were people who appeared to be very religious. They were, in fact, in Jerusalem for the feast of the Passover. But they were *"hypocritical mockers in feasts"* (v. 16). And the deeds of hypocrites are most exasperating; for they appear righteous, but are, in fact, wicked to the core.

What about us? Shall we not examine ourselves whether our love for the Lord is sincere? Let us examine ourselves when we come to the feast of the Lord's Supper. But not only then. Let us—whenever we sing this Psalm and others of similar themes—remind ourselves of the heinousness of hypocrisy, that we may deign to cry out unto our Saviour to give us more faith and more love for Him.

If we would do so, and thus walk with the Lord with a contrite spirit, in humble reliance and gratitude unto Him, we shall share in the joy of the Lord. Such is the joy He anticipates for Himself and His people in the final section of this Psalm, which we are given to sing with Him. For, here we see His supplication, and assurance of answers to prayer.

3. Supplication (v. 17-28)

[17] Lord, how long wilt thou look on? rescue my soul from their destructions, my darling from the lions. [18] I will give thee thanks in the great congregation: I will praise thee among much people.

Our Lord was not impassive as He headed to the cross, as some suppose. He is flesh and blood and soul like us. He felt pain in His body. He felt pain in His soul. Indeed, He felt it more acutely than anyone of us has ever felt, since our spiritual senses, unlike His, are dulled by sin. Therefore, He pours out the desires of His heart unto the Father, that the Father will not allow the injustice against Him to prevail a day longer than needed.

He desires to pass from the time of torment quickly into the time of rejoicing when He shall praise the Father in the great congregation.

He was looking forward to joining us and to us joining Him to worship the Father together (cf. Heb 2:12). Our Lord valued public worship more than any of us!

But as He anticipated the joy of worship, His heart was grieved over the injustice that He was experiencing. His enjoyment of God is marred by reasons outside of Himself.

He must have been experiencing the same kind of feeling we get when we have to suffer unjustly due to no fault of our own. It is the feeling that gives rise to a temptation to take revenge. But our Lord, the God-Man, would never give in to temptation. Vengeance belongs unto the LORD.

Instead, He reiterates His desire to be vindicated against His enemies and the enemies of the Father.

[19] Let not them that are mine enemies wrongfully rejoice over me: neither let them wink with the eye that hate me without a cause.

Now, the rejoicing of the enemies of the Lord would cease at His vindication. His vindication would be displayed for all to see in His rising from the dead. For His resurrection would indicate how His sacrifice on behalf of the Church is sufficient to pay for the sin of His people: which also proves beyond doubt, that His enemies had no basis whatsoever, to raise charges against Him, not to mention clamour for His death.

But as mentioned, our Lord does not take His vindication for granted. He presents it unto His Father as a matter of prayer. And He desired the Father to act quickly and decisively against those who dealt with Him unjustly and remained unrepentant (v. 22-26).

The Father heard the Lord's prayer. He would indeed answer Him. He would answer His prayer in the destruction of Jerusalem in AD 70. He would also answer His prayer in the everlasting punishment of the wicked, and at the Great and Mighty Day of the LORD.

In that great and glorious day, all who love the Lord shall magnify the name of the LORD for all eternity. This was the day anticipated and prayed for by our Lord as He concludes this Psalm:

> [27] *Let them shout for joy, and be glad, that favour my righteous cause: yea, let them say continually, Let the LORD be magnified, which hath pleasure in the prosperity of his servant.* [28] *And my tongue shall speak of thy righteousness and of thy praise all the day long.*

This is the day that we must also look forward to. Today we look forward to every opportunity to worship the LORD. But we know in our heart of hearts that our worship is not as joyful and perfect as we desire it to be.

We are still hindered by sin, both our own sin, and the sin of others.

We desire to shout for joy, but our hearts are often very heavy.

We desire that the LORD's name be magnified, but we know that often times, we bring shame to the LORD's name by our failures.

We desire to praise the LORD all the day. But we know that true and complete joy will come in the day when we will be able to worship the LORD without sin and distraction. Today, no matter how we try, the cares of the world, the limitations of our bodies and many other distractions hinder our enjoyment of God and His worship.

Thank God that the day is coming when all these limitations will be eradicated!

As our heavenly Father heard the prayer of our Lord Jesus and raised Him from the dead, so He will hear His prayer to bring us—for whom He died—into everlasting glory and heavenly enjoyment of God.

Conclusion

May these thoughts fill our hearts as we sing these words with our Saviour, and as we look forward to each Lord's Day to enjoy a foretaste of our eternal, ever-blessed communion with Him and with His and our Father! Amen. Ω

Psalm 36:
The Righteous One Looking up
to the God of Grace
from a World of Darkness

Psalm 36 is a Psalm of highs and lows. In this Psalm, Christ—speaking through David—brings us into the depth of human depravity and then takes us by the hand to lead us unto the heights of God's mercy and faithfulness. We may entitle it *"The Righteous One Looking up to the God of Grace from a World of Darkness."* It is a Psalm given by the Righteous One for us to sing in union with Him, to deplore the darkness of human depravity; and to extol, in contrast, the brightness of God's mercy and faithfulness.

It has three parts:

1. v. 1-4   The Depth of Human Depravity
2. v. 5-7a   The Height of God's Mercy & Faithfulness
3. v. 7b-12   Our Response

1. The Depth of Human Depravity

¹ The transgression of the wicked saith within my heart, that there is no fear of God before his eyes.

That is, as one commentator puts it:

> "The dictum of depravity concerning the wicked man in my heart is, there is no fear of God before his eyes."[19]

Or as Hengstenberg puts it:

> "Transgression utters its oracle to the wicked in my heart! There is no fear of God before his eyes!"

Herein is the meditation and conclusion of our Lord concerning the wicked. Why does the wicked commit iniquity? Why does he persist to carry out his wicked deeds? It is because he has no fear of God: For if he fears God, he will know that God will call him to account for his life, and judge him for his sin. But because he has no fear of God, he is a law unto himself. He assumes that whatever he does is right. Verse 2:

² For he flattereth himself in his own eyes, until his iniquity be found to be hateful.

Like the first verse, this verse is difficult to translate and understand at first sight. But the essential idea is that the wicked flatters himself in his own eyes, and his eyes are blinded so that he does not see that his iniquities are hateful, until they are discovered and frowned upon with disgust by others. The point is: the eyes of the wicked do not see God. He sees only himself; and he does not see anything hateful about himself. He sees himself as perfect and right all the time. He may see the fault of others. He may ridicule others. But in his own eyes, he is perfect.

This is the reason why he has no qualms about sinning against God—in words, deeds, and thoughts. Verse 3:

---

[19] Attrributed to JA Alexander by Charles Hodge in his comments on Romans 3:18. Most likely Hodge's paraphrase of Alexander's rather complicated exegesis. See Joseph A, Alexander, *The Psalms Translated and Explained* (Edinburgh: A. Elliot and J. Thin, 1864), 163-4.

³ The words of his mouth are iniquity and deceit: he hath left off to be wise, and to do good. ⁴ He deviseth mischief upon his bed; he setteth himself in a way that is not good; he abhorreth not evil.

Such is the natural man. Having no fear of God coupled with a high view of himself, he lives a lawless life.

Such a life can be a vexation to the righteous—both to the Righteous One, Christ, and to the saints united to Him.

Such a life makes man the most miserable and abominable living thing around. By such a life, man becomes worse than rats and cockroaches—because these are irrational creatures that sin not against God. Whereas man is made in the image of God, and yet rebels against God. How low can man get?

But in contrast to the meanness of man is the greatness of God. When we are vexed by the depravity of man, it does not help to mourn over it, or to grumble about it. What does help is to turn our eyes to see the mercy and faithfulness of God.

So our Lord would have us to join Him to extol the mercy and faithfulness of God with Him...

2. The Height of God's Mercy
& Faithfulness

⁵ Thy mercy, O LORD, is in the heavens; and thy faithfulness reacheth unto the clouds. ⁶ Thy righteousness is like the great mountains; thy judgments are a great deep: O LORD, thou preservest man and beast. ⁷ How excellent is thy lovingkindness, O God!

What a contrast: from the dark and murky depths of human depravity to the bright and clear heights of God's perfection.

God's mercy reaches unto the clouds. To save us from our sin, He broke the bounds of human mercy. He sent His only begotten Son! His mercy reaches unto the clouds!

His righteousness is like the great mountain. It is broad and it stands firm. Nothing can shake the LORD's standard of righteousness. Indeed, to save us and to make us acceptable to Himself, He gave us His own righteousness through His Son.

His judgements and justice are like the immense ocean. It is deep and far-reaching. Our God does not compromise on His justice. To spare us, Christ His Son was punished on our behalf.

And God does not only take care of His children. For the sake of His children, He preserves men and animals. His lovingkindness, or as it may be rendered, His covenant lovingkindness is excellent.

It was in answer to His covenant lovingkindness that God sent a flood to destroy the world so that His people might not be swallowed up in iniquity. It was also in answer to His covenant lovingkindness, that He preserved men and beasts in the ark when He flooded the world in the days of Noah. So deep was the justice and judgement of God; and yet deeper still is His covenant lovingkindness towards His own.

Oh how our hearts should resound with praise and gratitude when we think of these things!

And thus our Psalm ends with an acknowledgement of what our response ought to be: that by it we may stir one another's heart to the right attitude as we worship in union with our Saviour.

3. Our Response

7b Therefore the children of men put their trust under the shadow of thy wings. 8 They shall be abundantly satisfied with the fatness of thy house; and thou shalt make them drink of the river of thy pleasures. 9 For with thee is the fountain of life: in thy light shall we see light.

God is dependable. He is faithful. He loves His people, and He has demonstrated His faithfulness towards us over and over again—in days of chastisement and in day-to-day life. He gives us of His Spirit and His word. In this way we enjoy the fatness of His house, and drink of the fountain of life.

In His light we see light: for we are made to glorify and enjoy Him. Man's greatest joy can, therefore, be found in Him and Him alone.

But we are dependent upon Him to make His face to shine upon us, or our days will be dark and wearisome.

So we join our Saviour to cry unto the Father, verse 10:

10 O continue thy lovingkindness unto them that know thee; and thy righteousness to the upright in heart.

We know Him because He first knew us. We love Him because He first loved us (1 Jn 4:19). We are beloved in Christ. In Christ we have tasted of God's covenant lovingkindness. But we must not be presumptuous that God will continue to bless us. He will indeed, but we must lovingly and gratefully ask Him to continue to extend His arms of covenant lovingkindness for Christ's sake.

In particular, in view of the fact that we are in this world, though not of this world (Jn 17:16), we must ask the Lord to protect us from the wicked.

11 Let not the foot of pride come against me, and let not the hand of the wicked remove me. 12 There are the workers of iniquity fallen: they are cast down, and shall not be able to rise.

The wicked stands in drastic contrast with God. While our hearts are lifted up in praise when we think about God, we grieve when we think about the sorrows and anguish that the wicked bring to our lives.

Thank God that we have recourse, for the wicked is not outside the dominion of God.

And so we can go to the Lord to ask Him to deal with the wicked on our behalf. And He will indeed deal with them, for He is a loving, covenant-keeping God. He will not suffer the wicked to triumph over any whom His Son purchased with His blood.

Conclusion

This is Psalm 36. It must surely have been one of the Psalms that our Lord meditated on as He struggled with the oppression of the wicked. Nothing helps a soul, afflicted by anguish on account of the wicked, as much as to meditate on the greatness of our heavenly Father, and to cast our burdens upon Him.

As the Father strengthens His Son with the Spirit and His word, and delivered Him, so He strengthens us with His Spirit and His word; and He will deliver us from all our tribulations. Only trust in Him. Amen. Ω

The Righteous One's
ABC's of Discernment Between
the Godly & the Wicked

Psalm 37 is one of the seven Acrostic Psalms found in the Psalter. It is a Wisdom Psalm that can be taken in the lips of all of God's children—whether only begotten or adopted.

But as you read the Psalm, you will notice how the words appear to flow out of the lips of our Lord, and how they describe Him.

Consider verses 30 and 31:

> *"The mouth of the righteous speaketh wisdom, and his tongue talketh of judgment. The law of his God is in his heart; none of his steps shall slide."*

Who would exactly fit these words other than our Lord? Indeed, it seems almost a full portrait of the Lord—who is altogether righteous in words, thoughts and deeds!

And consider verse 11:

> *But the meek shall inherit the earth; and shall delight themselves in the abundance of peace.*

And verse 22:

> *For such as be blessed of him shall inherit the earth; and they that be cursed of him shall be cut off.*

Are these not the words of the Lord, who says in the 3rd Beatitude:

> "Blessed are the meek: for they shall inherit the earth" (Mt 5:5)?

Or consider verse 10: *"For yet a little while, and the wicked shall not be..."*

Do these words not remind us of the Lord's words to His disciples:

> *"A little while, and ye shall not see me: and again, a little while, and ye shall see me, because I go to the Father. &c"* (Jn 16:16ff)?

In a little while, we shall see the Lord; and the wicked shall be no more. They shall not trouble us anymore.

It is hard not to see how Psalm 37 is the word of Christ given to us that we may join Him to sing, to teach and admonish one another in the way of the LORD (v. 34).

In particular, in this Psalm, our Lord teaches us not to fret or to become envious because of evildoers or workers of iniquity (v. 1). We may call it, *"The Righteous One's ABC's of Discernment Between the Godly and the Wicked."*

Now, this Psalm, as with most of the alphabetic Psalms, does not have a clear structure. When I started working on this sermon, I divided the Psalm into what appears to be four logical sections, as follows:

1. v. 1-7   Trust in the LORD and Fear Not

2. v. 8-22   The Wicked Will Be Punished

3. v. 23-31   The LORD Loves and Blesses the Righteous

4.   v. 32-40   The Conflict Between the Wicked and the Righteous

This is a fairly good outline, I think. But as soon as I started working on the first two verses, I found that the first two sections overlap so significantly, that it is really only one section. So I merged section 1 and 2 together and started working on three sections. But as soon as I finished working on the first section and began to work on the second section, I realise that the second section covers essentially the same things as the first section. The point is: this Psalm defies any attempt to break it up into distinct logical sections.

Though that may be the case, the principal thoughts in this Psalm may be organised under three simple questions: (1) What we should not do? (2) What we should do instead? And (3) Why?

This, then, is how we will study this Psalm.

1. What We Should Not Do?

The opening verse of the Psalm makes it very clear:

> ¹ *Fret not thyself because of evildoers, neither be thou envious against the workers of iniquity.*

Who are the evildoers? Who are the workers of iniquity? We have no doubt that they include the unconverted in the world. They would live without regard to the law of God; and they would not hesitate to take advantage of God's people.

But workers of iniquity would, no doubt, also include many who profess to be believers: for the Lord Jesus tells us that at the last day many will say unto Him, "Lord, Lord, have we not prophesied in thy name? and in thy name have cast out devils? and in thy name done many wonderful works?" But He would say unto them: "I never knew you: depart from me, ye that work iniquity" (Mt 7:22-23).

The word translated "iniquity" is the Greek "*anomia*" which means lawlessness.

Workers of iniquity are those who live without regard to the law of God—whether they profess to be believers or otherwise.

These would often become very rich in the world because they keep not the Sabbath, nor do they care about hurting others in the name of money making.

When they want to sell a Christian something, they may say: "Oh I am a Christian too." But when you have bought it, and discover some issues with the product, and you get back to them, they will say: "Ah, business is business; please don't mix religion with business!"

When you have to deal with such persons, how do you feel? Are you not tempted to feel vexed, frustrated and angry?

The wicked are often rich whereas God's people would often have to struggle to make ends meet. And the wicked would often take advantage of God's people, knowing that they would very rarely fight back as they seek to follow the Lord's example of meekness.

To make matters worse evildoers and workers of iniquity are often very well-to-do and respected in society. So, together with a temptation to feel vexed and angry about them, we sometimes feel envious of their wealth—why do honest people not do as well as them? Maybe they have it right, whereas we are hindering ourselves unnecessarily?

Well, what should we do when we are vexed by the behaviour of the workers of iniquity?

What should we do if we are tempted to be envious of their wealth and achievement?

Our Lord would have us remind one another with His word:

> [1] *Fret not thyself because of evildoers, neither be thou envious against the workers of iniquity.*

We must not allow ourselves to fret or to be vexed by them. The word of God has already warned us that there will be such persons in the world. Were it not for the grace of God, we would also be like them.

And so, we should neither fret nor be envious of them. We should rather pity them.

It is simply not worth allowing ourselves to be exasperated by the wicked, or to get angry (v. 8), or to be tempted to follow their example.

2. What We Should Do Instead?

Instead of fretting or being envious of the evildoers and workers of iniquity, we should:

- Continue to trust the LORD, and do good (v. 3).
- Continue to delight in the LORD (v. 4), and commit our ways to Him (v. 5).
- Rest in Him, and wait patiently upon Him (v. 7).
- Cease from anger (v. 8).
- Strive to be meek, as our Lord is meek. We should not retaliate or return evil for evil (v. 11).
- Delight ourselves in the abundance of peace (v. 11).
- Depart from evil, and do good (v. 27).
- Wait on the LORD, and keep His way (v. 34).
- And above all, we should *"Mark the perfect man, and behold the upright: for the end of that man is peace"* (v. 37).

Who is the perfect man? Surely, He is none other than our Lord Himself.

Instead of being vexed and frustrated by wicked and lawless persons, let us learn to turn our eyes unto the Perfect Man, our Lord and Saviour, the Prince of Peace. There is no better antidote from the vexations of this present life than to turn our eyes and look full into the wonderful face of our Saviour.

Did someone make your life miserable?

She may be a sales clerk at the supermarket you had to deal with.

He may be a stranger who drove recklessly and nearly caused you to have an accident.

He may be your boss.

She may be your colleague.

He may be a member of the same church.

She may be your mother-in-law.

He may be a fair-weather friend.

She may even be a loved one who simply does not understand the way of truth and therefore has made your life miserable.

What should you do when you feel so vexed and angry? It does not help to keep brooding over it. It always helps to turn your eyes to the Perfect Man. Know that it is because there is none perfect that He had to come to rescue you. Know that one day there will be perfect peace for your soul because your Saviour, the Perfect Man, will make sure that all who surround you for all eternity, are perfectly loving, and understanding, and caring.

But this is not the only reason why we should not fret over evildoers and workers of iniquity. Our Lord has given us several other reasons to meditate on—in songs—with Him.

3. Why?

Why should we not fret over evildoers, but continue to trust and wait upon the LORD?

The answer is found everywhere in this Psalm, but we may summarise it under seven points.

First and foremost, when we learn to trust in the LORD and to seek first His kingdom and righteousness, God promises to provide for all our needs (v. 3), and to give us the desires of our hearts (v. 4).

Secondly, the LORD will give success to our endeavours (v. 5). All things work together for the good of the righteous even in days of famine (v. 19); whereas a curse will attend the wicked in days of plenty (v. 20). The LORD will order our steps and enable us to delight in His way (v. 23). He will not allow us to fall beyond recovery (v. 24). This is something that experience testifies to be true (v. 25-26).

Thirdly, when we put our trust in Him instead of taking matters into our own hands, our Lord will grant us deliverance from all our sin and from all our troubles, verse 39:

> [39] But the salvation of the righteous is of the LORD: he is their strength in the time of trouble. [40] And the LORD shall help them, and deliver them: he shall deliver them from the wicked, and save them, because they trust in him.

Fourthly, vengeance belongs to the LORD. When we refuse to allow ourselves to sin because of anger and vexation against the wicked, we will see the day when the LORD will deal with the wicked on our behalf.

He will cut off the evildoers (v. 9-10, v. 34b, v. 38). He will laugh at them: for He sees their day of recompense coming (v. 13). He will destroy them with swift and perfect judgement (v. 14-15, 17).

They may be great in power. They may spread themselves like a green bay tree. But they will pass away, and all their wealth will be completely lost to them, in contrast to the eternal wealth of the righteous (v. 34-36).

Fifthly, and related to the fourth point, when we commit ourselves to the LORD's vengeance, the LORD will vindicate us openly (v. 6, 17b).

Sixthly, when we refuse to be envious of the wicked, the LORD will give us an everlasting inheritance. We shall inherit the earth (v. 9, 12, 22, and 29). Our inheritance is eternal, whereas the inheritance of the wicked will last no more than a lifetime (v. 18)

For this reason, the little that the righteous have is better than the riches of many wicked persons (v. 16). We should, therefore, never be envious of their wealth and status.

We should not allow ourselves to sink into depression because of the vexing ways of the wicked. We should rather pity them.

Finally, when we take heed to the instructions of this Psalm and turn our eyes unto the LORD to walk in the ways of the Lord, we shall more and more be like the Lord, the Perfect Man, and know the blessings of the Perfect Man (v. 6, 37, 40; cf. v. 30-33).

In short, when we refuse to allow ourselves to be vexed by evil doers and instead trust and wait upon the LORD in regard to our present circumstances, we will experience the Lord's richest blessings today and forever.

Conclusion

May the LORD grant us that we may take heed to the admonishments in this Psalm, and encourage one another to that end, as we sing it together with one another.

May He grant us that we may, in a very real way, experience the blessings that are outlined in this Psalm.

May the LORD grant us that as we learn to humble ourselves under His mighty hand through all the trials and disappointments, we may experience in our lives.

May we have many occasions to rejoice and to testify before the world: "The LORD reigns and He keeps His promises!" Amen. Ω

Psalm 38:
The Righteous One's
Abhorrence of the Leprosy of Sin

Psalm 38 is a penitential Psalm of one who is sick. David, in all probability, wrote this Psalm at a time when he was very ill.

But, this Psalm is, no doubt, a prophetic prayer of Christ. As the Church Father, Augustine, puts it: "It would be hard not to apply to Christ a Psalm that as graphically describes His passion as if we were reading it out of the gospels."

But what about the confession of sin, iniquities and foolishness in it (v. 3-5 & 18)?

Foremost, let us be clear that if these statements are to be taken as indicators that this is not a Messianic Psalm, then Psalm 40 should not be a Messianic Psalm: for we read in Psalm 40:12: "mine iniquities have taken hold upon me, so that I am not able to look up; they are more than the hairs of mine head." And yet, the New Testament, very clearly, indicates that Psalm 40 prophetically contains the words of the Messiah, and hardly any evangelical commentator will challenge that conclusion.

How do we explain these penitential statements, then? Well, it really should not be difficult for those who believe in the doctrine of the substitutionary atonement of Christ. For Christ did not take our guilt upon Himself in a theoretical way. He was wounded for our transgressions; He was bruised for our iniquities (Isa 53:5).

Though our Lord had no sin, He experienced all the effects of sin upon Himself. We do not know if He ever fell ill. Some believe that He never fell sick, because He had no actual sin; but that is to misunderstand the relationship between sin and sickness altogether. In the first place, God does not generally send particular illness to punish us for particular sins (cf. Jn 9:3). Sicknesses are the effects of sin. There are illnesses in this world because we are all experiencing the effects of the Fall. In the second place, all sinners must face the effects of the Fall, and Christ our Lord was a sinner by imputation of our sin upon Him.

Christ had no sin, but He was bearing our iniquities. He felt pain, He felt thirst, He bled and He experienced death because He was bearing our sin. I see no reason why He should be immune to illnesses.

Nevertheless, whether the Lord is speaking in the context of bodily illness, or spiritual pains, we can agree with Bonar that this Psalm shows us, "He was weary of wearing that poisoned garment of our sins; He was weary of having our leprosy appearing on His spotless person; He was weary and woe-begone, and longed for the time when He should, 'appear without sin,' (Heb 9:28)."

Christ our Lord suffered much because of our sin. He was longing for deliverance. But make no mistake. Our Lord never did fret nor grumble at His Lot. He has a fully human nature, no doubt; and so He felt grief as we all do. But His human will and attitude were entirely sanctified. He had joy in the midst of the most challenging circumstances.

So, even in such a Psalm as Psalm 38, we must not think that our Lord was praying in desperation and hopelessness. No, no; He was, no doubt, pouring out His heart to the Father and at the same time submitting to His will. Here is a prayer set in song, which we may entitle, *"The Righteous One's Abhorrence of the Leprosy of Sin."*

Let's look at this prayer. Since it is a prayer, we may not expect a very distinct structure, but we can roughly divide it into four parts.

1. v. 1-5   Confession of Affliction
2. v. 6-10   Description of Affliction
3. v. 11-14   Deliverance from Affliction

1. Confession of Affliction
(v. 1-5)

Our Psalm begins with a plea to the Father to withhold His hand of chastisement.

[1] O LORD, rebuke me not in thy wrath: neither chasten me in thy hot displeasure. [2] For thine arrows stick fast in me, and thy hand presseth me sore.

By this plea, our Lord is making it very clear that the afflictions that He was experiencing did not come by chance. They are the sovereign and wise appointments of God.

Why did our Lord have to suffer? He had to suffer because of our sin (v. 3) and our foolishness (v. 5). Our Lord was the embodiment of wisdom and righteousness. There was neither foolishness nor sin in Him.

He did not need to suffer. But He did. He took our chastisement upon Himself. God treated Him as He would treat a sinner. Indeed, the nearer He approached the cross, the heavier the burden was upon His shoulders and the more He experienced the wrath of the Father. The shadow of the wrath of God was lengthening upon His soul.

As David experienced a waxing of his bones (Ps 32:3), so our Lord found no rest in His bones (v. 3), and He felt the heavy burden pressing upon Him.

Verses 6-10 contain a more complete description of the affliction He was facing.

2. Description of Affliction
(v. 6-10)

He is troubled in His heart, so much so that He is, as it were, bowed down as He walks (v. 6).

He feels a loathsome disease or a searing pain down His lower back (v. 7). He feels weak and broken. There is grief in His eyes.

When did our Lord experience all these? Well, He might have experienced an illness that might be described in these terms, but we have no records in the Gospel. What is recorded in the Gospel is, however, our Lord's sorrow and affliction as He headed to the cross.

He is troubled. He is bowed down. He is feeling a lot of pain in His heart and in His body. He has been whipped and forced to wear the crown of thorns. He was deprived of sleep as well as food and water. He is feeble and sore broken. Like a sheep before her shearers, He is dumb and opens not His mouth (v. 13).

But there is, no doubt, a roaring in His heart, or perhaps even in His ears, since He was slapped and punched by His tormentors.

And yet, though His eyes are weakened and dimmed (v. 10), He does not lose sight of His Father, verse 9:

[9] Lord, all my desire is before thee; and my groaning is not hid from thee.

He knows that the Father is aware of His sufferings. So He is submitted to His Father's will.

But He has to drink the bitter cup to its dregs so that He can fill it with the blessing of God. The cup of blessing is also the cup of God's wrath.

So our Lord suffered pain upon pain; or more precisely, insult upon injury.

Consider the aggravation to His affliction that He experienced....

3. Aggravation of Affliction
(v. 11-14)

[11] My lovers and my friends stand aloof from my sore; and my kinsmen stand afar off. [12] They also that seek after my life lay snares for me: and they that seek my hurt speak mischievous things, and imagine deceits all the day long.

Did not our Lord experience all these things? Do we not read of how our Lord's closest friends "stood afar off" (Lk 23:49) in His hour of sorrow and pain (v. 11)? Do we not read of how the scribes and Pharisees, and even the Herodians, all sought His life? They made many attempts to trap Him (v. 12).

How did they get Him crucified in the end? It was through deceit. Even Pilate knew that.

But His enemies were not the only ones adding salt to His wounds. His friends and kinsmen did the same. He was betrayed by a trusted disciple and friend. He was betrayed with a kiss.

And when He was betrayed, all His friends who had moments earlier pledged to stick with Him even unto death, abandoned Him. Everyone of them! His most trusted disciple even denied Him three times.

And where were His kinsmen? They were standing at a distance watching Him even as He hung on the cross.

Our Lord did not complain.

[13] But I, as a deaf man, heard not; and I was as a dumb man that openeth not His mouth. [14] Thus I was as a man that heareth not, and in whose mouth are no reproofs.

Did not the prophet Isaiah say the same thing of Him?

"He was oppressed, and He was afflicted, yet He opened not His mouth: He is brought as a lamb to the slaughter, and as a sheep before her shearers is dumb, so He openeth not His mouth" (Isa 53:7).

But make no mistake: Silence before man does not mean silence before God. Our Lord was not silent before the Father, and neither must we ever be.

He cried for deliverance...

4. Deliverance from Affliction
(v. 15-22)

[15] For in thee, O LORD, do I hope: thou wilt hear, O Lord my God. [16] For I said, Hear me, lest otherwise they should rejoice over me: when my foot slippeth, they magnify themselves against me. [17] For I am ready to halt, and my sorrow is continually before me. [18] For I will declare mine iniquity; I will be sorry for my sin. [19] But mine enemies are lively, and they are strong: and they that hate me wrongfully are multiplied. [20] They also that render evil for good are mine adversaries; because I follow the thing that good is. [21] Forsake me not, O LORD: O my God, be not far from me. [22] Make haste to help me, O Lord my salvation.

Our Lord confesses His hope in the Father (v. 15).

He commits Himself to the vindication and protection of His Father (v. 16).

He pours out His sorrow and confesses His weakness (v. 17).

He acknowledges that God is just in dealing with Him as He did because He was bearing the sin of His people (v. 18).

Nevertheless, He appeals for justice because His enemies, who were tormenting Him, hated Him wrongfully and were rendering evil for good (v. 19-20).

And so He pleads with His Father not to forsake Him, but to deliver Him.

Thank God that He heard our Lord's prayer. He did not take away the bitter cup. Our Lord had to drink it. But as soon as the cup was empty, so soon was the Lord raised and exalted on high.

Conclusion

What is this Psalm to you, beloved brethren and children? I trust that this Psalm has given you yet another glimpse of our Lord's suffering for your sin.

I trust you are not tired of hearing it again, for this is the heart of the Christian faith. I trust that your heart is once again filled with love and gratitude to the Lord as you consider what He has gone through for your sake.

Let us, therefore, join our Saviour to sing this Psalm with gratitude in our hearts as we think about His suffering for us.

But let us also sing it prayerfully as a people united to Christ when we experience illness or afflictions, whether it is due to a particular sin or otherwise. As the Father heard the cry of His Son, so He will hear us when we cry unto Him with the words of His Son.

Have you been afflicted, dear child of God? Make this Psalm your own. Cry unto the Father with melody in your heart. The Father will not forsake you, nor will He be far from you. He will not fail to make haste to help you—for Christ your Saviour's sake. Amen. Ω

Psalm 39:
The Righteous One's
Funeral Psalm

Psalm 39 may be known as a Funeral Psalm. Referring to its liturgical use in the Church of England, George Horne remarks: "This Psalm is with the utmost propriety appointed by the church to be used at the burial of the dead, as a funeral is indeed the best comment upon it."

We do not know the occasion which prompted David to write this Psalm in the first place. But it appears that David had perhaps suffered a prolonged illness and was near unto death (see v. 5 and 13). As he thought about how his pilgrim journey was coming to an end, he began to reflect on his own life. And he began to contemplate on life on this side of eternity, in general. In this way, David was given to pen, under the inspiration of the Spirit of Christ, the cogitation of our Saviour as the time of His death drew near.

Would He not have meditated on it at the Garden of Gethsemane as He anticipated the end of His earthly mission?

We may call it *"The Righteous One's Funeral Psalm."* It is a Psalm appointed by the Righteous One for us to sing in union with Him, both to contemplate on His death on our behalf, as well as to steer our thoughts when our minds are most likely to be pulled in many directions, by grief and confusion, due to the death of a loved one.

It has three parts. From verses 1-2, we have the Righteous One's Resolutions to bridle His tongue. From verses 3-6, we have the Righteous One's Reflections before the Father. And from verses 7-13, we have the Righteous One's Requests to the Father. Thus, a simple outline would be:

1. v. 1-2   Resolutions

2. v. 3-6   Reflections

3. v. 7-13   Requests

1. Resolutions

This Psalm begins rather abruptly. It is an abruptness that reflects the words of someone who has kept silent through sorrow of heart.

> [1] *I said, I will take heed to my ways, that I sin not with my tongue: I will keep my mouth with a bridle, while the wicked is before me.* [2] *I was dumb with silence, I held my peace, even from good; and my sorrow was stirred.*

Our Lord was a man of sorrows. He wept when His friend Lazarus died. He cried as He thought about the horrors of the cross. He grieved as He saw the women weeping for Him, as He was pushed and shoved to the cross at Calvary. He said to them:

> "Daughters of Jerusalem, weep not for me, but weep for yourselves, and for your children" (Lk 23:28).

Our Lord experienced grief. But make no mistake. He never did entertain hard thoughts against the Father. There was never any bitterness in His holy heart. His grief was founded upon His compassion for a fallen world. His grief overflowed from His heart and found expression in His words.

But our Lord, like David of old, was careful with His words. He would indeed speak the truth at all times; and His speech was righteous at all times. He does not say one thing while feeling something else. His words are consistent with His heart.

But it is not enough to ensure that our words are righteous and consistent. It is necessary for us to ensure that our words do not give rise to occasion of misunderstanding and hard feelings against God.

Our Lord was sorely tried. His heart was brimming with strong emotions. But when wicked persons were about Him, He held a bridle over His mouth and remained silent so that the wicked would not have occasion to blaspheme the name of the LORD. This is what the first two verses of this Psalm teach us.

The children of God understand God's ways. God will sometimes bring trials to His children for their good. But the wicked, and all unbelievers, do not understand that. It was for this reason that our Lord held His peace, lest His words become occasions for sin.

It is for this reason that we must also learn to hold our peace before unbelievers when our hearts are brimming with emotions. We may indeed share with God's people, but it is foolish to try to gain sympathy amongst unbelievers. We ought rather to have the attitude of Ezra who was too ashamed to ask King Cyrus for an armed escort "because [he] had spoken unto the king, saying, The hand of our God is upon all them for good that seek him; but His power and His wrath is against all them that forsake Him" (Ezr 8:22).

We must always seek to preserve the great honour of our God. Sometimes, that may mean remaining silent until it is appropriate to speak.

Our Lord did just that. He kept silent until He was no longer in the hearing of the wicked.

Then the pent-up emotions in His heart overflowed with His prayerful reflections unto God.

2. Reflections

³ My heart was hot within me, while I was musing the fire burned: then spake I with my tongue,...

Talking is therapeutic. One of the best ways to deal with hurt is to talk about it. To express one's emotions is a very human thing to do. But we must always do so at the right time.

When the time was right, the Lord spoke. He spoke in audible prayer.

⁴ LORD, make me to know mine end, and the measure of my days, what it is; that I may know how frail I am. ⁵ Behold, thou hast made my days as an handbreadth; and mine age is as nothing before thee: verily every man at His best state is altogether vanity....

This was the musing of the Lord: Man's life on earth is so brief compared to eternity. And it is so insignificant compared to the glory of God. Even the life of the best of ordinary man in his best state is altogether vanity compared to the weight of God's glory.

⁶ Surely every man walketh in a vain shew: surely they are disquieted in vain: He heapeth up riches, and knoweth not who shall gather them.

Man is like a phantom or a mist. He appears but for a moment. He *"walketh in a vain shew."* He is busy for nothing. He heaps up riches which he cannot bring into eternity. Often, he does not even know whom he is gathering his riches for.

Such is the life of the ordinary man.

Why would our Lord withhold Himself from saying these things in the hearing of the wicked? Perhaps it is because it might sound like He was complaining—when in fact, He is stating a fact that all men should be aware of.

Our Lord would, particularly, have to be careful about saying words that sound like complaints in the ears of the wicked, because of the sorrows attending His life.

Naturally, when someone is facing severe trials, what he says would sound like complaints to those who do not know him. But complaints against God by God's children dishonour His name. So our Lord withheld His tongue lest He be perceived to be complaining against the LORD.

So we must learn to do the same, even as Solomon puts it in His wisdom: "There is a time to keep silence, and a time to speak" (Ecc 3:7).

Honesty does not require us to say in the hearing of man everything that is in our hearts at all times. But we can be honest with God at all times.

We can make our requests known unto the Father before the saints. Consider our Lord's requests.

3. Requests

7a And now, Lord, what wait I for?

If man's life is a vanity, what should I look forward to in my life?

As He asks the question, so He answers:

7b My hope is in thee.

The Christian's hope is not merely wishful thinking. It is faith in God in regard to the future. It is a certain confidence in regard to the future.

Our Lord's hope is in the Father. He came to do the Father's will. He knew the purpose of His life. He knew what He came to do. His life is not without meaning.

He came to bear our transgressions. He came to deliver us from our sin.

He has no sin, but He was bearing our sin. He was being chastised for our sin. He was the reproach of the foolish because they did not understand what He was doing.

8 Deliver me from all my transgressions: make me not the reproach of the foolish. 9 I was dumb, I opened not my mouth; because thou didst it. 10 Remove thy stroke away from me: I am consumed by the blow of thine hand. 11 When thou with rebukes dost correct man for iniquity, thou makest His beauty to consume away like a moth: surely every man is vanity.

Our Lord had to deal with a very complex set of emotions.

He delights to do His Father's will and He knows He has to face punishment in the hand of the LORD. Yet He, obviously, does not enjoy pain.

He knows that He has no sin, and yet He has to submit Himself to be treated as a sinner.

He knows that when the Father deals with Him for the sin of His Church, His appearance will, as it were, consumed away like a moth. Yet, He, no doubt, desires to bear the image of God, including His glory.

He knows He has to suffer injustice; and yet to allow the foolish to reproach Him is to allow them to blaspheme the Father.

So He cries out "*make me not the reproach of the foolish.*" Our Lord is submitted to the will of His Father, but that does not mean that He must be silent in prayer. His Father delights to hear the outpouring of His heart.

So He concludes His prayer:

> [12] *Hear my prayer, O LORD, and give ear unto my cry; hold not thy peace at my tears: for I am a stranger with thee, and a sojourner, as all my fathers were.* [13] *O spare me, that I may recover strength, before I go hence, and be no more.*

Our Lord was a stranger and pilgrim in this world more than anyone of us. But more than anyone of us, He needed strength to fight the good fight and to complete the race.

He is going to face death and God's wrath for His Church. He is not going to "*be no more*" or to be annihilated. David was not expecting annihilation either. It was an expression that describes the finality of death.

Death spells the end of this present life. Death seals up one's work of this present life.

When our Lord prayed the prayer in this Psalm, He had not completed the race. Whether it was when Lazarus died, or in the Garden of Gethsemane, our Lord needed a restoration of emotional strength to continue on to the end. It was a way that would get more and more difficult. It would be a journey towards death.

It was a journey our Lord would not presume to undertake without the Father's presence and blessings. It was a painful journey that He had to undertake with tears.

Conclusion

Death is very poignant. This Psalm reflects the thoughts of our Lord as He anticipated His own death. We too can use this Psalm when we think about our own death.

But especially, let us reflect on the thoughts in this Psalm when we grieve over the death of a saint who has gone ahead of us.

Let us grieve when the life of a brother or sister has come to an end, but let us refrain from complaining or suggesting that it is unfair that God should cut his or her life short. Rather, let us take the opportunity to reflect on our own life: of the rest of the race we must complete. Let us ask the Lord to give us grace and strength to live and die in such a way as to bring glory to His name. This is how we must deal with our grief. For as someone puts it, "if our mourning goes beyond sorrow into bitterness, then we have allowed pain to abscess and become poison."

Let us pray, as the Lord did, that we may not be a reproach to the wicked. Let us pray, as the Lord did, that the Father may give us strength to continue the good fight, and to complete the race, in a way that will best bring glory to His great and holy name.

Let us do so, especially as death has lost its sting for us; and one day we shall rise from the dead together with all our loved ones in the Lord, just as Christ our Lord rose from the dead. Amen. Ω

Psalm 40:
The Righteous One's
Psalm of Personal Sacrifice

Psalm 40 is a well-known Messianic Psalm. Almost every commentator, including modern ones, agree that it is Messianic because verses 6-8 are quoted in the New Testament in Hebrews 10:6-9 in regard to the sacrifice of Christ. And it is quoted in such a way that the first person pronoun "I" is taken as referring to the Lord Himself. It is the Lord Jesus who says: *"Lo, I come in the volume of the book it is written of me. I delight to do Thy will, O my God"* (Ps 40:7-8).

Nevertheless, there are some who object to taking this Psalm as Messianic in its entirety especially because of verse 12: *"For innumerable evils have compassed me about: mine iniquities have taken hold upon me..."* (Ps 40:12a). Christ is sinless, He could never have owned up to evils and iniquities, it is claimed.

As a result of this objection, four different ways have been proposed for looking at this Psalm.

a. The first way is to read this Psalm as originally and exclusively the words of David. But to read this Psalm this way is to deny the inspiration and inerrancy of the book of Hebrew, for how ever you read it, the quotation in Hebrew 10:6-9 clearly takes Psalm 40:6-9 as referring to Christ. You can't even claim that the writer of Hebrew simply applied David's words in Psalm 40:6-9 to Christ as that would essentially be to accuse him of reading into the word and misapplying the text.

b. The second way of reading this Psalm is to see parts of it as David's words, while other parts as the Lord's words. So, for example verse 12 would be David's words, whereas verses 6-9 would be the words of Christ. But the problem with this view is that it would make the interpretation of this Psalm very arbitrary as there is no internal indicators to suggest that the "I" of verse 9 and the "I" of verse 12 refer to a different person.

c. The third way of looking at this Psalm is to see this Psalm as the words of David, but everywhere susceptible to double application. That is, though they are originally David's words and record his experience, David wrote as a type of Christ, and every verse of this Psalm has a reference to Christ, the anti-type of David.

d. The fourth way of looking at this Psalm is to see this Psalm as originally and exclusively the words of Christ. According to this view, David wrote prophetically in the Spirit of Christ, so that his experience is bypassed, and every word in this Psalm is solely the word of Christ.

Which of these 4 views is correct? I personally think that it has to be between the third and fourth. And I think it is not only true here, but in all the Psalms. However, there are some Psalms in which the type stands out much more than the antitype, such as Psalm 51; whereas there are some Psalms, such as Psalm 22, in which the antitype so far outshines the type that there are places where it is quite impossible to determine with certainty how the verses refer to David. When we read such Psalms, I believe we may simply leave David aside, and interpret the first person pronouns as referring to Christ directly. Psalm 40, like Psalm 22, is such a Psalm.

Psalm 40 contains the words of Christ summarising what He came to do for our salvation. We may entitle it *"The Righteous One's Psalm of Personal Sacrifice."* It has three parts: Verses 1-5 contains the Lord's recollection of deliverance through the darkest hour of His passion. Verses 6-10 summarises what the Lord came to do. Verses 11-17 contains the Lord's prayer in those dark hours. This prayer is recorded for us, no doubt, not only that we may understand the degree of our Saviour's suffering for us, but also that we may know how we ought to pray at times when we are faced with the same kind of suffering.

Accordingly, we may outline the Psalm as follows:

1. v. 1-5   The Recollection
2. v. 6-10   The Purpose
3. v. 11-17   The Prayer

1. The Recollection

¹ I waited patiently for the LORD; and he inclined unto me, and heard my cry. ² He brought me up also out of an horrible pit, out of the miry clay, and set my feet upon a rock, and established my goings.

It is obvious from these words, that they are written from the perspective of our Lord after His sacrifice was completed. This is a song which would have been most appropriately taken up by our Lord as He ascended to heaven, having given up the ghost.

During the hours following our Lord's agony in the Garden of Gethsemane, He sank, as it were, deeper and deeper into a pit of *"miry clay."*

The hours were long. The night was dark. The pain and loneliness that He had to endure were excruciating.

But He never lost sight of His Father. Even when the Father, as it were, turned His face away in wrath because of our sin imputed to Him, our Lord did not grow despondent.

He waited patiently upon the Father, enduring the cross, and despising the shame.

The three hours of darkness was perhaps the most gruelling time for our Lord. He, as it were, tasted hell on our behalf. But when the three hours were ended, our Lord was able to say, no doubt, with deep relief in His heart: "It is finished! Father, into thy hands I commend my spirit!"

Our Lord's humiliation was not yet complete as His body must rest in the grave for the next three days. But for all intents and purposes, His sacrifice was sufficient. It was finished!

Three days later, His body was raised from the dead. Then when He had completed what He had to do, our Lord ascended up to heaven—as the God-Man: body and soul in hypostatic union with His divine nature.

The darkness, pain, and sorrow, were entirely left behind. Henceforth, our Lord was set on the right hand of the throne of God. His feet are now set *"upon a rock"*; and a new song of praise, in the words of this Psalm, must have overflowed from His heart.

The Lord suffered and died for us. So naturally, even as He overflowed with joyful song, He does not forget us. *"Many shall see it, and fear, and shall trust in the LORD,"* He says (v. 3). The elect for whom Christ came are those who are made to fear God and trust in Him. The anticipation of those who are redeemed singing with Him, no doubt, added to the joy of our Lord.

Our Lord is the man (v. 4) who makes the LORD His trust, and respects neither the proud, nor those who turn aside to lies. But He came to represent sinners like us, so that united to

Him, we can also enjoy God's blessings. So the Lord, in verse 5, changes the 1st person pronoun from singular to plural: from "me" and "I" to "us" and "usward". God, He is saying, is good towards us. His blessings upon us for the sake of Christ are innumerable. We should count our blessings, but we cannot really count them because they are *"more than can be numbered"* (v. 5).

So, let us move now to the purpose of our Lord's incarnation.

2. The Purpose

^{6} *Sacrifice and offering thou didst not desire; mine ears hast thou opened: burnt offering and sin offering hast thou not required.* ^{7} *Then said I, Lo, I come: in the volume of the book it is written of me,* ^{8} *I delight to do thy will, O my God: yea, thy law is within my heart.*

There are quite a lot of debates surrounding the wordings of verse 6. In Hebrews 10:5, which is based on the Septuagint, it is rendered:

"Sacrifice and offering thou wouldest not, but a body hast thou prepared me."

Many attempts have been made to try to reconcile the difference. In Psalm 40, the words are *"mine ears hast thou opened"*; whereas in Hebrews 10, the words are "a body thou hast prepared me."

What is the connection between the two versions? Well, in the first place we must understand that the writer of Hebrews did not make a mistake. He was writing under the inspiration of the Holy Spirit.

The fact is: the writer of Hebrews did not quote the Psalm word for word, but captured its essence very accurately. The man who would have his ear opened, pierced or bored, was a bondslave who had willingly submitted himself to the perpetual lordship of his master. This was in accordance to the Mosaic Law, in regard to a slave who was pleased to dwell with his master (Ex 21:6).

The point is: our Lord, who is the eternal Son of God, took the form of a servant, in order to die for us. For this purpose, He was given a body. Or to put it in another way: a body was prepared for Him that His ear might, as it were, be opened.

Christ and His redemptive work are spoken about throughout the Old Testament—from Genesis to Malachi. When our Lord was finally born in the fullness of time, it was without any reluctance whatsoever. In fact, He delighted to do the Father's will. The fulfilment of the word of God was His joy.

And He delighted to be able to proclaim righteousness to His people. He came to procure righteousness for us, even a righteousness that is acceptable to God. So, He preached righteousness during His earthly ministry; and so He preaches righteousness through His Spirit working through His ministers, verse 9:

^{9} *I have preached righteousness in the great congregation: lo, I have not refrained my lips, O LORD, thou knowest.* ^{10} *I have not hid thy righteousness within my heart; I have declared thy faithfulness and thy salvation: I have not concealed thy lovingkindness and thy truth from the great congregation.*

It is because our Lord kept His promise that today we can enjoy the love and compassion of God as His children. It was, after all, through the preaching of the Gospel that we knew about God's righteousness, faithfulness, lovingkindness, truth and salvation.

These are the things that make us what we are as believers. These are the things we will continue to talk and sing about for all eternity as part of the great congregation of Christ.

But before the celebration, there was a hurdle of great suffering, which must be crossed by prayer.

Consider the Lord's prayer:

3. The Prayer

[11] *Withhold not thou thy tender mercies from me, O LORD: let thy lovingkindness and thy truth continually preserve me.*

As our Lord was suffering on the cross, in order to share with us something of the lovingkindness and truth of God, He was Himself in need of the same goodness of God.

This was especially so, as He was facing the effects of sin, having taken our guilt upon Himself.

[12] *For innumerable evils have compassed me about: mine iniquities have taken hold upon me, so that I am not able to look up; they are more than the hairs of mine head: therefore my heart faileth me.*

Our Lord had no sin. He needed not to feel the burden of guilt. Nor need He experience the effects of sin. But He was our representative. Our guilt was credited to Him. He had more arrows of guilt piercing His heart than any man in the history of mankind. As a result, God's wrath was heaped upon His head and at the same time, He faced the torment of men which all result from sin in general.

That does not mean that His tormentors were justified in what they did. But our Lord would not take vengeance into His own hands. He committed Himself to the Father and asked Him to deal with them:

He sought the Father's deliverance:

[13] *Be pleased, O LORD, to deliver me: O LORD, make haste to help me.*

Though He delighted to do the Father's will, our Lord did not hesitate to pour out His heart's desire to be delivered.

He sought the Father's justice against His enemies:

[14] *Let them be ashamed and confounded together that seek after my soul to destroy it; let them be driven backward and put to shame that wish me evil.* [15] *Let them be desolate for a reward of their shame that say unto me, Aha, aha.*

The enemies of Christ are the enemies of God. He is not ashamed to ask God to judge them.

On the other hand, however, He sought the Father's blessings upon those who seek Him:

[16] *Let all those that seek thee rejoice and be glad in thee: let such as love thy salvation say continually, The LORD be magnified.*

He came precisely for those who seek the LORD. He was thinking about us in His darkest hour.

Verse 17:

[17] *But I am poor and needy; yet the Lord thinketh upon me: thou art my help and my*

deliverer; make no tarrying, O my God.

Our Lord, who is infinitely rich, became poor, and needy, in order that He might represent us, and have compassion towards us.

But we must not imagine that He suffered stoically, or that it was a breeze for Him. No, no; as the God-Man our Lord would have suffered immensely through those hours of pain and misery on the cross.

Yet, even as He suffered, He never lost sight of the purpose for which He went to the cross. He went to the cross for us. He suffered for us. He died for us.

He could have called upon a million angels to bring Him down from the cross. But He would not. Being truly human, the Lord would have desired to be delivered from the pain He had to endure, but His constant prayer unto the Father must have been, "Yet not my will, but thy will be done."

Conclusion

Psalm 40 brings us to the cross in a theological and practical way.

Theologically, we see the purpose of the Lord's going to the cross. We see that it was not an accident in history, but something that God had planned from all eternity, and had spoken about from the beginning of history. We see from the volume of the Scriptures, that God's people, searching the Scriptures, had been waiting for His incarnation for centuries. We see that Christ our Lord took on our nature, in order to suffer and die for our sin, that we might enjoy fellowship with God.

Practically, we see the pain and sorrow that our Lord experienced; and how despite that, He was thinking about us. Through this Psalm we are brought face to face with our Lord in His deep compassion and love towards us.

Let us sing and meditate on this Psalm with a prayer in our hearts that the Lord will increase our love for Him. Let us also learn to use this Psalm at times when we ourselves experience the sinking feeling of being trapped in the mire. Let us look to the LORD for deliverance, with eyes of faith believing that He does all things right, and will hear our cry in His compassion: for our Lord went through much worse than us and was delivered for our justification. Amen.

Psalm 41:
The Righteous One's
Meekness in Betrayal

Psalm 41 appears to be another song written by David at a time of bodily afflictions (cf. Ps 38, 39). During those days, his enemies took advantage of his situation not only to wish him ill, but also to create trouble for him. Amongst all those who were his enemies was one whom he had regarded as familiar friend. Could it have been Ahithophel? Could it be that the uprising of Absalom took place at a time when David was also suffering some illness? We do not know. But it must have been an extremely vexing time for David. Nevertheless, he trusted in the justice and mercy of the LORD, believing that the LORD would protect and restore him.

Is this Psalm Messianic? Some deny that this Psalm can be Messianic because of verse 4: *"I said, LORD, be merciful unto me: heal my soul; for I have sinned against thee."* Our Lord could not have taken these words upon his lips, it is suggested.

However, we must not forget that in the night the Lord Jesus was betrayed, when He was celebrating His last Passover meal with His disciples, our Lord quoted verse 9 of this very Psalm. He said to the disciples:

> "I speak not of you all: I know whom I have chosen: but that the scripture may be fulfilled, He that eateth bread with me hath lifted up his heel against me" (Jn 13:18).

The Lord is referring to Judas Iscariot who is about to betray Him. And notice how He quotes the verse! "That the scripture may be fulfilled," He says. Essentially, what that means is that the Lord is not simply applying or adapting the Psalm to His own situation. He is suggesting that the Psalm is ultimately prophetic about His experience. David was but a type, whereas Christ is the substance. The suffering speaker in the Psalm is ultimately Christ. Verse 9 is ultimately referring to Judas Iscariot, whoever the type might have been.

With this in mind, let us look at this Psalm again and see how it fits so beautifully into the experience of the Lord under the theme *"The Righteous One's Meekness in Betrayal."*

There are three parts in this Psalm:

1. v. 1-4   The Blessedness of the Merciful
2. v. 5-9   The Wretchedness of the Traitor
3. v. 10-13   The Favour of the LORD

1. The Blessedness of
the Merciful

¹ Blessed is he that considereth the poor: the LORD will deliver him in time of trouble. ² The LORD will preserve him, and keep him alive; and he shall be blessed upon the earth: and thou wilt not deliver him unto the will of his enemies.

May not these words be summarised in the 5th beatitude of our Lord, "Blessed are the merciful: for they shall obtain mercy" (Mt 5:7)? Are the two statements not essentially synonymous?

The time of trouble is the Day of the Wrath of the Lamb and all the days of judgement that are precursors to it. But that day will also be a day when the merciful will obtain mercy and be delivered out of trouble. Did not our Lord tell us in His parable of the Sheep and Goat that He would say unto His sheep in that day:

"Come, ye blessed of my Father, inherit the kingdom prepared for you... For I was an hungred, and ye gave me meat: I was thirsty, and ye gave me drink: I was a stranger, and ye took me in: Naked, and ye clothed me: I was sick, and ye visited me..." (Mt 25:34b-36)?

Truly blessed are the merciful. But those who are merciful, do not need to wait till that Great Day of trouble to experience God's mercy, for our Lord has promised, verse 3:

³ *The LORD will strengthen him upon the bed of languishing: thou wilt make all his bed in his sickness.*

Those who are merciful can expect to experience the LORD's mercy in His providence when they are afflicted. They can expect to find strength in the LORD, emotionally and spiritually, and often times, even physically. This, I believe, is the experience of many a child of God.

God does not promise us exemptions from sorrows and sickness; but He has promised us strength and comfort to carry us through our trials. Those who have themselves been the LORD's instrument of mercy towards others in their hour of need, will inevitably experience a reciprocation of their kindness. This is God's promise. And this is also our experience. We experience mercy and comfort especially from those who have been helped by our ministry.

But our Lord, who is most merciful, ironically, experienced the least mercy through reciprocation. Those whom He showed kindness to, abandoned Him in His hour of need.

Why did this happen? This happened because He came to bear our sin; and He must bear it alone.

⁴ *I said, LORD, be merciful unto me: heal my soul; for I have sinned against thee.*

Our Lord had no sin: therefore, when He takes these words in His holy lips, He must be understood as confessing not His own sin, but the sin of those He came to represent.

Because He is bearing the sin of His people, He is in need of mercy from the Father. No one else will show mercy to Him. They have forsaken Him. And many of them are ready to render evil for good instead.

Consider their wretchedness...

2. The Wretchedness of the Traitor

⁵ *Mine enemies speak evil of me, When shall he die, and his name perish?*

Did not this happen exactly as described in our Lord's ministry? While He was doing good, His enemies were speaking evil of Him behind His back and before Him. "Thou hast a devil," they accused Him over and over again (Jn 7:20; 8:48 etc).

So they were constantly wishing He would die and His name would perish with Him. We are told of how the chief priests and Pharisees gathered together to discuss what they should do to the Lord. He was doing many miracles, they acknowledged. But they hated it that a multitude of people was following. They could not wait to get rid of Him (cf. Jn 11:47; 12:19).

So they kept sending out spies to trap Him. Luke tells us:

"And they watched him, and sent forth spies, which should feign themselves just men, that they might take hold of his words, that so they might deliver him unto the power and authority of the governor" (Lk 20:20).

Was this not prophesied in verse 6?

> *⁶ And if he come to see me, he speaketh vanity: his heart gathereth iniquity to itself; when he goeth abroad, he telleth it. ⁷ All that hate me whisper together against me: against me do they devise my hurt. ⁸ An evil disease, say they, cleaveth fast unto him: and now that he lieth he shall rise up no more.*

Their fury against the Lord heated up more and more as the Lord approached the cross so much so that towards the end, even before they handed Him over to Pilate, they had already decided that He should die.

The high priest, Caiaphas, even pronounced:

> ...it is expedient for us, that one man should die for the people, and that the whole nation perish not" (Jn 11:49-50).

A judgement of death penalty was already determined in the minds of those who hated Him.

Their hatred for the Lord became clearer and clearer until they cast off any pretence completely.

> "*⁹ Yea, mine own familiar friend, in whom I trusted, which did eat of my bread, hath lifted up his heel against me," says our Lord.

"The Son of man goeth as it is written of him: but woe unto that man by whom the Son of man is betrayed! it had been good for that man if he had not been born" (Mt 26:24), adds the Lord.

Judas Iscariot was a familiar friend. He was appointed an apostle together with the other eleven. He travelled with them, ate with them, worshipped with them. He was trusted enough to be appointed as the treasurer of the apostolic band. But even as they sat down to enjoy the Passover meal together, he was thinking of how to betray the Lord.

He betrayed the Lord with a kiss for thirty pieces of silver.

Such was the lot of our Lord.

Very few of us will be required to endure the same kind of betrayal because of the general principle which we have seen earlier, that the merciful will experience blessedness not only in the future but in this life.

However, it is not a promise that we shall be spared from such wicked betrayals. And so, if the LORD deems it necessary that you should experience what our Lord experienced, remember that "the disciple is not above his master, nor the servant above his lord" (Mt 10:24). "If the world hate you, ye know that it hated me before it hated you," reminds our Lord (Jn 15:18).

So dear child of God, if you experience betrayal from friends or foes, remember the Lord's example of meekness. And remind yourself of the Father's mercy as our Lord did in the final section of this Psalm.

3. The Favour of the LORD

¹⁰ But thou, O LORD, be merciful unto me, and raise me up, that I may requite them. ¹¹ By this I know that thou favourest me, because mine enemy doth not triumph over me.

The Lord knew that He was headed for the cross. He warned His disciples about it. He knew that when His familiar friend lifted up His heel against Him, He would have to die.

But the justice and mercy of God demanded that our Lord would not remain in the grave. He must arise from the dead for the justification of His saints. He must arise that He might sit in judgement against His foes who are the enemies of God.

So He prays, *"raise me up, that I may requite them."* Raise me up that I may know *"that thou favourest me."*

All of God's providential dealings with His saints in this life are designed to give them substance for praise and gratitude. Even the trials that God sends their way, together with the deliverances packaged in, are designed for them to experience God's favour—so that for all eternity they may have reasons to rejoice in Him.

Our Lord's suffering and victory served the same purpose. Through the experience of deliverance, our Lord, the God-Man learned experimentally of the Father's favour.

This then is one of the reasons why God appoints suffering for us. God sends trials into our lives for our good. These trials will never harm us. In fact, He upholds us through our trials, as He did to our Lord who testifies finally:

12 And as for me, thou upholdest me in mine integrity, and settest me before thy face for ever. 13 Blessed be the LORD God of Israel from everlasting, and to everlasting. Amen, and Amen.

Every step of the way, our Lord experienced the favour of the Father. Through the suffering which He must endure for our sakes, the Father upholds Him. When His atonement was accomplished, the Father raised Him up and seated Him at His right hand, one day to return as King and Judge over all the world—to execute justice upon His enemies, and the enemies of His people.

Conclusion

What a Psalm! As our Lord experienced the favour of His Father through the persecution and betrayal that He suffered on our behalf, may we also experience His favour.

At least, let us remember that dark providences in our lives are no indication of a withholding of God's favour and love. On the contrary, they are often sent in order that we may for all eternity sing of His love. His favour and love will be the theme of our song for all eternity. May we learn to sing it today—in the words of such a Psalm as this! Let us sing it, in remembrance of what our Lord went through for us. Let us sing it, at times when we suffer similar betrayal or persecution, understanding that Christ our Lord was tempted like as we are, yet without sin. Amen.

Psalm 42:
The Righteous One
in His Weariness,
Looking up

Psalm 42 was, no doubt, written by David under the inspiration of the Holy Spirit, at a time when he was facing severe discouragement and perhaps depression.

Commentators believe that David was, at this time, fleeing from his son Absalom and wandering in the wilderness beyond Jordan (cf. v. 6; 2 Sam 15-18).

It is, as such, a Psalm that is particularly comforting and instructive for those who are suffering spiritual depression or doldrums.

Depression and discouragement is something that is very real in the life of Christians. In fact, it is part of fallen human nature to experience depression. Yes, when we are perfected in glory we shall no more feel down, but while we live in this fallen world, we will experience it.

Is it sinful to feel depressed? Well, I do not think so. A failure to trust in God is sin. But it is possible to feel depressed while still trusting in God. To trust in God is an act of the will, on the basis of knowledge. Depression and discouragement has to do with emotions or feelings.

It is important for us to understand that it is no sin to be depressed or to be discouraged. One of the worst thing to do to a depressed or discouraged believer is to admonish him for his sin—whether of feeling depressed or of something that you perceive may be leading to the depression. It will exacerbate his feelings of guilt. He may not be guilty, but if you admonish him, he will certainly feel a terrible sense of guilt.

There is, of course, a place for loving admonishment, but it must be done with gentleness and at the right time.

And so dear brother or sister in the Lord, if you are feeling discouraged or depressed, you must remember that you are not alone and the LORD has not forsaken you.

You are amongst the many, many godly believers who have at some point experienced discouragement and depression. I think of Moses, David, Elijah and Jeremiah. I think of Luther, Owens, Edwards, Brainerd, Timothy Rogers, Spurgeon, Lloyd-Jones, etc. Yea, I think of the Lord Himself.

Indeed, I believe that this Psalm is not only about David. David wrote in the Spirit of Christ, so that what is recorded in this Psalm provides us with a glimpse of the Lord's thoughts and emotions during His incarnation. I believe Andrew Bonar is right in calling this Psalm: "*The Righteous One in His Weariness, Looking up to the Father for Refreshment.*" It is given by the Righteous One, that those who are righteous in Him may sing with Him: not only to experience fellowship in His sufferings; but also to encourage themselves, and each other in their discouragement.

This Psalm has two stanzas, each ending with the refrain, "*Why art thou cast down, O my soul &c*" (v. 5 and 11). It is believed that Psalm 43 is actually the third stanza of Psalm 42, because it ends with the same refrain.

If this is so, then this is a three-part Psalm. The first part, verses 1-5 contains an outpouring of the heart in regard to its longing and discouragements; the second part, verses 6-11 contains an outpouring of the heart in regard to the sorrows and confusion that it is experiencing. Psalm 43, on the other hand, contains an outpouring of the heart's desire unto the LORD to send forth His light to dispel the darkness of the soul.

Nevertheless, our Worshipper-in-Chief has deemed it fit that the two Psalms should be arranged separately. Thus, it behoves us to study them separately. Let us, therefore, consider first, Psalm 42, which we may outline as follows:

1. v. 1-5   An Outpouring of Longing and Exasperation

2. v. 6-11   An Outpouring of Sorrow and Confusion

1. An Outpouring of Longing
& Exasperation

¹ As the hart panteth after the water brooks, so panteth my soul after thee, O God. ² My soul thirsteth for God, for the living God: when shall I come and appear before God?

A hart is a deer. But the picture painted here is not an idyllic one, of a deer nibbling quietly by the lakeside in the misty cool of the morning. Think, rather, of a deer being hunted and running for its life. It is thirsty. It needs a drink badly, but there is no water to be found. It longs for water to quench its thirst.

David was being pursued by his son Absalom. But what was his longing? Not simply safety! His longing was God, or a sense of God's favourable presence.

Our Lord, especially, experienced the same longing as He was arrested and driven to the cross.

It is the Passover season. It should be a time of joyous religious observance and celebrations. But our Lord is bound, and deprived of freedom to appear before the Father with the people.

And moreover, He is bearing the sin of His people. The shadow of God's wrath cast over His soul is lengthening by the minute.

Our Lord is feeling depressed and discouraged. His divine will is one and the same as that of His Father and the Spirit, so there can be no discord. But His human will is another matter. He has no sin, and therefore, His human will is always in concert with, and acquiesces with His divine will. But being fully man, His human will cannot be dichotomised from the emotions He feels. Emotions, *per se*, have no moral quality, but they can tempt. This is why our Lord said to the Father in the Garden of Gethsemane, "not my will, but thine, be done" (Lk 22:42). His emotions are real. His tears, no doubt, flowed freely.

³ My tears have been my meat day and night, while they continually say unto me, Where is thy God?

Over and over again, our Lord was ridiculed: "If thou be the Son of God" save thyself, come down from the cross (Mt 27:40). "He saved others; himself he cannot save" (Mk 15:31). "He trusted on the LORD that he would deliver him: let him deliver him, seeing he delighted in him" (Ps 22:8).

"Where is thy God?" they taunt. Tears cannot wash away the exasperation of hearing God's name blasphemed, and not being able to defend it.

Our Lord longs for the vindication of God's name, and He longs to be able to worship the Father with the people who fear and love Him.

This feeling of longing and exasperation is intensified each time He recalls the blessedness of joyful praise and worship with the multitude—such as during his triumphal entrance into Jerusalem when a multitude welcomed Him by singing "Hosanna to the Son of David" (Mt 21:9).

> [4] *When I remember these things, I pour out my soul in me: for I had gone with the multitude, I went with them to the house of God, with the voice of joy and praise, with a multitude that kept holyday.*

That is to say: My heart overflows with emotion each time I recall the joy of worship with God's faithful people.

Have you ever felt this way, dear child of God? Perhaps you were prevented from joining God's people in worship due to illness or circumstance. Perhaps you are feeling very low and have lost the joy of worship. Tell your soul that the Lord felt the same longing and exasperation.

And talk to your soul as our Lord does, verse 5:

> [5] *Why art thou cast down, O my soul? and why art thou disquieted in me? hope thou in God: for I shall yet praise him for the help of his countenance.*

The child of God does not need to be downcast. Our hearts can be at peace. Raw emotions will arise, rather inexplicably, to cause us to feel discouraged and depressed. Often we cannot help when sad feelings overwhelm us. But we can help our souls by talking to our souls, and exhorting ourselves to continue to hope in God, and to look forward to the day when we shall yet worship the Lord joyfully, with the multitude who keep holy day. And that day will, surely, come—sooner or later.

2. An Outpouring of Sorrow & Confusion

> [6] *O my God, my soul is cast down within me: therefore will I remember thee from the land of Jordan, and of the Hermonites, from the hill Mizar.* [7] *Deep calleth unto deep at the noise of thy waterspouts: all thy waves and thy billows are gone over me.*

David was deep in the woods, hiding at the base of a waterfall in the land of Jordan, and of the Hermonites from the hill Mizar. As he heard the roaring noise of the water cascading down the face of the rock, and saw wave after wave of water and the billows or breakers rushing down the brook, he found expression for the pain that he was feeling.

His heart was full of confusion. There was a roaring in his soul. And wave after wave of sorrow was sweeping over his soul.

Our Lord feels the same, only more intensely, as He is driven to the cross. He is a man of sorrow. He is exasperated.

But He does not lose sight of His Father. Not once! He knows that behind the dark cloud is a loving Father.

> [8] *Yet the LORD will command his lovingkindness in the daytime, and in the night his song shall be with me, and my prayer unto the God of my life.* [9] *I will say unto God my rock, Why hast thou forgotten me? why go I mourning because of the oppression of the enemy?*

Our Lord knows the answer to His question, of course. He came to do His Father's will. He came to be our sin-bearer. This is why He must go mourning because of the oppression of the enemy. It must be so. In the volume of the book it is written of Him that it must be so. The Shepherd must be smitten that the Father's hand of blessing may be turned upon the lambs.

But sad feelings are inexplicable. And it is aggravated by what others say, however untrue they may be:

10 *As with a sword in my bones, mine enemies reproach me; while they say daily unto me, Where is thy God?*

Anyone who has felt depressed or discouraged would have experienced this. Here we are dealing with sorrows and discouragement, and there they are stabbing us with sharp words, thrusting their sword of cutting words between our ribs and twisting it.

I remember the experience many times. Many times, for me, it has to do with preaching. I struggle to be clear and faithful, and I get discouraged because I see very little result. Then comes someone who has an axe to grind. What does he tell me? "I have never benefited from a single of your sermons," he says. "I was just tolerating all this time!"

Oh how that felt like a stab and a twist in the heart!

Our Lord felt it more keenly than any of His servants could ever feel. But for Him it was always the taunting question: "Where is thy God?" that did it.

The reason is obvious. He is the eternal Son of God, only begotten and beloved of the Father. But because He is bearing our sin, His sense of the Father's favour is fading by the hour as He approaches the darkness of the cross.

It has to be so because our Lord must experience the full brunt of the Father's wrath for our sin. He must come to the point where He will have to endure the full wrath of God against our sin. He must taste hell on our behalf. Hell is not the absence of God. Hell is hell because God is there in His perfect wrath.

Our Lord would have to endure the darkness of the Father's countenance during those three hours of darkness when even the sun refused to shine.

During the three hours, the words of His tormentors, "*Where is thy God?*", no doubt, played itself over and over again in His soul, threatening to drive Him to despair—so that despite His faith in His Father, the feelings of being forsaken grew more and more intense.

It is no wonder that at the end of the three hours, our Lord cried out: "My God, my God, why hast thou forsaken me?"

Now, we must make no mistake. Our Lord was not just feeling that the Father had forsaken Him. The wrath of God that He experienced was real, just as the pains of hell will be real for all who remain unrepentant.

But our Lord knew and believed that the Father would receive Him back again once the sacrifice was completed. Never did our Lord doubt His Father. Doubt is sin. Our Lord had no sin. He never doubted.

But equally real is our Lord's feelings of sorrow and confusion. It is to give expressions to these feelings that our Lord would have us sing these words.

And it is to address these feelings of sorrow that our Lord asks again:

> [11] *Why art thou cast down, O my soul? and why art thou disquieted within me? hope thou in God: for I shall yet praise him, who is the health of my countenance, and my God.*

There is no reason to be cast down. I must hope in God, for it is a fact that I will yet praise the LORD. It is a fact that I will again experience the nourishing grace of the Father's love.

The Father will never leave me nor forsake me. He is a faithful God who will keep His promises.

Conclusion

What is this Psalm to you, dear child of God?

This Psalm has been a tremendous encouragement to me. It is so, firstly, because it assures me that our Lord experienced the feelings of deep sorrow, and therefore understands the depressive and discouraging feelings that I am sometimes overwhelmed with.

It is so, secondly, because I find the way that the Lord dealt with the feelings of discouragement most helpful. I will remember the next time I feel discouraged or depressed to talk to my soul as our Lord did.

Finally, this Psalm is tremendously encouraging to me because when I sing it, I am again brought to a wholehearted realisation of how much my Lord went through for me, and therefore how much He loves me. Amen.

Psalm 43:
The Righteous One
Anticipating the Father's
Heavenly Smile

Many commentators, modern and ancient, believe that Psalm 43 was originally part of Psalm 42. This may be so, or they may be two separate Psalms as reflected in our Bible. But whatever the case may be, notice that they are indeed related for they share a common refrain: *"Why art thou cast down, O my soul &c."*

This refrain is found in Psalm 42, verses 5 and 11. It is also the concluding verse of Psalm 43:

> [5] *Why art thou cast down, O my soul? and why art thou disquieted within me? hope in God: for I shall yet praise him, who is the health of my countenance, and my God.*

We saw that Psalm 42 was, no doubt, written by David under the inspiration of the Holy Spirit at a time when he was facing severe discouragement and perhaps depression. Many commentators believe that David was at this time fleeing from his son Absalom and wandering in the wilderness beyond Jordan (cf. v. 5; 2 Sam 15-18). We can imagine the tears, sense of loss, sorrow, pain, and confusion that must have overwhelmed David's soul.

But David's experience is not unique to him. All through the ages, the sons of man have experienced the same kind of discouragement though their circumstances might be different.

In fact, one man, the Son of Man, the Lord Jesus Christ, experienced the sorrows that David wrote about in a way that David could not have imagined. Indeed, we have little doubt that David wrote under the inspiration of the Spirit of Christ in a way that gave prophetic expression to the sorrows and meditations of Christ, our Lord, as He suffered for our sins.

In this way, this Psalm contributes to our understanding of the thought life and inner struggles of our Saviour.

But this Psalm must not only be used in an intellectual way. It is appointed by Christ for us to sing with Him: not only to experience fellowship in His suffering; but also to encourage ourselves, and each other in our trials. What is true of Psalm 42 is also true of Psalm 43.

In the first five verses of Psalm 42, we see how we are to pour out our hearts and talk not just to God, but to our soul about our feelings in times of despondency.

From verses 6-11, we learn that we must speak to God and to our own soul about why we are feeling what we feel. We learn to question our soul in a way that will make us realise how unreasonable it is for us to continue to feel despondent.

In Psalm 43, on the other hand, we are taught to pour out our hearts unto the Lord to send forth His light to dispel the darkness of our soul. We may use the title that Andrew Bonar proposes, namely, *"The Righteous One Claiming His Right to Full Refreshment."* Or we could call it, *"The Righteous One Anticipating the Father's Heavenly Smile."*

This Psalm has three parts:

1. v. 1-2   A Plea for Vindication
2. v. 3-4   A Petition to Send Forth the Light and the Truth
3. v. 5   A Refrain to Exhort Self

1. A Plea for Vindication

¹ Judge me, O God, and plead my cause against an ungodly nation: O deliver me from the deceitful and unjust man.

David, as we saw, was probably running away from Absalom. Perhaps he felt that the whole nation also turned against him for they had enthroned Absalom to be king.

In the case of our Lord, the unjust and deceitful man is not Absalom, but Judas Iscariot, the traitor. And indeed the ungodly nation had turned against Him. David would return to the throne when Absalom died; but the greater David was banished from the nation. The kingdom was taken away from them and given to the Gentiles, just as Hosea prophesied:

"²³ And I will sow her unto me in the earth; and I will have mercy upon her that had not obtained mercy; and I will say to them which were not my people, Thou art my people; and they shall say, Thou art my God" (Hos 2:23).

So as David appealed to God to come to his defence against the unjust man and ungodly nation, our Lord cried the same to His Father.

But on what basis?

² For thou art the God of my strength: why dost thou cast me off? why go I mourning because of the oppression of the enemy?

On the basis that you are the God of my strength! I have committed myself to your care as my stronghold, and I know that you are my strength. In you, I live, and move, and have my being. All that happens to me is in your sovereign hand. You are in control. When the traitor betrayed me, when the nation rejected me, it was not without your permission and sovereign foreordination.

My head tells me that Thou will never leave me nor forsake me, but my heart troubles me. I know it is irrational, but the feeling of being abandoned troubles me. I feel cast away and forsaken. I feel a sense of indignation that I have to go about mourning because of the oppression of the enemy when Thou art sovereign and just.

Dear child of God, have you not often felt the same way? It is no sin to feel this way. David grappled with such feelings; and so did our Lord who was tempted in all points like as we are, yet without sin.

What shall we do when we feel this way? Let us learn to petition the Father.

2. A Petition to Send Forth the Light & the Truth

³ O send out thy light and thy truth: let them lead me; let them bring me unto thy holy hill, and to thy tabernacles.

What a beautiful prayer! *"Send out thy light and thy truth!"* But what does it mean?

At first sight, it appears to be a prayer for God to send His illuminating Spirit and His word to lead us in the way we should go. However, this does not appear to be what the light and the truth refer to in the context. The context suggests, rather, that the "light" refers to light of God's countenance of favour; whereas the "truth" refers to God's faithfulness in keeping his promises.[20] This is a prayer for God's favour and an assurance of His faithfulness.

The depressed soul is shrouded in darkness. It is discouraged. It feels quite lost. What does it need most? It needs the light of God's countenance. It needs to see through eyes of faith, God's heavenly smile. It needs also the assurance that God's promises are true. It needs to be reminded that God is faithful and will keep His word.

God's light and truth alone will meet the deepest desire of the child of God—to worship and enjoy God.

> [3] *O send out thy light and thy truth: let them lead me; let them bring me unto thy holy hill, and to thy tabernacles.* [4] *Then will I go unto the altar of God, unto God my exceeding joy: yea, upon the harp will I praise thee, O God my God.*

The holy hill and the tabernacle are symbolic of joyful congregational worship of God's people. God's people enjoy God not only in informal worship, but in formal worship. Indeed, formal public congregational worship should be the epitome of our enjoyment of God!

It is there we must especially offer the incense of prayer at the altar. It is there we must offer the calves of our lips in corporate praise. It is there we must employ our harps, for it is there we must strum our heartstrings in harmony with God's people. It is there we may have a foretaste of the eternal worship in heaven, even heaven, which Christ our Lord was, no doubt, anticipating when He took up those words in His lips. It is there that our Lord would especially have us feel as He felt, as we sing His song in union with Him.

When the child of God is facing discouragement and spiritual depression, such an experience of enjoying God is one of his chiefest desires. This is what makes him cry out: "*O send forth thy light and thy truth...*"

But alas, the answer does not come immediately. Indeed, very often those who are suffering deep depression are unable to pray, and are sometimes even confused as to what they desire.

At such times, let us learn to talk to ourselves as the Psalmist does in the final refrain of this Psalm.

3. A Refrain to Exhort Self

[5] *Why art thou cast down, O my soul? and why art thou disquieted within me? hope in God: for I shall yet praise him, who is the health of my countenance, and my God.*

Notice the difference between talking *to* yourself, and talking *with* yourself. When you talk with yourself, you are reasoning in yourself. This is not a good thing to do when you are feeling discouraged and depressed. Often, the more you talk *with* yourself, the more discouraged and tired you will feel.

No, no; you must talk *to* yourself. You must exhort yourself with the authority of God's truth.

This is why our Lord would have us sing to ourselves: "*Why art thou cast down, O my soul?*"

---

[20] "The term *light* is to be understood as denoting *favour;* for as adversities not only obscure the face of God, but also overcast the heavens, as it were, with clouds and fogs, so also, when we enjoy the divine blessing which makes rich, it is like the cheerful light of a serene day shining around us; or rather the light of life, dispelling all that thick obscurity which overwhelmed us in sorrow.... He adds *truth,* because he expected this light only from the promises of God" (Calvin, *comm. in loc*).

This is not a question that expects an answer. It is a rhetorical question that exclaims: "You have no reason to be cast down! You do not need to be disquieted. You must hope in God."

Look to Him. He is a faithful God. For a season you have come under a frowning providence; but God has promised He will never leave you nor forsake you.

The Father did for a moment, as it were, turned His face from His Son as He bore our sin on the cross. But the darkness has turned to light. The Sun of Righteousness has risen with healings in His wings. He is exalted on high. He is sending forth His healing rays. He laid down His life for you. Shall He abandon you? Shall the Father and His Spirit abandon you, when the Son has redeemed you with His blood?

No, no; God will never forsake you. He will restore you. He will bring you back unto the place of the joy of your salvation. Look at how the Psalm ends:

...for I SHALL yet praise him, who is the health of my countenance, and my God.

It is not "For I *may* yet praise him." It is not even, "For *I think I shall* yet praise him." It is "I *shall* yet praise him..." He is the health of my countenance and my God.

He will lift me up. He has never failed me. He understands my struggles though man may not. He has proven Himself faithful. He will yet prove Himself faithful.

As the Father never ceases to love His Son when He turned His face from Him, so I know that the Father still loves me and will restore me to the joy of communion with Him.

He will plead my cause. He will send forth His light and His truth. I shall yet praise Him who is the health of my countenance and my God.

Conclusion

May the Lord use these words to lift up the spirit of any one of us who may be discouraged and depressed as was David, and as was our Lord! Amen.

Psalm 44:
The Righteous One
Crying with His
Slaughtered Sheep

I believe all the Psalms are Christological. They may all be spoken of as the "word of Christ" (Col 3:16). However, not every Psalm is about the experience of Christ like Psalm 22. Some of the psalms are given by Christ for His Church that she may sing about Him whether in the second or third person. Psalm 45, or at least the first part thereof, is a case in point. But there are other psalms which focus on the experience of the Church with Christ as her Head. Psalm 44 is one such psalms. It may be entitled *"The Righteous One Crying with His Slaughtered Sheep."*

You will see a reference to the slaughter of the sheep in verses 11 and 22. And you will see the Righteous One speaking or singing in His capacity as Head of the Church in verses 4, 6, and 15, where first person singular pronouns are used.

This is a psalm about the sufferings of the Church. We do not really know the occasion for which it was first written. But we know that it is included in the hymnbook of the Shepherd so that He may sing with His flock, especially when they find themselves being, as it were, slaughtered like sheep.

This psalm has four parts:

1. v. 1-8   Past Blessings
2. v. 9-16   Present Crisis
3. v. 17-22   Ponderous Reflections
4. v. 23-26   Plea for Deliverance

1. Past Blessings
(v. 1-8)

Whenever we are troubled, whether as individuals or as a church, it is good for us not to focus all our attention on the present difficulties. It is good for us, whether in prayer or in contemplation, to diversify our attention.

In particular, it is good for us to recall the LORD's past goodness towards us. This is what we are led to do as we begin to meditate on, or sing this Psalm:

> [1] *We have heard with our ears, O God, our fathers have told us, what work thou didst in their days, in the times of old.*

What did God do for His people in the past? He redeemed them from Egypt. He led them to the Promised Land. He drove out the Canaanites from the Land (v. 2).

The Israelites were as grasshoppers in their own eyes when they first went to spy out the land. It is clear that they could not have possessed the land had the LORD left them to fight for themselves. It is clear that it was neither their arm, nor their sword, that brought them victory. It was the "arm" and "right hand" of the Lord, and the light of His countenance, or His favour and blessing, that gave them victory (v. 3).

But the history of God's deliverance must not be left in the history books. It must be translated to present assurance and future hope.

So we are given to sing in union with Christ our Head, verse 4:

> [4] Thou art my King, O God: command deliverances for Jacob. [5] Through thee will we push down our enemies: through thy name will we tread them under that rise up against us.

Christ, the Prince of Peace, is the King of the Church; yet God Triune, represented by the Father is, as it were, King overall (1 Cor 15:25-28). Thus, it is perfectly meaningful for our King to address God as King; and to plead with Him to command deliverances for Jacob. Who is Jacob but Christ and His Church!

In union with our Head, we must ride upon past deliverances to trust God rather than our own abilities, or the means we have on hand. Our Head has appointed means: whether they be weapons of war, or means of grace for use in our battles. But these are not what ultimately save us. Thus, we are given to sing with our Head: "*I will not trust in my bow, neither shall my sword save me*" (v. 6). Instead, we must boast in the LORD all day long (v. 8)—not vacillating between doubt and faith, but constantly looking to the LORD, trusting Him. He has done well; He is perfectly able to do it again.

The battles we have to fight today can be very sore and discouraging; but let us remember how God had, for Christ's sake, given victory to our fathers in the faith, in days past, and perhaps even in our own life. Let us remember, as we meditate on this Psalm, that we are more than conquerors in Christ.

But that does not mean that we should not think, or talk about the present crisis.

2. Present Crisis
(v. 9-16)

It is good to talk. It is important to talk about the crisis we are facing. But it is important not just to talk, but to speak of them in prayer, with a right perspective. What is the right perspective?

Notice how it shows itself in the Lord's statement of prayer beginning at verse 9:

> [9] But thou hast cast off, and put us to shame; and goest not forth with our armies.

> [10] Thou makest us to turn back from the enemy...

> [11] Thou hast given us like sheep appointed for meat; and hast scattered us among the heathen.

> [12] Thou sellest thy people for nought...

> [13] Thou makest us a reproach to our neighbours...

> [14] Thou makest us a byword among the heathen...

Do you see the point? Things do not happen by chance or by some bad luck. They happen according to God's sovereign will and providential hand.

When bad things happen to us: never, never forget that God's hand is in it. Satan may have a hand in it—by permission of the LORD. Circumstances may play a part. But ultimately, whatever happens is in the hand of God. We must not forget that. We must not neglect that in our prayers.

And neither should we forget that Christ, our Head, is going through every trial with us. "Saul, Saul, why persecutes thou me?" asked our Lord (Acts 9:4, etc) when Saul was persecuting the Church. We are never alone in our trials. What we experience as a church, Christ as our Head feels personally, verses 15-16:

[15] *My confusion is continually before me, and the shame of my face hath covered me,* [16] *For the voice of him that reproacheth and blasphemeth; by reason of the enemy and avenger.*

The flock of Christ had many enemies and trials, which would have given rise to perplexities expressed in these words. The church that continues to follow after Christ in this dark and dreary time will also be faced with the same confusions.

It may be a national disaster. It may be a disappointing departure into the world of a prominent member of the church. It may be a church split, or merely dissension between brethren. It may be overt persecution by those outside the church. Whatever it may be, our Head feels with us, and would have us sing with Him to soothe our weary souls.

Oh may it be that our hearts beat with the same rhythm as our Saviour's, that we may share His indignation because of those who take advantage of the situation to blaspheme God. Oh may it be that we have faith sufficient to acknowledge that God is ultimately in control.

But for that to be so, it is good for us to consider the reasons for which God sends afflictions. This consideration is implied in the third section of this psalm, which we may entitle:

3. Ponderous Reflections
(v. 17-22)

We live in such a busy world that we often fail to pause to reflect. But reflect we must: especially when God sends trials and tribulations into our lives—whether corporately or individually.

One of the first things we must reflect on is whether the tribulation was sent because of any particular sin we have committed.

The apostle to the Hebrews says:

"For whom the Lord loveth he chasteneth, and scourgeth every son whom he receiveth" (Heb 12:6).

God, out of His love for us, will chastise us when necessary. He chastises us to cultivate the peaceable fruit of holiness for our sanctification. He does not punish true believers. Christ was punished for us. So we would not be punished again. But God does chastise us, in order that we might be holy, as He is holy.

So it is needful, as we reflect upon the hand of God, to consider how the Lord is dealing with us. What sinful attitude in me is He dealing with? Is it pride? Is it stubbornness, high-mindedness, selfishness, idolatry, laziness, covetousness, disobedience, or unbelief?

These are questions we must ask especially when God's chastisement has come upon the church as a whole.

When that happens, the faithful remnant must especially plead for the LORD's mercy. And this psalm is especially inspired for the faithful remnant to use.

This is the reason why instead of confessing that the sin of the church had occasioned the chastisement, there is a mention of their steadfastness, and the seeming injustice that had fallen upon them.

So we are given to sing:

> [17] *All this is come upon us; yet have we not forgotten thee, neither have we dealt falsely in thy covenant.* [18] *Our heart is not turned back, neither have our steps declined from thy way;* [19] *Though thou hast sore broken us in the place of dragons, and covered us with the shadow of death.*

Now, this sounds almost like a self-righteous Pharisee lamenting God's harsh chastisement. But we must understand that these words are the reflections of our covenant Head and His faithful remnant. This is not a Psalm of national confession. National confessions are found in other Psalms, such as Psalm 106, where we are given to sing:

> "We have sinned with our fathers; we have committed iniquity; we have done wickedly."

But here in Psalm 44, we are calling upon the LORD to hear the cry of the faithful remnant, of the sheep of Christ who are being slaughtered. Christ's sheep are His elect. These are the words that Christ has appointed for His faithful remnant to sing with Him unto His Father, for the sake of the Church.

Taking the cue from the Apostle Paul who quotes verse 22 in Romans 8:36, we see this Psalm as not only giving us a song to sing, but teaching us to pray:

> "Lord, we know that we have sinned as a nation, and as a church. We know that we deserve Thy chastisement. But, O Lord, wilt Thou have mercy upon thy people for the sake of Thy elect remnant—who love Thee and bear Thy name with all sincerity.

> We know that Thou dost search our hearts. We know that our sin cannot escape Thy knowledge (v. 21).

> Thou dost know, O Lord, how we love Thee, and sought to walk according to Thy covenant. We did not turn from Thy ways.

> And yet LORD, Thou hast chastised us with those who sinned.

> We know that all things work together for good to them that love Thee, and are called according to Thy purpose.

> We know that nothing shall separate us from Thy love that is in Thy Son—though we be killed all day long and are counted as sheep for the slaughter.

> For this reason, we come boldly to Thy throne..."

Yes, beloved child of God, if you love the Lord, you may come to Him boldly and pray as the psalmist teaches us. You may do so when you are made to suffer with the church. You may also do so when you undergo trials individually. You must not be afraid to claim the promises that all things will work together for your good and that nothing shall separate you from the love of God that is in Christ Jesus.

Indeed, it is with this confidence that you can plead with God according to the final stanza of this Psalm.

4. Plea for Deliverance
(v. 23-26)

[23] *Awake, why sleepest thou, O Lord? arise, cast us not off for ever.* [24] *Wherefore hidest thou thy face, and forgettest our affliction and our oppression?* [25] *For our soul is bowed down to the dust: our belly cleaveth unto the earth.* [26] *Arise for our help, and redeem us for thy*

mercies' sake.

Only someone who loves the LORD, and walks close to Him, can petition Him in prayer in such a confident manner. Does it not sound almost like a complaint that we are being forgotten despite our righteousness? Which one of us dares so to pray?

Thank God that Christ our Great High Priest qualifies to do so; and it is He who has given us these words to sing unto the Father in union with Him!

Let us, therefore, sing boldly to appeal to the Father with Him, in the words that He has given for us to use.

Conclusion

Both experience and the word of God teach us that "we must through much tribulation enter into the kingdom of God" (Acts 14:22). This is true of us, both individually and corporately, as a church. And this is why our Saviour has, by His Spirit, appointed this Psalm for us to sing with Him to give expression to our struggles, our faith, our desires and our hopes.

Thank God that we are more than conquerors through Him who loves us with an everlasting love! Thank God that He came to represent us, not only to save us, but also to lead us to worship the Father in union with Him.

For this reason, we must not sing and pray like those who have no forgiveness and no confidence. We must not sing or pray like one who is constantly watching his navel and is constantly unhappy about it. We must rather sing and pray with confidence as those who look unto Christ.

Amen.

Psalm 45:
The Righteous One's Wedding Hymn

Psalm 45 is indisputably a Messianic Psalm. In fact, in the Church of England liturgy, it is appointed for use on Christmas day!

Many commentators believe that this Psalm was written originally on the occasion of the wedding of Solomon. Did David, the sweet psalmist of Israel write it in his old age for his son? We do not know.

But one thing is certain, this Psalm is written under the inspiration of the Spirit of God as a hymn of celebration of the wedding between the Son of God and His bride, the Church.

The New Testament makes it clear that this Psalm contains the words of God the Father to God the Son. Look at Hebrews chapter 1. Here, the writer of Hebrews is comparing Christ with the angels.

He says in verse 5:

"For unto which of the angels said he at any time, Thou art my Son, this day have I begotten thee?" (Heb 1:5a)

Then in verse 8, he says:

"But unto the Son he saith, Thy throne, O God, is for ever and ever: a sceptre of righteousness is the sceptre of thy kingdom. Thou hast loved righteousness, and hated iniquity; therefore God, even thy God, hath anointed thee with the oil of gladness above thy fellows" (Heb 1:8-9).

These words are taken from Psalm 45:6-7.

So it is clear how we are to regard this Psalm when we sing it. We must not sing it as a wedding song for Solomon, but for Christ and His Bride. We may entitle it *"The Righteous One's Wedding Hymn."*

This Psalm has four parts:

1.   v. 1   Prologue
2.   v. 2-9   Praise to the Son
3.   v. 10-15   A Word to the Bride
4.   v. 16-17   Conclusion

1. Prologue

[1] *My heart is inditing a good matter: I speak of the things which I have made touching the king: my tongue is the pen of a ready writer.*[21]

---

[21] This is an enigmatic statement. Is it part of the hymn to be sung, or should we leave them out like the way we leave the title statements of the psalms when we sing them? I believe there are good reasons for us to sing them. But if so, who should we understand the "I" to be? Should we take it as the human author? If so, we are singing his feeling. But why should his feeling matter to us that we should sing it? Or should we take it as ourselves individually? If so, can we all say that our hearts are all overflowing on the subject? Perhaps, then, the best way for us to apprehend the "I" is to see it as intended to refer to Christ, by whose Spirit David writes what he wrote (1 Pet 1:10). This will be consistent with the fact that this is also the "word of Christ" (Col 3:16) given by Christ for us to sing in union with Him. Yes, the song contains the words of the Father to the Son and His bride, but they are revealed and appointed for worship by the Son, our Mediator. And there is really no contradiction or awkwardness in thinking of the Son leading us to sing a song that addresses Himself and ourselves.

The word *"inditing"* speaks of a boiling over or an overflowing.

This Psalm is about the King. And he is no ordinary king, for He is the King of kings and Lord of lords. For this reason, the heart that contemplates the subject on hand, will surely overflow with joyous and glorious thoughts.

God the Father, whose thoughts underlie this Psalm, is no doubt deeply pleased as He contemplates the wedding of His beloved Son. The Son—who received of the Father, and appointed these words for us to sing in union with Him, about Him and about ourselves— would have overflowed with joy as He contemplated the subject matter on hand. Indeed, His joy would extend beyond the moment of inspiration and the penning of these words by David. His words anticipate the overflowing joy that He experiences when His Church, as it were, sings these words in union with Him through His Spirit.

Thus, each of us taking this Psalm in our lips will also find our hearts filling up and overflowing, so that we sing with spontaneous joy about our King.

2. Praise to the Son

2 Thou art fairer than the children of men: grace is poured into thy lips: therefore God hath blessed thee for ever.

Our Lord is fairer not because of His physical appearance, for we are told by the prophet Isaiah that "his visage was so marred more than any man" (Isa 52:14). Our Lord is fairer than the children of men in the eyes of all in whose heart is the Spirit.

And indeed grace is poured into His lips. For when He first began to preach in the synagogue, we are told, "And all bare him witness, and wondered at the gracious words which proceeded out of his mouth" (Lk 4:22). Even the unbelieving officers of the Jews who were sent to trap the Lord were compelled to say: "Never man spake like this man" (Jn 7:46).

Our Lord's word is like a "two-edged sword" (Heb 4:12) proceeding from His mouth (Rev 1:16). It is, at once, meek and gracious, and quick and powerful. It comforts, convicts, converts and conquers.

So we sing, verse 3:

3 Gird thy sword upon thy thigh, O most mighty, with thy glory and thy majesty. 4 And in thy majesty ride prosperously because of truth and meekness and righteousness; and thy right hand shall teach thee terrible things. 5 Thine arrows are sharp in the heart of the king's enemies; whereby the people fall under thee.

In the vision of John, the Lord Jesus, the King of kings, is going forth upon a white horse, "conquering, and to conquer" (Rev 6:2). He has conquered. He conquered at the cross. And He is conquering and shall conquer by His word and Spirit.

And He will accomplish all that He sets out to do, for He is God, even the Son of God. So we echo the words of the Father:

6 Thy throne, O God, is for ever and ever: the sceptre of thy kingdom is a right sceptre. 7 Thou lovest righteousness, and hatest wickedness: therefore God, thy God, hath anointed thee with the oil of gladness above thy fellows.

Christ our God and King will rule forever and ever. He will rule in righteousness and justice.

Because He came to do His Father's will out of love of righteousness and hatred for wickedness, God has anointed Him with the Spirit without measure (cf. Jn 3:34).[22] And because He humbled Himself and became obedient unto death, God has highly exalted His name above every name (Phil 2:9).

His greatness and glory can hardly be described. Verse 8 describes it metaphorically with the sight and smell associated with a majestic earthly king.

Everything about Him is so great and glorious that one day when we see Him face to face, we will surely exclaim with the words of the Queen of Sheba when she saw Solomon: "Behold, the half was not told me: thy wisdom and prosperity exceedeth the fame which I heard" (1Kgs 10:7). For He who is greater than Solomon is come.

But that which redounds most greatly to the glory of our King is no doubt His Queen, who stands at His right hand arrayed in the gold of Ophir (v. 9).

Who is this Queen? Surely she is none other than His Church redeemed by His precious blood (Eph 5:25).

3. A Word to the Bride

What shall we say to the Queen? What does God our Father remind us, which our Husband wants us to rehearse with Him?

He says:

> [10] *Hearken, O daughter, and consider, and incline thine ear; forget also thine own people, and thy father's house;* [11] *So shall the king greatly desire thy beauty: for he is thy Lord; and worship thou him.*

That is to say: Let us forget about the world. And let us love our Lord, our Husband, single-mindedly. Our Lord Himself says:

> "He that loveth father or mother more than me is not worthy of me: and he that loveth son or daughter more than me is not worthy of me" (Mt 10:37).

He is not telling us to hate or disown our parents. He is teaching us to love Him above all other relations. We must give ourselves wholly unto Him as a bride gives herself wholly to her husband. We must love Him and serve Him. So shall we be His delight.

Then shall we have favour before God and men.

> [12] *And the daughter of Tyre shall be there with a gift; even the rich among the people shall intreat thy favour.*

The daughter of Tyre and the rich, I believe refers to unbelievers in the world. As the Church walks close to the Lord, the world will see and they will recognise her beauty and will be prepared to ask for her help and intercession.

If as the bride of Christ, we fail to show that we love and obey Christ, why would the world want to have anything to do with Christ?

But if we love the Lord and serve Him with all our hearts, then what a wonderful entrance we shall have into the wedding banquet of the Lamb!

> [13] *The king's daughter is all glorious within: her clothing is of wrought gold.* [14] *She shall be brought unto the king in raiment of needlework: the virgins her companions that follow*

---

[22] Notice how the doctrine of the Trinity is hinted here.

her shall be brought unto thee. [15] *With gladness and rejoicing shall they be brought: they shall enter into the king's palace.*

This beautiful picture can be very confusing until we recall the Lord's Parable of the Ten Virgins. You will realise that in the Parable, the virgins are the companions of the bride. If you like, the bride or queen represent the Church as a whole; whereas the virgins or the companions of the bride represent the individual believers.

If we would follow the Lord wholeheartedly, then what a glorious entrance it will be for every believer who seeks the Lord with us!

Then what a joy it will be for all of us in that great and glorious day of the Wedding Supper of the Lamb, as the heaven resounds with the voices of ten thousand times ten thousand, and thousands upon thousands of angels singing together:

Worthy is the Lamb that was slain to receive power, and riches, and wisdom, and strength, and honour, and glory, and blessing" (Rev 5:12).

Oh may the Lord grant us that we may be as the wise virgins individually that together with the Church we may, at the Great Wedding Supper of the Lamb, enjoy the everlasting joys and honours of the glorious Bride.

But now, we must conclude with the Father's closing remarks to the Son.

4. Conclusion

[16] *Instead of thy fathers shall be thy children, whom thou mayest make princes in all the earth.* [17] *I will make thy name to be remembered in all generations: therefore shall the people praise thee for ever and ever.*

This is a promise. It is a promise that the Church will endure.

It is a promise that from generation to generation, men, women and children will be enrolled as prophets, priests and kings.

It is a promise that the name of Christ will endure forever and ever, from generation unto generation, and for all eternity.

And this promise will be kept because He who has spoken is none other than God the Father, the Creator of the heavens and the earth.

Thank God for this great privilege of sharing in this glorious eternity with Him, who is our Great God and Saviour! Amen. Ω

Psalm 46:
The Righteous One's
Mighty Fortress
in the Storm

Psalm 46 is a very well-known and comforting Psalm. It is well known that Martin Luther would sing it when he felt discouraged or sore-tried in his fight against Rome. We read that there were moments when Luther would feel something akin to despair, and he would ask with the Psalmist: "Why art thou cast down, O my soul?" In such hours, he would say to Melanchthon, "Come, Philip, let us sing the 46th Psalm" and the two friends would sing it together using Luther's famous paraphrase of it.

But this Psalm is not only a comfort in times of ecclesiastical or political conflict; it is of great comfort whenever we are facing an uncertain tomorrow, or anticipate a severe trial.

Every Christian may sing this Psalm, for this Psalm is given by our Lord, that we may sing in union with Him. It may be understood as a conversational Psalm where sometimes the Church with Christ as Head speaks (e.g. v. 1-6); sometimes, the Church speaks about Christ (v. 7-9); and once Christ speaks of Himself apart from the Church (v. 10). It may also, as we shall see, be recognised as a Trinitarian Psalm with the three Persons of the Godhead extolled in the three strophes demarcated by the "selahs." But it is best known as a Psalm of great comfort which we may entitle, in tribute to Luther, but with recognition that it is not his song: *"The Righteous One's Mighty Fortress in the Storm."*

How does this Psalm comfort us in the storms? It comforts us by encouraging us to (1) *Fear Not* because God is our refuge and strength (v. 1-3); (2) *Move Not* because the Spirit is in our midst (v. 4-7); and (3) *Be Still* because Christ, the LORD of Host, the Captain of our salvation is God (v. 8-11).

1. v. 1-3   Fear Not

2. v. 4-7   Move Not

3. v. 8-11   Be Still

1. Fear Not

We need not fear because God is our strength and very present help in trouble.

¹ God is our refuge and strength, a very present help in trouble. ² Therefore will not we fear, though the earth be removed, and though the mountains be carried into the midst of the sea; ³ Though the waters thereof roar and be troubled, though the mountains shake with the swelling thereof. Selah.

Every child of God will experience different kinds of trials. It could be wars or quarrels. It could be church splits or severe disagreements. It could be natural disasters or political turmoil. It could even be personal struggles—conflict in the soul or the prospect of an impending trial, be it an examination or a court case.

Whatever it is, it can be very fearful to think about what will happen next. Indeed, very often we will think of the worst scenario, and we can get unduly worried.

But remarkably, our Lord does not comfort us by having us insist that it will not be as bad as we think. The fact is: we do not know what will happen tomorrow, and what happens may indeed be as bad if not worse than what we anticipate it to be. It is foolish, therefore, to comfort ourselves by saying, "Peace, peace; when there is no peace" (Jer 6:14).

What then shall we do? Well, instead of the best possible outcome, our Lord would have us think of the worst. What else would we mean when we sing:

> *"...though the earth be removed, and though the mountains be carried into the midst of the sea; ³ Though the waters thereof roar and be troubled, though the mountains shake with the swelling thereof"?*

How else could we imagine a worst scenario—than the earth being knocked out of orbit, the mountains blown off, and cast into the sea, when there are gigantic tsunamis and earthquakes everywhere. We are speaking metaphorically, of course. But is it not true that sometimes when terrible things happen to us, we feel the whole world crashing around us, and everything appears to be in turmoil?

But what shall we do if the worst should indeed happen? The Lord, by His Spirit, would remind us that we need not fear. We need not fear because we have God to be our refuge and our strength. When everything crumbles around us, when the whole world crumbles beneath our feet, we will still have somewhere to hide, and someone who will give us strength.

> ¹ *God is our refuge and strength, a very present help in trouble.*

God our heavenly Father loves us and will always be there for us, to hide us, to strengthen us and to help us, no matter how bad things may turn out for us. He will never leave us nor forsake us (Heb 13:5). "My Father, which gave *them* me, is greater than all; and no *man* is able to pluck *them* out of my Father's hand. I and *my* Father are one," says our Lord (Jn 10:29-30).

Therefore, we need not fear. Rather let us learn to run to Him, to hide in Him and to find strength in Him even as Christ our Head found strength in Him in His hour of need. "I am not alone because the Father is with me," says our Saviour (Jn 16:32).

But not only should we not fear, we also need …

2. Move Not

> ⁴ *There is a river, the streams whereof shall make glad the city of God, the holy place of the tabernacles of the most High. ⁵ God is in the midst of her; she shall not be moved: God shall help her, and that right early. ⁶ The heathen raged, the kingdoms were moved: he uttered his voice, the earth melted. ⁷ The LORD of hosts is with us; the God of Jacob is our refuge. Selah.*

What is it to be moved? It is to be shaken. It is to despair and to give up. It is to allow Satan to have victory. When a kingdom is moved as in verse 6, the kingdom is destroyed or displaced; and the people are scattered, and brought to despair of ever returning to their home land.

If the church is moved, she is shaken from her moorings of truth. She begins to doubt the purpose of her existence. Her members begin to scatter. Her leaders are too discouraged to do anything.

If a Christian is moved, he is in despair. He loses confidence not only in himself, but in God. He doubts God. He is tempted to forget about living a righteous and holy life. Indeed, he is tempted to leave the faith altogether.

But we need not be moved. We need not be moved because God is in us (v. 5), and with us (v. 7). He will help us. He will help us early when we are in need of help (v. 5).

How is God in us, and with us? Verse 4 gives us a clue.

⁴ There is a river, the streams whereof shall make glad the city of God, the holy place of the tabernacles of the most High.

What is this river? It has been suggested that it could represent God the Father (Jer 2:13); and God the Son (Zech 13:1). But it appears to me that this river is very likely a reference to the Holy Spirit and the blessings that He brings to His people. The Lord Jesus is referring to the Holy Spirit when He says:

"He that believeth on me, as the scripture hath said, out of his belly shall flow rivers of living water" (Jn 7:38).

One of the verses that the Lord is referring to, I believe, is Zechariah 14:8, which reads:

"And it shall be in that day, that living waters shall go out from Jerusalem…" (Zech 14:8a).

God is with us, and in us, by His Spirit. For this reason, we shall not be moved. For He will never leave us, nor forsake us; and as the Apostle John puts it, we have overcome, and will overcome, because greater is He that is in us, than he that is in the world (1 Jn 4:4).

The believer, in whom the Spirit dwells, will not be moved; therefore, the church which comprises believers, in whom the Spirit dwells, will not be moved.

Let us therefore pray for the Spirit as the Lord teaches us to:

"If ye then, being evil, know how to give good gifts unto your children: how much more shall your heavenly Father give the Holy Spirit to them that ask him?" (Lk 11:13).

If we want to remain steadfast in the midst of adversity, let us learn to pray for the Spirit and rely upon the Spirit.

Finally, in the midst of adversity, let us learn to…

3. Be Still

⁸ Come, behold the works of the LORD, what desolations he hath made in the earth. ⁹ He maketh wars to cease unto the end of the earth; he breaketh the bow, and cutteth the spear in sunder; he burneth the chariot in the fire. ¹⁰ Be still, and know that I am God: I will be exalted among the heathen, I will be exalted in the earth. ¹¹ The LORD of hosts is with us; the God of Jacob is our refuge. Selah.

"Be still, and know that I am God." What is the meaning of being still? It is not to sit down, and be inactive. It is, essentially, to fret not, and not to allow emotional turmoil to overwhelm us.

But why are we to be still? The reason is very simple: namely, that the Lord, He is God. "Be still, and know that I am God." Who is this "I"? This "I" is He who identifies Himself with us when we sing "us" and "we" in the context, but He is also God. Who is this "I", but Christ Himself?

The writer of Hebrews tells us:

"² [God] Hath in these last days spoken unto us by his Son, whom he hath appointed heir of all things, by whom also he made the worlds; ³ Who being the brightness of his glory, and the express image of his person, and upholding all things by the word of his power, when he had by himself purged our sins, sat down on the right hand of the Majesty on high" (Heb 1:1-3).

Christ has been appointed the heir of all things; and by the word of His sovereign power, He is bringing all things to pass.

The natural disasters in the earth, the wars and peace in the world do not come by chance. They are ordained by the LORD, and brought to pass by His sovereign power. They are all the works of the Lord (v, 8-9).

Why does He bring all things to pass? He brings all things to pass for His own glory (v. 10), and for our sakes, which is the reason we can confess, "*The LORD of hosts is with us*" (v. 11).

Therefore, in the midst of turmoil in our souls and in our lives, let us learn to be still and know that He is God. Let us cease to fret; let us cease from frantic activity. Let us be still and let God be God, to taste and see that He is good; and He will see to it that His name will be exalted, and good will come out of the turmoil.

Conclusion

Dear child of God, are there occasions when you are tempted to despair? Are you going through a particular trial at the moment?

Fear not: for God is our strength and very present help in trouble. He will never leave us nor forsake us. He does not stand by to watch. He is ever present to help us, moment by moment: so that help is but a prayer away. Meditate, therefore, on the greatness of the Father's love.

Move not: for God is in us and with us by His Spirit. We are not powerless, for He who dwells In us, not only comforts us with a sense of our Father's love, but gives us the strength that we need to cling on to the promises of our LORD. Pray, therefore, for the Spirit.

Be still: for God the Son is our God and Conqueror. He who is God and our Sovereign LORD is also our compassionate Great High Priest, who was tempted in all points like as we are and yet without sin. He has been through a trial far more intense than any of us will ever experience. He understands and He cares. He is interceding for you. He will see to it that your trial will work out for your good and redound to our Father's glory. Rest therefore upon Christ in your turmoil. And sing with Him His song, that the dread in your soul may be driven away. Amen. Ω

Psalm 47:
The Righteous One's
Glorious Sunshine
After the Storm

Psalm 47 and Psalm 46 are distinct Psalms. But the Holy Spirit has so put these two Psalms together that it is, I believe, very profitable to look at Psalm 47 in the context of Psalm 46.

Psalm 46 is set in a climate of great anxiety. The people of God are experiencing great turmoil of heart and mind; and things are expected to get worse. Our Lord gives us this Psalm that we may sing at such times. He exhorts us to be still and know that he is God. He would have us fear not, because God is our refuge and our strength, a very present help in trouble, even if the worst calamity were to happen. But we come to Psalm 47, and it is a very joyful Psalm. *"O clap your hands, all ye people; shout unto God with the voice of triumph,"* we are enjoined (v. 1).

Thus, against the background of Psalm 46, we may entitle it *"The Righteous One's Glorious Sunshine after the Storm."*

But should we sing Psalm 47 as a celebratory song only when the troubles are all over? Not really; for if you look at verses 3 and 4, you will see that this song is to be sung in anticipation of victory and rest, and not merely in celebration of victory. Notice the future tense. The enemies are not yet subdued. The war is still raging. Our inheritance is yet to be enjoyed.

Psalm 47, in other words, is not an inappropriate song to sing even when the church is going through severe trials.

Indeed, it is a Psalm, I believe, that God's children throughout the ages can sing, to praise the Lord and encourage themselves through all the pains and struggles that they face in this present life.

Let us look at this Psalm.

This Psalm has a very unique structure. It has two parts that are separated by a key verse, namely verse 5. In each of these parts, there is a call to praise the LORD followed by the reasons to do so. Thus its outline would be:

1. v. 1-4   The First Call to Praise
2. v. 5   The Key
3. v. 6-9   The Second Call to Praise

Let's look at the key verse first: for this is central to this Psalm.

1. The Key

⁵ *God is gone up with a shout, the LORD with the sound of a trumpet.*

What is this verse referring to? Some think that this is referring to the ark of God being brought into a battlefield like in the days of Eli. But most commentators agree that it is a reference to the ark being brought up into Jerusalem by David.

But why is this event important to us? This event is important to us because the New Testament teaches us that it has a very important typical significance. It pointed to the ascension of Christ into heaven after His crucifixion and resurrection!

This is what the Apostle Paul alludes to in Ephesians 4:8, where he quotes Psalm 68:18.

What about the reference to a shout and the sound of a trumpet? There were shouts and trumpets when the ark was brought up to Jerusalem (1 Chr 15:28); but we don't hear of the same at the ascension of Christ.

How do we reconcile the apparent mismatch? One way is to say that the shouts and trumpets, as with many things in the Psalms, must be understood metaphorically simply to express excitement and joy. But perhaps a better way is to see that at the second coming of Christ, there will be shouts and trumpets, as Paul says:

> "For the Lord himself shall descend from heaven with a shout, with the voice of the archangel, and with the trump of God..." (1Th 4:16).

What has this shout and trumpet to do with the ascension of Christ? It has everything to do with the ascension, because as the angel told the disciples:

> "This same Jesus, which is taken up from you into heaven, shall so come in like manner as ye have seen him go into heaven" (Acts 1:11).

I am not sure if there were trumpets and the shout of the archangel at the ascension of Christ. But one thing is certain: the ascension of Christ and His return are intricately tied events. Christ will return because He ascended. Christ's ascension signalled the beginning of the God-Man's triumphal rule as God and King.

To put it in another way: The ascension of Christ is one of the most significant bases of the Christian hope. The cross is important. But had Christ not risen and ascended to heaven, we would have no basis to hope that there will ever be perfect peace and perfect joy in this sin-scarred world.

With this in mind, I believe we can begin to get an idea of what the Spirit is seeking to do in our hearts and mind, as we sing this Psalm, in union with Christ our Head, to praise God and to exhort one another.

The Spirit would have us look unto Jesus in His ascension; and He would have us to think of all the things that He has done for us, so that everything in the world begins to pale into insignificance and become strangely dim. The Spirit would have us to bask in the glory of our ascended Lord, that our hearts may be filled with praise and thanksgiving for what He has done. The Spirit would have us celebrate the victory and peace that the Lord our King— whose song we sing—has wrought for us.

With this in mind, consider the first half of this Psalm, which is ...

2. The First Call to Praise

¹ O clap your hands, all ye people; shout unto God with the voice of triumph.

This is not a call for us to clap our hands in worship. No one in his right mind, throughout the history of the people of God from Moses, to David, to Pentecost, to the Reformation, would clap their hands in formal worship. Certainly, no one would clap their hands while singing this Psalm! And never would the temple be filled with the voice of shouting except during war.

No, no; this is a call to lift up our hearts to rejoice in the LORD. Christians must not be defeatists, whatever troubles and difficulties may attend us.

Why? For us, who are looking back, it is because Christ our King has conquered and ascended up on high. He is seated at the right hand of the Father upholding all things by the word of His power.

For the Old Testament saints, who were looking forward, it would be because Messiah their great King would conquer and would ascend up on high.

> [2] *For the LORD most high is terrible; he is a great King over all the earth.* [3] *He shall subdue the people under us, and the nations under our feet.* [4] *He shall choose our inheritance for us, the excellency of Jacob whom he loved.*

These words seem to look back to the conquest of Canaan, but notice the future tense. The conquest of Canaan is but a type of the great spiritual war that our Lord fought and is fighting for us.

There is a war of ages in progress. Everything in this world, including all its pains and suffering, great or small, are battles in this war. The enemy is sin, and Satan, and everything that seeks to rob us of peace and joy in the Lord.

So all family quarrels and church divisions; all relationship breakups; all deaths and illnesses; all job-losses; and indeed all things that bring a sigh and a tear to our eyes, are part of the war of ages.

But we thank God that Christ has conquered. He is risen. He is ascended. He will return. The Old Testament saints saw it with eyes of faith and hope; we see it partly in history, and partly with eyes of hope.

Our LORD will see to it that however powerful the enemies of our souls are, they will be trampled under our feet. "The God of peace shall bruise Satan under your feet shortly" (Rom 16:20), says the Apostle Paul. Christ has conquered. He conquered on the cross and His victory is sealed with His resurrection and ascension. The victory is secure. The serpent's head is crushed and will be crushed. He is in his dying throes seeking to sweep as many into damnation with him as possible, which is the reason why there is still no perfect peace, as yet. This is why Christians must put on the spiritual armour and fight. We must fight till the serpent is stilled, and we have, as it were, to "fill up that which is behind of the afflictions of Christ" (Col 1:24). For our crushing of Satan's head is one with the Lord's crushing of his head, for we are one with Him.

So fear not, dear soldier of the cross, whatever trials may come your way. They are part of the war of ages which Christ has conquered.

They are there that we may learn little by little, more and more, to trust Him who is our King.

But consider now…

3. The Second Call to Praise

[6] *Sing praises to God, sing praises: sing praises unto our King, sing praises.*

The word translated "sing praise" may also be translated "sing psalms" as in Psalm 105:2.

"Is any among you afflicted? let him pray. Is any merry? let him sing psalms," says James (Jas 5:13). Psalm singing is one of the best ways of expressing joy. Psalm singing is also one of the best ways of boosting our confidence in the LORD.

Four times in this one verse, we are exhorted to sing Psalms, in praise unto our God and

King.

When are we to sing Psalms? We are to do so when we are filled with joy. But not only so, for the reason that is given for us to sing is an unchanging reason:

> [7] *For God is the King of all the earth: sing ye praises with understanding.* [8] *God reigneth over the heathen: God sitteth upon the throne of his holiness.* [9] *The princes of the people are gathered together, even the people of the God of Abraham: for the shields of the earth belong unto God: he is greatly exalted.*

Why should we sing? How can we sing with understanding, unless we know why we should sing?

We should sing, v. 8, because *"God reigneth over the heathen: God sitteth upon the throne of his holiness."* We should sing because our God is the sovereign King of all the earth. He is in absolute control over everything in the universe including the heathen.

But to what purpose does He rule the earth? He rules the earth for the sake of His people — even the people of the God of Abraham. He rules that they may be gathered together as the trophies of His redeeming grace.

He rules that one day it may be declared:

> "The kingdoms of this world are become the kingdoms of our Lord, and of his Christ; and he shall reign for ever and ever" (Rev 11:15b).

Conclusion

Every Christian ought to be joyful when going through the trials and turmoil of this life.

The reason we are not is because we have a tendency to look at the wind and the waves surrounding us. If only we would think more and meditate more on the great things in this Psalm, then we shall be able to stay our minds upon Jehovah and remain joyful in whatever situation that the Lord brings us through.

Let us, therefore, sing this Psalm to remind ourselves. Let us sing it with understanding. Let us sing it to exhort one another in union with Christ our Lord, whose ascension gives us hope of final victory. Amen. Ω

Psalm 48:
The Righteous One's
Acclamation of His Church

Like Psalm 47, Psalm 48 is a very joyous Psalm. It is also a Psalm of celebration. On the surface, it is a Psalm of praise in celebration of Mt Zion, or Jerusalem. So it speaks of the palaces, towers and bulwarks of Jerusalem; as well as her victories over enemies that ventured to conquer her.

But let us not forget that Jerusalem and Mount Zion are but a type of the Church. So this Psalm is not really about Jerusalem *per se*. And therefore, when we sing this Psalm, we do not think of Jerusalem in Palestine, and certainly not of the Dome of the Rock that stands on the temple site today.

No, no; when we sing or meditate on this Psalm, our eyes must be lifted up to our Great God and King, as well as the Church He has purchased with His blood.

In the Church of England liturgy, this Psalm is appointed for use on Whitsunday, which is to commemorate Pentecost or the day of the outpouring of the Spirit of Christ upon the Church, after the ascension of Christ. Why? Well, to paraphrase Bishop Horne, this Psalm is thought to contain a snapshot of the glory, beauty and strength of the Church, immediately after she was rescued from her enemies. The outpouring of the Spirit upon the Church is like a reclamation of the Church after she was highjacked by the legalistic ideologies of the unbelieving Jews.

This is an interesting thought. However, we wonder if the attempt to fit the Psalm into a liturgical calendar that has no biblical sanction may have perhaps skewed the esteemed commentator in an eisegetical direction. It seems better to think of this Psalm simply as a hymn of praise that Christ our Lord has given us, to sing in union with Him, as He contemplates on the glory of the Church, and how she glorifies God who beautifies her. With this in mind, we may entitle it as *"The Righteous One's Acclamation of His Church."* And it has four parts:

1.   v. 1-3   Mt Zion is Glorious Because of the LORD

2.   v. 4-8   Mt Zion is Victorious Because of the LORD

3.   v. 9-11   Mt Zion is Joyous Because of the LORD

4.   v. 12-14   Mt Zion is Commendable Because of the LORD

1. Mt Zion Is Glorious
Because of the LORD

[1] *Great is the LORD, and greatly to be praised in the city of our God, in the mountain of his holiness.* [2] *Beautiful for situation, the joy of the whole earth, is mount Zion, on the sides of the north, the city of the great King.* [3] *God is known in her palaces for a refuge.*

Mount Zion is the Church of Christ, the city set upon a hill to show forth the praises of God. She is beautiful and glorious, not in herself: for by herself, she is wretched, full of spots and wrinkles and blemishes of all sorts (Eph 5:27). But when she stands in the arms of her Husband and Head, Christ the great King, she is altogether lovely.

This is why, even as this Psalm of celebration of the Church begins, it is not the Church, but the Head of the Church that receives the first accolade: *"Great is the LORD, and greatly to be praised in the city of our God..."*[23]

The Church, the city and bride of our great God and King is glorious and beautiful *because* of the glory of the LORD, our Great God and King. The words *"beautiful for situation"* speak of her loftiness. Just as Jerusalem of old was on an elevated plane geographically, the Church must be on an elevated plane morally and spiritually.

Indeed, she is beautiful; and she is a joy of the world when she is shining forth for Christ, as a city on a hill.

How does she shine forth for Christ? She shines forth for Christ today, not through the grandeur of architecture, but the preaching of the Gospel, and the practical demonstrations of His love and compassion to the world (cf. Jn 13:35). Moreover, she shines forth for Christ when she is victorious in trials.

This is what the second part of this Psalm is about.

2. Mt Zion Is Victorious
Because of the LORD

The biggest trial that the people of God in earthly Zion experienced would be war. We remember how Sennacherib laid siege on Jerusalem and kept Hezekiah, in his own words, like a bird in a cage.

But God's people need never fear, for when the LORD is with them, their enemies will return in fear and shame:

> [4] *For, lo, the kings were assembled, they passed by together.* [5] *They saw it, and so they marvelled; they were troubled, and hasted away.* [6] *Fear took hold upon them there, and pain, as of a woman in travail.* [7] *Thou breakest the ships of Tarshish with an east wind.* [8] *As we have heard, so have we seen in the city of the LORD of hosts, in the city of our God: God will establish it for ever.*

Today, this truth remains. Many things, in the hand of Satan, threaten to shake us loose, and separate us from the love of God. But our Lord will not allow it to happen. He has established the Church in His love forever.

Nothing shall separate us from His love: neither wars, nor sword, nor famine, nor persecution, nor tribulation. None of these shall separate us from the love of God which is in Christ Jesus. We are more than conquerors through Him who loves us (cf. Rom 8:35-39).

So Satan and his cohorts and agents are frustrated. They return from their attempts, defeated and troubled. The gates of hell cannot prevail against the Church (cf. Mt 16:18): for the King of kings has established it forever.

So the Church rejoices. This is what the third part of this Psalm is about...

---

[23] The LORD (Jehovah) here refers to God Triune, usually represented by God the Father so that we can almost always replace "LORD" with "the Father," and we will make sense of what we are singing. But our Lord has said "I and my Father are one" (Jn 10:30); and that "he that hath seen me hath seen the Father" (Jn 14:9). For this reason, in a number of Psalms, such as Psalm 23 and 48, our eyes naturally turn to Christ even as we worship the Father in union with the Son. In Psalm 23, the Shepherd is Jehovah, but He is a shepherd to us in Christ, so we cannot help but look to Christ as we sing praise unto God with Christ. In Psalm 48, similarly the Great God and King is Jehovah, but He is our King in Christ (cf. Rev 15:3; 19:16), and therefore even as we sing unto the LORD God Triune as our God and King, our eyes are set upon our Worshipper-in-Chief, Christ, who is, as it were, leading us in praise.

3. Mt Zion Is Joyous
Because of the LORD

⁹ We have thought of thy lovingkindness, O God, in the midst of thy temple. ¹⁰ According to thy name, O God, so is thy praise unto the ends of the earth: thy right hand is full of righteousness. ¹¹ Let mount Zion rejoice, let the daughters of Judah be glad, because of thy judgments.

The world sees the work of the LORD, but does not apprehend the purpose behind it. In fact, even believers sometimes get discouraged when they see the wicked prospering, while they are not doing so well. This thought is found in Psalm 73, which begins on a gloomy note that the wicked often prosper more than the righteous. But the Psalm begins to brighten towards the end when we are given to confess:

"Until I went into the sanctuary of God; then understood I their end" (Ps 73:17).

Going into the sanctuary of the LORD is a symbolic way of speaking about spiritual meditation and reasoning. It is only when we think carefully about what God is doing from a spiritual and eternal perspective, that we begin to see things clearly.

This is the case in our text, verse 9. Some of the things that happen in this world are hard to understand. Some have asked: "If there is God, why is there evil?" Others ask: "How can a righteous God allow the righteous to suffer while letting the wicked go free?"

But the children of God, in whom dwells the Spirit of Christ, know that God is righteous in all that He does. Indeed, the children of God desire that God be praised throughout the world—by an understanding that His right hand is full of righteousness. All that He does arises out of His heart of compassion and love, and is always righteous.

The children of God must be the first to acknowledge this truth. But not only are we to acknowledge it; we must also rejoice in His righteousness, as we see His great hand in all the things that are happening in the world, and especially in His Church.

Indeed, let us not only rejoice to see what the LORD is doing in the Church; but let us study it and talk about it. This is what the final section of this Psalm is about.

4. Mt Zion Is Commendable
Because of the LORD

¹² Walk about Zion, and go round about her: tell the towers thereof. ¹³ Mark ye well her bulwarks, consider her palaces; that ye may tell it to the generation following. ¹⁴ For this God is our God for ever and ever: he will be our guide even unto death.

Taken literally, these words instruct us to go to Jerusalem, to walk about the city, to observe the towers, the bulwarks or fortifications and her palaces. We are to note down what we see so that we may talk about them to our children and grandchildren.

But certainly, this cannot be the meaning: for otherwise, we will never be able to do as we are commanded to do today. For most of the towers, bulwarks and palaces of Jerusalem are long gone.

What then does the Holy Spirit want us to do? No doubt, He wants us to see what He has done, in building up the Church in history and in our own times.

He wants us to tell the story of the Church to our children. We must read the Bible for the inspired history of the church. But we should also read church history books. We should talk about the great work of God in the history of the Church. Talk about His great work of redemption and deliverance. Talk about the servants of the Lord and their exploits—of Martin Luther, John Calvin, John Knox, Jonathan Edwards, David Brainerd, Hudson Taylor, about the two Margarets, about the dairyman's daughter, about the little kitchen maid, etc.

And we should also talk about what the Lord is doing in our own time. Talk about how the Lord saved and delivered us. Talk about how He saw us through various trials. Speak of the Dorcases and the Lazaruses. Tell of lives transformed.

Tell it to our children. Tell them of things that will evoke praise. Don't tell them of our grievances and disagreements unless there has been reconciliation and mutual forgiveness. Do not make them despise the Church because of her spots and wrinkles. But lead them to love the Church because Christ loves her. Tell them, therefore, of the great work of God. Tell them so they may know that:

...God is our God forever and ever: he will be our guide even unto death [and beyond].

It is because of our LORD God, that we are what we are. It is because of the LORD that it is meaningful to talk about the Church.

And our LORD is well pleased when we talk about what He is doing in the lives of His people. Malachi puts it this way:

"Then they that feared the LORD spake often one to another: and the LORD hearkened, and heard it, and a book of remembrance was written before him for them that feared the LORD, and that thought upon his name" (Mal 3:16).

Conclusion

What a blessing it is to be in this glorious and victorious Church of Christ: to rejoice and to talk about what Christ is doing in our midst and how that glorifies God.

May the LORD help us, that we may truly find it a blessing to be in the Church of Christ, and truly able to see with spiritual eyes that she is beautiful and glorious in Christ who is altogether lovely. Amen. Ω

Psalm 49:
The Righteous One's
Encouragement when Bullied

Psalm 49 is not a very well-known Psalm. It is also not a Psalm that is generally regarded as Messianic. However, we have reason to agree with Andrew Bonar that the speaker in this Psalm is first and foremost the Messiah.

We read in Matthew 13:34-35:

"³⁴ All these things spake Jesus unto the multitude in parables; and without a parable spake he not unto them: ³⁵ That it might be fulfilled which was spoken by the prophet, saying, I will open my mouth in parables; I will utter things which have been kept secret from the foundation of the world."

Matthew is referring to the teaching ministry of the Lord Jesus. He is, essentially, saying that the Lord spoke in parables according as it was prophesied. What prophecy is he referring to? He is referring particularly to Psalm 78:2, which reads: "I will open my mouth in a parable: I will utter dark sayings of old."

What Matthew is saying is that the "I" is Christ. Now, it happens that the "I" in Psalm 49 says basically the same thing as the "I" in Psalm 78! Look at verses 3 and 4.

Bonar is right, I believe, when he says:

The Redeemer himself speaks this "parable," this weighty discourse, which in its topics is to the world no better than an unintelligible enigma—"a dark saying."

What is this Psalm about? Well, the thesis of this Psalm is found in verse 5:

⁵ Wherefore should I fear in the days of evil, when the iniquity of my heels shall compass me about?

But what does He mean? A quick check with the commentaries will confirm that we are not the only ones confounded! This verse is recognised as the key to this Psalm of dark sayings, but dark is our understanding.

Well, what does it mean? Leaving the spadework behind, let me give you the excellent paraphrase of verse 5 by Bishop George Horne:

Why should I give way to fear and despondency, in time of calamity, when the wickedness of my wealthy and powerful adversaries [see verse 6] compasses me about, to supplant and overthrow me?

This Psalm, in other words, reflects the Messiah's thoughts and encouragement as He suffered in the hands of His powerful enemies. We may entitle it *"The Righteous One's Encouragement when Bullied."* It is a Psalm appointed by our Saviour for us to sing with Him that we may better appreciate the intensity of His sufferings on our behalf. It is also a Psalm that all believers, being united with Christ may have recourse to, whenever they feel themselves persecuted or bullied by the rich and powerful of the world.

We may outline it as follows:

1. v. 1-5   Prologue & Thesis

2. v. 6-15   Why we Need Not Fear Bullies?

    a.   Temporal Weath and Power is Limited (v. 6-9)

     b.   Temporal Wealth and Power Perishes (v. 10-13)

     c.   Temporal Weath and Power Will be Trounced (v. 14-15).

3.   v. 16-20   Conclusion

1. Prologue & Thesis

The Psalm begins with a prologue followed by the thesis statement which we have just considered.

> [1] *Hear this, all ye people; give ear, all ye inhabitants of the world:* [2] *Both low and high, rich and poor, together.* [3] *My mouth shall speak of wisdom; and the meditation of my heart shall be of understanding.* [4] *I will incline mine ear to a parable: I will open my dark saying upon the harp.* [5] *Wherefore should I fear in the days of evil, when the iniquity of my heels shall compass me about?*

This is a Psalm of instruction. It is for all people—whether rich or poor, great or small. When we sing it, we must sing it with the view of admonishing one another in the fear of the LORD.

We must sing it to encourage one another to take courage when the powerful people in the world lift themselves up against us to intimidate us because of Christ whom they hate (Jn 15:18-19).

But why should we not fear them?

2. Why We Need Not Fear Bullies?

Our Lord gives us three reasons:

a. Temporal Wealth &
Power Is Limited

[6] *They that trust in their wealth, and boast themselves in the multitude of their riches;* [7] *None of them can by any means redeem his brother, nor give to God a ransom for him:* [8] *(For the redemption of their soul is precious, and it ceaseth for ever:)* [9] *That he should still live forever, and not see corruption.*

The point is: The rich and powerful have a false sense of power. But the simple reality is that with all their wealth, they cannot save a person from death and the judgement of God.

So why should we fear them? We should rather fear God.

Our Lord is essentially saying the same thing in the New Testament when He counsels:

> "And fear not them which kill the body, but are not able to kill the soul: but rather fear him which is able to destroy both soul and body in hell" (Mt 10:28).

Let us fear God rather than man: for temporal wealth and power are limited. Let us not allow the fear of man to dictate how we feel, what we think, and what we do, or do not do, especially when such feelings, thoughts and actions cause us to sin against God. Let us remember rather to fix our eyes on the LORD.

Secondly, we should not fear those rich and powerful oppressors of this world because...

b. Temporal Wealth &
Power Perishes

[10] *For he seeth that wise men die, likewise the fool and the brutish person perish, and leave their wealth to others.* *[11]* *Their inward thought is, that their houses shall continue forever, and their dwelling places to all generations; they call their lands after their own names.* *[12]* *Nevertheless man being in honour abideth not: he is like the beasts that perish.* *[13]* *This their way is their folly: yet their posterity approve their sayings.*

Fallen man will die. It is appointed unto man once to die. Even the rich and powerful can observe that (v. 10). But yet they sometimes live as if they will be rich and powerful forever.

To preserve their honour they would do many things, including naming parcels of land after themselves (v. 11). Remember how Emperor Nero wanted to name part of Rome Neropolis? Today the same display of self-exaltation persists with less abashed persons naming corporations, buildings and streets after themselves.

But whatever they do, they will perish. Their honour will go down to the grave with them. However great and powerful, the wicked will return to the dust like animals. If they live like animals, without regard for God, then they will die like animals (v. 12). How foolish to live such a life! How foolish it is to envy such a life, and even follow in the footsteps of those who have gone that way.

Should we fear them? Shall we not, rather, fear God, who is unchanging? Fear not the rich and powerful bullies of the world for their wealth and power is here today and gone tomorrow.

Thirdly, let us not fear the rich and powerful enemies of God for…

c. Temporal Wealth & Power
will Be Trounced

[14] *Like sheep they are laid in the grave; death shall feed on them; and the upright shall have dominion over them in the morning; and their beauty shall consume in the grave from their dwelling.*

We have seen how the wicked, however rich, and powerful, will die. They will die as animals will die. They are, in that sense, no better than the beasts, whatever they may think of themselves.

But there is something else that distinguishes the brute beasts from the wicked persons who are rich and powerful. This difference is hinted in verse 14: *"the upright shall have dominion over them in the morning."*

The fact is: man unlike animals is created in the image of God. We will face the judgement of God. And there will come a day when our bodies will be raised from the dead. In that day, which is heralded by the Resurrection Morning of the Lord Jesus Christ, the poor and the weak of Christ will triumph over the rich and powerful of the world. For in that day, the righteous in Christ will be raised with a body incorruptible, and fitted for glory; whereas the wicked would be raised with a corruptible body, fitted for eternal punishment.

Our Lord is He who alone is upright. So in a certain sense, verse 14 is about the Lord triumphing over the wicked. But all who believe in Him are united to Him and are upright in Him. Thus the Apostle Paul referring to Genesis 3:15 tells the Roman believers: "And the God of peace shall bruise Satan under your feet shortly.…" (Rom 16:20).

Thank God for our union with Christ. Our Lord knew that He needed not be afraid of His powerful foes because He would rise again from the dead, verse 15:

[15] *But God will redeem my soul from the power of the grave: for he shall receive me.*

So we too who are united to Christ need not fear those who oppress us, because we too will be raised from the dead and will be as kings and priests with Christ. We shall be vindicated. Our sorrows and mourning will turn to joy: for we are more than conquerors through Him who loves us, for vengeance belongs to Him.

3. Conclusion

Here then are the three reasons why those who are united to Christ need not fear the rich and powerful of this world who may bully them. They need not fear them for the wealth and power of this world is limited, will perish, and will be trounced by the power and honour that the Church will be given.

With this, we must conclude our study of this Psalm. And what better way than to use the conclusion appointed in this Psalm itself: for verse 16 to the end of the Psalm is really a conclusion and recapitulation of the reasons why we need not be afraid of the wicked who are rich and powerful:

[16] *Be not thou afraid when one is made rich, when the glory of his house is increased; [17] For when he dieth he shall carry nothing away: his glory shall not descend after him. [18] Though while he lived he blessed his soul: and men will praise thee, when thou doest well to thyself. [19] He shall go to the generation of his fathers; they shall never see light. [20] Man that is in honour, and understandeth not, is like the beasts that perish.*

We need not be afraid of the wicked rich and powerful because their power and wealth are limited and temporal, and because they will be overcome by death and judgement. In one sense *"Man that is in honour, and understandeth not, is like the beasts that perish"* (v. 20). In another sense, he is worse than the beasts.

On the other hand, those who are in Christ will rise with Him, and will triumph over Satan and his cohorts.

Do you feel discouraged because you feel that you have been bullied by your company, or by someone? Do you work for a boss who is rich, but cares not about your welfare? Do you sense that your classmates look down upon you because you are not as well-to-do as they are? Do you feel a sense of inferiority because you see others doing well in their careers, whereas you perceive that you have been sidelined due to your Christian principles?

If so, you must not wallow in self-pity. You must look to the cross. Christ laid down His life for you. Shall He not vindicate you; and shall not the Father give you all things needful for you? Envy not and fear not those who bully you. Pity them rather and pray for them. Amen.
Ω

Psalm 50:
The Righteous One's Case
Against His People

Psalm 50 is one of the most interesting of the Psalms. It is written like a lawsuit and may be entitled *"The Righteous One's Case Against His People."* It is a suit against His people primarily. But as the Apostle Peter reminds us:

> "For the time is come that judgment must begin at the house of God: and if it first begin at us, what shall the end be of them that obey not the gospel of God?" (1 Pt 4:17).

God's judgement against Jerusalem and Israel is a figure and harbinger of His judgement against the world.

This Psalm is therefore a passionate call, given by the King of the Church and the Judge of the World—to the Church to sing with Him: to warn her members and the world to wake up from their slumber and to live with a fear of God. For who is the Judge, but the Lord Himself: "For the Father judgeth no man, but hath committed all judgment unto the Son," says our Lord (Jn 5:22).

Thus, we can take the primary singer of this Psalm as Christ, the Righteous One. So He addresses "our God" with us in verse 3. But He also sings as the "I" in the words attributed directly to God in verses 5, 7-15 and 16b-21. We sing these verses as quotations of God's words to us; whereas He sings them with ownership as His words! Yet He is also the speaker in the concluding words, verse 22-23, where God is referred to in the third person. He is the God-Man, fully God, fully man.

This Psalm begins with a picture of the courtroom in which the charges are filed (v. 1-6). This is followed by the charges against God's people who are still willing to listen to Him but have grown complacent (v. 7-15). And finally, there is a charge against those who have grown hardened by the deceitfulness of sin (v. 16-23).

Thus, a simple outline would be:

1. v. 1-6   The Courtroom Scene
2. v. 7-15   A Plea to the Complacent
3. v. 16-23   A Plea to the Hardened

1. The Courtroom Scene

As we enter into this Psalm we enter into a courtroom. Let us read the introduction to the case being heard:

> [1] *The mighty God, even the LORD, hath spoken, and called the earth from the rising of the sun unto the going down thereof.*

The case being heard concerns the whole world. The charges are directed against the Church. But the world—as it lies from the rising of the sun to the going down thereof—must take heed.

Judgement will proceed from Zion; but the Judge is the God of glory, before whom all the world should tremble:

> [2] *Out of Zion, the perfection of beauty, God hath shined.* [3] *Our God shall come, and shall not keep silence: a fire shall devour before him, and it shall be very tempestuous round*

about him.

This is the Judge, great in glory, mighty in power. As the Judge enters into the courtroom, let us bow in humble adoration and fear.

Listen, the Judge is calling the court into Session:

⁴ *He shall call to the heavens from above, and to the earth, that he may judge his people.*

This is a courtroom of cosmic proportion. It is a case of cosmic implications. Who are the plaintiff and the defendant?

Here are the defendants:

⁵ *Gather my saints together unto me; those that have made a covenant with me by sacrifice.*

God's covenant people are the defendants. Who are those who have made a covenant with Him by sacrifice? They are all who were circumcised in the old covenant. So the defendants are the visible people of God. Today, the visible people of God is the Church, which comprises believers, and their children bearing the sign of the covenant, namely baptism.

Who is the plaintiff or complainant? Who is filing the lawsuit against the Church? Verse 6:

⁶ *And the heavens shall declare his righteousness: for God is judge himself.*

God is the Judge! So the heavens is the plaintiff. The heaven is bringing the charges against the people on behalf of the Lord.

Of course, this is a metaphorical picture. The idea is that God has a very serious charge against His people. He is bringing this charge against them in a formal way.

Let us consider first, His plea or charge against the complacent:

2. A Plea to the Complacent

What is the LORD's charge against the people who have become complacent?

⁷ *Hear, O my people, and I will speak; O Israel, and I will testify against thee: I am God, even thy God.* ⁸ *I will not reprove thee for thy sacrifices or thy burnt offerings, to have been continually before me....*

The charge is that the people had become legalistic and superstitious in their relationship with God.

Consciously or unconsciously, they have begun to relate to God as if they are doing Him a favour when they worship Him. They are feeding a hungry god, with their sacrifices, they seem to think.

But every beast of the forest belongs to God and He owns the cattle upon a thousand hills (v. 9-11). All that the people offer in sacrifice belongs to Him. How foolish for the people to think that they are doing God a favour. And how foolish for them to think that God needs them! God does not get hungry. He has no need. God is being sarcastic when He says, "If I were hungry, I would not tell thee..." (v. 12).

One wonders how many of us have this false notion about God—that He needs our worship, or our money, or our talents.

Make no mistake. God does not need us. He does not need you. Neither does He need me.

He does not need our talents, or our money, or our time. Let none of us entertain this false notion that we are doing God a favour when we serve Him.

No, no; when we serve Him, it is a privilege. And let none of us entertain this false notion that we need to pay for God's blessings by serving Him, or by giving our tithe.

No, no; that is not the Christian life. This is precisely what God is seeking to correct in His suit against Israel and against us!

God wants us to serve Him gratefully as a people who love Him and as those who cheerfully keep our vows unto Him. Look at verse 14:

> [14] *Offer unto God thanksgiving; and pay thy vows unto the most High:* [15] *And call upon me in the day of trouble: I will deliver thee, and thou shalt glorify me.*

God is pleased with those who serve Him and who return their tithes and offerings to Him; but His pleasure is not in their giving or service. It is rather in their gratitude and love for Him. Paul says:

> "Every man according as he purposeth in his heart, so let him give; not grudgingly, or of necessity: for God loveth a cheerful giver" (2Cor 9:7).

God will bless. He will deliver us out of trouble that we may glorify Him, not because He owes us anything, and certainly not because we can do Him any favour.

He will bless us in His love. He will reciprocate our love for Him. For indeed, we love because He first loved us.

Let us, therefore, disabuse our mind of the idolatrous notion that God needs us. Let us rather serve Him gratefully and cheerfully, as a privilege, rather than as a favour to the LORD.

But is there anyone who does not even care about the LORD? Is there anyone who says in his heart, there is no God? Is there anyone who is hardened by the deceitfulness of sin?

Listen to His plea to you.

3. A Plea to the Hardened

[16] *But unto the wicked God saith, What hast thou to do to declare my statutes, or that thou shouldest take my covenant in thy mouth?* [17] *Seeing thou hatest instruction, and castest my words behind thee.*

What is the charge? The charge is that they who are the wicked amongst God's people are simply hypocrites—or whited sepulchres, as our Lord puts it. They speak about the law of God. They claim to be in the covenant, and pride themselves as God's people. But in reality, they hate biblical instruction, and cast God's words behind them.

I trust that if you have a mind to read this study up to this point, that you probably do not have such an attitude. But if you have somehow gone off-tangent, and you perceive that the Holy Spirit is speaking to you, then you must wake up from your slumber.

If you despise the instruction from the word of God; if like the Thessalonians, you reject the word of God, and cast it behind you, or let it fall to the ground, then you must seriously go to the LORD in humble repentance.

Do not continue to fool yourself. You may fool man; but you can never fool God. He sees the depth of your heart. He is not blind to your hypocrisy. The fact that He has not dealt with you, does not mean that He is unaware, or that He does not care.

In fact, this is precisely what the LORD wants you to know. The fact that your sin does not bother you, does not mean that God is not concerned about it. Do not think that God is like you.

You may see someone stealing something, and it does not shock you. In fact, you may even join him if the opportunity arises (v. 18). Or you may hear someone speak about his fornication and adultery, and instead of being shocked, you indulge in the story. Or you may use deception and slander freely (v. 19-20).

You may imagine that since God did not deal with you for these, that He must be thinking like you, that these are inconsequential.

But this is far from the reality:

> [21] *These things hast thou done, and I kept silence; thou thoughtest that I was altogether such an one as thyself: but I will reprove thee, and set them in order before thine eyes.*

The wicked, especially among professing believers, who are hardened by the deceitfulness of sin, tend to create an idol in their mind. They begin to imagine how God must view their sin according to how they themselves view it with all their excuses.

But the day will come when God will set them straight. That day may be too late for repentance.

Therefore, let us, while there is yet time for repentance, wake up from our slumber and remember God:

> [22] *Now consider this, ye that forget God, lest I tear you in pieces, and there be none to deliver.*

If you love not the LORD, and therefore do not serve Him with gratitude, you must fear Him for His wrath: for He will call you to account for your life one day. May this thought shut you up to Christ, to seek salvation in Him!

Conclusion

The LORD has spoken. His charge sheet has been read. The heavens bear testimony of what has been spoken.

What shall we do?

The question we must ask ourselves is: Have we become complacent? Is our Christianity an outward religiosity, having a form of godliness, but denying the power thereof? Is our worship and attendance at the ordinances formal and mechanical?

Will you not humbly examine your heart once again? Are you serving to please men? Are you doing what you do as a believer only because it is expected of you? Are you doing what you do in the hope that God will overlook your secret sins?

Or are you serving Him out of gratitude and love? Oh will you not take time to be alone with the LORD, to ask the LORD to change your perspective and attitude. Do not allow yourself to continue to serve the Lord legalistically when you can truly enjoy serving Him with joy and gratitude.

Or have you been hardened through the deceitfulness of sin, living a hypocritical life? Oh will you not repent of your hardness and unbelief. Will you not disabuse your mind of the idol that you have made God to be? God is not like you. He is great and holy. He will not tolerate sin. But He is full of compassion and mercy. How else can we interpret God's provision of His Son to suffer and die for our sin, that we might enjoy His Fatherly fellowship. God is not like us. He will not overlook sin. In order that He might forgive us and receive us into His fellowship, He paid for our sin. Mercy and justice kissed each other at the cruel cross for our redemption.

Shall we not, therefore, seek to serve Him with our lips, our hearts, and with our lives? This Psalm ends beautifully with the words:

> ²³ *Whoso offereth praise glorifieth me: and to him that ordereth his conversation aright will I shew the salvation of God.*

These are the words of Christ our Mediator. Those who worship the LORD in sincerity, and live for His glory will know the salvation of God. They will persevere unto the day of everlasting rest, when they will glorify and enjoy God without any hindrance of sin or sinners.

May the LORD grant us the help of His spirit to offer praise with our lips, our hearts, and our lives. Let us by His grace, seek to live gratefully for Him in imitation of and in gratitude towards Him, whose body was broken and whose blood was shed for us. Amen. Ω

Psalm 51:
The Righteous One's Prayer
of Confession

Psalm 51 is one of the most famous Psalms. Very few of us would not know off-hand that it was written on the occasion of David's sin of adultery with Bathsheba.

The title of the Psalm reads:

> *To the chief Musician, A Psalm of David, when Nathan the prophet came unto him, after he had gone in to Bathsheba.*

One day when David's army had gone to war, David was idling upon the rooftop of his palace, when he spied Bathsheba taking a bath in a pool nearby. He summoned for her, and committed adultery with her. Then to cover up his sin, he summoned Uriah her husband back from the battlefield: in order that he might sleep with her, so that no one would suspect that the child she was bearing was his.

His plan did not work because Uriah—who was a principled man and a loyal soldier—could not get himself to sleep with his wife while his men were suffering in the field.

Adding sin upon sin, David then commanded his general Joab to put Uriah where the fighting was fiercest. It was a plot to have Uriah killed. David, essentially, murdered Uriah so that he might marry his wife.

A year later, the LORD revealed what had happened, to the prophet Nathan. Nathan approached David, with a parable about a rich man who killed the beloved lamb of a poor man, to entertain a traveller. David had responded with anger that the rich man must pay fourfold. It was then that Nathan said: "Thou art the man!" David was immediately struck in his conscience and cried, "I have sinned against the LORD" (2 Sam 12:13).

From that moment David was under deep conviction for his sins. In the days following, David wrote two Psalms, namely Psalms 32 and 51. Most likely, Psalm 51 was written immediately after Nathan the prophet rebuked him, whereas Psalm 32 was probably written later when he had fully confessed his sins, knew that he was forgiven, and so was ready to keep his promise to teach transgressors the LORD's ways (cf. v. 13).[24]

This is a Psalm that every believer may use when he is grieved due to sin in his life.

But the question may be asked—especially to those of us who believe that the Psalms are all Messianic—whether this Psalm could even be taken up in the lips of our Holy Saviour, who was tempted in all points like as we are, and yet without sin?

Could our Lord have sung it? Could it reflect the experience and thought life of our Saviour? Well, I must confess that I have not read any commentator who would venture to say that Psalm 51 reflects the thoughts and experience of our Saviour. Andrew Bonar wrote a beautiful statement to show how Psalm 32 could apply to Christ. He says:

> We generally take up this Psalm as if it was for the members of Christ alone; but we should not forget that the Head himself traversed the way of forgiveness. He stood for us, in our room, in our very place. He stood as substitute, and all the sins of all "that great

---

[24] "Most commentators suppose that David composed this Psalm when he obtained forgiveness from God after his adultery with Bathsheba, and the death of Uriah, to which that sin led. The correctness of this view can scarcely be called in question" (*Hengstenberg's Commentary on the Psalms*, [T&T Clark, 1869], 508).

multitude which no man can number" were upon him.... In this state He acknowledged our sin; it was only ours he had to acknowledge; he spread it out before God on the cross; he continued to do so till it was forgiven him as our substitute.

Yet when it comes to Psalm 51, which is almost certainly written on the same occasion, Bonar denies that it could have been taken up by our Lord. I think the verse that tipped the scale must be verse 5:

> [5] Behold, I was shapen in iniquity; and in sin did my mother conceive me.

But is it true that the Lord could not have identified with these words? The question we need to ask is: What does "in iniquity" and "in sin" mean? Whose sin and iniquity is David referring to? I am inclined to think, on the basis of the parallelism in the verse, that he is thinking of the sin of his parents, or that of his mother, in particular. Of course, he is not saying that he was conceived out of wedlock. Rather, he is saying that he was conceived and shapened or formed in the womb of a sinner! Clearly, the Lord Jesus could have taken these words on His lips: for it is true. Mary was a sinner. And the verse itself does not mention the father. It is in the womb of the mother that the baby is conceived and shapened.

Well, some, like John Gill, opine that David is thinking about his own iniquity in the first part of the verse. I do not think he is right. But suppose he is, then David would probably have in mind as he wrote these words, that from that moment, he was not only guilty but had a propensity to sin. Even so, what would our Lord be thinking when He, by His Spirit, inspired the words, or when He took it up in His lips? Surely He would not confess a propensity to sin, for He had none. But surely, it would be right to say that He was guilty at conception and birth because He came for that very purpose: Even that He might bear the sin of His people! Thus, we need have no doubt that these words, even if interpreted in this way, could have been taken up by our Lord—just as our Lord sought baptism though He had no sin, nor needed repentance. Thus we agree with Belcher that:

> "Jesus can pray Psalm 51 as our representative and priest before God.... As our sin-bearer he prayed for renewal and that God would not cast us away from his presence because of the sin he bore (Mt 27:46)."[25]

In any case, we may appropriately entitle this Psalm as *"The Righteous One's Prayer of Confession."* It is the song of the Righteous One given to righteous ones united to Him, to sing with Him in recognition of how their sin brings deep grief to God and to their own hearts.

When we have sinned grievously, or when a sense of sinfulness overwhelms our hearts, we may take up this Psalm, prayerfully, with reference to our own sin to express our guilt and grief. But let us do so knowing that we are singing the words of Christ as He confesses our sin on our behalf and pleads forgiveness for us on the basis of His sacrifice for us on our behalf.

But now, when we sing this Psalm in unison, in public worship, the corporate significance of the words proffered cannot refer to our individual sin: for that is unknown to one another; nor can it refer to David's sin: for which we cannot own. Rather, it must refer to all our sins imputed to Christ, the leader of the song. In other words, ultimately, the first person pronoun in this Psalm would be Christ!

---

[25] Richard P. Belcher Jr, *The Messiah and the Psalms: Preaching Christ from all the Psalms* (Ross-shire: Christian Focus Publications, 2006), 87-88.

Practically, nevertheless, even when we sing this Psalm corporately, it is inevitable that we will recall our own sin, if we are to sing affectionately and not dispassionately. And we should always sing affectionately, else we will be guilty of having God in our lips but not in our hearts (cf. Isa 29:13; Mt 15:8; Mk 7:6). This being so, it is helpful for us when singing this Psalm to think of every first person pronoun as referring to "Christ and I." In this way, we will be moved to keep an eye on the Lord, thanking God that our Saviour and Head was tempted in all points like as we are, and therefore felt for us what we do not feel, in regard to the abhorrence of our sin.

This Psalm has three stanzas corresponding to the three simple responses that the conviction of sin should provoke in the heart of a child of God:

1. v. 1-6   A Plea for Mercy
2. v. 7-13   A Plea for Restoration
3. v. 14-19   A Plea for Forgiveness

1. A Plea for Mercy

This is essentially what we are given to do in verses 1-6:

> [1] *Have mercy upon me, O God, according to thy lovingkindness: according unto the multitude of thy tender mercies blot out my transgressions.*

Sin makes us abominable and disqualifies us from every blessing. Therefore, the first thing we should do when we are convicted of sin, should be to acknowledge our unworthiness, and appeal to the lovingkindness and tender mercies of the LORD.

What shall we desire of the LORD? Shall we not desire for Him to blot out our transgressions so that we may not be hindered from fellowship with Him?

> [2] *Wash me thoroughly from mine iniquity, and cleanse me from my sin.* [3] *For I acknowledge my transgressions: and my sin is ever before me.* [4] *Against thee, thee only, have I sinned, and done this evil in thy sight: that thou mightest be justified when thou speakest, and be clear when thou judgest.*

Think of these words as they applied originally to David. He had sinned grievously against Bathsheba and especially against Uriah. But notice how he says, "*Against thee, thee only, have I sinned.*" David is certainly not saying that he did not wrong Bathsheba and Uriah. But sin ultimately is a transgression of God's law. David recognises, that above and beyond the wrong and hurt that he had inflicted upon Bathsheba and Uriah and his loved ones, he had sinned against God.

Very few of us have sinned as grievously as did David. So, very few of us have recognised the severity of our sin, as we should. Therefore, even when we confess our sin, we fall short of the sincerity that would be acceptable to the transcendently holy God whom we worship. But thank God for the Lord Jesus Christ, who took all our sin, individually and corporately, upon Himself, to confess them as they should be confessed, to plead for mercy, as we should.

Yet, as imitators of Christ enabled by the Spirit of Christ, let us not fail to learn this very important aspect of contrition. It is one thing to be sorry to those whom we sinned against. And indeed, we must be sorry. But it is quite another thing to acknowledge to the LORD how we had betrayed His love and sinned against Him.

And if we recognise that we have sinned against the LORD, then we must also, as we are taught in this Psalm, acknowledge that whatever chastisement or punishment that the LORD may mete out to us, will definitely be just. For God is merciful and kind. He does not "[deal] with us after our sins; nor [reward] us according to our iniquities" (Ps 103:10).

And we have sinned from the time we were born into this world. We have not followed God's commandments, contrary to His will. We have not pleased God, but rather have brought shame to His name. And worse still, we tend to be defensive and blind to our own faults when sin is exposed. But the LORD would have us to be totally honest when we come to confession:

> [5] Behold, I was shapen in iniquity; and in sin did my mother conceive me. [6] Behold, thou desirest truth in the inward parts: and in the hidden part thou shalt make me to know wisdom.

David, we must understand, is not trying to shift blame to his mother. He is simply acknowledging that he was acquainted with sin from conception and birth (v. 5), though it might not be obvious (v. 6). Which baby looks like a guilty sinner?[26] But God is not mocked, and therefore, David comes to Him with an open heart that he may be led in the way of wisdom, honesty and full contrition.

Let us learn to do the same—not giving excuses, not minimising our sin, not bargaining with God about what He may or may not do to us, because of our sin. Let us be wholehearted in our confession, especially as the Spirit of Christ has opened our eyes to see the true sinfulness of our sin. Let us learn to plead sincerely even when we realise that due to the remnant of corruption, we may not feel grief for our sin as much as we should, for Christ the greater David did fill up that which is lacking in our sorrows when He took our sin upon Himself.

And let us not only plead for mercy, but let us also plead for restoration ...

2. A Plea for Restoration

Many professing believers ask God for forgiveness when they fall into a particular sin. But they proceed no further: for they perceive no loss, apart from a loss of face.

I mean, they are living a life of hypocrisy and practical atheism. Sin takes nothing away from them except their honour in the eyes of man. Sin punctures their pride, but does nothing more. A chicken will never understand what the eagle loses when it breaks its wings.

The child of God, having experienced the love of God, knows better. He knows what he has lost by his sin and is seeking to be restored. He has experienced the blessing of fellowship with God. He has known the joy of salvation. He has known what it is to be living a life of enjoying and glorifying God. He has known the thrill of leading sinners to the LORD as He showed them the way of righteousness.

So he cries:

> [7] Purge me with hyssop, and I shall be clean: wash me, and I shall be whiter than snow. [8] Make me to hear joy and gladness; that the bones which thou hast broken may rejoice. [9] Hide thy face from my sins, and blot out all mine iniquities. [10] Create in me a clean heart, O God; and renew a right spirit within me. [11] Cast me not away from thy presence; and take not thy holy spirit from me. [12] Restore unto me the joy of thy salvation; and uphold

---

[26] Note that our Lord was guilty because He was bearing our sin, but He had no propensity for sin.

me with thy free spirit. [13] *Then will I teach transgressors thy ways; and sinners shall be converted unto thee.*

What about you, dear child of God? Do you understand the concerns and desires expressed in these words? Do you know what *"the joy of salvation"* means? If not, may I encourage you to go to the LORD to ask Him to open your eyes, and to plead with Him sincerely with these appointed words, that He might give you the joy and blessings that every child of God should experience.

And likewise, if you have lost that joy, and know that it is due to a particular sin, then I would beseech you not to wallow in sin, but to go to the LORD to lift you up. He is a merciful God who forgave David, even David, for the gross sins that he committed.

Yes, go to Him not because you are good enough, or that you deserve forgiveness. Go to Him to plead for forgiveness and restoration, on account of Christ whose sacrifice on your behalf has been accepted, and whose grief for sin and plea for restoration, on your behalf, have been heard.

Plead, moreover, as we are taught to do in the final stanza of this Psalm:

3. A Plea for Forgiveness

[14] *Deliver me from bloodguiltiness, O God, thou God of my salvation: and my tongue shall sing aloud of thy righteousness.* [15] *O Lord, open thou my lips; and my mouth shall shew forth thy praise.* [16] *For thou desirest not sacrifice; else would I give it: thou delightest not in burnt offering.* [17] *The sacrifices of God are a broken spirit: a broken and a contrite heart, O God, thou wilt not despise.*

David knew that He was guilty. He knew that he deserved to be pursued and punished for his sin. But he also understood, albeit in a shadowy way, how there is forgiveness for the true worshipper, in order that we may fellowship with God.

This is the reason why the Messiah must come. All the Old Testament sacrifices pointed to the one sacrifice of the Messiah, the Lamb of God who takes away the sin of the world.

This is the reason why David said that God does not desire sacrifice. Indeed, the offences that David committed were so heinous and high-handed (cf. Num 15:30), that there was no sacrifice appointed for his atonement. The sin offerings were for sins of ignorance (see Lev 4:1, 13, 22; 5:15), not for wilful sins such as what he committed. He had no recourse, but to cast himself completely at the mercy of the LORD. Only the sacrifice of the antitype would be sufficient. All Old Testament sacrifices pointed to the Messiah's sacrifice. So, animal sacrifices without repentance and faith in the Messiah are meaningless. On the other hand, those who worship in union with the Messiah are enabled to worship in spirit and in truth, so that out of their contrite hearts and lips would pour forth sweet savour sacrifices pleasing to the LORD. In fact, this is the mission of Christ; for did He not say in Psalm 22:22, in regard to what He would do on the basis of His crucifixion: "I will declare thy name unto my brethren: in the midst of the congregation will I praise thee." Is this not exactly what we are given to sing in union with Christ in verse 15: *"O Lord, open thou my lips; and my mouth shall shew forth thy praise"*?

David's heart was beating to the same rhythm as that of the greater David, only that the latter's heart is still beating loud and strong as His mouth shows forth God's praise through the Church, His body!

David is, indirectly, seeking the forgiveness of the LORD on the basis of the perfect sacrifice of the Messiah. And even as he pleads for forgiveness, he takes up the plea of the Messiah to bless His Church, for that is the reason why the Messiah came. Christ came to redeem His bride, the Church. He came to save her from her sins (cf. Eph 5:25).

> *18 Do good in thy good pleasure unto Zion: build thou the walls of Jerusalem. 19 Then shalt thou be pleased with the sacrifices of righteousness, with burnt offering and whole burnt offering: then shall they offer bullocks upon thine altar.*

The sacrifice of the Church is only as acceptable as the sincerity of the members of the Church.

Every member of the Church must be mindful that his sin is not a private matter, for when one suffers all suffer. When Achan sinned, Israel could not defeat Ai.

Today, it is the same. For this reason, we must not only seek forgiveness for the sake of our personal enjoyment of God. We must seek forgiveness for Christ's sake—who is the Head of the Church of which we are members. Indeed, we must plead for forgiveness in union with Christ who took our guilt upon Himself.

Conclusion

Let us, beloved brethren and children, learn from David and the greater David. Let us abhor ourselves when we sin against the LORD. Let us plead His mercy. Let us plead for restoration and let us seek forgiveness, on the basis of what Christ has done for us, and in imitation of what He teaches us to do in this Psalm. Indeed, let us sing this Psalm with Christ our head singing with us that we may have the assurance that the Father will indeed hear our pleas, for they are also the pleas of His Son on our behalf. Amen. Ω

Psalm 52:
The Righteous One's Hope
in a Sea of
Malicious Tongues

Psalm 52 was penned at the time when David heard the news, that Doeg the Edomite had reported to Saul, that he had seen him at the house of Ahimelech the priest.

David was at that time in the service of King Saul as one of his army captains. Saul had become very jealous because David was doing very well, and becoming very popular, particularly amongst the women. So he wanted to kill him off.

When David finally confirmed that this was Saul's intention, he decided to flee.

One of the first places he ran to was Nob, a city where the priests of the LORD were residing. There, he met with Ahimelech who was ministering in the tabernacle of the LORD.

David lied to Abimelech that he was on a mission on behalf of Saul, and because the king's business required haste, he did not bring any food, or weapons with him. Ahimelech gave him the showbread in the tabernacle and the sword of Goliath.

But Doeg, the Edomite, happened to be there. David had an uncomfortable feeling about it, but did nothing.

Subsequently, it was told David that Doeg had reported his meeting with Ahimelech to Saul and even lied that Ahimelech had inquired of the LORD for him (1 Sam 22:10).

Saul summoned Ahimelech and his entire household, and had them slaughtered by Doeg. Then he went down to the city of Nob and there he slew all the men, women and children, and even the animals.

By the providence of God, one of the sons of Ahimelech, Abiathar by name, escaped and brought the terrible news to David.

We are not sure if it was at this point when David wrote this Psalm, or whether it was written earlier before he got news of the slaughter at Nob.

But in any case, while this Psalm was occasioned by the destruction that spewed forth from the malicious tongue of Doeg, it is written under the inspiration of the Spirit of Christ. As such, it is a Psalm that points us to the sufferings of the Lord under the pall of many malicious wagging tongues—some ready to accuse, some spreading lies about Him, some mocking Him, some expressing hurtful opinions, etc.

We may entitle this Psalm *"The Righteous One's Hope in a Sea of Malicious Tongues."* It reflects the anguish and hope in the heart of our Lord, as He faced the slander and malice of those who clamoured for His death. It is appointed by our Saviour for us to sing with Him that we may better appreciate His anguish as He lived and suffered for us. This feeling of anguish when found in David's heart was, no doubt, mingled with unrighteous thoughts; but in the heart of our Saviour, it was perfectly righteous; and therefore, His sentiments are worthy of our ownership and imitation.

Indeed, apart from using it in corporate worship, this Psalm may be used by all righteous ones—believers united to Christ—who are suffering under similar circumstances.

I agree with Andrew Bonar that it was natural to place this Psalm after Psalm 51. Indeed, I think it is so by divine appointment. The reason is that anyone who experiences the trauma that is described in Psalm 51 will probably also experience, in the aftermath, the troubles described in Psalm 52. No doubt, even after David repented of his sin, a multitude of people would have clamoured for his blood. Many of these would act like Doeg.

So this Psalm is particularly fitting for the encouragement of anyone of us who may be in a situation where we have to face with malicious wagging tongues after a traumatic fall, and deliverance by the LORD.

Let's look at this Psalm briefly. This Psalm has three stanzas, according to the divisions created by the "selahs" or pauses.

In the first stanza, verses 1-3, the malicious boaster is condemned for his wickedness. In the second stanza, verses 4-5, the malicious boaster is warned against judgement to come. And finally, the Righteous One reflects on His exasperation in the hearing of the LORD and His Church, verse 6 to the end. A simple outline may be given as follows:

1. v. 1-3   The Condemnation
2. v. 4-5   The Admonition
3. v. 6-9   The Reflection

The Condemnation

¹ Why boastest thou thyself in mischief, O mighty man? the goodness of God endureth continually. ² Thy tongue deviseth mischiefs; like a sharp razor, working deceitfully. ³ Thou lovest evil more than good; and lying rather than to speak righteousness. Selah.

Doeg was a *mighty man* in so far as the world was concerned. He was powerful and strong. He had access to and influence upon the king. He could be of great use in the kingdom of God if only he would humble himself to serve Him.

Instead, he lifted himself up, and took pride in doing evil. In doing so, he was directly opposed to the LORD whose *goodness endures continually*.

Everything that man does, he does in service of God, or in opposition against God. Doeg was an enemy of God. He used his tongue to devise mischief, to cause trouble, to destroy and cut down. He had no qualms about speaking lies to accomplish his intentions, for he loved evil more than good. He cared not to speak righteously. He cared not about peace and edification.

That Doeg, who troubled David, is gone. He is suffering just recompense for his wickedness, and will never trouble God's people ever again. But in his place many mighty men have arisen, who are proudly following in his footsteps.

Our Lord was faced with many such Doegs. They slandered His name, spoke lies against Him, mocked Him, cast doubts about His character and clamoured for His blood. Shall we who are His disciples be spared from the same trials?

The Lord Himself says:

"If the world hate you, ye know that it hated me before it hated you" (Jn 15:18).

So let us be prepared to face our Doegs. We cannot do anything to them except to commit them to the LORD.

They will speak against us at every opportunity. They will express their opinions in the grapevine of gossip. They shall use their tongues in the papers, in Facebook, in Twitter and private chatgroups to make sure that the world knows of any suspicion of blameworthiness on our part. Like Doeg, they do not really care about the facts. They have no compassion. They want to make their opinions known. They want things to be done their way. They will clamour for our blood. We are guilty, unless proven innocent, irrefutably to their shame.

Let us not be surprised, nor be overtaken with grief and guilt when this happens. We must commit ourselves to the LORD. Our Lord who was tempted in all points like as we are, and yet sinned not, has given us righteous words to express ourselves under such circumstances. David was able to pen those words against his own experience. He acknowledged that he had contributed to the slaughter at Nob. It must have pricked his conscience, but he knew that he had no malice when he went to Ahimelech. The malice was in Doeg's heart and tongue. He could, therefore, speak out against Doeg with the righteous words of the Lord. And so too if we are not guilty as charged by our critics, we may indeed plead with the LORD against them.

But let anyone who perpetuates evil with his tongue take heed. God is not mocked. Listen therefore to the Lord's warning.

2. The Admonition

4 Thou lovest all devouring words, O thou deceitful tongue. 5 God shall likewise destroy thee forever, he shall take thee away, and pluck thee out of [thy] dwelling place, and root thee out of the land of the living. Selah.

The deceitful tongue loves to devour or to destroy. Words can hurt and words can tear down. So the tongue can cause terrible damage like in the case of Doeg's.

As James puts it:

"... the tongue is a little member, and boasteth great things. Behold, how great a matter a little fire kindleth!" (Jas 3:5).

Doeg told a half truth about David's visit to Ahimelech. It resulted in the slaughter of the city of Nob.

So too we must be mindful of how easily our tongues can cause great pain and sorrow. It must make us very reluctant to express negative opinions about things and decisions for which we do not have the full picture.

Think about how much talk there is on the internet whenever anything negative happens, whether it is a train breakdown or a rat infestation or a viral outbreak. How many have clamoured for the resignation of certain government officers? How many have offered their opinion as if their opinion is what really matters?

Many tongues are wagging. Many tongues want to be heard. Many suppose that they are wiser, and more righteous than those who are working round the clock to solve the problems.

We must take care not to fall into that sins of the tongue by which we tear down rather than build up. We must especially be careful lest by our tongue, we touch an apple of God's eye, and condemn those whom God has justified.

For when that happens, God will vindicate and condemn.

5 God shall likewise destroy thee forever, he shall take thee away, and pluck thee out of thy dwelling place, and root thee out of the land of the living.

If a tongue destroys a child of God, God will destroy the tongue forever. "The tongue is a fire, a world of iniquity... and it is set on fire of hell," says James (Jas 3:6).

God's children can take comfort that God Himself will vindicate them and take action against those who by their tongue seek to destroy them.

Those who use their tongues against God's children, especially when they know them to be believers, should take heed and know that He—who will require us to account for every idle word—will not leave destructive words unpunished.

He will punish in the day of judgement. He may even punish in this life. He will punish so that the righteous may see and fear. This is part of the reflection of the Righteous One on this matter.

3. The Reflection

⁶ The righteous also shall see, and fear, and shall laugh at him: ⁷ Lo, this is the man that made not God his strength; but trusted in the abundance of his riches, and strengthened himself in his wickedness.

Those who speak proudly against God's children, as it were, without giving face to the God they serve, can expect a very severe public judgement against them.

They may laugh at the righteous in this life. They may mock at them for trusting in the LORD. They may boast of what they can do without the LORD. But the last laugh will be reserved for God's children.

The enemies of God and their children will face everlasting destruction. In contrast, God's children will enjoy the blessings of the LORD in this life and in the life to come:

⁸ But I am like a green olive tree in the house of God: I trust in the mercy of God forever and ever.

Who is this "I" who is like a green olive tree? This "I" could refer to David, or it could refer to Israel or the Church. But is it not the case that Christ alone can most fittingly appropriate these words?

He is, indeed, like a green olive tree in the house of God. He is perfectly righteous and perfectly fruitful. It is in union with Him that the Church is known as the olive tree in Romans 11. The Visible Church has many branches that are decayed or are fruitless, and need to be trimmed. But Christ is forever a green olive tree, and so are the elect united to Him in the Church Invisible.

Our Lord was slandered and mocked. But He does not allow the pain and sorrow to hinder Him from God's work. Indeed, He recognises that all things, including painful ones, come from the hand of the LORD. And thus He concludes:

⁹ I will praise thee forever, because thou hast done it: and I will wait on thy name; for it is good before thy saints.

This statement seems so out of place. In the context of this Psalm, David had just experienced the wickedness of Doeg. Likewise, the Lord had to endure the malicious wagging tongues of the unbelieving Jews that eventually led Him to the cross. Yet, this Psalm concludes with a word of praise for what the LORD has done and a statement of trust in Him.

How could this be possible, except there be a firm recognition of God's sovereignty and goodness in everything?

So it is for us. We may lament about the actions of others that bring pain and sorrow to us. We may take comfort in God's Word that He will vindicate. We may sing words of imprecations and warning which our Lord has provided for us.

But ultimately, we must not allow anger and discontentment to eat into us. We must still turn our eyes to the LORD, and see that the LORD is good, and that He brought all the pains and sorrows we have experienced to pass for our good. And so we must trust Him still.

Conclusion

Have you been hurt by the tongues of man, dear child of God? Do not allow yourself to become despondent or to take revenge. Leave the matter to the LORD, trusting that He will see to your vindication and your good.

Go to the Lord Jesus for comfort. Sing the words He has provided you. He will sing with you. He is your compassionate Great High Priest. He was tempted in all points like as you are and yet without sin. He understands, and He cares. He went through a more terrible time under malicious wagging tongues than you can ever imagine. Amen. Ω

Psalm 53:
The Righteous One's
Answer to Atheism

Christians, redeemed by the blood of Christ, are *in* this world, but not *of* this world (Jn 17:15-16). We were born again by the Spirit that we might one day dwell in the celestial city where righteousness prevails. We are "strangers and pilgrims on the earth" (Heb 11:13; cf. 1 Pet 2:11).

For this reason, despite the corruption of our nature, many Christians will find it baffling to dwell in this world where wickedness and atheism prevail. "We know that we are of God, and the whole world lieth in wickedness," says the Apostle John (1 Jn 5:19).

It is perhaps for this reason that Christ our Saviour appointed for us two almost identical Psalms to be, as it were, spectacle lenses for us to see what God thinks of the world and its foolishness.

I am referring to Psalms 53 and 14. These two Psalms are well known to New Testament believers because they are quoted by the Apostle Paul to support the doctrine of the Total Depravity of man in Romans 3.

Contentwise, they are almost identical—just like the two lenses in our spectacles. The two main differences are, firstly, in the way God is addressed. In Psalm 14, the name of God, *Jehovah*, is used, whereas in Psalm 53, the word *"Elohim"* is used. *Elohim* emphasises the might and power of God. This is consistent with the second significant difference between these two Psalms, which is in verse 5.

What is the difference? The difference is that in Psalm 14, verse 6 is addressed to the wicked; whereas the counterpart in Psalm 53, i.e. the second part of verse 5, is addressed to believers.

In Psalm 14, the emphasis is that God will deal with the wicked for their wickedness towards His people. In Psalm 53, the emphasis is that God's people will triumph over the wicked.

So as someone puts it: Psalm 14 refers to God's enemies and their alarm, whereas Psalm 53 refers to God's people and their interest. Psalm 14 contemplates judgements against God's enemies; whereas Psalm 53 contemplates vindication for God's people.

So Andrew Bonar entitled Psalm 14 as "The Righteous One's view of the earth and its prospect," and Psalm 53 as "The Righteous One's view of the earth and the victory of God's people." We may entitle it simply, *"The Righteous One's Answer to Atheism,"* in contrast to Psalm 14, which we entitled *"The Righteous One's Censure of Atheism."* The Righteous One, of course, is Christ, who alone is righteous, and therefore is alone able to give a wise, objective and righteous judgement of the foolishness of the world. It is His song that we are singing when we sing this Psalm in union with Him.

Let us take a fresh look at this Psalm, bearing this in mind.

We can divide this Psalm into two parts. In the first part, verse 1-4, we have an explanation of why the world is in such a state of moral chaos and wickedness; whereas in the second part, verses 5-6, we are given a glimpse of the solution to the problem.

1. v. 1-4   The Problem
2. v. 5-6   The Answer

1. The Problem

¹ The fool hath said in his heart, There is no God. Corrupt are they, and have done abominable iniquity: there is none that doeth good. ² God looked down from heaven upon the children of men, to see if there were any that did understand, that did seek God. ³ Every one of them is gone back: they are altogether become filthy; there is none that doeth good, no, not one. ⁴ Have the workers of iniquity no knowledge? who eat up my people as they eat bread: they have not called upon God.

Man is made in the image of God. There are no natural atheists. Every man knows by nature that God exists.

But fallen man hates God, and so he tries his best to hold down the truth in unrighteousness (Rom 1:18). He tries to convince himself that there is no God. This is what he is doing when he says in his heart, *"There is no God."*

His heart tells him that there is God, but he is trying to convince himself that there is no God.

He succeeds to an extent. At least, he succeeds sufficiently to disregard God's laws, and His righteousness and holiness. And so he lives as if God does not exist.

And as he lives without the love of God and His fear, nothing he does can be acceptable to God. Instead, he becomes corrupt and does abominable iniquity.

Who are we referring to? Are we referring only to terrorists, robbers, adulterers and murderers? No, no; we are talking about every man.

Notice how the Spirit emphasises this fact:

¹ ...there is none that doeth good....³ Every one of them is gone back: there is none that doeth good, no, not one.

Whose conclusion is this? It is God's conclusion. This is what Christ is saying when He would have us confess with Him that God is looking down from heaven to seek out any that *"did understand, [or] that did seek God"* (v. 2). But he finds none. If anyone can find a righteous man upon the earth, it must be God who knows all things and sees all things. And yet we are told that it is God's conclusion that there are none righteous, no not one (v. 3). Not one of the natural sons of man can meet up to God's standard of righteousness.

The Apostle Paul confirms this doctrine, not only by quoting from our text (Rom 3:10-12), but declaring: "For all have sinned, and come short of the glory of God" (Rom 3:23).

The fact is: without love for God and a fear of Him, we cannot glorify God. Therefore, we will fall short of His glory.

But how bad is the problem? Is it just a case of a touch of naughtiness that affects some men, at some time, in some things that they do? Well, no, for as the Spirit of Christ declares emphatically:

³ Every one of them is gone back: they are altogether become filthy; there is none that doeth good, no, not one.

Man is altogether become filthy because of the Fall. He sinned in Adam and is guilty in him. He inherits original sin, and a corrupt nature. All that he does, says, or thinks, is therefore tainted with sin. Even his most righteous acts are impure. All our righteousnesses are as filthy rags in the sight of God, says Isaiah (Isa 64:6).

This explains—does it not—all the trouble, pains and sorrows that exist in the world. If every man loves and fears the LORD, would there be any of the pains and sorrows in the world? No, no; it would be paradise on earth!

Foolishness is a disease that affects all men. But make no mistake: none of us should be complacent about this disease.

In fact, we should live such a distinct life from the world that, in some ways, the world which believe not God finds us offensive. This distinction is implied in verse 4, where the workers of iniquity are condemned for persecuting and taking advantage of God's people. Why do they do so? One of the major reasons is that they hate God and therefore they hate those who love and know Him.

Therefore as believers, we should not be neutral to the atheism of the wicked, or worse, applaud them for their way of life. God has declared those who live atheistically to be fools. The fool has said in his heart, "There is no God."

They may think themselves to be very wise because they know rocket science, nanotechnology, geology, archaeology or palaeontology. But if they say in their heart, "There is no God," they are fools.

The world may not regard them to be fools, but God does; and one day, He will openly condemn them for foolishness and He will vindicate the saints whom the world regards to be fools.

2. The Answer

[5] *There were they in great fear, where no fear was: for God hath scattered the bones of him that encampeth against thee: thou hast put them to shame, because God hath despised them.*

These words are directed to God's children who are persecuted for righteousness' sake. These are comprehended in the word "*thee*", which is really Christ and those united to Him.

The world today may be without the fear of God. The world may trample underfoot righteousness; and look upon God's people with disdain; and persecute them by vehemently denouncing them as fools, or politely hinting that they are fools.

They seem to be able to get away with it. But not for long! The day of judgement is coming. God will vindicate His people. He will avenge His people. He will condemn the wicked by showing that His people are right.

That day will be a day of great fear. The wicked are foolish, proud and self-sufficient. But they will cringe in fear and call upon the mountains and the rocks to cover them for the day of the wrath of the Lamb is come.

What shall we do as we anticipate that day? Let us not look forward to it like the Pharisees who are full of condemnation for the wicked. Let us, rather, remember that we too are by nature foolish, and have need of deliverance.

So let us sing in union with our Saviour, the alone Righteous One, verse 6:

[6] *Oh that the salvation of Israel were come out of Zion! When God bringeth back the captivity of his people, Jacob shall rejoice, and Israel shall be glad.*

Oh that the salvation of Israel were come out of Zion! Oh that the LORD would redeem His

Church through the ministration of the word coming out of Zion. When that happens, then Christ and His Church—here referred to as Jacob and Israel—shall rejoice and be glad.

We have seen at the beginning of this Psalm that there are none righteous, no not one, except Christ. We are all fools by nature. There is no exception. "Foolishness is bound in the heart of a child," says Solomon (Prov 22:15). We were all children of the world and if God does not intervene we will remain spiritually childish.

But God can change us. He can change us by redeeming us through the blood of Christ and transforming us through the renewing of our minds in the knowledge of Christ by His Spirit and by His word.

He can, in this way, bring us unto salvation. Is this not what the Apostle Paul is alluding to in 2 Timothy 3:15? We are fools by nature, but Christ can by His word and Spirit make us wise unto salvation.

And we need to be wise. We should long to be wise.

We began our study of this Psalm by talking about the problems of the world that result from foolishness. Do you realise, dear child of God, that most, if not all your problems in the Christian life, and in the church have their origin in foolishness?

If we were wise, we would not make foolish choices which make us practical atheists and bring pain and sorrow to ourselves.

If we were wise, and did not entertain foolish thought patterns, we would be able to overcome many of the pains and sorrows surrounding relational problems, with our friends, colleagues and church mates.

We need, therefore, to pray for wisdom.

> "If any of you lack wisdom, let him ask of God, that giveth to all men liberally, and upbraideth not; and it shall be given him. [6] But let him ask in faith, nothing wavering. For he that wavereth is like a wave of the sea driven with the wind and tossed" (Jas 1:5-6).

We need to pray for it unwaveringly. We need to ask the LORD to help us to apply His word to our hearts. We must be determined to be wise, first by recognising that we are, by nature foolish, and have need of the wisdom that God alone can give; and secondly, by pursuing after the knowledge of Christ in His fear.

Conclusion

The fool hath said in his heart, there is no God. Let us not be fools. Let us rather remind ourselves that unless we are made wise unto salvation by the word and Spirit of Christ, we shall remain foolish, and we shall reap our foolishness in pain and sorrow.

Let us therefore pray. Let us pray for wisdom. Let us pray that the Lord will revive us, and change all our wrong thinking into biblical and godly ways of thinking.

We must not allow ourselves to be consumed by the foolishness of the world; for otherwise, in the day that God deals with foolishness, we shall be as the foolish virgins who are shut out of the wedding banquet of the Lamb. Let us be wise, and be prepared for His coming, by seeking true knowledge, and true ways of thinking about God, about ourselves, and about one another. Only in this way will we be able to glorify God, and enjoy him and one another. Amen. Ω

Psalm 54:
The Righteous One's
Response to Betrayal

Betrayal is one of the most painful experiences that a person has to endure. Those of us who have experienced it, would understand the intense pain and bewilderment that comes with it.

Psalm 54 is about betrayal. It was written at a time when David was experiencing betrayal from some people he thought were his friends. He was being pursued by Saul, and had gone to the wilderness of Ziph to hide out with some of his men. While he was there, David and his men, no doubt, sought to be of service to the people there, such as protecting them from raiders. But the men of Ziph were apparently unappreciative. They went to Saul to report to him that he was dwelling in the woods in their midst (1 Sam 23:14-20). Saul and his men went down to pursue David and was about to close in on him when the LORD intervened by sending the Philistines to invade the land; and so Saul's attention was diverted.

David moved on to the wilderness of Engedi. But later he returned to the wilderness of Ziph again; and again the Ziphites betrayed him; and Saul came again after him (1 Sam 26:1-3). David must have been deeply grieved. It was apparently upon this second betrayal that David wrote this Psalm. If this is so, then the last verse of this Psalm is probably referring to the first instance when God delivered him just when Saul was closing in on him and his men. But whatever the case might be, one thing is sure. This Psalm is not just a personal poetry of grief. It was inspired by the Spirit of Christ for the Church to sing in union with Him.

We can see how this Psalm could easily have been taken up by the Lord Jesus Christ as He began to sense a growing opposition to His ministry, which made it more and more dangerous for Him to minister in the open (cf. Jn 11:8). This sense of hostility even from those who were once His followers, and those who were helped by Him (Jn 6:66), no doubt, translated into a sense of betrayal, which would culminate with the treachery of Judas Iscariot (cf. Jn 6:71).

The betrayal of Judas Iscariot will be addressed in the next Psalm, but so clearly does this Psalm lead us to the LORD that it is appointed for liturgical reading on Good Friday in the Church of England. Good Friday is the day that Rome and most churches today commemorate the Lord's death. We should, of course, commemorate the LORD's death, rather, at the LORD's Supper.

But is this Psalm primarily about David and only to be applied secondarily to Christ and Christians? Or is David merely a type whose experience reflected what our Lord experienced in the Passion Week? I believe it is the latter. I believe this Psalm reflects the anguish of our Lord as He suffered betrayal. For this reason, we may sing it in corporate worship to meditate on the sufferings of our Saviour. But for the same reason, all believers united to Christ may use this Psalm whenever they experience betrayal of some sort. We may entitle it *"The Righteous One's Response to Betrayal."*

It has two obvious stanzas separated by the "Selah." In the first stanza, the Righteous One cries unto the LORD for help against those who have risen against Him. In the second stanza, He acknowledges the LORD's past and future helps.

1. v. 1-3   Prayer for Help
2. v. 4-6   Praise for the Helper

1. Prayer for Help

¹ Save me, O God, by thy name, and judge me by thy strength.

"Save me, O God, by thy name!" Does this not remind us of our Lord's petition in His high priestly prayer?

"Holy Father, keep through thine own name those whom thou hast given me, that they may be one, as we are" (Jn 17:11b).

But what does it mean to be kept or saved by the name of God? To understand what it means, we must understand that the name of God is really a shorthand which refers to all the perfections of God such as His wisdom, power, holiness, justice, goodness and truth.

When the Lord cries, "*Save me... by thy name,*" He is really appealing to the Father to exercise His wisdom, power and goodness, etc, for His deliverance. And so He adds, "*judge me by thy strength*" or "vindicate me by thy might."

In times when we feel betrayed, we feel that we can no longer trust man or look to man. This is so because man is imperfect. Man fails; he sins; he is foolish; he is weak; he is selfish. Because we can see and hear fellow men, we tend to rely on them. But when we experience betrayal, we realise that only the LORD can help us. He alone is reliable. He alone can vindicate us.

So David and the Lord cried out:

² Hear my prayer, O God; give ear to the words of my mouth. ³ For strangers are risen up against me, and oppressors seek after my soul: they have not set God before them.

The Ziphites and men of Saul rose up against David. Judas and the Jews rose up against our Lord. Most of them were strangers to our Lord and to His gospel. Were they not strangers to the gospel, God would be before their eyes and they would not persecute the righteous.

But since they did, it is clear that nothing was going to stop them from their wickedness. No amount of talking and persuasion would help. Only God could help.

What then shall we do, when we feel betrayed by man, but to cry out unto the LORD? He will hear us. He will comfort us and He will deliver us.

But let us not stop at petitions. Rather, let us learn to praise Him as our LORD does in the second stanza of this Psalm.

2. Praise for the Helper

⁴ Behold, God is mine helper: the Lord is with them that uphold my soul. ⁵ He shall reward evil unto mine enemies: cut them off in thy truth.

God is perfectly righteous and just. He will help the righteous. He will defend those who are unjustly treated by his enemies. He will render evil unto the wicked. He will demonstrate that truth will prevail.

The Jews, who clamoured for the blood of the Lord, ought to be the friends of the Lord since they were His covenant people. Instead, they became His enemies. They hated Him; and they loved neither truth nor righteousness. God eventually cut them off and transferred the blessing of the covenant to the Gentiles.

Today, this promise holds true. God is the helper of all who are united to Christ, who are on His side, who would have upheld His soul in prayer had they witnessed His afflictions.

Do you feel yourself slandered and betrayed, dear child of God? Seek not your own vindication: for the more you try, the more likely you will sin against the LORD. So leave it to the LORD. He will see to it that justice is done for Christ's sake.

What was true for our Lord, will be true for you. And so let your response to a sense of betrayal be as our Lord's response, rather than one of defeat and despair.

What is our Lord's response? It is in the final two verses:

> [6] I will freely sacrifice unto thee: I will praise thy name, O LORD; for it is good. [7] For he hath delivered me out of all trouble: and mine eye hath seen his desire upon mine enemies."

David could have written this as he reflected on how the LORD delivered him out of trouble the first time the Ziphites betrayed him.

But these words have a timeless significance. Our Lord must have taken them upon His lips in perfect anticipation of His deliverance at the resurrection.

We may take these words with the same hope. Our Lord was fully vindicated, so we too will be fully vindicated.

Shall we then wait for the day of full vindication before we worship the LORD? No, no; the sacrifice of Christ is complete; and He rose from the dead. Victory is secured for us. Justice is sure. Vindication for God's children is a matter of when, not if.

Shall we not, therefore, in anticipation and certainty of hope, worship the LORD freely? Let us offer unto the LORD the calves of our lips. Let us praise Him in sincere hope that He will do what is right and will one day deliver us fully from all our troubles.

Conclusion

Our Lord, when faced with a sense of betrayal and opposition from those who might have benefited from His ministry, did not take matters into His own hand by dealing with them. Instead, He committed His grief to His Father, and looked to Him in praise knowing that He would vindicate Him and deliver Him out of His troubles. Shall we not learn to do likewise? Shall we not take His words in our lips in recognition that He understands our grief because He has experienced something worse? Shall we not also take up His words in union with Him in corporate worship, not only that we may feel with Him what He has suffered for us, but that we may encourage one another with His example? Amen. Ω

Psalm 55:
The Righteous One's
Response to Treachery

Psalm 54 was about betrayal. David was betrayed by the Ziphites when he was being pursued by Saul. But the betrayal experienced by David when he wrote Psalm 54 is small compared to what he experienced when he wrote Psalm 55. Compared to what he experienced in Psalm 54, what he experienced here is treachery.

Psalm 55 was apparently written by David at the time when his favourite son Absalom rose against Him. That was bad enough. But to make matters worse, one of his best friends and counsellors, Ahithophel, cast in his lot with Absalom and was advising him on how to defeat his father! What could be worse?

It was under such a dark cloud over his soul that David wrote this Psalm.

But make no mistake, this Psalm is not just a song of personal lament, but it was written under the inspiration of the Holy Spirit and appointed for the Church to sing in worship, in union with Christ the greater David.

Andrew Bonar puts it well when he says:

> "We may read these strains as expressing David's feelings in some peculiar seasons of distress, and as the experience of Christ's Church in every age; for we find much, very much, that accords altogether with humanity in a state of intensely stirred emotion, and affection wounded to the quick. Yet still it is in Jesus, the Man of Sorrows, that the Psalm finds its fullest illustration. He was the soul that was stirred to its lowest depth by scenes such as are described here."

When our Lord told his disciples about His betrayal by Judas Iscariot, He spoke of it as fulfilling Scripture:

> "I speak not of you all: I know whom I have chosen: but that the scripture may be fulfilled, He that eateth bread with me hath lifted up his heel against me" (Jn 13:18).

He is quoting Psalm 41:9. Psalm 41 was written, apparently, under the same circumstance as Psalm 55. So the "familiar friend" referred to in Psalm 41:9 is none other than Ahithophel, who is referred to as "*a man mine equal, my guide, and mine acquaintance*" in verse 13 of our text.

We have no doubt, therefore, that Psalm 55 finds its fullest fulfilment in Christ. We may entitle it "*The Righteous One's Response to Treachery.*"

This Psalm can be divided into three parts plus a conclusion. Each of the three parts begins with a prayer or petition, followed by explanations or arguments supporting the request:

1. v. 1-8   A Plea out of Sorrow
2. v. 9-14   A Request out of Anguish
3. v. 15-19   An Imprecation out of Indignation
4. v. 20-23   A Conclusion out of Sympathy

1. A Plea out of Sorrow

¹ Give ear to my prayer, O God; and hide not thyself from my supplication. ² Attend unto me, and hear me: I mourn in my complaint, and make a noise...

Like David, our Lord experienced deep sorrow when He was betrayed by a trusted friend. Though our Lord knew who he was "who should betray him" (Jn 6:64), He would not relate to him according to His secret knowledge nor did He reveal it to His disciples. He treated him as a trusted disciple and related to him according to his present conduct and apparent disposition. This is evidenced by the fact that he was appointed as the treasurer of the band.

So when Judas began to manifest himself as the betrayer, oh what deep sorrow must have filled our Lord's heart! Our Lord, we must remember, is fully man even as He is fully God.

He heart was *"sore pained within him"* (v. 4); and no doubt a sense of *"fearfulness and trembling"* (v. 5) came upon Him.

In the Garden of Gethsemane, He prayed with great drops of sweat upon His forehead as He cried out unto His Father, "If it be possible, take this cup away from me..."

It is not inconceivable, therefore, that He thought in the words of verse 6, *"Oh that I had wings like a dove! for then would I fly away, and be at rest."*

Is this not how we sometimes feel too? When the storm is brewing, oh what temptation fills our hearts, but to fly away, to *"escape from the windy storm and tempest"* (v. 8) and *"remain in the wilderness"* (v. 7). Oh how often have I felt like that, and how intense the feeling!

I thank God that I am not alone. Our Lord suffered the same sense of betrayal of friendship—though at a level I could never comprehend. When a friend or a loved one leaves me, I know I am partly at fault, but when Judas betrayed the Lord, and when His disciples forsook Him, it was not because of any wrong He has done.

But as our Lord suffered the same grief, I know He understands and He will intercede for me as I cry unto the Father with the words He provided for me.

But now, in the second part of our text, we see our Lord's request to the Father with respect to those who had risen against Him.

2. A Request out
of Anguish

[9] *Destroy, O Lord, and divide their tongues: for I have seen violence and strife in the city....*

When David wrote these words, he must have been thinking about the counsel that Ahithophel was giving to Absalom. As he saw the lawlessness, chaos and destruction in Jerusalem in the aftermath of the uprising of his son, his heart was filled with anguish. He knew that if he allowed it to continue, there would be disaster in the land.

And so he desired of the LORD that He might confuse the rebels and make their plans of none effect, just as He confounded the tongues of the people when they tried to build the tower of Babel.

This prayer was all the more urgent because the man who was advising his son was one who was close to him—who knew him well, and knew his weaknesses. This is what the verses 12-14 are all about.

Indeed, from the historical accounts, we see that had God not confused Ahithophel's counsel through the counter-suggestions of Hushai, then Absalom would have defeated

David.

Our Lord would have prayed the same prayer. Judas knew where He would be, his betrayal would be effective unless the Father intervened.

But we must understand that His prayer was always qualified with, "Yet not as I will, but thy will be done."

And so both their prayers were heard, but in different ways. David was delivered from Absalom. Our Lord was delivered to be crucified according to the will of the Father.

I thank God for the godly example of how to pray for deliverance, for thereby I am also encouraged to pray for deliverance when I know that I have been unfairly plotted against.

But personal deliverance is not the only thing to pray for in such circumstance, so we see thirdly in this Psalm…

3. An Imprecation out of Indignation

[15] Let death seize upon them, and let them go down quick into hell: for wickedness is in their dwellings, and among them….

When tumult arises against the anointed of the LORD, it is not only a matter of personal dispute. It is an affront against God, for the anointed is the LORD's representative.

So Absalom and Ahithophel's rebellion is a rebellion against God. So Judas' betrayal was a betrayal against God. Their sin indicates that they have no fear of God (v. 19). If they feared God, they would not have fought against the LORD's anointed.

I don't think David liked Saul; but he feared God, and therefore he refused to hurt Saul: for he was the anointed of the LORD.

Those who fear not God and would rebel against Him deserve not only to be confounded by the LORD, but also to be dealt with severely by the LORD.

Even as God hears the cries of the righteous and delivers them, He will punish those who refuse to repent of their ways. *"Because they have no changes"* (v. 19) simply means, "because they repent not."

As a servant of the Lord who has many faults myself, I must confess that I dare not use imprecations against those who show disregard for the office that the Lord has vested upon me.

But I thank God that as our Lord had prayed, I know He is deeply concerned when troubles arise in His Church; and I know that He will see to it that for His name's sake, good will come out of the trials we experience.

Let us, therefore, not be discouraged when we see debilitating politics and disregard for the church and her authority. As our Lord was forsaken, so His servants must experience the same. So Demas forsook Paul, and so throughout the ages, the servants of the Lord face desertions from departures and rebellion.

4. A Conclusion out of Sympathy

[20] He hath put forth his hands against such as be at peace with him: he hath broken his

covenant. ²¹ The words of his mouth were smoother than butter, but war was in his heart: his words were softer than oil, yet were they drawn swords.

David thought Ahithophel was his friend; the Lord thought that Judas was His friend; Paul thought that Demas was his friend. Every servant of the Lord who ever experienced similar trial thought that those who turned against him were his friends, when in fact, they had other motives in their heart.

Throughout the ages, the experience of David and of our Lord has repeated itself. There will be covenant-breakers or those who care not for their vows. They will speak peace when there is war in their heart. They will speak smooth words, which are laced with poison.

What should those who are afflicted by such troubles do? Our Lord exhorts us, and would have us exhort one another with the words, verse 22:

²² *Cast thy burden upon the LORD, and he shall sustain thee: he shall never suffer the righteous to be moved.*

The Apostle Peter is probably paraphrasing this verse when he reminds us:

"[Cast] all your care upon him; for he careth for you" (1 Pet 5:7).

What is the context in which Peter used those words? He used it in the context of the pain and sorrow that come through the anguish of church politics!

Peter reminds us of the devices of the devil to disrupt peace and to devour whom he may. The ancient serpent which provoked Absalom and Ahithophel to rebel, and Judas to betray the Lord, and Demas to forsake Paul, is still at work.

But we need not be afraid. So long as we are seeking to walk with the LORD, we may cast our burden upon Him, and He will sustain us: for He will never suffer the righteous to be moved.

So let us trust in the LORD. When men for whatever reasons treat us in unchristian ways, let us not give in to the temptation to respond in the same way. Let us, rather, seek to respond in a righteous way, and the LORD will see to it that our name is vindicated and His glory is upheld.

Conclusion

Not every one of us will experience the kind of betrayal that David and the Lord experienced. But some of us will, no doubt, feel like flying away like a dove from all the troubles we face—whether at work, at home or in church. If this is the case, this Psalm is for you too. Pray for deliverance as the Lord did. Trust the Lord to do that which is right. Leave it to Him to vindicate. Cast your burdens upon Him, and He shall sustain you: He will never suffer the righteous to be moved. Amen. Ω

Psalm 56:
The Righteous One's
Rest upon the Word of God

Psalm 56, as the title suggests, was occasioned by David's capture by the Philistines after he ran away from Saul. David, I am sure was trying to keep a low profile in Gath, but the servants of Achish, king of Gath, recognised him, apprehended him and brought him to the king (1 Sam 21:10ff). They said unto the king:

"[11] ...Is not this David the king of the land? did they not sing one to another of him in dances, saying, Saul hath slain his thousands, and David his ten thousands?" (1 Sam 21:11)

David feared for his life and instinctively pretended to be a mad man. The ruse apparently worked. King Achish thought that he was indeed a mad man, and released him. David would reflect on how the Lord delivered him at this time in Psalm 34. Psalm 56 was apparently also written after the occasion. I doubt David would have time during his arrest to write the Psalm. But it is written in such a way as to reflect on the thoughts and prayers of David during those terrifying hours or days.

We have no doubt, nevertheless, that David wrote under the inspiration of the Spirit of Christ so that these words reflect not only what he experienced, but also what Christ our Lord experienced when the Jews were clamouring for His death. Bishop George Horne says it well:

The same words are applicable to the situation and circumstance of David, pursued by his enemies; of Christ persecuted by the Jews; of the church, afflicted in the world; and of the soul encompassed by enemies, against whom she is forced to wage perpetual war.

We may entitle this Psalm *"The Righteous One's Rest upon the Word of God."* It is a Psalm which we may use both to feel something of our Saviour's inner battles as He bore our sin, and to exhort one another to trust in the LORD and His promises when we are faced with similar anxieties as our Saviour (see Col 3:16).

This Psalm does not have a distinct structure; but we may look at it as containing five ideas, each expressed in a couple of verses:

1. v. 1-2   An Expression of Distress
2. v. 3-4   An Expression of Strength
3. v. 5-7   An Expression of Grief
4. v. 8-11   An Expression of Trust
5. v. 12-13   An Expression of Hope

1. An Expression of Distress

[1] *Be merciful unto me, O God: for man would swallow me up; he fighting daily oppresseth me.* [2] *Mine enemies would daily swallow me up: for they be many that fight against me, O thou most High.*

David was persecuted by Saul; but now he is in the rough hands of the Philistines, who were ready to avenge the death of their country-men. He is surrounded by enemies ready to swallow him up.

Our Lord was in the same situation especially after His arrest. David had Saul, and king Achish and his henchmen. The greater David had Judas, and Annas and Caiaphas, and all the men who agreed with them, all clamouring for His blood.

What would have been in the mind of our Lord during those chaotic hours after Judas betrayed Him with a kiss? Our Lord was no stoic. We must not imagine that He felt nothing. I am sure it was partly in anticipation of the suffering under the hands of cruel men that our Lord cried out in the Garden of Gethsemane, "If it be possible take this cup from me."

What then would be the thought in our Lord's heart? No doubt, it was as expressed in this Psalm. No doubt He prayed unto His Father, "*Be merciful unto me, O God.*" Our Lord knew that whatever man might do to Him was in the hand of His Father. He knew that man could not help Him, but the Father could.

Oh may we learn, likewise, to take our distress unto the Father. Let us cry as our Lord did: "*Be merciful unto me, O God.*"

And then let us learn to find strength in the Lord and His word.

2. An Expression of Strength

³ What time I am afraid, I will trust in thee. ⁴ In God I will praise his word, in God I have put my trust; I will not fear what flesh can do unto me.

Verse 3 is a beautiful archaic expression. It simply means, "Whenever I am afraid, I will trust in thee."

To fear is human. David was a courageous warrior who slew thousands of Philistines; but there were times when he was afraid too. Our Lord was the God-Man. He could summon a thousand angels to His aid in an instant; but there were certainly times when He was afraid too. The capacity to fear is human. Before the Fall, man need not fear; but in a fallen world, a sense of fear is essential for survival. It is not necessarily sinful.

But especially at times of great anxiety, fear would often threaten to overwhelm the heart to respond in a sinful way. What would our Lord do when fear begins to flood His heart? He would trust in the Father. Trust is an act of the will. It is an act of the will that is helped by remembering the word of God.

Our Lord would call to mind the promises of God in His word. By the word, He found the strength and courage to trust the Father to do all things well. As a sense of the Father's care fills His heart, so any sense of the fear of men, and of circumstances, also abated.

No doubt, Christian men and women, boys and girls who put their trust in the word of God, will also have the greatest strength of character to face up to the abuses and attacks of fellow men.

What time you are afraid, turn to the LORD: recall His promises that He will never leave you, nor forsake you. Remember that all things will work together for good to them that love God. It is in this way that you will find the strength of our LORD to go through the most difficult times.

I do not know what sort of difficult times you have gone through. But for David and our Lord, it was often when they were misquoted and when they found their enemies trying to trap them at their words. Consider their thoughts in the expression of grief.

3. An Expression of Grief

⁵ Every day they wrest my words: all their thoughts are against me for evil. ⁶ They gather themselves together, they hide themselves, they mark my steps, when they wait for my soul. ⁷ Shall they escape by iniquity? in thine anger cast down the people, O God.

Although David wrote this Psalm as he reflected on his own thoughts during his time in Gath, he recognises that his fears, grief, anxieties and exasperation often arise out of a more common situation. This is the situation that involves people misunderstanding or twisting his words, or misquoting him. Such is the case when his enemies try to trap him at his word.

Why does God give him such experiences? I have, no doubt, that it is so that he might be a type of Christ, for indeed our LORD suffered by having his words twisted? Did he say, "I will destroy this temple that is made with hands, and within three days I will build another made without hands" (Mk 14:58)? Did not the Pharisees and Sadducees keep attempting to trap him? Show us a sign from heaven! Do we need to pay tax? Moses commands that we should stone such a woman: but what do you say (Lk 20:25; 11:16; Jn 8:6 etc)?

Are you facing this kind of trial? Have you experienced it before? I am sure you will know how exasperating it is. You are rumoured to have said certain things which you did not say. You wonder why no one came up to you to clarify them when they were so outrageous, that you would have been shocked yourself if you had said them. The disciple is not greater than his master! Pour out your heart to the LORD, knowing that your Lord suffered in the same way, and so He understands.

Did you weep, and did He not?

4. An Expression of Trust

⁸ Thou tellest my wanderings: put thou my tears into thy bottle: are they not in thy book?

God cares. Your teardrops are not lost. God has bottled them up. Your sighs do not vanish into the air. God has recorded them in His book.

This is not just a cute idea. It is an expression of God's love. Because David knew that God cares, he knew that God will answer his prayers. This is why he says:

⁹ When I cry unto thee, then shall mine enemies turn back: this I know; for God is for me.

David experienced it many times. Saul could not capture him because God intervened. King Achish let him go, not because David was a great actor, but because the LORD heard his cry. Our Lord had the same experience before His time was up. Yes, when it was time for Him to go to the cross as our representative, the Father would not spare Him the intense suffering. But even then, the Father would deliver Him, even if not immediately.

This is important for us to remember. Experience of past deliverances may encourage us to rest in the LORD; but let us remember that God can answer our prayer in a different way each time. So our confidence must not be based on experience. It must be based on the word of God.

And this is what we are told in the next verse:

¹⁰ In God will I praise his word: in the LORD will I praise his word. ¹¹ In God have I put my trust: I will not be afraid what man can do unto me.

Does this sound familiar? We just heard that in verses 3 and 4! This point is so important that our Lord repeats it.

As our Lord put His trust in the word of God, so let us do so!

And as we trust Him, let us hope in Him even when things are uncertain and the future seems bleak. Does not the future look bleak when we are facing persecution? But we must live by faith and not by sight.

5. An Expression of Hope

[12] *Thy vows are upon me, O God: I will render praises unto thee.* [13] *For thou hast delivered my soul from death: wilt not thou deliver my feet from falling, that I may walk before God in the light of the living?*

We do not know what vows David made unto God. It is possible that he is referring to a promise he made that he would render special praise to God if He would deliver Him. Or he may be referring to an expression of gratitude for deliverance (cf. Acts 18:18; 21:23-24).

Whatever the case may be, we know that our Lord's covenant was to die for His people in order that they may glorify and enjoy God. He knew that it is through the cross that He would praise God with the congregation. Psalm 22:25:

> "My praise shall be of thee in the great congregation: I will pay my vows before them that fear him."

Our Lord knew that the Father would deliver Him: for otherwise, how would He glorify and enjoy the Father with the people entrusted to Him?

And so, we see how this Psalm, as with many others, ends with a note that suggests that God has already delivered.

Remember that David is writing about his thoughts when he was confronted by Achish. Remember that his thoughts served to reflect the thoughts of our Lord during His arrest and interrogation. Deliverance was yet future at that time. And yet, it is spoken of in the past tense. Why?

Because God's Word will not return unto Him void. God keeps His promises. Has He said? Will He not bring it to pass? Our Lord knew that He would rise again from the grave that He might *"walk before God in the light of the living"* (v. 13).

Oh that the Lord will give us the same firm hope when we look to Him for deliverance from all our fears.

Conclusion

Our Lord went to the cross for us. Once again we see that He went not as an intrepid or senseless lamb. He went with a heart full of fears and anxieties. His suffering was real. But our Lord's fears and anxieties did not cripple Him. No, no; His faith in the word of God, and His hope in God triumphed over His fears. He found strength to do the Father's will. He found courage to keep His vow unto the Father.

For this cause we can today enjoy God's love and worship. Shall we not, therefore, learn from our Lord's example? As we remember His death, let us remember that everything He suffered, He suffered for wretched sinners like you and me. He suffered for us not just to redeem us from sin, but also to set us an example to follow (1 Pet 2:21), that we may also glorify and enjoy God through the pains and sorrows that we experience in this life. Amen.
Ω

Psalm 57:
The Righteous One
Under the Wings in Calamities

Psalm 57 is one of the Psalms appointed by the Church of England to be sung at Easter—the day[27] on which they celebrate the resurrection of Christ.

The reason for this assignment would be quite obvious if you read this Psalm with a Christological eye. This Psalm as the title suggests, was composed by David on the occasion of his escape from Saul in the cave at Engedi (1 Sam 24:1ff). David had earlier taken cover in the caves of Adullam. But at that time, Saul had not started to pursue him in earnest. Later, however, after the slaughter at Nob, the Ziphites betrayed David; and David was forced to flee. He went to the wilderness of Engedi.

Engedi is the largest oasis on the Western shore of the Dead Sea. It is there that one of the only two freshwater springs along the Western shore of the Dead Sea is found. It was a place where wild goats or ibex roamed, which is why it is called Engedi: literally, "the spring of the kid (goat)."

David stayed at one of the many caves at Engedi. When Saul heard that David was there, he brought his men down to hunt him out. David was, no doubt, filled with apprehension. Would Saul find him? And to add to his anxiety was the perplexity arising from the four hundred men who were with him. What kind of men were they? They were certainly not well-disciplined warriors! We are told, in 1 Samuel 22:2:

> "And every one that was in distress, and every one that was in debt, and every one that was discontented, gathered themselves unto him; and he became a captain over them: and there were with him about four hundred men."

With such a motley gang of people, we can expect anything but peace in the cave! David says:

> *4 My soul is among lions: and I lie even among them that are set on fire, even the sons of men, whose teeth are spears and arrows, and their tongue a sharp sword.*

I do not think he is referring to Saul and his men. He was not lying amongst them. David is clearly speaking about Saul in verse 3 and about Saul and his men in verse 6, but I believe that he is speaking about his own men here in verse 4! They would have been quarrelsome, and full of opinions, which they would make known to each other; and probably only David could subdue them. We think of how they wanted to kill Saul when he wandered into the cave; and how David had to restrain them (1 Sam 24:6-7).

What did David do under such an exasperating circumstance? He wrote a song. But this is no ordinary song. It was a Psalm, an inspired song. God had so ordered David's life and experience that his feelings would reflect the feelings of our Lord. David was being pursued by King Saul and his men; the greater David was being pursued by the prince of the power of the air, and the people blinded by him.

As David was perplexed by his followers, so the Lord was often perplexed by His own disciples. Remember how they bickered over who was greatest (Lk 9:46; 22:24). And

---

[27] Or days. Easter, to some Anglicans, covers the remembrance of the events of the week leading up to and including Christ's crucifixion; with Easter-Sunday as the day of celebration. Then the events of the week following the Resurrection are remembered. In other words, for these, Easter covers a two-week period, and not just a day.

remember how the Lord had to rebuke Peter for suggesting that He should not go to the cross. "Get thee behind me, Satan: thou art an offence unto me: for thou savourest not the things that be of God, but those that be of men," He said to Peter (Mt 16:23).

And did not the Lord express the sentiments found in this Psalm as He went to the cross? He said:

"[27] Now is my soul troubled; and what shall I say? Father, save me from this hour: but for this cause came I unto this hour. [28] Father, glorify thy name...." (Jn 12:27-28)

So closely fitted to Christ is this Psalm that Andrew Bonar confidently asserts: "Christ is the chief Speaker, entering into his own difficulties and those of his church."

We may entitle it *"The Righteous One Under the Wings in Calamities."* It is appointed by our Lord for us to sing in union with Him that we may meditate on His inner thoughts and struggles as He suffered for us; as well as to give expression to our own struggles as a church and as individuals. As we sing it together, let us exhort one another to learn from our Saviour an infallible example of how we must direct our thoughts when we are facing similar calamitous situations in our lives.

It has three stanzas divided by the two selahs in verse 3 and verse 6. The first stanza is a cry for mercy with firm assurance that God will hear. The second stanza is a call to the Father to glorify Himself in the midst of dangers and perplexities. The third stanza is a confident hope and resolution to praise the Father amongst the nations.

1. v. 1-3   A Cry for Mercy
2. v. 4-6   A Call to Glorify God
3. v. 7-10   A Confident Resolve

1. A Cry for Mercy

[1] *Be merciful unto me, O God, be merciful unto me: for my soul trusteth in thee: yea, in the shadow of thy wings will I make my refuge, until these calamities be overpast.* [2] *I will cry unto God most high; unto God that performeth all things for me.* [3] *He shall send from heaven, and save me from the reproach of him that would swallow me up.*

This beautiful paragraph can hardly be commented on without marring its beauty. David was hiding in a cave, so we might expect him to use the analogy of hiding in the cleft of a rock as he does in other Psalms. But no, he does better here. He is not cringing in fear, hiding away. He is snuggled under the protective wings of the mother eagle, which is facing the storm fearlessly!

Our Lord, facing great fears and exasperation, would have used the same words—which were inspired by His Spirit—to cry out unto His Father to have mercy upon Him. Notice how He does not say, "Save me from this hour," for it was for this hour He was born (Jn 12:27). Rather, our Lord cries, *"Be merciful unto me,"* and to underscore the urgency of the plea, He repeats the same.

Now, in calling unto the Father to have mercy upon Him, our Lord is not only saying that the whole trial upon His soul is in the sovereign hand of the Father, but also that He is, in a sense, not worthy of the LORD's blessing. Why is He not worthy? He is not worthy, not because He falls short of the glory of God, but because the sins of His people were imputed to Him. Though He had no sin, He is heading to the cross as one guilty before the LORD because of the sins of His people.

On what basis then, does He pray? He prays on the basis of His faith in the Father, and His Father's faithfulness. *"My soul trusteth in thee"*, *"He shall send from heaven, and save me."*

What a beautiful paragraph! Are you facing a storm, dear child of God? Take the words of the Lord in your lips. Sing them from the bottom of your heart.

> ¹Be merciful to me, O God;
> thy mercy unto me
> Do thou extend; because my soul
> doth put her trust in thee:
> Yea, in the shadow of thy wings
> my refuge I will place,
> Until these sad calamities
> do wholly overpass. [28]

The Lord was worthy; but because He bore our sin, He cried for mercy. You are not worthy; but because the righteousness of Christ covers you, you can go to the Father confidently and hide in Him.

2. A Call to Glorify God

It is easy to focus on ourselves when we are suffering affliction. But the right thing to do is not only to ask for mercy; but also to ask God to glorify Himself. Man's chief end, after all, is to glorify God and to enjoy Him forever. In asking for His mercy and protection, we are asking Him to enable us to enjoy Him. But that is not enough; we must also ask Him to glorify Himself through the trial we are going through. So our Lord says:

> *³ God shall send forth his mercy and his truth. ⁴ My soul is among lions: and I lie even among them that are set on fire, even the sons of men, whose teeth are spears and arrows, and their tongue a sharp sword. ⁵ Be thou exalted, O God, above the heavens; let thy glory be above all the earth. ⁶ They have prepared a net for my steps; my soul is bowed down: they have digged a pit before me, into the midst whereof they are fallen themselves.*

My soul is vexed and perplexed. I am surrounded by fierce lions, and fire, and sharp spears, and arrows. And then there are those who are pursuing after me, trying to trap me with all their hard questions. But does it matter? Thou, O LORD, shall send forth Thy mercy and truth. Thou, O LORD, art my refuge and my help. I will hide under the shadow of Thy wings. Thou wilt send forth from heaven to help me.

What else do I desire from this trial?

> *⁵ Be thou exalted, O God, above the heavens; let thy glory be above all the earth.*

I desire Thy glory. "Father, glorify thy name," says our Lord (Jn 12:28). One of the best ways to encourage ourselves in the midst of tribulation is to focus on the glory of the LORD. When we do so, all our trials will become strangely dim and insignificant. Thus, when Peter was looking at the Lord, basking in His glory, he was able to walk on water. But as soon as he took his eyes off from the Lord to observe the wind and the waves, he began to sink.

So let us look to the LORD. Let us look to Him by looking to our Lord Jesus Christ. "He that hath seen me hath seen the Father," He says (Jn 14:9). Let us desire His glory even when we

---

[28] Psalm 57:1 from *The Psalms of David in Metre* According to the Version approved by the Church of Scotland and appointed to be used in worship.

are in the midst of personal perplexity and trials. Then will we get a right perspective of the problems. Then will our hearts be overwhelmed with gratitude to our heavenly Father who names the stars and the galaxies and yet feeds the sparrows and takes care of us.

3. A Confident Resolve

If we desire God's glory, then what must we do but stir ourselves up to glorify Him. So the Psalm ends with a confident resolve:

> [7] My heart is fixed, O God, my heart is fixed: I will sing and give praise. [8] Awake up, my glory; awake, psaltery and harp: I myself will awake early. [9] I will praise thee, O Lord, among the people: I will sing unto thee among the nations.

What should occupy our hearts when we are undergoing trials? Not our sorrows and our griefs, but the glory of the LORD

So our Lord sets us an example. He tells us of His resolution to praise the LORD, come what may. His heart is fixed. He is not allowing Himself to sway to and fro in the midst of the storm. And He is not going to change His mind about praising the LORD even if the LORD would not deliver Him. His heart is fixed. I will sing and give praise! Yes, my soul is in perplexity and grief. Yes, it is hard to sing praise in such situations. But it is not impossible if I would stir my heart to sing sincerely.

> [8] Awake up, my glory; awake, psaltery and harp: I myself will awake early.

Neither David nor the Lord is referring to musical instruments, but to the musical ability of the soul. He is calling upon all to join Him in praise. He is exhorting Himself, and is calling upon all who are united to Him to rejoice in the LORD. Rejoice in the LORD, therefore. Let not your emotional turmoil reign over you. Reign rather over your emotions.

> [9] I will praise thee, O Lord, among the people: I will sing unto thee among the nations.

This prophecy is fulfilled not in David, but in the Lord Jesus Christ, for He indeed praises the LORD among the people. He indeed sings unto the Father, among the nations, whenever believers gather together to worship God, using His words. He joins them by His Spirit after His resurrection.

> "I will declare thy name unto my brethren: in the midst of the congregation will I praise thee" (Ps 22:22).

What of His name does our Lord declare? He will declare His mercy. He will declare His truth and faithfulness. He will declare His glory:

> [10] For thy mercy is great unto the heavens, and thy truth unto the clouds. [11] Be thou exalted, O God, above the heavens: let thy glory be above all the earth.

Conclusion

What a Psalm! The occasion of deepest gloom and sorrow must give rise to the highest praise. So it was with our Lord; so it must be for us.

Occasions of calamity or of perplexity and grief must not become occasion of self-pity and morbid speculations. They should rather become occasion of praise unto God. We may not forget to praise and worship Him when He has granted us deliverance. But we must stir up our hearts to worship Him while the fire burns: for it is then that we need, for our joy and comfort, to praise Him most. May the Lord help us! Amen. Ω

Psalm 58:
The Righteous One's
Warning Against the Wicked

Psalm 58 is one of the several imprecatory Psalms found in our Psalter, the most famous of which is Psalm 69. Commentators are not agreed on when this Psalm was written. Some suppose that it was written during the time David was pursued by Saul, and perhaps after the massacre at Nob due to Doeg's evil report. Others suppose that it was written against Joab—David's general—after he murdered Abner, the general of the ten northern tribes who had come to seek peace with David.

In any case, we can see how the words in this Psalm should be taken as the word of Christ, just as the words in Psalm 69 are attributed to Christ in the New Testament.

How can these be the words of Christ when the title, which appears in the Hebrew manuscript, suggests that this is a "Michtam of David"? Well, not only did David write in the Spirit of Christ, but we note that Psalm 69 is also known as a Psalm of David, and yet the Apostle Paul, writing under inspiration, quotes the words as the words of Christ. He says in Romans 15:3:

> "For even Christ pleased not himself; but, as it is written, The reproaches of them that reproached thee fell on me" (Rom 15:3).

Paul is quoting from Psalm 69:9.

And so we have a good basis to take Psalm 58 as the word of Christ. And besides, who but Christ could have spoken the words of imprecation in this Psalm with perfect sincerity: for there is none amongst man who is truly righteous except Christ. This Psalm, as such, may be entitled *"The Righteous One's Warning Against the Wicked."*

It has three parts:

1. v. 1-5   A Description of the Wicked
2. v. 6-9   An Imprecation Against the Wicked
3. v. 10-11   The Vindication of the Righteous

1. A Description of the Wicked

¹ Do ye indeed speak righteousness, O congregation? do ye judge uprightly, O ye sons of men?

The first part of this verse has been variously translated. The word translated "congregation" is related to the word for "silent" (אֵלֶם, *êlem*). It is not the usual word for "congregation" (עֵדָה, *êdâh*; or קָהָל, *qâhâl*). However, our translation does give a good sense.

The Lord is calling upon all men—Jews or Gentiles, Christian or non-Christians, churched or unchurched, who are present to hear the word sung—to examine themselves.

Do you indeed speak righteousness? Do you judge uprightly? Now, if we are honest with ourselves, we can only answer: "No, our speech is far from righteous. There is none righteous, no, not one. Our thoughts are far from perfect uprightness, for none of us can claim to be without prejudice in any judgement we have to make."

Our Lord agrees, and would have us to sing with Him to remind one another, verse 2:

> *² Yea, in heart ye work wickedness; ye weigh the violence of your hands in the earth.*

We are by nature wicked. We inherited a sinful nature from Adam. Left to ourselves, we will work wickedness. We only restrain ourselves because we realise—when we weigh it in our hearts (deliberately or instinctively)—that the cost of violence and wickedness is not worth the pleasure. We will, in other words, do it if we think we have nothing to lose and everything to gain.

The fact is: we are totally depraved. We are, in nature and principle, as wicked as we can be, though in our acts and practice, we are restrained. Apart from grace, we are, by nature, no different from the wicked and hardened people in the world: for though they may be less restrained than we are, their wickedness arose from the same source.

³ *The wicked are estranged from the womb: they go astray as soon as they be born, speaking lies.* ⁴ *Their poison is like the poison of a serpent: they are like the deaf adder that stoppeth her ear;* ⁵ *Which will not hearken to the voice of charmers, charming never so wisely.*

The wicked here stands for those who remain in unbelief, who will continue in their sin. They received their sinful nature in the womb, and as soon as they are born they begin to speak lies and to do wickedness. Worse yet, there will be those in the congregation who have the privilege of listening to the Lord to be instructed by Him, but they will not. They are like the snake charmers' serpents which have, as it were, stopped their ears so that they cannot hear the music of their charmers.

Shortly after our Lord began His ministry, He began to upbraid the people for their unbelief. This is what He says in Matthew 11:

¹⁶ *But whereunto shall I liken this generation? It is like unto children sitting in the markets, and calling unto their fellows,* ¹⁷ *And saying, We have piped unto you, and ye have not danced; we have mourned unto you, and ye have not lamented.*

"We have piped unto you, and ye have not danced." Is there not a significant parallel to what the Lord is saying in verse 4 and 5 of our text? The snake is supposed to dance harmlessly when the pipe is played. But the stubborn and unresponsive reptile will refuse and will rather continue to threaten with his poison.

How did the Lord respond to the hardness of heart in Matthew 11? He does not simply let them be. He upbraids the cities of Chorazin and Capernaum, telling them that their judgement will be more severe than that of Sodom and Gomorrah.

A similar sentiment is expressed in our text, for the Lord calls out an imprecation against the wicked that remains in sin and hardness of heart.

2. An Imprecation Against the Wicked

⁶ *Break their teeth, O God, in their mouth: break out the great teeth of the young lions, O LORD.* ⁷ *Let them melt away as waters which run continually: when he bendeth his bow to shoot his arrows, let them be as cut in pieces.* ⁸ *As a snail which melteth, let every one of them pass away: like the untimely birth of a woman, that they may not see the sun.* ⁹ *Before your pots can feel the thorns, he shall take them away as with a whirlwind, both living, and in his wrath.*

Strong and graphic words! Our Lord calls upon the Father to deal with the wicked. He curses them with six imageries. (1) *"Break their teeth, O God."* They are proud like lions, ready to tear their prey apart; but knock out their teeth, O LORD. Take away their pride and ability.

(2) *"Let them melt away as waters."* As the torrents of water that flow down the mountain side may make a mighty noise, so let them clamour all they want, but dissipate them and their noise, that they be remembered no more. (3) When they *bend their bow to shoot their arrows*, let their arrows splinter into pieces. That is, frustrate their efforts, that they accomplish nothing, however focused they may be. (4) Let them melt away like a *snail* or a slug. Snails and slugs come out in the night, because once the sun begins to beat down on them, they begin to dry up, and as it were, melt away. Let it be so for the wicked. Remove them, that they trouble no more the vineyard of the LORD. (5) Let them experience the *"untimely birth of a woman."* That is, they may be filled with expectation as a pregnant woman expects a child, but let their expectation end with a miscarriage. Give them no reason to rejoice. (6) Let them be like pots that are swept away by the whirlwind before the food can be cooked. Don't just blow out the fire, but sweep the pots away! Give them astonishment and fear and frustration.

Our Lord has no sympathy for the wicked, especially for those who have the opportunity to hear the word and yet refuse to repent. He wants the Father to deal with them, since they have blasphemed the Father's name.

What about us?

3. The Vindication of
the Righteous

[10] *The righteous shall rejoice when he seeth the vengeance: he shall wash his feet in the blood of the wicked.* [11] *So that a man shall say, Verily there is a reward for the righteous: verily he is a God that judgeth in the earth.*

Who is the righteous? The righteous is none other than Christ, for there is none righteous but Christ. But Christ came to represent His people and to purchase righteousness for them so that all who are united to Him by faith are also seen as righteous in the eyes of God.

Christ will rejoice when He sees vengeance exacted against the wicked. And so will all believers in union with Him. Christ crushed the head of the serpent on the cross; so saints will bruise Satan under their feet shortly (Rom 16:20). Christ and His Church will, as it were, wash their feet in the blood of the wicked, even the serpent and his seed.

When this happens, then will the justice of God be openly vindicated and magnified.

In that day, the righteous, whose reasoning power and affection is fully restored, will see the goodness of God. They will rejoice that God has swept away wickedness which has hitherto marred God's creation. They will thank God for His love, by which He frees His children from any contamination by sin and wickedness.

Conclusion

Psalm 58 contains a strong warning against the wicked. It shows us our Lord's attitude towards those who remain in unbelief and refuse to take heed to God's Word.

Psalm 58, however, gives no warrant for believers to boast or to despise the wicked, for right from the beginning, we are reminded by our Lord that we are, by nature, no different from the wicked. We should use this Psalm, therefore, not only as a warning against the wicked, but as a reminder and warning to ourselves, lest we take sin lightly and sin against the LORD. Amen. Ω

Psalm 59:
The Righteous One's
Appeal Against Heathenish Israelites

Like Psalm 58, Psalm 59 is an imprecatory Psalm. An imprecatory Psalm is a song by which the singer calls upon the LORD to deal with his enemies who are also the enemies of God.

This Psalm was written by David: as the title suggests, at a time when Saul, his father-in-law, had sent some soldiers to watch his house to look for an opportunity to kill him. We can read the account in 1 Samuel 19. There, we see how Saul had tried to kill David with a spear. David managed to escape, and went back to his house. But that night Saul sent some men to watch him and to slay him when he came out in the morning. When Michal, David's wife, found out, she let him down by a back window so that he could escape. David fled to Samuel the prophet; and it was perhaps while staying with Samuel that he wrote this Psalm.

So David penned this Psalm. But notice how the words of this Psalm was given by the Spirit of Christ to express the thoughts and feelings of the greater David, when He Himself was being pursued by His enemies who had risen up against Him.

Consider the opening verses of this Psalm:

*1 Deliver me from mine enemies, O my God: defend me from them that rise up against me.
2 Deliver me from the workers of iniquity, and save me from bloody men. 3 For, lo, they lie in wait for my soul: the mighty are gathered against me; not for my transgression, nor for my sin, O LORD.*

Do not these words fit perfectly the experience of our Lord? Are we not told of His enemies "laying [in] wait for Him" as they sought to catch something He might say, that they might accuse Him (Lk 11:54)?

And are we not told of the mighty, the powerful priests and their guards gathering themselves against our Lord? And was it for His transgression? No, no; He was pursued unto death not for His transgression, for He had none. He was pursued because of our transgressions.

And what does our Lord call the enemies of God who are outwardly God's people—like those who were pursuing after David? Did He not call them "workers of iniquity" as in verse 2? The Lord says, "I profess unto them, I never knew you: depart from me, ye that work iniquity" (Mt 7:23; see Lk 13:27).

And did not the Jews who pursued the Lord eventually say to Pilate to whom they had delivered the Lord to be crucified: "His blood be on us, and on our children" (Mt 27:25)? Were they not "bloody men" as they are called in verse 2?

And consider the closing verses of this Psalm. Look at verse 16:

16 But I will sing of thy power; yea, I will sing aloud of thy mercy in the morning: for thou hast been my defence and refuge in the day of my trouble.

David might have sung and meditated on these words, but their significance would have been very limited and general. What power? The Lord did not demonstrate His power in an extraordinary way to deliver David. David was lowered out of the window using perhaps bedsheets. What about the morning? What special morning could David be talking about?

But does not this verse fit into our Lord's anticipation of the resurrection morning? On the morning of the resurrection, our Lord was indeed delivered by the extraordinary power of God so that there was great cause to praise the Father for His mercy. Indeed, every time the Lord's people gather for worship on the Resurrection Day, the Lord joins us to praise the Father. "This is the day which the LORD hath made; we will rejoice and be glad in it" (Ps 118:24).

Can you see how this Psalm is so much richer when we consider how it expresses the thoughts and feelings of our Lord as He was persecuted for our sakes?

But so much for this lengthy introduction. What is this Psalm about? This Psalm—as the introductory words suggest—is *"The Righteous One's Appeal Against Heathenish Israelites."* It is a Psalm appointed by our King for us to sing in union with Him, to cry out to the Father to deal with false professors of the faith.

Despite the two "selahs", it is difficult to discern very distinct structure in this Psalm. But roughly: In verses 1-5, we are given to complain about workers of iniquity; in verses 6-10, we express our confidence that the LORD will triumph over them; in verses 11-13, we are given to plead that God will deal with them in the way that will conduce to the benefit of the Israel of God; and we are given to conclude in verses 14-17, that God will not allow the wicked to triumph but will give us reasons to praise Him despite the present troubles.

1. v. 1-5   Complaint Against Workers of Iniquity in Israel
2. v. 6-10   Confidence that the LORD Will Triumph over Them
3. v. 11-13 Cry to the LORD to Deal Justly for Israel's Good
4. v. 14-17 Conclusion that the Righteous Will Triumph

These sections are so tightly bound that it is hard to speak about each section distinctly. Nevertheless, there are three ideas that thread through them: Appeal, Adversaries and Assurance. Although there is some overlap, most of the verses in this Psalm can be classified under one of these ideas. For example, in verses 1-2, we have part of the Appeal; in verses 3-4 we have the Adversaries described and in verses 8-9, we have a word of Assurance.

Let's look at the content of this Psalm under these three categories briefly.

1. Adversaries

This Psalm begins with the plea: *"Deliver me from mine enemies."* Who are the enemies or adversaries? As mentioned earlier, they are not strangers to the covenant or people outside the Church of God. David was being pursued by Saul and his men. Our Lord was being pursued by none other than the Jews, the covenant people of God at that time.

But these are Jewish "workers of iniquity" or "bloody men" (v. 2) who would call a curse upon themselves as they proudly declared that the blood of Christ be upon them and their children.

These are wicked men who knew the law of God and yet laid in wait for the blood of the Lord although all He had done was righteousness.

> ³ *For, lo, they lie in wait for my soul: the mighty are gathered against me; not for my transgression, nor for my sin, O LORD.* ⁴ *They run and prepare themselves without my fault...*

That is, they persecuted me, though I had not done anything wrong, nor had I any fault worthy of their hatred.

Indeed, their wicked pursuit of the LORD shows clearly that though they were outwardly Jews, inwardly they were children of the devil (cf. Rom 2:28-29).

So our Lord condemns them as children of the devil. "if ye were Abraham's children, ye would do the works of Abraham. But now ye seek to kill me... Ye are of *your* father the devil, and the lusts of your father ye will do" (Jn 8:39b-40a, 44a).

So they are called "heathen" in verse 5. They are not heathen out of the commonwealth of Israel. They are, as one commentator puts it, "heathenish Israel." Indeed, they were so thirsty for the blood of the Lord that they became like stray dogs, noisily running around the city looking for food (v. 6).

Are you a professing believer and therefore a member of the covenant? If so, do you love the Lord and His word? If not, you have become a heathenish Christian who in the eyes of the Lord is no better than a wild dog.

2. Appeal

The appeal is for deliverance (v. 1-2). But more than that, the appeal is for vengeance upon the wicked transgressors.

> [5] *Thou therefore, O LORD God of hosts, the God of Israel, awake to visit all the heathen: be not merciful to any wicked transgressors.*

As the Son of Man, our Lord would not vindicate Himself. He would commit Himself to His Father, and call upon Him to take vengeance.

But even as He calls His Father to deal with them, He thinks of His people. He does not want His Father to exterminate them. He desires Him to deal with the wicked in such a way that His people would see and take warning just like the way He dealt with Cain.

So we read, verse 11:

> [11] *Slay them not, lest my people forget: scatter them by thy power; and bring them down, O Lord our shield.* [12] *For the sin of their mouth and the words of their lips let them even be taken in their pride: and for cursing and lying which they speak.* [13] *Consume them in wrath, consume them, that they may not be: and let them know that God ruleth in Jacob unto the ends of the earth. ...*

Has not our Lord's request in regard to apostate Israel been heard? Israel had proudly called a curse upon herself; and Israel had followed the devil in promoting lies about the Messiah (cf. Jn 8:44; Mt 28:15).

So God dealt with them severely. This happened especially in A.D. 70. So severe was their chastisement that the Apostle Paul declares in his letter to the Thessalonians that "wrath is come upon them to the uttermost" (1 Th 2:16).

But as our Lord requested, God did not destroy them completely. Israel continued to suffer tremendously in the centuries that followed, even when they were scattered throughout the world (v. 13). They suffered as a reminder to the people belonging to Christ, the Israel of God, of how seriously God viewed the sins of His people; and how jealous He was of His Son and His beloved people (v. 11).

Where is Israel today? She is back in the land which God promised Abraham. I wonder if this return has anything to do with our Lord's request in verses 14-15:

> [14] *And at evening let them return; and let them make a noise like a dog, and go round*

about the city. ^{15} Let them wander up and down for meat, and grudge if they be not satisfied.

Whatever the case may be, one thing is certain. Those who refuse to acknowledge Christ, will never have peace and satisfaction in this world or the world to come.

On the other hand, those who trust in the Lord will have the LORD's...

3. Assurance

Our Lord suffered immensely, but that did not extinguish His hope and assurance in the Father.

There are two paragraphs expressing our Lord's hope and assurance in this Psalm. Notice how both paragraphs begin with the word "but." Our Lord's hope and assurance was despite and in spite of the trials He was facing.

^{8} But thou, O LORD, shalt laugh at them; thou shalt have all the heathen in derision. ^{9} Because of his strength will I wait upon thee: for God is my defence. ^{10} The God of my mercy shall prevent me: God shall let me see my desire upon mine enemies.

The wicked may do all they want. They may shoot out words of scorn (v. 7). They may ridicule: "He trusted in God; let him deliver him now, if he will have him: for he said, I am the Son of God" (Mt 27:43). But I will still trust in Thee. Thou shalt have the last laugh. Thou shalt have them in derision. Thou art my defence. Thou art the lifter up of my head. Thou wilt vindicate and let me see my desire upon mine enemies.

Thou wilt deal with them In thy wrath.

^{16} But I will sing of thy power; yea, I will sing aloud of thy mercy in the morning: for thou hast been my defence and refuge in the day of my trouble. ^{17} Unto thee, O my strength, will I sing: for God is my defence, and the God of my mercy.

Our Lord was delivered over to be crucified; but He rose victorious on the third day. And He has since been singing praises with His children unto His Father who was His defence, refuge and strength. He has been doing so from the first resurrection morning until now.

Conclusion

What a wonderful Psalm! But what is this Psalm to you?

Imprecatory Psalms are very difficult to apply into our lives if we focus on the imprecations. However, if we focus on how the Father loves His children and would take vengeance on their behalf, then we shall find these Psalms to be of tremendous comfort—especially when we face trials that result from those who profess to be Christian, but have acted in unchristian ways.

Our Lord has said: "The disciple is not above his master, nor the servant above his lord" (Mt 10:24). If He faced severe trials from covenant apostates, then His disciples may expect to face the same kind of trials at one time or another. But whatever trials we may face, let us remember how our Lord prayed; and how the Father heard. And let us follow the example of our Lord to look forward to the Father's vindication and final deliverance at the resurrection. Our hope is not an empty hope. As our Lord rose from the dead to rejoice in the Father ever more, so we who are united to Him will rise again one day—fully vindicated and fully made ready to enjoy God forever and ever. Amen. Ω

Psalm 60:
The Righteous One's
Prayer for Victory for His People

Psalm 60 may be known as a didactic Psalm as its superscription suggests. A didactic Psalm is one that is designed for teaching. But Psalm 60 is not the usual kind of didactic Psalm such as Psalms 1, 19 and 25, which are not founded upon any particular occasion. Rather it is written as a prayer at a time of war.

There was war in Israel during the days of the Judges up to the days of King Saul. In particular, under the reign of King Saul, the man after the people's heart, the people suffered massive defeat in the hand of the Philistines, so much so that Saul and his son were killed in battle and the troops were scattered.

But things were looking better under the leadership of David, the man after God's heart. Under David, the people were able not only to repel foreign powers, but actually fight against them on their own turf. On one occasion, recorded in 2 Samuel 8, David led his men up North to Syria to fight against the army of Zobah and the Syrian army, which had come to help the king of Zobah. David and his man won a convincing victory (2 Sam 8:5).

But while they were away, the Edomites, apparently, began to gather themselves to invade Judah. David and his generals, Joab and Abishai, rushed back and fought against them in the Valley of Salt, South-West of the Dead Sea and North of Edom. The Edomites were soundly defeated. 12,000 of their troops were killed (as indicated in the superscription of this Psalm).

Having defeated the Edomite army, David and his generals began to prepare to march into Edom to conquer the land (cf. v. 9).

Apparently another 6,000 Edomites were killed in the invasion; so altogether, 18,000 of the Edomite army were killed (cf. 1 Kgs 11:15-16; 1 Chr 18:12).

David, probably, wrote this Psalm during the days before they marched into Edom. Although the historical record is lacking, it is not difficult to infer that David's troops suffered significant losses too, and many of his men baulked at the idea of taking the campaign into Edom, and some probably abandoned their posts (see v. 1, 9).

David wrote, perhaps, to encourage his troops to trust in the LORD who had turned the tide against their enemies and begun to restore the glory of Israel.

But David wrote, no doubt, in the spirit of Christ so that this Psalm is not only his word, but the word of Christ; and the praying singer of this Psalm is not merely David, but the greater David united to His people. Therefore, this Psalm may be used by God's people united to the greater David, the Righteous One of God, as we attempt great things for the Lord (cf. Ps 126:2-3).

We may entitle this Psalm *"The Righteous One's Prayer for Victory for His People."*

This Psalm has three parts:

1. v. 1-5   Petition for Deliverance
2. v. 6-8   Assurance of Victory
3. v. 9-12   Hope of Confidence

1. Petition for Deliverance

Every prayer for victory and restoration must begin with an acknowledgement of the causes of loss and defeat. So our Psalm begins with such an acknowledgement.

> [1] *O God, thou hast cast us off, thou hast scattered us, thou hast been displeased; O turn thyself to us again.* [2] *Thou hast made the earth to tremble; thou hast broken it: heal the breaches thereof; for it shaketh.* [3] *Thou hast shewed thy people hard things: thou hast made us to drink the wine of astonishment.*

During the days of Saul, Israel was in disarray. The people were divided and scattered. But why? Because God was displeased. Why was God displeased? Because God's people have turned aside from following Him and every man did that which was right in his own eyes. We need only to read the book of Judges to know how bad the situation had become.

So the LORD brought disasters upon His own people. He made them suffer defeat, hardship and astonishment. But now that David is king, Israel is doing better; yet it is not altogether without trouble, for as we noted, it is likely that during the battle in the Valley of Salt, they suffered some casualties and some of David's troops, no doubt, deserted him when they were told that they were going to push ahead into Edom itself. Such a scenario would have been quite perplexing to David and could have brought about the sentiments expressed in the opening words of this Psalm.

But as the LORD brought defeat, so He can bring victory to His people. And thus David pleaded for deliverance with confidence.

So let us, as we face similar trials in our battles as the army of Christ, cry with the words of David and of the Captain of our salvation, *"O turn thyself to us again"* (v. 1); and *"heal the breaches thereof"* (v. 2).

But on what basis should the Father heal and restore the people? The answer, I believe is found in verses 4-5:

> [4] *Thou hast given a banner to them that fear thee, that it may be displayed because of the truth.* [5] *That thy beloved may be delivered; save with thy right hand, and hear me.*

What is this banner? The banner is none other than Christ Himself!

In numbers 21:9, we read:

> "And Moses made a serpent of brass, and put it upon a pole, and it came to pass, that if a serpent had bitten any man, when he beheld the serpent of brass, he lived."

The brass serpent represented Christ. But do you realise that the words translated "it upon a pole" are from a Hebrew word that is translated "banner" in our text. What Moses essentially did was to lift the brazen serpent up as an ensign to represent Christ.

Similarly, in Isaiah 11:10, we read:

> "And in that day there shall be a root of Jesse, which shall stand for an ensign of the people; to it shall the Gentiles seek: and his rest shall be glorious." (Isa 11:10)

The word translated "ensign" is the same word as that translated "banner" in our text. The "root of Jesse" is none other than Christ. So the banner that is given to them that fear God is, no doubt, a reference to Christ.

> [4] *Thou hast given a banner to them that fear thee, that it may be displayed because of the truth.*

Now, the word "truth" here is not the usual word for "truth". Rather it is a word that literally means "bow" as in "bow and arrow." The truth is that Israel deserved God's wrath and curse for their sin. And so God's wrath is, as it were, arrows primed on a bow ready to shoot at His people.

But God has given them a banner, even Christ, to be lifted up against the attack. Christ stands as a representative of all them that fear the LORD. He stood in our place as our shield so as to take all the arrows of God's wrath shot towards us.

So Christ our mediator, the only mediator between God and man, petitions the Father on our behalf:

> [5] *That thy beloved [i.e. thy beloved people] may be delivered; save with thy right hand, and hear me.*

The "beloved" is in the plural in the Hebrew, so it is a reference to God's people. Our Lord is pleading on behalf of His people for a powerful deliverance for His sake.

Thank God for Christ our banner. For His sake, though the Father will try the Church because of her sin, He will always preserve her and save those who fear His name.

Therefore, as we petition the Father for deliverance, we can always have the assurance of victory.

2. Assurance of Victory

Indeed, the Father Himself has given us assurance: *"God has spoken in his holiness"* (v. 6). What did God say?

Most modern translations including the NIV, NASB and even the NKJV translate the second part of verse 6 all the way to verse 8 as the direct speech of God. In other words, they would take the punctuation after "God hath spoken in his holiness" as a colon rather than a semi-colon.

Which version is correct? Well, personally, I think the way that our translators have it, makes more sense. The "I" in verse 6 is the same as the "me" in verse 5.

If this is right, and I believe it is, then we must ask: What did God say in his holiness?

Well, the answer is found in another Psalm, in Psalm 89:35:

> "[35] *Once have I sworn by my holiness that I will not lie unto David.* [36] *His seed shall endure for ever, and his throne as the sun before me"* (Ps 89:35-36).

God has sworn in his holiness that David's throne will be established and his seed will endure forever.

On the basis of this, David writes:

> [6] *...I will rejoice, I will divide Shechem, and mete out the valley of Succoth.* [7] *Gilead is mine, and Manasseh is mine; Ephraim also is the strength of mine head; Judah is my lawgiver;* [8] *Moab is my washpot; over Edom will I cast out my shoe: Philistia, triumph thou because of me.*

Israel was at war. The nation was unstable. The Northern tribes had just recently acknowledged David as king. And the Syrians, the Edomites, the Moabites and the Philistines all wanted a piece of the land.

David, on the basis of God's promise, could confidently assert that all the tribes and cities in the North and East—Shechem, Succoth, Gilead, Manasseh, Ephraim—are his to rule and to apportion as king. Ephraim would be the strength of his head. It would provide military might. And he would rule from Judah. *"Judah is my lawgiver,"* he says.

And David claimed victory over Moab, Edom and Philistia. Moab would be like a washbasin given to the conqueror to refresh himself. Edom would pick up his shoes like a slave and the Philistines would look to him for success.

But wait a minute! Is this all about David? Is this all about the tribes and cities in the Old Testament? Is this all about Edom, Moab and Philistia?

No, no; if it were all about David and the tribes and enemies of Israel, then this song would not be very meaningful for New Testament singing.

But no; we noted that the "I" of verse 6, is also the "me" of verse 5. Who is the "me" of verse 5? Not just David, but the greater David. The lesser David no longer intercedes for his people; but the greater David continues to do so at the right hand of the throne of God.

Indeed, what God has sworn in his holiness pertains to the greater David, for as Dr Luke, citing Psalm 89, puts it: "Of this man's seed hath God according to His promise raised unto Israel a Saviour, Jesus" (Acts 13:23).

Christ, more than David, had the right to claim ownership and sovereignty over His people, and victory over His enemies.

Christ has secured the victory. He secured it at the cross. But it pleases God to leave the complete and final victory for a future day. "For he must reign," says the Apostle Paul, "till he hath put all enemies under his feet" (1 Cor 15:25).

But victory is certain. Christ has laid claim to His people and all the heavenly blessings that the Promise Land typified. Christ has declared victory over His enemies. His word will not fail.

Spiritual Gilead, Succoth, Manasseh, Ephraim and Judah are His to apportion. And the people signified by the people who dwelt in these lands are His to rule. He who has begun a good work in every congregation in the Israel of God will perfect it unto the day of His revelation. Spiritual Edom, Moab and Philistia will be conquered, for He has conquered and is conquering (cf. Rev 6:2). He is conquering sin by His Spirit. He is conquering sinners by His Gospel. One day, every knee will bow and every tongue will confess that Jesus is Lord and King. God has spoken in his holiness. It will happen.

And so our King would have us to join Him to sing the words of His confidence...

3. Hope of Confidence

⁹ Who will bring me into the strong city? who will lead me into Edom? ¹⁰ Wilt not thou, O God, which hadst cast us off? and thou, O God, which didst not go out with our armies? ¹¹ Give us help from trouble: for vain is the help of man. ¹² Through God we shall do valiantly: for he it is that shall tread down our enemies.

David of old could have confidence that the Father would restore the glory of his people and lead him into Edom. He understood that vain is the help of man, but through God he would do valiantly.

How much more does the greater David have such confidence! As man, He must pray unto the Father, as God He must fulfil the prayer. He is the God-Man. "All power is given unto me in heaven and in earth," He says (Mt 28:18). Our Lord will not fail because God is on His side.

So as His people, we too will not fail if we are fighting His battles. We must be sure that we are fighting His battles and not our own. But if we are sure, and we are fighting in His strength and confidence, we can have every reason to believe that He will grant us success.

Conclusion

Look at the Church at large. Does it not feel like we are in the early days of David? God has given us victory, but things are unsettled, and there are many battles to fight. Do we need to feel weak and discouraged? No, no; let us rely on the LORD. Vain is the help of man; but through God we shall do valiantly. If the Lord be for us, who can be against us? If we are seeking to do His work, in His ways, in obedience to our King, we can have the firm confidence that we shall have the victory.

Let us, therefore, sing this Psalm corporately to encourage each other in our battles together. And likewise, let us individually find encouragement in this Psalm.

I don't know about you, but sometimes I feel that my life is full of uncertainty like Israel in the early days of David. And there are battles to be fought and conquests to be made. Is this how your life is at the moment? If it is, cry unto the Father in the words of this Psalm. As our Lord used this Psalm, so we who are united to Him may use it. Cry unto the Father for His help! He will send his Son and His Spirit, for says our Lord, "I will be with you always, even unto the end of the world."

Vain is the help of man, but with God you will do valiantly. You will tread down your enemies: be they your sin and weakness, or be they obstacles that stand in the way of holiness and the enjoyment and glory of God. Amen. Ω

Psalm 61:
The Righteous One
Reaching up to the Rock Higher than Him

Psalm 61 was written at a time when David was facing persecution from his enemies, and driven into hiding away from the comforts of home. There were two occasions when that happened. The first time was when King Saul was pursuing him because he was jealous of his growing popularity. The other time was when his son Absalom rose up in rebellion against him.

Most commentators believe that this Psalm was written on this second occasion because verse 6 suggests that David was already king at this time. If so, the suffering of David at this time must have been most intense. What could be worse than having your beloved son and one of your best friends turn against you and turn others against you?

Well, nothing may be worse amongst mere men, but something worse happened to the God-Man. David's persecution in the hand of his son was largely a result of his own failures as a father and a king. The greater David's persecution was entirely on account of the sin of His people. While David was persecuted by a son who hated him; the greater David was persecuted by people who claimed to love His Father.

Indeed, I am convinced that God had so ordered David's life that he would suffer intensely, yet only sufficiently to give him a taste of what the Son of God would experience. This is so that the Psalms that he would write by the inspiration of the Spirit of Christ would accurately portray the experiences and thoughts of our Lord in His days of suffering.

So Psalm 61 gives us an expression of the anguish and hope of our King of kings when He was being persecuted for our sakes.

What about David's own experience? Well, David could use this Psalm not only because he was a type of Christ, but because he was a member of Christ. I think this is perhaps why when he talks about the king in verses 7 and 8, it is in the third person. What I am saying is that when Christ used this Psalm, the whole Psalm is about His experience; but when David sang this Psalm, verses 7-8 refer to Christ, whereas for the rest of the verses, he can apply to himself as one united to Christ.

So too for us: We can sing this Psalm and apply it to our own situation when we sing the first person pronouns. But as we apply it, we must remember that we can use it only because we are united to Christ, and that Christ experienced what is expressed in this Psalm for our sakes. Unbelievers may not use this Psalm with any sincerity or assurance.

But with that introduction, let us look at the Psalm as it applies to our Lord. We may entitle this Psalm *"The Righteous One Reaching up to the Rock Higher than Him."*

This Psalm has essentially two stanzas separated by a Selah in verse 4. In the first stanza, we see the Righteous One's confidence in the Father expressed in prayer and words of faith. In the second stanza, we see the Righteous One's hope on the basis of the Father's faithfulness.

1.   v. 1-4   The Righteous One's Confidence
2.   v. 5-8   The Righteous One's Hope

1. The Righteous One's

Confidence

[1] Hear my cry, O God; attend unto my prayer. [2] From the end of the earth will I cry unto thee, when my heart is overwhelmed: lead me to the rock that is higher than I.

David wrote this Psalm while driven from his beloved Jerusalem where the temple of God was. Wherever he might be, it was too far away for him. He had been, as it were, exiled to the end of the earth, from whence he cried unto God.

Our Lord would have had the same experience. Since He started His ministry, He was forced to wander from place to place. "The foxes have holes, and the birds of the air have nests; but the Son of man hath not where to lay his head," says our Lord (Mt 8:20).

But as the shadow of the cross lengthened, things became even more difficult for Him. It became impossible for Him to go about freely, especially in Judea, "because the Jews sought to kill him" (Jn 7:1; 11:8).

The Lord was forced to minister in Galilee, which was known as Galilee of the Gentiles. Our Lord was, as it were, in exile from the beloved city Jerusalem and from the "multitude that kept holyday" (Ps 42:4). So great was His desire to be in Jerusalem, the city of the temple, that it appears like He was at *"the end of the earth."*

It was, therefore, as it were, from the end of the earth, that our Lord cried unto His Father to hear His prayers. What did He pray? He prayed that the Father would hear His cries and lead Him to the Rock that is higher than Him.

Our Lord is a Rock Himself as the Apostle Paul reminds us (1 Cor 10:4). But there is a Rock that is higher, the Rock which is the First Person of the Godhead, unto whom the Son, the God-Man, must find His hope and confidence. "My Father is greater than I," says the Son (Jn 14:28).

Though the Son is equal in power and glory to the Father, He is economically subordinate to the Father, and especially in His humiliation, He must depend on His Father for comfort and strength:

[3] For thou hast been a shelter for me, and a strong tower from the enemy. [4] I will abide in thy tabernacle for ever: I will trust in the covert of thy wings.

The Father was to our Lord a shelter in the storm; and a fortress against the enemy. Who is the enemy? Externally, the devil, and those that did the devil's bidding, were His enemies. But internally, all the fears, and apprehensions that attempted to assault his soul, were His enemies.

For this reason, our Lord resolved that He would remain in the tabernacle, or tent, of the LORD: that is, to remain under His care. And He would continue to trust in the covert of the Father's wings: that is, to trust that the Father would protect Him as the eagle would protect her eaglets under her wings.

Our Lord needed the support of His Father! What does this tell us about His suffering? Does it not tell us that it was real and intense? Our Lord was tempted in all points like as we are, and yet without sin. Emotionally, He would have suffered as David did, and as all of us would, when we are faced with storms in our life.

Thank God for our Lord Jesus Christ. He suffered in order that one day we would be free from suffering. He suffered so that today we may confidently rest in the Father, knowing that we have a sympathetic elder brother to intercede for us as our Great High Priest.

But now, our Lord did not only rest in the Father, He enjoyed a firm hope of deliverance.

2. The Righteous One's Hope

⁵ For thou, O God, hast heard my vows: thou hast given me the heritage of those that fear thy name.

Our Lord entered into a covenant with the Father to deliver us from sin. The cutting of this covenant was made in eternity, but enacted in the ceremony before Abraham, recorded in Genesis 15. The Father was represented by the burning furnace; while the son was represented by the smoking lamp that passed between the pieces. In the covenant, our Lord vows to lay down his life for us according as it is written in the volume of the book.

The Father heard His vow; and the Father has reciprocated with His own oath to give Him the heritage of those that fear His name. The oath that God made with Abraham in Genesis 15 was not really made with Abraham, for Abraham was sleeping (v. 12). The oath was made with the Seed of Abraham, Christ. The writer of Hebrews tells us that God "willing more abundantly to shew unto the heirs of promise the immutability of his counsel, confirmed it by an oath," which oath involves two immutable things (Heb 6:17).

So the Lord Jesus told His disciples: "I appoint unto you a kingdom, as my Father hath appointed unto me" (Lk 22:29). The word translated "appoint" literally means "assign unto by covenant."

The Father heard and reciprocated the Son's vow with His own promissory oath, for which reason, the Son could have an infallible hope that the Father would deliver Him. So we read:

⁶ Thou wilt prolong the king's life: and his years as many generations. ⁷ He shall abide before God for ever: O prepare mercy and truth, which may preserve him.

Christ is the King. He must suffer and He must die, for He came to bear the iniquity of us all. But He would yet live. He would live on for generation to generation. He would abide before God forever.

Thus we read also in Isaiah 53:10-11:

"¹⁰ Yet it pleased the LORD to bruise him; he hath put him to grief: when thou shalt make his soul an offering for sin, he shall see his seed, he shall prolong his days, and the pleasure of the LORD shall prosper in his hand. ¹¹ He shall see of the travail of his soul, and shall be satisfied: by his knowledge shall my righteous servant justify many; for he shall bear their iniquities."

Those whom He justified are united to Him. He would praise God with them; they would praise God with Him, forever and ever. So the Psalm ends:

⁸ So will I sing praise unto thy name for ever, that I may daily perform my vows.

What is the vow of the Lord? It was, no doubt, to redeem a people who would glorify God and enjoy Him forever and ever!

Thank God that the Lord kept His promise. Thank God that the Father kept His promise. Thank God that our Lord rose from the dead even as He had hoped in this Psalm. Our Lord suffered and died for us, but He rose for our justification. His sacrifice is complete. His atonement was sufficient. He has won for us the right to be the sons and daughters of God and the privilege of praising the Father with Him for all eternity.

Conclusion

What is this Psalm to you, dear child of God? Are you able to identify with the suffering of the Lord? Christ our Lord suffered not only physically, but also emotionally and spiritually.

Indeed, a large part of His suffering was emotional and spiritual. For this reason, even those of us who may not be suffering physical pains today, should be able to identify with Him: for do not most of us suffer emotionally on a very regular basis?

Is not our life like, as Andrew Bonar describes so well in his introduction to Psalm 61:

> In this life, every member of the Church has a varied lot—now at rest, then troubled; now hopeful, then fearful; now a conqueror, then a combatant. Seated as he is on the Rock of Ages, immovably seated, he sees at one time a fair sky and a bright sun; then the thick cloud spreads over nature; soon, the beam struggles through again, but soon it is mist once more.

Is this your experience? If it is, this Psalm is for you. It is for the Church to sing in union with Christ to meditate on His sufferings. But it is also for you to sing especially in the moments when dark clouds envelop your soul.

When dark clouds envelop your soul, go to the Lord; cry unto Him who is the Rock higher than you. Go to Him with the understanding that as He was delivered by the Father, He will deliver you. Amen. Ω

Psalm 62:
The Righteous One
upon the Rock, Unmoved
by Blasts of Threats

Psalm 62, like most of the Psalms from Psalm 52 onwards (apart from Psalm 60), was written at a time when David was facing persecution. There were two occasions when David was being persecuted. In Psalm 61, the occasion was probably his persecution at the hand of his son Absalom, but the rest were probably written during the times when he was pursued by Saul, and he had to hide in the caves of Adullam (1 Sam 22:1ff) and Engedi (1 Sam 24:1ff).

We don't really know when Psalm 62 was written. But the occasion and location at which it was written is not as important as the content of the Psalm, and how it fits into the experiences and thoughts of the greater David in His days of persecution. This Psalm, like all the others, was written in the Spirit of Christ to give us a glimpse of the thoughts and suffering of our Lord on our behalf. "We have here," as Andrew Bonar puts it, "the soul of the Righteous One—Christ and his members—resorting to Jehovah while iniquity surrounds them, and persecution tries them."

This Psalm would fit very well with the time after our Lord was arrested and He was being tried before the Sanhedrin and before Pilate. We may entitle it *"The Righteous One upon the Rock, Unmoved by Blasts of Threats."*

It may be divided into three stanzas of four verses each according to the two "selahs" in verses 4 and 8. It is difficult to distinguish the theme of each of these stanzas in a meaningful way. But using the comforting words in each stanza, we may outline the Psalm thus:

1. v. 1-4   He Is My Rock and My Salvation
2. v. 5-8   He Is My Expectation and My Glory
3. v. 9-12   He Is My Strength and My Reward

1. He Is My Rock &
My Salvation

¹ Truly my soul waiteth upon God...

As King David waited upon God when he was under persecution, so our Lord waited upon His Father when His enemies were breathing out threats against Him during His trials.

What is it to wait upon God? It is to rest in Him and trust that He will do what is right in answer to prayer. It is not about inactivity. It is about peace and calm in the soul. *"My soul waiteth upon God,"* says our Lord. The word rendered "waiteth" here literally means "silence" (דּוּמִיָּה, *dûmîyâh*). In Psalm 39:2, we read, "I was dumb with silence, I held my peace." The word rendered "with silence" and the word "waiteth" is the same word.

Remember how our Lord largely did not reply to the charges against Him. Indeed we are told that before Pilate, "he answered him to never a word; insomuch that the governor marvelled greatly" (Mt 27:14). "As a sheep before her shearers is dumb, so he openeth not his mouth" (Isa 53:7).

Our Lord had peace and calm in His heart and was committing all things to the Father though He was silent before man. He was waiting upon the Father in the midst of the assaults upon His soul.

But on what basis was He able to wait?

> [1b] *from him cometh my salvation.* [2] *He only is my rock and my salvation; he is my defence; I shall not be greatly moved.*

Our Lord would wait upon the Father because He knew that deliverance must come from Him. He is His rock, and salvation, and defence. He could cling on to His Father like a man threatened by a gale could cling on to a sturdy rock. He is His safety.

But more than that, He knew the Father would deliver in His time, and His Father would defend Him. He is like a fortress to protect Him from anything outside His plan. Though it is human to fear, our Lord need not worry what man could do to Him. His Father was in control. So He would not be greatly moved or shaken.

And so instead of taking matters into His own hands, which He could, our Lord waited upon the Father, and implicitly rebuked His tormentors:

> [3] *How long will ye imagine mischief against a man? ye shall be slain all of you: as a bowing wall shall ye be, and as a tottering fence.* [4] *They only consult to cast him down from his excellency: they delight in lies: they bless with their mouth, but they curse inwardly.*

Our Lord is the God-Man. Those who persecuted Him, were not persecuting an ordinary man. God would see to it that vengeance is exacted on them. They have raised themselves up and abused their power against the Son of Man. They spoke lies about Him. They consulted not so that they might treat Him fairly. They consulted to "*cast Him down from his excellency.*" They smeared His reputation; they disregarded His position of excellency as the Son of God.

They blessed with their mouth, but cursed Him inwardly. So, a few days before, the multitude were singing "Hosanna to the son of David." But now, they are crying, "Away with him. Crucify him." So Pilate pronounced Him innocent but executed Him anyway.

Those who remain unrepentant will face the judgement of God. Who can stand before the wrath of God? They will be slain, they will be cast down like a tilting wall and a tottering fence. When they persecute the Lord, they are full of pride, but when they face the avenger of our Lord's blood, they cannot even stand by themselves. A little push and they would crash into everlasting death.

Let us, therefore, wait upon the Father as our Lord did. He is our rock and our salvation. He is our defence and our vindicator.

But He is also our expectation of glory even as our Lord expresses in the second stanza of this Psalm.

2. He Is My Expectation
& My Glory

> [5] *My soul, wait thou only upon God; for my expectation is from him.* [6] *He only is my rock and my salvation: he is my defence; I shall not be moved.* [7] *In God is my salvation and my glory: the rock of my strength, and my refuge, is in God.*

At times when we face severe assaults upon our souls, when there is no one to sympathise with us or to comfort us, one of the things we must do is to talk to ourselves.

What does our Lord say to His own soul? He reminds Himself of who the Father is to Him. He is His Rock, His Salvation, and His Defence. And not only that: He is also His Expectation, His Glory, His Strength, and His Refuge.

- *"My expectation is from him"* (v. 5). He is my expectation. While I cannot expect much from man, I can expect much from Him: for He is a prayer hearing God. Therefore, I will wait upon Him.

- He is *"my rock"* (v. 6). I will cling on to Him for safety.

- He is *"my salvation"* (v. 6). I will trust Him to deliver me.

- He is *"my defence"* (v. 6). He is my fortress. I will hide in Him. I will not be shaken. He is my security.

- He is *"my glory"* (v. 7). My honour is in His hand, He will vindicate me.

- He *"is the rock of my strength."* That is: He is the rock upon which I derive my strength. He is my strength.

- He is *"my refuge."* I can hide in Him when my heart is overwhelmed.

What shall we do in the face of such overwhelming assurances?

[8] Trust in him at all times; ye people, pour out your heart before him: God is a refuge for us.

Since God is so great and so good to us, let us trust in Him at all times, through thick and thin, through peace and war. Let us learn to pour out our hearts to Him, and hide in Him.

Moreover, let us recognize, as our Lord would have us sing with Him, that He is our reward.

3. He Is My Strength
& My Reward

[9] Surely men of low degree are vanity, and men of high degree are a lie: to be laid in the balance, they are altogether lighter than vanity. [10] Trust not in oppression, and become not vain in robbery: if riches increase, set not your heart upon them.

Man is constantly tempted to look to man to seek riches, honour, and approval. If they cannot gain riches, honour, and approval by looking to the rich and powerful, they might attempt oppression to gain respect and approval, and robbery to gain riches.

But to do so is foolishness: for as our Lord warns us, *"men of low degree are vanity."* In other words, those who are poor and have no honour in society are nothing. They are as good as a puff of steam that appears for a moment and then disappears.

What about men of high degree? Well, they are a lie. They are lighter than vanity! When you weigh them on a balance, vanity tips the scale!

How foolish it is then to seek honour and riches from man. Those who put their trust in the rich and powerful are trusting in a lie. Those who fear them, fear a lie. Those who oppress the poor and the weak to gain honour and riches are more insignificant than vanishing steam, in the eyes of God.

But God is almighty. He is to be trusted, to be feared, and to be loved.

[11] *God hath spoken once; twice have I heard this; that power belongeth unto God.* *[12]* *Also unto thee, O Lord, belongeth mercy: for thou renderest to every man according to his work.*

God has spoken once, twice must we hear—not only because we have two ears, but because it is so important. We must hear it with the ears of our body; we must hear it with the ears of our soul.

Power and authority belong to God. All things come to pass according to His sovereign power. But mercy and love also belong to God.

What does this mean? This means that He will protect His people; and He will vindicate them. He will see to it that justice is done. Those who are persecuted for His sake, will be handsomely rewarded. Those who persecute His saints, will be severely punished: for those who persecute the saints, persecute Christ.

God's people, therefore, need not fear what man can do to them. God's people need not be overwhelmed by the devices of man.

Conclusion

These are the sentiments we are given to confess with the Righteous One in Psalm 62. As our Lord waited on the Father, so we too can wait upon Him. Let us learn to rest in Him and wait upon Him at all times. He is our expectation, our rock, our salvation, our defence, our glory, our strength, our refuge, our reward and our King. Amen.

Psalm 63:
The Righteous One's
Refreshment in the Wilderness

Psalm 63 is a very lovely Psalm written by David at a time when he was in the wilderness of Judah. The wilderness of Judah is a vast wasteland west of the Dead Sea. David was known to have camped out there on two occasions. Once, he was fleeing from Saul. Another time, he was fleeing from his son Absalom. But which of these two occasions gave rise to this beautiful Psalm is not as important as the spiritual and emotional experience of David on which this Psalm took roots and grew.

This experience was, I believe, given to David as a foretaste of what the greater David, Christ, would experience in His earthly ministry. It was an experience that enabled David to express—by the inspiration of the Spirit of Christ—the very feelings and thoughts of our Lord during His earthly sojourn.

And these thoughts and feelings of our Lord would also be experienced by every believer at one time or another. Indeed, the Psalms would not only have been used by our Lord in His incarnation, they are intended for our use as those united to Him and bear His name. They are, as such, not songs which can be used by unbelievers meaningfully.

But what is the spiritual and emotional soil on which this Psalm springs? Well, the answer is hinted in the prologue of this Psalm: it is a wilderness experience or an experience of spiritual thirst. We may entitle this Psalm *"The Righteous One's Refreshment in the Wilderness."*

This Psalm may be divided into three parts. The first part (v. 1-2) contains an expression of longing; the second part (v. 3-6) contains an expression of satisfaction; while the third part (v. 7-11) contains an expression of confidence.

Shall we not see these as expressions of the Lord? As Andrew Bonar puts it:

> When we read all this as spoken of Christ, how much does every verse become enhanced. His thirst for God! His vision of God! His estimate of God's lovingkindness! His soul satisfied! His mouth full of praise! His soul following hard after God!

With this in mind, we may outline this Psalm thus:

1. v. 1-2   The Lord's Longing
2. v. 3-6   The Lord's Satisfaction
3. v. 7-11   The Lord's Confidence

1. The Lord's Longing

¹ O God, thou art my God; early will I seek thee: my soul thirsteth for thee, my flesh longeth for thee in a dry and thirsty land, where no water is; ² To see thy power and thy glory, so as I have seen thee in the sanctuary.

David would have taken these words in his lips with sincerity, but in whom but the Lord Jesus Christ could these words find their fullest meaning.

In His high priestly prayer, our Lord pleaded with His Father:

> "And now, O Father, glorify thou me with thine own self with the glory which I had with thee before the world was" (Jn 17:5).

Our Lord, more than anyone else, would have seen the power and glory of God in the heavenly sanctuary. What is it to see the glory of God, but to see the brightness of God's face, as our Psalter has it? David would have seen but a shadowy display. Indeed, we have no record of David seeing anything extraordinary by way of the power of God in the sanctuary. David must be speaking about what he saw through eyes of faith; whereas our Lord saw the substance of the great power and glory of God.

Our Lord, more than anyone else, thirsted to be filled with a sense of the presence, favour and glory of God. Our Lord, more than anyone else, longed for the fellowship of His Father every morning. We are told of how He would rise up a great while before day to pray in a solitary place (Mk 1:35).

Oh, that we may imitate His example! Oh, that by His Spirit we may also thirst after the LORD—that we may sing this Psalm with a true yearning in our hearts. Shall we not, therefore, whenever we sing this Psalm, ask the LORD to give us this thirst and yearning. Only those who hunger and thirst after the LORD will know the blessing of being filled by the LORD.

But let us be careful, children of God, that we do not become overly dependent on feelings so that we become despondent when we do not sense the LORD's presence in our lives.

2. The Lord's Satisfaction

³ Because thy lovingkindness is better than life, my lips shall praise thee. ⁴ Thus will I bless thee while I live: I will lift up my hands in thy name. ⁵ My soul shall be satisfied as with marrow and fatness; and my mouth shall praise thee with joyful lips: ⁶ When I remember thee upon my bed, and meditate on thee in the night watches.

Notice, that while He speaks of His thirst in the first part of the Psalm, here in this second part, He is essentially saying that His thirst and hunger is actually being met by the LORD. *"My soul shall be satisfied as with marrow and fatness,"* He says in verse 5. We must not mistake the apparent future tense (rendering of the Hebrew imperfect tense) here as referring to a distant future conditioned upon what God would do. No, no; the imperfect tense is used here to express the fact that the needs of His soul are being met by God, so that there is a spontaneous and continuous response of gratitude and praise.

But how? How is the desire of His soul being met? It is being met by a simple thought of the lovingkindness of the LORD for His covenant people! That is what the Hebrew word translated "lovingkindness" (חֶסֶד, *chêsêd*) means. Whenever it is used in the Old Testament to describe God, it describes His lovingkindness, or special covenant love, towards His people.

"Thy lovingkindness is better than life," muses our Lord. Life is universally acknowledged as the greatest of earthly blessings. Every other blessing on earth is included in life, and depends on life. For this reason, Satan insinuates in Job 2:4: "Skin for skin, yea, all that a man hath will he give for his life."

But our Lord does not think like the world: *"Thy lovingkindness is better than life,"* He declares. To know God's lovingkindness is more important and more comforting to Him than to experience a life of ease and plenty.

In other words, our Lord is not looking to any mystical experience when He speaks about the thirst in His soul. Neither is He saying that His soul was empty until He enjoyed fully the presence of God. No, no; while He longs to enjoy the love of His Father in close fellowship,

His soul was satisfied even while waiting for the day to come.

His soul is satisfied merely by the thought that God is merciful, loving and kind. Therefore, He would praise Him with joyful lips. Therefore, He would fill His mind with the thought of God in the night when He finds Himself awake. Indeed, the lovingkindness of God is so much better to Him than life, that He willingly laid down His life in order that His people might enjoy the love of God as He did.

Herein is a secret, dear reader. Whenever your soul has reason to fret or to become discontented, do not think about how bad things are, or how good they could be. If you fill your hearts with these thoughts, you shall become more and more discontented, and more and more fretful and fearful. What then should you think about? Learn from the example of our Lord. Meditate on the lovingkindness of God! Think of how the love of God was brought to you by the Lord in His death so that nothing shall separate you from God's love.

Be careful! When you do so, you may be kept up all night with excitement and joy (v. 6). But at least you will not be kept up all night with worries and regret. Indeed, I believe that as the LORD gives His beloved sleep, so those who meditate on the lovingkindness of the LORD will not lack sleep. They will sleep peacefully and joyfully, they will awake with fresh expectancy and confidence as they look to the LORD for a new day of challenges.

And consider…

3. The Lord's Confidence

7 Because thou hast been my help, therefore in the shadow of thy wings will I rejoice. 8 My soul followeth hard after thee: thy right hand upholdeth me.

God is our ever-present help. Sometimes, He helps us by delivering us out of a danger or out of a difficult situation. Other times, He helps us by His Spirit working powerfully in our hearts, and assuring us of God's lovingkindness.

Our Lord in His earthly sojourn experienced the Father's help over and over again, just as David must have experienced deliverance and encouragement many times. Thus, He is not afraid of any storm ahead. He learned to rejoice in the shadow of His Father's wings and sought to follow after Him, even when the way ahead might be difficult and fraught with danger.

He knew that the Father would uphold Him even in the darkest hours (v. 8).

He knew also that those who sought His destruction and everything else that brings pain and sorrow to His heart would be dealt with by the Father, verse 9:

9 But those that seek my soul, to destroy it, shall go into the lower parts of the earth. 10 They shall fall by the sword: they shall be a portion for foxes.

That is to say, they will be dealt with dramatically and powerfully by the Father.

On the other hand, verse 11:

11 But the king shall rejoice in God; every one that sweareth by him shall glory: but the mouth of them that speak lies shall be stopped.

Who is this king? David has long ceased to be king. But there is yet a king who reigns. He is none other than the King of kings and Lord of lords, the Lord Jesus Christ. All who name the name of Jehovah, the living and true God, and swear by His name will glory in the King.

We will rejoice with Him today. We will rejoice in Him forever and ever.

But all who speak lies will forever be stopped, as will their father, the devil. No, they will not be silenced completely, for in hell, there is weeping and gnashing. There is groaning and regrets. But they shall no longer be able to afflict God's people with their lies.

Conclusion

Dear child of God, what is this Psalm to you? For me, it is one which I turn to very often. It is a Psalm that automatically fills my heart when anxiety and fears begin to cloud my thoughts in the morning. It is a Psalm which our family will use when troubles cloud our minds and we long for the relief of the LORD.

The love of God towards me, or His lovingkindness towards His people is very precious to me. If I have not the assurance of His love, I shall have no strength to live another day in the face of all the trials and discouragement that often assault my soul.

Sing this Psalm, therefore, beloved Christian. The Lord your Saviour will sing with you by His Spirit when you do so, whether corporately or privately. Sing it to encourage yourself and to encourage one another as you journey together to see the brightness of the face of your King. Amen. Ω

Psalm 64:
The Righteous One's
Assurance as Arrows Fly

Psalm 64 is short but not very well known. Most of us will know Psalm 63 and Psalm 65, but we will probably draw a blank when asked about Psalm 64. What is its most memorable feature? It is, no doubt, its reference to archery! Yet it is a very useful Psalm—not so much to encourage archery—but to encourage ourselves when we are confronted with arrows of vicious words flying in our direction; or when fears seem to pierce our hearts like stray arrows.

It has been conjectured that this Psalm might have been written by David, when he was a young man who had just entered into the service of King Saul.

David, who had no political experience, was cast into political limelight by his defeat of Goliath; and by the honours that the king and his son Jonathan accorded him. Those who are in the political limelight, especially those who are godly and principled, can expect many arrows and secret darts to fly in their direction.

We think of what happened to Joseph amongst his brothers. We think of Daniel in the court of King Nebuchadnezzar. But most of all, we think of the experience of our Lord Jesus, in whose Spirit David wrote this Psalm.

Those who would imitate the Lord, and seek to be righteous as He is righteous, will experience the fears and exasperation that our Lord experienced, which are expressed in this Psalm.

We may entitle this Psalm *"The Righteous One's Assurance as Arrows Fly."*

This Psalm has two parts. In the first part, we see arrows flying towards the Righteous One. In the second part, we see the arrow of God flying towards the wicked.

1.   v. 1-6   Arrows of the Wicked Targeting the Righteous
2.   v. 7-10   Arrow of God Targeting the Wicked

1. Arrows of the Wicked Targeting
the Righteous

¹ Hear my voice, O God, in my prayer: preserve my life from fear of the enemy.

Fear is a very human emotion. He who has no fear is not human. Our Lord feared in the days of His humiliation. He is fully God and fully Man.

What shall we do when we fear? Our Lord prayed. He prayed with "strong crying and tears,… and was heard in that he feared" (Heb 5:7). He subdued His fear of the creature with a fear of God.

We must follow the example of our Lord to pray. How to pray? We may pray in two ways in regard to our fears.

Firstly, we may pray for the removal of that which causes our fear. But when we do so, it must always be conditioned upon the Father's will. Our Lord prayed in the Garden of Gethsemane, "Take this cup from me, yet not my will, but thy will be done."

Secondly, we may pray that God will help our fears by increasing our faith, our courage, and our strength. In this case, we may pray absolutely, for it is always God's will for believers to have victory over the fear of man and circumstances (cf. Gal 1:10).

This is the prayer offered by David and the greater David when He says: *"preserve my life from fear of the enemy."*

And so too the subsequent verses:

> *2 Hide me from the secret counsel of the wicked; from the insurrection of the workers of iniquity: 3 Who whet their tongue like a sword, and bend their bows to shoot their arrows, even bitter words: 4 That they may shoot in secret at the perfect: suddenly do they shoot at him, and fear not. 5 They encourage themselves in an evil matter: they commune of laying snares privily; they say, Who shall see them? 6 They search out iniquities [i.e. they plot and scheme]; they accomplish a diligent search: both the inward thought of every one of them, and the heart, is deep.*

Who are the wicked and the workers of iniquity? They are the Devil and his seed. Some are overtly haters of God, whereas others are covertly so. There are many who will call unto the Lord, in the last day saying, "Lord, Lord, have we not prophesied in thy name?" who will hear the Lord say, "I know you not ...depart from me, all ye workers of iniquity" (Lk 13:27).

In this life, they will target the righteous. They targeted the Lord Jesus. They will continue to target those who are united to Him, even those who are righteous because He is righteous, and known as perfect because He is perfect.

How do they target the Righteous One and His disciples? They use their tongues like swords and arrows. Sometimes, they slash with their swords (v. 3a). Other times, they shoot out arrows secretly (v. 3b-4). They spread rumours and slander. They scheme and plot to assassinate the character of the righteous.

Did it not happen in the days of our Lord? How did so great a multitude eventually turn against the Lord? There were arrows flying from all directions against Him, many surreptitiously, so that He had no opportunity to defend Himself.

Today, things are not different, only that the arrows are quicker and more sophisticated, such as emails and SMSes, WhatsApp, Telegram, Instagram, Twitters, Facebook etc. And yes, they are often shot anonymously. They shoot in secret, and fear not. They encourage themselves, saying, *"Who shall see them?"* (v. 4-5).

As our Lord suffered, so did David, so did Joseph, so did Daniel, so will all who follow the Lord. But God will not sit by idly when His sons and daughters are being shot at.

So we see in the second part of this Psalm...

2. Arrow of God Targeting
the Wicked

> *7 But God shall shoot at them with an arrow; suddenly shall they be wounded. 8 So they shall make their own tongue to fall upon themselves: all that see them shall flee away.*

The enemies of the Righteous One shoot their arrows. The righteous ones cannot shoot back. If their enemy had used a sword in unjust criticism, they would have the right to fight back with the sword of the Spirit. But if the enemy shoots arrows of rumours, gossips and anonymous slanders, then the righteous ones may not respond in kind.

But the LORD who says, "Vengeance belongs to me," will not stand idly by. He will, as it were, shoot back.

God's arrows are precisely aimed. He knows exactly who shot the arrows at His children. He would even pick up their arrows to shoot back. *"So they shall make their own tongue to fall upon themselves"* (v. 8).

History is replete with illustrations of how God deals with His enemies. The Assyrians who tormented the people of God in the North were defeated by the Babylonians. The Babylonians who slaughtered the people of God in the South were defeated by the Persians, etc.

And so Jerusalem that shot arrows against the Righteous One and His disciples was overrun by the Roman army under the leadership of General Titus.

And likewise, at the individual level, it often happens that those who persecute God's children, find themselves the object of God's temporal judgement: as Solomon observed, "Whoso diggeth a pit shall fall therein: and he that rolleth a stone, it will return upon him" (Prov 26:27).

Wherefore? Verse 9:

> ⁹ *And all men shall fear, and shall declare the work of God; for they shall wisely consider of his doing.*

Those who remained hardened in sin will tremble for fear of judgement. But those with eyes of faith, shall see the hand of God in the events of this present life. A godly fear will arise in their heart as they declare that it is God who brings all things to pass by His wisdom, and sovereign power, and His jealousy for His children. They shall replace their fear of persons and circumstances, with a fear of God. The fear of God shall subdue their fear of persons and circumstances. Our Lord was heard in that He feared God (Heb 5:7).

But complete justice will be reserved for the final day.

> ¹⁰ *The righteous shall be glad in the LORD, and shall trust in him; and all the upright in heart shall glory.*

The righteous, being assured of God's vindication, shall be glad in Him and trust Him.

The righteous, seeing God's providential vindication, shall have their faith strengthened.

The righteous and the upright in heart, seeing God's perfect justice being enacted on behalf of His children at the general judgement, shall praise and glorify God, forever and ever.

Conclusion

When our Lord was suffering for us, He suffered in many ways—physically, spiritually and emotionally. One of the ways He suffered was through the sharp arrows of the enemies of God which, as it were, flew by night. Our Lord committed Himself to the Father, and looked to Him to allay His fears.

Today, as the disciples of Christ, we are also confronted by sharp arrows—of sharp tongues and pointing fingers. The servants are not greater than their master. But thank God, we can have the assurance that not only our Master understands, but that our Master will see to it that justice be done for those who seek to remain meek for His name's sake. And we are given a Psalm to sing in union with our Master to soothe our anxieties, and to strengthen our confidence that all is well. Amen. Ω

Psalm 65:
The Righteous One's
Joyful Praise
for the Prayer-Hearing God

Psalm 65 is a familiar Psalm. I suspect that it is especially familiar to, and beloved by Psalm singers because of its lively theme and the lively tune that is usually associated with it.

It is the first Psalm that clearly breaks from the previous twelve or thirteen Psalms in its tone. The previous twelve or thirteen Psalms tend to be heavy-hearted as they were borne out of the soil of persecution. Psalm 65, on the other hand, is a joyous Psalm flowing out of a heart of gratitude and praise.

David apparently wrote this Psalm to be sung annually at one of the harvest feasts celebrated by the people of God, such as the Feast of Firstfruits in which the first sheaves of the barley harvest were waved before the LORD as a dedication offering (see Lev 23:9-14; cf. v. 9, 13). So it is a harvest Psalm to celebrate the goodness of God in hearing the prayers of His people for His blessing. However, David, no doubt, wrote it in the Spirit of Christ so that God's people throughout the ages might sing it with meaning, even if they have no harvest to celebrate. But to sing it meaningfully, we must associate the first person pronouns in it not with David (he is dead and far removed from us), but with the greater David, Christ (who is alive and united to us). This must be how His Spirit would have us sing it.

With this in mind, we must understand the "me" in this Psalm (v. 3) as Christ, the Righteous One. And the "we" (everywhere), accordingly, would be the righteous ones united to Christ, even Zion, the Church of Christ.

This then, is a Psalm of joyful praise which our Head has given for us to sing in union with Him to extol our great God of salvation and blessings. We may entitle it *"The Righteous One's Joyful Praise for the Prayer-Hearing God."*

What should we praise God for? This Psalm gives us three reasons:

1.   v. 1-4   Praise God for His Salvation

2.   v. 5-8   Praise God for His Mighty Power

3.   v. 9-13   Praise Him for His Provision

1. Praise God for His
Salvation

[1] *Praise waiteth for thee, O God, in Zion: and unto thee shall the vow be performed.*

Mt Zion was where the temple of God resided. Zion was the place where true worship and praise ascended daily unto the living and true God. Zion was where vows were paid. But earthly Zion has given way to the heavenly Zion, the Church of Christ (Heb 12:22).

For as soon as the stone which the builders rejected was made head-corner stone, in His resurrection, so soon did the old temple begin to cease its former function.

Zion today is not located in Palestine. It is located everywhere in the world. Where the citizens of heaven are, there, the city of God is. And there praises await, like runners poised and waiting at the starting line, ready to take off at the drop of a hat.

There, in spiritual Zion, vows are being performed. Nay, more than that, there in Zion, *the vow* (v. 1) is being performed. What is the vow? The vow is that one vow that makes all the other vows possible. It is the vow of the man that God has chosen to live and die for the redemption of His people, in order that they might have fellowship with God, and glorify and enjoy Him forever. It is a vow that a people should be saved from their sin to serve God in prayer and praise.

In that the people are rejoicing in Him and praising God, the vow is being performed. The vow of this man chosen of God is being performed.

This one man opened the way for us to approach God at His throne. It is by Him we may confess, verse 2:

> *2 O thou that hearest prayer, unto thee shall all flesh come.*

Our God is a prayer-hearing God. But He does not hear the prayers of everyone. "The sacrifice of the wicked is an abomination to the LORD: but the prayer of the upright is his delight" (Prov 15:8). But there is none upright amongst fallen men. How then can we come before God?

We can come before God because Christ our Lord made it possible by taking our guilt upon Himself. He paid for our transgressions by His blood, so that they are purged away. Notice the representative principle in verse 3:

> *3 Iniquities prevail against me: as for our transgressions, thou shalt purge them away.*

Our iniquities were imputed to Him who gave us this Psalm. By His blood our transgressions have been purged away.

Blessed be this man and all men united to Him, for by Him we shall enjoy the praise and worship of God, forever and ever, verse 4:

> *4 Blessed is the man whom thou choosest, and causest to approach unto thee, that he may dwell in thy courts: we shall be satisfied with the goodness of thy house, even of thy holy temple.*

Who is this man whom the Father has chosen? He is none other than Christ, the elect chief corner stone of Zion (1Pt 2:6). It is in union with Him that we shall be satisfied with the goodness of the LORD's house. That is to say, it is by Him, that we might enjoy all the blessings of salvation, of worship and of joy in the LORD.

O that we may fully grasp what this Psalm is saying! If we do, then our hearts should be ready to leap to praise the LORD as we confess: "*Praise waiteth for thee in Zion, O God!*"

We must praise Him for salvation so rich and free in Christ Jesus. But we must also praise God for His mighty power as the second part of this Psalm reminds us to do.

2. Praise God for His
Mighty Power

5 By terrible things in righteousness wilt thou answer us, O God of our salvation; who art the confidence of all the ends of the earth, and of them that are afar off upon the sea: 6 Which by his strength setteth fast the mountains; being girded with power: 7 Which stilleth the noise of the seas, the noise of their waves, and the tumult of the people. 8 They also that dwell in the uttermost parts are afraid at thy tokens: thou makest the outgoings of the morning and evening to rejoice.

Our God is a prayer-hearing God. For this reason, we should praise Him. But He is not just a prayer-hearing God! He not only hears, but answers our prayers.

Of course, being infinitely wise and loving, God does not always answer our prayers according to our desire. But He delights in doing so, and it would be a great dishonour to Him if we come to Him for anything and doubt that He can do it.

We must therefore bear in mind whenever we approach Him that He is almighty. He has power to answer our prayers wherever we may be, and whatever our prayers may be, so long as it is in accordance to His will. He will answer according to His wisdom, righteousness and power.

His power is displayed in the creation of the mighty mountains and in calming the boisterous sea (v. 7a)—just as demonstrated by the Lord Jesus who commanded the wind and the waves, "Peace, be still" (Mk 4:39).

His power is also manifested in His ability to bring peace out of war or to still the tumult of the people in an instant (v. 7b).

Yea, indeed, His power is manifested even unto the uttermost parts of the world through the great wonders of nature. We think of lightning and storms, earthquakes and volcanoes, and even the simple process of sunrise and sunset (v. 8).

Do not these things call forth praise in the hearts of man? Even those who do not know the LORD are awed by the display of His power, and are sometimes moved to worship whatever they perceive to be the source of power.

As believers we know better. We know that power belongs to Him (Ps 62:11) who is our God and Saviour.

For this reason, He is *"the confidence of all the ends of the earth, and of them that are afar off upon the sea"* (v. 5). Who are they? They are those who are united to the Lord, wherever they may be on the earth. They may be exiled to a foreign land, or they may be sailing in the ocean with no sight of land or people. Yet, the LORD is with them and they may hope and trust in Him.

So too for all of us! Do you who feel like you have been driven to the ends of the earth? Do you feel that you are being tossed to and fro on the high seas?

Remember that the God we serve is the Creator of the mountains and the seas. No mountain is too great that He cannot overcome. No sea is too rough that He cannot calm. No tumult amongst man is too great that He cannot still.

The LORD can bring peace. He is the God of peace. And your Mediator is the prince of peace. Go therefore to the Father in the name of your Mediator, and you shall find peace and rest for your souls.

Then praise Him. Praise Him for His mighty power. Praise Him as He fills your heart with confidence and hope in Him who is our almighty God, who answers our prayers in His righteousness and power.

And praise Him too for He is the LORD who provides....

3. Praise God for His Provision

⁹ Thou visitest the earth, and waterest it: thou greatly enrichest it with the river of God, which is full of water: thou preparest them corn, when thou hast so provided for it. ¹⁰ Thou waterest the ridges thereof abundantly: thou settlest the furrows thereof: thou makest it soft with showers: thou blessest the springing thereof. ¹¹ Thou crownest the year with thy goodness; and thy paths drop fatness. ¹² They drop upon the pastures of the wilderness: and the little hills rejoice on every side. ¹³ The pastures are clothed with flocks; the valleys also are covered over with corn; they shout for joy, they also sing.

Israel was an agricultural people. They understood that all the material blessings they received came from the LORD. He is the one who provides the rain and the sunshine. He is the one who gives a bountiful harvest. He is the one who makes the flock healthy and prolific.

He is the one, not the farmer, nor the shepherd, nor the earth, which deserves the praises of His people when the year is crowned with goodness and our paths drop fatness.

Today, we are not an agricultural people. How do we appreciate this final stanza? We must appreciate it by believing that God will provide everything that we need, both temporal and material, as well as eternal and spiritual.

In fact, the reference to the "river of God" (v. 9), should lead us to understand that the emphasis in this Psalm is not really the temporal and material, but the spiritual and eternal.

The picture given here is that of a barren and dry land rendered fruitful by the bountiful rain that God sends and by the "river of God."

Both the rain and the "river of God" signify the Spirit of God and the spiritual blessings that He brings.

God's children must look to God for the spiritual blessings that He brings to the congregation of His people.

In union with our Head, we must look to Him to do a mighty work in our Church. We must praise Him when we see His blessings upon the Church.

Conclusion

Let us learn to praise Him joyfully. Praise Him for salvation so rich and free. Praise Him for His mighty power in answer to prayer. Praise Him for His provisions for His people. And as we praise Him, let us learn to ask of Him, believing that He is perfectly able to hear and answer our prayers.

"Call unto me, and I will answer thee, and shew thee great and mighty things, which thou knowest not" (Jer 33:3).

May the LORD help us to pray and to praise. May He so hear and answer our prayers that we have reason to exchange our prayers for praise. Amen. Ω

Psalm 66:
The Righteous One's Praise
for Answered Prayer

Psalm 66 is a solemn and yet joyful Psalm. It is a song of joyful praise unto God for prayers answered (see verses 19-20).

Whose song is it? Who is the "I" in this song? Well, the "I" at first sight is the writer of this Psalm. Who is the writer of this Psalm? We are not told. He is probably King David, "the sweet psalmist of Israel" (2 Sam 23:1). But is this how we are to understand the "I"? If so, then would not we simply be singing someone else's experience, so that when we sing "God hath heard me" (v. 19), we cannot mean what we sing? We can only mean "God heard David"!

Well, could it be that the "I" is intended to be anyone who sings this song? Well, it cannot be, because it is meaningless for an unbeliever to sing this song!

What then? It is not difficult to see that if this is a Kingdom Song intended for the Church to sing in corporate worship, then the "I" in this Psalm must be taken as the Lord Jesus Christ, in the first place; and all who are mystically united to Him, in the second place. Christ and His Church are one. Christ is the head of the Church, and the Church is the body of Christ.

This Psalm is written in the Spirit of Christ (1 Pet 1:10-11; Col 3:16). It is a Psalm of praise of Christ and His Church for answered prayers. It may be entitled *"The Righteous One's Praise for Answered Prayer."* It is a Psalm for the Church comprising righteous ones to sing in union with Christ, the Righteous One, to extol God for hearing their cries.

But it is fitting for the Church to use on all occasions. When God has heard a specific prayer of the church or a member of the church, we may sing this Psalm in confident praise. But even when we do not know of any specific prayer being answered, we may use this Psalm, because it is always true in Christ!

This Psalm has five parts:

1. v. 1-4   A Call to Praise God for His Greatness
2. v. 5-7   A Call to Consider God's Work of Redemption
3. v. 8-12   A Call to Praise God for His Providential Care
4. v. 13-15   A Resolution to Praise God
5. v. 16-20   A Testimony to Our Prayer-Hearing God

Let's consider these five parts briefly.

1. A Call to Praise God
for His Greatness

[1] Make a joyful noise unto God, all ye lands: [2] Sing forth the honour of his name: make his praise glorious. [3] Say unto God, How terrible [awesome] art thou in thy works! through the greatness of thy power shall thine enemies submit themselves unto thee. [4] All the earth shall worship thee, and shall sing unto thee; they shall sing to thy name.

The God we worship is great in His power and awesome in His works. He alone is worthy of our adoration and praise. Indeed, so great and glorious is He that we cannot but desire that all the earth join us to praise Him with a joyful noise!

What is a joyful noise? Well, phrase "make a joyful noise" (v. 1) comes from a Hebrew word that is usually translated as "shout" in the Old Testament, such as in Psalm 47:1: "O clap your hands, all ye people; shout unto God with the voice of triumph." Perhaps our translators rendered it as "make a joyful noise" because we can't shout when we sing!

But the idea is that as we think about God, our hearts must be filled with such strong affections that we cannot but sing loudly and zealously, with all our hearts.

It is as simple as that: If we believe God and we are not apathetic to all that He has done for us, we shall not simply mumble in praise of Him. Indeed, I believe it is a great sin for us to sing the praise of God in a half-hearted way! If we sing in a half-hearted way, what are we telling the heathen? Are we not saying to them: God is not worthy of our praise? What are we saying to God? Are we not saying to Him: "You are not really that great!"

Ah, we all have our excuses: We have sorrows of heart. Was not our Lord a man of sorrows? Yet this is His song. He, no doubt, sang it wholeheartedly in His humiliation. And He is calling us to sing heartily unto His Father with Him! And what about not knowing the tune, not knowing the meaning, or being distracted by the cares of the world? O what excuses can we have? Some of us had the privilege of visiting the reforming churches in North Eastern China. There, we heard some of the heartiest of praises unto God! Were they without the cares of the world? Did they understand everything they sang? Did they care that they were not musically trained? No! Yet, they sang their hearts out because they knew they were praising God with His own words!

Oh let us cease from our mumbling. Let us praise God from the bottom of our hearts. And let the joyful shout of triumph with God's Word encourage us that He who has begun a good work in us "will perform it unto the day of the Lord Jesus Christ" (Phil 1:6). And let us believe and look forward to the day when every knee shall bow and every tongue confess that He is Lord! And let us stir our hearts to serve Him to the end that we might be instrumental in conquering the world for God as we worship and live by His power (see v. 4).

But how do we worship and live by this power? We must do so by considering God's mighty work of redemption.

2. A Call to Consider God's Work of Redemption

5 Come and see the works of God: he is terrible in his doing towards the children of men. 6 He turned the sea into dry land: they went through the flood on foot: there did we rejoice in him. 7 He ruleth by his power forever; his eyes behold the nations: let not the rebellious exalt themselves.

The exodus of God's people out of Egypt was not just a historical event. It is, in God's plan, intended to be a drama to teach His people the power of His redeeming grace.

Think of the greatness of His power manifested against the heathen in the ten plagues (v. 5). Think of how God parted the Red Sea for His people to pass on dry land (v. 6).

Put yourself in the shoes of the Israelites who passed through the Red Sea and "rejoice in Him."

But more than that, think of what He has done in redeeming you through the blood of Christ. Think of how hardened in sin you were. Think of how God had to break you down little by little. Think of how by the power of the Spirit of Christ, you were brought out of spiritual death and darkness and planted onto the path that leads to life.

Were it not for the power of God manifested in your life, would you be what you are today? Were it not for the power of God manifested in the lives of our fathers in the faith, would the world in terms of her advancements be what it is today?

You need only to visit a country which has had strong Christian influence, and then parts of the third world, which have not enjoyed any Christian influence, to notice the difference. Though many of these Christian nations are no longer Christian, the effect of the Gospel in all aspects of life is still being enjoyed by the people. Not so in places where the Gospel influence was severely curtailed or limited.

When we contemplate this, shall we not lift up our hearts to praise the LORD, and shall we not call unto the rebellious to lay down their arms (v. 7)? Anyone, and any nation which exalt themselves against God do so to their own detriment (cf. Prov 14:34)!

So, let the people of God praise Him! Let all who have been redeemed by the blood of Christ, join Him to praise God for redemption!

3. A Call to Praise God
for His Care

[8] *O bless our God, ye people, and make the voice of his praise to be heard:* [9] *Which holdeth our soul in life, and suffereth not our feet to be moved.* [10] *For thou, O God, hast proved us: thou hast tried us, as silver is tried.* [11] *Thou broughtest us into the net; thou laidst affliction upon our loins.* [12] *Thou hast caused men to ride over our heads; we went through fire and through water: but thou broughtest us out into a wealthy place.*

Why should we bless our God? Why must we make the voice of His praise heard? We must because of His care for us. He is a mighty God, but He has condescended to pity us and to show His love towards us.

He sustains our life. In Him we live and move and have our being. But more than that, He suffers not our feet to be moved. That is, He does not allow us to slip and fall.

I think of the experience some of us had recently, when we had to make use of cesspools and dung holes in China. I think of what disastrous consequence there would be had any of us fallen into any of these pools. Thank God that none of us slipped. When I told my mum about dung pits, she related to me of how in olden days in Singapore, there were such pits, and chickens attracted by the maggots would fall into them and drown in a most malodorous way.

So it is in our lives. There are many cesspools baited with the morsels of this world. We are easily drawn to them and can quickly slip and fall into them. But God takes care of us. He preserves us.

Yes, sometimes, He brings us through difficult circumstances or slippery places to try us as silver is tried (v. 10). In such circumstances, we may feel trapped like a bird (v. 11). We may feel like men are riding roughshod over us (v. 12). We may feel like we are going through fire or through a flood (v. 12).

But God always brings us out and sets us in a wealthy place as He did our Head.

A wealthy place is a place of abundance. God will never allow His children to be deprived of spiritual needs. Those who trust in Him will know His blessing. He will not allow them to die of spiritual famine. He preserves them. He takes care of them.

This is how He deals with us who have been adopted as His sons and daughters on account of His only begotten Son. Shall we not, therefore, praise Him? Shall we not, therefore, make sure that others know our gratitude towards Him by singing His praise heartily, and so make the voice of His praise to be heard (v. 8)?

And not only so, but shall we not imitate our Lord to praise the Father?

4. A Resolution to Praise God

[13] *I will go into thy house with burnt offerings: I will pay thee my vows,* [14] *Which my lips have uttered, and my mouth hath spoken, when I was in trouble.* [15] *I will offer unto thee burnt sacrifices of fatlings, with the incense of rams; I will offer bullocks with goats.*

Because of who our God is, we must worship Him and we must keep our vows.

Our Lord did so. He did not go to the Father with burnt offerings. He went to the Father with what the burnt offerings signified. "Sacrifice and offering thou wouldest not, but a body hast thou prepared me" (Heb 10:5). He kept His vow to suffer and die for our sin.

For this reason, we do not need to go to the Father with burnt offerings. But we go to Him with what the burnt offerings represented. We go to Him with "the calves of our lips" (Hosea 14:2). We can "offer the sacrifice of praise to God continually, that is, the fruit of our lips giving thanks to his name" (Heb 13:15). We do so by Him who is signified by the burnt offerings.

Shall we not do so? Shall we not praise Him? Those of us who are baptised have taken a vow to walk in the way of the Lord. While baptism signifies the promise of God to us, it is—as Calvin would remind us—a sacrament, such that those who receive it also pledge allegiance unto Christ. Shall we not offer our lives a living sacrifice (Rom 12:1-2) for the glory of God in Christ?

And shall we not especially bear witness of our Father's love for us as did our Lord?

5. A Testimony to Our
Prayer-Hearing God

[16] *Come and hear, all ye that fear God, and I will declare what he hath done for my soul.* [17] *I cried unto him with my mouth, and he was extolled with my tongue.*

Testimonies are important, but it is important that we know whom we are testifying about too. Our Lord is testifying of what God has done for Him as the God-Man. He is testifying of how the Father heard His prayer so that He had occasion to extol Him with His tongue. But who is He testifying to?

He is testifying to those who *"fear God"* (v. 16). Perhaps it is more important to testify to those who fear God, that God is a hearer of prayer, than to those who fear Him not. For what does it matter to those who fear not God, that God hears prayers? Most times, the testimony will fall by the way side or it would be cynically brushed aside. Indeed, even if the testimony is believed, the unbeliever, without a fear of God, will turn to God as they would turn to an idol—with superstitious fear and selfish desires, rather than love and honour. That will not do.

So testimonies are best spoken to those who fear the LORD. Those who fear the LORD are deeply encouraged whenever they hear about God hearing prayers.

But we must not leave the impression that God will always attend to our prayer. This is not true. There is one condition that will make our prayer hateful to God, namely that we harbour unconfessed and unrepented sin in our hearts.

So our Lord says:

> [18] *If I regard iniquity in my heart, the Lord will not hear me:*

This is a beautiful statement that we must bear in mind constantly. God is a prayer-hearing heavenly Father. He is not an unprincipled grandfather who will spoil his grandchildren. God will refuse to hear and answer our prayers if we regard iniquity in our hearts. He hears and answers our prayers if we walk in obedience and pray according to His will.

So if anyone of us were to say: "I have no experience of having God answer my prayer," then it must be that he or she has not been praying, or praying amiss, or praying in sin.

Our Lord was tempted in all points like as we are, yet without sin. His prayer was always heard and answered, verse 19:

> [19] *But verily God hath heard me; he hath attended to the voice of my prayer.* [20] *Blessed be God, which hath not turned away my prayer, nor his mercy from me.*

Can you say these words with all honesty? Thank God that our Saviour can, so that we can sing these words with sincerity even if we struggle with doubt. But may the Lord grant us the experiences that we need, that we may sing these words in sincerity and solidarity with Him.

Conclusion

The Apostle Paul urges us to sing psalms, hymns and spiritual songs to exhort and encourage one another. This is one of the songs of the Spirit which Paul must have had in mind. May the Lord grant us help as we seek to encourage one another to praise the LORD, by meditating on His power and goodness together, by singing His praise zealously and by testifying to one another of how God heard our Saviour's prayer, and how for His sake, He has heard our prayers. Amen. Ω

Psalm 67:
The Righteous One's
Missionary Psalm

Psalm 67 is known as an evangelical Psalm. We may call it *"The Righteous One's Missionary Psalm."* It is a Missionary Psalm because it expresses the desire of the Messiah and His people to see the name of God glorified in all the world. This, ultimately, must be the purpose of mission and evangelism of the Church of Christ. While compassion must motivate us to bring the Gospel to the lost, our higher goal must still be to see God's name magnified, as sinners join us to return joyful praise unto Him.

Psalm 67 expresses this desire. Through it, Christ, the Righteous One, leads and joins His people to look expectantly to the heavenly Father for His blessing upon them and upon the world, that His name may be exalted in the hearts and lips of all men upon the earth.

It is not difficult to see that there are three parts in this Psalm. Each part expresses a plea unto God from our hearts, followed by an argument or reason for our desires. These three pleas may be summarised according to the simple outline as follows:

1. v. 1-2   Bless Us that All the World May Know Thy Blessing
2. v. 3-4   Let all People Bless Thee, for Thou Art Worthy
3. v. 5-7   Let all People Bless Thee that We May Enjoy Thy Blessing

1. Bless Us that All the World
May Know Thy Blessing

[1] God be merciful unto us, and bless us; and cause his face to shine upon us; Selah.

What is our plea? Our plea is that God may look down upon us to show us mercy, and to bless us, and to make His face to shine upon us.

We know that we do not deserve God's favour, because we have nothing to commend ourselves to Him. We are but poor and unlovely creatures of dust; whereas He is the infinite God of glory. Indeed, we know that we deserve God's frown rather than God's smile because of our sin against Him. By ourselves, we have no right to take these words upon our lips. But thanks be to God, we are not given to sing these words by ourselves: for we are but lively stones of the temple, and the Chief Corner Stone is worthy!

We are united to Him. He has promised never to leave us, nor to forsake us. Not only does His righteousness cover us, but His Spirit works in us to enable us to do righteousness, and promises to intercede for us as our Sympathetic Great High Priest. Therefore, we can always take these words of petition in our lips by faith. The Father will hear us. He will bless us for the sake of His Son!

Bless and pity us, LORD, for the sake of Thy Son. Make thy face to shine upon us. Grant us that we may know Thy heavenly smile through thy dealings with us. Grant that Thy mercy, blessing and heavenly smile may be evident not only to us, but to all who behold us.

But why? Why should it be so?

[2] That thy way may be known upon earth, thy saving health [or salvation] among all nations.

Bless us, in other words, not only for our good; but bless us that all the earth may know

Thee through Thy blessing. Bless and pity us and make Thy face to shine upon us so that the world may know that Thou art a great God of mercy, ready to pardon and save. Bless and pity us, and make Thy face to shine upon us, so that the world may turn to Thee and glorify Thy great name, and so be provoked to seek Thy salvation.

This is the first plea.

The second is like unto the first...

2. Let All People Bless Thee,
for Thou Art Worthy

³ Let the people praise thee, O God; let all the people praise thee. ⁴ O let the nations be glad and sing for joy: for thou shalt judge the people righteously, and govern the nations upon earth. Selah.

In our first plea, we ask the LORD to bless and pity us. But here in the second plea, we are given to express our desire that the entire world joins us to bless the LORD.

Herein is the purpose of the church's missionary endeavour. We do want people to be saved; but we want people to be saved, not just because we have sympathy for the perishing; but because we desire that God's great name be magnified. We are not satisfied to praise Him alone. We want the whole world to join us to praise Him, for He is worthy.

A sense of gratitude, love and adoration for our Great God for salvation so rich and free in Christ, should automatically translate to a deep desire to see His name honoured by the whole world.

This is all the more so, because we see that the LORD is worthy of all honour and praise: for we know that He will *"judge the people righteously, and govern the nations upon earth [justly]."* Indeed, we are convinced that only under God and His Son's kingship, will the world experience righteousness and peace.

Therefore, the more we see the chaos and wars, the greed and wickedness in the world, the more we long for the day when every knee shall bow and every tongue confess allegiance to the King of kings, and Lord of lords, even the Prince of Peace. Wars and political turmoil, economic collapse, terrorism, riots, chloroform in fish and Melamine in milk are just the tip of the ice-berg in the culture of selfishness, greed and materialism. These things may provoke anger in our hearts; but should it not provoke also a longing for the day of peace under the rule of Christ? Only Christ can put an end to all these sorrows. Only in Christ will there be righteousness and justice.

And so our heart's desire is that all people praise the LORD: for He is worthy. All who truly worship the LORD, will do so only in union with Christ.

Finally, it is also our desire that all people bless the LORD in order that He might bless us together with all the earth.

3. Let All People Bless Thee
that We May Enjoy
Thy Blessing

⁵ Let the people praise thee, O God; let all the people praise thee. ⁶ Then shall the earth yield her increase; and God, even our own God, shall bless us. ⁷ God shall bless us; and all the ends of the earth shall fear him.

In our first plea, we ask the LORD to bless and pity us that His name may be known in all the world. In the second plea, we express our desire that all the world join us to bless the LORD. But now in the third plea, we come a full circle. We again express our desire that all the world may join us to worship the LORD: for we know that when that happens, not only will the world be blessed, but we, especially, will experience God's blessing.

The world may not understand; but as God's people who have tasted of the goodness of the LORD, we understand.

We have seen how lives are transformed under the beneficent rule of Christ. We have seen how families and societies have benefited from the rule of Christ. We know that even without the extraordinary blessings of the LORD, land cultivated by those whose lives have been transformed by gratitude and prayer will often have a more productive yield. Matthew Henry is correct, isn't he, when he says: "The success of the gospel sometimes brings outward mercies along with it; righteousness exalts a nation."

The gospel changes the way that people think and instils an attitude of diligence which must ultimately bear fruit. This is part of the reason why the Lord would have us confidently assert: "I have been young, and now am old; yet have I not seen the righteous forsaken, nor his seed begging bread" (Ps 37:25).

The effect of the Gospel, when it is felt, is enjoyed not only by those who are newly added to the covenant body; it is enjoyed by those who are already in it.

The effect of the conversion of the Gentiles, therefore, is as expressed in verse 7: "*God shall bless us; and all the ends of the earth shall fear him.*"

As sinners are brought into the fold, so those already in the fold enjoy God's blessing; and those outside, unto the ends of the world, cannot but marvel at the power of the LORD, and so fear him. Or as Calvin puts it:

> "...the consequence would be, to increase the fear of [God's] name, since all ends of the earth would, by what they saw of his fatherly regard to His own, submit themselves with greater cheerfulness to His government."

Conclusion

Psalm 67 is no doubt a favourite Psalm of most Psalm-Singing Churches. We have, no doubt, sung it countless times as we look with expectant hearts unto the LORD to bless and pity us. But what many of us do not realise, is its evangelical appeal. This Psalm, very beautifully, expresses what our attitude should be when it comes to the work of evangelism and missions. The modern idea of missions and evangelism is man-centred, which explains all the extravagant man-honouring methods that are often adopted today. The biblical idea of mission and evangelism is God-centred. Even the conversion of man is for the glory of God.

May the Lord help us to serve Him with this attitude which He is enjoining in this Psalm that He has given us to sing, to praise and petition His Father with Him! Amen. Ω

Psalm 68:
The Righteous One's
Ascension as the Victorious King

Psalm 68 is known as an Ascension Psalm. Most commentators agree that this Psalm was written to commemorate the occasion or occasions when the Ark of the Covenant was brought into Jerusalem.

Some believe that it is a song which celebrates the return of the ark every time it was brought out when Israel went into battle. The reason for this idea is that this Psalm is indeed a battle song! But there is little or no evidence that the ark was routinely brought out to battle apart from the time of Eli when the ark was captured by the Philistines! It is possible 2 Samuel 11:11 is a reference to the ark being brought out to battle,[29] but there is no record of any celebration related to the ark returning from battle in the historical accounts.

Therefore, I believe that this Psalm was really written to celebrate the occasion when it was finally brought into Jerusalem by King David. After David conquered Jerusalem and made it his capital, one of the first things he did, was to bring the ark into Jerusalem. But the first attempt failed because David had imitated the Philistines by carrying the ark on a bullock cart. This was contrary to the law of God, and God struck dead a man by the name of Uzzah who tried to hold the ark steady when he thought it was about to fall to the ground. After the calamity, David decided to leave the ark in the home of Obed-Edom the Gittite. It was to remain there for three months until David decided to bring the ark back again. This time the ark was carried on the shoulders of the priests as required by the Law.

The book of Samuel describes the event in these words: "So David went and brought up the ark of God from the house of Obed-Edom into the city of David with gladness" (2 Sam 6:12).

Notice the reference to going up? Jerusalem is situated on a mount, 750 m above sea-level: so when the ark was brought into Jerusalem, it literally ascended. So in verse 18, we read, *"Thou hast ascended on high."* The ark represents the presence of God.

But if this Psalm is about the ascension of the ark in Old Testament days, then what is its relevance to us today? To answer this question, we must realise that the ascension of the Ark of the Covenant is a type of the ascension of Christ!

We say that because the Apostle Paul actually makes use of Psalm 68:18 to describe the ascension of Christ! He says in Ephesians 4:8: "Wherefore he saith, When he ascended up on high, he led captivity captive, and gave gifts unto men." Now, if you read carefully, you will realise that Psalm 68:18 speaks about receiving gifts whereas Ephesian 4:8 speaks of giving gifts. The reason for this difference is that Paul—writing under the inspiration of the Holy Spirit—felt it necessary to clarify that Christ did not receive gifts from men, but rather received them from the Father in order to give them unto men.

So this Psalm is about Christ! It is about the battles that Christ led His people to fight, and about the significance of His ascension as the Captain of their salvation.

With this in mind, we may entitle this Psalm *"The Righteous One's Ascension as the Victorious King."* It is a Psalm appointed by our King to sing in celebration with Him about His conquest and ascension for our sakes.

---

[29] But is it not more likely a reference to the fact that the ark was at this time kept in a temporary tabernacle? See 2Samuel 7:2, 6!

Most of the words in this Psalm may be words provided by Christ for His Church to sing in union with Him unto God Triune as represented by the Father. But remember that Christ is God Himself, so there are portions in this Psalm where we have words that should be understood as being directed to Him. We think of verses 28-29:

> *Thy God hath commanded thy strength: strengthen, O God, that which thou hast wrought for us.* [29] *Because of thy temple at Jerusalem shall kings bring presents unto thee.*

Clearly, the second person pronoun *"thy"* here refers to Christ, even Christ who is addressed as "God" in the phrase *"O God"* (cf. Ps 45:6).

This is a rather large Psalm with many sections, so we will only endeavour to give a very brief introduction to it. We may divide the Psalm into five sections.

1. v. 1-6   The King's Greatness
2. v. 7-14   The King's Conquest
3. v. 15-21   The King's Enthronement
4. v. 22-31   The King's Victories
5. v. 32-35   The King's Glory

1. The King's Greatness

Our Psalm begins by extolling the greatness of our King and how He is to be feared by His enemies. Our King is God Triune. The exercise of His Kingship is mediated through the Son, the second person of the God-head. In Isaiah 9:6, where He is spoken of as the Prince of Peace upon the throne of David, and called "the mighty God." But it is proper for Him as the God-Man to lead us to praise God.

> [1] *Let God arise, let his enemies be scattered: let them also that hate him flee before him.* [2] *... let the wicked perish at the presence of God.*

God is to be greatly feared by His enemies because He is a holy and righteous God, who will deal in perfect justice. He will fight against all unrighteousness. But those who are righteous, or those who have His righteousness, need not fear. They may instead rejoice and be glad in Him.

> [3] *But let the righteous be glad; let them rejoice before God: yea, let them exceedingly rejoice.* [4] *Sing unto God, sing praises to his name: extol him that rideth upon the heavens by his name JAH, and rejoice before him.*

Our King is the "I AM" (cf. *JAH*), the alone self-existent, living and true God. And yet, He understands all our pains and sorrows. In Christ, He took on our flesh and suffered for us. He would be a father to the fatherless and a loving judge to the widows who will put their trust in Him. He blesses all who acknowledge Him as King, frees them from the bondage of sin, and covers them with His righteousness, that they may be known as *"the righteous"* (v. 3). Therefore, as His righteous ones, we have reasons to be exceedingly glad in Him.

On the other hand, those who rebel against Him, despite all that He has done, will know only cursing and sorrow. They will dwell, as it were, on dry, thirsty land (v. 6).

2. The King's Conquest

> [7] *O God, when thou wentest forth before thy people, when thou didst march through the wilderness &c...*

God our King has, in Christ, led His people through the ages. He is the Captain of our salvation. He led our fathers out of Egypt and provided for them in the wilderness (v. 7). He gave them the Law at Mount Sinai in the midst of thunder and lightning and earthquakes (v. 8). He led them to the Promised Land. He gave them victory over their enemies. He sent rain to refresh the land as the people began to settle into it. He blessed the poor with His goodness (v. 9-10). He defended them against their enemies and gave them victory in their conquests (v. 11).

Our King is the Captain of our salvation. He has been doing the same for us. He redeemed us out of spiritual Egypt. He gave us His word. He is leading us by His word and Spirit. He provides for us in our spiritual battles. He gives us victory and rest in the assurance of His love. He will lead us to our everlasting rest; He will turn our afflictions into glory and joy which will culminate in the day of the wrath of the Lamb:

> [13] *Though ye have lain among the pots, yet shall ye be as the wings of a dove covered with silver, and her feathers with yellow gold.* [14] *When the Almighty scattered kings in it, it was white as snow in Salmon.*

Today we are like doves lying amongst the pots, having our feathers blackened by the soot of suffering and affliction. But the day is coming when we shall be, as doves adorned with gold and silver. "For our light affliction, which is but for a moment, worketh for us a far more exceeding and eternal weight of glory," says the Apostle Paul (2Cor 4:17).

That day of our vindication is also the day of the wrath of the Lamb, when kings shall be scattered and righteousness shall cover the earth like snow in Salmon. For this reason, we must press on, following our King, as we march to the Celestial City.

But make no mistake. Our King has already conquered, and is enthroned as we see in the third part of this Psalm...

3. The King's Enthronement

Jerusalem or Mount Zion was favoured by the King of kings to be the mount on which His throne, the ark of God, would ascend (v. 15-17). The Church, the antitype of Jerusalem, is favoured to be the capital of the King of kings.

Our Lord is seated enthroned and "upholding all things by the word of his power." He is sitting at "the right hand of the Majesty on high" after "he had by himself purged our sins" (Heb 1:2-3). From there our Lord has sent His Spirit, and continues to send us the gifts of the Spirit that we may build one another up in the Church. Verse 18:

> [18] *Thou hast ascended on high, thou hast led captivity captive: thou hast received gifts for men; yea, for the rebellious also, that the LORD God might dwell among them.*

The Apostle Paul, as we mentioned, quotes this verse in Ephesians 4:8 to show how, when Christ ascended to heaven, He received gifts from the Father to give unto the Church. His principal gift is none other than the Holy Spirit, by whom the LORD God dwells amongst us (v. 18); by whom we, who were rebellious, are made little by little, more and more like our Elder Brother, the King.

Oh may we learn to praise Him for His benefits as we are exhorted to do in verse 19:

> *Blessed be the Lord, who daily loadeth us with benefits, even the God of our salvation.....* [20] *He that is our God is the God of salvation; and unto GOD the Lord belong the issues*

from death.[30]

Our King knows who are His. He blesses them daily with a life abundant and free. But let not any person who *"goes on still in his trespasses"* think that His benefits are for everyone: for our King does not bless hypocrites. He will, rather, punish them (v. 21).

But make no mistake, for the Spirit is an earnest of our inheritance. We have not received complete rest in Him. The war is won, but there are still battles to be fought. He has conquered and is conquering. In Him we shall be more than conquerors.

4. The King's Victories

[22] *The Lord said, I will bring again from Bashan, I will bring my people again from the depths of the sea:* [23] *That thy foot may be dipped in the blood of thine enemies, and the tongue of thy dogs in the same.* [24] *They have seen thy goings, O God; even the goings of my God, my King, in the sanctuary &c.*

Our King will fight for us and deliver us. When we follow after Him obediently, we shall have the victory. "We are more than conquerors through him that loved us" (Rom 8:37). "Thanks be to God, which giveth us the victory through our Lord Jesus Christ" (1Cor 15:57).

As we experience victory in each battle we fight, let us sing with joy amongst God's people (v. 25). Let us exhort and encourage one another, great or small, young or old, to fight valiantly with the praise of God—on our lips (v. 26); with the promise that our King will be victorious—in our minds (v. 27-30); and with the assurance—in our hearts that all those who are appointed to salvation will come to Him (v. 31).

Indeed, let us seek, as we are taught in the previous Psalm, to call unto the world to join us to worship the LORD. This is the call in the final part of this great Psalm...

5. The King's Glory

[32] *Sing unto God, ye kingdoms of the earth; O sing praises unto the Lord...* [33] *To him that rideth upon the heavens of heavens, which were of old; lo, he doth send out his voice, and that a mighty voice.* [34] *Ascribe ye strength unto God: his excellency is over Israel, and his strength is in the clouds.*

As the people redeemed and led by the King of kings, we must sing praises unto Him. But we must not stop there: for gratitude demands that we make Him known to others, that others may praise Him too. So let us call upon the kingdoms of the earth to join us to ascribe glory and strength unto our Lord.

Let us acknowledge how great He is. But let us not forget, ourselves, to bless His holy name for all that He has done for us:

[35] *O God, thou art terrible [thou art awesome] out of thy holy places: the God of Israel is he that giveth strength and power unto his people. Blessed be God.*

Conclusion

War is not a popular or pleasing subject to discuss. But war is the central theme in the Scripture. Indeed, it may be argued that all the wars in the world are the offspring of the

---

[30] Notice how these words are directed to Christ? But isn't He supposed to be leading us in praise when we sing this psalm? Yes, He is, but because He is the God-Man and worthy of praise too, there are portions in this psalm where He has given the Church words to praise Him with. We will see the same in verses 28-29.

mother of all wars: the War of the Ages, even the war between the Seed of the Serpent and the Seed of the Woman.

Psalm 68 is a celebration of the victory of the Seed of the Woman. The Lord Jesus, the King of kings and Lord of lords, is *the* Seed of the woman. He secured victory in the War by His sacrifice on the cross of Calvary, and His resurrection from the grave. But the war is not complete yet. There are battles still to fight.

Therefore, we thank God for this Psalm. This Psalm was used whenever Christians went out to war for the sake of Christ. It was the favourite Psalm of Charlemagne (747-814 AD), the father of Europe, and one of the most pious of the Christian emperors who sought to conquer Europe for Christ. We can only imagine how much more good he could have done in the continent had he not been grossly misled by the superstitions and ambitions of Rome. More appropriately, though poignantly, it was also the battle song of the French Huguenots, who were persecuted for their biblical faith. And it was the favourite Psalm of Oliver Cromwell, the Puritan general who led the battles to uphold the true Protestant faith which was under threat from Romanists during the days of the Westminster Assembly.

But make no mistake, this Psalm is not only for times of religious wars for Christ: for there is a constant battle raging, for which the Apostle Paul instructs us to fight with the full armour of God. This Psalm, therefore, should be sung by all of us to encourage ourselves in all our battles, in the knowledge that Christ has secured the victory. He is sitting on the right hand of the majesty on High. He has given us the Spirit, and He continues to give us whatever we need for our battles. Let us therefore fight on bravely, looking unto Jesus, the Captain of our salvation, until the day when we shall rest with Him in the Celestial City, never ever to fight again. Amen. Ω

Psalm 69:
The Righteous One's Passion,
a Savour of Life & Death

Psalm 69 is an Imprecatory Psalm. An Imprecatory Psalm is a Psalm where the singer calls upon God to deal with his enemies severely.

But Psalm 69 is also recognised almost universally as a Messianic Psalm. A Messianic Psalm is a Psalm that speaks of the Messiah, or a Psalm that contains the words and experiences of the Messiah, Christ, in a prophetic way.

Commenting on Psalm 69, the commentator E.W. Hengstenberg remarks that...

> In the New Testament there is no one Psalm, with the exception of the 22nd, which is so frequently quoted and applied to Christ, ... not only by the Apostles, but also by Christ Himself [as the one before us].

The Lord Jesus told His disciples that the Jews would hate Him "without a cause" (Jn 15:25) according as it was prophesied in Psalm 69:4.

When He cleared the temple area of buyers and sellers, the disciples remembered that it was prophesied in Psalm 69:9, "The zeal of thine house hath eaten me up" (Jn 2:17).

The Apostle Paul referring to the same verse exclaims:

> "For even Christ pleased not himself; but, as it is written, The reproaches of them that reproached thee fell on me" (Rom 15:3).

Then when the Lord was crucified, the soldiers gave Him vinegar mixed with gall as a kind of painkiller (Mt 27:34). Our Lord would not take it. But their action fulfilled the first part of Psalm 69:21. Later on, however, in order to fulfil the second part of the verse, the Lord said, "I thirst" (Jn 19:28). In fact, we are told that he said "I thirst" not so much because he needed a drink, but so as to fulfil Scripture! He was thirsty, no doubt. But more important than having His thirst quenched, was having Scripture about Himself fulfilled!

Clearly, then, Psalm 69 is not merely the word of David. At the very least, it contains the word of Christ. To what extend does it contain the word of Christ? Some commentators feel that it is only "partly typological of Christ," which is to say that the Psalm is not about Christ, but a few verses were selected to be applied to Christ in the New Testament. However, such a view will make the New Testament use of this Psalm rather dubious and subjective. So it appears to me that the only consistent way of looking at this Psalm is to see it as fully and finally the word of Christ, the Righteous One. It was written by David as a type of Christ under the inspiration of the Spirit of Christ, but the experiences and emotions recorded in it, no doubt, find their fullest expression at the cross.

Thus Bishop George Horne confidently declares that the content of this Psalm, and the way in which the church has always used it, "direct us to consider it as uttered by the Son of God, in the day of His passion."

Our Lord might not have said the words in this Psalm audibly. However, it is not difficult for us to see as we read this Psalm, how the words must have filled our Lord's heart as He hung on the cross. We may entitle it *"The Righteous One's Passion, a Savour of Life and Death."* The "Passion" (from Latin *passionem*, "suffering") refers, of course, to the intense sufferings of the Lord from His final visit to Jerusalem to His crucifixion at Calvary.

We may divide this Psalm roughly into four parts:

1. v. 1-12   The Lord describes the situation He was in
2. v. 13-21   He prays for deliverance
3. v. 22-28   He calls upon God to deal justly with His enemies
4. v. 29-36   He anticipates God's deliverance

Let's look at these four parts briefly. We shall not be able to scrutinise every verse, but I trust we will get a peek into our Lord's heart as He hung on the cross.

1. The Situation (v. 1-12)

¹ Save me, O God; for the waters are come in unto my soul. ² I sink in deep mire, where there is no standing: I am come into deep waters, where the floods overflow me. ³ I am weary of my crying: my throat is dried: mine eyes fail while I wait for my God. ⁴ They that hate me without a cause &c.

Our Lord is in deep mire and deep waters.

In the Garden of Gethsemane, the night before, He had cried with strong crying and tears as He anticipated what was going to happen. And the worst has indeed happened. A multitude of people unjustly clamoured for His blood. He was buffeted left and right. He had false accusations hurled against Him, for which He could not defend Himself. He was sentenced to death by crucifixion even though no crime worthy of death was found in Him.

He is now hanging on the cross. His throat is dry. His eyes fill with tears. Speaking, or even breathing, is excruciatingly difficult.

But our Lord is not on the cross for His own sake. He is there for our sake. The foolishness and sins that He confesses in verse 5 are not His own: for if they are, His enemies would indeed have just cause to hate Him.

But no, our Lord was imputed with our sin, and He is being punished for our sin. And He is still thinking about us on the cross. He desires that those who wait upon the Father be not ashamed or confounded for His sake. He is praying for His disciples that the Father will preserve them through the great trial that has come upon them. And He prays that His zeal for the Father's house may not become occasion for shame and confusion for His disciples. Like an elder brother who loves His siblings, He does not want them to suffer on His account!

But as the suffering is intense, so He prays also for deliverance.

2. Plea for Deliverance (v. 13-21)

¹³ But as for me, my prayer is unto thee, O LORD, in an acceptable time: O God, in the multitude of thy mercy hear me, in the truth of thy salvation. ¹⁴ Deliver me out of the mire, and let me not sink...

Our Lord is still in the mire and water (cf. v. 1). His suffering on the cross is real and intense. He is facing the consequence of our sins alone. He is heart-broken, full of heaviness in His heart, and He is alone: for none could share His burden (v. 19-20).

He is not suffering for His sin. Nevertheless, He appeals not to His righteousness in His prayer for deliverance: for He is bearing our sin. He appeals, rather, to the Father's lovingkindness and tender mercy.

¹⁶ *Hear me, O LORD; for thy lovingkindness is good: turn unto me according to the multitude of thy tender mercies.*

Here is how we must pray for deliverance! Never pray as if you deserve to be delivered. If there is anyone who ever deserved to be delivered, it is our Lord. And yet He appeals to the lovingkindness and mercies of the Father.

But our Lord, in His perfect righteousness, also does something which most of us may find difficult to imitate: for He calls for judgement upon His enemies.

3. Call for Judgement & Justice
(vv. 22-28)

²² *Let their table become a snare before them: and that which should have been for their welfare, let it become a trap.* ²³ *Let their eyes be darkened, that they see not; and make their loins continually to shake. &c.*

These are frightful words, which none of us will dare to take on our lips against our enemies. But our Lord is perfectly just. His enemies are not only His enemies, but also God's enemies. In that they had rejected the Son of God and crucified Him, they had rejected the alone living and true God, and the only way to be saved.

All this is despite the great privilege that they had of having the law of God; of hearing His teachings; and of seeing the miracles He performed. It is no wonder our Lord is so angry with them.

Yes, our Lord is not only loving and forgiving. He is capable of being angry too. Remember how He made a scourge and drove out all the money changers and sellers of doves in the temple? Remember how He even overthrew their tables (Mt 21:12; Mk 11:15; Jn 2:15)?

These words of imprecation are, therefore, not inconsistent with our Lord's character, as some claim. Our Lord was zealous for holiness and truth. He does not fit into the modern idea of a loving person, which is a person with no backbone and principles, who never gets angry with anyone for any reason.

Our Lord shows sympathy to those who were misled. He prays for them for their forgiveness. But for those who are hardened, who ought to know and yet reject Him, He pulls no punches. They deserve eternal damnation. He calls upon His Father to glorify Himself by displaying His wrath and justice. He would have them blotted out of the Book of Life: not that they would have been in the Book in the first place, but that they might be sharply distinguished from the righteous who would enjoy life, eternal and free, in Him.

And so, as He concludes the Psalm, He turns again to seek the good of His people as He expresses...

4. Hope of Deliverance
(v. 29-36)

²⁹ *But I am poor and sorrowful: let thy salvation, O God, set me up on high.* ³⁰ *I will praise the name of God with a song, and will magnify him with thanksgiving.* ³¹ *This also shall please the LORD better than an ox or bullock that hath horns and hoofs. &c.*

Our Lord came to save His people. He knows that His Father will receive His sacrifice and hear His prayers. He knows that His Father will raise Him from the dead. He knows that He will praise the Father in union with the people whom He came to save.

Together they will offer the calves of their lips. Their worship will please the Father better than the Old Testament animal sacrifices.

The proud Jews who rejected Him, and remained hardened in their unbelief, will suffer God's judgement.

But the humble will see, and understand, and be glad. They will seek the Father, verse 32:

> [32] *The humble shall see this, and be glad: and your heart shall live that seek God.*

And the Father will hear their prayers and free them from their bondage to sin, verse 33:

> [33] *For the LORD heareth the poor, and despiseth not his prisoners.*

God will, in this way, build up Zion, or the Church of Christ (v. 35). He will do so from generation to generation. For His own glory, He will fill spiritual Zion with all who love His name.

Let, therefore, heaven and earth, and all creatures great and small praise His holy name (v. 34)!

Conclusion

Psalm 69 is well known as an imprecatory Psalm. But as we can see, it is much more than an imprecatory Psalm. It is rather, an out-pouring of our Lord's heart as the savour of life unto life for the saints; and the savour of death unto death for the unbelieving.

Let us be reminded of the severity and goodness of the Father, such as we see in this Psalm. For the Father loves His Son, but punished Him severely because of our sin.

So, those for whom the Lord suffered and died can enjoy an abundant life, which includes deliverance from sin, union and communion with Christ, and everlasting joy.

On the other hand, those who remain in unbelief and hardness of heart, and trample underfoot the blood of Christ, can expect the everlasting judgement of God.

Your sins must either have already been punished in Christ, or you shall be punished for them. Those of us whose sins have been punished in Christ, can sing about the sufferings of Christ in Psalm 69 with gratitude and a full realisation that we are the ones who deserve to suffer the heartache, heaviness of heart and loneliness which our Lord experienced on the cross. Amen. Ω

Psalm 70:
The Righteous One's Petitions
in His Darkest Hours

Psalm 70 is really an extract from Psalm 40. There is very little material difference between Psalm 70 and Psalm 40:13-17.

Psalm 40 is almost universally regarded as a Messianic Psalm. It is the Psalm in which Christ speaks of His taking on a human body, to offer Himself as a sacrifice to fulfil prophecy. So Psalm 70 may be taken expressly as the words of Christ, though as with most, if not all of the Psalms, all believers united to Christ may appropriate them to themselves when they experience similar circumstances in their lives.

But why is this extract made? Why is it placed here in the Psalter? Some believe that it is placed here to serve as a prayerful extension of Psalm 69, which is another Messianic Psalm quoted regularly in the New Testament to reflect the suffering of our Lord on the cross. This may be so. But whether read in the context of Psalm 40 or Psalm 69, these are petitions of our Lord as He hung on the cross of Calvary for our sakes. We may entitle it *"The Righteous One's Petitions in His Darkest Hours."*

It contains three prayers:

1. v. 1, 5   A Prayer for Deliverance
2. v. 2-3   A Prayer for Justice
3. v.4   A Prayer for Blessing

1. A Prayer for Deliverance

¹ Make haste, O God, to deliver me; make haste to help me, O LORD.

The Righteous One is on the cross. His suffering is real and intense. He has a reason to be there. He is doing the will of His Father. He must pay for the sin of His people if He is to redeem them.

But our Lord is no stoic. He feels the pain, and He desires to be delivered from it. He prayed in the Garden of Gethsemane, "O my Father, if it be possible, let this cup pass from me: nevertheless not as I will, but as thou wilt" (Mt 26:39).

Our Lord knew that He had to go to the cross, though His human feelings cringed from it. This is why our Lord prayed the way He did. For though His divine will is the same as the Father's will, there is an emotional aspect to His human will, which lagged behind. So we can imagine that our Lord's constant prayer unto His Father must have been: "Not my will, but thy will be done."

It is for this same reason that our Lord prays, *"Make haste, O God, to deliver me; make haste to help me, O LORD."*

He knows that He is suffering for His people. He knows that He needs to suffer God's curse, in order that His people may enjoy God's blessings. For this reason, immediately after He prays for the LORD's blessing to be upon His people (v. 4), He repeats His prayer for deliverance in these words:

⁵ But I am poor and needy: make haste unto me, O God: thou art my help and my deliverer; O LORD, make no tarrying.

Our Lord is *"poor and needy"* because He is suffering for us. "For ye know the grace of our Lord Jesus Christ, that, though he was rich, yet for your sakes he became poor, that ye through his poverty might be rich" (2Cor 8:9). Our Lord was poor and needy for our sakes. Nevertheless, every moment when He suffered poverty and need, was a moment too long—for the suffering was intense!

But our Lord does not only pray for deliverance. He prays for justice as well.

2. A Prayer for Justice

² *Let them be ashamed and confounded that seek after my soul: let them be turned backward, and put to confusion, that desire my hurt.* ³ *Let them be turned back for a reward of their shame that say, Aha, aha.*

The enemies of Christ are the enemies of God. Because He is perfectly just, He knows that His enemies, who are persecuting Him, ought to know they are one hundred percent wrong for doing so.

It is true that not all who persecuted Him knew what they were doing. Our Lord prayed for those who were misled: "Father, forgive them for they know not what they do." His prayers are always heard, for His prayers are always fully in accordance with the Father's will.

The same is true for His prayers of imprecation against those who ought to know, but yet persecute Him. The scribes and Pharisees, and the priests were certainly included in the number.

They are those who refused to take heed to His call to repent of their sin of unbelief and hypocrisy. They are those who would persecute Him out of jealousy, indignation, and hatred: for they took umbrage against Him for exposing their wickedness.

Our Lord minces no words in His prayers against them. He seeks to please God and not man. He cares not for political correctness. He cares not about offending sinners. He prays courageously.

None of us can pray an imprecation with the same confidence as our Saviour: for none of us are without sin. But if we are to imitate the Lord, we must also learn to be fearless in praying for the glory of the Father against those who would bring shame to His name.

But let us be careful not to become cynical and negative in our prayers: for our Lord would always balance his imprecations with prayers for blessings, as we see in the third petition of this Psalm.

3. A Prayer for Blessing

⁴ *Let all those that seek thee rejoice and be glad in thee: and let such as love thy salvation say continually, Let God be magnified.*

Our Lord came for His people. In particular, He came for the needy, the poor, the sick, the downcast and the sinners. He came for those who recognise that they are nothing, have nothing and deserve nothing but the wrath of God.

They are those who would seek the LORD: for those who are self-sufficient and self-righteous would not seek Him.

They are those who know that they can have no real joy except they know that the Father is pleased with them.

They are those who know they need a Saviour to deliver them out of their sin, and out of the wrath of God.

Our Lord calls upon the Father to bless them. He desires that they would know the joy and gladness of the LORD. He desires that they be saved so that forever and ever, their lives and their lips will *"say continually, Let God be magnified."*

This was our Lord's deepest desire, even as He suffered on the cross for our sin. So great was His suffering that His cries for deliverance envelope this Psalm. But so great is His love for His people that He does not forget them in the midst of His suffering.

Conclusion

What is this Psalm to you, dear child of God? I trust that this Psalm has given you another glimpse of our Saviour's inner thoughts—even His pain, His zeal for the glory of God, and His desires for us.

But may this Psalm also encourage us to imitate our Lord in prayer in our darkest hours—to pray not only for deliverance, but for the glory of God and for the good of His people. May the Lord help us! Amen. Ω

Psalm 71:
The Righteous One's
Confidence of Hope
to the End

Psalm 71 is a song for old age. The psalmist, probably David, must have penned it in his old age. We can see this from verse 9: "*Cast me not off in the time of old age...*" and verse 18: "*Now also when I am old and grayheaded, O God, forsake me not...*"

We like the title proposed by Andrew Bonar, "*The Righteous One's Confidence of Hope to the End.*" He suggests that though our Lord never reached old age, He experienced the sorrows, pains and anxieties of old age. The prophet Isaiah spoke of how our Lord's "visage was so marred more than any man, and his form more than the sons of men" (Isa 52:14). He must have looked older and suffered more than one would expect for His 33 years of age. So we read in verse 7: "*I am as a wonder unto many...*"

We may say that David's experience at old age foreshadowed our Lord's experience as He drew near to the grave. Therefore, this Psalm—that David wrote under the inspiration of the Spirit of Christ—expresses the feelings and experiences of our Lord in His final days on earth.

In any case, our Lord can sing this Psalm in sympathy with us when we sing it in our old age; and we can sing it in our youth in sympathy with Him, and with our elderly members.

This Psalm has an interesting structure:

1. v. 1-4   1st Petition
2. v. 5-8   1st Expression of Confidence: Upon What God has Done
3. v. 9-13   2nd Petition
4. v. 14-17   2nd Expression of Confidence: Upon What God is Doing
5. v. 18   3rd Petition
6. v. 19-24   3rd Expression of Confidence: Upon What God Will do

1. First Petition (v. 1-4)

^{1} In thee, O LORD, do I put my trust: let me never be put to confusion. ^{2} Deliver me in thy righteousness, and cause me to escape: incline thine ear unto me, and save me.

The word rendered "confusion" (בּוּשׁ, *bûsh*) is usually rendered "ashamed" or "shame" in the Old Testament. The experience of old age is usually underlined by a fear of indignity and confusion.

Though most of us will not experience the assaults of the wicked one in the way that David did, and particularly in the way our Lord did (see v. 4), yet we will in our old age face many enemies.

Not only will we be suffering the ravages and illnesses of old age, we will also have many fears, not the least because of increasing disability and the anticipation of death round the corner. At such times, the wicked one will also play on our fears to make us confused and doubt the LORD.

But thank God we can always resort to Him as our "*strong habitation*", our rock and our fortress. Thank God that He is never hard of hearing as some of us are. He will always hear our prayers as He heard our Saviour in the day when He experienced our fears, and was tempted in all points like as we are.

But what is the basis of our confidence?

2. First Expression of Confidence
(v. 5-8)

This is an expression of confidence based on what God has done.

> [5] *For thou art my hope, O Lord GOD: thou art my trust from my youth.* [6] *By thee have I been holden up from the womb: thou art he that took me out of my mother's bowels: my praise shall be continually of thee.*

Andrew Bonar speaks of these verses together with verse 17 as being "precious glimpses given us of Messiah's childhood." And we can see how this must be the case if this Psalm contains the sentiments of our Lord.

Our Lord can rest in His Father, for He had experienced His loving protection and care from the day He was born. He knows that His Father will not forsake Him. Even as the shadow of the cross lengthens, and the moment when He will bear the brunt of God's wrath for us approaches, our Lord has the confidence that His lips will be filled with praise and honour for His Father (v. 8).

And so let us rest in the same confidence. When we are old and fearful, let us remember how the LORD has kept us, and trust Him to continue to keep us.

3. Second Petition (v. 9-13)

> [9] *Cast me not off in the time of old age; forsake me not when my strength faileth.* [10] *For mine enemies speak against me; and they that lay wait for my soul take counsel together...*

Our Lord did not experience old age physically as David did; but did He not experience the burdens of old age as His enemies plotted to get rid of Him?

"*God hath forsaken him*" they say (v. 11). "He saved others; let him save himself, if he be Christ, the chosen of God" they cried (Lk 23:35).

What was our Lord's response? "*Cast me not off... forsake me not... O God, be not far from me: O my God, make haste for my help.*"

And so when we are confronted with old age, when we are feeling lonely and forsaken, when everything seems to be falling apart, let us learn to go to the Father in prayer. Let us implore Him to stay close to us (v. 11-12); let us plead with Him to deal with the enemies of our soul (c.f. v. 13), that we may find comfort in Him.

Let us hope in God continually as our Lord expresses in His...

4. Second Expression of Confidence
(v. 14-17)

> [14] *But I will hope continually, and will yet praise thee more and more.* [15] *My mouth shall shew forth thy righteousness and thy salvation all the day; for I know not the numbers thereof....*

This is an expression of confidence by way of a resolution. And what a beautiful resolution, worthy of our imitation!

I will hope continually. I will praise Thee more and more. I will talk about Thy righteousness and salvation all the day because I don't know how much more time I have!

The Apostle Paul instructs us to "Walk in wisdom towards them that are without, redeeming the time" (Col 4:5).

This is what our Lord is doing in these words. This is what we must do more, and more, even as we realise more, and more, that time is short.

We must speak of God's grace and mercy to us all the days of our life. We must go and do so in His strength (v. 16). What does it mean to go in His strength? It is to depend upon Him to give us the courage and energy to do what we resolve to do.

If we would resolve to be a witness for the Lord, let us ask Him for strength and He will give it to us.

This is what we are directed to ask for in the...

5. Third Petition (v. 18)

[18] *Now also when I am old and grayheaded, O God, forsake me not; until I have shewed thy strength unto this generation, and thy power to everyone that is to come.*

Again, our Lord did not grow old and grayheaded outwardly, as David did. But He was surely, in a sense, growing old and grayheaded in His soul as He faced persecution, and a looming cross.

What was His prayer under such a circumstance? It is the same as before, only expressed in a different way. In His first petition, He asks for deliverance. In the second, He asks not to be cast away in old age. In this third petition, He asks to be given the opportunity to testify of God's strength and power in the remaining time that He has.

What a prayer! How many of us will make such a petition?

But why?

6. Third Expression of Confidence
(v. 19-24)

This is an expression of confidence based upon what God will do:

[19] *Thy righteousness also, O God, is very high, who hast done great things: O God, who is like unto thee!* [20] *Thou, which hast shewed me great and sore troubles, shalt quicken me again, and shalt bring me up again from the depths of the earth.* [21] *Thou shalt increase my greatness, and comfort me on every side.*

Can you see how verses 20-21 are about the resurrection and exaltation of our Lord? Everyone united to Christ, will also be raised unto glory at the Last Day.

And therefore, we can sing these same words with confidence. Whether we are young or old, death is but a grim portal into glory. In glory, we shall be able to worship God and enjoy Him in praise forever and ever, without ever being hindered by sin and sinners or by human frailties.

Our Lord was looking forward to the end of His suffering and the beginning of His exaltation, and an eternity of praising the Father.

After three days in the tomb, He rose from the dead. Forty days later, He ascended to heaven in the sight of His disciples.

But our Lord is still with us by His Spirit, who is given as an earnest of our eternal inheritance. By His Spirit, our Lord, as our covenant Head, worships with us whenever we sing His words.

Our Lord, in other words, has begun to do what He expected to do in verse 22 to the end of the Psalm:

> [22] *I will also praise thee with the psaltery, even thy truth, O my God: unto thee will I sing with the harp, O thou Holy One of Israel.* [23] *My lips shall greatly rejoice when I sing unto thee; and my soul, which thou hast redeemed.* [24] *My tongue also shall talk of thy righteousness all the day long...*

One day, we will all rest from all our troubles. But we must not wait for that day to rejoice. We must greatly rejoice today for Christ our Lord has already conquered death.

Conclusion

Death has lost its sting. We need not fear what death—which is our most fearsome enemy today—will do to us. Therefore, we need not fear old age or the approach of death. Let us, rather, learn to live joyfully before the Lord even before the days we arrive at our old age.

Let us learn to *"go in the strength of the Lord GOD"* (v. 16), our Sovereign King. Let us ask for the LORD's grace that we cease to saunter and begin to run as we head towards the Celestial City. Let us give Him the glory by living a joyful Christian life that is characterised by holiness, hope and assurance of His love in Christ. Amen. Ω

Psalm 72:
The Righteous One's
Glorious Reign

Psalm 72 was probably written by King David for his son Solomon as he passed the sceptre over to him.

But Solomon was a type of Christ. God would not allow David to build the temple partly because He would have the Son of David to build it. The son of David, Solomon, would build the shadow of the true temple in earthly Jerusalem. The greater son of David, Christ Jesus, would build the substance or antitype of the temple in heavenly Jerusalem.

Thus, when God had told David that he would not build the temple, He said to him through Nathan:

> "[12] And when thy days be fulfilled, and thou shalt sleep with thy fathers, I will set up thy seed after thee, which shall proceed out of thy bowels, and I will establish his kingdom. [13] He shall build an house for my name, and I will stablish the throne of his kingdom forever" (2 Sam 7:12-13).

The New Testament makes it clear that this prophecy is not ultimately referring to Solomon, but to Christ, the greater son of David, the greater Solomon (Lk 1:32-33; Acts 2:30; 13:22-23).

And so Psalm 72 is not ultimately about Solomon, but about the greater Solomon. Indeed, if this Psalm were only about Solomon, we would not be able to sing it meaningfully, for it would make little sense, and would have little enduring value.

The esteemed commentator Hengstenberg is so sure that this Psalm is Messianic that he says:

> "The Psalmist would have rendered himself ridiculous, if he had promised such a dominion to any of the ordinary posterity of David, and no such thing ever took place.... The violent assumptions which must be made, by those who do not adopt the Messianic interpretation, shew how imperatively that interpretation is demanded by the contents of the Psalm."

With this sentiment we agree.

Psalm 72 concerns the glorious reign of Messiah, the King. We may entitle it *"The Righteous One's Glorious Reign."*

This Psalm has two unequal parts. Verses 1-17 describes the reign of the Messiah, the Righteous One. Verses 18-19 is a doxology. Verse 20 is not really a part of this Psalm, but the ending marker of the second division of the book of Psalms (which begins at Psalm 42). A simple outline of this Psalm will be:

1. v. 1-17   The Reign of Christ

          a. Its Righteousness (v. 1-7)

          b. Its Universality (v. 8-11)

          c. Its Benevolence (v. 12-14)

          d. Its Perpetuity (v. 15-17)

2. v. 18-19   The Doxology

1. The Reign of Christ

This is really the body of this Psalm even though many Psalm singers are more familiar with the doxology that follows. In any case, we are here given words to sing in union with Christ our King to extol His reign from four perspectives, namely: (1) Its Righteousness (v. 1-7); (2) Its Universality (v. 8-11); (3) Its Benevolence (v. 12-14); and (4) Its Perpetuity (v. 15-17).

a. Its Righteousness (v. 1-7)

¹ Give the king thy judgments, O God, and thy righteousness unto the king's son.

Our Psalm opens with a plea to the Father to endow our King with righteousness and justice. Every king may claim righteousness and justice, but ultimately only the righteousness and justice of God matters, for He is the Lawgiver. No one has the right to define what is right and just, but He who is the Lawgiver.

Christ our King, as the God-Man was endowed with true and perfect righteousness and justice. As such, His reign is characterised by righteousness and peace:

² He shall judge thy people with righteousness, and thy poor with judgment. ³ The mountains shall bring peace to the people, and the little hills, by righteousness. ⁴ He shall judge the poor of the people, he shall save the children of the needy, and shall break in pieces the oppressor. ⁵ They shall fear thee as long as the sun and moon endure, throughout all generations.

What a beautiful picture of peace and tranquillity is brought about by righteousness and justice! Look at the mountains and the hills in the distance. Peace and righteousness seem to be flowing from them, like a refreshing mist. It will touch the lives of everyone. The poor will not be neglected; the children of the needy will be delivered. The oppressors will be punished. This reign of righteousness and justice shall last forever and ever—as long as the sun and the moon shall endure.

Again, this righteousness will come upon the earth like a shower that refreshes the land.

⁶ He shall come down like rain upon the mown grass: as showers that water the earth. ⁷ In his days shall the righteous flourish; and abundance of peace so long as the moon endureth.

This righteousness would come when Messiah comes. Today as we sing this Psalm, Messiah has come: His kingdom is established and righteousness and peace have begun to flourish. But it is not yet in full bloom. That must await His second coming. So, what was true for our fathers in the Old Covenant when they first sang this Psalm, is still true for us.

When Christ comes, His kingdom will be established forever and ever. The prophet Isaiah expressed these same truths in prophecy some 300 years after this Psalm was penned. He says concerning the Messiah, Isaiah 9:7:

"Of the increase of his government and peace there shall be no end, upon the throne of David, and upon his kingdom, to order it, and to establish it with judgment and with justice from henceforth even forever. The zeal of the LORD of hosts will perform this."

And again, Isaiah 11:4:

"But with righteousness shall he judge the poor, and reprove with equity for the meek of the earth: and he shall smite the earth with the rod of his mouth, and with the breath of his lips shall he slay the wicked."

This rule of righteousness and justice and peace has already begun. It began in the heart of his people and it will last for all eternity.

And this reign of peace is not only found in a small piece of land like in earthly kingdoms, it is a universal reign.

b. Its Universality (v. 8-11)

[8] *He shall have dominion also from sea to sea, and from the river unto the ends of the earth.* [9] *They that dwell in the wilderness shall bow before him; and his enemies shall lick the dust.* [10] *The kings of Tarshish and of the isles shall bring presents: the kings of Sheba and Seba shall offer gifts.* [11] *Yea, all kings shall fall down before him: all nations shall serve him.*

No earthly Jewish king, not even Solomon, fulfilled this prophecy. Only Christ the King has fulfilled and is fulfilling these words.

Today, His reign extends from sea to sea as His subjects in every period, nation, tongue and clime bow down to Him in humble adoration.

It is true that His kingdom today is largely hidden, though it is no less real. But the day is coming when every knee will bow and every tongue will confess that "Jesus Christ is Lord, to the glory of God the Father" (Phil 2:10-11 Rom 14:11).

Herein is the universality of Christ's reign. Everywhere in the world today, there are those who will confess Him as King. And it will be so until Christ returns again, when His rule will be acknowledged by all.

But consider now the benevolence of His reign.

c. Its Benevolence (v. 12-14)

[12] *For he shall deliver the needy when he crieth; the poor also, and him that hath no helper.* [13] *He shall spare the poor and needy, and shall save the souls of the needy.* [14] *He shall redeem their soul from deceit and violence: and precious shall their blood be in his sight.*

We have already seen aspects of this when we spoke about the justice and righteousness of the reign of Christ, but here is more.

Our Lord is not an absent king. He does not only provide the people with a righteous rule and access to justice, He hears the cries of the needy. He helps those who are in need. He delivers them from deceit and violence. He does not shut his bowels of compassion against them.

He hears our prayer, and we can be sure He is doing something about it.

Yes, He may not immediately remove every injustice we suffer, for the kingdom of Christ is not of this world (Jn 18:36). But let us be sure that He hears our cries and He will not allow any sense of injustice in the heart of His children to remain forever. He will see to it that the meek will inherit the earth (Mt 5:5). He will see to it that those who are persecuted for righteousness' sake, shall know everlasting blessedness (Mt 5:10).

And He is able to give this guarantee: for His reign will know no end, which is the fourth attribute of his reign.

d. Its Perpetuity (v. 15-17)

[15] *And he shall live, and to him shall be given of the gold of Sheba: prayer also shall be made*

for him continually; and daily shall he be praised. ¹⁶ *There shall be an handful of corn in the earth upon the top of the mountains; the fruit thereof shall shake like Lebanon: and they of the city shall flourish like grass of the earth.*

Here is another beautiful picture of Christ's eternal reign.

It is a picture of perfect blessedness as those who have been blessed by Him, cast their crowns of gold before Him and praise and thank Him forever and ever (v. 15).

It is also a picture of overflowing blessings (v. 16). The reference to the "handful" of corn must not be misunderstood. The original word (פִסַּת, *pissâh*) signifies abundance. It is a picture of a mountain carpeted with fruitful grain crop swaying in the wind.

The city of the Lord will flourish (v. 17), but her citizens will be fully provided for, unlike in the case of many large cities around the world.

Such is the reign of Christ the King that we may confidently sing:

> ¹⁷ *His name for ever shall endure;*
> *last like the sun it shall:*
> *Men shall be bless'd in him, and bless'd*
> *all nations shall him call.*

Does not the hope and thrill of these words chase away the deepest gloom in our soul? Thank God for Christ our Lord. Thank God that He is our King today and forevermore.

But such a thrill in our hearts cannot be contained. It must find expression in our tongues. And what better way to express our praise, then to lift up our hearts and voices together using the doxology in our metrical version.

2. The Doxology

> ¹⁸ *Now blessed be the Lord our God,*
> *the God of Israel,*
> *For he alone doth wondrous works,*
> *in glory that excel.*
> ¹⁹ *And blessed be his glorious name*
> *to all eternity:*
> *The whole earth let his glory fill.*
> *Amen, so let it be.*

What more shall we say? This is our desire. This is our hope. This is our future. This is our joy.

May the Lord fill the earth with His glory! May we bask in His glory forever and ever!

Conclusion

The world that we live in, has been wrecked by sin. Bad news and grief confront us every step of the way so that it appears that we cannot enjoy a moment of happiness without a sustained period of grief. But let us not lose heart. Let us learn rather to rejoice in the midst of adversities—for we know that Christ our King is reigning. And the day is coming when all our tears and sorrows will be replaced by songs of joy.

Therefore let us lift up our heads and look to our King, and live by faith and hope, not by sight. Blessed are those who believe and who will walk in this hope. Amen. Ω

Psalm 73:
The Righteous One's
Sympathetic Anguish on the
Prosperity of the Wicked

Psalm 73 begins the 3rd division of the Book of Psalms. It also begins a collection of Psalms that were attributed to Asaph. Who is this Asaph? We normally think of Asaph as the Asaph the seer who is spoken of in 2 Chronicles 29:30, which reads:

> "Moreover Hezekiah the king and the princes commanded the Levites to sing praise unto the LORD with the words of David, and of Asaph the seer...." (2 Chr 29:30a).

This Asaph was a descendant of Gershom, the son of Levi (1 Chr 6:39, 43). He was a contemporary of David. At the time when the ark was brought back to Jerusalem, he was appointed by the chief Levites as a leading singer to use the cymbals (1 Chr 15:17, 19). David, subsequently, made him the leader of the choral worship services before the ark of the covenant (1 Chr 16:4-5). It was probably in this capacity as royal cantor, that Asaph served as the king's poet to write his songs, or to edit them for singing by the Levites, or by the congregation of Israel. This is probably why he is known as "the seer" (2 Chr 29:30).

But Asaph's contribution to royal psalmody did not end with him: for history tells us that he trained his sons, and perhaps others, to perform his role down through the generations. This resulted in a musical guild named after him as the "sons of Asaph" (1 Chr 25:1). These, we are told, "prophesied according to the order of the king" (1 Chr 25:2) as Asaph did. For this reason, it is very likely that when a Psalm is attributed to Asaph, it is really a Psalm authorised by, or originated from, the king; and prepared for singing by Asaph or his sons.

Altogether twelve Psalms in the Psalter are attributed to Asaph: namely, Psalms 73-83 and Psalm 50. Some, as we shall see, are really Psalms of David, while others are probably initiated by subsequent Davidic kings.

Regardless, we have, no doubt, that Asaph, like David, laboured in the Spirit of Christ, so that every one of the songs attributed to him in the Psalter, may be sung meaningfully as the "word of Christ" (Col 3:16) by those who are united to Christ. They sometimes express the sentiments of Christ (e.g. Pss 75, 77, 78, 81) that we can sing in union with Him as our Head. At other times, they express the desires and conflicts of the Church in a way that Christ our Head may sing in union with us as His body.

Psalm 73 is one such Psalm. It is not directly about the Messiah, but about "His people" (v. 10). It expresses the conflict and perplexity that the average child of God will experience as he walks in this world. Our Lord understands, as He was tempted in all points like as we are, and yet without sin. He has, therefore, given us a song to sing to express our hearts that He may sing with us; and we with Him. We may entitle it *"The Righteous One's Sympathetic Anguish on the Prosperity of the Wicked."*

Very broadly, this Psalm has three parts:

1. v. 1-16   The Saint's Anguish
2. v. 17-22   The LORD's Answer
3, v. 23-28   The Saint's Assurance

1. The Saint's Anguish

Anguish or perplexity usually begins with an expectation. If we have no expectation, we will have no perplexity. But expectations have their proper place in the Christian life. While we should not entertain too much expectation from man, it is right and proper for us to expect much from God. Indeed, we have reasons to expect great things from the LORD because He is sovereign, good and just; and He has promised to bless those who walk in holiness.

This is the assertion that we are given to confess as we begin this Psalm:

> [1] *Truly God is good to Israel, even to such as are of a clean heart.*

This is a biblical truism: which is why it begins with the word "truly". God is always good, and His goodness always extends to His covenant people Israel. He is especially kind to those who are sincere and holy in their walk.

But experience teaches us, does it not, that things are not always so smooth and clear-cut? Sometimes, while we are seeking to walk in all honesty, we get into all sorts of trouble, whereas unbelievers who live without regard for God, seem to be enjoying God's blessing.

When this happens, it can be a matter of perplexity, and often anguish, to the point that we may even be tempted to give up walking with the LORD:

> [2] *But as for me, my feet were almost gone; my steps had well nigh slipped.* [3] *For I was envious at the foolish, when I saw the prosperity of the wicked.*

Why continue to walk with purity of heart, when there does not seem to be any benefits: whereas those who care not for God, seem to be prospering in life?

> [4] *For there are no bands in their death: but their strength is firm.*

We expect that the wicked would at their deathbed feel tormented with guilt and frustrations like having constricting bands around their body and soul. But no, many of them seem to die with dignity.

Indeed, the wicked often seem to be free of the common problems that plague mankind (v. 5). And so they become proud, and self-confident, and continue to do wickedness and violence (v. 6). And they become rich in the things of this world (v. 7), continue to do wickedly (v. 8), and even have the audacity to blaspheme God (v. 9).

It is no wonder then, that the LORD's people—especially those who have been hurt by the conduct of the wicked—are tempted to look back at their life and wonder if it is worth it to walk the way they did, verse 10:

> *Therefore his people [i.e. the LORD's people] return hither: and waters of a full cup are wrung out to them.* [11] *And they say, How doth God know? and is there knowledge in the most High?*

They, the LORD's people, try so hard to walk in righteousness, and yet they have been rewarded with tears enough to fill a full cup! Does God not know? Does He care about what is going on?

Who are those who prosper in the riches of this world? Who are those who have to suffer? It seems so incongruous:

> [12] *Behold, these are the ungodly, who prosper in the world; they increase in riches.* [13] *Verily I have cleansed my heart in vain, and washed my hands in innocency.* [14] *For all the day long have I been plagued, and chastened every morning.*

This does not seem right! It seems unfair! But to talk about it like that seems to border on blasphemy, and can be a stumbling block to children. This is painfully perplexing, verse 15:

> *If I say, I will speak thus; behold, I should offend against the generation of thy children.* [16] *When I thought to know this, it was too painful for me;*

Is this your perplexity too? Is there an answer to our perplexity? Surely there is. For consider...

2. The LORD's Answer

The answer came for the psalmist, not through a still small voice; but rather through the preaching of God's Word, or through the work of the Holy Spirit bringing to remembrance something else that God says elsewhere. This reminder was triggered by the use of the means of grace in public worship, verse 17:

> *Until I went into the sanctuary of God; then understood I their end.*

What is the answer?

> [18] *Surely thou didst set them in slippery places: thou castedst them down into destruction.* [19] *How are they brought into desolation, as in a moment! they are utterly consumed with terrors.* [20] *As a dream when one awaketh; so, O Lord, when thou awakest, thou shalt despise their image.*

The answer is found in the fact that things are not always as they appear. Or—in the words of the book of Ecclesiastes—there is more to life than what is visible "under the sun."

The fact is: God, in His longsuffering, often allows the wicked to go unpunished in this life. So He appears to be sleeping. But God never sleeps. "Behold, he that keepeth Israel shall neither slumber nor sleep" (Ps 121:4). The day will come when He will rise in judgement like a man waking from his sleep.

When that happens, He will deal with the wicked with perfect justice and an unmistakable finality. They will be cast into destruction, consumed by terror, and made to experience the wrath of God for all eternity.

Indeed, we may infer that the wealth and prosperity of the wicked would, as it were, serve as weights to sink them down into the lake of fire. Everyday that the wicked do not repent of their sin, everyday that they do not acknowledge God, they are treasuring up wrath against the day of wrath and revelation of the righteous judgement of God.

The psalmist continues:

> [21] *Thus my heart was grieved, and I was pricked in my reins.* [22] *So foolish was I, and ignorant: I was as a beast before thee.*

What a sobering thought! How foolish it is to envy the wicked and to question God.

But thank God that He does not cast us away despite our foolishness. Consider therefore, finally,...

3. The Saint's Assurance

[23] *Nevertheless I am continually with thee: thou hast holden me by my right hand.* [24] *Thou shalt guide me with thy counsel, and afterward receive me to glory.*

While the wicked may enjoy wealth and prosperity for a season, the righteous are continually before the LORD and constantly being upheld by the power of God. They are led by the counsel of God that ensures that all things work together for their good at every moment in their lives. And not only so, but they are being led to the Celestial City where they will, one day, enjoy the weight of eternal glory forever and ever.

For this reason, the child of God may enjoy the deepest assurance that there can be no greater, or more lasting, blessedness, than to trust in the LORD, and to serve Him:

> [25] *Whom have I in heaven but thee? and there is none upon earth that I desire beside thee.* [26] *My flesh and my heart faileth: but God is the strength of my heart, and my portion for ever.* [27] *For, lo, they that are far from thee shall perish: thou hast destroyed all them that go a whoring from thee.* [28] *But it is good for me to draw near to God: I have put my trust in the Lord GOD, that I may declare all thy works.*

There is little that needs to be said to explain this beautiful concluding refrain. The saint—whose sins are forgiven in Christ, who is thinking aright—can find no greater joy in anyone or anything, whether in heaven or in earth, besides the Lord GOD. Heaven would be joyless without the LORD. Earth would be meaningless without Him.

Let us learn, in moments when our hearts fail, to turn to the LORD, and rest in Him. Let us be assured that He will see to it that the saints will be vindicated, and the wicked punished. So let us confidently draw nigh to Him to trust Him, to live for Him honestly, and to testify of Him to all who will hear.

Conclusion

Thank God for this Psalm. Thank God for answering the anguish and perplexity in our hearts when we see the wicked prospering while the godly are suffering. Thank God for giving us the words to express our vexation and also our confidence in the LORD. May the Lord use this Psalm to encourage us whenever we are confused by the wind and the waves, and the roaring of the prowling lion, as we journey together to the Celestial City! Amen. Ω

Psalm 74:
The Righteous One's
Lamentation & Plea
for the Church

Psalm 74 is another Psalm attributed to "Asaph", which as we noted previously may be regarded as a pen name, which may be used by one or more persons in the same godly tradition of royal cantors started by Asaph the seer (2 Chr 29:30).

This is especially important for us to know, as Psalm 74 appears to refer to a time when the temple was destroyed by the enemies of God (v. 3-7). The first time the temple was destroyed was in 586 BC, more than 400 years after the original Asaph was appointed chief cantor by King David (1 Chr 16:4-5).

Of course, it is possible that Asaph the Seer was writing prophetically about the destruction of the temple even before the temple was built. But it is unlikely. More probably, this Asaph refers to a member of the musical guild named after him as the "sons of Asaph" (1 Chr 25:1).

This Asaph must have written this Psalm sometime after 586 BC, and perhaps a few years after Jeremiah died, or after he was carried away to Egypt. *"There is no more any prophet: neither is there among us any that knoweth how long,"* says Asaph (v. 9).

Our Asaph was perhaps standing by the ruins of the temple, recalling the days when the Babylonian came to strip off the cedar panelling and carved works of the temple, before setting the building on fire. As tears streamed down his eyes, he began to sing the words of this Psalm as they were given to him by the inspiration of the Spirit of Christ. Though it was not directly authorised by the king then, since he has been sent to exile, it was authorised by the King of kings that it might express His grief at the sight of the ruinations in His Church which was typified by the temple.

As Andrew Bonar puts it beautifully:

> The Head of the Church, who wept over Jerusalem on the Mount of Olives, and lamented their too sure ruin, could use these strains, and pour them into the Father's ear.

But He would sing it, no doubt, not merely with reference to the destruction of Jerusalem of old. He would, rather, have us to join Him to use these strains to lament how sin has brought devastation to the Church even in our day.

We may entitle it *"The Righteous One's Lamentation and Plea for the Church."*

It has four parts. The first part, verses 1-3, is a call unto the LORD to remember His people. The second part, verses 4-11, is a description of the present desolation. The third part, verses 12-17, is a declaration of the power of God. The fourth part, verses 18-23, is a plea to the LORD to defend His own name.

For our study, we may outline this Psalm using the key phrase occurring in each part:

1. v. 1-3   "Remember thy Congregation" (v. 2)
2. v. 4-11   "O God, how long?" (v. 10)
3. v. 12-17   "God is my King of old" (v. 12)
4. v. 18-23   "Arise, O God, Plead Thine Own Cause" (v. 22)

1. Remember Thy Congregation

The psalmist, as I mentioned, must have penned this Psalm as he beheld the desolation of the land. Perhaps the smoke was still rising from the houses that were burned down. The people who were left alive, were scattered and terrified. The fields that used to be covered with beautiful flocks, were barren with a few frightened sheep huddled at a corner. Could this pathetic sight have given rise to the opening words of this Psalm?

¹ O God, why hast thou cast us off for ever? why doth thine anger smoke against the sheep of thy pasture?

But Israel is no ordinary people. They belong to the LORD. They were purchased at a great price. Has the LORD forgotten?

² Remember thy congregation, which thou hast purchased of old; the rod of thine inheritance, which thou hast redeemed; this mount Zion, wherein thou hast dwelt. ³ Lift up thy feet unto the perpetual desolations; even all that the enemy hath done wickedly in the sanctuary.

Israel of old was, as it were, purchased and redeemed out of slavery in Egypt. She was made the rod or tribe of Jehovah's inheritance. She was appointed the dwelling place of God. Would not the LORD remember Israel? Would not the LORD lift up His feet and step into the land to see the destruction and desolations that the enemy has poured on the Land, and especially of the temple?

Today, the Israel of God is likewise purchased and redeemed out of bondage to Satan. We have been redeemed by the blood of Christ, and made the dwelling place of God.

And look: do we not see how the Israel of God is today suffering much desolation and destruction? Churches that are faithful to the word are few and troubled by many difficulties. Churches that have departed from the truth, appear to be fat and flourishing. Has God forgotten? No, no; God does not forget.

But perhaps we have forgotten to pray as our King would teach us to pray: "Remember Thy congregation, O LORD; behold the desolation that Thy enemy hast wrought. Remember, O LORD, Thy redeemed people for the sake of Thy Son who shed His blood to purchase her."

And let us not allow ourselves to grow used to the sorry situation, but learn to cry out unto the LORD, "How Long?" as we are given to do in the second strophe.

2. O God, how Long?

⁴ Thine enemies roar in the midst of thy congregations; they set up their ensigns for signs. ⁵ A man was famous according as he had lifted up axes upon the thick trees. ⁶ But now they break down the carved work thereof at once with axes and hammers.

The Babylonian soldiers must have roared and laughed as they stripped the temple of God of her cedar carvings and gold. They congratulate one another for how well they were dismantling the temple of God! What a contrast with the days when brave men were applauded for how they were able to cut down huge trees for the temple of the Lord.

But not satisfied with plundering the temple, they set it on fire and tore it down:

⁷ They have cast fire into thy sanctuary, they have defiled by casting down the dwelling place of thy name to the ground. ⁸ They said in their hearts, Let us destroy them together: they have burned up all the synagogues [or meeting places] of God in the land. ⁹ We see not our signs: there is no more any prophet: neither is there among us any that knoweth how long.

So thorough was their work of destruction that every meeting place which God's people used, and not just the temple, was burned up. The symbols of the faith were destroyed. The prophets and teachers were killed or exiled. There was no one left who can say how long this humiliation would last.

[10] O God, how long shall the adversary reproach? shall the enemy blaspheme thy name for ever? [11] Why withdrawest thou thy hand, even thy right hand? pluck it out of thy bosom.

It is not wrong to ask the LORD, "How long?" No, no; we are not expecting an answer in words. When we ask "How long?", we are essentially expressing our desire that God will soon intervene. So as we pray "how long?" with the Psalmist, we pray at the same time, "Maranatha!" with the Apostle Paul. Come quickly, O LORD! Pluck out thy right hand from thy bosom for the sake of Thy people.

God is able to do exceedingly above what we may think or imagine, for He is our King, or as we are given to sing in the third part of this Psalm:

3. God Is My King of Old

[12] For God is my King of old, working salvation in the midst of the earth. [13] Thou didst divide the sea by thy strength: thou brakest the heads of the dragons in the waters. [14] Thou brakest the heads of leviathan in pieces, and gavest him to be meat to the people inhabiting the wilderness. [15] Thou didst cleave the fountain and the flood: thou driedst up mighty rivers. [16] The day is thine, the night also is thine: thou hast prepared the light and the sun. [17] Thou hast set all the borders of the earth: thou hast made summer and winter.

Nothing is impossible with God. He is the King, the Creator and Redeemer. He is the governor of all things upon the earth. Notice the eightfold "thou." He alone is in control. All things that come to pass upon the earth, come to pass according to His sovereign providential power. The great leviathans, and dragons, or dinosaurs, may inspire the imagination of man because of their strength and power; but they are nothing in the hand of the LORD. Even the mighty rivers, and the sea, and the seasons are in His hands.

All things in the universe are ordered by God's power for the salvation of His people (cf. Eph 3:9-11).

God, of course, knows that. But in prayer, God is glorified when we appeal to His power and sovereignty. Such is the argument for the petition in the last part of this Psalm, which is:

4. Arise, O God, Plead Thine Own Cause

[18] Remember this, that the enemy hath reproached, O LORD, and that the foolish people have blasphemed thy name.

When the Babylonians desecrated the temple of God, they blasphemed the name of the LORD. Today, when atheists (i.e. *"the foolish people"*) and those of false religions speak evil of the word of God and His people, they blaspheme the name of the LORD.

When the name of God is blasphemed, then the people of God would inevitably suffer mockery and injustice. So we must appeal to the compassion of the LORD for His people:

[19] O deliver not the soul of thy turtledove unto the multitude of the wicked: forget not the congregation of thy poor forever. [20] Have respect unto the covenant: for the dark places of

the earth are full of the habitations of cruelty. ²¹ *O let not the oppressed return ashamed: let the poor and needy praise thy name.*

The LORD is a loving and compassionate God. He will not sit idly while His covenant people are being persecuted or taken advantage of by the world.

But let us also not forget to appeal to the LORD to vindicate His own name: for the blessedness of the people of God is very much tied to the glory of God's name in the world. So let us cry with our Saviour:

²² *Arise, O God, plead thine own cause: remember how the foolish man reproacheth thee daily.* ²³ *Forget not the voice of thine enemies: the tumult of those that rise up against thee increaseth continually.*

Is it not true that the tumults of those who rise against the LORD are increasing continually? Year by year, we see atheists and those who care not for the LORD or His Law, getting louder and louder in their opposition to God and His ways. We see it in the West where Christianity once had an almost all-pervasive influence. We see it also in the East where Christianity has begun to make significant inroads, only in relatively recent times.

So year by year, we see Christian influences being eroded and evolutionistic humanism swaying entire populations of people away from God and old-fashioned biblical values.

Shall we not cry out unto the LORD to arise, to plead His own cause: for He alone can put a stop to the rapid declension of society and the desecration of His name throughout the world?

Conclusion

This is Psalm 74. It contains an urgent and needful prayer. The Church that would not pray as our Head would have us pray, must be blind to what is happening in the world.

But this Psalm must also encourage us to trust in the LORD. In the midst of the ruins we see, and the sufferings we may experience as God's people, let us learn to turn our eyes to the LORD our King, for He is God unchanging and omnipotent. He will, in His own time, arise for our deliverance and vindication. Only let us remember to look to Him rather than allow ourselves to become discouraged or apathetic. Amen. Ω

Psalm 75:
The Righteous One's Rejoinder
to the Saints' Maranatha

Psalm 75 is another Psalm of Asaph. It was written by Asaph under the inspiration of the Holy Spirit. But unlike the previous two Psalms of Asaph, it is written in such a way that it is more clearly Messianic, even though it is not generally recognised as Messianic by those who hold strictly to the historical-grammatical method, without giving weight to subsequent revelation and the canonical context. Neither is it accepted as Messianic by those who would regard a Psalm as Messianic only if it is explicitly attributed to Christ in the New Testament. It has even been suggested that the Christological approach to the Psalms—that sees every Psalm as explicitly or implicitly the word of Christ, which Christ might have sung or meditated on, or that His people may sing in union with Him—is a modern innovation.

But listen to the Church Father Augustine in his opening comments on this Psalm:

> ...Hear ye now the words of Christ. For these seemed not as it were to be His words... But whether [the] Head speaketh or whether [the] members speak, Christ speaketh: He speaketh in the person of the Head, He speaketh in the person of the Body.... He is speaking therefore as One, let us hear Him, and in Him let us also speak. Let us be the members of Him, in order that this voice may possibly be ours also.[31]

Augustine is speaking about how we must sing the Psalm in union with Christ and how sometimes the words of various verses in the Psalms may clearly appear to be the words of Christ, while at other times, they may appear more to be the words of His body, the Church.

This is especially so in Psalm 75. Though in the opening verse of this Psalm, we do not have Christ speaking singularly, verses 2-3 have the first person singular pronoun.

> [2] *When I shall receive the congregation I will judge uprightly.* [3] *The earth and all the inhabitants thereof are dissolved: I bear up the pillars of it.*

Who is this "I"? Commentators have some difficulty answering. We know it cannot be "Asaph" who was a Levite. So three different options are suggested: David, God and the Messiah. W.S. Plumer says: "That person is either David as king of Israel, or Messiah as typified by David, or God as Judge of the whole earth."

But if God is the speaker, would it not be quite arbitrary and confusing since verse 1 addressed God in the second person, whereas in verse 9, the speaker addresses God in the third person!

> [9] *But I will declare for ever; I will sing praises to the God of Jacob.*

Who alone upholds the pillars of the earth (v. 3) and also sings praises to God (v. 9)? Who alone can both sing "I" (v. 2) and "we" (v. 1) with us? When we have searched the Scripture, we will not be able to find a more fitting answer than the Son of God, the Messiah, the Righteous One!

We may entitle this Psalm *"The Righteous One's Rejoinder to the Saint's Maranatha."* It is a Psalm appointed by our King that we may sing with Him unto the Father as we anticipate the Coming Day of Judgement.

---

[31] Augustine, in *Nicene And Post-Nicene Fathers*, first series, vol. 8—"Augustin: Expositions on the Book of Psalms," ed. Philip Schaff (Peabody: Hendrikson Publishers, reprinted 2004 [1888]), 351,

It has four parts:

1. v. 1 — Ascription of Thanks by Messiah and His Saints
2. v. 2-5 — Acknowledgement of Messiah the Judge
3. v. 6-8 — Affirmation that Messiah's Judgement is Approved of God
4. v. 9-10 — Annoucement that the Goal of Messiah's Judgement is God's Glory

1. Thanksgiving of Messiah
& His Saints

[1] *Unto thee, O God, do we give thanks, unto thee do we give thanks: for that thy name is near thy wondrous works declare.*

The "we" in this Psalm, as we noted, is not just anyone who sings this Psalm. An unbeliever may not sing this Psalm meaningfully: for he cannot identify with the "we." The "we" refers to Christ and His Church in union with Him.

As our Lord teaches us to pray in the first petition, "Our Father which art in heaven, hallowed be thy name," so here we pray with our Lord: "*Unto thee, O God, do we give thanks for that thy name is near...*"

Even as we think about the solemn subject of judgement, it is important for us to approach it with thanksgiving, "*for that [God's] name is near [His] wondrous works declare.*" That is to say, God's wondrous works everywhere declare the name of God, that it is praiseworthy.

Is it not true that if we look closely enough, God's signature is in everything that He has made? And so everything that God has made, declares His wondrous name.

The world did not come about by random chance. There is a Creator. And if there is a Creator, there will be a judgement. Solomon reminds us: "Remember now thy Creator... For God shall bring every work into judgment" (Ecc 12:1, 14).

Who is our Judge? Our Judge is none other than Christ Jesus: for He says, "the Father judgeth no man, but hath committed all judgment unto the Son" (Jn 5:22).

And so in verses 2-5, we have our Lord's acknowledgement of His role as Judge.

2. Acknowledgement of Messiah
the Judge

[2] *When I shall receive the congregation I will judge uprightly.* [3] *The earth and all the inhabitants thereof are dissolved: I bear up the pillars of it.*

Christ is upholding all things by the word of His power (Heb 1:3). In so far as all things were created for the sake of the Church, all things are being, as it were, borne up by their pillars, by the Lord, until the Day of Judgement.

That Great Day of Judgement is the day when the Lord receives the whole number of His congregation. The Apostle Peter says that "the Lord [is] not willing that any should perish, but that all should come to repentance" (2 Pet 3:9). Only when the full number of His elect has come in, will Christ formally receive His congregation; and only then will He bring about the Judgement.

That day will also be known as the "day of wrath" (Rom 2:5), for on that day, the earth and all her inhabitants shall, as it were, be dissolved. "The elements shall melt with fervent heat, the earth also and the works that are therein shall be burned up," says Peter (2 Pet 3:10). The earth will be renovated and there will be a new heaven and new earth (2 Pet 3:13).

This is a great and terrible day for those who remain unrepentant and in unbelief. Therefore, the Lord is today warning and calling for repentance through the preaching of the Gospel:

> *4 I said unto the fools, Deal not foolishly: and to the wicked, Lift not up the horn: 5 Lift not up your horn on high: speak not with a stiff neck.*

To lift up the horn is to be proud and to refuse to listen to admonishment and instruction. In the day of the wrath of the Lamb, the proud and stiff-necked will cry unto "the mountains and rocks, Fall on us, and hide us from the face of him that sitteth on the throne, and from the wrath of the Lamb" (Rev 6:16).

He that sitteth upon the Throne is the Lamb. But He is also the God-Man. His judgement is the judgement of God. Therefore, we have an affirmation that...

3. Messiah's Judgement
is Approved of God

> *6 For promotion cometh neither from the east, nor from the west, nor from the south. 7 But God is the judge: he putteth down one, and setteth up another.*

We are all familiar with these two verses. Many of us would refer to them to thank God when we get a promotion at work. Or we might use them to encourage someone to seek first the kingdom of God rather than worry about his promotion.

But these two verses are not only about job promotion. It is about the perfect justice of God. He deals with all men—by His providential power—according to His perfect justice today. He will reward those who walk righteously, and chastise, or punish those who walk lawlessly.

God is longsuffering, and slow to wrath. Therefore, He gives time for man to repent, and does not deal with man according to what our sins deserve in this life.

But one day, God will deal with sinners with the full fury of His wrath.

> *8 For in the hand of the LORD there is a cup, and the wine is red; it is full of mixture; and he poureth out of the same: but the dregs thereof, all the wicked of the earth shall wring them out, and drink them.*

Christ, our Lord, we must remember, has been appointed by the Father to judge and to execute judgement. This is why the day of judgement is called the day of the wrath of the Lamb (Rev 6:16).

The judgement of Christ is the same as the judgement of God, for Christ is God. Indeed, the purpose of Christ's judgement is ultimately the glory of God, as we see it in His own declaration...

4. The Goal of Messiah's Judgement
Is God's Glory

> *9 But I will declare for ever; I will sing praises to the God of Jacob. 10 All the horns of the wicked also will I cut off; but the horns of the righteous shall be exalted.*

The appellation, "God of Jacob," speaks of God as the covenant-keeping God, for the name

Jacob or Israel is used in the Old Testament as a short form for "the covenant people of God."

Christ will judge perfectly; and for all eternity, He will sing praises unto the Father in union with His people. For all eternity, the mercy of God for the elect and His justice against the reprobate will be clearly shown and become a subject of everlasting praise and meditation.

Conclusion

In this world, we will have much tribulation. We must through much tribulation enter into the kingdom of God. And the more tribulation we experience—whether physical, emotional or spiritual—the more we cry out with the Psalmist "How long, O LORD?" (cf. Ps 79:5; Ps 89:46, Ps 90:13; etc). And the more we cry out "Maranatha!" (1 Cor 16:22).

Christ our Lord has heard our prayer. He will come. He will come when the full number of His elect has been brought in. And when He comes, He will set all things in order and correct all injustice, unfairness, cynicism, and wrongs.

Let us, beloved brethren, therefore, wait patiently, cling on to our Lord, and run the race with His strength, patience, hope, and joy. Let us not allow any sense of grief or injustice to entangle us, and make us weary in the race. Amen. Ω

Psalm 76:
The Righteous One's
Proclamation of
God's Sovereignty in Judgement

Psalm 76 is a Psalm of Asaph. Who is this Asaph? Again, he could be Asaph the seer (2 Chr 29:30) or one of the "sons of Asaph" (1 Chr 25:1). We may regard "Asaph" as a pen name which was used by one or more persons in the same godly tradition as Asaph the Seer.

Psalm 76 is not a very well-known Psalm in that most of us would not be able to say off-hand what it is about. But just as there is a famous verse in Psalm 75, there is one famous verse in Psalm 76.

The famous verse in Psalm 75 is verse 6: "For promotion cometh neither from the east, nor from the west, nor from the south." It speaks of God as being fair and just; so the Psalm is about the Messiah coming to restore fairness and justice.

Correspondingly, the famous verse in Psalm 76 is verse 10: *"Surely the wrath of man shall praise thee: the remainder of wrath shalt thou restrain."* From this verse we can see how this Psalm speaks of the sovereignty and power of the God of Jacob. We may call it *"The Righteous One's Proclamation of God's Sovereignty in Judgement."*

It is a Psalm inspired by the Spirit of Christ that He and His covenant people may sing as one in praise of the Father for His sovereignty displayed in judgement.

There are three stanzas in this Psalm, each ending with the word "Selah," the famous musical notation to instruct us to pause to think.

1.   v. 1-3   Declaration that God's Judgement is Covenantal
2.   v. 4-9   Proclamation that God's Judgement is Awesome
3.   v. 10-12   Confession that God's Judgement is to be Feared

1. God's Judgement Is
Covenantal (v. 1-3)

¹ In Judah is God known: his name is great in Israel. ² In Salem also is his tabernacle, and his dwelling place in Zion. ³ There brake he the arrows of the bow, the shield, and the sword, and the battle.

At first sight, these opening words do not seem to be related to what we say is the theme of this Psalm, namely the display of God's sovereignty in His Judgement. But we must remember that all that God does in the world, He does for His people.

His judgement is displayed in His sovereign acts in the world whether they be wars or natural disasters. Not everyone sees His hand in the acts. Some attribute the things that happen to nature, or to chance. Others attribute them to false gods, or simply to human power.

But God is known in Judah. His name is great in Israel. God's people can see His hand in judgement. Indeed, God's people know that His judgement is often meted out in support of His covenant people: for God has chosen to dwell amongst His people. He pitched His tabernacle in Salem and made Zion His dwelling place.

The name Salem is, no doubt, used here intentionally. The reference is to Jerusalem. But

Salem means peace. The apostle to the Hebrews reminds us that Melchizedek is "the King of Peace" since he is "the King of Salem" (Heb 7:2). Melchizedek was a type of Christ, *the Prince of Peace*.

For Christ's sake, God preserves peace for His people by defending them from His and their enemies. He does so by rising in judgement against their enemies. He does so also by breaking the shields, arrows and swords of their enemies who encamp against them (v. 3).

God's judgement, in other words, is not a series of random acts displaying His power. Rather, His judgement is designed to display His own glory, and directed according to His covenant love for His people.

We may think of God's judgement, whether in national crises, or natural disasters, as being all directed for the good of His covenant people. God's people or His Church, after all, thrives best under suffering which tries them that they may come forth as gold.

2. God's Judgement Is
Awesome (v. 4-9)

⁴ Thou art more glorious and excellent than the mountains of prey. ⁵ The stouthearted are spoiled, they have slept their sleep: and none of the men of might have found their hands [i.e. they have become powerless]. ⁶ At thy rebuke, O God of Jacob, both the chariot and horse are cast into a dead sleep.

Our great and glorious God does not often break out in dramatic display of His power on behalf of His people. But He has done so in the history of His people, and will continue to do so whenever necessary.

We think of His intervention during the days of Hezekiah when the Assyrian army of Sennacherib surrounded Jerusalem, and almost forced a surrender. But God intervened. The Angel of the LORD went forth, and in one night 185,000 of the Assyrian army died.

The next day, the people of God came out to plunder (or to *spoil*, v. 5) the dead invaders, and so averted the starvation of the city. This is what we are given to celebrate in verses 5 and 6.

God's judgement is awesome, is it not?

⁷ Thou, even thou, art to be feared: and who may stand in thy sight when once thou art angry? ⁸ Thou didst cause judgment to be heard from heaven; the earth feared, and was still, ⁹ When God arose to judgment, to save all the meek of the earth.

His awesome judgement is for the meek of the earth. Who are the meek? They are none other than God's covenant people. "But the meek shall inherit the earth; and shall delight themselves in the abundance of peace" (Ps 37:11).

God is yet able to do awesome things for His people. We live in a day of small things. We have grown accustomed to becoming overwhelmed by the spinter in our toe. We are all consumed and terrified by a little wind and waves. Our prayers do not reach beyond the little concerns that irritate us. Like babies having interest only on their navel, we have forgotten that there is much more in the Christian life. We have forgotten to look where we should be looking. No, no; dear child of God, God is able to do great things. We must learn to expect great things from the LORD. He will yet rise up on behalf of His people and His Son.

But as we see God's sovereignty displayed in His judgement, let us humble ourselves and acknowledge that...

3. God's Judgement Is to
be Feared (v. 10-12)

[10] *Surely the wrath of man shall praise thee: the remainder of wrath shalt thou restrain.*

This is a famous verse as we mentioned. But what does it mean? What it means is that God is sovereignly in control over the affairs of man!

Proud man may think that they can do what they want to do with impunity, without any regard for God; but in reality they are accomplishing God's will. The Babylonians and the Assyrians were cruel and greedy. They sought to conquer Judah and Israel. They thought their god was greater than Jehovah. But what was happening? What was happening was that they were doing God's will! They were His sword of chastisement (cf. Jer 20:4; Isa 8:7, etc). This explains why when it was not time for Jerusalem to be overthrown yet, God restrained the Assyrian's wrath by a display of His sovereign power.

Can you see how greatly to be feared His power is?

What shall our response be?

[11] *Vow, and pay unto the LORD your God: let all that be round about him bring presents unto him that ought to be feared.* [12] *He shall cut off the spirit of princes: he is terrible to the kings of the earth.*

If God is so great as to be in control, even of the wrath of man, what should our response be to Him, but to serve Him in fear?

We must not take His name lightly. When we have vowed, we must not forget to pay the vow. In this way, we can have the assurance that God will not deal with us in the way He deals with the princes and kings of the earth that have no regard for Him. Obedience is the key to the assurance of God's love, which is why the Lord teaches us: "If ye love me, keep my commandments" (Jn 14:15). If we keep God's commandments sincerely, we can be assured that we do love Him, and if we have the assurance that we do love Him, then we can be assured that God by His sovereign power is working all things together for our good.

Conclusion

God's judgement is covenantal, awesome and to be feared. His judgement is awesome: for His power is beyond human imagination. The destruction of Sennacherib's army is but a hiding of God's power and yet we are astounded. Who may stand in God's sight if He reveals the fullness of His power?

But God displays His sovereign power not indiscriminately, but rather out of love and consideration for His people.

What shall we do with this knowledge, but to fear Him and serve Him? Let us not fear man, or look to man for our comfort. Let us not trust in our own abilities. Let us, rather, cling on to Christ, and look to Him who is unchanging, come what may in our lives. Amen. Ω

Psalm 77:
The Righteous One
Finding Strength Through Remembrance

Psalm 77 is another Psalm which churches and individual believers may use when dark clouds appear over our lives. It is attributed to Asaph, who is most probably, one of the sons of Asaph. Hengstenberg suggests that this Psalm was written during the days of King Josiah. His reason is that this Psalm bears a very striking resemblance to the Song of Habakkuk, recorded in the third chapter of his prophecy. He says:

> Our Psalm is related in such a striking manner to the 3rd chapter of Habakkuk, that the agreement can only be explained by the supposition that the one writer made use of the expressions of the other.

Habakkuk ministered during the days of Josiah. He had dedicated his song "to the chief singer on my string instruments" (Hab 3:19). It is very probable that Asaph as the appointed cantor edited the song to include it in the book of Psalms, the official hymnbook of the Church. While Habakkuk's song is inspired and remains in his prophecy, it is not inspired for the church to sing in public worship in that form. The form that it finally took for public worship is in Psalm 77.

Who then is the first person, "I" in this Psalm? Is it Habakkuk or is it Asaph with the authority of the king? Well, whoever the penman is, this Psalm is no doubt inspired by the Spirit of Christ, and may be used by God's people corporately or individually. We may use it in union with Christ, who must have sung and meditated on this Psalm during the dark days that He went through.

Andrew Bonar expresses this thought beautifully:

> "Asaph's harp's strings are moaning to the chilly night-wind. Instead of triumphing in the Mighty One, whom all must fear, Asaph is full of unkindly fears, fears arising from clouds around his soul. Our Lord on earth had such changes in his soul as we find in this Psalm. One day, under the opened heavens at Jordan; another, in the gloom of the howling wilderness; one evening, ascending the Transfiguration hill; another entering Gethsemane. And so with every member of his body. Not that the love of their God varies towards them, and not that they themselves feel that love exhausted; but providences and trials of strange sort, and temptations buffeting the soul, hide the sun by their dark mists."

This Psalm is especially encouraging when we find our soul enveloped by dark clouds, when the only comfort we can find, is the remembrance that beyond what we can see, is the Sovereign God doing well. We may entitle it *"The Righteous One Finding Strength Through Remembrance."* The Righteous One is first of all Christ, and by extension, the Church of Christ and every member who is united to Him by grace through faith. This Psalm is not for non-Christians. Only a Christian can identify with the sentiments expressed in it.

It has, essentially, two parts. In the first part (verses 1-9), we sing of our problem, which is the distress in our soul. In the second part (verses 10-20), we sing of the solution, which is the remembrance of what God has done.

Thus, an outline will be as follows:

1. v. 1-9   The Problem
2. v. 10-20   The Solution

1. The Problem

We often think of problems in terms of the trials that afflict us. But if you think about it, you will realise that the real problem is not the trial, but how we react to the trial. After all, if we believe in the word of God, then we must be convinced that all things are working together for our good. If that is so, how can it really be a problem? What then is the problem? It must be our reaction to trials, isn't it?

This is what we are taught in this Psalm.

[1] I cried unto God with my voice, even unto God with my voice; and he gave ear unto me. [2] In the day of my trouble I sought the Lord: my sore ran in the night, and ceased not: my soul refused to be comforted.

It is good and right for a child of God to cry out to the LORD in prayer when he is faced with troubles. Likewise, it is good and right for the church to be earnest in prayer, when faced with particular trials such as during the days of Josiah.

However, while God hears our prayers, He does not always bring immediate relief. Indeed, are there not times when God appears to withhold His hand of mercy so much so that the more we pray, the more anxious we get? Look at verse 3:

[3] I remembered God, and was troubled: I complained, and my spirit was overwhelmed. Selah.

The word "selah" reminds us to pause to think about it. Is it not true that sometimes the more we complain to the Lord, the more our spirit gets overwhelmed? And is it not true that often, the more we think about it, the more sleepless nights we get, and the more perplexed we get, verse 4:

[4] Thou holdest mine eyes waking: I am so troubled that I cannot speak. [5] I have considered the days of old, the years of ancient times. [6] I call to remembrance my song in the night: I commune with mine own heart: and my spirit made diligent search.

One of the best remedies for insomnia for the child of God is not counting sheep, but prayer. But is it not true that sometimes we are so troubled that we do not know what to say even though we cannot sleep, because we keep thinking about an issue that troubles us (cf. v. 4)?

We think about all that the LORD has done in the past for us (v. 5). We think about our prayers and songs (v. 6). We check our hearts, and search to see if we are asking amiss (v. 7). But instead of comfort, we get more questions. Notice the many questions from verses 7-9:

[7] Will the Lord cast off for ever? and will he be favourable no more? [8] Is his mercy clean gone for ever? doth his promise fail for evermore? [9] Hath God forgotten to be gracious? hath he in anger shut up his tender mercies?

Is this not the way we think, whenever we are perplexed? The more we think, the more questions we raise, and more doubts begin to arise in our hearts. And as we begin to doubt God and His favour, mercy, grace and promise, we begin to spiral further and further into a pit of anxiety in our mind.

Herein is the problem. It is a problem of wrong thinking. The problem is not that of asking questions, or else our Saviour would not have used these questions, which He has given us to meditate in song. Now, our Lord was tempted in all points like as we are, yet without sin.

He would not have entertained doubt, but the questions that tempt Him to doubt would almost certainly have flooded His holy soul. Except that, instead of giving birth to doubt, they actually strengthened His faith as He meditated on the answer to His questions as given in the second part of this Psalm.

Now, the line between temptation and sin is not so clear for us. Most, if not all of us, when faced with temptation to doubt, will actually fall into doubt at least momentarily. And so we add guilt to our perplexity; and it becomes easy for us to spin into depression. Indeed, I sometimes wonder if some of us fall into depression because we feel that the LORD is not answering our prayers or that the LORD is looking upon us with disfavour and anger rather than with mercy and love.

We must realise that this is our problem. God never changes. Jesus Christ the same yesterday, today and tomorrow. He will never leave us nor forsake us. He does not love us yesterday and hate us today. But the problem remains. How to deal with the problem? Consider the solution in the second part of this Psalm:

2. The Solution

The first step of the solution to the problem is none other than recognition of the problem, verse 10:

> ^{10a} And I said, This is my infirmity:

Now, the Hebrew of this statement has been variously understood. Albert Barnes, I believe, summarises its meaning well when he says, "The Hebrew means, 'This makes me sick;' that is, 'This distresses me; it afflicts me; it overwhelms me." How apt! Such questions in the heart are deeply troubling to the soul and could lead to great discouragements if not answered. How many believers are suffering pain and sorrow in their soul with apparently no way out because they fail, in the first place, to recognise the need to find the right answers to their questions. So instead solving the grief in their soul by steering their thoughts in the right direction, they run around trying to deal what they perceive to be the causes of their trouble.

The Lord, by His Spirit, shows us a different way. The solution simply stated is to remember who the LORD is and what the LORD has done in the history of redemption. Now, take note that it is not merely remembering what the LORD has done for us individually, but what the LORD has done for the Church in days of old. What the LORD has done for us individually, may encourage us to some degree. But very often in times when we are already discouraged and doubting God, those experiences of past deliverance may not help that much. Why? Because we begin to wonder if it is a co-incidence that we were helped or if the present situation warrants help from the LORD, etc, etc.

On the other hand, remembering what God has done in canonical history helps us to see God objectively. So verse 10b:

> ^{10b} but I will remember the years of the right hand of the most High. ^{11} I will remember the works of the LORD: surely I will remember thy wonders of old. ^{12} I will meditate also of all thy work, and talk of thy doings. ^{13} Thy way, O God, is in the sanctuary [i.e. in holiness]: who is so great a God as our God? ^{14} Thou art the God that doest wonders: thou hast declared thy strength among the people.

When we are confronted with problems and perplexities in our souls, it is important for us to turn away from the wind and the waves, and from others and from ourselves, to look at the LORD. It is important to think about Him and to talk about Him (v. 12). "A meditative man must be a talker otherwise he is a mental miser," says Spurgeon. We must meditate and talk or sing about the greatness of our God. Only God is unchanging and perfectly reliable. Only God has the power to do what is right all the time. Who is so great as our God?

And it is important, not only to think in general terms what the Lord has done. It is necessary for us, rather to recall in very specific terms what He has done. So our Lord would have us to meditate with Him specifically on the great events surrounding God's redemption of His people out of Egypt.

> [15] Thou hast with thine arm redeemed thy people, the sons of Jacob and Joseph. Selah. [16] The waters saw thee, O God, the waters saw thee; they were afraid: the depths also were troubled. [17] The clouds poured out water: the skies sent out a sound: thine arrows also went abroad. [18] The voice of thy thunder was in the heaven: the lightnings lightened the world: the earth trembled and shook. [19] Thy way is in the sea, and thy path in the great waters, and thy footsteps are not known. [20] Thou leddest thy people like a flock by the hand of Moses and Aaron.

The Exodus was a very great event. God worked in a very mighty way to redeem His people out of Egypt. Not only did He send the Ten Plagues, He parted the Red Sea in a very dramatic display of His power. There was, as it were, mighty lightnings and thunders. The earth trembled and shook. But God led His people through the Red Sea upon dry land. The people were like a precious flock being led by their shepherds, Moses and Aaron. Did the people deserve what He did for them? No, not at all! Remember how even after they were redeemed, they were full of murmuring and complaints. God led them out because He loved them as His covenant people.

Today, we may look at the Exodus event and get encouraged—not only by what God did for our fathers in the Faith, but by our own redemption from spiritual Egypt. How does meditating on the Exodus account help us, when it seems so remote to us? How does thinking about how God redeemed us help us? How do they help us when we are troubled individually or as a church? They help us because they remind us of the power of God and of His covenant love. God was at work in the lives of His people. He is still at work in the lives of His people. He worked redemption in all cases, not according to how much His people deserve His intervention, but according to His great love for them. While individually, we may not see any dramatic interventions of God in our life, we must know that He is the same God who redeemed Israel out of Egypt. If He does not deliver us from our trials according to our petition, we must still believe that He is able to do great things, and that He is indeed doing great things for us. As we are given to sing in verse 9, we may not be able to see His footsteps as He leads us, but with eyes of faith, we must see that He is indeed leading us with great love and compassion. Only in this way, can the problem of our hearts be truly solved.

Conclusion

What is this Psalm to you, dear reader? Are you facing a discouraging problem in your life? Remember that the solution is neither to be found in introspection, nor in murmuring and grumbling. It is to be found, rather, in remembering. Remember all that the LORD has done for His people. Remember all that the LORD has done for you. Learn to rejoice in what He has done. Learn to see His power and the big picture of what He is doing. Herein is the solution to many of the problems that make us discouraged, weak and weary Christians. Let us remind ourselves of this solution by singing this Psalm with our Lord, with understanding. Amen. Ω

Psalm 78:
The Righteous One's
Parable of Covenant History

One day, during the earthly ministry of the Lord Jesus, He preached a number of parables including the Parable of the Sower, the Parable of the Wheat and the Tares, the Parable of the Mustard Seed and of the Leaven. When the apostle Matthew has recorded all these, he remarks:

"^{34} All these things spake Jesus unto the multitude in parables; and without a parable spake he not unto them: ^{35} That it might be fulfilled which was spoken by the prophet, saying, I will open my mouth in parables; I will utter things which have been kept secret from the foundation of the world" (Mt 13:34-35).

Who is this prophet? Where is the prophecy recorded? This prophet is the writer of Psalm 78. Matthew is quoting from Psalm 78:2:

^{2} I will open my mouth in a parable: I will utter dark sayings of old...

Andrew Bonar, observing Matthew's use of Psalm 78, remarks:

"We are led to conclude that Asaph here was directed to foreshadow Messiah, the Prophet, disclosing the mind and ways of God, where these were hidden from the gaze of the common eye."

But how did Matthew in the first place come to conclude that Psalm 78 is referring to the Lord's ministry of parables? We believe it is because Matthew, together with the other apostles, saw the Psalms as the word of Christ, and so they instinctively and generally took the first person singular pronouns in the Psalms as having an ultimate reference to Christ.

In Psalm 78, the first two verses makes much more sense when understood as the word of Christ than as the word of Asaph, for Asaph, as far as we know, had no right to be a lawgiver.^{32} What about the first person plural pronoun, "we" in verse 3? Again, it makes much more sense to think of it as Christ in union with His Church, doesn't it? When we think of it in this way, we may sing this Psalm as members of the body whose history we are recounting.

In ancient days, this long Psalm was probably chanted rather than sung the way that we do today. If we read it or chant it through, we will not fail to notice the recounting of the history of God's people from Egypt to Jerusalem, from Moses to David. But we will also get the idea that this Psalm is not merely to recount history. Rather, it is to teach something more profound. Indeed, as Hengstenberg puts it, there is in every part of this historical Psalm, "a concealed background of instruction." The historical narrative, in other words, is to convey deeper lessons, just as the parables are intended to teach deeper spiritual truths. We may entitle it "The Righteous One's Parable of Covenant History."

It has four parts:

(1) Verses 1-8 is a call to respond gratefully to God's faithfulness. We are to respond by loving obedience to our Lord's instruction and to teach it to our children, and our children's

---

^{32} He is most probably one of the sons of Asaph who lived after the kingdom was divided. We suspect this is the case because of the reference to the apostasy of Ephraim and the contrast to Judah in this Psalm (see v. 9, 10, 68). This son of Asaph would have been the editor and poet of the king to prepare the king's song for publication and use by the congregation of Israel.

children.

(2) Verses 9-11 gives us the occasion for the writing of this Psalm. It appears that the occasion is the rebellion of Ephraim and the Northern Ten Tribes.

(3) Verses 12-64 recounts the history of God's people in their cycle of divine blessing, rebellion, repentance, mercy, etc. In this account, a great contrast is drawn between the ingratitude and stiffneckness of God's people, and God's faithfulness and compassion.

(4) Verses 65-72 concludes by stating how God has chosen Judah instead of the tribes of Joseph to experience His special love.

In this short study, we will not be able to cover this Psalm exhaustively. But we may get a sense of what our Lord wants us to learn and exhort one another with it by considering 4 lessons, one from each of the four sections of this Psalm:

1. v. 1-8   The Tradition of Instruction: Respond Gratefully to God's Faithfulness
2. v. 9-11   The Disobedience of Ephraim: Refuse to Rebel like Ephraim
3. v. 12-64   The Faithfulness of God: Remember Our Tendency to Be Like Our Fathers
4. v. 65-72   The Prerogative of God: Relish the Love of God for Our King's Sake

1. Respond Gratefully to God's Faithfulness

This is the purpose of this Psalm. So our Lord through Asaph says:

¹ Give ear, O my people, to my law: incline your ears to the words of my mouth....

The Lord's law in this context includes, no doubt, His teachings recorded for us throughout the Scriptures such as in the Pentateuch, the historical books, the poetic books, the prophecies, the Gospel and the letters.

What is the purpose of Christ's instruction? It is not only for the sanctification of the redeemed; it is so that God's people down the generations may know the LORD, and praise Him and obey Him gratefully.

For this reason, our response to God's faithfulness must not only include words of praise; it must also include faithful instruction of our children (v. 5) with a humble prayer that they will not forget God, but be grateful and obedient unto Him unlike their parent's generation, which is *"a stubborn and rebellious generation"* (v. 6-8).

2. Refuse to Rebel Like Ephraim

It is likely, from verses 9-11, that the occasion for this Psalm is the rebellion of the Northern ten tribes after Solomon passed away.

The Northern Tribe, represented by Ephraim *"kept not the covenant of God, and refused to walk in his law"* (v. 10). In this way, they demonstrated their forgetfulness and ingratitude (v. 11).

As God's covenant people, we must resist the same temptation. The Northern Kingdom under the leadership of Jeroboam, broke away from Judah and began to worship Jehovah using Golden Calves in Dan and Bethel. What was the reason for their departure? It was mainly convenience and political expediency.

History has repeated itself and demonstrated how easily a church or denomination can take the same path by introducing popular innovations into God's worship which are not appointed by the LORD.

Oh may the Lord grant us help that we may refuse to rebel like Ephraim!

3. Remember Our Tendency
to Be Like Our Fathers

We are one with the people of God in the Old Testament. They were our fathers in the faith. Let us remember the history of our fathers that we may not repeat the same mistakes.

God did marvellous works to redeem Israel out of Egypt (v. 12). He parted the Red Sea (v. 13). He led them with a pillar of cloud by day and a pillar of fire by night (v. 14). He quenched their thirst with water out of the rock (v. 15-16).

And yet they sinned against the LORD by murmuring against Him and His servant. God gave them manna and water, but they were not satisfied. They wanted the leeks and cucumber and fish of Egypt. They would rather trade their freedom to satisfy the lust of their flesh. They cried for meat (v. 18).

God, therefore, sent them quails to eat, and at the same time chastised them severely for their murmuring and grumbling (v. 19-31).

But still they refused to remember. *"For all this they sinned still, and believed not for his wondrous works"* (v. 32).

Each time the Lord chastised them, they turned back and remembered that He is their Rock and Redeemer (v. 34-35). But very quickly they forgot again (v. 36), instead of *"remaining stedfast in His Covenant"* (v. 37).

> *"But [God], being full of compassion, forgave their iniquity, and destroyed them not: yea, many a time turned he his anger away, and did not stir up all his wrath"* (v. 38).

He remembers that they are *"but flesh"* (v. 39). By contrast they provoked Him and grieved Him (v. 40), and tempted Him and limited Him (v. 41), and refused to remember all that He had done for them (v. 42). For example, they forgot the ten plagues that He wrought in Egypt for their deliverance (v. 43-51). They forgot how God led them like a flock (v. 52). They forgot how God led them step by step until they were able to conquer the Promised Land (v. 53-55).

So they *"tempted and provoked the most high God, and kept not his testimonies"* (v. 56).

They provoked God to anger and jealousy with their idols (v. 57-58) so much so that God caused their army to be defeated, and the ark to be captured by the Philistines (v. 59-64).

Let us remember that though God is patient, His patience does not last forever. For the sake of His own name, He will often send His people great troubles. What should our response be when God sends troubles to us? Should not our response be to humble ourselves and to return to the old paths? And shall we not learn from history, how prone to wander we are, and how bent on backsliding we are? Shall we not check ourselves, and constantly remind ourselves to remain faithful to the LORD?

4. Relish the Love of God
for Our King's Sake

Despite the failures of the people, when God had sufficiently chastised them, He again arose to intervene on behalf of His people (v. 65). He smote their enemies (v. 66).

Moreover (v. 67), God in His sovereignty and wisdom rejected the house of Joseph, and therefore the great tribe of Ephraim, as the base to establish His kingdom on earth in preparation of the coming Messiah. He chose Judah instead: for as the Chronicler puts it, "Judah prevailed above his brethren, and of him came the chief ruler; but the birthright was Joseph's" (1 Chr 5:2).

So, God in His mercy and covenant faithfulness towards His inheritance, prepared the tribe of Judah to receive His special blessing, including having His temple built in her, and raising up a man from the tribe to be king over His people (v. 68-71).

This man is none other than King David, the forefather and type of the greater David. David led his people with integrity and skill (v. 72).

Today, King David has passed from the scene. How is his appointment important to us? Of course! It is important to us because it serves as a type of the greater David, Christ.

Indeed, the only reason, we can expect God to continue the good work in us despite our repeated failures against Him, is that the Lord Jesus is our King.

As the Israelites of old often look back to King David as they anticipated the Messiah, shall we not look back to what Christ our King has done as we anticipate what He will do for us?

"He which hath begun a good work in [us] will perform it until the day of Jesus Christ" (Phil 1:6).

Conclusion

History keeps repeating itself, for the church is made up of sinners saved by grace, not yet perfected. Let us therefore hide the lessons of this Psalm in our hearts as we continue in our journey towards the Celestial City as a church.

1. Let us respond gratefully to God's faithfulness. Let us take heed to the Lord's word always to cultivate gratitude in our own heart and the heart of our children.

2. Let us refuse to rebel like Ephraim. It is easy to give in to expediency and convenience and fall into the sin of the Northern Kingdom—to worship God according to man's invention rather than God's appointment.

3. Let us remember our tendency to be like our fathers. We are a forgetful and ungrateful people. Let us not crave the leeks and cucumbers of Egypt. Hitherto has the Lord led us! Shall we despise His mercy and faithfulness and refuse to serve Him cheerfully?

4. Let us relish the love of God for our King's sake. Christ is the King of the Church. Let us look to Him constantly, thanking God that we can be His Judah, His kinsmen, to share in the blessings that God has given Him to bestow upon His people. Let us therefore run the race, looking unto Him, the Author and Finisher of our faith, knowing that with Him as the Captain of our salvation, the gates of hell shall not prevent our advance from glory unto glory despite all our failures. Amen. Ω

Psalm 79:
The Righteous One's
Plea with and for Widowed Zion

Psalm 79 is closely related to Psalm 74. Both of these Psalms are about the destruction of Jerusalem. It is attributed to Asaph. It is possible that Asaph the Seer, who lived in David's time, was writing prophetically about the destruction of the temple (v. 1). But the temple was not even built yet.

Therefore, more probably, this Asaph refers to a member of the musical guild known as the "sons of Asaph" (1 Chr 25:1). This Asaph must have written Psalm 79 sometime after 586 BC when the Babylonians destroyed the temple at Jerusalem, and slaughtered many of the Jews.

Andrew Bonar has a beautiful title for this Psalm. He calls it "The Cry of Widowed Zion to the Righteous Judge." For consistency, and to highlight the fact that the Psalms are kingdom songs meant for us to sing in union with Christ as our chief singer, we may call it: *"The Righteous One's Plea with and For Widowed Zion."* It is a Psalm which the Church may sing whenever she reflects on her impoverished and aggrieved state.

It has three parts:

1. v. 1-4   Lament over Jerusalem
2. v. 5-6   Plea for Divine Interposition
3. v. 7-13   Arguments to Support the Plea

1. Lament over Jerusalem

[1] O God, the heathen are come into thine inheritance; thy holy temple have they defiled; they have laid Jerusalem on heaps.

Jerusalem was the holy city. It symbolised the Church and pointed to God's special love for His people. The temple, likewise, represented the Church and God's favourable presence in her through the Messiah.

But beginning from 606 BC, the Babylonians began to oppress Jerusalem and her residents. The wicked King Jehoiakim was on the throne in those days. Nebuchadnezzar had him arrested and sent to exile to Babylon together with many others including the Prophet Daniel. Most of the implements of worship found in God's temple were also carried away then.

In 597 BC, another group of Jews including the Prophet Ezekiel was sent to exile.

But it was in 586 BC, that the worst atrocities were perpetrated. In that year, the Babylonians burned down the temple, looted the palaces, sent many to exile, while massacring most of the rest of the people.

There were so many dead bodies in Jerusalem that they could not be cleared, and their blood soaked the ground of Jerusalem everywhere, verse 2:

[2] The dead bodies of thy servants have they given to be meat unto the fowls of the heaven, the flesh of thy saints unto the beasts of the earth. [3] Their blood have they shed like water round about Jerusalem; and there was none to bury them.

What a tragedy! What sadness! How and where could the people of God find comfort in such times? They could find it only in the presence of the LORD, especially when they come before Him in prayer and the singing of Psalms.

Now, the event recorded in this Psalm happened a long time ago. But is not this Psalm still relevant to us? Even if we do not experience the same atrocities recorded in this Psalm, do we not from time to time suffer calamities of one sort or another in the Church? Are there not the relationship flare-ups that leave many hurting? Are there not the court cases, which leave bodies as it were in the streets for all to see? Are there not times when the heathen ridiculed the people of God? Are there not times, when we are confounded by what happened within the congregation: such as when suicide or a shameful crime is committed by one of us? Do we not experience the shame that our fathers in the faith endured?

⁴ *We are become a reproach to our neighbours, a scorn and derision to them that are round about us.*

Shall we not, at such times learn to pray as our King teaches us to? Shall we not unite our hearts to sing with Him this Psalm, which He has appointed for us to use at such a time?

Shall we not plead with the LORD according to the second part of this Psalm?

2. Plea for Interposition

⁵ *How long, LORD? wilt thou be angry for ever? shall thy jealousy burn like fire?* ⁶ *Pour out thy wrath upon the heathen that have not known thee, and upon the kingdoms that have not called upon thy name.*

Very often when the people of God experience great troubles, it is because God is angry. Like a father who loves his children, God does get angry with us when we walk in disobedience, when we fear Him not, or when we squabble with one another.

Sometimes in His anger, God would chastise His people. Very often He would chastise them by afflicting them through the heathen. Israel, the Northern Kingdom in Old Testament days was chastised by Assyria. Judah, in the south was chastised by Babylon.

The prophet Habakkuk was perplexed by why the LORD who is of purer eyes than to behold evil, should make use of a people more wicked than His own, to chastise them. God's answer was that the just shall live by faith alone. God's people who sin grievously, despite knowing God's word, cannot claim to be better than the heathen.

But the faithful remnant of God's people can always cry to the Father. When under affliction, we may always pray: *"How long, LORD?"* We must not pray with impatience; but we must pray with importunity. We must plead with the LORD to show mercy to His people, to deliver them, and to recompense the heathen who take advantage of the situation.

But on what basis may we pray, when we know that the troubles that have come upon us, are in some ways brought about by our own sin, in the first place?

Our Lord gives us six arguments to confess in the final part of this Psalm.

3. Arguments to Support the Plea

The Lord Himself and James teach us that when we pray, we must pray with faith (Mt 21:22; Jas 1:6). The Apostle John teaches us that when we pray according to God's will, God will hear us and give us the desire of our hearts (1 Jn 5:14-15). This is why it is important for us to learn the art of using godly arguments in prayer. When we use arguments, we assure ourselves that our prayer is in accordance to God's will, and we strengthen our faith that

God will hear our cries.

What then are the arguments that our Lord would have us to appeal with Him in His prayer, on behalf of God's people, suffering on account of their sin?

The first argument is an appeal for mercy on the basis of the extent and intensity of the affliction of God's people. Jacob has been devoured and his dwelling place has been laid waste (v. 7). We may enlarge the cry thus: "Thy people have suffered greatly. They have not only been afflicted, they have been devoured. The very land which they must depend on for their life has been laid waste. Have mercy, O Lord!"

The second argument is a plea for speedy deliverance on the basis that those who are presently suffering, are not those who bear primary responsibility for the iniquities that brought God's wrath. *"O remember not against us former iniquities [or the iniquities of our fathers]"* (v. 8). Is it not true that the church often suffers for the sin of a few individuals, who would often walk away after creating the havoc?

The third argument is an appeal to the glory of God before the heathen.

⁹ Help us, O God of our salvation, for the glory of thy name: and deliver us, and purge away our sins, for thy name's sake. ¹⁰ Wherefore should the heathen say, Where is their God? let him be known among the heathen in our sight by the revenging of the blood of thy servants which is shed.

God's name is closely tied to the prosperity of His people. When the heathen mock God's people, they blaspheme God's name. Therefore, God's people can always plead to God to defend His own name.

The fourth argument is an appeal to the LORD's compassion. *"Let the sighing of the prisoner come before thee..."* (v. 11). Our heavenly Father is "full of compassion, and gracious, longsuffering, and plenteous in mercy and truth" (Ps 86:15). As God's children, we can always draw near to the Father to appeal to His compassion. God, of course, does not forget, nor does He change. But He is pleased when His people acknowledge the same in prayer.

Finally, in conclusion to the whole Psalm, we are given to appeal to the hope that God's people will have occasions to praise God.

¹³ So we thy people and sheep of thy pasture will give thee thanks for ever: we will shew forth thy praise to all generations.

The glory of God is the chief end of man, and of the Church. Therefore, let us be mindful to appeal to God's glory with a desire to glorify Him in our petitions before His throne of grace.

Conclusion

The word of God, history and our own experience have shown that there will always be occasions for the LORD's chastisement. We are, after all, a body of sinners saved by grace. We have the privilege of relating to God because God's Son has paid for our sin. But it pleases God that the Spirit should not make us perfect in this life. Therefore, we will sin. And as a people, we are prone to wander, bent on backsliding.

As such, this Psalm will never cease to be relevant to us until the Perfect Day. Until then, shall we not gladly use it and learn from it how to plead with God for restoration? Amen. Ω

Psalm 80:
The Righteous One's
"Turn Us Again, O God!"

Psalm 80 is another Psalm of Asaph. As with Psalms 74 and 79, it was probably written after 586 BC when the Babylonians razed Jerusalem.

Is Psalm 80 a Messianic Psalm? Curiously, it has not made it to the list of 13 Psalms considered to be Messianic by many commentators. However, it will be quite hard for any untrained reader or singer of this Psalm *not* to see a reference to Christ in verse 17:

> "Let thy hand be upon the man of thy right hand, upon the son of man whom thou madest strong for thyself" (Ps 80:17).

Who is this man of God's right hand? Who is this son of man? Some commentators suggest that it referred to a temporal king reigning at that time.[33] Others argue that the man of God's right hand refers to "Benjamin" whose name means "son of my right hand"; whereas "son of man" refers to Israel as a nation.

But it would seem much more intuitive to see in the terms a reference to Christ who is in a figure seated at the right hand of the throne of God today, and who always referred to Himself as the "son of man" during His incarnation. Whether or not the terms had a reference to a type of Christ at the time the Psalm was written is not really the most important point. The point is they appear to have ultimate reference to the Lord Jesus Christ. Thus, "Many interpreters, both Jewish and Christian," says Matthew Henry, "apply this to the Messiah, the Son of David, the protector and Saviour of the church and the keeper of the vineyard."

The Church Father Augustine, for example, says: "The song here is of the Advent of the Lord and of our Savior Jesus Christ, and of His vineyard."[34] Dr JA Alexander suggests that the words *"let thy hand be upon"* can be understood as implying favour or wrath, and adds that "The only way in which both senses can be reconciled is by applying the words to the Messiah, as the ground of the faith and hope expressed. Let thy hand fall not on us but on our substitute."[35] It is no wonder that WS Plumer could assert that "the best commentators admit that this refers to Christ."[36]

We may entitle this Psalm *"The Righteous One's 'Turn Us Again, O God!'"* This is a Psalm which we may especially use when as a church we experience God's severe chastisement as Israel of old did. But it is also a Psalm for all ages and times, for us to sing in union with our King, for there will never be a time when the Church Visible is not suffering and not in need of repentance. That will have to wait till the day of our King's return.

It is not difficult to see the three natural strophes in this Psalm, for each one ends with a refrain that begins with the words, "Turn us again, O God" (cf. v. 3, v. 7 and v. 19). In the first strophe (v. 1-3), we see a plea that God would hear the cry of His saints. In the second strophe (v. 4-7), we see an expression of the longing of the people. Finally, in the third strophe (v. 8-

---

[33] Though if our dating of this psalm is correct, King Zedekiah has already been sent into exile.

[34] Augustine, *op. cit.*, 386

[35] JA Alexander, *Comm. in loc.*

[36] For a scholarly, though meandering discussion that ultimately leads to the same conclusion, see O. Palmer Robertson, *The Flow of the Psalms: Discovering their Structure and Theology* (Phillipsburg: P&R Publishing, 2015), 132-4.

19), we have a petition for full restoration argued upon our union with the Son of Man.

We may study this Psalm briefly with an outline based on the key words that occur in each of the three strophes:

1. v. 1-3   "Give Ear" (v. 1)
2. v. 4-7   "How Long?" (v. 4)
3. v. 8-19   "Visit this Vine" (v. 14)

1. Give Ear

[1] *Give ear, O Shepherd of Israel, thou that leadest Joseph like a flock; thou that dwellest between the cherubims, shine forth.* [2] *Before Ephraim and Benjamin and Manasseh stir up thy strength, and come and save us.*

Who is the Shepherd of Israel? Bishop Horne suggests that:

> The Christian Church is now become the "Israel" of God. Jesus Christ is the "Shepherd" of this Israel, who leadeth his people "like a flock;" he dwelleth in the midst of them by His spirit, as of old He dwelt in the holy places, "between the cherubims."

Well, this is a very nice thought that fits with the analogy of Scripture in which Christ is often called the Shepherd of His people. However, the content of this Psalm suggests that it is a plea to the Father in the name of the Son. As such, it is perhaps better for us to think of the Shepherd here as referring to the Father. The Father is inseparable from the Son, and indeed it is in the Son, that the Father shepherds us.

Nevertheless, we ought to cry to the Father, as the Lord Jesus teaches us to. Our Father's ears are open to our cries not because we deserve to be heard, but because of Christ our Mediator. The Father dwells, as it were, between the cherubim in the Holy of holies. But the body of Christ was broken for us that the curtain separating us from the Holy of Holies might be torn, so that we may come boldly before His throne of grace.

Like as Israel of old went to Him, so we may go to Him. We may go to Him in Christ to seek His favour and blessing. This is what the plea to "shine forth" or to cause His face to shine forth (v. 3) means. The children of God can find no greater blessedness in this life than to know that God's face is shining upon them, especially in times of distress.

But at such times, we would desire not only to know His heavenly smile, but also to know His heavenly guidance. And so we are given to cry out to Him as in verse 2, "*stir up thy strength, and come and save us.*"

During the days in the wilderness, whenever the people moved from place to place, the Ark of God would lead the way; and all the people would march in a tribal formation appointed by the LORD. The tribes Manasseh, Benjamin and Ephraim were to march together as the rear column (Num 2:20-24). They were marching in the rear because Benjamin and Joseph were the sons of Rachel and favoured by Jacob. When Jacob went to meet Esau after His exile in Paran, Joseph and Benjamin were placed last in the convoy, because Jacob wanted to ensure maximum safety for them.

This picture lends us a wonderful mental image: for though we be furthest from the favourable presence of God represented by the ark, we may know that we are there because we are most beloved.

And so when we, as a church, are in a wilderness of chastisement, we may cry out unto the

Father confidently to ask Him to make His face to shine upon us, and to lead us unto a full restoration of His blessing and joy. And so let us learn to cry with our King:

3 Turn us again, O God, and cause thy face to shine; and we shall be saved.

2. How Long?

If God loves us and we know He does, then surely, He will hear us when we come to Him to show Him the wounds in our soul that He has afflicted. I think of how a child who has received a spanking from her father, might come to him, after she has repented, to show him the weal from the spanking, and so to seek some comfort and restoration. The father who loves the child will, no doubt, be grieved by what he sees, even though the punishment had been necessary. Though he might have refused to talk to the child before, he will now hear her cries and comfort her.

And so when we have been chastised and have repented of our sin, we may go to the Father to seek His comfort and reassurance:

4 O LORD God of hosts, how long wilt thou be angry against the prayer of thy people? 5 Thou feedest them with the bread of tears; and givest them tears to drink in great measure. 6 Thou makest us a strife unto our neighbours: and our enemies laugh among themselves. 7 Turn us again, O God of hosts, and cause thy face to shine; and we shall be saved.

God is angry with the prayer of His people when they disregard His law. "If I regard iniquity in my heart, the Lord will not hear me" (Ps 66:18). "He that turneth away his ear from hearing the law, even his prayer shall be abomination" (Prov 28:9).

We will experience God's chastisement when that happens. But as soon as we repent of our sin, God opens His arms to us when we come to Him. Go to Him, therefore, with your tears. Go to Him with your grief regarding the enemies' laughter.

The Lord will hear our cries and show us again His heavenly smile. But let us go to Him not only with sorrows, but with the confidence that Christ affords.

3. Visit This Vine

Let us go to the LORD, confessing how we are a vine plucked out of Egypt, and how it was by His mercies that we were able to prosper:

8 Thou hast brought a vine out of Egypt: thou hast cast out the heathen, and planted it. 9 Thou preparedst room before it, and didst cause it to take deep root, and it filled the land. 10 The hills were covered with the shadow of it, and the boughs thereof were like the goodly cedars. 11 She sent out her boughs unto the sea, and her branches unto the river.

Go to Him also to complain about the robbers who break down our hedges, to pluck our fruits: "Why hast thou then broken down her hedges, so that all they which pass by the way do pluck her?" (v. 12). Go to Him to complain about the wild boar of the woods, that waste it: "The boar out of the wood doth waste it, and the wild beast of the field doth devour it" (v. 13). This verse became famous in the time of the Reformation, when in 1520, the Pope wrote a papal bull to excommunicate Martin Luther, calling him the wild boar which destroyed the Lord's vineyard!

But far from being the wild boar, Luther was being used by the Lord as a fellow-labourer of the vinedresser to prune the vine.

The wild boar is the devil and all that do his will, which would destroy the Church of Christ throughout the ages. We must cry unto the Father against the wild boar whenever we find him wandering into the vineyard and bringing pain and sorrow.

Then we cry with our Head, verse 14:

> Return, we beseech thee, O God of hosts: look down from heaven, and behold, and visit this vine;

Plead with the LORD for mercy, acknowledging that He is the one who planted the vine and made her to grow: "*And the vineyard which thy right hand hath planted, and the branch that thou madest strong for thyself*" (v. 15). And go to Him confessing that all the troubles that the vine experienced, have come about because we have angered Him:

> [16] *It is burned with fire, it is cut down: they perish at the rebuke of thy countenance.*

And as soon as we make that acknowledgement, let us appeal to the LORD for grace on account of our Saviour:

> [17] *Let thy hand be upon the man of thy right hand, upon the son of man whom thou madest strong for thyself.* [18] *So will not we go back from thee: quicken us, and we will call upon thy name.*

Who is this man of God's right hand or the son of man, but the Lord Jesus Christ, the Captain of our salvation? It is in His strength that we are strong. It is because He deserves God's blessings that we are blessed. Matthew Henry puts it beautifully when he says:

> The stability and constancy of believers are entirely owing to the grace and strength which are laid up for us in Jesus Christ, Ps 68:28. In Him is our strength found, by which we are enabled to persevere to the end.

The Father will, no doubt, not lift His hand of blessings that is upon His Son our Lord. But let us humbly plead with Him, nevertheless, to keep His hand there, in recognition of the fact that we can receive no blessing, but through Christ, to whom we are united by faith. And so let us plead that God may quicken us, that we may have faith to believe, and to walk in newness of life.

Do we not need to pray this prayer often? We are so prone to wander, so bent on backsliding. Shall we not come to Him to seek His strength through Christ, whenever we find ourselves wandering and fruitless?

Shall we not plead once again:

> [19] *Turn us again, O LORD God of hosts, cause thy face to shine; and we shall be saved.*

Conclusion

Christ loves His Church Universal, but we cannot love the Church Universal until we love the church local. What will you do when you see that there are great needs in the church? Will you not come to the Lord often to pray, to plead with the Father, as the Lord has taught us in this Psalm?

Let us not only pour out our complaints. Let us pour it out in recognition of our own failures, and how we deserve God's chastisement. But let us also confidently plead God's intervention for the sake of His Son. The church, we must remember, belongs not to the elders or pastors. She belongs to Christ. We can always plead His name as we call unto the Father to turn us again, to revive and restore us that we may bear more fruit for His glory. Amen. Ω

Psalm 81:
The Righteous One's
"O My People!"

Psalm 81 is another Psalm of Asaph. We have no reason to think that this is any other than "Asaph the Seer" (2 Chr 29:30) who lived during David's time. And this Psalm, like Psalm 75, which was clearly edited or set by Asaph the Seer, is also unusual in its use of the first person pronouns.

Who are the "I"s and "we"s in this Psalm? A variety of views is offered by commentators. Most will say that from verse 6 onwards, the speaker is God. But the "selah" which divides the Psalm into two is in verse 7! This means that if we take this view, then in the first division of this Psalm, we have confusion of first person pronouns. One moment the "we" and "I" is Asaph or Israel; and the next moment it is God! There is, after all, no indication that verse 6 onwards is to be understood as a quotation rather than the direct words of the speaker in verse 5.

Much more satisfying is the view of Andrew Bonar:

> In the first verses, is it the voice of Israel we hear? Is it not rather the voice of the Church's Head and Israel's, identifying Himself with us and them? Is it not Messiah, the lawgiver and redeemer of Israel? To understand the speaker throughout to be He, gives beautiful unity and force to the whole.

This then is how we will expound this Psalm. This is probably the least confusing and arbitrary, and biblically the most natural approach. Christ, the God-Man alone can speak as one with His people, or as the LORD of His people.

It is thought that this Psalm was written for the celebration of the Passover; or as Luther supposed, for the Feast of Tabernacles. However, as W.S. Plumer puts it, "the fact is, this ode is fit to be sung on any joyous occasion of worship in Israel."

We may entitle this Psalm *"The Righteous One's 'O My People!'"* or more fully, "The Righteous One's Remonstration to His People to be Faithful & Grateful." This is one of those Psalms which is heavy in admonishment: which is given to the Church that we may, in union with Christ, admonish one another with His word (cf. Col 3:16). It has, as we mentioned, two parts. From verses 1-7, we see the Lord, the Righteous One calling His people to grateful and faithful worship. From verses 8-16, we have a warning by the Lord of the consequence of ingratitude and unfaithfulness. An expository outline would then be:

1. v. 1-7   Call to Gratitude and Faithfulness
2. v. 8-16   Warning Against Ingratitude and Unfaithfulness

1. Call to Gratitude
& Faithfulness

¹ Sing aloud unto God our strength: make a joyful noise unto the God of Jacob. ² Take a psalm, and bring hither the timbrel, the pleasant harp with the psaltery. ³ Blow up the trumpet in the new moon, in the time appointed, on our solemn feast day.

Christ our covenant Head is one with us. When we worship the Father, our worship is only acceptable if it is offered in His name and in union with Him. When He says, "*Sing aloud unto God our strength*," He is calling us, is He not, to worship God in union with Him?

Now, in Old Testament days, the people would worship the LORD with musical instruments. Four kinds of instruments were used in the temple in formal worship: cymbals, psaltery, harp and trumpets (2 Chr 29:25; 1 Chr 25:6; 2 Chr 5:12). Timbrels were used in more informal occasions (e.g. Ex 15:20; Jdg 11:34). But these instruments were no longer used in New Testament worship. The Apostle Paul teaches us to strum our heartstrings. This is the literal meaning of Paul's call to "[make] melody in your heart to the Lord" (Eph 5:19).

We must, therefore, obey our Lord's call not by way of taking up musical instruments for worship, but rather by heartily and joyfully singing unto the Lord; and perhaps as Augustine suggests to us, by loudly and boldly preaching the word of God. "Be not affrighted!" he says, for "as the prophet says in a certain place, 'Cry out, and lift up as with a trumpet thy voice.'"

We must worship the Father both in private and in public, in obedience and grateful response to all that the Lord has done for us. As the Lord puts it, verse 4:

> [4] *For this was a statute for Israel, and a law of the God of Jacob.* [5] *This he ordained in Joseph for a testimony, when he went out through the land of Egypt: where I heard a language that I understood not.* [6] *I removed his shoulder from the burden: his hands were delivered from the pots.* [7] *Thou calledst in trouble, and I delivered thee; I answered thee in the secret place of thunder: I proved thee at the waters of Meribah. Selah.*

God's people should serve Him in grateful obedience because this is what the Lord appointed for them to do after His mighty act of redeeming them (v. 4-6). They were in bondage in Egypt. It was a foreign land. The people spoke a foreign language. The Jews in their enclave in Goshen continued largely to speak in Hebrew. Our Lord identifying with the people spoke of the Egyptian language as a language He understood not (v. 5).

But He heard the cries of His people and delivered them. He led them in the wilderness. He provided water for them out of the rock despite the people's ingratitude and grumbling. This is why the place was called Meribah (v. 7, cf. Num 20:11). "Meribah" means "strife." There at Meribah, Moses, in anger struck the rock, which symbolised Christ Himself (1 Cor 10:4). Despite that, the LORD gave them water, though Moses forfeited his privilege of entering the Promised Land.

All these have symbolic and typical significance. The Apostle Paul says: "Now all these things happened unto them for examples: and they are written for our admonition, upon whom the ends of the world are come" (1 Cor 10:11). As God redeemed His people of old out of Egypt, so He has redeemed us out of spiritual bondage to sin and Satan. As He was longsuffering towards His people of old despite their sin, murmuring and ingratitude, so He is longsuffering towards us. Indeed, Christ our Lord was punished for our sin that we may enjoy life abundant and free without being bogged down by guilt.

What would be a reasonable response for us, but to praise Him and worship Him gratefully and joyfully with our lips and our life according to His commandments? *"Sing aloud unto God our strength: make a joyful noise unto the God of Jacob"* (v. 1).

We shall, no doubt, enjoy God's heavenly favour and blessing when we respond to His love in this way. But knowing our propensity to backsliding, let us take heed to the Lord's warning:

2. Warning Against Ingratitude & Unfaithfulness

[8] *Hear, O my people, and I will testify unto thee: O Israel, if thou wilt hearken unto me;* [9]

There shall no strange god be in thee; neither shalt thou worship any strange god. ¹⁰ I am the LORD thy God, which brought thee out of the land of Egypt: open thy mouth wide, and I will fill it.

When our LORD led Israel out of Egypt, He led them to Mount Sinai where He gave them the Ten Commandments in their hearing. He reminded them that He was the LORD their God who brought them out of Egypt and charged them that they should have no other gods before Him, and gave them nine other commandments.

If they would walk in His ways, they would be His people, and He would be their God. He would fill their mouth, however wide they open it. He would bless them exceedingly abundantly above all they could ask or think. But sadly the people refused to hear His voice. Wickedly, they ignored God. And so the LORD decided to give them over to their own evil inclination that they might taste the sorrow of walking lawlessly and without the Lord's favour (v. 11-12).

What was our LORD's attitude towards His people's rebellion? Did He entertain a vindictive, serve-them-right attitude? No, no; far from it. Our Lord was, no doubt, grieved:

> ¹³ *Oh that my people had hearkened unto me, and Israel had walked in my ways! ¹⁴ I should soon have subdued their enemies, and turned my hand against their adversaries. ¹⁵ The haters of the LORD should have submitted themselves unto him: but their time should have endured forever. ¹⁶ He should have fed them also with the finest of the wheat: and with honey out of the rock should I have satisfied thee.*

Consider how similar in tone these words are to our Lord's lament recorded in the Gospel:

> "O Jerusalem, Jerusalem, thou that killest the prophets, and stonest them which are sent unto thee, how often would I have gathered thy children together, even as a hen gathereth her chickens under her wings, and ye would not!" (Mt 23:37).

If these words were spoken by the Father, we would speak of the sentiment of regret and longing as "anthropopathic." But our Lord has a human nature in order that He might be our compassionate High Priest. He was tempted in all points like as we are, yet without sin.

His longing for us is actual and literal. As He longed for the people of old to enjoy His blessings by way of grateful obedience; so He, no doubt, longs the same for us.

Conclusion

When we sing this Psalm and hear it being sung, let us remind ourselves of our Lord's longing for us. He paid for our redemption from Egypt with His own blood. He suffered the pains of hell for us that we may begin to experience heaven today and forever.

We will never enjoy heaven tomorrow if we do not begin to enjoy God today. How to enjoy God today? By walking according to God's way in worship and life (v. 12). If we stubbornly continue to walk in our own ways (v. 13), we shall not only experience our Lord's chastisement, but we shall experience the fruit of sorrow of our own doing.

Oh may we not take a new look at our own life! What are some things we have to change? What are some priorities we have to set right? Let us courageously make the changes with the Lord's help. Then shall we know a new joy in worship; then shall we enjoy the Lord's blessing in a way we have never experienced. "But seek ye first the kingdom of God, and his righteousness; and all these things shall be added unto you," says our Lord (Mt 6:33). Amen.
Ω

Psalm 82:
The Righteous One's
Solemn Charge as the Judge of Judges

In John 10, we have a record of the Jews confronting the Lord Jesus about who He is. "If thou be the Christ, tell us plainly," they charge (v. 24).

The Lord Jesus admonishes them saying that He has already told them so, but they would not believe. They would not believe, He tells them, because they are not His sheep. His sheep would hear His voice and follow Him. But in order to make sure they understand clearly who He is claiming to be, our Lord adds: "I and *my* Father are one" (v. 30).

This time, the Jews catch it, for they immediately take up stones to stone Him (v. 31).

The Lord asks them with a holy sarcasm: "Many good works have I shewed you from my Father; for which of those works do ye stone me?" (v. 32).

The reason I say it is sarcasm is because I believe the Lord knew that they were not stoning Him for good works, but really for claiming He is God.

And they confirm it by saying: "For a good work we stone thee not; but for blasphemy; and because that thou, being a man, makest thyself God" (v. 33).

The Jews understood that the Lord is claiming to be God.

But at this point the Lord says something rather mysterious:

> "Is it not written in your law, I said, Ye are gods? [35] If he called them gods, unto whom the word of God came, and the scripture cannot be broken; [36] Say ye of him, whom the Father hath sanctified, and sent into the world, Thou blasphemest; because I said, I am the Son of God?" (Jn 10:34-36).

Now, those who deny the deity of Christ, will pluck out what the Lord says here and exclaim: "There you have it: the Lord Himself is disclaiming deity. The Jews had jumped to the wrong conclusion. Claiming to be equal with the Father, and claiming to be the Son of God are not the same as claiming to be God!"

But is this what the Lord is saying? Well, no; not at all! Our Lord is not disclaiming deity, or the whole passage will make no sense, and it will make our Lord guilty of double-talk.

No, if you think about it carefully, you will realise that what the Lord is really telling the Jews, is that they ought not to stone Him merely because of what He says, for words can easily be misunderstood. They should rather consider what He is doing. So He adds:

> [37] If I do not the works of my Father, believe me not. [38] But if I do, though ye believe not me, believe the works: that ye may know, and believe, that the Father *is* in me, and I in him.

But now the deity of Christ is not really the direct subject of our study. Rather, we came to this incident because the words "I said, Ye are gods," which our Lord quoted comes from this Psalm.

We shall perhaps understand better what the words he quoted mean as we study this Psalm together. But we may entitle it *"The Righteous One's Solemn Charge as the Judge of Judges."*

This Psalm has an interesting structure. It paints the scene where the Chief Judge, the Judge of judges, addresses the judges or the magistrates of the world before a congregation. It begins with an introductory statement that sets the scene.

¹ God standeth in the congregation of the mighty; he judgeth among the gods.

This is followed by the speech of the Chief Justice, and concludes with a rejoinder by the congregation to call upon the Judge to arise to execute justice.

⁸ Arise, O God, judge the earth: for thou shalt inherit all nations.

Who is this Chief Justice, who is also called God, and would inherit all nations?

He is, no doubt, the one whom the Father addresses in Psalm 45:6:

"Thy throne, O God, is for ever and ever: the sceptre of thy kingdom is a right [or righteous] sceptre" (cf. Heb 1:8).

He is the one to whom the Father tells in Psalm 2:8:

"Ask of me, and I shall give thee the heathen for thine inheritance, and the uttermost parts of the earth for thy possession" (Ps 2:8).

He is the one to whom the judgement of the world is committed (Jn 5:22).

Who is He, but the only begotten Son of God, the Messiah? "For the Father judgeth no man, but hath committed all judgment unto the Son" (Jn 5:22).

So the picture here is that of Messiah the Judge addressing the judges of the earth. These are called "mighty" as they are the powerful men of society. They also are called "gods" in verses 1 and 6. Why are they called "gods"? Not because they are truly gods, for there is but one living and true God only. Rather, it is because they are representatives of God. They are the magistrates or ministers of the sword ordained by God to execute justice in the world (Rom 13:1ff).

They are supposed to act as the conscience of society, the deputy of God in the soul of the world. They are to judge the world and steer the world in the right way today, before the Day of Judgement.

Unfortunately, these deputies of God, or ministers of the sword, often fail in their duty, and must be summoned before the Judge of judges to be admonished by the Chief Justice.

Now, of course, this meeting does not actually happen today. There will indeed be a day when the judges will have to give an account of what they have done, but in that day there will be no more opportunity for them to repent and to correct their failures.

What then is this Psalm about? Well, this Psalm serves two purposes. First, it is for the Church to cry out unto the Lord to arise to vindicate His people (v. 8). Secondly, it is for the very purpose of the meeting painted in it. It is for God's people, to stand in union with Christ in song, to admonish the judges and civil magistrates of the land.

Now, of course, in today's secular and pluralistic society, the judges and magistrates will hardly get the opportunity to hear this Psalm. Does this mean that we should therefore not sing it? Of course not!

What it means is that all the more, we should promote it and make it known, especially if we find injustice being tolerated in the land.

But other than that, as we sing this Psalm to admonish one another, we remind ourselves that our Lord is the Lord of justice. He hates injustice and unfairness. He loves justice and righteousness. And so we are reminded to practice justice and fairness in all spheres of our life—at home, at work, in school and in church.

Likewise, we are reminded to pray for our civil and church government that there be justice and fairness. And again, we are given the assurance that our Lord is not blind to the injustice and unfairness that we suffer in this life. Rather, He will hear our cries. He will arise and vindicate His people when they are unfairly treated in this world, especially when it is for His name's sake.

Essentially, the Lord does three things. First, He accuses the unjust judges (v. 2); secondly, He commands them to do what is right (v. 3-5); and thirdly, He warns them of judgement against them (v. 6-7). Thus an expository outline for the whole Psalm would be:

0. v. 1   The Courtroom
1. v. 2   The Accusation
2. v. 3-5   The Command
3. v. 6-7   The Warning
4. v. 8   The Rejoinder

We have already considered the opening and closing verses. Let us now look briefly at what the Lord would say to the judges of the world.

1. The Accusation

² How long will ye judge unjustly, and accept the persons of the wicked?

Now, this is not really a question. It is an accusation!

The judges have perverted justice. They have accepted bribes, and freed the wicked and guilty at the expense of those who were taken advantage of. The rich and connected are let off for serious crimes whereas the poor and lonely are severely punished for a loaf of bread.

The Lord is asking: How long are you going to continue doing what you are doing?

Don't you know that I see? "Can any hide himself in secret places that I shall not see him?" (Jer 23:24).

Don't you know that though I appear to tolerate what you are doing, I am angered by your failures? For "*It is* not good to accept the person of the wicked, to overthrow the righteous in judgment" (Prov 18:5).

Don't you know that you are storing up "wrath against the day of wrath" (Rom 2:5)?

"How long will ye imagine mischief against a man?" (Ps 62:3)

"How long wilt thou refuse to humble thyself before me?" (Ex 10:3)

How long will it be before you begin to do that which is right?

There is yet time for you to repent before my patience runs out. Oh will you not cease from your wickedness!

2. The Command

³ Defend the poor and fatherless: do justice to the afflicted and needy. ⁴ Deliver the poor and needy: rid them out of the hand of the wicked. ⁵ *They [the wicked] know not, neither will they understand; they walk on in darkness: all the foundations of the earth are out of course.*

The judges and magistrates of the land are appointed by the LORD to be ministers of God, not to be "a terror to good works, but to the evil" (Rom 13:3).

As such, they have a duty to defend and deliver the poor, the fatherless, the needy, and the afflicted, who are being oppressed by the wicked.

The judges' eyes should be opened to their plight, and their ears should be opened to their cries, just as our heavenly Father sees our grief and hears our cries.

The wicked, on the other hand, do not care. They are blinded in their ease, their pride and their wealth. They walk in darkness. Selfishly, they turn the natural course of justice, and the order and compassion of society upside down. In this way, they destroy the foundations of the moral fabric, and the law, and order of society.

Justice as a result is denied for the righteous. "If the foundations be destroyed, what can the righteous do?" (Ps 11:3). The society becomes lawless. Children are taught not that honesty pays, but that crime and deceit are fair game. Honesty and righteousness get you nowhere, they are taught. You got to learn to be shrewd. You got to learn to look after yourself.

The society begins to crumble when that happens. We think of how this has happened in so many places in the world. We think of the situation in parts of Mexico, Somalia, Zimbabwe, Nicaragua, Congo, parts of India and Pakistan, etc.

Those who are called to be judges and magistrates in the land, must take heed to uphold a high standard of justice, or they would be instrumental in the destruction of the nation. And not only so, they would also have to answer to the Lord, the King of kings, and Judge of judges.

This is the warning that our Lord would have us join Him to issue.

3. The Warning

⁶ *I have said, Ye are gods; and all of you are children of the most High.* ⁷ *But ye shall die like men, and fall like one of the princes.*

When our Lord appoints judges and magistrates, they are appointed as His ministers whether they are conscious of it or not. They are vested with great powers. They are called, as it were, "gods". They are given great privileges like the *"children of the most High."*

But privileges come with responsibilities; and a failure to fulfil responsibility, comes with the LORD's chastisement or punishment.

The mighty judges and leaders of this world will all die. They will die like all men. They must not forget that. Every prince in this world, however great, has fallen and died.

Some have died terrible deaths that bear the marks of divine judgement (cf. 2Chr 21:18-19; Acts 12:23). Others have died less violently. But regardless of how they died, they will have to come before the Judge, before whom they have to give an account of what they had done with the great power vested upon them in their office.

Let all who aspire to positions of power take heed to the Lord's remonstration.

Let all who have been unjustly afflicted, cry out unto the LORD as in the final words of this Psalm:

"Arise, O God, judge the earth: for thou shalt inherit all nations" (Ps 82:8).

May the Lord of justice whose ears are open to the cries of the widows and fatherless, hear our cries and vindicate His people!

Conclusion

The God of gods, the Judge of judges has spoken. We have been admonished. We have been encouraged. How shall we respond apart from conveying His message to the world by singing His words? But beyond that, shall we not pray that God will raise up more righteous and godly leaders in our land? Shall we not pray for our existing leaders? It does not take much for the devil to tempt an unbelieving judge or magistrate to commit injustice so long as it can be done secretly. Therefore, if we are given the opportunity, shall we not render any assistance we may, to believers in the world who are persecuted for their faith because of evil judges and magistrates in their country. May the Lord help us! Amen. Ω

Psalm 83:
The Righteous One's
Plea for the Hidden Ones

Psalm 83 is an imprecatory Psalm with a twist. It is the prayer of the Church, led by her Head,[37] to the covenant God to deal with their enemies who had risen up against them. It is a prayer to punish the enemies; but at the same time, it is a prayer to convert them! This is the twist.

In this Psalm, we will find some specific enemies of Israel, the Church underage, mentioned explicitly. These were the enemies of the Church when Asaph or one of the sons of Asaph prepared the Psalm for singing. But all believers and the Church throughout the ages may use this Psalm meaningfully in our spiritual battles that in this life.

As Bishop George Horne puts it:

> While the world endureth, there will be a church, and while there is a church, she will have her enemies, who are to increase upon her as the end approacheth, [therefore] this Psalm can never be out of date. And to the spiritual adversaries of his soul every private Christian may apply it at all times.

We may entitle this Psalm "*The Righteous One's Plea for the Hidden Ones.*" The saints are called the "hidden ones" in verse 3. We will see why in a moment.

This Psalm has two parts, divided by the "Selah". The first part (v. 1-8) is a call to the LORD to arise to deal with the enemies. It contains a plea to the LORD, and then paints the background for the call for intervention. The second part (v. 9-18) contains five specific petitions, each of which is augmented with a reason for the petition, or an elaboration of the petition.

1. v. 1-8   The Plea to Arise
2. v. 9-18   The Petitions to Destroy & Build Up

1. The Plea to Arise

¹ Keep not thou silence, O God: hold not thy peace, and be not still, O God. ² For, lo, thine enemies make a tumult: and they that hate thee have lifted up the head.

The enemies of the Church are the enemies of God, for the Church is married to Christ, the Son of God. She is His bride. He is her husband. Therefore, her enemies are God's enemies. Those who hate her hate God.

We need not be ashamed to speak of those who persecute or seek to destroy the Church as the haters of God. We need not be inhibited to ask God to arise for our defence and vindication when His enemies appear to be plotting against us. Thus, our Head would have us join Him to complain to the Father:

³ They have taken crafty counsel against thy people, and consulted against thy hidden ones.

"God's people are his hidden ones, hidden," says Matthew Henry,...

"(1) In respect of secrecy. Their life is *hid with Christ in God; the world knows them not; if*

---

[37] See the first person singular pronoun in verse 13.

they knew them, they would not hate them as they do. (2) In respect of safety. God takes them under his special protection, hides them in the hollow of his hand."

It is "in defiance of God and his power and promise to secure his people" that the enemies of God conspire to put them to shame. Because ultimately they hate God, "they resolve to destroy those whom God resolves to preserve."

In the days of Asaph, they sought to obliterate the nation of Israel (v. 4). They were a disparate group of people who would generally have nothing to do with one another. There were Edomites, Ishmaelites, Hagarenes, Gebalites, Amalekites, Philistines, the Phoenicians, the Assyrians, and the children of Lot, Moabites and Ammonites (v. 5-8).

Never mind that some of them were related to Israel. Never mind that they did not know each other. Never mind that they were at odds with one another. What mattered was that they had a common enemy: God and His favoured people.

Is it not often the case that those who have a common enemy become friends? But when their enemy is God, their marriage is but a marriage of convenience with no commitment and love.

It was so during the earthly ministry of the Lord too. Pharisees and Sadducees would normally have nothing to do with one another for one is legalistic separatists, while the other is liberal. And yet they went together to tempt the Lord (Mt 16:1). Likewise, the Herodians would have nothing to do with the Pharisees who opposed the Roman occupation, and yet they could gang up to try to trap the Lord (Mk 12:13). Need we mention about Pilate and Herod who "were made friends together" when before "they were at enmity between themselves" (Lk 23:12)?

Today, is not the problem the same? Abortionists, evolutionists, atheists, gay rights activists, embryonic stem cell advocates, and liberal film stars and rock musicians—these may have little to do with one another, but they have a common enemy: the Lawgiver and His Church which tries to hinder progress in their eyes.

Is there not an almost concerted attempt to blot out true religion—through education, government, publication, entertainment, etc? What can God's people do against this onslaught? We must educate and we must pray.

We may ask God to arise in defence of His people and His own name. We may also pray specific petitions like as we are given to do in the second part of this Psalm.

2. The Petitions to Destroy & Build Up

Here are five petitions:

- Firstly, recompense them for their wickedness:

⁹ Do unto them as unto the Midianites; as to Sisera, as to Jabin, at the brook of Kison: ¹⁰ Which perished at Endor: they became as dung for the earth.

The Midianites had conspired with the Moabites to destroy Israel by seducing the men (Num 25:6). The Canaanite King Jabin conquered the Israelites, and his captain Sisera, "mightily oppressed" them for twenty years (Jdg 4:2-3). God rose up in judgement against them during the time of Moses (Num 25:16-17), and during the time of Balak and Deborah, when a woman by the name of Jael was used by the LORD to execute justice on Sisera (Jdg 4:21).

- Secondly, deal with their leaders sternly:

> ¹¹ *Make their nobles like Oreb, and like Zeeb: yea, all their princes as Zebah, and as Zalmunna:* ¹² *Who said, Let us take to ourselves the houses of God in possession.*

Again Oreb and Zeeb were Midianite princes (Jdg 8:3); and Zeba and Zalmunna were Midianite kings (Jdg 8:12ff). They hated Israel and incurred the judgement of God through Gideon.

- Thirdly, frustrate their plans:

> ¹³ *O my God, make them like a wheel [i.e. tumbleweed]; as the stubble [or chaff] before the wind.* ¹⁴ *As the fire burneth a wood, and as the flame setteth the mountains on fire;* ¹⁵ *So persecute them with thy tempest, and make them afraid with thy storm.*

These who exalt themselves and are puffed up against God's people, have caused hurt and sorrow amongst God's people. But God can destroy them as by fire, or make them ineffective in all that they do so that they become like tumbleweed and chaff in their attempts to destroy the Church. God can also cause them to feel what the Church experienced, even persecution in the face of a frightening storm.

- But fourthly, humble them to seek Thee:

> ¹⁶ *Fill their faces with shame; that they may seek thy name, O LORD.*

Now, this is the twist of this Psalm. We may pray that the LORD will deal strongly with His and our enemies. But we should also have compassion for them!

So it must be our desire to see repentance on the part of God's enemies that they may seek the LORD and be converted. We must not entertain the attitude of Jonah who wanted only to see the destruction of Nineveh. We must long for the repentance even of God's enemies.

- But what if they remain stubborn? Then consider the fifth petition, namely, confound them that others may take warning:

> ¹⁷ *Let them be confounded and troubled for ever; yea, let them be put to shame, and perish:* ¹⁸ *That men may know that thou, whose name alone is JEHOVAH, art the most high over all the earth.*

We must ask the LORD to deal firmly with all who remain stubborn and hardened in rebellion, so that others may take warning and know that there is a living and true God, who will not sit idly as His people are tormented and His name trampled underfoot.

Conclusion

Do we not wonder why the Lord has not dealt with the unbelief, lawlessness, and immorality that is sweeping across the world in this day and age?

We wonder if the Lord is holding back His hand of wrath so that the world will store up wrath against the day of wrath, like in the case of the Canaanites before the conquest led by Joshua (cf. Rom 11:25; Dt 32:25)?

But could it be that the LORD is not doing anything because God's people have made no request for Him to intervene? God is pleased to act in response to the pleas of His people.

Let us remember, therefore, to pray for the destruction of the kingdom of Satan as we pray for the advancement of the kingdom of grace. Let us learn from this Psalm to pray that God will deal firmly against His enemies, and let us pray that in this way, many will also turn to Him.

But let us also learn to apply this Psalm in our own lives to pray against the sin that affect us individually, as families and as a church. Israel of old had their Edomites, Ishmaelites, Amalekites, Moabites and Ammonites, etc. What about us?

We have militant evolutionists, gay right activists, abortionists and atheists, etc. Shall we not forget to pray for them that their raging may come to naught and that they may be humbled before the Lord to seek Him while He may be found?

But is that all? Do we not also have pride, worldliness, materialism, individualism, selfishness, indifference, unbelief, hardness of heart, etc? Are not these sins also the enemies of the Church, and of the hidden ones of God? We cannot pray for the conversion of these sins, but shall we not learn to pray and to labour for their destruction? For "little sins" left to fester unchecked may prove eventually to be as destructive to the Church as the more scandalous sin which we do not tolerate. Amen. Ω

Psalm 84:
The Righteous One's Longing
for the Tabernacles of God

Psalm 84 is one of the most beautiful Psalms in the Psalter. Although the writer's name is not stated, I agree with almost every commentator I have read that it breathes of David's excellent spirit. And it appears to me that the majority of commentators are right that this Psalm was probably written by David during the time when he was driven away from Jerusalem by his son Absalom. During this period of time, David also wrote Psalm 42, which is another beautiful Psalm expressing his desire to be found with God's people in public worship at the Tabernacle, or wherever God's people are gathered.[38] But David wrote not as a private person, but as the anointed king; and he wrote it in the Spirit of the Righteous One, even the Anointed One (cf. v. 9), so that this is a song that all who are united to Him may sing with Him, to express their longing which is wrought in their heart by His Spirit.

This then is how we will understand this Psalm. We may entitle it *"The Righteous One's Longing for the Tabernacles of God."*

It has, essentially, three parts, according to the division provided by the two selahs in verse 4 and 8.

From verses 1-4, we have an expression of how lovely the prospect of dwelling in the tabernacles of God is to the anointed soul. We may subtitle this "The Sparrow's Bliss."

From verses 5-8, we have a description of how the anticipation of being found in the tabernacles of God brings joy to the pilgrim on his journey, and makes him a blessing to others in the world. Here we have "The Pilgrim's Cheer."

From verses 9-12, is a plea to the LORD to look down upon us with favour for the sake of the Anointed One, so that those who trust in Him may find grace to enjoy His blessing today and forever more. Here we have "The Anointed's Favour."

Assigning a succinct subtitle to each stanza, we have an expository outline as follows:

1. v. 1-4   The Sparrow's Bliss
2. v. 5-8   The Pilgrim's Cheer
3. v. 9-12   The Anointed's Favour

1. The Sparrow's Bliss

[1] *How amiable [or loved and lovely, i.e. beloved] are thy tabernacles, O LORD of hosts!* [2] *My soul longeth, yea, even fainteth for the courts of the LORD: my heart and my flesh crieth out for the living God.*

The temple had not yet been built in David's time; so it is fitting that David should speak of the tabernacle as the place of worship.

But let us take note that the tabernacle of the LORD is but a symbol of His worship. God is omnipresent, but the tabernacle symbolises His favourable presence. It is not so much a meeting place for the congregation, as it is a symbol of the LORD's delight in His people, especially when they are united in corporate worship. He "loveth the gates of Zion more

---

[38] The word "tabernacles" is given in plural in verse 1 apparently because the tabernacle and temple in the Old Covenant were partitioned into sections or rooms.

than all the dwellings of Jacob" (Ps 87:2).

David therefore speaks of his deepest inner longing for the courts of the LORD's tabernacle. But really his desire is to worship the LORD with his people, and to commune with Him. He says it clearly in verse 2: "*my heart and my flesh crieth out for the living God.*"

David desired after the LORD in his whole being. So deprived was he, and so deeply did he long to meet with the LORD in worship that he expresses a playful envy for the birds that dwell in and around the tabernacle, near the altars of the LORD.

> *3 Yea, the sparrow hath found an house, and the swallow a nest for herself, where she may lay her young, even thine altars, O LORD of hosts, my King, and my God.*

This beautiful verse has been variously interpreted. Hengstenberg believes that David is referring to himself as the sparrow and a swallow; the birds, after all, could not possibly make their nest on the altars in the tabernacle. But it appears to me that it would be strange for David to speak of himself as a bird laying her young if he is indeed speaking about his own bliss in metaphor.

It appears to me that as David envisioned in his mind the tabernacle, he is reminded of the birds that fly freely around the courts of the tabernacle. Did he see a swallow or sparrow fleeting by as he thought about the tabernacle and the joy of worship in it? Did David imagine in his mind's eye, how the birds are making their nests on the altars? How he envied the birds!

But as George Horne puts it:

> It is evidently the design of this passage to intimate to us, that in the house, and at the altar of God, a faithful soul findeth freedom from care and sorrow, quiet of mind, and gladness of spirit; like a bird, that has secured a little mansion for the reception and education of her young. And there is no heart, endued with sensibility, which doth not bear its testimony to the exquisite beauty and propriety of this affecting image.

This must be so, for David no doubt was not only thinking about the tabernacle as a happy place to be in. He must rather be thinking of the happiness of being in the presence of God to praise and worship Him. This is surely what he means in verse 4:

> *4 Blessed are they that dwell in thy house: they will be still praising thee.*

What a joy it is to be amongst those who dwell in the temple, whose daily employment is to serve and worship the LORD directly.

David had, at best, tasted a hint of the bliss of communion with God, through the typical modes of worship of the Old Covenant. Yet, he longed for it. How much more profound would be our Saviour's longing when He sang those words? For the joy of perfect worship that He looked forward to, was a joy unspeakable and incomparable. It is this beatific experience that our Lord would have us yearn for, when He would have us join Him to sing these, His words.

Oh what a joy it will be one day, when we shed this earthly tabernacle (cf. 2 Cor 5:4) to worship the Father whom we love (Heb 8:5, 9:11), in the heavenly tabernacle,.

And the anticipation of that day must surely quicken our steps and bring a smile despite our present trials.

2. The Pilgrim's Cheer

David says:

[5] Blessed is the man whose strength is in thee; in whose heart are the ways of them [or as clarified in the NKJV—"Whose heart is set on pilgrimage"]. [6] Who passing through the valley of Baca make it a well; the rain also filleth the pools. [7] They go from strength to strength, every one of them in Zion appeareth before God.

From within the tabernacle, David's mind wanders to a holy day when God's people are streaming towards Jerusalem to worship the LORD at the tabernacle or to celebrate the Passover.

He sees the smile on the faces of the pilgrims. He sees the spring in their stride. Their heart is filled with anticipation. They go from strength to strength, determined to reach the tabernacle to worship the LORD.

And yea, because of the joy that they are looking forward to, they, as it were, become a blessing to those they pass by.

The picture that David paints is that as they pass through the valley of Baca, which is the valley of weeping, they make it into a well or a spring, and the rain follows and fills the pools with water. The valley, which is dry and arid, which was watered only by the tears of farmers lamenting their crop failures and animal losses, is suddenly transformed into a lush landscape, filled with watering holes for the animals to graze and drink.

Listen to the poetic rendering of this paragraph by a Mr Merrick as quoted by Bishop Horne:

> Bless'd, who, their strength on thee reclined,
>> Thy seat explore with constant mind,
> And, Salem's distant tow'rs in view,
>> With active zeal their way pursue;
> Secure the thirsty vale they tread,
>> While, call'd from out their sandy bed
> (As down in grateful show'rs distill'd
>> The heav'ns their kindlest moisture yield),
> The copious springs their steps beguile,
>> And bid the cheerless desert smile.
> From stage to stage advancing still,
>> Behold them reach fair Sion's hill,
> And prostrate at her hallowed shrine,
>> Adore the Majesty divine.

What a beautiful picture of blessing that the pilgrims and strangers of the LORD may bring to the land through which they traverse, as they head towards the Celestial City. Oh may the Lord grant us that we too may be a blessing to many today, as we follow the footsteps of our Saviour, with the hope of everlasting fellowship with Him!

For David, this thought brought him again to cry out to the LORD to hear His plea to bring him speedily back to the holy city:

[8] O LORD God of hosts, hear my prayer: give ear, O God of Jacob.

And it led to his appeal to the LORD to show him favour on account of the Anointed One, even He who in His own pilgrimage longed, more than anyone else, for the glory and joy He shared with His Father from all eternity (cf. Jn 17:5).

3. The Anointed's Favour

⁹ Behold, O God our shield, and look upon the face of thine anointed.

The anointed or the anointed one is literally the "messiah" in Hebrew. This could be a reference to David himself who was anointed as king over his people, unlike Absalom. But David stood as a type of Christ, who is truly our shield—to shield us from the assaults of God's enemies and from the wrath of God himself.

So David's longing for the tabernacles of God, found its fulfilment in the Messiah's longing to return to the true tabernacle to worship together with the people He came to redeem.

And this longing is imprinted in the heart of all anointed ones—even all in whom the Spirit of Christ dwells. Such is the case, that every child of God longs to be found in worship with God's people, both today in public worship, and in the day to come when we shall worship God forever and ever, with God's people redeemed through all ages.

This was our Saviour's attitude. This must be our attitude. David, like our Saviour, longed to spend his time in worship.

¹⁰ For a day in thy courts is better than a thousand. I had rather be a doorkeeper in the house of my God, than to dwell in the tents of wickedness.

Pastor Jeff O'Neil has a very beautiful comment on this verse:

Although a king, yet he would exchange places with a doorkeeper. He did not think of that as a sacrifice, for he reckoned service in the house of God was superior to the throne. The tents of wickedness were not to be compared with the tent or tabernacle of grace. One day of opening and shutting the doors of God's house is supremely greater than a thousand days of worldly pursuits. A full day will give a full blessing.

Is this your longing too, dear child of God?

"One thing have I desired of the LORD," says David in another Psalm, "that will I seek after; that I may dwell in the house of the LORD all the days of my life, to behold the beauty of the LORD, and to enquire in his temple" (Ps 27:4).

But why should the saints so delight to be in the presence of the LORD? The answer is given for us to confess in verse 11 onwards:

¹¹ For the LORD God is a sun and shield: the LORD will give grace and glory: no good thing will he withhold from them that walk uprightly. ¹² O LORD of hosts, blessed is the man that trusteth in thee.

The LORD God is our all in all. He is our joy and our protection. As our Sun, He chases away the ignorance, gloom, darkness, danger and suffering in our lives. He did these for our Saviour when He bore our guilt and griefs; then when our Saviour was risen from the dead, He manifested His blessing especially through Him, the Sun of Righteousness who has risen with healing in His wings (Mal 4:2).

Likewise as our shield, God protects us from all the darts of the evil ones and indeed from the wrath of God to come. Again He does so through Christ, who became a curse for us, to take the arrows of divine wrath for our sin that we might experience divine blessing.

As our Sun and Shield, the LORD gives us grace and glory. He gives us grace as a preparation for glory to come. Indeed where he gives grace, he will give glory, "for grace is glory begun and is an earnest of it" (Matthew Henry).

Grace and Glory: these are the two great things that most conduce to our joy today and in eternity. Therefore, if God would give us grace and glory, we know He will not withhold anything good from the man that walk uprightly.

Therefore, the man who trusts in the Lord, and is able to worship the LORD with God's people, is truly blessed, and has no need of anything else to add to His blessing.

Is this your attitude towards life in this world, dear Christian?

Conclusion

Oh may the LORD grant us that we may truly look forward to assembling with the saints to worship the LORD on the Sabbaths.

And may He grant us that we may so experience a foretaste of heavenly worship on the Sabbath that we long for the eternal Sabbath.

And may we live with such anticipation of joy to come that all the things of this present world may become strangely dim.

And may we so overflow with joy that we become a blessing to fellow pilgrims and others in this life.

May we indeed find true blessedness as pilgrims and strangers heading towards the Celestial City as we look "unto Jesus the author and finisher of our faith; who for the joy that was set before him endured the cross, despising the shame, and is set down at the right hand of the throne of God" (Heb 12:2). Amen. Ω

Psalm 85:
The Righteous One's
Plea for Revival for the Church
OR THE CHURCH'S SENDING & RECEIVING
THE DOVE OF PEACE

Psalm 85 is probably a post-exilic Psalm together with Psalm 126 and possibly Psalm 147, whereas Psalm 137 was probably written in the early years of the captivity.

We don't know who the writer is, but he had possibly returned from exile with Zerubbabel or Ezra. Now, as we can imagine, during those years, things were still very difficult for the returnees. The seventy years appointed by the LORD for the chastisement of the nation was coming to an end. But tokens of the LORD's displeasure were still evident everywhere. The population was decimated. The city needed to be rebuilt. The pains and sorrows of the earlier years were still being felt.

It was in this context that the psalmist both praised the LORD for deliverance and petitioned Him for further restoration.

Matthew Henry likens the situation that the people of God were under to that of Noah in the ark when the rain had stopped and the water started to subside. He likens the first part of this Psalm, verses 1-7, to Noah sending out the dove; and the second part of the Psalm, verses 8-13, as the dove returning with an olive branch in her beaks.

This is a beautiful picture, isn't it? And does it not also help us to see how relevant this Psalm is to us today? For are we not like Noah in the ark? The wrath of God is over for us, but the power and consequence of sin is everywhere present, and threatens to cast a pall of gloom over us. Oh how we need the LORD's assurance through the dove with her olive branch! And this is what the Lord provides us with, when we sing this Psalm in union with Him, to plead with the Father to revive us (cf. v. 6).

We may entitle this Psalm *"The Righteous One's Plea for Revival for the Church."* Or if you like, "the Church's Sending and Receiving the Dove of Peace," which may better explain the outline we have adopted:

1. v. 1-7   The Dove Sent
2. v. 8-13   The Dove Returns

It is a song given by the inspiration of Christ that the Church may sing in union with Him as she awaits the day of her full redemption.

1. The Dove Sent

[1] *LORD, thou hast been favourable unto thy land: thou hast brought back the captivity of Jacob.* [2] *Thou hast forgiven the iniquity of thy people, thou hast covered all their sin. Selah.* [3] *Thou hast taken away all thy wrath: thou hast turned thyself from the fierceness of thine anger.*

The Jews returning from exile have much to thank God for: for the LORD had not dealt with them after their sin; nor rewarded them according to their iniquities (Ps 103:10). Instead, He has forgiven their iniquity and covered their sin (v. 2). He has set aside His anger and wrath. He looks upon them with favour and love.

Is this not also our own experience individually and corporately? We were children of God's wrath deserving eternal damnation for our sin against Him. We were under the bondage of sin and Satan. But God in His mercy has redeemed us by the blood of Christ, and freed us from captivity, and given us the assurance that His anger has been turned from us. We are no longer children of God's wrath, but His adoptive sons and daughters; no longer aliens from the commonwealth of Israel, but citizens of heaven.

But like the Jews of old, we have not reached heavenly rest. There remains a rest unto the people of God. There remains evident tokens of God's wrath in our lives, individually and corporately. Are there not the struggles against sin? Are there not the assaults of the wicked one? Are there not quarrels and disharmony?

Shall we not, stand behind our Saviour as He, with and for us, sends out the dove?

> *⁴ Turn us, O God of our salvation, and cause thine anger towards us to cease. ⁵ Wilt thou be angry with us for ever? wilt thou draw out thine anger to all generations? ⁶ Wilt thou not revive us again: that thy people may rejoice in thee? ⁷ Shew us thy mercy, O LORD, and grant us thy salvation.*

This must be our plea. Turn us; revive us; show us mercy; grant us salvation!

Though we have the assurance that we have been reconciled to God, the flood waters have not receded. The serpent whose head was crushed at the cross is still thrashing about seeking to destroy whom he may.

And at the same time, there is also the remnant of corruption in us. As such we will still sin against the LORD. Therefore, although we are judicially forgiven, we will still incur God's Fatherly displeasure.

What child who loves his father, will merely endure the father's loving chastisement and not seek the father's mercy and help that he may enjoy him more?

And so let us send our dove. Let us cry: Turn us; revive us; show us mercy; grant us salvation! Change us; increase our zeal and love for Thee. Forgive and save us. We desire, heavenly Father, to rejoice in thee more and more (v. 6).

2. The Dove Returns

She is returning with an olive branch of peace in her beaks:

> *⁸ I will hear what God the LORD will speak: for he will speak peace unto his people, and to his saints: but let them not turn again to folly. ⁹ Surely his salvation is nigh them that fear him; that glory may dwell in our land.*

"I will hear." But who is this "I"? Who but Christ can be one of us when we sing "we" and "us," who is also God's prophet to convey God's word to us?

What does the Christ hear? He hears that God will show compassion to His people. He will speak peace to us. But listen, there is a "but"... "But let them not turn again to folly." Let us, therefore, gratefully take heed not to turn again to folly, and so incur the Lord's displeasure.

If we walk in His fear, we will know His salvation. That is, we will know His help to grow in grace. We will bask in His glory and have the firm hope of ourselves being glorified one day.

Why is this so? This is so because God has graciously brought together mercy [or grace] and truth, righteousness and peace; and bestowed them upon us.

> *¹⁰ Mercy and truth are met together; righteousness and peace have kissed each other. ¹¹ Truth shall spring out of the earth; and righteousness shall look down from heaven.*

How did God do that? Listen first to the Apostle John in John 1:14:

> And the Word was made flesh, and dwelt among us, (and we beheld his glory, the glory as of the only begotten of the Father,) full of grace and truth.

Mercy or grace and truth are met together in the Lord Jesus Christ.

What about righteousness and peace? Did they not also kiss each other in the Lord Jesus Christ, the Great High Priest after the order of Melchizedek? What did the writer of Hebrews say concerning Melchizedek? His name, says the writer is "by interpretation King of righteousness, and after that also King of Salem, which is, King of peace" (Heb 7:2).

> "All the promises of God in him are yea, and in him Amen, unto the glory of God by us" (2Cor 1:20).

Through Him, we have grace and mercy, because it is for His sake we are not consumed. It is for His sake, the wrath of God towards us is replaced by love.

And through Him, truth and justice are upheld, for He suffered and died to pay for our sin.

Because of Him, we can have both mercy and truth. Were it not for Him, we may have either but not both. If we have mercy, truth will be violated because sin has to be overlooked. If we have truth, then mercy must be forfeited because our sin must be punished or else justice is destroyed. But because of Christ, the Son of God, mercy and grace do not violate truth and justice; and truth and justice do not preclude mercy and grace.

Christ was punished as the God-Man, and our covenant representative, on our behalf. We deserve everlasting hell for our sin against God; but Christ our Lord, the Son of God, suffered the equivalent of everlasting hell while on the cross for us. Did He not experience the terror of being forsaken of the Father on the cross? Hell is not where God is not. It is where there is an absence of the favourable presence of God, and a pervasive presence of His infinite wrath. Christ our Lord experienced that for a full three hours when the sun could not shine. For three hours, all that the eternal Son of God saw of His Father, was His burning wrath. At the end of the three hours, our Lord cried out "My God, my God, why hast thou forsaken me!"

It is because Christ our Lord was punished on our behalf that we will never be punished again. In Him is mercy and truth.

And likewise, Christ is our righteousness, for He kept the law perfectly on our behalf so that His righteousness, which is the righteousness acceptable to God, is imputed to us.

And Christ is our peace, for through Him we have peace with God and with one another.

Christ is our mercy and truth, and our peace and righteousness.

It is because of Christ that we can have the assurance that all things, including things that do not appear so good to us, are working together for our good.

> "He that spared not his own Son, but delivered him up for us all, how shall he not with him also freely give us all things?" asks the Apostle Paul (Rom 8:32).

And look at verse 12:

> *12 Yea, the LORD shall give that which is good; and our land shall yield her increase. 13 Righteousness shall go before him; and shall set us in the way of his steps.*

What good will the Father withhold from us, when He withheld not His only begotten Son from us?

Whatever struggles we may experience, let us run on in the Christian race with this assurance. For Christ's sake, the Father will bless us. We shall grow in grace and strength. We will continue to bear fruit unto His glory.

He who is the Sun of Righteousness will lead us in the paths of righteousness, as *"righteousness shall go before him."* Righteousness went before Him not only in that the preacher of righteousness, John the Baptist, prepared His way. Righteousness went before Him also in that His path to glory was the highway of righteousness.

Conclusion

Dear child of God, what is Christ to you? Is the Lord your all in all? He is appointed by the Father to be the One in whom mercy meets with truth, and righteousness and peace kissed each other.

He is not only the basis of our Christian life; He is our hope and assurance.

Without Him, the Christian life is meaningless and without hope. Indeed, had He not died for us, we would have no Christian life, for we would have no mercy nor peace. It is for this reason, we must remember His death for us often.

May the Lord grant us His help not only to remember His love for us, but to follow "in the way of his steps" that we may glorify Him with our lives. Amen. Ω

Psalm 86:
The Righteous One
Desiring a Token for Good
from the Father

Psalm 86 is, as the title suggests, "A Prayer of David." From its content, it looks like David must have been experiencing some distress. We do not know what the occasion was, but David, together with all the saints, and especially with the greater David, would have experienced many occasions of distresses, sufferings and persecution. Indeed, this Psalm, written under the inspiration of the Spirit of Christ, no doubt, expresses our Lord's own meditation, as He hung on the cross—perhaps after the three hours of darkness during which He experienced hell on our behalf. In verse 13, we read, *"thou hast delivered my soul from the lowest hell."* For David and for all believers, these words when applied to themselves, would refer to deliverance from eternal death. But for our Lord, this could only be a reference to His experience of suffering the wrath of God on our behalf.

Whatever the case may be, we may, based on the unique request in verse 17, entitle this Psalm *"The Righteous One Desiring a Token for Good from the Father."*

The Righteous One is Christ, and in Him all who are united to Him by faith, who sings this Psalm in union with Him.

This Psalm is a prayer; and it is notoriously difficult to discern the structure of heartfelt prayers. As a result, almost every commentator, regardless of whether he is familiar with Hebrew poetry or not, will propose a different structure from another.

We may break the Psalm up into five parts.

From verses 1-7, there is a series of petitions to the Father, to bow down His ear.

Verses 8-10 is a statement of faith, that God is the alone living and true God.

Verses 11-13 is a request to be taught the way of the LORD.

Verses 14-15 is a statement of confidence in the mercies of the LORD against the backdrop of persecution.

In verses 16-17, we have another series of petitions: this time to ask the LORD to grant an evident token of His mercy.

With this in mind, an expository outline, using the key phrase in each stanza, would be:

1. v. 1-7   Bow Down Thine Ear
2. v. 8-10   Thou art God Alone
3. v. 11-13   Teach Me Thy Way
4. v. 14-15   Thou art a God Full of Compassion
5. v. 16-17   Show Me a Token for Good

1. Bow Down Thine Ear

[1] *Bow down thine ear, O LORD, hear me: for I am poor and needy.* [2] *Preserve my soul; for I am holy: O thou my God, save thy servant that trusteth in thee.* [3] *Be merciful unto me, O Lord: for I cry unto thee daily.* [4] *Rejoice the soul of thy servant: for unto thee, O Lord, do I lift*

up my soul. ⁵ For thou, Lord, art good, and ready to forgive; and plenteous in mercy unto all them that call upon thee. ⁶ Give ear, O LORD, unto my prayer; and attend to the voice of my supplications. ⁷ In the day of my trouble I will call upon thee: for thou wilt answer me.

Notice that this stanza contains a series of petitions, each one with a reason attached, "Bow down thine ear" (v. 1a): "for I am poor and needy" (v. 1b); "Preserve my soul" (v. 2a): "for I am holy" (v. 2b); "Be merciful unto me" (v. 3a): "for I cry unto thee daily" (v. 3b), etc.

This is the art of prayer. Prayer is not only about asking, but about persuading. Of course, God does not need to be persuaded, but we need to be persuaded and encouraged that God will hear our prayers.

Here, in this paragraph we are given an example of how we may, in prayer, appeal to our present needs (v. 1); our holiness (v. 2); our importunity (v. 3); our desire to praise the Lord (v. 4); and also God's goodness and mercy (v. 5).

Of course, there is none holy but Christ: for which reason, Christ would be most qualified to take these words on His lips. But we may appeal to the righteousness of Christ imputed to us, to our being set apart unto God, and to our integrity in seeking to be holy as God is holy.

Those who strive to walk in holiness, can have great assurance that the Father will hear their cries, as they are brought to Him through the mediatorship of Christ. On the other hand, those who live in hypocrisy or refuse to walk in the way of the Lord, can have no confidence that their prayers will be received by the Father.

2. Thou Art God Alone

⁸ Among the gods there is none like unto thee, O Lord; neither are there any works like unto thy works. ⁹ All nations whom thou hast made shall come and worship before thee, O Lord; and shall glorify thy name. ¹⁰ For thou art great, and doest wondrous things: thou art God alone.

Although the major part of prayer may, indeed, consist largely of petitions, as our Lord demonstrates in the Lord's Prayer, we must not forget that prayer is basically our soul's conversation with our heavenly Father.

Therefore, even when we use the Lord's Prayer, for example, we should enlarge the petitions, to speak with love and gratitude with our Father to acknowledge who He is to us.

In fact, we may use this second stanza as an elaboration of the first petition in the Lord's Prayer: "Hallowed be thy name"!

Let us learn to do so, acknowledging God's greatness and power, and that He is the alone living and true God, and therefore worthy of all honour, glory and praise.

But now we come to another petition...

3. Teach Me Thy Way

¹¹ Teach me thy way, O LORD; I will walk in thy truth: unite my heart to fear thy name. ¹² I will praise thee, O Lord my God, with all my heart: and I will glorify thy name for evermore. ¹³ For great is thy mercy towards me: and thou hast delivered my soul from the lowest hell.

This is a petition that all believers should learn to make: "Teach me thy way, O LORD; I will walk in thy truth: unite my heart to fear thy name."

As God's children, we must desire to glorify Him, especially when He has shown us great mercy in redeeming us, when we were hitherto children of wrath.

How may we glorify God? Only if we walk in His fear in the way that He has appointed for us! If our lives are no different from the rest of the world, then how do we glorify Him? A pauper who has been made a prince by a benevolent king would surely honour him by walking with dignity as a generous prince, rather than as a needy beggar, or as a miserly snob. If an unbelieving friend were to stay at your home for a week, what will his impression be at the end of the week? Will He think that your family is no different from the average unbelieving family; or will He think that there is something different in your home?

May it be the latter! But if we fear that it will be the former, then it is clear that we need to pray this petition more. We should pray this petition not only in times of trial, but as a regular part of our prayer for ourselves.

We need to learn to walk in the way of the LORD, in His fear, both in our public engagements, and in private.

But thank God that despite our failures, He continues to show us mercy: for He is full of compassion.

4. Thou art a God
Full of Compassion

[14] O God, the proud are risen against me, and the assemblies of violent men have sought after my soul; and have not set thee before them. [15] But thou, O Lord, art a God full of compassion, and gracious, longsuffering, and plenteous in mercy and truth.

All the trials and sufferings that we experience in this life come upon us because of sin, whether personal or imputed. Whether we are suffering on account of persecution, or on account of illnesses, the suffering can be traced to sin. Christ our Lord had no sin, but He was bearing our sin. He was suffering the consequences of sin on our behalf. He did not deserve to suffer at all. But He put Himself into harm's way, for our sake.

The rest of us, on the other hand, deserve the pain and sorrow that we experience in our lives because we have sinned against God. And God would chastise us in order that we may be beautiful vessels of His redeeming grace.

But God's chastisement is always tempered with grace, compassion, longsuffering, mercy and truth. And we should also acknowledge it. We should not only talk about our pains and sorrows, we should acknowledge God's mercy and compassion, even that He has not dealt with us according as our sin deserves.

This is how we will be able to give thanks in all circumstances as the Apostle Paul teaches us. We may not be able to thank God for the pain. That would be very unnatural and hypocritical. If we are honest, we want to be freed of all pains. But it is good for us to acknowledge in prayer that the LORD has not dealt with us as we deserve.

But that does not mean we cannot plead for mercy. God will indeed show mercy to His children: for it pleases Him to dispense mercy in answer to prayer. Thus, we see in the final stanza of this Psalm another petition.

5. Show Me a Token for Good

[16] O turn unto me, and have mercy upon me; give thy strength unto thy servant, and save the son of thine handmaid. [17] Shew me a token for good; that they which hate me may see it,

and be ashamed: because thou, LORD, hast helped me, and comforted me.

I am always intrigued by the phrase *"son of thine handmaid."* I know this is a common Hebrew expression, but when it is used in Sacred Scripture, it begs the question, does it not? Who is this, the LORD's handmaid? David's mother is hardly known, and many believers have unbelieving parents. Who then is this handmaid of the LORD, both here and in Psalm 116? I believe the answer may be found in Luke 1:38, in Mary's response to the angel Gabriel when he told her that she would conceive and bear the Son of God. What was Mary's reply? Mary said, "Behold the handmaid of the Lord; be it unto me according to thy word."

I believe that the phrase "son of thine handmaid" both in our text, and in Psalm 116, is intended by the Holy Spirit to be, ultimately, a reference to Christ, the God-Man.

But in any case, we may certainly use our Lord's petition. He had it written for our use with Him. Because of our mystical union with Christ, we may legitimately speak of ourselves as the "sons of thine handmaid," not because we have any direct relationship with Mary, but because "we dwell in [the Son], and he in us" (1Jn 4:13).

So let us learn to cry for mercy and strength. But let us also learn to ask for *"a token for good."* What is a token for good? A token for good is basically a sign or a turn of event that shows that the Lord is working on our behalf.

Those of us who have been believers for a while, will know it as a fact that very often, we may have no indication of God's answer to our prayer for long seasons. We pray that the LORD will move the government of our land to deal with sin. We pray for the church that she may grow in grace and in numbers. We pray for the conversion of a loved one. We pray for healing from a debilitating illness. We pray for reconciliation with a friend who has fallen out with us due to a misunderstanding. But years past, and God does not seem to be answering our prayers.

What do we do? Shall we not learn to pray that the LORD will show us tokens for good in regard to our prayer—even if He does not give us a fuller reply?

A short message by a wayward son indicating that he visited a conservative church, a new family visiting the church, a government initiative to discourage abortion, a simple "hello" from an offended brother: these are the kind of tokens that often bring much cheer to the heart. Shall we not learn to pray for them?

But sometimes, God's tokens may not be spotted so quickly. Could the ugly political fiasco occupying the front page everyday be, in fact, a token for good, to wake up the government, and Christians from our complacency? Could the sudden loss of job after years of complacency be in fact a token for good to bring us to rely and hope in the LORD again? Could a nasty letter from the offended brother be a token for good in answer to prayer for reconciliation? Could the increase in attendance at prayer meeting be a token for good in answer to prayer for growth in the church?

David, and the greater David, prayed for a token that their enemies might see and be ashamed, in the realisation that they are up against one who is on the LORD's side.

May the Lord grant us tokens of good not only that His enemies may see and be ashamed that they are fighting against the LORD, but that we may be encouraged to continue to trust the LORD through all the trials that the LORD may bring along our way, both corporately and individually.

Conclusion

This is Psalm 86. May we sing it prayerfully with our Saviour especially when we find our souls distressed by present circumstances! May we also learn to pray as we are taught herein, with expectation, adoration, humility, assurance and faith! Amen. Ω

Psalm 87:
The Righteous One's
Appraisal of Zion

Psalm 87 is a short Psalm, but it is a very cryptic and profound Psalm. Most of us would know snippets of this Psalm. Those of us who were from uninspired hymn-singing background would be familiar with verse 3, because it is found in the hymn of John Newton—"Glorious Things of Thee Are Spoken":

> Glorious things of thee are spoken,
> Zion, city of our God;
> He whose word cannot be broken
> Formed thee for His own abode.

Those of us who have come to embrace Psalm singing, on the other hand, would probably be familiar with verse 2: *"The LORD loveth the gates of Zion more than all the dwellings of Jacob."* We know from Matthew Henry that this means that while private family worship is pleasing to God, and must not be neglected, yet "when they come in competition, public worship [other things being equal] is to be preferred before private."

But that is just a couple of verses. What about the rest of the Psalm? I suspect that most of us have very little idea what it is about. We can probably read it five or six times and still do not know what it is saying. Try it! Could it be that the author was very distracted, or not of sound mind when he wrote it?

Of course not! But it is true that this Psalm is difficult to understand. Yet however difficult it is, it is part of the inspired word of God; and so it beckons us to study it to see what the Lord would teach us.

Now, while it is difficult to understand at first sight what this Psalm is saying, it is clear that it is about Zion. Matthew Poole summarises the scholarly consensus on the occasion of its composition quite well:

> "This psalm was doubtless composed after the building of the temple; and as learned men think, and it seems probable, when the people were newly returned out of Babylon, and laboured under many discouragements about the return of most of their brethren, and the difficulties which they met with in the rebuilding of their temple and city."

But be as that may or may not be the case, we may be sure that the *sitz im leben*[39] is not as important as the timeless spiritual meaning of the Psalm. The things that happened to our fathers in the faith, after all, are divinely designed for "our admonition upon whom the ends of the world are come" (1 Cor 10:11). With this in mind, we may entitle it *"The Righteous One's Appraisal of Zion."* Zion is, of course, not just a physical city, but a type of the Church; and should, therefore be understood as such in our meditation of this Psalm.

Quite clearly, this Psalm has three strophes or poetic movement of unequal length—as the two selahs in verses 3 and 6 indicate:

1. v. 1-3   Worship of Zion, Beloved of the LORD

2. v. 4-6   Membership of Zion, Established by the LORD

3. v. 7   Delight in Zion, Acknowledged by the LORD

---

[39] I.e., its setting in life at the time of its composition.

1. Worship of Zion,
Beloved of the LORD

[1] His foundation [LXX: Οἱ θεμέλιοι αὐτοῦ, Hoi themelioi autou] is in the holy mountains. [2] The LORD loveth the gates of Zion more than all the dwellings of Jacob. [3] Glorious things are spoken of [or by] thee, O city of God.

Now, immediately as we enter into this Psalm, we are confronted with a unique feature of this Psalm that makes it difficult to interpret it: for notice the abruptness and brevity. The Psalm begins with a third person pronoun that is not even defined.

But we have no difficulty understanding that it is the LORD. The LORD's foundation is in the holy mountains. But what is this foundation?

I believe this foundation refers to Christ.

- "Therefore thus saith the Lord GOD, Behold, I lay in Zion for a foundation a stone, a tried stone, a precious corner stone, a sure foundation [LXX: θεμέλιος]: he that believeth shall not make haste" (Isa 28:16).
- "For he looked for a city which hath foundations (GK: θεμέλιος], whose builder and maker is God" (Heb 11:10).
- "For other foundation [GK: θεμέλιος] can no man lay than that is laid, which is Jesus Christ" (1Cor 3:11).

The city of Zion is, as it were, built upon Christ. It is significant and beloved for Christ's sake.

It is for the same reason that the LORD loves the gates of Zion more than the dwellings of Jacob (v. 2). We noted how this verse has to do with the worship of God's people.

Family worship is of course important. But nothing exalts God's name more than the public worship of God's people as they are gathered together in the name of Christ and sounding their praises together in union with Him: "I will declare thy name unto my brethren: in the midst of the congregation will I praise thee," declares Christ our Lord (Ps 22:22).

The worship of Zion is especially beloved of the LORD because it is the corporate worship of the people purchased by the precious blood of the Son of God. Such public worship best reflects the people as a holy nation, or as the temple of God comprising living stones built upon the foundation, the chief corner stone, Christ, to offer up spiritual sacrifices acceptable unto God.

Such are the "glorious things" that are spoken of, or by, Zion, the city of God. Oh what a privilege it is to be led by our King to speak such glorious things that brings great delight and honour to our God and King!

And what a great privilege it is to be part of this City of God, for consider how...

2. Membership of Zion,
Established by the LORD

[4] I will make mention of Rahab and Babylon to[40] them that know me: behold Philistia, and Tyre, with Ethiopia; this man was born there. [5] And of Zion it shall be said, This and that man was born in her: and the highest himself shall establish her. [6] The LORD shall count, when he writeth up the people, that this man was born there.

---

[40] Heb. ?, also "for", or "as", or "amongst" – see BAGD.

No part of this Psalm is more cryptic than this second stanza. What does it mean? Well, we may fill in the blanks and add some clarifying words to read it thus:

> [4] *I will make mention of Rahab and Babylon [as amongst] them that know me: behold [also] Philistia, and Tyre, with Ethiopia; [and I shall say] this man was born there [in Zion].* [5] *And of Zion it shall be said, This and that man was born in her: and the highest himself shall establish her.* [6] *The LORD shall count, when he writeth up the people, that this man was born there.*

But even with these clarifying words, most of us would still have trouble with it. What is needed is really for us to use our imagination to think of what circumstance will lead to these words being spoken. This Psalm is enigmatic because we are expected to fill in the blanks.

It's like, if you hear on radio someone saying: "Oh, what a beautiful place this is! What majesty! What grandeur! Oh how it thrills my heart to behold this breathtaking view!"

Where do you think the speaker is standing? What do you think he is seeing? You will no doubt imagine, won't you, that he is standing in front of a majestic scenery? Perhaps he is standing at the edge of the Grand Canyon, or maybe he is looking across Yosemite Valley. Whatever it is, from his words, we can imagine where he is.

So it is with our text. Now, we have no reason to doubt that the speaker here is the Lord, the Righteous One. But what is the context of His saying these things?

The picture painted appears to be that the Lord is standing at the gate of Zion (cf. v. 2), and beholding the people coming to join Him to worship the Father. He is seeing and recording, and therefore making mention of the people coming in.

He sees not only those who are Jews. He sees Egyptians (that is what Rahab refers to). He sees Babylonians. He sees Philistines and Sidonians or Tyrians, and Ethiopians. He sees all the different nationalities in the world! But behold they are come to join together in worship with the Jews! They are all united in Christ!

Oh what a delight it is to our Lord! Oh what a delight it must be to the Father.

What does He say of them? He says of each one of them: This man is born there in Zion! This man is one of mine! This man is part of the commonwealth of Israel. This man is no more strangers of the covenant for he has joined himself to my Son. He is a citizen of Zion!

Can you see now the meaning of this second stanza!

Christ Himself will establish Zion. The LORD, the Father, will declare her membership (v. 6). He will draw them from the four corners of the world! The LORD says to His Son, in Isaiah 49:6:

> It is a light thing that thou shouldest be my servant to raise up the tribes of Jacob, and to restore the preserved of Israel: I will also give thee for a light to the Gentiles, that thou mayest be my salvation unto the end of the earth.

Jews and Gentiles—saved together in Christ! This is the vision painted in our Psalm.

Oh what a great privilege we enjoy, dear fellow-citizen, of being part of this glorious city of God!

And it is this city that affords the greatest delight to the LORD.

3. Delight in Zion, Acknowledged by the LORD

⁷ As well the singers as the players on instruments shall be there: all my springs are in thee.

Zion is God's royal priesthood and holy nation. There in Zion, will God be praised with the calves of the lips. There in Zion, will be the highest praises. Under the Old Covenant, when the people were waiting for Christ in the shadow, there were the musical instruments; but now in the New Covenant, when the Spirit has been poured out, we have heartstring tuned to heavenly strains.

There in Zion is the Lord's delight. "All my springs are in thee," says the Lord. God's people in ancient times would understand the value of springs of water, and the delight they bring.

When Isaiah would persuade the people to seek first the kingdom of God and His righteousness, he encouraged them with the blessings and joy they would experience if they did so. He says...

"And the LORD shall guide thee continually, and satisfy thy soul in drought, and make fat thy bones: and thou shalt be like a watered garden, and like a spring of water, whose waters fail not" (Isa 58:11).

Springs of waters are synonymous with spiritual delights. All of the LORD's springs are in Zion. And the LORD's greatest delight is when the people praise and glorify Him in worship.

Conclusion

Dear Christian, can you appreciate this Psalm better now? Can you see what a great privilege we have to be part of Zion, the city of God, that we may be instruments of God's delight?

The Lord has redeemed us with His precious blood, that we may be instruments of God's praise. Oh may the Lord grant us that we may be filled with such gratitude to Him, that our praise will never more be a mere going through the motion!

May the Lord grant us that we will never again drag our feet to worship! Never again, may we refuse to sing His praise. Never again may we despise God's goodness in accounting us members of Zion. Amen. Ω

Psalm 88:
The Righteous One's
Dark Lamentations

Psalm 88 is a very dark Psalm. It has been suggested that the only bright spot in this Psalm is the opening words, *"O LORD God of my salvation."* After that, it contains line after line, wave after wave, of heaviness and dismay. Well, I believe, if we know where to look, we will see a couple more bright spots. But it is true that, overall, this is a rather gloomy Psalm.

Nevertheless, this Psalm is recognised by many ancient, and not so ancient commentators, as Messianic. Augustine says, "The Passion of our Lord is here prophesied... Let us therefore now hear the voice of Christ singing before us in prophecy." Luther says: "This is a prayer, as in the person of Christ and of all the saints." The Church of England appointed this Psalm to be sung on Good Friday. The learned bishop Samuel Horsley calls this Psalm, "the Lamentation of Messiah." Bishop Horne says, "We hear in these words the voice of our suffering Redeemer.... [We see] His unexampled sorrows both in body and soul; his desertion in the day of trouble; his bitter passion, and approaching death; with his frequent and fervent prayers for the accomplishment of the promises, for the salvation of the church through him, and for the manifestation of God's glory." Andrew Bonar entitled this Psalm, "The sorrowful days and nights of the Man of Sorrows."

I am inclined to think on the basis of verses 6, 7 and 14, that this Psalm contains prophetically, the meditations of our Lord during the three hours of darkness when He experienced the intense wrath of God on our behalf. Of course, in so far as our Lord suffered for us not only on the cross, but also throughout His whole lifetime, this Psalm refers to His suffering from youth upwards. And so this Psalm is also very useful for us to give expression to our own sufferings as those united to Christ in our pilgrim journey. We may entitle it simply as: *"The Righteous One's Dark Lamentations."*

This Psalm has two selahs which means that it has three strophes when it was sung or chanted in Hebrew. But since this is a prayer of lamentation that wells up from a heart of sorrow, it is not so helpful for the purpose of appreciating the Psalm to break it up into divisions.

Rather, I think it will be helpful for us to enumerate and comment briefly on some of the sentiments expressed in it.

Let me highlight nine of them:

1. v. 1-2   The Prayerful Constancy of Our Lord
2. v. 3   The Depth of Our Lord's Sorrow
3. v. 4-5   Our Lord's Sense of Helplessness
4. v. 6-7   His Experience of Hell
5. v. 8   His Sense of Abandonment
6. v. 9   His Tears
7. v. 10-12 Our Lord's Yearning for the Resurrection
8. v. 13-14 The Lord's Hopeful Prayer
9. v. 15-18 The Reality of Our Lord's Suffering

1. The Prayerful Constancy
of Our Lord

¹ O LORD God of my salvation [or deliverance], I have cried day and night before thee: ² Let my prayer come before thee: incline thine ear unto my cry;

Our Lord was a man of sorrows and a man of prayer. Were He not a man of prayer, the intensity of the sorrow He had to endure would have overwhelmed Him: for who else could understand His struggles more than His heavenly Father. If anyone would be Christlike, let him first learn to be constant in prayer.

2. The Depth of Our
Lord's Sorrows

³ For my soul is full of troubles: and my life draweth nigh unto the grave.

When sorrow attends our soul and grief would break our hearts, it is difficult for us to see that we are not alone in suffering. But let us remember that our Lord suffered to a depth that none of us could fully appreciate: *"my soul is full of troubles: and my life draweth nigh unto the grave,"* He says. "My soul is exceeding sorrowful, even unto death," He told His disciples as He entered the Garden of Gethsemane to pray (Mt 26:38).

However painful our suffering may be, there is one who understands.

3. Our Lord's Sense
of Helplessness

⁴ I am counted with them that go down into the plt: I am as a man that hath no strength: ⁵ Free [or separated] among the dead, like the slain that lie in the grave, whom thou rememberest no more: and they are cut off from thy hand.

Our Lord was helpless. He was bound and tormented, helpless to deliver Himself. Well, He was not really helpless in that He could have called upon "twelve legions of angels" at any time (Mt 26:53). But our Lord was suffering for us. He willingly laid down His life to suffer what we deserve to suffer. Through it, He experienced being treated like one who is given up for dead—like a man who is buried alive and forgotten.

Has anyone of us ever felt such a sense of helplessness? But His experience went deeper.

4. His Experience of Hell

⁶ Thou hast laid me in the lowest pit, in darkness, in the deeps. ⁷ Thy wrath lieth hard upon me, and thou hast afflicted me with all thy waves.

Because we are creatures with a body and soul, Christ our representative must suffer not only physical torment, but spiritual torment as well.

Our Lord suffered in His soul throughout His earthly ministry. But His suffering was especially intense, during those three hours of darkness when the sun could not shine. During those three hours, our Lord was experiencing hell on our behalf. Hell is not merely darkness and fire. Hell is where the wrath of God burns. Our Lord was experiencing the wrath of God on our behalf.

It was the most intense suffering that any man could ever endure. And it was sweeping over His soul in waves.

5. His Sense of
Abandonment

[8] Thou hast put away mine acquaintance far from me; thou hast made me an abomination unto them: I am shut up, and I cannot come forth.

Not only did our Lord experience hell; He experienced being abandoned by His disciples and friends. His disciples fled from Him when He was arrested. He could not communicate with them. He could not enjoy the company and comforts of His friends. Do not the poignant words of Luke 23:49 allude to verse 8 of our Psalm: *"And all his acquaintance, and the women that followed him from Galilee, stood afar off..."*?

None of us can claim that no one understands our pain of loneliness, for our Lord felt it far more keenly than anyone of us would in our most lonely moments.

6. His Tears

[9] Mine eye mourneth by reason of affliction: LORD, I have called daily upon thee, I have stretched out my hands unto thee.

This hardly needs any comment. Our Lord was fully man. He cried. The writer of Hebrews tells us that our Lord "offered up prayers and supplications with strong crying and tears unto him that was able to save him from death" (Heb 5:7). His prayers were not stoical and unemotional. He felt the grief and it manifested itself on His face and body.

7. Our Lord's Yearning
for the Resurrection

[10] Wilt thou shew wonders to the dead? shall the dead arise and praise thee? [11] Shall thy lovingkindness be declared in the grave? or thy faithfulness in destruction? [12] Shall thy wonders be known in the dark? and thy righteousness in the land of forgetfulness?

I believe that this sentiment expresses our Lord's yearning for the resurrection: for our Lord had perfect hope and perfect faith. So He could not think of the hopelessness of death, without thinking about the resurrection.

But if our Lord was suffering the darkness of the pains of hell, we can understand why He spoke of the hope of resurrection, by way of questions that sounds almost despairing.

Yet if we look at these six questions, and understand that our Lord was not looking to have them answered negatively, but positively, then we shall understand something of the hope, in the hopelessness that our Lord experienced.

[10] Wilt thou shew wonders to the dead?

Yes; I shall raise thee, and I shall raise those whom I have given to thee to save.

...shall the dead arise and praise thee?

Assuredly yes; for I have promised. I will keep my covenant.

[11] Shall thy lovingkindness be declared in the grave?

No; but I will raise Thee and Thy elect, and Thou and Thy church, shall declare my lovingkindness for all eternity.

...Or [shall] thy faithfulness [be declared] in destruction?

Not ordinarily; but in the punishment that my son will endure, I will declare my faithfulness by requiring no more from those who are His.

12 Shall thy wonders be known in the dark?

No; but the resurrection morning will soon dawn.

...and [shall] thy righteousness [be known] in the land of forgetfulness?

No; but it is sin and sorrows that will be forgotten when death is swallowed up in victory!

These must have been some of the thoughts that encouraged our Lord and gave Him confidence to look to the Father. This explain, does it not,...

8. The Lord's Hopeful
Prayer

13 But unto thee have I cried, O LORD; and in the morning shall my prayer prevent thee. 14 LORD, why castest thou off my soul? why hidest thou thy face from me?

In Psalm 22:1, our Lord asks, "My God, my God, why hast thou forsaken me?" Here He asks the same: *"LORD, why castest thou off my soul? why hidest thou thy face from me?"*

This is not a question of indignation. It is an expression of grief, as well as confidence in the Father, for it is in confidence that our Lord could say *"in the morning shall my prayer prevent thee."* I know the morning will come; and you shall hear my prayer of thanksgiving.

But hope does not minimise...

9. The Reality of Our
Lord's Suffering

15 I am afflicted and ready to die from my youth up: while I suffer thy terrors I am distracted. 16 Thy fierce wrath goeth over me; thy terrors have cut me off. 17 They came round about me daily like water; they compassed me about together. 18 Lover and friend hast thou put far from me, and mine acquaintance into darkness [or literally as Hengstenberg puts it: "The dark kingdom of the dead is [sic] instead of all my companions, has come near to me, while they have gone back."].

Suffering has a tendency to distract us. It turns our eyes away from God's mercy and grace and tempts us to indulge in self-pity. This was no different for our Lord.

But in the midst of all the pain and sorrow, our Lord had hope. It is because of this hope, that this Psalm can be a source of encouragement to us in our darkest hours.

Conclusion

What is this Psalm to you, dear suffering saint? This is not a Psalm which we would normally turn to, is it? But can you see how this Psalm can be a comfort in times of despair?

No one ever experienced the temptation to despair as much as our Lord did. No one suffered as deeply as He did. But no one triumphed over darkness as well as did our Lord.

Let us learn from this Psalm, that nothing can be that bad as to be without hope. Christ has conquered the worst for us. There can be nothing worse remaining for those who are His. Trust Him. Believe in Him. Learn from Him. Cast your cares upon Him, when there appears to be no hope, remember that our Lord hoped: *"in the morning shall my prayer prevent thee."* Amen. Ω

Psalm 89:
The Righteous One's Reflection
upon God's Covenant Faithfulness

Psalm 89 is commonly accepted as one of the thirteen or so Messianic Psalms by commentators who approach the Psalms purely from a Historical-Grammatical Method. The difference between the Historical-Grammatical Method and the Christological or Grammatical-Canonical Approach is that the former sees Christ in a Psalm only if there is no other choice; whereas the latter sees Christ in a Psalm unless there is no other choice. And the former tends to see Christ in isolated verses that can appear out of context with the surrounding verses; whereas the latter tends to see Christ in the whole Psalm. In any case, Psalm 89 is almost universally regarded as Messianic because of its emphasis on God's covenant faithfulness towards David, which—all evangelical readers will agree—finds its fulfillment in the Kingdom of Christ.

Calvin was working with the Historical-Grammatical Method when he says concerning verse 30-36:

> "To limit what is here said to the ancient people of Israel, is an exposition not only absurd, but altogether impious.… If we set Christ aside, where will we find that everlasting duration of the royal throne of which mention is here made?"

To this sentiment we heartily agree, though we think that the Psalm is so much more meaningful when we see Christ throughout—the way that the apostles apparently did. But seeing Christ in the Psalm does not mean that we should throw away all the rules of hermeneutic and simply ignore the context. And therefore, it is wrong to say that every first person pronoun in the Psalm must be Christ speaking. Sometimes the "I" is God the Father speaking. Sometimes the "I" could even be the sheep of Christ or the Church speaking. And so very careful thought must be made to decipher what each of the pronouns points to.

I bring this up in the exposition of this Psalm, because it is especially needful for our understanding of it. But before we go into some details, let me give you a working title and structure for this Psalm. We may entitle this Psalm *"The Righteous One's Reflection upon God's Covenant Faithfulness."* It was penned under the inspiration of the Spirit of Christ by Ethan the Ezrahite who was known as a wise man who lived around the time of Solomon (1 Kgs 4:30-31). We do not know the exact occasion that prompted its composition. Some suggest that it was occasioned by one of the various military defeats suffered by Judah, such as during the campaign by Shishak, king of Egypt (1 Kgs 14:25). But regardless of whether this is correct, such times of perplexity and sense of defeat have recurred in the Church both under the Old Covenant and the New. This Psalm is suitable for Christ-honouring meditation at all such times. There are three main parts in it, which we may outline:

1. v. 1-37   The Promise
2. v. 38-45   The Present
3. v. 46-62   The Plea

1. The Promise

Now, this is the major division of this Psalm. It begins in a rather interesting fashion, not unique in the psalter, namely, with a word of praise:

a. Praise to the Father (v. 1-2)

¹ I will sing of the mercies of the LORD for ever: with my mouth will I make known thy faithfulness to all generations. ² For I have said, Mercy shall be built up for ever: thy faithfulness shalt thou establish in the very heavens.

Who is the speaker of these words? Well, this Psalm is attributed to *"Ethan the Ezrahite."* Who is he? He is a wise man to whom Solomon is compared with (1 Kgs 4:31). It is not probable that the Davidic king who is contemporaneous with him, knew him, and when he had read this song which he had composed, gave approval (under inspiration) for it to be used in temple worship.

Were it not so, it would be quite meaningless for Israel and the Church to sing these words in the first person. But with the royal and inspired approval of the Psalm, we can assuredly conclude that Ethan penned the words of Christ for the Church to sing in union with Him. Only Christ is capable of making God's faithfulness known to all generations (v. 1). Only Christ could honestly assert: *"I have said..."* (v. 2). Christ, our Lord, would have us join Him to extol the Father for His covenant faithfulness.

b. The Father's Response (v. 3-4)

As the Son speaks, so the Father replies:

³ I have made a covenant with my chosen, I have sworn unto David my servant, ⁴ Thy seed will I establish for ever, and build up thy throne to all generations.

Hardly any commentators will dispute that these are the words of God the Father, though there is an obvious change in the meaning of the first person pronoun between verses 1-2 and 3-4. God has made a covenant with David to establish his seed and his throne forever. The covenant, no doubt, was the promise of the Messiah who would descend from David. Remember how the angel Gabriel announced unto Mary, that "the Lord God shall give unto [the son she shall bear] the throne of his father David...and of his kingdom there shall be no end" (Lk 1:32-33).

This brings us to the first "selah", which beckons us to pause and consider the greatness of what God has promised.

c. The People's Rejoicing (v. 5-18)

⁵ And the heavens shall praise thy wonders, O LORD: thy faithfulness also in the congregation of the saints....

Who is the speaker of these words? The speaker, I believe, is intended to be the Church. Here is one of the few places in the Psalms where our Saviour gives words to the Church to sing to the Father in reference to Himself as their King. For look at verse 18: *"For the LORD is our defence; and the Holy One of Israel is our king."*

The Church, knowing the covenant promises of the Father, cannot but praise Him for who He is, for what He has done, and for His Son. We must praise Him for His glory and power (v. 17) as displayed in creation and providence (v. 9-12). We must praise Him for His justice and judgement, and for His mercy and truth (v. 14). But we must especially praise Him for His Son. Notice the indirect exaltation of the Son even as the Father is extolled:

⁶ For who in the heaven can be compared unto the LORD? who among the sons of the mighty can be likened unto the LORD?

⁸ O LORD God of hosts, who is a strong LORD like unto thee?...

[18] For the LORD is our defence; and the Holy One of Israel is our king.

What does the Father say to these questions and intimation?

d. The Father's Rejoinder (v. 19-37)

[19] Then thou spakest in vision to thy holy one [i.e. the Church], and saidst, I have laid help upon one that is mighty; I have exalted one chosen out of the people. *[20]* I have found David my servant; with my holy oil have I anointed him:...

These are the words of our Saviour which quotes God the Father. God has found David. And He made a covenant with David. But certainly, He did not only have David, the son of Jesse in mind, for as Matthew Henry observed, ...

> [This covenant] certainly... looks at Christ, and has its accomplishment in him much more than in David; nay, some passages here are scarcely applicable at all to David, but must be understood of Christ only (who is therefore called *David our king,* Hos. 3:5), and very great and precious promises they are which are here made to the Redeemer, which are strong foundations for the faith and hope of the redeemed to build upon. The comforts of our redemption flow from the covenant of redemption; all our springs are in that, Isa. 55:3. *I will make an everlasting covenant with you, even the sure mercies of David,* Acts 13:34.

The Father says many things relative to the covenant He has made, but let us highlight a few verses.

[26] He shall cry unto me, Thou art my father, my God, and the rock of my salvation. *[27]* Also I will make him my firstborn, higher than the kings of the earth. *[28]* My mercy will I keep for him for evermore, and my covenant shall stand fast with him. *[29]* His seed also will I make to endure for ever, and his throne as the days of heaven.

[33] ...my lovingkindness will I not utterly take from him, nor suffer my faithfulness to fail. *[34]* My covenant will I not break, nor alter the thing that is gone out of my lips. *[35]* Once have I sworn by my holiness that I will not lie unto David.

God's covenant with David and the greater David is an unconditional, eternal covenant. He will chastise the children of David, i.e. all believers, if they stray from the commandments of the Lord, but He will never forsake His covenant.

It is for this reason that we can continue to trust in the Lord through all the ups and downs, and all the pains and struggles, in our battles as the Church of Christ. The Father has promised. The Son has kept the covenant. The gates of hell shall not prevail against the Church (Mt 16:18).

But what of the present reality faced by the Church at every age...

2. The Present

[38] But thou hast cast off and abhorred, thou hast been wroth with thine anointed. *[39]* Thou hast made void the covenant of thy servant: thou hast profaned his crown by casting it to the ground, etc.

We do not know when this Psalm was written. We know Ethan the Ezrahite was a very wise man (1 Kgs 4:31), but we don't know when he lived. Very possibly, he lived to see the destruction of Jerusalem and the humiliation of the Davidic kings by the Babylonians.

Whatever the case might be, the present reality on the ground appears to contradict God's covenant promises. The crown has been cast to the ground. The walls and palaces are torn down. The homes are plundered. A multitude has been killed. Shame covers Jerusalem.

Can we not sing the same words today to describe the situation of our day? The church is small and decimated. The crown of Christ is not represented in the nations. There are few faithful churches and few in faithful churches. Shame has shrouded many churches due to scandalous sin and worldly behaviour.

What could be the reason? Well, were we under under the Old Covenant, we could explain that the Covenant did not guarantee that the line of David would not be cut off in any sense at all; for the full fulfilment of the Covenant awaited Christ. But today, Christ has come, and yet in some sense, the kingdom in its outward manifestation is not much better than in the days after the Babylonian captivity. How do we explain that? Well, we must explain, I believe, by the fact that the kingdom of Christ is not of this world. This is what the Lord says: "My kingdom is not of this world: if my kingdom were of this world, then would my servants fight" (Jn 18:36).

The kingdom of Christ is a heavenly kingdom. During the period of time until the final manifestation of His kingdom, there will be ups and downs. There will be periods of prosperity and periods of declension brought about by disobedience. This will be so till the Last Day. But the promises of God stand sure.

For this reason, we may come to the Father in union with the Son to plead with Him as we are taught in the last part of this Psalm.

3. The Plea

46 How long, LORD? wilt thou hide thyself for ever? shall thy wrath burn like fire? Etc.

We must go to the Father to present our grief. We must come to Him to plead with Him according to His covenant mercies:

49 Lord, where are thy former lovingkindnesses, which thou swarest unto David in thy truth?

We know from retrospect and from comparing Scripture with Scripture that God does not promise prosperity even for the Church in this world. But we know that God is pleased to hear the cries of His people so that very often, He would pour down His blessing in such a way that the glory of His kingdom emanates through the church visible, and is visible to the world.

May the Lord grant us the heart so to pray! I am personally not persuaded that the postmillennial vision that things will get better and better in the world is scripturally or historically sustainable; but I think we should share an optimism in God's answer to prayer. We must not assume things will get better with or without prayer because God has promised. No, no; it is because God has promised, we must pray.

Conclusion

Let us refuse to resign to the state of things when we see the crown of Christ trampled underfoot in this world. Let us remind ourselves that He is reigning. He is reigning at the right hand of the throne of God. And He will be pleased to manifest His power in prayer until the great and glorious day when every knee will bow and every tongue confess that Jesus is Lord.

52 Blessed be the LORD for evermore. Amen, and Amen. Ω

Selected Bibliography

Adams, James E. *War Psalms of the Prince of Peace*. Phillipsburg: P&R Publishing, 1991.

Alexander, Joseph A. *The Psalms Translated and Explained*. Edinburgh: A. Elliot and J. Thin, 1864.

Augustine. *Augustin: Expositions on the Book of Psalms*. Nicene And Post-Nicene Fathers, first series. Vol. 8. Ed. Philip Schaff. Peabody: Hendrikson Publishers, reprinted 2004 [1888].

Beeke, Joel R. & Selvaggio, Anthony T., editors. *Sing a New Song: Recovering Psalm Singing for the Twenty-First Century*. Grand Rapids: Reformation Heritage Books, 2010.

Belcher, Richard P., Jr, *The Messiah and the Psalms: Preaching Christ from all the Psalms*. Ross-shire: Christian Focus Publications, 2006.

Bonar, Andrew A. *Christ and His Church in the Book of Psalms*. Stoke-on-Trent: Tentmaker Publications. Reprinted 2002 [1859].

Bushell, Michael. *The Songs of Zion: A Contemporary Case for Exclusive Psalmody*. Pittsburgh: Crown & Covenant Publications, 2nd ed., 1993 [1977]

Calvin, John. *Joshua, Psalms 1-35*. Calvin's Commentaries. Vol. 4. Trans. Henry Beveridge. Grand Rapids: Baker Book House, reprinted 1989.

Calvin, John. *Psalms 36-92*. Calvin's Commentaries. Vol. 5. Trans. Henry Beveridge. Grand Rapids: Baker Book House, reprinted 1989.

Calvin, John. *Psalms 93-150*. Calvin's Commentaries. Vol. 6. Trans. Henry Beveridge. Grand Rapids: Baker Book House, reprinted 1989.

Chrysostom, John. *Commentary on the Psalm*. Trans. Robert Charles Hill. Brookline, Massachusetts: Holy Cross Orthodox Press, 1998.

Delitzsch, Franz. *Psalms*. Commentary on the Old Testament. Vol. 5. Trans. James Martin. Grand Rapids: William B. Eerdmans Publishing Company, reprinted 1991.

Dickson, David. *A Commentary on the Psalms*. Edinburgh: The Banner of Truth Trust, reprinted 1985 [1653-5].

Eveson, Philip. *Psalms: From Suffering to Glory*. Vol. 1: Psalms 1-72 The Servant King. Darlington: EP Books, 2014.

Eveson, Philip. *Psalms: From Suffering to Glory*. Vol. 2: Psalms 73-150 God's Manual of Spirituality. Darlington: EP Books, 2014.

Futato, Mark D. *Interpreting the Psalms: An Exegetical Handbook*. Grand Rapids: Kregel Publications, 2007.

Hengstenberg, Ernst Wilhelm. *Hengstenberg's Commentary on the Psalms*. Edinburgh: T&T Clark, 1869

Henry, Matthew. *Job to Song of Solomon*. Commentary on the Whole Bible. Vol. 3. Peabody: Hendrikson Publishers, reprinted 1992.

Horne, George. Commentary on the Psalms. New Jersey: Old Paths Publication, reprinted 1997 [1771].

Johnston, S. Philip & Firth, David God. *Interpreting the Psalms: Issues and Approaches*. Illinios: Inter-Vasity Press, 2005.

Kenneth Stewart, editor. *Songs of the Spirit: The Place of Psalms in the Worship of God.* Glasgow: Reformation Scotland Trust, 2014.

LeFebvre, Michael. *Singing the Songs of Jesus: Revisiting the Psalms.* Ross-Shire: Christian Focus, 2010.

McNaughter, John. *The Psalms in Worship.* Edmonton: Still Waters Revival Books, reprinted 1992 [1907].

O'Neil, Jeffery. *God's Hymn Book: Composed by the Sweet Psalmist of Israel.* Singapore: Pilgrim Covenant Church, 2007.

Plumer, W.S. *Psalms: A Critical and Epository Commentary with Doctrinal and Practical Remarks.* Edinburgh: The Banner of Truth Trust, reprinted 1990 [1867].

Poole, Matthew. *Psalms to Malachi.* Commentary on the Holy Bible. Vol. 2. Peabody: Hendrikson Publishers, reprinted n.d. [n.d.].

Prothero, R.E. *The Psalms in Human Life.* London: John Murray, 1904.

Robertson, O. Palmer. *The Flow of the Psalms: Discovering their Structure and Theology.* Phillipsburg: P&R Publishing, 2015.

Robertson, O. Palmer. *Psalms in Congregational Celebration.* Darlington: Evangelical Press, 1995.

Shwertley, Brian H. *Exclusive Psalmody: A Biblical Defence.* Haslett: Covenanted Reformation Press, 2002.

Spurgeon, Charles H. *The Treasury of David.* Peabody: Hendrikson Publishers, reprinted n.d. [1869].

Waltke, Bruce K.; Houston, James M.; & Moore, Erika. *The Psalms as Christian Worship: A Historical Commentary.* Grand Rapids: William B. Eerdmans Publishing Company, 2010.

Waltke, Bruce K.; Houston, James M.; & Moore, Erika. *The Psalms as Christian Lament: A Historical Commentary.* Grand Rapids: William B. Eerdmans Publishing Company, 2014.

Ward, Rowland S. *The Psalms in Christian Worship: A doctrinal, historical and expository Guide.* Victoria: Presbyterian Church of Eastern Australia, 1992.